THE
RHODODENDRON
SPECIES

Open situations in northwest Yunnan. Photo J. F. Rock.

THE RHODODENDRON SPECIES

VOLUME III • ELEPIDOTES continued
Neriiflorum–Thomsonii,
AZALEASTRUM and CAMTSCHATICUM

H. H. Davidian
B.A., B.Sc. (Hons.)

TIMBER PRESS
Portland, Oregon

ISBN 0-88192-168-8
Printed in Hong Kong

TIMBER PRESS, INC.
9999 SW Wilshire, Suite 124
Portland, Oregon 97225

Library of Congress Cataloging-in-Publication Data
(Revised for vol. 2)

Davidian, H. H.
    The rhododendron species.

    Includes indexes.
    Contents: v. 1. Lepidote -- v. 2-   . Elepidotes.
    1. Rhododendron--Classification. I. Title.
SB413.R47D258 1982   583'.62   81-23232
ISBN 0-91730-471-3 (v. 1)

Contents

Colour plates 1–161 follow page 240.

A Note on Vols. II and III

VOLUME II consists of the Series Arboreum, Argyrophyllum, Auriculatum, Barbatum, Campanulatum, Falconeri, Fortunei, Fulgens, Fulvum, Grande, Griersonianum, Irroratum, and Lacteum.

VOLUME III comprises the Series Neriiflorum, Parishii, Ponticum, Sherriffii, Taliense, Thomsonii. AZALEASTRUM—Albiflorum, Ovatum, Semibarbatum, and Stamineum. CAMTSCHATICUM—Camtschaticum.

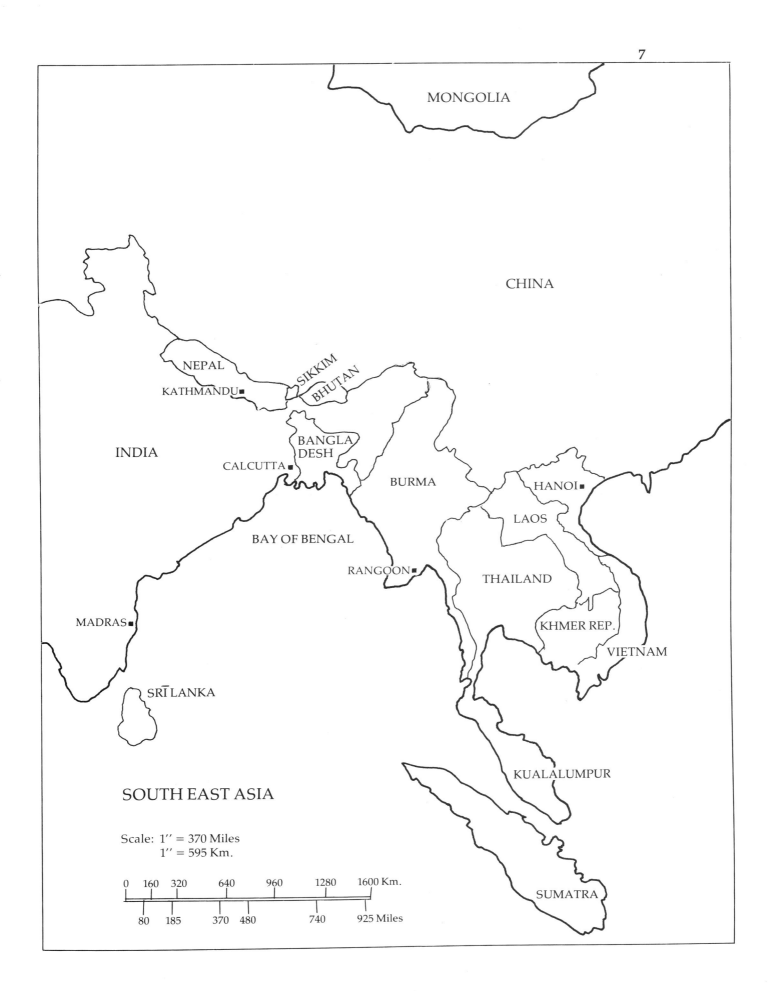

MONGOLIA

CHINA

NEPAL

SIKKIM

BHUTAN

KATHMANDU ■

INDIA

BANGLA DESH

CALCUTTA ■

BURMA

HANOI ■

LAOS

BAY OF BENGAL

RANGOON ■

THAILAND

KHMER REP.

VIETNAM

MADRAS ■

SRĪ LANKA

KUALALUMPUR

SOUTH EAST ASIA

Scale: 1″ = 370 Miles
       1″ = 595 Km.

0	160	320	640	960	1280	1600 Km.
	80	185	370 480		740	925 Miles

SUMATRA

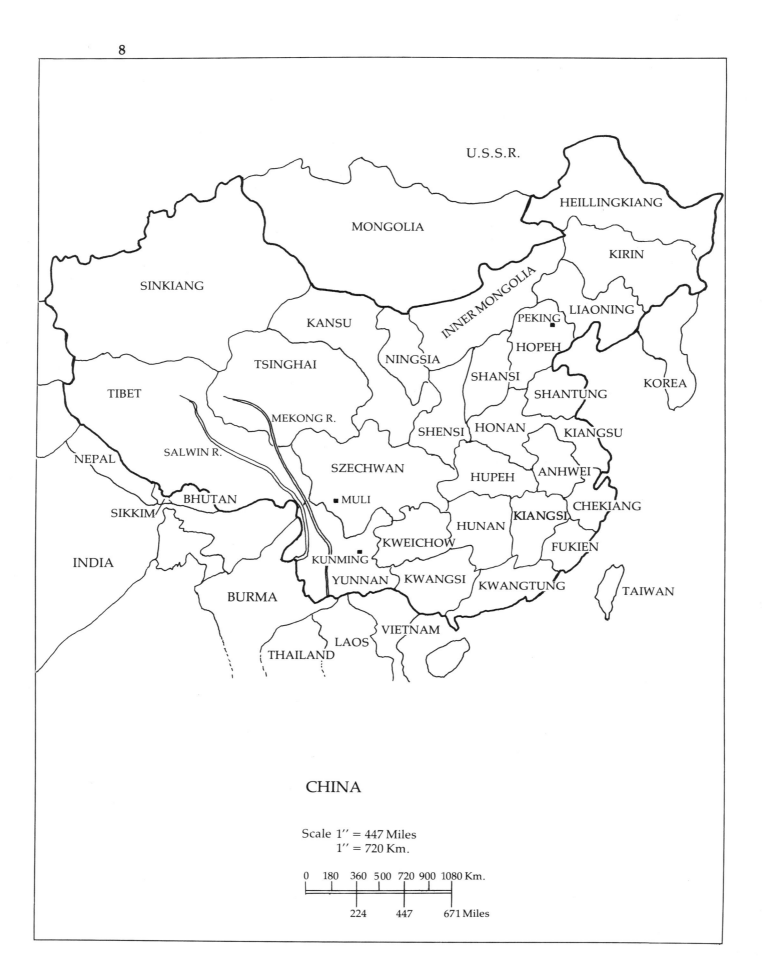

CHINA

Scale 1″ = 447 Miles
1″ = 720 Km.

| 0 | 180 | 360 | 500 | 720 | 900 | 1080 Km. |

| | 224 | | 447 | | 671 Miles |

Old and New Names of Provinces in China

Sinkiang. Xinjiang
Tibet. Xizang
Mongolia. Mongolia
Heillingkiang. Heilongjiang
Kansu. Gansu
Ningsia. Ningxia
Inner Mongolia. Nei Mongol
Hopeh. Hebei
Liaoning. Liaoning
Kirin. Jilin
Tsinghai. Qinghai
Shansi. Shanxi
Shantung. Shandong
Shensi. Shaanxi

Honan. Henan
Kiangsu. Jiangsu
Szechwan. Sichuan
Hupeh. Hubei
Anhwei. Anhui
Chekiang. Zhejiang
Yunnan. Yunnan
Kweichow. Guizhou
Hunan. Hunan
Kiangsi. Jiangxi
Fukien. Fujian
Kwangsi. Guangxi
Kwangtung. Guangdong
Taiwan. Taiwan

J. F. Rock's camp in northwest Yunnan. Photo J. F. Rock.

List of Colour Plates

144. Rhododendrons at Brodick Castle, Isle of Arran.
145. Rhododendrons in Corsock House garden, Kirkcudbrightshire.
146. Rhododendrons in Corsock House garden, Kirkcudbrightshire. Photo W. R. Hean.
147. Rhododendrons at Galloway House, Wigtownshire.
148. Rhododendrons at Lochinch, Wigtownshire.
149. Rhododendrons at entrance to Achamore House, Isle of Gigha. Photo Dr. Florence Auckland.
150. Rhododendrons in Deer Dell, Mr. J. McQuire's garden, Farnham, Surrey.
151. Rhododendrons in Deer Dell, Mr. J. McQuire's garden, Farnham, Surrey.
152. Rhododendrons at Trengwainton, Cornwall.
153. Rhododendrons at Howth, Eire.
154. Rhododendrons in Mr. Cecil Smith's garden, Newburg, Oregon, U.S.A.
155. Rhododendrons in Mr. & Mrs. W. Berg's garden, Oregon, U.S.A.
156. Rhododendrons in Mr. Barfod's garden, Denmark.
157. Rhododendrons in Mr. Barfod's garden, Denmark.
158. *R. caucasicum* in East Turkey.
159. Collecting area in Bhutan.
160. Collecting area at Hpuginhka, North Burma.
161. Collecting area, Mt. Omei, Sichuan.

List of Black and White Photographs

by J. F. Rock

List of Line Drawings

Acknowledgments

My sincere thanks are extended to my lawyer Mr. William D. Davidson, W.S. who made all the required arrangements with the publisher.

I wish to express my deepest gratitude to Mrs. Eileen M. D. Wood for her excellent typing of the whole manuscript, and for devoting so many hours to the reading of the proofs.

My special thanks and appreciation are due to Mrs. Rodella A. Purves for her most beautiful line drawings of the species.

I am also most grateful to all others who supplied beautiful colour slides.

Classification

It would be of interest to refer to the classification of Rhododendrons.

The presence or absence of scales on rhododendrons has long been regarded as a fundamental distinction in the classification of Rhododendrons into two large divisions. Let us evaluate the merits of this classification.

First. According to the presence or absence of scales, we have two large divisions of Rhododendrons of almost equal size, namely, Lepidote (scaly) and Elepidote (non-scaly). These are two large natural divisions, therefore, a natural classification.

Second. All Rhododendron seeds belong to one of three well-marked types: 1. Alpine type. 2. Forest type. 3. Epiphytic type. (See Volume I pages 26–27). All Lepidote (scaly) Rhododendrons have Alpine or Epiphytic type of seed (except a few species of the Maddenii Series), and all Elepidote (non-scaly) Rhododendrons (except the Azaleastrums—Albiflorum, Ovatum, and Stamineum Series, and part of Azaleas) have the Forest type of seed. Therefore, we have two large natural divisions of Rhododendrons, namely, Lepidote (scaly) and Elepidote (non-scaly).

Third. There are two types of bud-construction in rhododendrons, convolute in Lepidote species, and revolute in Elepidote species. (See Volume I page 15). It is maintained that in the division of Rhododendrons based on the presence or absence of scales, the bud character is equally a fundamental one, and that these two characters, scales and bud-construction, are related one to the other. Therefore, we have two large natural divisions of Rhododendrons based on bud-construction, Lepidote (scaly) and Elepidote (non-scaly).

Fourth. The hybridizer knows well that he cannot cross Lepidote with Elepidote. So far as is known only one authentic hybrid between a Lepidote and an Elepidote species has ever been successful, namely, *R. griersonianum* × *R. dalhousiae* 'Grierdal'. It is possible that one or two other hybrids between Lepidote and Elepidote species have been produced, but not officially recognised. Many attempts have been made to cross the two groups, but unsuccessfully. It is apparent that Lepidote and Elepidote rhododendrons repel one another and will not cross; they are incompatible. Therefore, we have two large natural divisions of Rhododendrons, Lepidote (scaly) and Elepidote (non-scaly).

Fifth. In 1946 Dr. J. Hutchinson gave an account of "The Evolution and Classification of Rhododendrons" in *The Rhododendron Year Book* 1946, pp. 42–48. According to the "family tree" which he illustrated, it will be seen that Lepidote (scaly) and Elepidote (non-scaly) Series are two large natural divisions of Rhododendrons.

Sixth. Another interesting distinction between Lepidote and Elepidote Rhododendrons is polyploidy. It will be seen that all the Elepidote Series (excluding *R. canadense* and *R. calendulaceum* in the Azalea Series) are diploids, $2n = 26$. But in the Lepidote Series, it is noted that polyploids occur in 8 out of the 24 recorded Series. Altogether 78 polyploids have been found representing more than a third of the species in which counts had been made. It has been shown that the degree of polyploidy ranges from triploids $2n = 39$ to dodecaploids $2n = 156$, and that the most prevalent type is the tetraploid $2n = 52$. It is apparent that polyploidy is an important aid in classifying Rhododendrons into two large natural divisions, Lepidote (scaly) and Elepidote (non-scaly).

Therefore, it is convincingly clear that there are two large natural divisions of Rhododendrons of almost equal size, namely, Lepidote (scaly) and Elepidote (non-scaly), a natural classification.

In *The Species of Rhododendron,* the species are classified into groups known as Series. It has been acknowledged that within most of the Series there is considerable variation in habit and height of growth, in leaf shape and size, in flower shape, size and colour, and in other characters. The degree of variation is so great, and the fact that the Series merge into each other to such an extent that it was impossible to draw hard and fast lines between them. It was this linkage, and indeed it was this merging or continuity between the Series which made the making of a concise Key to the Series impracticable in *The Species of Rhododendron.* Although I produced a Key on page 42 of *The Rhododendron Species,* Volume I, and on page 62, Volume II, I had to introduce most of the Subseries in more than one section of each Key.

Accordingly Sir William W. Smith and his assistants had no hesitation in retaining the word "Series" for each group of species. They knew well the meaning of the word "Series" which means "join, succession, continuity, one group merging into another group." What better term is there to denote this unity, succession, merging or continuity of these groups of Rhododendrons than "Series"?

Glossary

Acuminate. Tapering into a point.
Acute. Pointed.
Adpressed. Lying flat.
Agglutinate. Glued.
Alveola. Cavity.
Anther. The part of the stamen containing the pollen grains.
Apex. Tip.
Appressed. See adpressed.
Aristate. Awned; tipped by a bristle.
Auricle. An ear-like appendage.
Axillary. Arising in the angle formed by the junction of leaf and stem.
Bistrate. With two layers or strata.
Bullate. Puckered or blistered.
Campanulate. Bell-shaped.
Capitate. Collected in a dense knob-like head or cluster.
Chromosome. Rod-like portion of the cell-nucleus which determines hereditary characteristics.
Ciliate. With fine hairs.
Ciliolate. Minutely ciliate.
Clone. The vegetatively produced progeny of a single individual.
Contiguous. Touching.
Convolute. Rolled up longitudinally.
Cordate. With two round lobes at the base forming a deep recess at the base.
Coriaceous. Leathery.
Crenulate. Margin notched, with rounded teeth, scalloped.
Cultivar. Cultivated variety as distinct from other varieties.
Cuneate. Wedge-shaped.
Decurrent. Extended below the point of insertion.
Deflexed. Bent downwards.
Dichotomous. Divided in pairs.
Eciliate. Without fine hairs.
Eglandular. Not glandular.
Elepidote. Not scaly.

Emarginate. With a notch at the end.
Entire. Margin undivided.
Epiphyte. A plant growing on another plant without being parasitic.
Epiphytic. Growing on another plant without being parasitic.
Fastigiate. With erect branches.
Filament. The stalk bearing the anther.
Floccose. With soft woolly hairs.
Glabrous. Without hairs.
Glandular. With glands.
Glaucous. Covered with greyish waxy bloom.
Globose. Spherical.
Hirsute. Covered with stiff long erect hairs.
Imbricate. Overlapping each other at the margins.
Indumentum. A hairy covering, particularly of the lower surface of the leaves.
Lamina. Blade.
Lepidote. Scaly.
Mucro. A hard sharp point.
Mucronate. Terminated by a hard sharp point.
Nectary. A gland through which a solution of sugar is secreted.
Obtuse. Blunt.
Papillate. Pimpled; covered with minute pimples.
Pedicel. Flower-stalk.
Petiole. Leaf-stalk.
Pilose. Covered with soft long hairs.
Plastered indumentum. Indumentum skin-like with a smooth polished surface.
Polyploid. With more than the diploid (2n) number of chromosomes.
Precocious. Flowers produced before the leaves appear.
Puberulous. Minutely pubescent.
Pubescent. Hairy with short soft hairs.

Punctulate. Minutely dotted.
Racemose. Flowers borne on an unbranched main stalk.
Recurved. Curved backwards.
Reflexed. Bent abruptly backwards.
Reticulate. Netted, like a network.
Revolute. Rolled backwards; margin rolled towards the lower side.
Rhachis. The part of the inflorescence bearing the flowers.
Rotate. A very short tube with spreading, almost flat petals.
Rugose. Wrinkled.
Rugulose. Somewhat wrinkled.
Salver-shaped. With a long slender tube, and flat spreading petals.
Scabrid. Rough to the touch.
Scale. Minute disc-like object found on branchlets, leaves and flowers.
Serrulate. Minutely saw-toothed.
Sessile. Without a stalk.
Setose. Bristly; with stiff hairs.
Spathulate. With a broadly rounded apex gradually tapering into the stalk.
Stigma. A small pollen-receptive surface at the tip of the style.
Stoloniferous. Bearing runners from near the base of the stem, often below the surface of the soil.
Strigillose. Hairs smaller in size than strigose.
Strigose. With stiff appressed hairs.
Style. The thread-like part of a gynoecium (pistil) between the ovary and stigma.
Tapered. Lengthening, gradually decreasing in breadth.
Terminal. At the end of a shoot.
Tomentum. Dense hair covering.
Truncate. Straight across.
Undulate. Having a wavy margin.
Unistrate. With one layer or stratum.
Ventricose. Swollen on one side.
Villous. With long soft straight hairs.
Zygomorphic. Flower of irregular shape which can be divided into equal halves along one vertical line only.

Leaf Shapes. Descriptions

Linear.	Narrow, with parallel opposite sides, the ends tapering, at least 10–12 times as long as broad, e.g. *R. trichostomum*.
Lanceolate.	Lance-shaped, widest below the middle, the length of the leaf about three times the breadth, e.g. *R. griersonianum, R. yunnanense.*
Oblanceolate.	Base tapering, apex broad, widest above the middle, the length of the leaf about three times the breadth, e.g. *R. fulvum, R. uvarifolium.*
Oblong.	The sides more or less parallel, the ends obtuse or somewhat rounded, the length of the leaf is twice the breadth, e.g. *R. selense, R. cerasinum.*
Elliptic.	The sides of the leaf are curved tapering equally to tip and base, widest at the middle, the length of the leaf is twice the breadth, e.g. *R. ciliatum* a form, *R. wallichii* a form.
Obovate.	The sides are curved, apex rounded, base narrower, widest above the middle, length is about twice the breadth, e.g. *R. lanatum* a form, *R. tsariense* a form.
Ovate.	The sides are curved, widest at the base, the tip narrowed, the length is greater than the breadth, e.g. *R. edgeworthii* a form, *R. wasonii.*
Oval.	The sides are curved, rounded at both ends, widest at the middle, longer than broad, e.g. *R. callimorphum, R. leucaspis* a form.
Orbicular.	Circular, e.g. *R. orbiculare.*

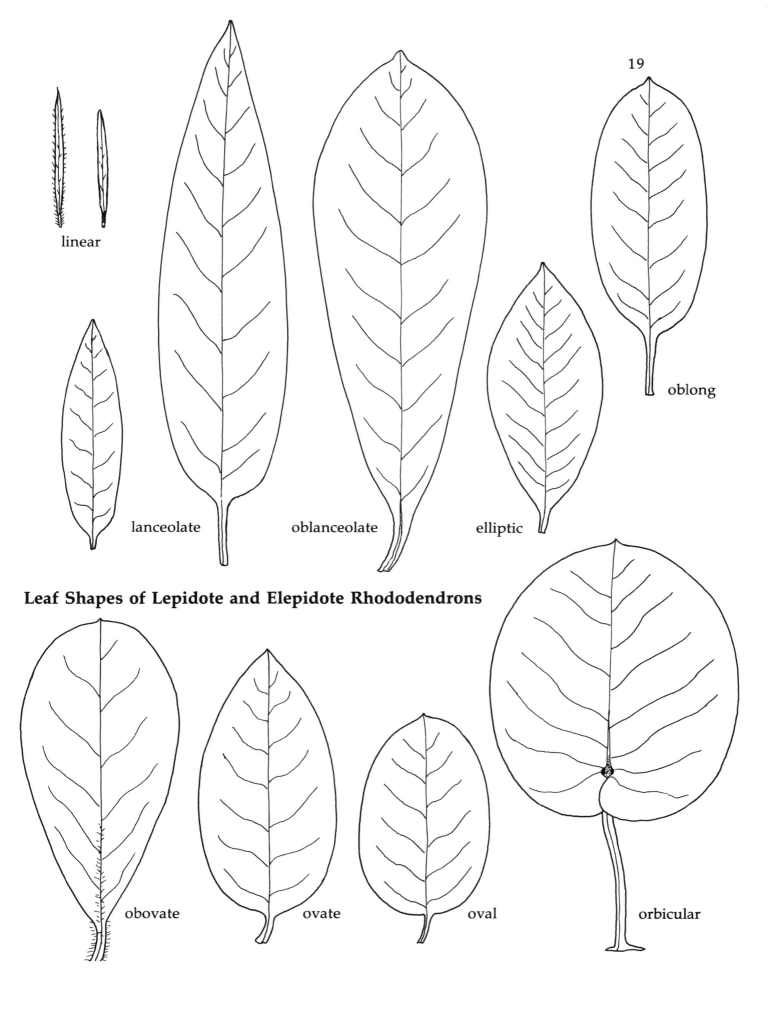

19

linear

lanceolate

oblanceolate

elliptic

oblong

Leaf Shapes of Lepidote and Elepidote Rhododendrons

obovate

ovate

oval

orbicular

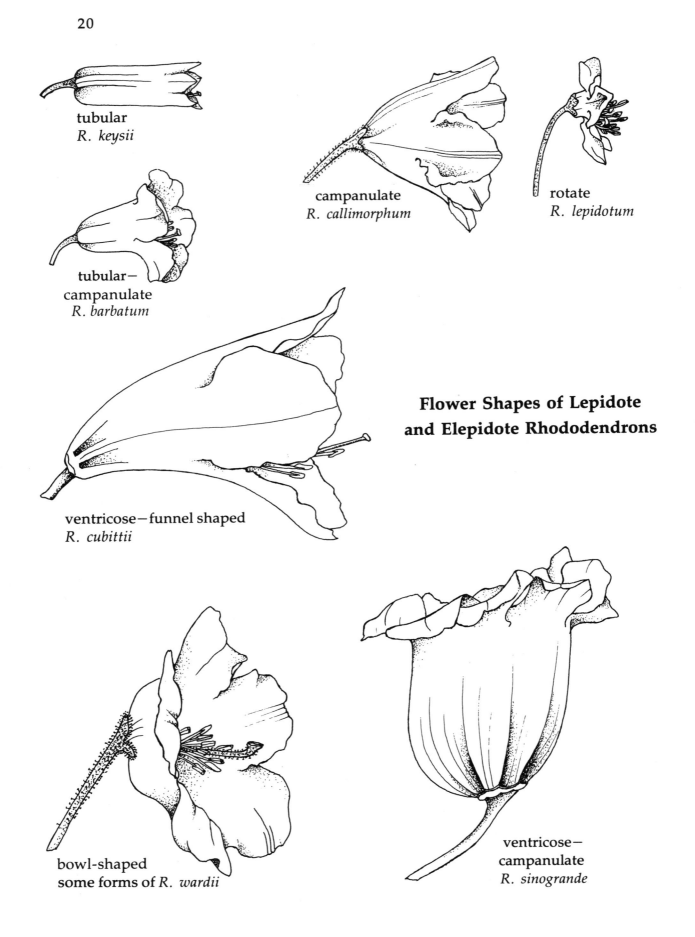

tubular
R. keysii

campanulate
R. callimorphum

rotate
R. lepidotum

tubular—
campanulate
R. barbatum

**Flower Shapes of Lepidote
and Elepidote Rhododendrons**

ventricose—funnel shaped
R. cubittii

bowl-shaped
some forms of *R. wardii*

ventricose—
campanulate
R. sinogrande

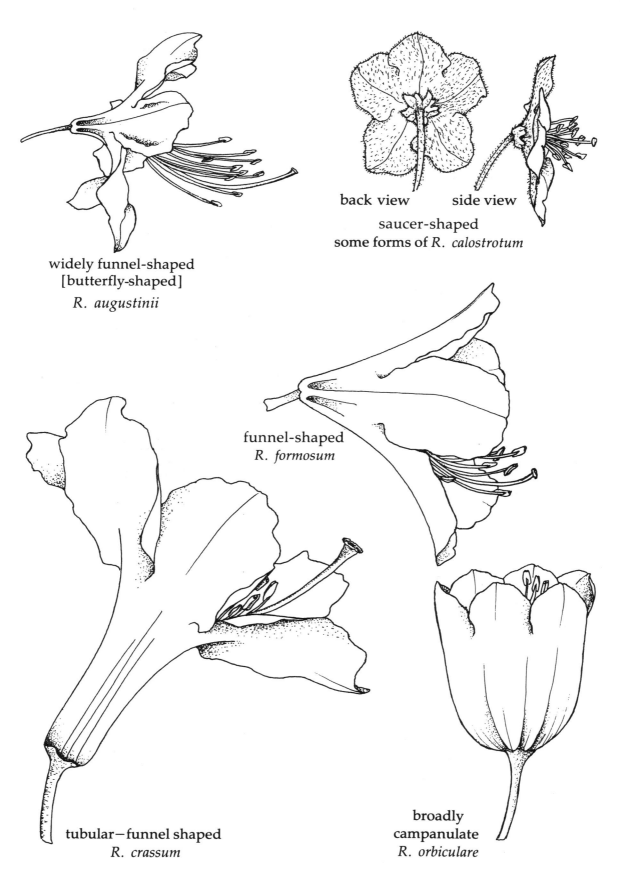

back view   side view

saucer-shaped
some forms of *R. calostrotum*

widely funnel-shaped
[butterfly-shaped]
R. augustinii

funnel-shaped
R. formosum

tubular—funnel shaped
R. crassum

broadly
campanulate
R. orbiculare

Scales

Entire: *R. crassum*

× 125
viewed from above

Undulate: *R. impeditum*

× 137
viewed from above

Lacerate: *R. anthopogon*

× 125
viewed from above

Crenulate: *R. saluenense*

× 125
viewed from above

Vesicular: *R. trichocladum*

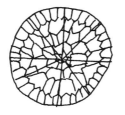

× 125
viewed from above

R. trichocladum

× 80
viewed from side

Seeds

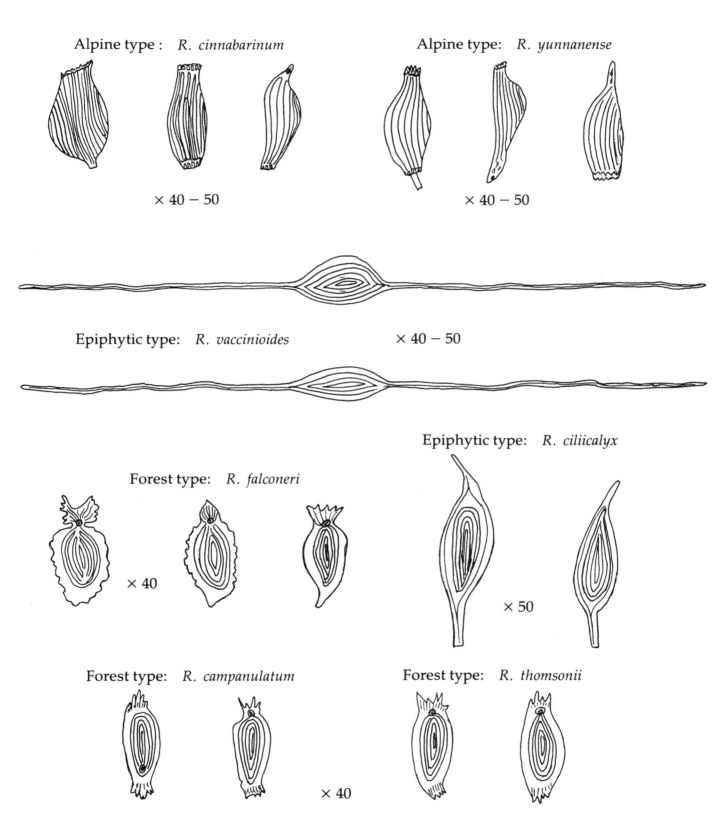

Alpine type : *R. cinnabarinum*

× 40 − 50

Alpine type: *R. yunnanense*

× 40 − 50

Epiphytic type: *R. vaccinioides*   × 40 − 50

Epiphytic type: *R. ciliicalyx*

Forest type: *R. falconeri*

× 40

× 50

Forest type: *R. campanulatum*

× 40

Forest type: *R. thomsonii*

Rhododendron Hairs

Some eighteen distinct different Types of Rhododendron hairs have been described. A detailed microscopic examination of the indumentum on the lower surfaces of all the specimens and of confirmed cultivated plants of all the species shows an extreme diversity of hair structure. At least 10 additional new Types of hairs will also be observed. It would serve no useful purpose to describe these new Types, but they will be regarded as "Forms" of the Types.

It should be noted that in some Series only a few hair Types are constant and characteristic, but in many other Series there is a considerable mixture of Types, and a certain Type of hair is common to several Series.

As to structural detail, each Type of hair shows a certain degree of variation. Moreover, there is a tendency for one Type of hair to merge into another Type. For instance, the most common hair structure is the Ramiform hair with long filamentous arms. It varies to such an extent both in shape and size that it merges into the Dendroid Type of hair of the Arboreum Series; the latter Type also exhibits several variant forms. It will be observed that some of the intermediates between these two Types of hairs (Ramiform and Dendroid) are so similar to both Types that they may be given either name.

It may be remarked that in various species the indumentum is bistrate or two-layered, an upper and a lower layer. The latter consists of small Rosulate hairs, often intermixed with much larger ones.

Hairs Drawn by H. H. Davidian

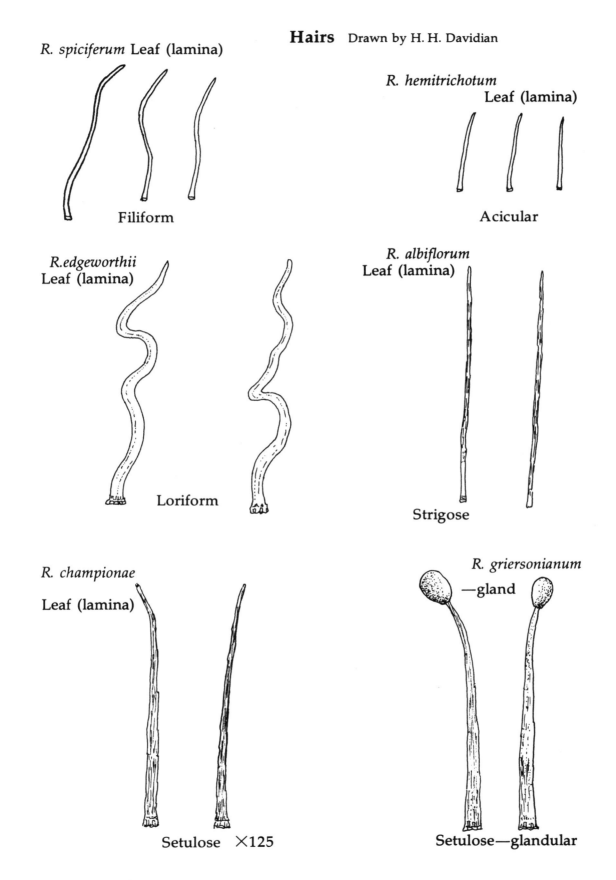

R. spiciferum Leaf (lamina)

Filiform

R. hemitrichotum Leaf (lamina)

Acicular

R.edgeworthii Leaf (lamina)

Loriform

R. albiflorum Leaf (lamina)

Strigose

R. championae Leaf (lamina)

Setulose ×125

R. griersonianum —gland

Setulose—glandular

Arboreum Series

R. arboreum

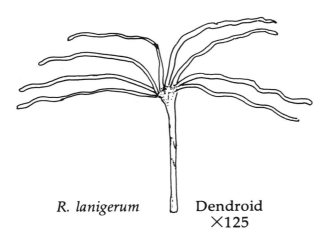

Small Large
Rosulate

A form of
Dendroid
×50

R. cinnamomeum

A form of Dendroid
×50

R. lanigerum Dendroid
×125

R. niveum

A form of Dendroid
or a form of Capitellate
×50

R. zeylanicum

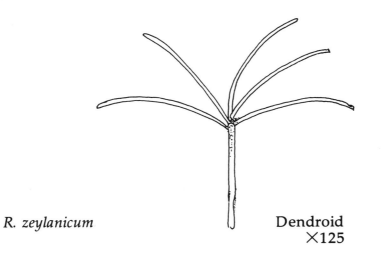

Dendroid
×125

Argyrophyllum Series

A form of Ramiform

R. chienianum
×50

Ramiform
Branches broad ribbon-like
R. farinosum   ×125

A form of Ramiform
R. floribundum

small

large
forms of Rosulate
R. hypoglaucum
×50

stem short

stem long
forms of Ramiform
R. pingianum
×50

Sometimes a form of Ramiform
R. simiarum
or a form of Dendroid

Barbatum Series

Barbatum Subseries

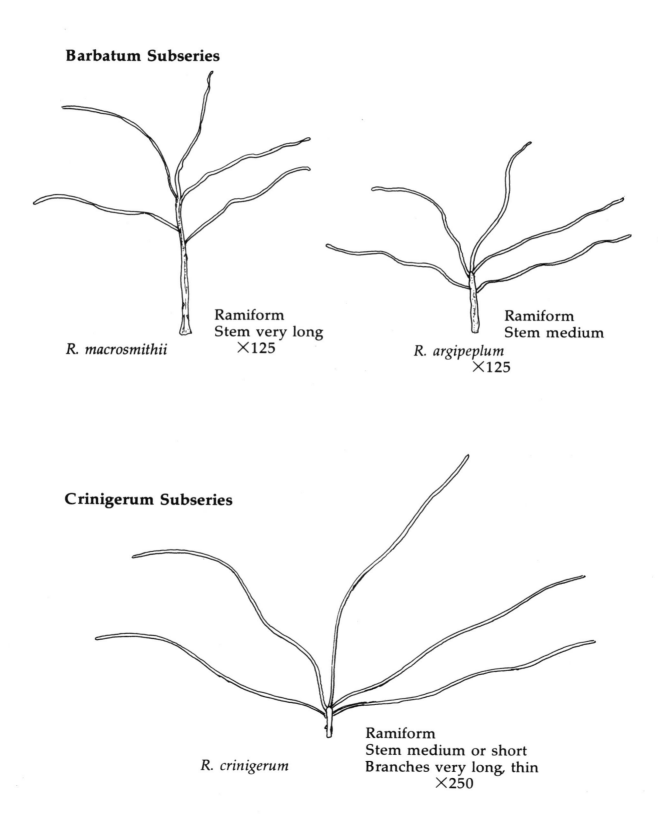

R. macrosmithii
Ramiform
Stem very long
×125

R. argipeplum
Ramiform
Stem medium
×125

Crinigerum Subseries

R. crinigerum
Ramiform
Stem medium or short
Branches very long, thin
×250

Campanulatum Series

Campanulatum Subseries

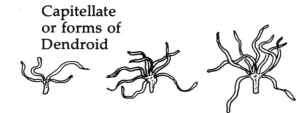

Capitellate
or forms of
Dendroid

When indumentum is thin, stem is short.

Capitellate
mop-like
×50

Capitellate
with long
stem

R. campanulatum

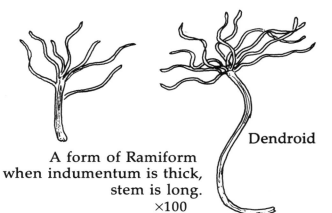

A form of Ramiform
when indumentum is thick,
stem is long.
×100

Dendroid

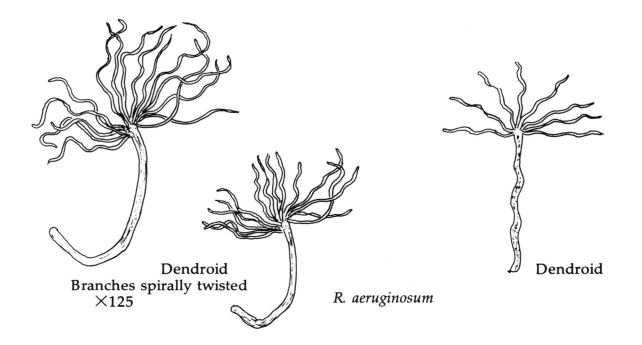

Dendroid
Branches spirally twisted
×125

R. aeruginosum

Dendroid

Campanulatum Series contd.

Campanulatum Subseries contd.

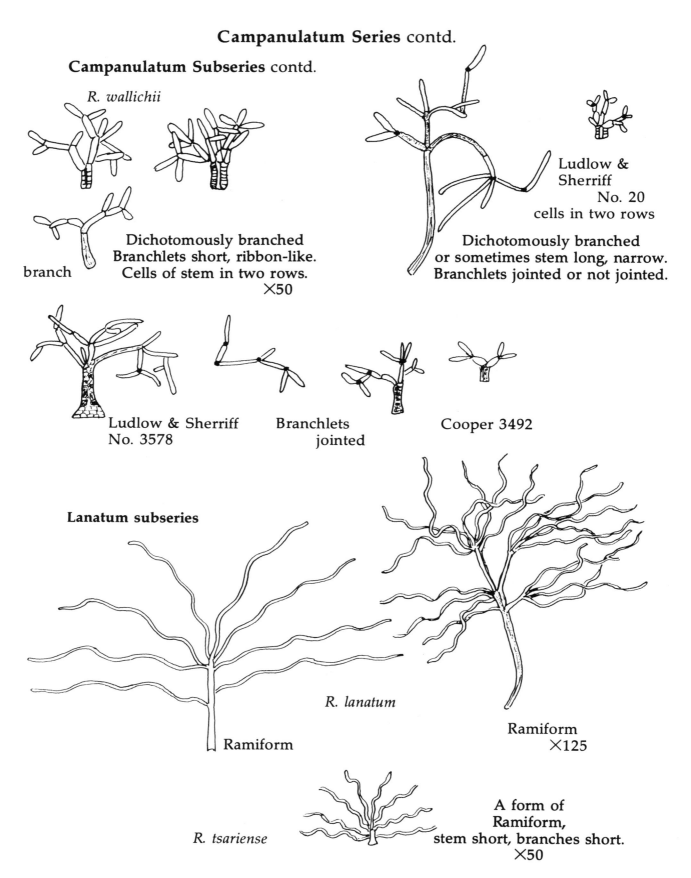

R. wallichii

branch

Dichotomously branched
Branchlets short, ribbon-like.
Cells of stem in two rows.
×50

Ludlow &
Sherriff
No. 20
cells in two rows

Dichotomously branched
or sometimes stem long, narrow.
Branchlets jointed or not jointed.

Ludlow & Sherriff
No. 3578

Branchlets
jointed

Cooper 3492

Lanatum subseries

R. lanatum

Ramiform

Ramiform
×125

R. tsariense

A form of
Ramiform,
stem short, branches short.
×50

Falconeri Series

R. falconeri

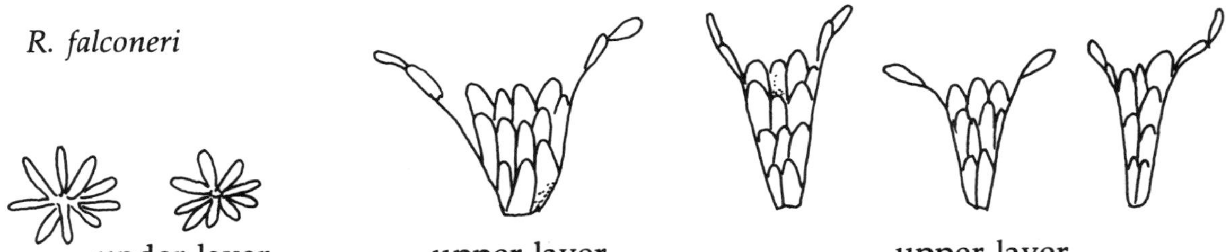

under layer
Rosulate

upper layer
Vase-shaped

upper layer
Funnel-shaped

R. fictolacteum

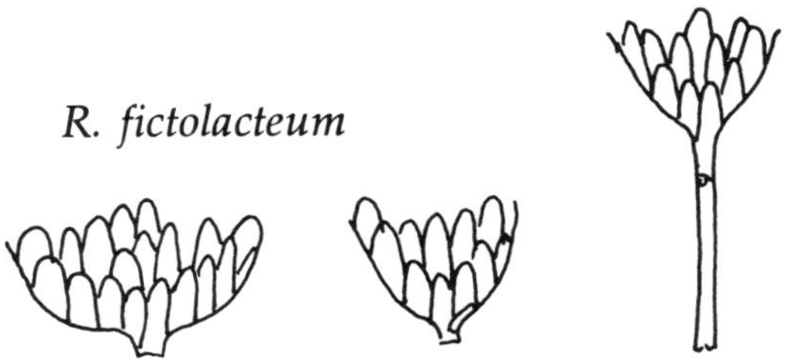

Short-stalked   Long-stalked
Cup-shaped

R. galactinum

Broadly   Narrowly
Funnel-shaped   Funnel-shaped

R. hodgsonii

Cup-shaped   Bowl-shaped
Cells of the wall isodiametric
×50

R. preptum

Narrowly Funnel-shaped    Broadly Funnel-shaped

Falconeri Series contd.

R. rothschildii

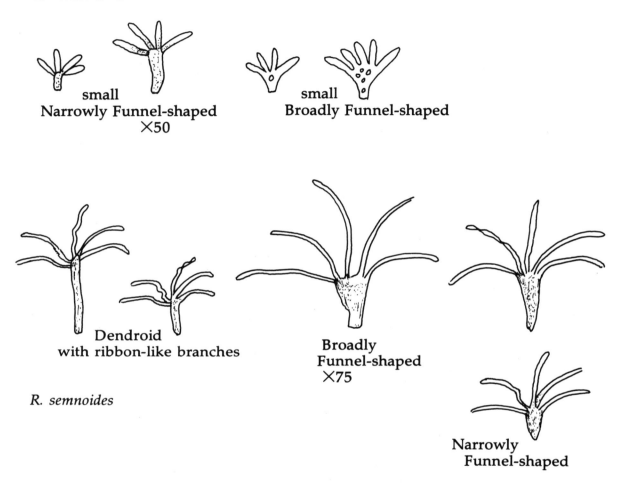

small
Narrowly Funnel-shaped
×50

small
Broadly Funnel-shaped

Dendroid
with ribbon-like branches

Broadly
Funnel-shaped
×75

Narrowly
Funnel-shaped

R. semnoides

R. sinofalconeri

Broadly
Funnel-shaped

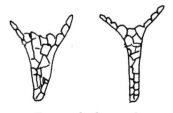

Funnel-shaped

×50

Fulgens Series

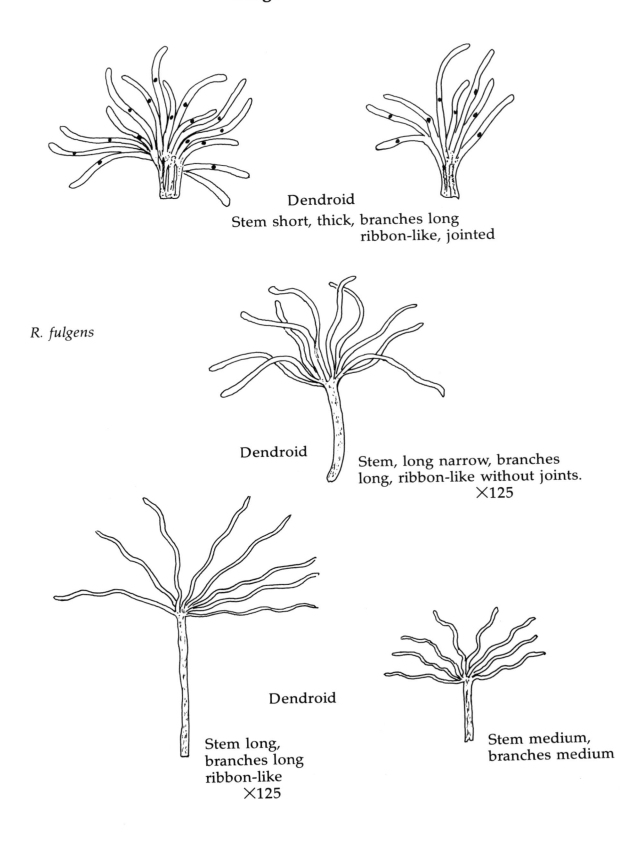

Dendroid
Stem short, thick, branches long
ribbon-like, jointed

R. fulgens

Dendroid

Stem, long narrow, branches
long, ribbon-like without joints.
×125

Dendroid

Stem long,
branches long
ribbon-like
×125

Stem medium,
branches medium

Fulvum Series

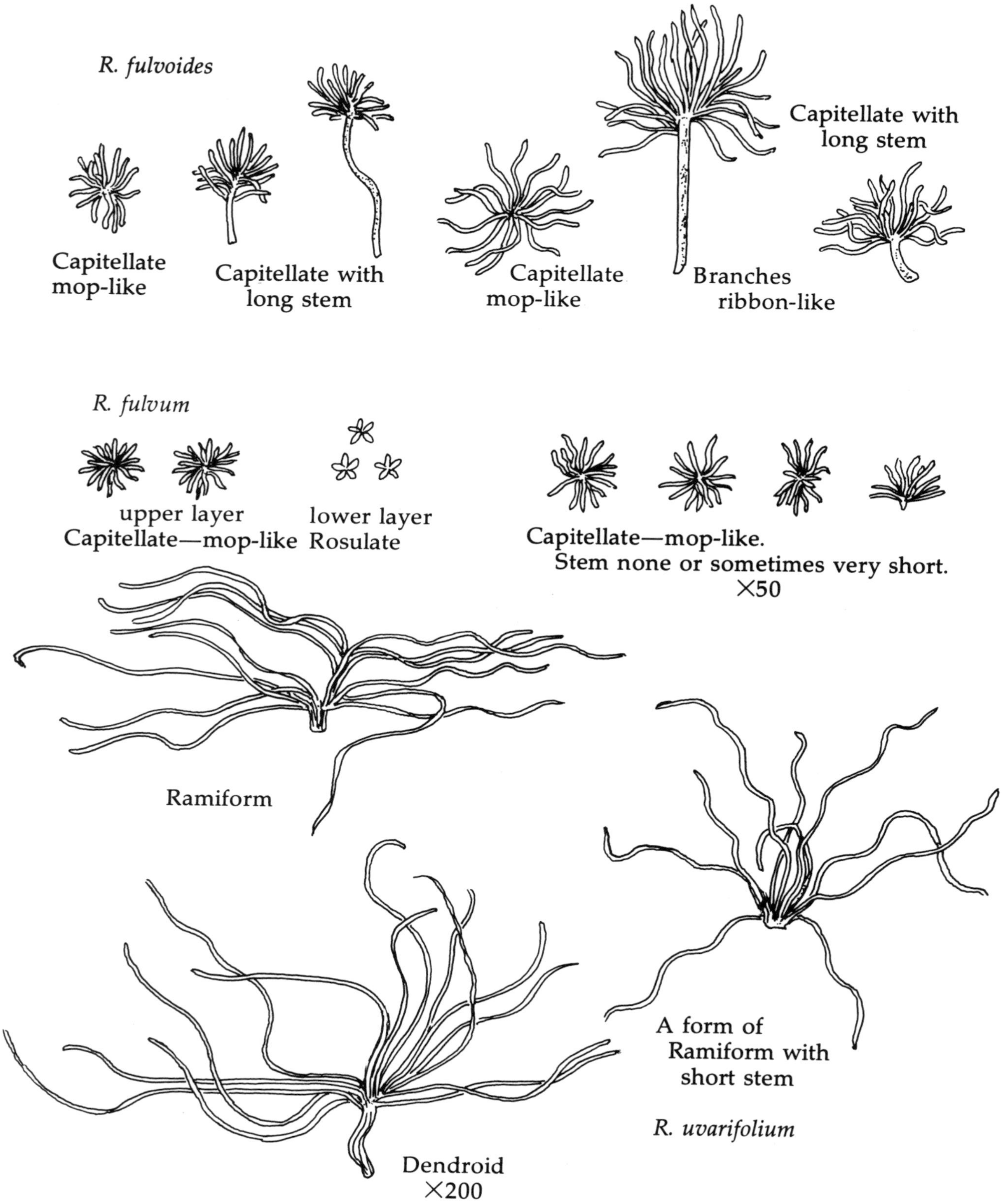

R. fulvoides

Capitellate
mop-like

Capitellate with
long stem

Capitellate with
long stem

Capitellate
mop-like

Branches
ribbon-like

R. fulvum

upper layer
Capitellate—mop-like

lower layer
Rosulate

Capitellate—mop-like.
Stem none or sometimes very short.
×50

Ramiform

Dendroid
×200

A form of
Ramiform with
short stem

R. uvarifolium

Fulvum Series contd.

R. uvarifolium contd.

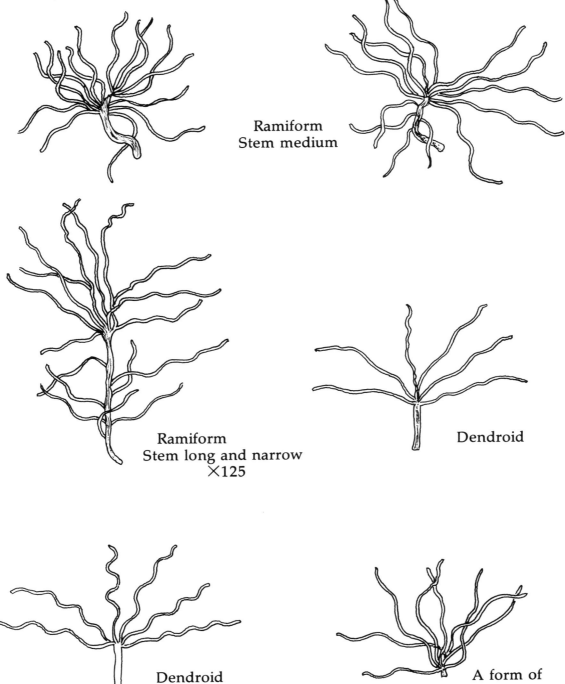

Ramiform
Stem medium

Ramiform
Stem long and narrow
×125

Dendroid

Dendroid
Branchlets curled

A form of
Ramiform
stem short

Fulvum Series contd.

R. uvarifolium cont.

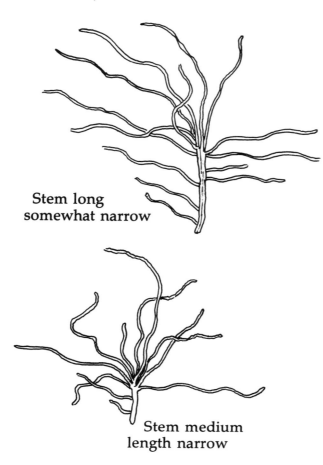

Stem long
somewhat narrow

Stem medium
length narrow

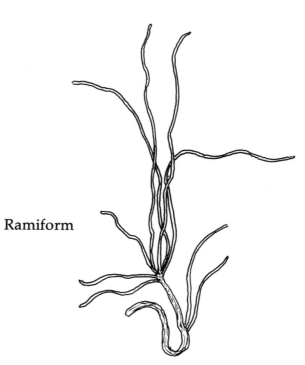

Ramiform

Stem long narrow.
Branchlets very long narrow
and thread-like.
×125

Grande Series

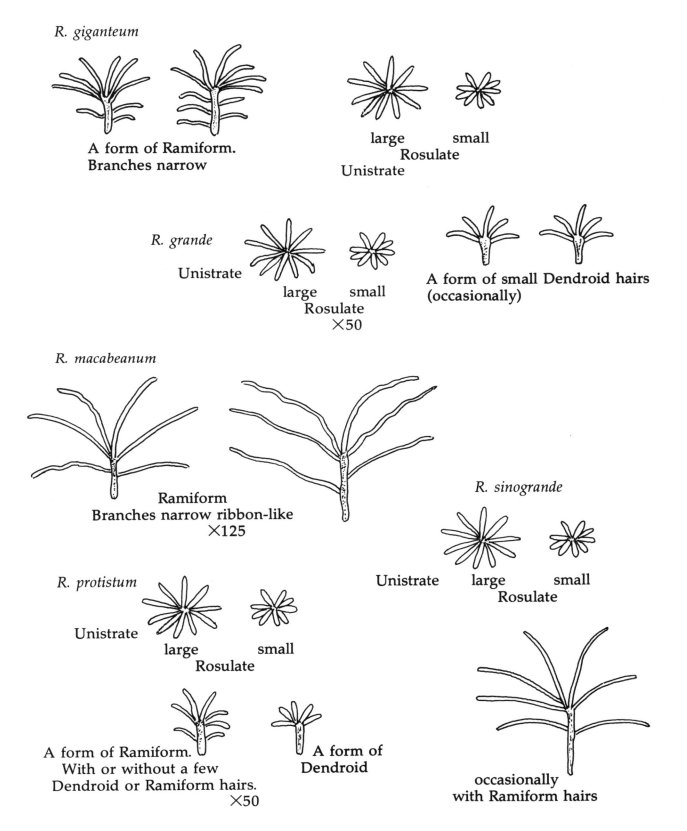

R. giganteum

A form of Ramiform.
Branches narrow

large   small
Rosulate
Unistrate

R. grande

Unistrate

large   small
Rosulate
×50

A form of small Dendroid hairs
(occasionally)

R. macabeanum

Ramiform
Branches narrow ribbon-like
×125

R. sinogrande

Unistrate   large   small
Rosulate

R. protistum

Unistrate

large   small
Rosulate

A form of Ramiform.
With or without a few
Dendroid or Ramiform hairs.
×50

A form of
Dendroid

occasionally
with Ramiform hairs

Lacteum Series

R. beesianum

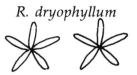

Radiate

R. dictyotum

Long-rayed

R. dignabile

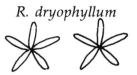

Radiate
×30

R. dryophyllum

Long-rayed
×50

R. lacteum

Radiate

R. nakotiltum

Bistrate

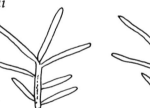

Upper layer
Long-rayed

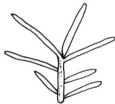

Lower layer
small Long-rayed

R. wightii

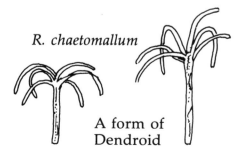

A form of Ramiform
Stem medium length, branches
ribbon-like.

R. traillianum

Neriiflorum Series

Haematodes Subseries

R. beanianum

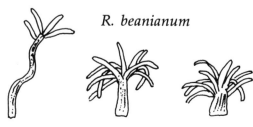

A form of Dendroid

R. chaetomallum

A form of
Dendroid

Branches ribbon-like
×50

Neriiflorum Series contd.

Haematodes Subseries contd.

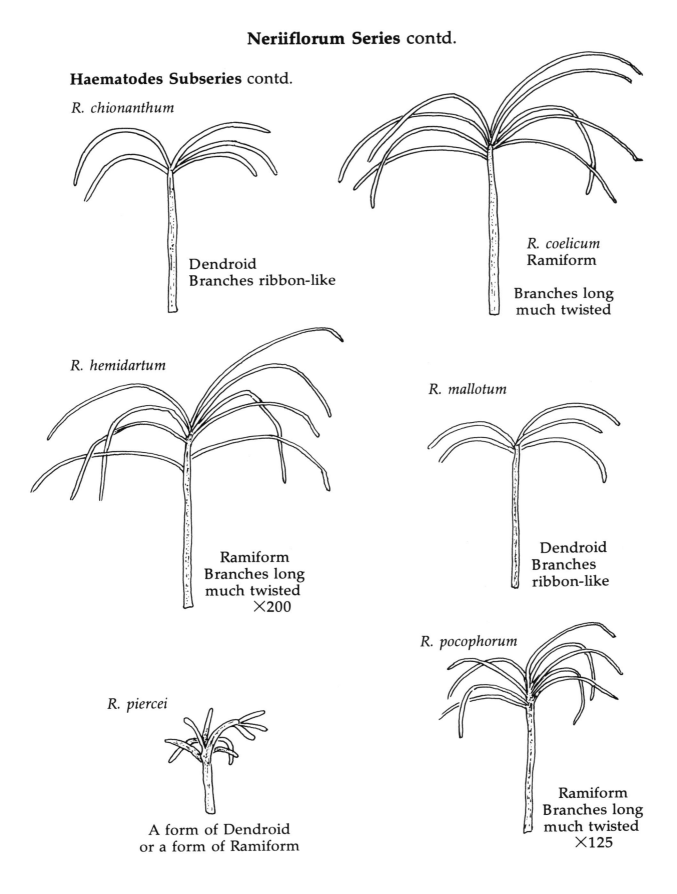

R. chionanthum

Dendroid
Branches ribbon-like

R. coelicum
Ramiform

Branches long
much twisted

R. hemidartum

Ramiform
Branches long
much twisted
×200

R. mallotum

Dendroid
Branches
ribbon-like

R. piercei

A form of Dendroid
or a form of Ramiform

R. pocophorum

Ramiform
Branches long
much twisted
×125

Neriiflorum Series contd.

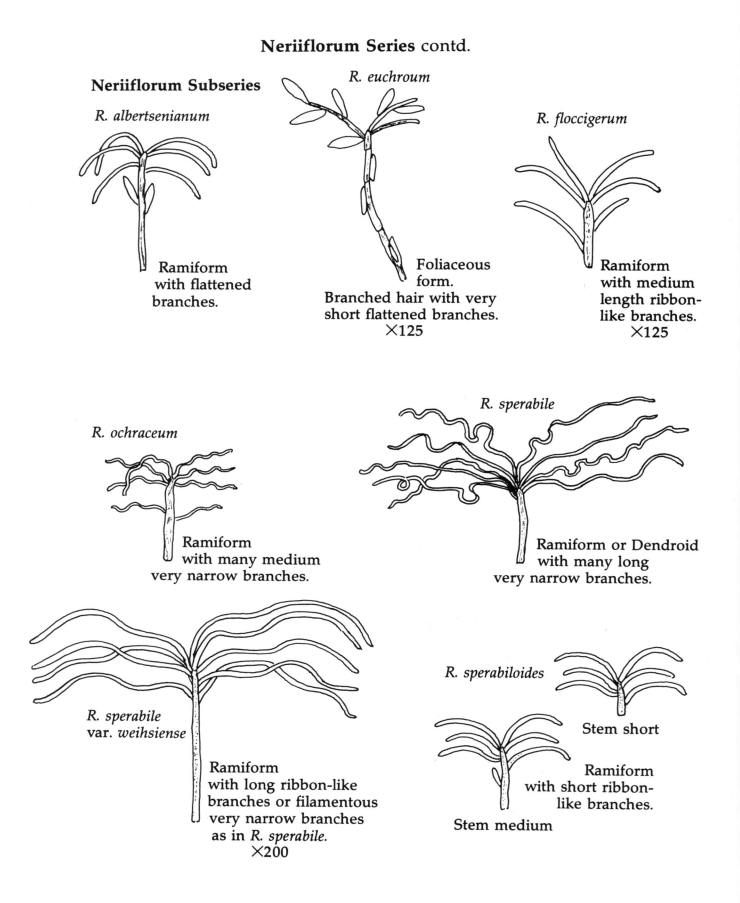

Neriiflorum Subseries

R. euchroum

R. albertsenianum

R. floccigerum

Ramiform
with flattened
branches.

Foliaceous
form.
Branched hair with very
short flattened branches.
×125

Ramiform
with medium
length ribbon-
like branches.
×125

R. ochraceum

R. sperabile

Ramiform
with many medium
very narrow branches.

Ramiform or Dendroid
with many long
very narrow branches.

R. sperabile
var. *weihsiense*

R. sperabiloides

Stem short

Ramiform
with long ribbon-like
branches or filamentous
very narrow branches
as in *R. sperabile*.
×200

Ramiform
with short ribbon-
like branches.

Stem medium

Neriiflorum Series contd.

Sanguineum Subseries

R. citriniflorum

Stem short,
a form of
Ramiform with curled branches.

R. didymum

Stem short,
a form of
Ramiform with
curled branches.

R. gymnocarpum

Stem short,
a form of
Ramiform branches long,
flat, ribbon-like not curled.
×125

R. himertum

Rosulate
Unistrate   arms long or short.

R. horaeum

Stem short
Ramiform with curled branches.
×50

Parishii Series

R. facetum

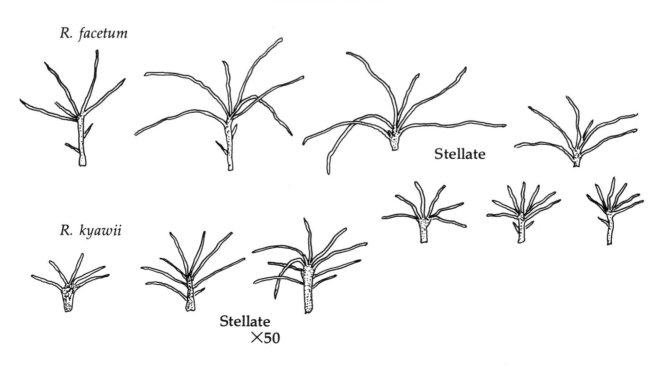

Stellate

R. kyawii

Stellate
×50

Ponticum Series

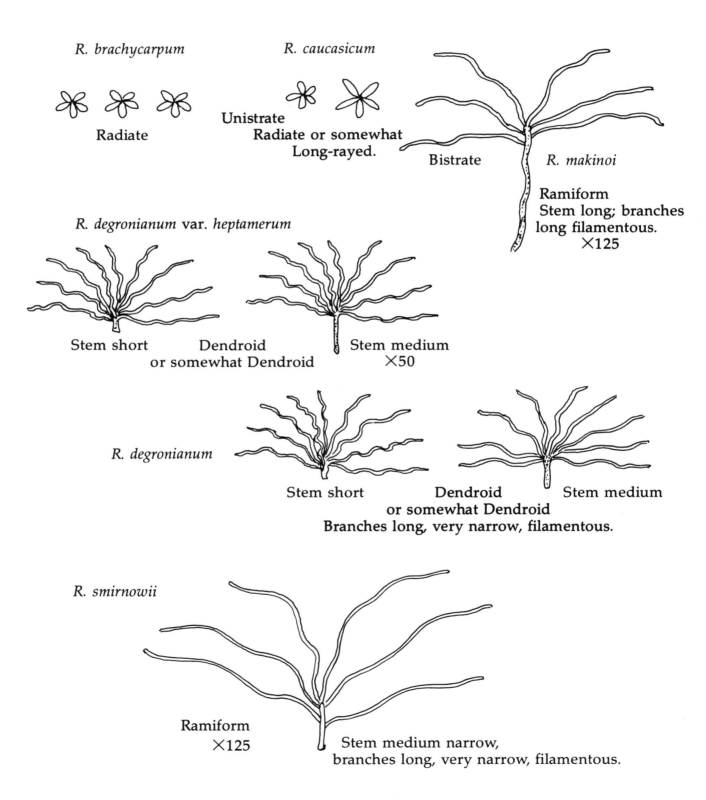

R. brachycarpum

Radiate

R. caucasicum

Unistrate
Radiate or somewhat
Long-rayed.

Bistrate   R. makinoi

Ramiform
Stem long; branches
long filamentous.
×125

R. degronianum var. heptamerum

Stem short   Dendroid   Stem medium
or somewhat Dendroid   ×50

R. degronianum

Stem short   Dendroid   Stem medium
or somewhat Dendroid
Branches long, very narrow, filamentous.

R. smirnowii

Ramiform
×125   Stem medium narrow,
branches long, very narrow, filamentous.

Ponticum Series contd.

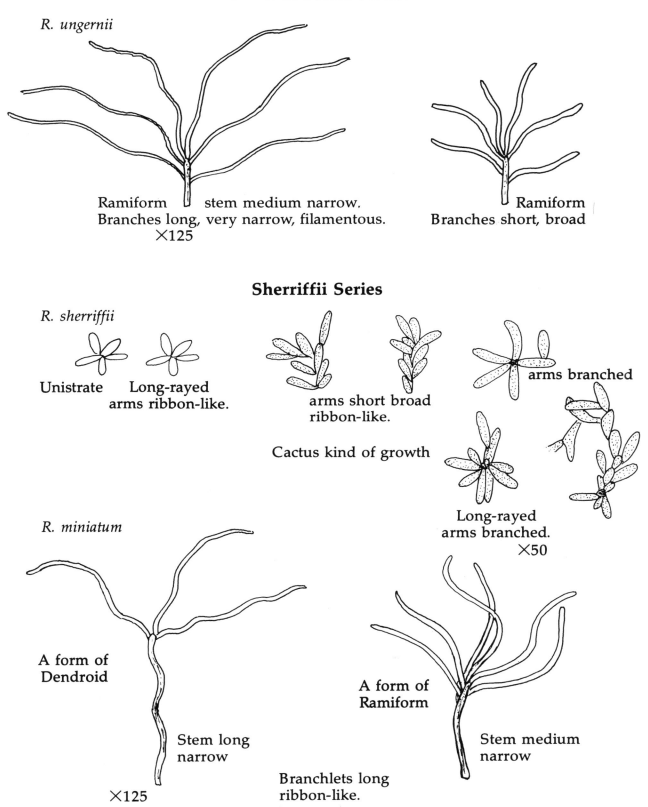

R. ungernii

Ramiform ⎍ stem medium narrow.
Branches long, very narrow, filamentous.
×125

Ramiform
Branches short, broad

Sherriffii Series

R. sherriffii

Unistrate   Long-rayed
arms ribbon-like.

arms short broad
ribbon-like.

Cactus kind of growth

arms branched

Long-rayed
arms branched.
×50

R. miniatum

A form of
Dendroid

Stem long
narrow

×125

Branchlets long
ribbon-like.

A form of
Ramiform

Stem medium
narrow

Taliense Series

Adenogynum Subseries

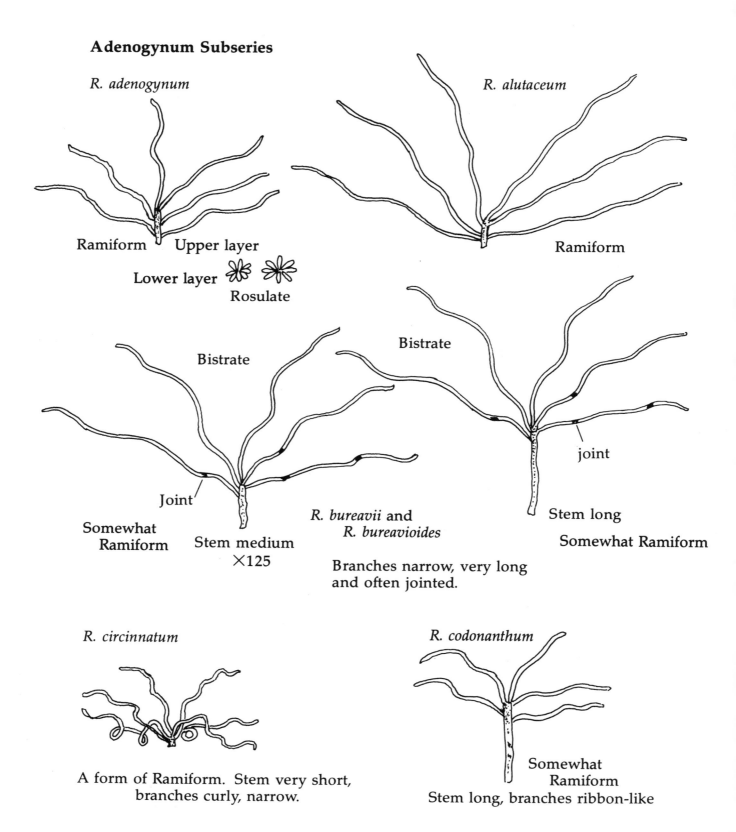

R. adenogynum

Ramiform   Upper layer

Lower layer   Rosulate

R. alutaceum

Ramiform

Bistrate

Bistrate

joint

Joint

Somewhat
Ramiform   Stem medium
×125

R. bureavii and
R. bureavioides

Branches narrow, very long
and often jointed.

Stem long

Somewhat Ramiform

R. circinnatum

A form of Ramiform. Stem very short,
branches curly, narrow.

R. codonanthum

Somewhat
Ramiform
Stem long, branches ribbon-like

Taliense Series contd.

Adenogynum Subseries contd.

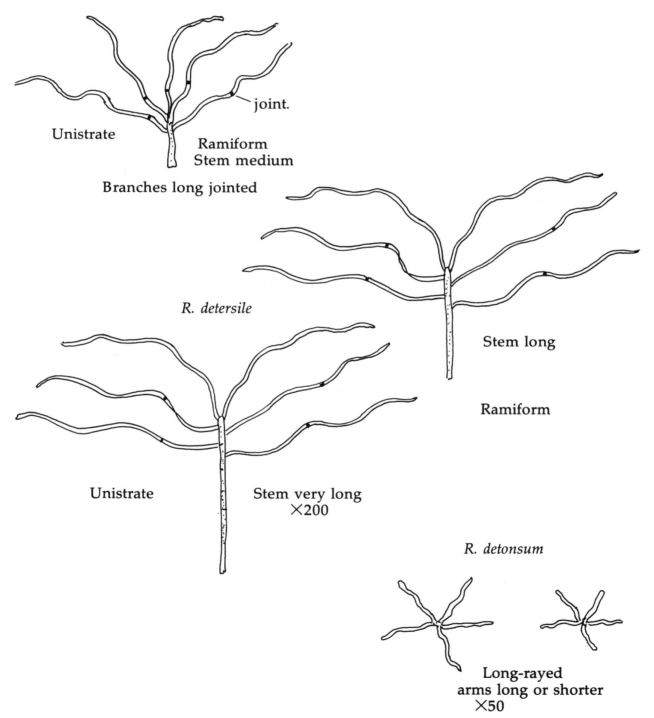

R. cruentum

Unistrate

joint.

Ramiform
Stem medium

Branches long jointed

R. detersile

Stem long

Ramiform

Unistrate

Stem very long
×200

R. detonsum

Long-rayed
arms long or shorter
×50

Taliense Series contd.

Adenogynum Subseries contd.

R. elegantulum

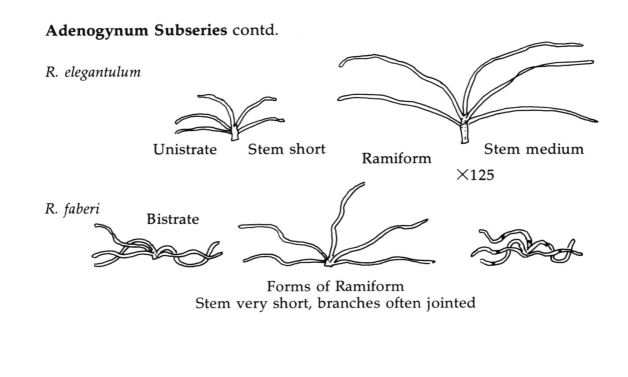

Unistrate   Stem short   Ramiform   Stem medium
×125

R. faberi   Bistrate

Forms of Ramiform
Stem very short, branches often jointed

R. mimetes

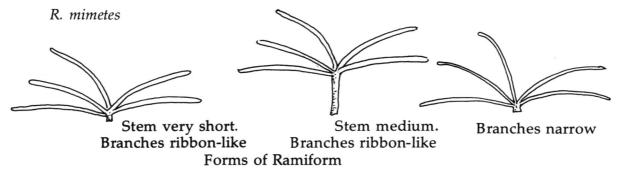

Stem very short.   Stem medium.   Branches narrow
Branches ribbon-like   Branches ribbon-like
Forms of Ramiform

R. prattii

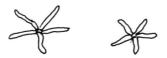

Unistrate Long-rayed
×40

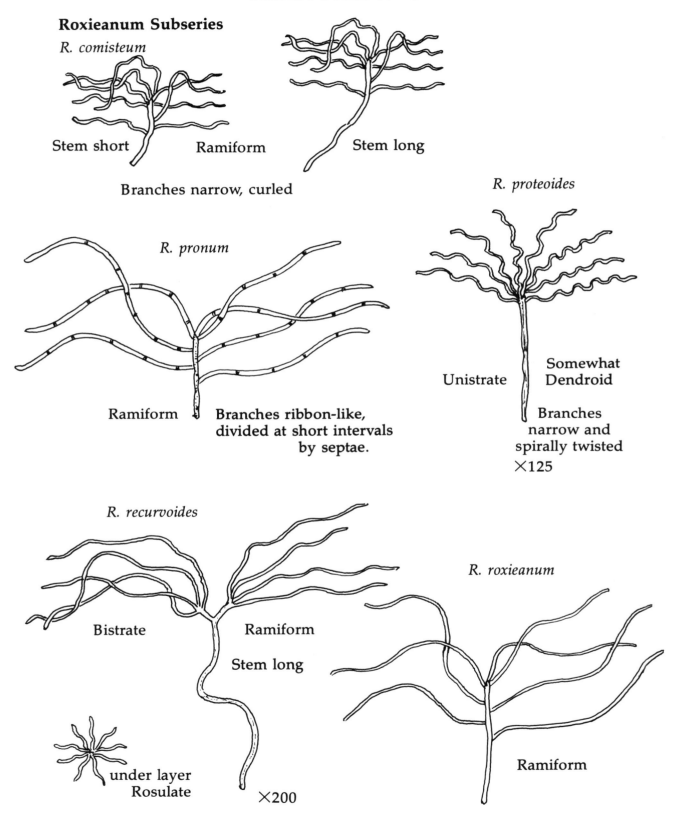

Taliense Series contd.

Roxieanum Subseries

R. comisteum

Stem short   Ramiform   Stem long

Branches narrow, curled

R. proteoides

R. pronum

Ramiform   Branches ribbon-like,
divided at short intervals
by septae.

Unistrate   Somewhat
Dendroid

Branches
narrow and
spirally twisted
×125

R. recurvoides

R. roxieanum

Bistrate   Ramiform

Stem long

under layer
Rosulate   ×200

Ramiform

Taliense Series contd.

Roxieanum Subseries contd.

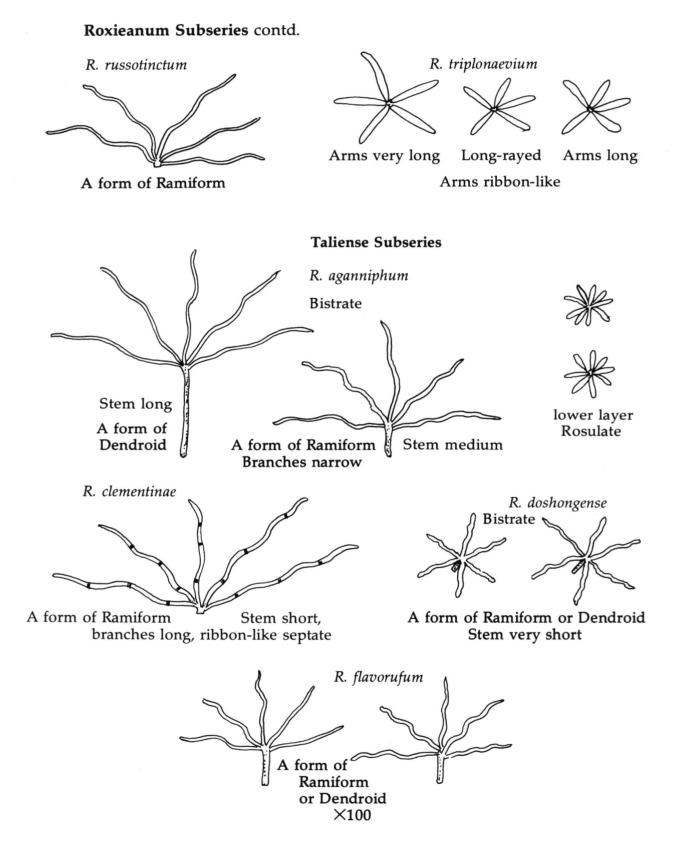

R. russotinctum

A form of Ramiform

R. triplonaevium

Arms very long   Long-rayed   Arms long

Arms ribbon-like

Taliense Subseries

R. aganniphum

Bistrate

Stem long

A form of
Dendroid

A form of Ramiform   Stem medium
Branches narrow

lower layer
Rosulate

R. clementinae

A form of Ramiform   Stem short,
branches long, ribbon-like septate

R. doshongense
Bistrate

A form of Ramiform or Dendroid
Stem very short

R. flavorufum

A form of
Ramiform
or Dendroid
×100

Taliense Series contd.

Taliense Subseries contd.

R. sphaeroblastum

Bistrate

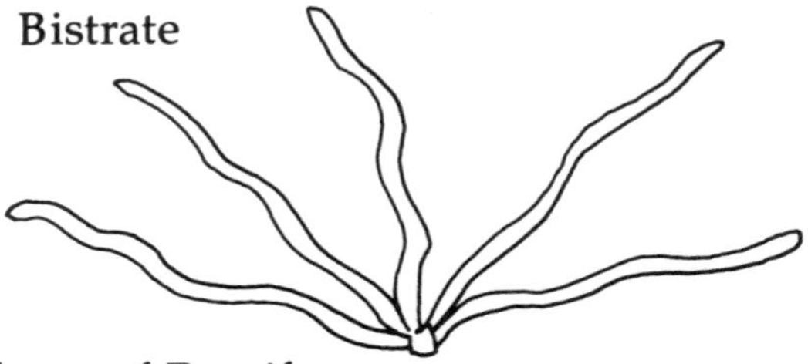

A form of Ramiform
Stem very short,
branches long, ribbon-like.

R. taliense

Bistrate

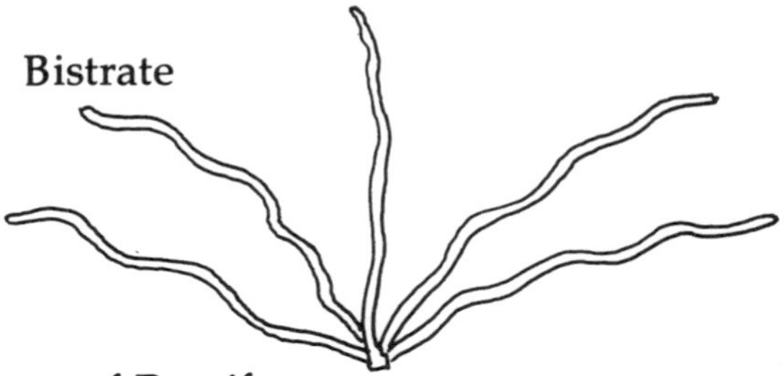

A form of Ramiform
Stem very short,
branches long, somewhat ribbon-like.

Wasonii Subseries

R. coeloneurum
Bistrate

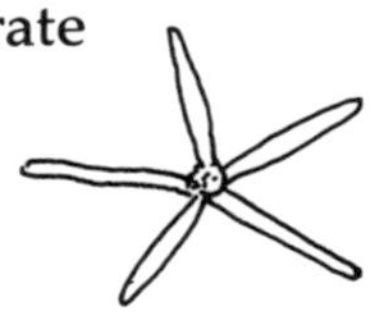

Upper layer—a form of Stellate.
Arms long, somewhat broad ribbon-like.

R. inopinum

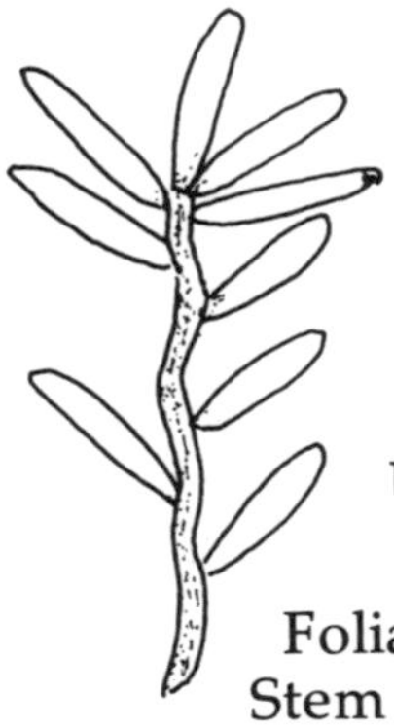

Unistrate

Foliaceous
Stem long,
branches broad, flat, ribbon-like
×100

R. wasonii

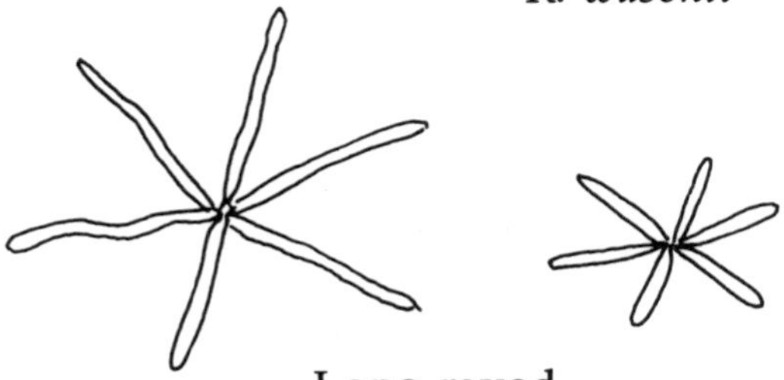

Long-rayed
Arms long, somewhat broad
ribbon-like
×50

A cultivated specimen
Arms short

Taliense Series contd.

Wasonii Subseries contd.

R. weldianum

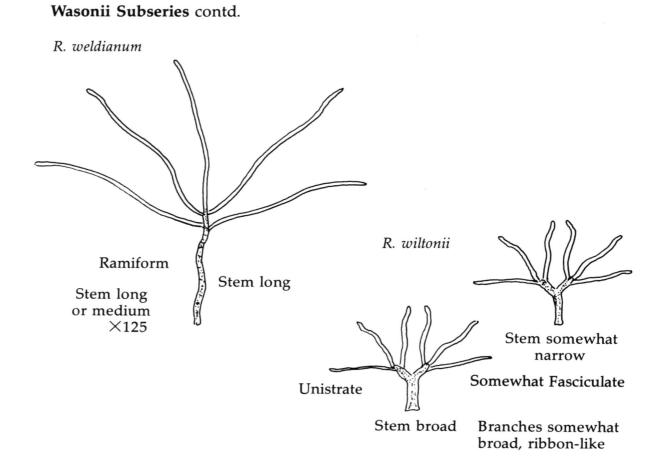

Ramiform

Stem long
or medium
×125

Stem long

R. wiltonii

Stem somewhat
narrow

Unistrate

Somewhat Fasciculate

Stem broad

Branches somewhat
broad, ribbon-like

Thomsonii Series

Thomsonii Subseries

R. hookeri

Fasciculate
×40

Hardiness

H4 Hardy anywhere in the British Isles.
H3 Hardy in the west, east and south, and inland but requires shelter.
H2 Suitable for sheltered gardens in the west coast.
H1 Usually a greenhouse plant.

Award Systems

BRITISH AWARDS

First Class Certificate. F.C.C. Given on the recommendation of the Rhododendron and Camellia Committee to rhododendrons of great excellence. Given at Shows or after trial at Wisley.

Award of Merit. A.M. Given on the recommendation of the Rhododendron and Camellia Committee to rhododendrons which are meritorious. Given at Shows or after trial at Wisley.

Preliminary Commendation. P.C. Given on the recommendation of the Rhododendron and Camellia Committee to a new plant of promise, whether a new introduction from abroad or of garden origin. Given at Shows only.

Award of Garden Merit. A.G.M. Given on the recommendation of the Award of Garden Merit Committee to plants which either are well known to the Council, Committees, Garden Staff and Fellows or have been tested and grown at Wisley in the same manner as they would have been grown in the open in a private garden, are of good constitution, and have proved to be excellent for ordinary garden decoration.

AMERICAN AWARDS

Preliminary Award. P.A. Given for a cut flower truss, with foliage, exhibited at a Show, evaluated by three official judges.

Award of Excellence. A.E. Given by a panel of three judges for a complete plant exhibiting superior foliage, flowers, and growth habit.

Test Garden Certificate. T.G.C. Given to a rhododendron which has been propagated vegetatively and seen in flower by three judges for at least two years in one of the recognised test gardens of the American Rhododendron Society.

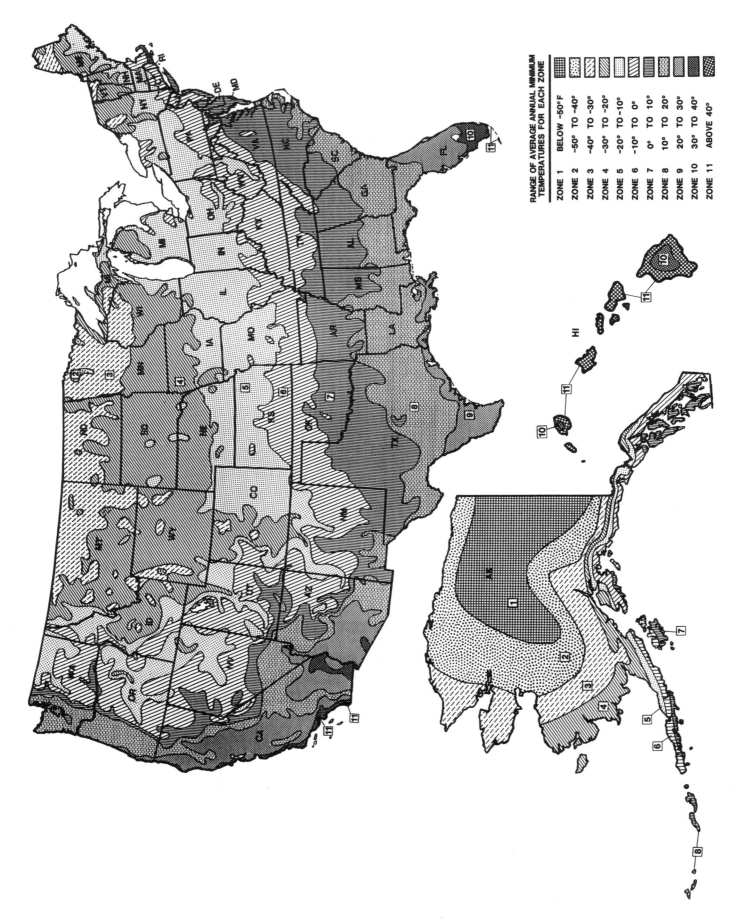

RANGE OF AVERAGE ANNUAL MINIMUM
TEMPERATURES FOR EACH ZONE

ZONE 1   BELOW -50°F
ZONE 2   -50° TO -40°
ZONE 3   -40° TO -30°
ZONE 4   -30° TO -20°
ZONE 5   -20° TO -10°
ZONE 6   -10° TO 0°
ZONE 7   0° TO 10°
ZONE 8   10° TO 20°
ZONE 9   20° TO 30°
ZONE 10   30° TO 40°
ZONE 11   ABOVE 40°

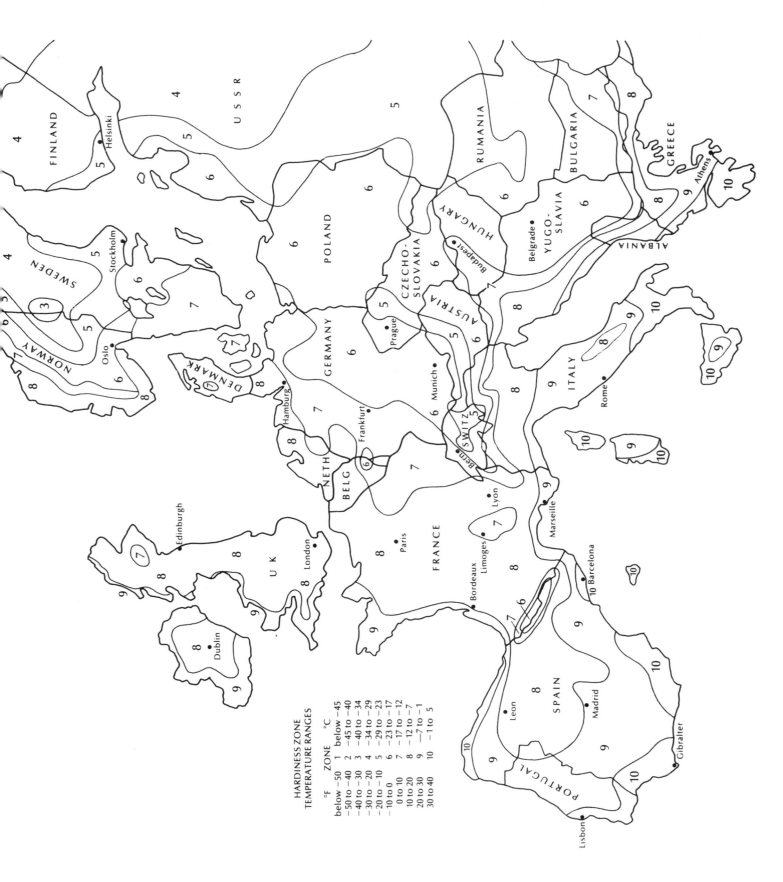

HARDINESS ZONE
TEMPERATURE RANGES

°F	ZONE	°C
below −50	1	below −45
−50 to −40	2	−45 to −40
−40 to −30	3	−40 to −34
−30 to −20	4	−34 to −29
−20 to −10	5	−29 to −23
−10 to 0	6	−23 to −17
0 to 10	7	−17 to −12
10 to 20	8	−12 to −7
20 to 30	9	−7 to −1
30 to 40	10	−1 to 5

SOVIET UNION

Heilongjiang

Mongolia

3

Jilin

4

4

Xinjiang

Liaoning

5

Gansu
Kansu

Inner Mongolia

PEOPLE'S REPUBLIC OF CHINA

4

5

KOREA

5

Hebei

6

Ningxia

Shanxi

Shandong
Shantung

JAP

Qinghai

5

5

6

7

4

Shaanxi
Shenshi

Jiangsu
Kiangsi

Tibet

6

Henan

Anhui

8

NEPAL

5

7

9

Hubei
Hupeh

SIKKIM

6

Sichuan
Szechuan

Zhejiang
Chekiang

9

BHUTAN

7

8

INDIA

ASSAM

Hunan

Jiangxi

BANGLADESH

9

Guizhou
Kweichow

Fujian
Fukien

BURMA

9

10

Yunnan

Guangxi
Kwangshi

Guangdong

TAIWAN

Tropic of Ca

10

VIETNAM

Kwangtung

LAOS

HAINAN

PHILIPPINES

THAILAND

CAMBODIA

HARDINESS ZONE
TEMPERATURE RANGES

°F	ZONE	°C
below −50	1	below −45
−50 to −40	2	−45 to −40
−40 to −30	3	−40 to −34
−30 to −20	4	−34 to −29
−20 to −10	5	−29 to −23
−10 to 0	6	−23 to −17
0 to 10	7	−17 to −12
10 to 20	8	−12 to −7
20 to 30	9	—7 to −1
30 to 40	10	−1 to 5

N. BORNEO

INDONESIA

MALAYSIA

MALAYSIA

List of Elepidote Rhododendron Species and Varieties in their Series

(Q = not known to be in cultivation)

ARBOREUM SERIES

arboreum *Sm.*
arboreum *Sm.* forma album *Wall.*
arboreum *Sm.* forma roseum (*Lindl.*) *Tagg*
campbelliae *Hook.f.*
cinnamomeum *Wall. ex G. Don.*
delavayi *Franch.*
delavayi *Franch.* var. albotomentosum *Davidian,* var. nov.
delavayi *Franch.* var. album *W. Watson*
lanigerum *Tagg*
lanigerum *Tagg* var. silvaticum (*Cowan*) *Davidian,* comb. nov.
nilagiricum *Zenker*
niveum *Hook. f.*
peramoenum *Balf. f. et Forrest*
zeylanicum *Booth*

ARGYROPHYLLUM SERIES

argyrophyllum *Franch.*
argyrophyllum *Franch.* var. cupulare *Rehd. et Wils.*
argyrophyllum *Franch.* var. nankingense *Cowan*
argyrophyllum *Franch.* var. omeiense *Rehd. et Wils.* Q
chienianum *Fang* Q
coryanum *Tagg et Forrest*
denudatum *Lévl.* Q
farinosum *Lévl.* Q
floribundum *Franch.*
formosanum *Hemsl.*
haofui *Chun et Fang* Q
hunnewellianum *Rehd. et Wils.*
hypoglaucum *Hemsl.*
insigne *Hemsl. et Wils.*
longipes *Rehd. et Wils.* Q
pingianum *Fang*
ririei *Hemsl. et Wils.*
rockii *Wils.* Q
simiarum *Hance*
thayerianum *Rehd. et Wils.*
youngae *Fang* Q

AURICULATUM SERIES

auriculatum *Hemsl.*

BARBATUM SERIES
BARBATUM SUBSERIES

argipeplum *Balf. f. et Cooper*
barbatum *Wall. ex G. Don*
erosum *Cowan*
exasperatum *Tagg*
imberbe *Hutch.*
macrosmithii *Davidian,* nom. nov.
shepherdii *Nutt.*

CRINIGERUM SUBSERIES

bainbridgeanum *Tagg et Forrest*
crinigerum *Franch.*
crinigerum *Franch.* var. euadenium *Tagg*

GLISCHRUM SUBSERIES

adenosum *Davidian*
diphrocalyx *Balf. f.*
glischroides *Tagg et Forrest*
glischroides *Tagg et Forrest* var. arachnoideum *Tagg et Forrest*
glischrum *Balf. f. et W.W. Sm.*
habrotrichum *Balf. f. et W.W. Sm.*
hirtipes *Tagg*
rude *Tagg et Forrest*
spilotum *Balf. f. et Farrer*
vesiculiferum *Tagg*

MACULIFERUM SUBSERIES

longesquamatum *Schneider*
maculiferum *Franch.*
monosematum *Hutch.*
morii *Hayata*
nankotaisanense *Hayata* Q
pachytrichum *Franch.*
pseudochrysanthum *Hayata*
strigillosum *Franch.*

CAMPANULATUM SERIES
CAMPANULATUM SUBSERIES

aeruginosum *Hook f.*
campanulatum *D. Don*
heftii *Davidian,* sp. nov.
wallichii *Hook. f.*

LANATUM SUBSERIES

flinckii *Davidian*
lanatum *Hook. f.*
luciferum (*Cowan*) *Cowan*
poluninii *Davidian*, sp. nov.
tsariense *Cowan*
tsariense *Cowan* var. magnum *Davidian*, var. nov.
tsariense *Cowan* var. trimoense *Davidian*, var. nov.

FALCONERI SERIES

arizelum *Balf. f. et Forrest*
arizelum *Balf. f. et Forrest* var. rubicosum *Cowan et Davidian*
basilicum *Balf. f. et W.W. Sm.*
coriaceum *Franch.*
eximium *Nutt.*
falconeri *Hook. f.*
fictolacteum *Balf. f.*
fictolacteum *Balf. f.* var. miniforme *Davidian*, var. nov.
galactinum *Balf. f. ex Tagg*
hodgsonii *Hook. f.*
preptum *Balf. f. et Forrest*
rex *Lévl.*
rothschildii *Davidian*
semnoides *Tagg et Forrest*
sinofalconeri *Balf. f.* Q

FORTUNEI SERIES
CALOPHYTUM SUBSERIES

asterochnoum *Diels* Q
calophytum *Franch.*
openshawianum *Rehd. et Wils.* Q

DAVIDII SUBSERIES

davidii *Franch.* Q
planetum *Balf. f.*
praevernum *Hutch.*
sutchuenense *Franch.*
sutchuenense *Franch.* var. geraldii *Hutch.*

FORTUNEI SUBSERIES

decorum *Franch.*
diaprepes *Balf. f. et W.W. Sm.*
discolor *Franch.*
faithae *Chun* Q
fortunei *Lindl.*
glanduliferum *Franch.* Q
hemsleyanum *Wils.*
houlstonii *Hemsl. et Wils.*
huianum *Fang* Q
platypodum *Diels* Q
serotinum *Hutch.*
vernicosum *Franch.*
vernicosum *Franch.* forma araliiforme (*Balf. f. et Forrest*) *Tagg*

vernicosum *Franch.* forma euanthum (*Balf. f. et W.W. Sm.*) *Tagg*
vernicosum *Franch.* forma rhantum (*Balf. f. et W.W. Sm.*) *Tagg*
vernicosum *Franch.* forma sheltonae (*Hemsl. et Wils.*) *Tagg*

GRIFFITHIANUM SUBSERIES

griffithianum *Wight*

ORBICULARE SUBSERIES

cardiobasis *Sleumer*
orbiculare *Decaisne*

OREODOXA SUBSERIES

erubescens *Hutch.*
fargesii *Franch.*
kwangfuense *Chun et Fang* Q
oreodoxa *Franch.*
praeteritum *Hutch.*

FULGENS SERIES

fulgens *Hook. f.*
succothii *Davidian*

FULVUM SERIES

fulvoides *Balf. f. et Forrest*
fulvum *Balf. f. et W.W. Sm.*
uvarifolium *Diels*
uvarifolium *Diels* var. griseum *Cowan*

GRANDE SERIES

giganteum *Forrest ex Tagg*
grande *Wight*
macabeanum *Watt ex Balf. f.*
magnificum *Ward*
montroseanum *Davidian*
praestans *Balf. f. et W.W. Sm.*
protistum *Balf. f. et Forrest*
pudorosum *Cowan*
sidereum *Balf. f.*
sinogrande *Balf. f. et W.W. Sm.*
sinogrande *Balf. f. et W.W. Sm.* var. boreale *Tagg et Forrest*
watsonii *Hemsl. et Wils.*

GRIERSONIANUM SERIES

griersonianum *Balf. f. et Forrest*

IRRORATUM SERIES

aberconwayi *Cowan*
adroserum *Balf. f. et Forrest*
agastum *Balf. f. et W.W. Sm.*
anhweiense *Wils.*
annae *Franch.*
anthosphaerum *Diels*

anthosphaerum *Diels* var. eritimum (*Balf. f. et W.W. Sm.*) *Davidian*, comb. nov.
araiophyllum *Balf. f. et W.W. Sm.*
brevinerve *Chun et Fang* Q
ceraceum *Balf. f. et W.W. Sm.*
cerochitum *Balf. f. et Forrest* Q
epapillatum *Balf. f. et Cooper* Q
hardingii *Forrest*
irroratum *Franch.*
kendrickii *Nutt.*
laxiflorum *Balf. f. et Forrest*
leptopeplum *Balf. f. et Forrest*
lukiangense *Franch.*
mengtszense *Balf. f. et W.W. Sm.* Q
ningyuenense *Hand.-Mazz.* Q
papillatum *Balf. f. et Cooper* Q
pennivenium *Balf. f. et Forrest*
pogonostylum *Balf. f. et W.W. Sm.* Q
ramsdenianum *Cowan*
spanotrichum *Balf. f. et W.W. Sm.* Q
tanastylum *Balf. f. et Ward*

LACTEUM SERIES

aberrans *Tagg et Forrest* Q
agglutinatum *Balf. f. et Forrest*
beesianum *Diels*
colletum *Balf. f. et Forrest*
dictyotum *Balf. f. ex Tagg*
dignabile *Cowan* Q
dryophyllum *Balf. f. et Forrest*
dumosulum *Balf. f. et Forrest*
lacteum *Franch.*
nakotiltum *Balf. f. et Forrest*
phaeochrysum *Balf. f. et W.W. Sm.*
pomense *Cowan et Davidian* Q
przewalskii *Maxim.*
traillianum *Forrest et W.W. Sm.*
wightii *Hook. f.*

NERIIFLORUM SERIES
FORRESTII SUBSERIES

chamaethomsonii (*Tagg et Forrest*) *Cowan et Davidian*
chamaethomsonii (*Tagg et Forrest*) *Cowan et Davidian* var. chamaethauma (*Tagg*) *Cowan et Davidian*
erastum *Balf. f. et Forrest* Q
forrestii *Balf. f. ex Diels*
forrestii *Balf. f. ex Diels* var. repens (*Balf. f. et Forrest*) *Cowan et Davidian*
forrestii *Balf. f. ex Diels* var. tumescens *Cowan et Davidian*
porphyrophyllum *Balf. f. et Forrest* Q
pyrrhoanthum *Balf. f.*
trilectorum *Cowan* Q

HAEMATODES SUBSERIES

beanianum *Cowan*
catacosmum *Balf. f. ex Tagg*
chaetomallum *Balf. f. et Forrest*
chaetomallum *Balf. f. et Forrest* var. chamaephytum *Cowan* Q
chaetomallum *Balf. f. et Forrest* var. hemigymnum *Tagg et Forrest*
chaetomallum *Balf. f. et Forrest* var. xanthanthum *Tagg et Forrest*
chionanthum *Tagg et Forrest*
coelicum *Balf. f. et Farrer*
haematodes *Franch.*
hemidartum *Balf. f. ex Tagg*
hillieri *Davidian*
mallotum *Balf. f. et Ward*
piercei *Davidian*
pocophorum *Balf. f. ex Tagg*

NERIIFLORUM SUBSERIES

albertsenianum *Forrest*
bijiangense *T.L. Ming* Q
dimitrum *Balf. f. et Forrest*
euchroum *Balf. f. et Ward* Q
floccigerum *Franch.*
floccigerum *Franch.* var. appropinquans *Tagg et Forrest*
neriiflorum *Franch.*
neriiflorum *Franch.* var. agetum (*Balf. f. et Forrest*) *Davidian*, comb. nov.
neriiflorum *Franch.* var. euchaites (*Balf. f. et Forrest*) *Davidian*, comb. nov.
ochraceum *Rehd. et Wils.* Q
phaedropum *Balf. f. et Farrer*
sperabile *Balf. f. et Farrer*
sperabile *Balf. f. et Farrer* var. weihsiense *Tagg et Forrest*
sperabiloides *Tagg et Forrest*

SANGUINEUM SUBSERIES

aperantum *Balf. f. et Ward*
aperantum *Balf. f. et Ward* var. subpilosum *Cowan*
apodectum *Balf. f. et W.W. Sm.*
brunneifolium *Balf. f. et Forrest*
citriniflorum *Balf. f. et Forrest*
cloiophorum *Balf. f. et Forrest*
cloiophorum *Balf. f. et Forrest* var. leucopetalum (*Balf. f. et Forrest*) *Davidian*, comb. nov.
cloiophorum *Balf. f. et Forrest* var. mannophorum (*Balf. f. et Forrest*) *Davidian*, comb. nov. Q
cloiophorum *Balf. f. et Forrest* var. roseotinctum (*Balf. f. et Forrest*) *Davidian*, comb. nov.
dichroanthum *Diels*
didymum *Balf. f. et Forrest*

eudoxum *Balf. f. et Forrest*
fulvastrum *Balf. f. et Forrest*
fulvastrum *Balf. f. et Forrest* var. gilvum (*Cowan*) *Davidian,* comb. nov.
glaphyrum *Balf. f. et Forrest*
glaphyrum *Balf. f. et Forrest* var. dealbatum (*Cowan*) *Davidian,* comb. nov.
gymnocarpum *Balf. f. ex Tagg*
haemaleum *Balf. f. et Forrest*
haemaleum *Balf. f. et Forrest* var. atrorubrum (*Cowan*) *Davidian,* comb. nov.
haemaleum *Balf. f. et Forrest* var. mesaeum (*Balf. f. ex Cowan*) *Davidian,* comb. nov.
herpesticum *Balf. f. et Ward*
himertum *Balf. f. et Forrest*
horaeum *Balf. f. et Forrest*
horaeum *Balf. f. et Forrest* var. rubens (*Cowan*) *Davidian,* comb. nov.
mesopolium *Balf. f. et Forrest*
microgynum *Balf. f. et Forrest*
parmulatum *Cowan*
sanguineum *Franch.*
sanguineum *Franch.* var. consanguineum (*Cowan*) *Davidian,* comb. nov.
sanguineum *Franch.* var. didymoides *Tagg et Forrest*
sanguineum *Franch.* var. sanguineoides (*Cowan*) *Davidian,* comb. nov.
scyphocalyx *Balf. f. et Forrest*
scyphocalyx *Balf. f. et Forrest* var. septendrionale *Tagg ex Davidian,* var. nov.
temenium *Balf. f. et Forrest*
trichomiscum *Balf. f. et Forrest*

PARISHII SERIES

agapetum *Balf. f. et Ward*
cookeanum *Davidian*
elliottii *Watt. ex Brandis*
facetum *Balf. f. et Ward*
kyawii *Lace et W.W. Sm.*
parishii *C.B. Clarke* Q
schistocalyx *Balf. f. et Forrest*
sikangense *Fang*
venator *Tagg*

PONTICUM SERIES

adenopodum *Franch.*
aureum *Georgi*
brachycarpum *D. Don ex G. Don*
brachycarpum *D. Don ex G. Don* var. tigerstedtii (*Nitzelius*) *Davidian,* comb. nov.
catawbiense *Michaux*
caucasicum *Pallas*
degronianum *Carr.*
degronianum *Carr.* var. heptamerum (*Maxim.*) *Sealy*
fauriei *Franch.*

hyperythrum *Hayata*
hypopitys *Pojarkova* Q
macrophyllum *D. Don ex G. Don*
makinoi *Tagg*
maximum *Linn.*
ponticum *Linn.*
ponticum *Linn.* forma album (*Sweet*) *Zab.*
smirnowii *Trautvetter*
ungernii *Trautvetter*
yakushimanum *Nakai*

SHERRIFFII SERIES

miniatum *Cowan* Q
sherriffii *Cowan*

TALIENSE SERIES
ADENOGYNUM SUBSERIES

adenogynum *Diels*
alutaceum *Balf. f. et W.W. Sm.*
balfourianum *Diels*
balfourianum *Diels* var. aganniphoides *Tagg et Forrest*
bureavii *Franch.*
bureavioides *Balf. f.*
circinnatum *Cowan et Ward* Q
codonanthum *Balf. f. et Forrest*
cruentum *Lévl.* Q
detersile *Franch.* Q
detonsum *Balf. f. et Forrest*
elegantulum *Tagg et Forrest*
faberi *Hemsley*
mimetes *Tagg et Forrest*
mimetes *Tagg et Forrest* var. simulans *Tagg et Forrest*
nigroglandulosum *Nitzelius*
prattii *Franch.*
wuense *Balf. f.* Q

ROXIEANUM SUBSERIES

bathyphyllum *Balf. f. et Forrest*
comisteum *Balf. f. et Forrest*
cucullatum *Hand.-Mazz.*
globigerum *Balf. f. et Forrest*
iodes *Balf. f. et Forrest*
lampropeplum *Balf. f. et Forrest*
pronum *Tagg et Forrest*
proteoides *Balf. f. et W.W. Sm.*
recurvoides *Tagg et Ward*
roxieanum *Forrest*
roxieanum *Forrest* var. oreonastes (*Balf. f. et Forrest*) *Davidian,* comb. nov.
roxieanum *Forrest* var. parvum *Davidian,* var. nov.

roxieanum *Forrest* var. recurvum (*Balf. f. et Forrest*) *Davidian*, comb. nov.
russotinctum *Balf. f. et Forrest* Q
triplonaevium *Balf. f. et Forrest*
tritifolium *Balf. f. et Forrest*

TALIENSE SUBSERIES

aganniphum *Balf. f. et Ward*
clementinae *Forrest*
doshongense *Tagg*
flavorufum *Balf. f. et Forrest*
glaucopeplum *Balf. f. et Forrest*
principis *Bur. et Franch.* Q
purdomii *Rehd. et Wils.*
sphaeroblastum *Balf. f. et Forrest*
taliense *Franch.*
vellereum *Hutch.*

WASONII SUBSERIES

coeloneurum *Diels* Q
inopinum *Balf. f.*
pachysanthum *Hayata*
paradoxum *Balf.f.*
rufum *Batalin*
wasonii *Hemsl. et Wils.*
wasonii *Hemsl. et Wils.* var. rhododactylum (*Hort.*) *Davidian*, comb. nov.
weldianum *Rehd. et Wils.*
wiltonii *Hemsl. et Wils.*

THOMSONII SERIES
CAMPYLOCARPUM SUBSERIES

callimorphum *Balf. f. et W.W. Sm.*
caloxanthum *Balf. f. et Farrer*
campylocarpum *Hook. f.*
myiagrum *Balf. f. et Forrest*
panteumorphum *Balf. f. et W.W. Sm.*
telopeum *Balf. f. et Forrest*

CERASINUM SUBSERIES

bonvalotii *Bur. et Franch.* Q
cerasinum *Tagg*

SELENSE SUBSERIES

calvescens *Balf. f. et Forrest*
dasycladoides *Hand.-Mazz.* Q
dasycladum *Balf. f. et W.W. Sm.*
erythrocalyx *Balf. f. et Forrest*
esetulosum *Balf. f. et Forrest*
eurysiphon *Tagg et Forrest*
jucundum *Balf. f. et W.W. Sm.*
martinianum *Balf. f. et Forrest*
selense *Franch.*
selense *Franch.* var. pagophilum (*Balf. f. et Ward*) *Cowan et Davidian*
selense *Franch.* var. probum (*Balf f. et Forrest*) *Cowan et Davidian*
setiferum *Balf. f. et Forrest*

vestitum *Tagg et Forrest*

SOULIEI SUBSERIES

litiense *Balf. f. et Forrest*
puralbum *Balf. f. et W.W. Sm.*
souliei *Franch.*
wardii *W.W. Sm.*

THOMSONII SUBSERIES

cyanocarpum (*Franch.*) *W.W. Sm.*
eclecteum *Balf. f. et Forrest*
eclecteum *Balf. f. et Forrest* var. bellatulum *Balf. f. ex Tagg*
eclecteum *Balf. f. et Forrest* var brachyandrum (*Balf. f. et Forrest*) *Tagg*
hookeri *Nutt.*
hylaeum *Balf. f. et Farrer*
lopsangianum *Cowan*
meddianum *Forrest*
meddianum *Forrest* var. atrokermesinum *Tagg*
populare *Cowan*
stewartianum *Diels*
stewartianum *Diels* var. tantulum *Cowan et Davidian*
thomsonii *Hook. f.*
thomsonii *Hook. f.* var. candelabrum (*Hook. f.*) *C.B. Clarke*
viscidifolium *Davidian*

WILLIAMSIANUM SUBSERIES

williamsianum *Rehd. et Wils.*

AZALEASTRUM

ALBIFLORUM SERIES

albiflorum *W.J. Hooker*

OVATUM SERIES

hongkongense *Hutch.*
leptothrium *Balf. f. et Forrest*
ovatum (*Lindl.*) *Maxim.*
vialii *Delavay et Franch.* Q

SEMIBARBATUM SERIES

semibarbatum *Maxim.*

STAMINEUM SERIES

cavaleriei *Lévl.* Q
championae *W.J. Hooker*
ellipticum *Maxim.*
esquirolii *Lévl.* Q
feddei *Lévl.* Q
hancockii *Hemsl.* Q
henryi *Hance* Q
latoucheae *Franch.* Q
mackenzianum *G. Forrest*

moulmainense *W.J. Hooker*
pectinatum *Hutch.*
siamense *Diels* Q
stamineum *Franch.*
taiense *Hutch.* Q
tutcherae *Hemsl. et Wils.* Q
wilsonae *Hemsl. et Wils.*

CAMTSCHATICUM

CAMTSCHATICUM SERIES

camtschaticum *Pallas*
camtschaticum *Pallas* var. albiflorum *Koid-zumi*
glandulosum (*Standley ex Small*) *Millais* Q
redowskianum *Maxim.* Q

Moorland in the Shweli-Salwin Divide, western Yunnan. Photo J. F. Rock.

Introduction to Keys and Descriptions

Included in Volume III are a Key to the Series and Subseries followed by Descriptions of Species. It contains 11 Series arranged in alphabetical order. Each Series comprises general characters, distribution, affinity with other Series, a Key to its species, and descriptions of the species.

Each species is given a detailed description based on herbarium specimens and plants in cultivation, with the more important characteristics appearing in italics. The description is followed by notes on the species in relation to the discoverer, collectors, distribution, native habitats and altitudes, affinity with other species, an account of the plant in cultivation, awards, hardiness, and flowering months.

KEY TO THE SERIES AND SUBSERIES

1. Flowers borne on special buds.
    2. Flowers in terminal buds.
        3. Corolla 7–10- (or sometimes 6-) lobed; stamens 12–25 (rarely 10); ovary 6–18-celled.
            4. Corolla usually 8–10-lobed, ventricose campanulate; stamens usually 16–20; truss many-flowered 15–30; leaves very large.
                5. Indumentum on the under surface of the leaves thick, woolly, hairs usually Cup-, Vase- or Bowl-shaped . . . *Falconeri Series*
                5. Indumentum on the under surface of the leaves thin, plastered, or absent, hairs Rosulate (except in *R. macabeanum,* thick woolly, hairs Ramiform) . . . *Grande Series*
            4. Corolla 6–7-lobed, usually funnel-campanulate; stamens often 14; truss usually few-flowered 2–15; leaves medium to large.
                6. Under surface of the leaves glabrous, eglandular, (or rarely with a few hairs or glands).
                    7. Inflorescence 5–15-flowered; medium or large often broadly upright shrubs or trees; leaves (laminae) large, 5–30 cm. long.
                        8. Leaves oblong, oblong-oval, oval or orbicular; ovary glandular or eglandular; corolla 5–7 cm. long . . . . *Fortunei Series* (part)
                        8. Leaves oblong; ovary eglandular; corolla 4–5 cm. long . . . . *R. anthosphaerum*
                    7. Inflorescence usually 2–3-flowered; small or sometimes medium-sized compact rounded shrub; leaves (laminae) smaller, 1.5–4.2 cm. long . . . . *Williamsianum Subseries*
                6. Under surface of the leaves densely hairy with isolated flexuous long hairs and glands or densely covered with a continuous indumentum of hairs.
                    9. Under surface of the leaves densely hairy with isolated flexuous long hairs and glands; foliage-buds and flower-buds conical tapered, the outer scales with long tips; ovary densely glandular with short-stalked glands; style glandular throughout to the tip . . . . *Auriculatum Series*
                    9. Under surface of the leaves densely covered with a continuous indumentum of hairs; foliage-buds and flower-buds rounded, the outer scales rounded; ovary eglandular; style eglandular.
                        10. Leaves oblong, oblanceolate or oblong-lanceolate; ovary densely tomentose. From Japan . . . . *R. degronianum* var. *heptamerum*
                        10. Leaves oval, oblong-oval, ovate, elliptic or oblong-elliptic; ovary glabrous. From Yunnan and Sichuan . . . . *R. clementinae*
        3. Corolla 5-lobed; stamens 5–10; ovary 5–10-celled.
            11. Inflorescence very compact, 15–30-flowered; corolla usually with 5 nectar pouches at the base.
                12. Branchlets and petioles not bristly, not bristly-glandular.

13. Leaves usually lanceolate, oblong-lanceolate or oblanceolate.
  14. Indumentum on the under surface of the leaves thin plastered or sometimes thin woolly; corolla with 5 nectar pouches at the base; inflorescence 10–50-flowered; trees or large shrubs . . . . *Arboreum Series*
  14. Indumentum on the under surface of the leaves usually thick woolly; corolla without nectar pouches at the base; inflorescence 6–20-flowered; usually small or medium shrubs . . . . *Roxieanum Subseries*
13. Leaves oval, oblong-oval, obovate or oblong-obovate.
  15. Flowers crimson, deep scarlet or scarlet; indumentum on the under surface of the leaves thick, woolly or absent; ovary glabrous . . . . *Fulgens Series*
  15. Flowers white, white tinged pink, or yellow; indumentum on the under surface of the leaves thin, suède-like; ovary often densely or moderately tomentose . . . . *Lacteum Series*
                    (part)
12. Branchlets and petioles bristly and bristly-glandular . . . . . *Barbatum Series*
11. Inflorescence lax, not compact, 3–15-flowered; corolla usually without nectar pouches at the base.
  16. Under surface of the leaves covered with a thick or sometimes thin woolly, continuous indumentum of hairs.
    17. Ovary glabrous, eglandular.
      18. Hairs of the indumentum Capitellate, mop-like (except in *R. uvarifolium*, Dendroid form).
        19. Leaves usually oblanceolate or oblong-obovate; inflorescence compact or fairly compact, globose (8–20-flowered). From Yunnan, Sichuan, Tibet, and east Burma . . . . *Fulvum Series*
        19. Leaves oval, elliptic, obovate or oblong-oval; inflorescence racemose umbel, lax (6–12-flowered). From Nepal, Sikkim, Bhutan, Kashmir, Punjab . . . . *R. campanulatum*
      18. Hairs of the indumentum Ramiform, Dendroid, Radiate or dichotomously branched, not Capitellate (not mop-like).
        20. Inflorescence candelabroid, pedicels long, very unequal, varying much in length, elongating in fruit, rhachis elongate; corolla often widely funnel-shaped or funnel-campanulate . . . . *Ponticum Series*
                    (part)
        20. Inflorescence racemose umbel, somewhat rounded, pedicels short, somewhat equal, elongating little in fruit; rhachis short; corolla usually campanulate.
          21. Indumentum suède-like, continuous, hairs Dendroid, or consisting of numerous individual hair tufts, hairs dichotomously branched. . . . *Campanulatum Subseries*
          21. Indumentum not suède-like; thin, hairs Long-rayed or Radiate, or thick woolly hairs Ramiform.
            22. Indumentum thin, hairs usually Long-rayed or Radiate; ovary densely or moderately tomentose or glabrous . . . . *Lacteum Series*
                    (part)
            22. Indumentum thick woolly or spongy (except in *R. doshongense*, thin plastered); hairs Ramiform; ovary glabrous . . . . *Taliense Subseries*

    17. Ovary densely tomentose, glandular or eglandular.

23. Flower-bud and foliage-bud long, tapered, the outer scales with long tapering tips; young shoots, petioles, rhachis of the inflorescence, and pedicels setulose-glandular; corolla funnel-campanulate . . . . *Griersonianum Series*

23. Flower-bud and foliage-bud rounded or oblong, the outer scales with rounded or obtuse tips; young shoots, petioles, rhachis of the inflorescence, and pedicels not setulose-glandular; corolla campanulate or tubular-campanulate.

    24. Hairs of the indumentum Long-rayed or Radiate (except in *R. miniatum*, Fasciculate).

        25. Flowers white, white tinged pink, pink, creamy-white or yellow.

            26. Indumentum unistrate, hairs Radiate or Long-rayed; leaves oval, ovate, elliptic, oblong, oblanceolate or lanceolate.

                27. Indumentum thin, hairs Radiate or Long-rayed; leaves oval, oblong-oval, oblong-lanceolate or lanceolate, base rounded, obtuse or tapered . . . . *Lacteum Series* (part)

                27. Indumentum thick, woolly, hairs Long-rayed, often with somewhat broad ribbon-like arms; leaves ovate, base rounded or cordulate . . . . *R. wasonii*

            26. Indumentum bistrate, upper layer Long-rayed with long ribbon-like arms (except in *R. russotinctum*, Ramiform), often detersile, falling off in large or small patches, under layer Rosulate or Radiate; leaves lanceolate, oblanceolate, oblong-lanceolate or rarely oblong . . . . *Roxieanum Subseries*

        25. Flowers deep carmine . . . . *Sherriffii Series*

    24. Hairs of the indumentum Rosulate or Ramiform or a form of Ramiform or Dendroid.

        28. Indumentum plastered or thin tomentose or a thin veil of hairs; hairs of the indumentum Rosulate, or sometimes Ramiform or a form of Ramiform.

            29. Corolla white, pink, rose or purple, without nectar pouches at the base (except in *R. ririei* with 5 nectar pouches); inflorescence 4–20- or sometimes 30-flowered; calyx 1–2 mm. or rarely 3–5 mm. long; shrubs or trees 92 cm.–12 m. (3–39 ft.) high . . . . *Argyrophyllum Series*

            29. Corolla black-crimson, crimson, scarlet, orange, yellow, rose, pink, white, with 5 nectar pouches at the base; inflorescence 2–8-flowered; calyx 1 mm.–2.5 cm. long; small or medium-sized shrubs, 30 cm.–2.44 m. (1–8 ft.) or sometimes 8–15 cm. (3–6 in.) high . . . . *Sanguineum Subseries*

        28. Indumentum thick, woolly; hairs Dendroid or Ramiform.

            30. Branchlets, petioles, pedicels, calyx and ovaries densely tomentose, not bristly, eglandular; hairs of the indumentum often Dendroid; calyx minute 0.5–2 mm. long; inflorescence usually few-flowered. Usually from the Himalayas . . . . *Lanatum Subseries*

            30. Branchlets, petioles, pedicels, calyx and ovaries glabrous or densely tomentose or bristly, glandular or eglandular; hairs of the indumentum Ramiform or Dendroid; calyx 1 mm.–2.5 cm. long; inflorescence many- to few-flowered. Usually from Tibet, Sichuan, Yunnan and Burma.

31. Corolla deep crimson, crimson, scarlet, or sometimes deep rose, yellow or white, with 5 nectar pouches at the base; hairs of the indumentum Ramiform or Dendroid........ .... *Neriiflorum Series*

31. Corolla white, creamy, yellow, pink, rose, pinkish-purple or reddish-purple, without nectar pouches at the base; hairs of the indumentum Ramiform. .... *Taliense Series*

16. Under surface of the adult leaves, except sometimes midrib, glabrous or sometimes sprinkled with isolated hairs.

32. Hairs on the ovaries, branchlets, petioles and under surface of the leaves Stellate .... *Parishii Series*

32. Hairs on the ovaries, branchlets, petioles and under surface of the leaves not Stellate.

33. Midrib on the under surface of the leaves densely or moderately floccose .... *Maculiferum Subseries*

33. Midrib on the under surface of the leaves glabrous.

34. Low-growing or prostrate or dwarf shrubs, 3–60 cm. (1 in.–2 ft.) high; inflorescence 1–4-flowered.

35. Leaves not in whorls on the branchlets, under surface pale glaucous green; leaf-bud scales usually deciduous; inflorescence usually 1–2-flowered; prostrate or creeping or compact shrubs, 3–60 cm. (1 in.–2 ft.) high .... *Forrestii Subseries*

35. Leaves clustered in whorls at the end of the branchlets, under surface glaucous white; leaf-bud scales markedly persistent; inflorescence 4–5-flowered; compact shrub usually 60 cm. (2 ft.) high........................... *R. aperantum*

34. Medium-sized or large shrubs or trees, 92 cm.–4.58 m. (3–15 ft.) high; inflorescence 4–30-flowered.

36. Inflorescence candelabroid, pedicels long, very unequal, varying much in length, elongating in fruit, rhachis elongate; corolla often widely funnel-shaped or funnel-campanulate............................. *Ponticum Series* (part)

36. Inflorescence racemose umbel, somewhat rounded, pedicels usually short, somewhat equal, elongating little in fruit; rhachis short; corolla campanulate or tubular-campanulate.

37. Leaves large, laminae 10–30 cm. long; corolla large 5–7 cm. long........................... *Fortunei Series* (part)
Davidii Subseries
Griffithianum Subseries

37. Leaves smaller, laminae 3–8 cm. long; corolla smaller, 3–5 cm. long.

38. Leaves lanceolate, oblong-lanceolate, oblanceolate or oblong-elliptic, apex usually acute or acuminate; corolla tubular-campanulate.

39. Ovary conoid, apex truncate; corolla without or with 5 nectar pouches at the base, white, pink, rose, purple-crimson, crimson-rose, scarlet, crimson, crimson-magenta........ .... *Irroratum Series*

39. Ovary slender, tapering to the base of the style; corolla with 5 nectar pouches at the base, crimson........ *Neriiflorum Subseries*

          38. Leaves orbicular, oval, ovate, elliptic or oblong, apex rounded or broadly obtuse; corolla usually broadly campanulate, campanulate, bowl- or saucer-shaped. . . . . *Thomsonii Series*

2. Flowers in axillary buds . . . . *Azaleastrum*

    40. Leaves deciduous.

        41. Stamens 10, unequal; corolla rotate-campanulate or campanulate; branchlets and petioles moderately or rather densely hairy with long, appressed pointed hairs . . . . *Albiflorum Series*

        41. Stamens 5, very unequal, dimorphic; corolla rotate; branchlets and petioles rather densely or moderately pubescent . . . .
. . . . *Semibarbatum Series*

    40. Leaves evergreen.

        42. Stamens 5; corolla rotate somewhat flat, or almost bowl-shaped, or tubular slightly widened towards the top, 1.6–3.2 cm. long; calyx 2–9 mm. long; ovary ovate or conoid, 1–3 mm. long; capsule ovoid or conoid, 4–6 mm. long; inflorescence 1–2-flowered. . . . . *Ovatum Series*

        42. Stamens 10, rarely 8, 11 or 13; corolla tubular-funnel-shaped, 2.5–7.8 cm. long; calyx minute, 0.5–1 mm. long; ovary slender, 4 mm.–1.1 cm. long; capsule slender or sometimes oblong, 2–6.5 cm. long; inflorescence 1–8-flowered . . . . *Stamineum Series*

1. Flowers borne on leafy shoots of current year. . . . . *Camtschaticum*
Camtschaticum Series

NERIIFLORUM SERIES

General characters: creeping or prostrate or small or medium-sized or large shrubs, rarely small trees, 3 cm.–6 m. (1 in.–20 ft.) high. Leaves evergreen, linear-lanceolate, lanceolate, oblong to obovate, orbicular, lamina 0.6–16 cm. long, 0.4–8 cm. broad; under surface with a thick, woolly continuous or sometimes interrupted indumentum or with a thin continuous plastered indumentum or with a thin veil of hairs or glabrous; petiole 0.1–3.6 cm. long. Inflorescence terminal, a racemose umbel of 1–20 flowers; pedicel 0.5–3.6 cm. long, densely or moderately tomentose or glabrous, not bristly or sometimes bristly, glandular or eglandular. Calyx 5-lobed or rarely an undulate rim, 0.1–2.5 cm. long. Corolla tubular-campanulate or campanulate, 2–5.3 cm. long, deep crimson, black-crimson, scarlet, rose, pink, yellow, orange or white, 5 nectar pouches at the base; lobes 5. Stamens 10. Ovary conoid, oblong or ovoid, 0.2–1 cm. long, 5–10-celled, densely or moderately tomentose or sometimes glabrous, densely or moderately glandular or eglandular; style glabrous or sometimes tomentose at the base. Capsule oblong, ovoid, conoid or slender, 0.6–3 cm. long, 0.3–1.2 cm. broad, densely or moderately tomentose or glabrous, not bristly or sometimes bristly, moderately or densely glandular or eglandular.

Distribution. South-east and east Tibet, north-west, west, mid-west and north-east Yunnan, western Sichuan, north, north-east and Upper Burma, Burma-Tibet Frontier, Assam and Bhutan.

This large Series consists of dwarf, small, medium-sized, and large shrubs or rarely trees. It varies considerably in habit and height of growth, in leaf shape and size, in the presence or absence of indumentum of hairs on the lower surface of the leaves, in the colour of the flowers, and in the glandular or eglandular features. Accordingly, the Series is divided into four Subseries, namely, Forrestii Subseries, Haematodes Subseries, Neriiflorum Subseries, and Sanguineum Subseries.

KEY TO THE SUBSERIES

A. Dwarf creeping or prostrate or compact shrubs, usually 3–60 cm. (1 in.–2 ft.) high; leaves small, laminae usually 0.6–5 cm. long, under surface glabrous or with a thin discontinuous indumentum of hairs; inflorescence usually 1–3-flowered . . . . *Forrestii Subseries*

A. Large, medium-sized or small shrubs, rarely trees, usually 75 cm.–6 m. (2½–20 ft.) high; leaves large, laminae usually 5–16 cm. long, under surface with a thick woolly or thin plastered continuous indumentum or sometimes with a thin veil of hairs or glabrous; inflorescence usually 3–20-flowered.

   B. Ovary usually slender, tapered to the base of the style; capsule slender, usually curved; leaves oblong, oblong-lanceolate, lanceolate or oblanceolate . . . . *Neriiflorum Subseries*

   B. Ovary conoid, ovoid or oblong, truncate; capsule conoid, ovoid or oblong, straight; leaves obovate, oblong-obovate, oblong to lanceolate.

      C. Under surface of the leaves with a thick woolly continuous or sometimes interrupted indumentum; leaves broadly obovate or oblong-obovate, 1.6–8 cm. broad; indumentum on the under surface brown, dark brown or cinnamon-coloured; corolla fleshy . . . . . . *Haematodes Subseries*

      C. Under surface of the leaves usually with a thin plastered continuous indumentum or with a thin veil of hairs or glabrous; leaves obovate, oblong-obovate, oblong, oblanceolate, oblong-lanceolate or lanceolate, 0.6–4.5 cm. broad; indumentum on the under surface white, fawn, brown or dark brown; corolla thin or fleshy . . . . . *Sanguineum Subseries*

FORRESTII SUBSERIES

General characters: *dwarf, creeping or prostrate or compact* shrubs, *3–92 cm. (1 in.–3 ft.)* high, branchlets glandular or eglandular. Leaves obovate, orbicular, elliptic, oblong, lanceolate, oblanceolate, linear-lanceolate, lamina 0.6–9 cm. long, 0.4–4 cm. broad; *under surface glabrous or with a thin discontinuous indumentum of hairs;* petiole 0.2–1.6 cm. long, glandular or eglandular. Inflorescence 1–5-flowered; pedicel 0.6–3 cm. long, glandular or eglandular. Calyx 5-lobed, 0.5–5 mm. long, eglandular or sometimes glandular. Corolla tubular-campanulate or sometimes campanulate, 2.2–5 cm. long, deep crimson, crimson, scarlet, rose-crimson, carmine, rose or yellow, 5 nectar pouches at the base; lobes 5. Stamens 10. Ovary conoid, oblong or ovoid, truncate, 3–6 mm. long, 5-celled, densely or moderately tomentose or glabrous, densely or moderately glandular or eglandular; style glabrous. Capsule oblong, 0.8–2.5 cm. long, 3–8 mm. broad, straight, densely or moderately tomentose or glabrous, moderately or densely glandular or eglandular.

KEY TO THE SPECIES

A. Creeping or prostrate shrub, or sometimes dome-shaped, the outer branches creeping, usually 3–30 cm. (1 in.–1 ft.) high.
> **B.** Flowers crimson, scarlet, carmine, pale or deep rose; leaf base usually not decurrent on the petiole; ovary usually densely tomentose; stamens often glabrous.
>> **C.** Flowers crimson, scarlet or carmine; leaves obovate, orbicular, elliptic or oblong-elliptic .... *forrestii*
>> **C.** Flowers pale or deep rose; leaves lanceolate or linear-lanceolate to elliptic.
>>> **D.** Leaves usually lanceolate, oblong, oblong-obovate or elliptic, usually 1–2.6 cm. broad.................... *porphyrophyllum*
>>> **D.** Leaves narrowly lanceolate or oblanceolate or linear-lanceolate, 4–8 mm. broad....................................... *erastum*
> **B.** Flowers pale yellow or pale lemon-yellow, flushed pale pink; leaf base decurrent on the petiole; ovary glabrous; stamens densely puberulous towards the base .... *trilectorum*

A. Compact or broadly upright shrubs, 30–92 cm. (1–3 ft.) high.
> **E.** Broadly upright or compact shrub up to 60 cm. (2 ft.) across; leaves obovate, oblong-obovate or oblong; inflorescence 1–2—or sometimes 3–5-flowered.. *chamaethomsonii*
> **E.** Very compact spreading shrub up to 92 cm. (3 ft.) across; leaves usually elliptic or oblong-elliptic; inflorescence 4–5-flowered ..... *pyrrhoanthum*

DESCRIPTION OF THE SPECIES

R. chamaethomsonii (Tagg et Forrest) Cowan et Davidian in The Rhododendron Year Book (1951–52) 70.
> Syn. *R. repens* Balf. f. et Forrest var. *chamaethomsonii* Tagg et Forrest in Notes Roy. Bot. Gard., Edin., Vol. XLI (1931) 206; The Sp. of Rhod., (1930) 514.

A broadly upright shrub with ascending stems or a compact shrub, *30–92 cm. (1–3 ft.) high,* or *rarely semi-prostrate* 15 cm. (6 in.) high, branchlets glabrous or hairy, glandular with short-stalked glands or eglandular, leaf-bud scales persistent or deciduous. *Leaves* obovate, oblong-obovate or oblong, *lamina rigid, 3–9 cm. long,* 2–4 cm. broad, apex rounded or rarely obtuse, emarginate or not emarginate, mucronate, base obtuse or rounded; upper surface dark green, glaucous or not glaucous, glabrous or with vestiges of hairs, midrib grooved, primary veins 8–12 on each side, deeply impressed; margin recurved or flat; *under surface pale glaucous green or pale green, glabrous or with vestiges of hairs or with a thin discontinuous indumentum of hairs,* glandular with sessile or short-stalked glands or eglandular, midrib raised, primary veins slightly raised; petiole 0.4–1.6 cm. long, hairy or glabrous, glandular with short-stalked glands or eglandular. *Inflorescence* terminal, umbellate, *1–5-flowered,* bud-scales persistent at the base of the pedicel during flowering or deciduous; rhachis 0.5–1 mm. long, hairy or glabrous, glandular with short-stalked glands or eglandular; pedicel 0.8–3 cm. long, glabrous or sometimes hairy, glandular with short-stalked glands or eglandular. *Calyx* 5-lobed, 1–5 mm. long, lobes rounded or ovate, outside glabrous or rarely hairy, eglandular, margin hairy or glabrous, glandular with short-stalked glands or eglandular. *Corolla* tubular-campanulate, 2.6–5 cm. long, deep-crimson or crimson, with or without darker spots, 5 fleshy nectar pouches at the base; lobes 5, 0.8–1.2 cm. long, 1.3–2.7 cm. broad, rounded, emarginate. *Stamens* 10, unequal, shorter than the corolla, 1.5–3.4 cm. long; filaments glabrous or puberulous at the base. *Gynoecium* 1.8–4.5 cm. long; ovary conoid, 4–6 mm.

long, 5-celled, moderately or densely tomentose or glabrous, moderately or densely glandular with short-stalked glands or eglandular; style glabrous or rarely hairy at the base, eglandular. *Capsule* oblong, 1.3–2.3 cm. long, 4–8 mm. broad, straight, tomentose or glabrous, glandular with short- or medium-stalked glands, calyx-lobes persistent.

R. chamaethomsonii was discovered by Forrest in July 1921 in the Salwin-Kiu Chiang Divide, eastern Tibet. Further gatherings by him, Rock, Ludlow, Sherriff, Elliot, and Kingdon-Ward show that the plant is distributed in east and south-east Tibet, northwest Yunnan, and North Burma. It grows in moist rocky moorland, on ledges of cliffs, on boulders, on rocks, and in dense thickets, at elevations of 3,355–4,575 m. (11,000–15,000 ft.).

The main diagnostic feature of this plant is its broadly upright or compact rounded habit of growth up to 3 feet high. In this respect it is readily distinguished from *R. forrestii* and its varieties. It further differs usually in its larger leaves. It is also allied to *R. pyrrhoanthum* but is distinguished usually by its habit of growth, by the shape and smaller size of the leaves, and usually by the 1–2-flowered inflorescence.

R. chamaethomsonii was first introduced by Forrest in 1922 (No. 21723—the Type number, and No. 21900). It was reintroduced by Rock under four different seed numbers (Nos. 11036, 11169, 11597, 22050). Kingdon-Ward sent seeds from North Burma (Nos. 21073, 21074). In cultivation the species is a broadly upright shrub with ascending stems or a compact rounded shrub, usually 1½–3 feet high, rarely less. It is hardy outdoors with short rigid branchlets; moreover, it is easy to grow, and is most attractive with crimson flowers in trusses of 1–5. Kingdon-Ward's plant (No. 21073) introduced from the Triangle, North Burma in 1953 is generally considered to be the best form; it is compact, rounded, 3 feet high, with large leaves and large crimson flowers produced in great profusion. It is regrettable that some plants in cultivation under Kingdon-Ward No. 21073 have now been labelled "*R. coelicum* × *R. forrestii*".

Epithet. Dwarf *R. thomsonii*.
Hardiness 3. March–May.

R. chamaethomsonii (Tagg et Forrest) Cowan et Davidian var. **chamaethauma** (Tagg) Cowan et Davidian in The Rhododendron Year Book (1951–52) 71.
> Syn. *R. repens* Balf. f. et Forrest var. *chamaethauma* Tagg in Notes Roy. Bot. Gard. Edin., Vol. XVI (1931) 206; The Sp. of Rhod., (1930) 514.
> *R. repens* Balf. f. et Forrest var. *chamaedoron* Tagg et Forrest in Notes Roy. Bot. Gard. Edin., Vol. XVI (1931) 206; The Sp. of Rhod., (1930) 514.
> *R. chamaethomsonii* (Tagg et Forrest) Cowan et Davidian var. *chamaedoron* (Tagg et Forrest) Chamberlain in Notes Roy. Bot. Gard. Edin., Vol. 37 (1979) 332.
> *R. repens* Balf. f. et Forrest var. *chamaedoxa* nomen nudum.

This plant was first collected by Forrest in the Londre Pass, Mekong-Salwin Divide, south-east Tibet. It was later found by him, by Kingdon-Ward, and Rock in other localities in the same region and in north-west Yunnan. It grows amongst boulders, on rocks, amongst scrub on open rocky slopes, in stony alpine meadows, and in moist stony peaty moorland, at elevations of 3,355–4,575 m. (11,000–15,000 ft.).

In 1931, the name var. *chamaedoron* was applied to plants similar to *R. chamaethomsonii* var. *chamaethauma* but with a hairy leaf under surface. In cultivation, as confirmed by plants growing at Tower Court and at the Royal Botanic Garden, Edinburgh the leaves may be hairy or glabrous. Plants raised from the same seed pan under var. *chamaedoron,* have leaves which are hairy or glabrous. In *The Rhododendron Year Book* 1951–52 page 71, var. *chamaedoron* was placed in synonymy under *R. chamaethomsonii* var. *chamaethauma*. Var. *chamaedoxa* nomen nudum, is identical with var. *chamaethauma*.

The variety differs from *R. chamaethomsonii* in its smaller leaves, laminae 1.6–5 cm.

(usually 1.6–4 cm.) long, and 1–3 cm. (usually 1–2 cm.) broad.

The flower colour is very variable; it is deep crimson, crimson, deep crimson-rose, deep scarlet, rose-red, rose, apple-green, shell-pink or pale pink.

The plant was first introduced by Forrest in 1922 (Nos. 21768, 21916). It was reintroduced by Kingdon-Ward in 1924 (Nos. 5845, and 5847—the Type number). Rock sent seeds on four occasions. Two growth forms are in cultivation. Form 1. A compact rounded shrub up to 2 or 3 feet high. Form 2. A broadly upright shrub up to 2 feet high with ascending stems. There are two colour forms, deep crimson and rose-red. The flowers appear in March or April, and are liable to be destroyed by early spring frosts. Like its ally *R. forrestii*, it is a slow grower and many years are required before it flowers freely. Although hardy, it should be given a sheltered position along the east coast.

The variety was given an Award of Merit when shown as *R. repens* var. *chamaedoxa* by Lady Aberconway and the Hon. H. D. McLaren, Bodnant, in 1932.

Epithet of the variety. Marvellous dwarf plant.

Hardiness 3. March–May.

R. erastum Balf. f. et Forrest in Notes Roy. Bot. Gard. Edin., Vol. 11 (1919) 60.

A *creeping shrub*, 6–9 cm. (2½–3½ in.) high, branchlets densely tomentose, eglandular; leaf-bud scales persistent. *Leaves narrowly lanceolate, oblanceolate or linear-lanceolate*, lamina 1.8–3 cm. long, *4–8 mm. broad*, apex obtuse or acute, mucronate, base tapered, decurrent or not decurrent on the petiole; upper surface dark green, semi-rugulose, with vestiges of hairs, midrib grooved, primary veins 7–9 on each side, deeply impressed; margin recurved; *under surface pale purple, with a thin discontinuous indumentum of hair tufts*, glandular with sessile glands, midrib raised, primary veins slightly raised; petiole 4–7 mm. long, densely tomentose, eglandular. *Inflorescence* terminal, umbellate, *1–4-flowered*, base of pedicel surrounded by bud-scales persistent during flowering; rhachis 1 mm. long, glabrous, sparsely glandular with sessile glands; pedicel 0.8–1 cm. long, densely floccose, sparsely glandular with short-stalked glands. *Calyx* 5-lobed, minute, 0.5–1 mm. long, lobes rounded or triangular, outside glabrous, eglandular, margin hairy or glabrous, eglandular. *Corolla* campanulate or tubular-campanulate, 2.2–2.4 cm. long, clear *rose* without markings, 5 fleshy nectar pouches at the base; lobes 5, 6–7 mm. long, 1 cm. broad, rounded. *Stamens* 10, unequal, shorter than the corolla, 1–1.3 cm. long; filaments puberulous at the base. *Gynoecium* 1.8 cm. long; ovary ovoid, 3 mm. long, 5-celled, densely tomentose, sparsely glandular with short-stalked glands; style glabrous, eglandular. *Capsule*:—

This plant was discovered by Forrest in July 1917 in the Mekong-Salwin Divide, north-west Yunnan, growing in stony alpine meadows, at an elevation of 4,270 m. (14,000 ft.).

A diagnostic feature of *R. erastum* is the narrowly lanceolate, oblanceolate or linear-lanceolate leaves by which it is usually readily distinguished from its nearest ally *R. porphyrophyllum*, and from all the other members of its Series. Other characteristics are the clear rose flowers without markings, in trusses of 1–4, and the pale purple lower surface of the leaves with a thin discontinuous indumentum of hair tufts and sessile glands.

The plant was introduced by Forrest in 1917 (No. 14373—the Type number). It has not been seen for a long time, and is possibly lost to cultivation.

Epithet. Lovely.

Not in cultivation.

R. forrestii Balf. f. ex Diels in Notes Roy. Bot. Gard. Edin., Vol. 5 (1912) 211.

Illustration. Bot. Mag. Vol. 153 t. 9186 (1930).

A *creeping or prostrate shrub*, 3–45 cm. (1 in.–1½ ft.) high, branchlets hairy or glabrous, glandular with short-stalked glands; leaf-bud scales persistent. *Leaves* obovate, orbicular, elliptic or oblong-elliptic, *lamina rigid,* 0.6–5.5 cm. long, 0.5–3.4 cm. broad, apex rounded or sometimes obtuse, emarginate or not emarginate, mucronate, base obtuse or rounded; upper surface dark green, semi-bullate, glabrous or with vestiges of hairs, midrib grooved, primary veins 5–14 on each side, deeply impressed; margin recurved or flat; *under surface deep purple-red,* glabrous or with vestiges of hairs, glandular with sessile or sometimes short-stalked glands, midrib raised, primary veins slightly raised; petiole 0.4–1.4 cm. long, floccose or rarely glabrous, glandular with short-stalked glands or rarely eglandular. *Inflorescence* terminal, umbellate, *1–2-flowered,* base of pedicel surrounded by bud-scales persistent during flowering; rhachis 0.5 mm. long, glabrous, sparsely glandular with sessile glands or eglandular; pedicel 0.6–2 cm. long, hairy or glabrous, glandular with medium or short-stalked glands or rarely eglandular. *Calyx* 5-lobed, 0.5–3 mm. long, lobes triangular or rounded, outside glabrous, glandular with short-stalked glands or eglandular, margin hairy or glabrous, glandular with short-stalked glands. *Corolla* tubular-campanulate, 2.5–4 cm. long, 5-lobed, *deep crimson, crimson, scarlet, light rose-crimson or carmine,* 5 fleshy nectar pouches at the base; lobes 5, 0.8–1.1 cm. long, 1.3–2.5 cm. broad, rounded emarginate. *Stamens* 10, unequal, shorter than the corolla, 1.3–2 cm. long; filaments glabrous. *Gynoecium* 1.7–2.9 cm. long; ovary conoid, 3–5 mm. long, 5-celled, densely or moderately tomentose or glabrous, densely or moderately glandular with short-stalked glands or eglandular; style glabrous, eglandular. *Capsule* oblong, 1–2.5 cm. long, 3–7 mm. broad, straight, densely tomentose or glabrous, densely to sparsely glandular with medium or short-stalked glands, calyx-lobes persistent.

This charming species was discovered by Forrest in June–July 1905 growing as a creeper on moist moss-covered rocks on the ascent of the Tsedjong pass, Mekong-Salwin Divide, south-east Tibet. Subsequently it was found by him and other collectors in south-east and east Tibet, north-west Yunnan, and north-east Upper Burma. It grows on rocks, boulders, in alpine meadow, and in open moist peaty moorland, at elevations of 3,050–4,423 m. (10,000–14,500 ft.).

R. forrestii shows a strong resemblance to *R. porphyrophyllum* in its creeping habit of growth and in the deep purple-red lower surface of the leaves, but differs markedly in its broadly obovate, obovate or orbicular leaves, and in the crimson, scarlet or carmine flowers.

The species was first introduced by Forrest in 1921 (No. 20027). It was reintroduced by him under four different seed numbers (Nos. 21724, 21786, 22923, 22924). Rock sent seeds under Nos. 11033, 11074. Yü introduced it under No. 19034. The plant is hardy outdoors, but is reputed to be difficult. It is a slow grower and requires many years to reach the flowering stage. However, a well-grown plant is of exquisite beauty when adorned with single or paired deep crimson tubular-campanulate flowers. The species is uncommon in cultivation, but should be a most valuable acquisition to any rock garden.

Epithet. After George Forrest, 1873–1932.
Hardiness 3. April–May.

R. forrestii Balf. f. ex Diels var. **repens** (Balf. f. et Forrest) Cowan et Davidian in The Rhododendron Year Book (1951–52) 69.

    Syn. *R. repens* Balf. f. et Forrest in Notes Roy. Bot. Gard. Edin., Vol. 11 (1919) 115.

        R. forrestii Balf. f. ex Diels subsp. *papillatum* Chamberlain in Notes Roy. Bot Gard. Edin., Vol. 37 (1979) 338.

        R. forrestii Balf. f ex Diels subsp. *forrestii* Repens Group R. H. S. in Rhod. Handb. (1980) p. 49.

This plant was first collected by Forrest in June 1917 in the Mekong-Salwin Divide, north-west Yunnan. Further gatherings show that the plant is distributed in north-west Yunnan, south-east and east Tibet, and north-east Upper Burma. It grows on moss-

1. **R. forrestii** var. **repens**.

nat. size.

a. leaf (lower surface). b. leaf (upper surface) c. capsule.
d. petals. e. section. f. ovary, style. g. stamen. h. flower.

covered boulders, on rocks, cliffs, in open moist stony pasture, in peaty meadows, in boggy stony moorland, and on open rocky hillside, at elevations of 3,325–4,575 m. (10,900–15,000 ft.). Farrer records it as forming quite flat carpets in moss in damp places at 10,000 feet in the Chaw Ji Pass, Upper Burma. According to Kingdon-Ward it is fairly common in the alpine region on granite or schistose cliffs and slopes at 14,000–15,000 feet above Tse-ku, north-west Yunnan. In their field note, Ludlow, Sherriff and Taylor describe it as being very common, covering large areas of open rocky hillside at Langong, south-east Tibet. Ludlow, Sherriff and Elliot have also found it growing in a swamp in south-east Tibet.

The variety differs from *R. forrestii* in the glaucous green lower surface of the leaves. (The relationship of var. *repens*, *R. forrestii* and *R. chamaethomsonii* was discussed in some detail in *The Rhododendron Year Book* 1951–52, pages 66–71).

R. forrestii Balf. f. ex Diels subsp. *papillatum* which was described by Chamberlain in 1979, is identical with *R. forrestii* var. *repens* under which it is now placed in synonymy.

R. forrestii var. *repens* was first introduced by Forrest in 1914 (No. 13259). It was reintroduced by him under No. 14011—the Type number, and Nos. 14138, 19515, 22922. Kingdon-Ward sent seeds in 1922 (No. 5417). It was introduced by Rock on five occasions, and by Yü under three different seed numbers. The plant is hardy outdoors, but requires a sunny aspect with some protection from wind, for the best results to be obtained. It varies in its freedom of flowering. Some forms produce the flowers freely, other forms moderately, but a few forms are shy flowerers and hardly produce more than one or two flowers every year. Like its species it is a slow grower and many years are required before it flowers freely. A free-flowering form gives an admirable display with its single or paired crimson flowers for which the dark green foliage provides an effective contrast. It is a creeper, and is a first class plant for the rock garden.

The plant was given a First Class Certificate when shown as *R. repens* by J. B. Stevenson, Tower Court, Ascot, in 1935.

Epithet of the variety. Creeping.

Hardiness 3. April–May.

R. forrestii Balf. f. ex Diels var. **tumescens** Cowan et Davidian in The Rhododendron Year Book (1951–52) 69.

This variety was first collected by Forrest in June 1922 in the Salwin-Kiu Chiang Divide west of Chamatong, south-east Tibet. It was found by him again later in July and October 1924 in the Mekong-Yangtze Divide, north-west Yunnan. Kingdon-Ward collected it in 1924 at Doshong La, south-east Tibet, and in 1926 in the Seinghku Valley, north-east Upper Burma. Yü found it in 1938 in north-west Yunnan.

The variety differs from *R. forrestii* in its dome-shaped habit with the outer branches creeping up to 2 feet in length, and in the glaucous green under surfaces of the leaves.

It was first introduced by Forrest in 1922 (No. 21718—the Type number). It was reintroduced by him in 1924 (Nos. 25524, 25961). Kingdon-Ward sent seeds in 1924 (No. 5846), and in 1926 (No. 6935). The plant is hardy in a sheltered position, and is a fairly robust grower. Like var. *repens*, some forms flower freely, but a few other forms are shy flowerers. The flowers are crimson or deep crimson, but a form introduced by Kingdon-Ward (No. 6935) from the Seinghku Valley, has bright pink or pinkish-purple flowers. The variety is well suited for the rock garden, and is most effective with its large, single or paired tubular-campanulate flowers.

The plant received an Award of Merit when exhibited by Mrs. R. M. Stevenson, Tower Court, Ascot, in 1957.

Epithet of the variety. Dome-shaped.

Hardiness 3. April–May.

R. porphyrophyllum Balf. f. et Forrest in Notes Roy. Bot. Gard. Edin., Vol. 11 (1919) 108.
Syn. *R. serpens* Balf. f. et Forrest in Notes Roy. Bot. Gard. Edin., Vol. 11 (1919) 135.

A *creeping or prostrate shrub*, 6–60 cm. (2½ in.–2 ft.) high, branchlets densely or moderately tomentose or glabrous, glandular with short-stalked glands or eglandular; leaf-bud scales persistent. *Leaves lanceolate, oblanceolate,* oblong, oblong-obovate or elliptic, lamina rigid, 1.5–5.7 cm. long, 0.5–2.6 cm. broad, apex obtuse, acute or rounded, mucronate, base tapered or obtuse, decurrent or not decurrent on the petiole; upper surface dark green, semi-rugulose, with vestiges of hairs, midrib grooved, primary veins 6–14 on each side, deeply impressed; margin recurved; *under surface deep purple-red or pale purple, with a thin discontinuous indumentum of hairs* or glabrous, glandular with sessile glands, midrib raised, primary veins slightly raised; petiole 0.4–1.2 cm. long, densely or moderately floccose, glandular with short-stalked glands or eglandular. *Inflorescence* terminal, umbellate, 1–3-flowered, base of pedicel surrounded by bud-scales persistent during flowering; rhachis 0.5–1 mm. long, glabrous, moderately or sparsely glandular with sessile glands or eglandular; pedicel 0.8–1.5 cm. long, floccose or rarely glabrous, sparsely glandular with short-stalked glands or eglandular. *Calyx* 5-lobed, minute, 0.5–1 mm. long, lobes rounded, outside glabrous or floccose, eglandular, margin hairy, eglandular. *Corolla* tubular-campanulate, 2.4–3.6 cm. long, *pale or deep rose,* unspotted, 5 fleshy nectar pouches at the base; lobes 5, 0.8–1 cm. long, 1.2–2.4 cm. broad, rounded, emarginate. *Stamens* 10, unequal, shorter than the corolla, 1.8–2.3 cm. long; filaments puberulous at the base. *Gynoecium* 2–2.3 cm. long; ovary oblong or conoid, 3–5 mm. long, 5-celled, densely tomentose, glandular with short-stalked glands or eglandular; style glabrous, eglandular. *Capsule* oblong, 8–9 mm. long, 3–4 mm. broad, straight, densely tomentose or glabrous, eglandular, calyx-lobes persistent.

Forrest discovered this species in July 1917 in the Mekong-Salwin Divide, north-west Yunnan. Subsequently he found it on several occasions in the same region and in south-east Tibet. Kingdon-Ward collected it in 1924 (No. 6090) also in south-east Tibet. It grows in open stony alpine pastures, in open moist alpine meadows, on ledges of cliffs, and in barren alpine moorland, at elevations of 3,965–4,575 m. (13,000–15,000 ft.).

In 1919, another species, *R. serpens* Balf. f. et Forrest was described from a specimen (No. 16698) collected by Forrest in south-east Tibet. The ample material now available shows that *R. serpens* is identical with *R. porphyrophyllum.*

R. porphyrophyllum shows a strong resemblance to *R. forrestii* in general appearance, but differs in that the corolla is pale or deep rose, unspotted, the leaves are often lanceolate or oblanceolate, and the lower surfaces of the leaves often have a thin discontinuous indumentum of hairs.

The species was introduced by Forrest in 1918 (No. 16695—the Type number). The plant is now possibly lost to cultivation.

Epithet. Purple-leaved.
Not in cultivation.

R. pyrrhoanthum Balf. f. in Notes Roy. Bot. Gard. Edin., Vol. 12 (1920) 154.

A *very compact spreading* shrub, 30–92 cm. (1–3 ft.) high, and as *much across,* branchlets pink, glabrous or floccose, eglandular or glandular with short-stalked glands; leaf-buds long, pointed, crimson, leaf-bud scales long, persistent. *Leaves elliptic or oblong-elliptic* or rarely obovate, lamina coriaceous, *5.5–8 cm. long,* 2.8–4 cm. broad, apex obtuse or rounded, mucronate, base obtuse; *upper surface* dark green, *convex,* somewhat shining, not glaucous, glabrous, midrib grooved, primary veins 10–14 on each side, deeply impressed; margin recurved; *under surface* pale green, *glabrous* or with vestiges of hairs, midrib prominent, moderately or sparsely floccose, moderately or sparsely glandular with minute glands, *primary veins markedly raised,* moderately or sparsely hairy with small floccose hairs, moderately or sparsely glandular with minute glands; petiole 1–2 cm. long, reddish, grooved above, glabrous or puberulous in the groove, moderately or sparsely glandular in the groove, elsewhere glabrous, eglandular. *Inflorescence* terminal, umbellate, *4–5-flowered*, flower-bud scales persistent during flowering; rhachis 5–6 mm. long, sparsely floccose, eglandular; pedicel 1.6–3 cm. long, pink, moderately or sparsely floccose, glandular with short-stalked glands or eglandular. *Calyx* 5-lobed, 2 mm. long, crimson, lobes rounded, outside glabrous, eglandular, margin shortly ciliate, glandular with short-stalked glands or eglandular. *Corolla* tubular-campanulate, 3.4–3.5 cm. long, *crimson,* without spots, tube fleshy, 5 nectar pouches at the base; lobes 5, 0.8–1 cm. long, 1.4–2 cm. broad, rounded, emarginate. *Stamens* 10, unequal, shorter than the corolla, 1.8 –2.5 cm. long; filaments glabrous or puberulous at the base. *Gynoecium* 3.2–3.5 cm. long, shorter than the corolla; ovary conoid, 3–6 mm. long, 5-celled, densely tomentose, eglandular or glandular with short-stalked glands; style glabrous, eglandular. *Capsule* oblong, 1.1–1.2 cm. long, 5–6 mm. broad, straight, tomentose or glabrous, glandular with short-stalked glands, calyx-lobes persistent.

In the course of years, a few new species were described from cultivated plants raised from collectors' seed of unknown origin. These species were later discovered in their country of origin, agreeing with the described species in all features. *R. pyrrhoanthum* falls into this category of plants.

It was described by Isaac Bayley Balfour in 1920 from a cultivated plant which appeared among seedlings of *R. repens* (now *R. forrestii* var. *repens*) raised by J. C. Williams; these were of doubtful origin, but believed to have come from Yunnan seed collected by Forrest. Three years later, in 1923, Rock discovered *R. pyrrhoanthum* on Mount Kenyichunpo, in the Salwin-Irrawadi watershed, in south-east Tibet, under No. 59174A. In cultivation plants raised under this number are identical with the original plant of *R. pyrrhoanthum* in every morphological detail.

The main characteristics of *R. pyrrhoanthum* are its very compact and spreading habit of growth up to 3 feet high and as much across, the large elliptic or oblong-elliptic convex leaves up to 8 cm. long, the markedly raised primary veins on the lower surface of the leaves, and the 4–5-flowered inflorescence. It is allied to *R. chamaethomsonii* but differs in distinctive features.

The plant is in cultivation in a few gardens. It is hardy outdoors, a robust grower, and is easy to cultivate.

Epithet. With red flowers.
Hardiness 3. April–May.

R. trilectorum Cowan in Notes Roy. Bot. Gard. Edin., Vol. 21 (1953) 144.

A prostrate shrub, 23–30 cm. (9 in.–1 ft.) high, branchlets reddish-brown, glabrous, leaves clustered at the upper end of the branchlets; leaf-bud scales persistent. *Leaves subsessile,* obovate or obovate-spathulate, lamina leathery, 1–3.2 cm. long, 0.6–1.8 cm. broad, apex rounded, conspicuously mucronate, *base obtuse, decurrent on the petiole;* upper surface dark green, glabrous, midrib deeply grooved, primary veins 8–10 on each side, deeply impressed; margin recurved; *under surface* pale green, shining, *glabrous,* eglandular, midrib raised, primary veins raised; *petiole very short, more or less winged* by the decurrent base of the lamina, glabrous or floccose, eglandular. *Inflorescence* terminal, umbellate, *2–5- (usually 3-) flowered;* rhachis 1 mm. long, glabrous; *pedicel 2–3 cm. long,* glabrous. *Calyx* 5-lobed, small, 1–3 mm. long, glabrous. *Corolla* funnel-campanulate or tubular-campanulate, 3–4 cm. long, *pale yellow or pale lemon-yellow, flushed pale pink;* lobes 5, 0.8–1 cm. long, 1.6–1.8 cm. broad, rounded, emarginate. *Stamens* 10, unequal, shorter than the corolla, 1.4–2.9. cm. long; *filaments* white, *densely puberulous towards the base. Gynoecium* 2.4–3.3 cm. long; *ovary* conoid, about 4 mm. long, *glabrous;* style glabrous. *Capsule:*—

This species was discovered by Ludlow, Sherriff and Taylor in June 1938 at Tsari Sama, Langong, south-east Tibet. It was found by them again three weeks later at Tum La, Nayii in the same region. The plant grows on rocks on open hillsides, at elevations of 3,660–4,270 m. (12,000–14,000 ft.).

R. trilectorum is a prostrate shrub, 9 inches to 1 foot high. It is allied to *R. forrestii* and to its var. *repens*, but differs from both in that the corolla is pale yellow or pale lemon-yellow, flushed pale pink, the base of the leaf lamina is decurrent on the very short petiole which is more or less winged on both sides, the ovary is glabrous, the pedicels are usually longer, and the filaments of the stamens are densely puberulous towards the base.

The plant has not been introduced into cultivation.

Epithet. Three collectors.

Not in cultivation.

HAEMATODES SUBSERIES

General characters: shrubs or rarely small trees, 60 cm.–4.58 m. (2–15 ft.) or rarely 30 cm. (1 ft.) high, branchlets densely or moderately tomentose or bristly or glandular (in *R. coelicum* usually glabrous eglandular). Leaves *obovate, oblong-obovate* or oblong, rarely elliptic or oblanceolate, lamina 3–16 cm. long, *1.6–8 cm. broad; under surface with a thick, woolly, continuous or sometimes interrupted indumentum of brown, dark brown or cinnamon-coloured Dendroid or Ramiform* hairs, or sometimes thin discontinuous or rarely absent; petiole 0.2–3.6 cm. long, densely or moderately tomentose or bristly or glandular (in *R. coelicum* usually glabrous eglandular). Inflorescence a racemose umbel of 2–20 flowers; pedicel 0.6–3 cm. long, densely or moderately tomentose or bristly or glandular. Calyx 5-lobed, 0.2–2.5 cm. long, lobes unequal (in *R. mallotum* triangular, minute 0.5 mm. long), usually crimson or red. Corolla tubular-campanulate or campanulate, usually fleshy, 2.8–5.3 cm. long, deep crimson, crimson or rarely black-crimson, or deep carmine, deep scarlet, crimson-rose, rarely red, deep rose, yellow or white, 5 nectar pouches at the base; lobes 5. Stamens 10. Ovary conoid or oblong, truncate, 3–7 mm. long, 5–10-celled, densely tomentose or glandular; style usually glabrous. Capsule oblong, ovoid or short stout, 0.8–2.8 cm. long, 0.5–1.2 cm. broad, usually straight, densely or moderately tomentose or bristly or glandular.

KEY TO THE SPECIES

A. Inflorescence very compact, 10–20 flowered; leaves very thick, upper surface markedly rugulose; calyx with 5 minute triangular lobes, 0.5 mm. long . . . . *mallotum*

A. Inflorescence lax, 2–10-flowered; leaves thick, upper surface not rugulose or minutely rugulose (except in *R. beanianum*, rugulose); calyx with 5 unequal, rounded, ovate, oblong or irregular lobes, 3 mm.–2.5 cm. long.

    B. Branchlets, petioles, pedicels, ovaries and capsules usually eglandular, densely or moderately tomentose or bristly with branched or unbranched bristles.

        C. Branchlets and petioles densely tomentose, not bristly.

    D. Calyx large, 1.6–2.5 cm. long, cup-shaped, divided a little from above .... *catacosmum*

    D. Calyx small, 3 mm.–1.4 cm. long, divided to the base or to about the middle.

        E. Upper surface of the leaves not rugulose or slightly rugulose; indumentum on the under surface of the leaves very thick, spongy; calyx 3 mm.–1.4 cm. long .... *haematodes*

        E. Upper surface of the leaves slightly rugulose; indumentum on the under surface of the leaves thick, woolly, not spongy; calyx 3–6 mm. long .... *piercei*

C. Branchlets and petioles densely or moderately bristly (setulose).

    F. Flowers deep crimson, crimson, black-crimson, sometimes pink or creamy-yellow flushed rose or rose; under surface of the leaves with a thick usually continuous or sometimes interrupted indumentum or with a thin veil of hairs or sometimes glabrous.

        G. A somewhat rounded or compact shrub; upper surface of the leaves not rugulose or minutely rugulose, usually matt, olive-green or dark green; under surface of the leaves with a thick or thin continuous or sometimes interrupted brown or dark brown indumentum, or a thin veil of hairs, or sometimes glabrous.

            H. Leaves (laminae) large, usually 5–12.5 cm. long, 3.5–5.5 cm. broad; indumentum on the under surface of the leaves thick woolly, continuous or sometimes interrupted or rarely absent, bistrate or unistrate; corolla large, usually 3.8–5.3 cm. long.... *chaetomallum* and var. *chamaephytum*

            H. Leaves (laminae) small, usually 3–4.5 cm. long, 1.6–3.1 cm. broad; indumentum on the under surface of the leaves thin, usually discontinuous, unistrate; corolla small, usually 2.8–3.5 cm. long............. *hillieri*

        G. A lax upright shrub with long ascending stems, or somewhat straggly; upper surface of the leaves rugulose, dark green, shining; under surface of the leaves with a thick continuous cinnamon-brown or brown indumentum ..... *beanianum* (part)

    F. Flowers white; under surface of the leaves with a thick interrupted indumentum of hairs, in shreds and patches ..... *chionanthum*

B. Branchlets, petioles, pedicels, and usually ovaries and capsules densely or moderately glandular (except in *R. coelicum* branchlets and petioles eglandular or sparsely glandular), usually not tomentose, not bristly (except in *R. beanianum* bristly).

    I. Under surface of the leaves with a thick interrupted indumentum of hairs in shreds and patches, or with scattered hairs, or with a thin veil of hairs, or rarely glabrous.

        J. Under surface of the leaves with a thick woolly interrupted indumentum of hairs in shreds and patches ...... *hemidartum*

        J. Under surface of the leaves with scattered hairs or with a thin veil of hairs or rarely glabrous .... *chaetomallum* var. *hemigymnum*

    I. Under surface of the leaves with a thick continuous indumentum of hairs.

        K. Branchlets, petioles and pedicels glandular with short-or medium-stalked glands; upper surface of the leaves not rugulose or slightly rugulose; compact or broadly upright shrubs.

L. Branchlets and petioles rather densely or moderately glandular.................................. *pocophorum*
L. Branchlets and petioles eglandular or sparsely glandular ....
.... *coelicum*
K. Branchlets and petioles bristly-glandular; upper surface of the leaves rugulose; a lax shrub with long ascending stems, or somewhat straggly.................................. *beanianum*
(part)

DESCRIPTION OF THE SPECIES

R. beanianum Cowan in New Flora & Silva, Vol. 10 (1938) 245.
Illustration. Bot. Mag. n.s. Vol. 169 t. 219 (1953).

A *lax upright shrub with ascending stems or somewhat straggly* or a tangled or bushy shrub, 92 cm.–3 m. (3–10 ft.) high, *branchlets* sparsely or moderately tomentose with a brown tomentum or not tomentose, *moderately or densely bristly* with branched or unbranched brown bristles, eglandular or *sparsely or moderately bristly-glandular,* those below the inflorescences 4–5 mm. in diameter; leaf-bud scales deciduous. *Leaves* oblong-obovate, obovate, oblong or oblong-elliptic, lamina thick, leathery, 4.8–10.3 cm. long, 2.3–4.6 cm. broad, apex rounded, mucronate, base obtuse or rounded; *upper surface* dark green, *rugulose,* glabrous or with vestiges of hairs, midrib grooved, bristly or not bristly, primary veins 8–12 on each side, impressed; margin recurved; *under surface* covered with a thick, woolly, continuous, brown or *cinnamon-brown, bistrate or unistrate indumentum of* hairs, *upper layer a form of Dendroid with short or long stem,* and *short ribbon-like branches, lower layer Rosulate continuous or absent,* when unistrate with only *a form of Dendroid hairs,* midrib raised, primary veins concealed; *petiole* 0.8–2 cm. long, grooved above, tomentose or not tomentose, *moderately or densely bristly* with branched or unbranched brown bristles, eglandular or *sparsely or moderately bristly-glandular. Inflorescence* terminal, a racemose umbel of 4–10 flowers; rhachis 4–9 mm. long, tomentose, bristly or not bristly, eglandular; pedicel 1–2 cm. long, densely or moderately tomentose with a brown tomentum or not tomentose, not bristly or densely or moderately bristly with branched bristly hairs, eglandular or sparsely or moderately bristly-glandular. *Calyx* 5-lobed, 0.2–2 cm. long, crimson, divided to about the middle or to the base, lobes unequal, ovate or irregular, outside glabrous, eglandular, margin glabrous or hairy, eglandular. *Corolla* tubular-campanulate, fleshy, 3–4.5 cm. long, deep crimson or crimson, 5 nectar pouches at the base; lobes 5, 1–1.5 cm. long, 1.4–2 cm. broad, rounded, emarginate. *Stamens* 10, unequal, shorter than the corolla, 1.6–3.4 cm. long; filaments crimson in the lower half or at the base, whitish above, glabrous. *Gynoecium* 2.8–3.8 cm. long; ovary conoid, truncate, 3–5 mm. long, 7–8-celled, densely tomentose with a brown tomentum, not bristly, eglandular; style hairy at the base, eglandular. *Capsule* oblong, 2–2.8 cm. long, 6–9 mm. broad, slightly curved, not tomentose, densely bristly with branched bristly hairs, eglandular, calyx-lobes deciduous.

Kingdon-Ward first collected this plant in June 1926 at Seinghku Wang, Upper Burma. He found it again in the Seinghku Valley in the same month. It grows in thickets, on the flanks of forests, and on steep granite gullies, at elevations of 3,050–3,355 m. (10,000–11,000 ft.).

The main characteristics of this plant are its lax or somewhat straggly habit of growth with ascending stems, the moderately or densely bristly and often bristly-glandular branchlets and petioles, and the rugulose upper surface of the leaves. In these respects, the species is readily distinguished from its ally *R. piercei.*

The plant was introduced by Kingdon-Ward in 1926 (No. 6805, and No. 6829—the

Type number). According to Kingdon-Ward, in its native home it is a small tangled shrub or a bushy undershrub or a bush of 3–6 feet with ascending branches. In cultivation it is a lax upright shrub up to 10 feet high. The bristly and often bristly-glandular branchlets and petioles are a diagnostic feature. Another characteristic is usually the cinnamon-brown thick woolly indumentum on the lower surface of the leaves. As in other species of its Series, the five dark nectar pouches at the base of the corolla-tube are distinctive. The species is hardy, fairly fast grower, with deep crimson flowers produced freely in trusses of 4–10.

The plant received an Award of Merit when exhibited by Col. Lord Digby, Minterne, Dorset, in 1953 (Kingdon-Ward No. 6805).

Epithet. After W. J. Bean, 1863–1947, former Curator, Royal Botanic Garden, Kew. Hardiness 3. March–May.

R. catacosmum Balf. f. ex Tagg in Notes Roy. Bot. Gard. Edin., Vol. 15 (1927) 307.

A rounded shrub, 1.22–2.75 m. (4–9 ft.) high, *branchlets* densely tomentose with a brown tomentum or rarely floccose, *not bristly*, eglandular, those below the inflorescences 5–9 mm. in diameter; leaf-bud scales deciduous. *Leaves* obovate, lamina thick, leathery, 5–11 cm. long, 2.5–5.3 cm. broad, apex rounded, mucronate, base obtuse; upper surface green, matt, minutely rugulose, glabrous or with vestiges of hairs, midrib grooved, primary veins 8–12 on each side, impressed; *under surface covered with a thick, woolly, continuous,* cinnamon-brown or dark brown or brown, *bistrate indumentum of hairs, upper layer Dendroid, lower layer Rosulate,* midrib raised, primary veins concealed; *petiole* 1–1.5 cm. long, grooved above, densely tomentose with a brown tomentum or rarely floccose, *not bristly,* eglandular. *Inflorescence* terminal, a racemose umbel of 4–9 flowers; rhachis 0.5–1.5 cm. long, tomentose with a brown or fawn tomentum, eglandular; *pedicel* 1.6–2.5 cm. long, densely tomentose with a brown tomentum, *not bristly,* eglandular. *Calyx* 5-lobed, *large, 1.6–2.5 cm. long, red or crimson, cup-shaped, irregularly lobed,* divided a little from above, lobes unequal, rounded or irregular, outside and margin hairy or glabrous, eglandular. *Corolla* broadly campanulate or tubular-campanulate, fleshy, 4–4.8 cm. long, crimson, crimson-rose or pink, 5 nectar pouches at the base; lobes 5, 1–1.3 cm. long, 1.8–2 cm. broad, rounded, emarginate. *Stamens* 10, unequal, shorter than the corolla, 1.9–3.4 cm. long; filaments puberulous at the base or glabrous. *Gynoecium* 3.4–3.8 cm. long; ovary conoid or oblong, truncate, 5 mm. long, 5-celled, densely tomentose with a brown tomentum, eglandular; style glabrous or rarely puberulous at the base, eglandular. *Capsule* ovoid or broadly oblong or short stout, 1–2.5 cm. long, 0.9–1.2 cm. broad, densely tomentose with a brown or cinnamon tomentum, *not bristly,* eglandular, calyx-lobes not persistent.

This species was discovered by Forrest in July 1921 in the Salwin-Kiu Chiang Divide, east Tibet. It was found by him again three months later in the same area, and in 1922 in the same region in south-east Tibet. In 1923 Rock collected it in south-east Tibet. It grows on the margins of rhododendron forest and amongst scrub in alpine side valleys, at elevations of 3,965–4,270 m. (13,000–14,000 ft.).

The most striking character of this plant is the very large cup-shaped, irregularly lobed calyx, 1.6–2.5 cm. long, which suggests a hose-in-hose form of a flower. In this respect, the species is readily distinguished from all other members of its Subseries. It is allied to R. *chaetomallum* which it resembles in habit and height of growth, in leaf shape and size, and in the size and colour of the corolla, but differs markedly in the very large cup-shaped calyx, and in the non-bristly branchlets, petioles, pedicels, and capsules. It should be noted that in R. *catacosmum* the indumentum on the lower surface of the leaves is bistrate; an upper layer of Dendroid hairs, and a lower layer of Rosulate hairs.

The species was first introduced by Forrest in 1921 (Nos. 20078, 20895). It was reintroduced by him in 1922 (No. 21727—the Type number). Rock sent seeds in 1923 (No.

11185 = 59543). In its native home it grows up to 9 feet high; in cultivation it is a rounded shrub up to about 5 feet. Two flower colour forms are in cultivation, crimson and crimson-rose. As it comes from elevations as high as 13,000–14,000 feet, it is hardy, and has proved to be of sturdy habit with thick branchlets. The crimson or crimson-rose flowers with large cup-shaped calyx about one-half the length of the corolla, are most attractive in trusses of 4–9. The plant is uncommon in cultivation but well deserves the widest possible recognition.

Epithet. Adorned.

Hardiness 3. April–May.

R. chaetomallum Balf f. et Forrest in Notes Roy. Bot. Gard. Edin., Vol. 12 1920 (95).

Syn. *R. chaetomallum* Balf f. et Forrest var. *glaucescens* Tagg et Forrest in Notes Roy. Bot. Gard. Edin., Vol. 16 (1931) 189; Tagg in The Sp. of Rhod. (1930) 520.

R. haematodes Franch. subsp. *chaetomallum* (Balf. f. et Forrest) Chamberlain in Notes Roy. Bot. Gard. Edin., Vol. 37 (1979) 333.

R. haematodes Franch. subsp. *chaetomallum* (Balf. f. et Forrest) Chamberlain *Glaucescens Group* R.H.S. in Rhod. Handb. (1980) p.49.

Illustration. Bot. Mag. n.s. Vol. 165 t. 25 (1948).

A somewhat rounded or compact, or broadly upright shrub, 60 cm.–3 m. (2–10 ft.) high, *branchlets* moderately or sparsely tomentose with a brown, pale brown or whitish tomentum or not tomentose, *densely or moderately bristly with branched or sometimes unbranched bristles* or rarely not bristly, *eglandular*, those below the inflorescences 4–7 mm. in diameter; leaf-bud scales deciduous. *Leaves* oblong-obovate or obovate, rarely elliptic or oblong, lamina thick, leathery, 4.2–12.5 cm. long, 2–5.5 cm. broad, apex rounded or sometimes obtuse, mucronate, base obtuse or rarely rounded; upper surface olive-green or pale green, matt, sometimes with a wax-like bloom, minutely rugulose, glabrous or with vestiges of hairs, midrib grooved, primary veins 8–14 on each side, impressed; *under surface with a thick, woolly, continuous or sometimes interrupted,* brown or dark brown or sometimes chocolate colour, *bistrate or unistrate* indumentum of hairs, *upper layer Dendroid with ribbon-like branches,* lower layer Rosulate, continuous or widely spaced or absent, when unistrate with only *Dendroid* hairs, midrib raised, primary veins concealed or sometimes exposed; *petiole* 0.4–1.6 cm. long, grooved above, rather densely or sparsely tomentose with a brown or pale brown or whitish tomentum, *moderately or densely bristly with branched or sometimes unbranched bristles, eglandular. Inflorescence* terminal, a racemose umbel of 4–7 flowers; rhachis 0.4–1 cm. long, tomentose with a brown tomentum, not bristly or bristly, eglandular; *pedicel* 1.3–3 cm. long, not tomentose or sometimes tomentose, *moderately or densely bristly with long, branched or sometimes unbranched* brown *bristly hairs, eglandular. Calyx* 5-lobed, 0.3–1 cm. or rarely up to 2 cm. long, crimson, pink or red, cup-shaped, divided to about the middle or to the base, lobes unequal, rounded, ovate or irregular, *outside* glabrous, *eglandular, margin* glabrous or hairy, *eglandular. Corolla* tubular-campanulate, fleshy at the base, 3.2–5.3 cm. or rarely 2.8 cm. long, deep crimson, crimson, black-crimson, deep carmine, scarlet, deep rose or pink, 5 nectar pouches at the base; lobes 5, 1.3–1.5 cm. long, 1.5–2.2 cm. broad, rounded, emarginate. *Stamens* 10, unequal, shorter than the corolla, 1.6–3.5 cm. long; filaments glabrous or rarely puberulous at the base. *Gynoecium* 2.3–4 cm. long; *ovary* conoid or oblong, truncate, 4–6 mm. long, 5–10-celled, densely tomentose with a brown tomentum, not bristly or sometimes bristly with bristly hairs, *eglandular;* style glabrous or sometimes hairy at the base, eglandular. *Capsule* oblong or ovoid or short stout, 0.8–2.3 cm. long, 0.6–1.2 cm. broad, tomentose or not tomentose, *densely or moderately bristly with* brown *bristly hairs, eglandular,* calyx-lobes not persistent.

This plant was first collected, in fruit, by Forrest in October 1917 on Mount Ka-gwr-pw, Mekong-Salwin Divide, south-east Tibet. Further gatherings by him and other collectors show that the species is distributed in south-east and east Tibet, north-

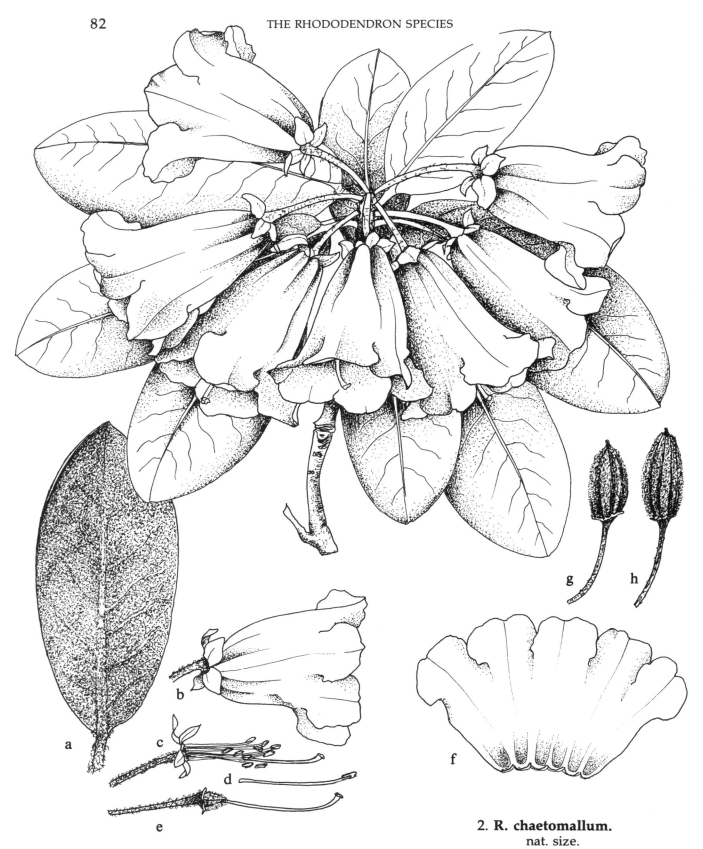

2. **R. chaetomallum.**
nat. size.
a. leaf (lower surface). b. flower. c. section.
d. stamen. e. ovary, style. f. petals. g. capsule. h. capsule.

east Upper Burma, and north-west Yunnan. It grows in very varied habitats, in open situations among rocks, on boulder strewn slopes, on rocky slopes, on cliffs and crags, in open thickets, among scrub, in cane brakes, and in open moorland, at elevations of 2,745–4,575 m. (9,000–15,000 ft.). Yü records it as being common, 1–2 feet high, in the Salwin-Kiu Chiang Divide, north-west Yunnan.

R. chaetomallum is very variable in general features due to the various environmental conditions in which it is found. It grows from 2–10 feet high; the leaves (laminae) are 4.2–12.5 cm. long, 2–5.5 cm. broad; the indumentum on the lower surface of the leaves is brown or dark brown or chocolate colour; and the flower colour is deep crimson, crimson, black-crimson, deep carmine, scarlet, deep rose or pink.

The species is allied to R. catacosmum. The distinctions between them are discussed under the latter. It is also related to R. haematodes, but is readily distinguished by well-marked characters. The indumentum on the lower surface of the leaves is often bistrate. The upper layer is Dendroid with ribbon-like branches. The lower layer of Rosulate hairs is continuous in very few specimens; it is widely spaced or absent, in most specimens.

R. chaetomallum was first introduced by Forrest in 1917 (No. 14987). It was reintroduced by him in 1918 (No. 16691—the Type number), and later under 24 different seed numbers. Rock sent seeds on 39 occasions. The plant was also introduced by Kingdon-Ward (No. 5431), and by Yü (Nos. 20609, 20738). Several distinct forms are in cultivation, including: Form 1. A large somewhat rounded shrub, 5–6 feet high, with scarlet flowers. Form 2. A somewhat compact shrub, 2–3 feet high, with larger crimson flowers. Form 3. A medium-sized shrub with black-crimson flowers. Form 4. A small, somewhat compact shrub with chocolate colour indumentum on the lower surface of the leaves. Form 5. A medium-sized shrub with brown indumentum and pink flowers. One of the chief merits of the species is that it flowers at a fairly young age. It often produces a few capsules containing good fertile seeds in plenty. The plant is hardy, free-flowering, and is easy to grow.

The species was given an Award of Merit when shown by E. de Rothschild, Exbury, in 1959 (Forrest No. 25601).

Epithet. With woolly hair.

Hardiness 3. March–May.

R. chaetomallum Balf. f. et Forrest var. **chamaephytum** Cowan in Notes Roy. Bot. Gard. Edin., Vol. 21 (1953) 147.

    Syn. (?R. forrestii × R. haematodes) Chamberlain in Notes Roy. Bot. Gard. Edin., Vol. 39 (1982) 408.

This plant was discovered by Ludlow, Sherriff and Taylor in May 1938 at Singo Samba, Lo La Chu, near Molo, south-east Tibet. It grows creeping over rocks in rhododendron and Abies forest, at an elevation of 3,965 m. (13,000 ft.).

The variety differs from the species in the prostrate, creeping habit of growth, 30–60 cm. (1–2 ft.) high, in the glabrous lower surface of the leaves, and in the non-bristly pedicels.

The plant has not been introduced into cultivation.

Epithet of the variety. Dwarf plant.

Not in cultivation.

R. chaetomallum Balf. f. et Forrest var. **hemigymnum** Tagg et Forrest in Notes Roy. Bot. Gard. Edin., Vol. 16 (1931) 189.

    Syn. R. × hemigymnum (Tagg et Forrest) Chamberlain in Notes Roy. Bot. Gard. Edin., Vol. 37 (1979) 333—R. pocophorum × R. eclecteum.

Forrest discovered this plant in June 1922 in the Salwin-Kiu Chiang Divide, Tsarong, south-east Tibet. He found it also in July 1924 on the western flank of the Salwin-Kiu Chiang Divide, north-east Upper Burma, and again in the same region in

October of that year. It grows in mixed scrub in quarries, on open rocky slopes, and in alpine scrub, at elevations of 3,355–4,270 m. (11,000–14,000 ft.).

The variety differs from *R. chaetomallum* in that the indumentum on the lower surface of the leaves consists of closely or widely scattered hairs or a thin veil of hairs or rarely glabrous, and usually in the bristly-glandular branchlets, petioles, pedicels and ovaries.

The plant was first introduced by Forrest in 1922 (No. 21728—the Type number, and No. 21837). It was reintroduced by him in 1924 (No. 25605). In cultivation it is a broadly upright shrub up to 6 feet high. It is hardy, a vigorous grower, with bright crimson flowers produced freely in trusses of 4–6.

It was given an Award of Merit when shown by Mrs. R. M. Stevenson, Tower Court, Ascot, in 1957 (Forrest No. 25605).

Epithet of the variety. Half glabrous leaf.

Hardiness 3. April–May.

R. chaetomallum Balf. f. et Forrest var. **xanthanthum** Tagg et Forrest in Notes Roy. Bot. Gard. Edin., Vol. 15 (1927) 308.

Syn. *R.* × *xanthanthum* (Tagg et Forrest) Chamberlain in Notes Roy. Bot. Gard. Edin., Vol. 39 (1982) 393.

This variety was discovered by Forrest in June 1922 in the Salwin-Kiu Chiang Divide, Tsarong, south-east Tibet. It was afterwards found by him again on several occasions in the same region. The plant grows among dwarf rhododendron scrub in moist alpine moorland, in alpine corries, and on ledges of cliffs, at elevations of 3,660–4,270 m. (12,000–14,000 ft.).

The variety differs from *R. chaetomallum* in that the flowers are creamy-yellow, flushed or striped and often margined pale rose or crimson.

The plant was introduced by Forrest in 1922 (No. 21725—the Type number, and Nos. 21729, 21745). In cultivation it is a somewhat rounded shrub, 3–5 feet high, usually with large calyx up to 1.3 cm. or rarely 1.7 cm. long, and large corolla up to 5.9 cm. long. It is hardy, a robust grower, and is easy to cultivate.

Epithet. With yellow flowers.

Hardiness 3. April–May.

R. chionanthum Tagg et Forrest in Notes Roy. Bot. Gard. Edin., Vol. 15 (1927) 309.

A somewhat rounded shrub, 60–92 cm. (2–3 ft.) high, branchlets tomentose with a pale brown tomentum or not tomentose, moderately or rather densely bristly with branched or unbranched bristles, eglandular, those below the inflorescences 3–4 mm. in diameter; leaf-bud scales deciduous or somewhat persistent. *Leaves* obovate or oblanceolate, lamina thick, leathery, 5–7.6 cm. long, 2.3–3 cm. broad, apex rounded or broadly obtuse, mucronate, base obtuse or tapered, decurrent on the petiole; upper surface dark green, minutely rugulose, glabrous or with vestiges of hairs, midrib grooved, primary veins 7–10 on each side, impressed; *under surface with a thick woolly, interrupted, in shreds and patches,* dark brown, *unistrate indumentum of Dendroid hairs with ribbon-like branches,* midrib raised, primary veins partly exposed; petiole 0.2–1 cm. long, grooved above, slightly ridged by the decurrent lamina, moderately or sparsely tomentose with a pale brown or whitish tomentum, bristly with branched or unbranched bristles, eglandular. *Inflorescence* terminal, a racemose umbel of 4–6 flowers; rhachis 4–5 mm. long, tomentose with a brown tomentum, not bristly, eglandular; pedicel 1.5–2 cm. long, not tomentose, bristly with long, branched or unbranched brown bristly hairs, eglandular. *Calyx* 5-lobed, 3–9 mm. long, divided nearly to the base or to the base, lobes unequal, oblong, ovate or rounded, outside glabrous, eglandular, margin hairy, eglandular. *Corolla* campanulate, 3.4–4 cm. long, *white,* 5 nectar pouches at the base; lobes 5, 1.3–1.4 cm. long, 1.5–2 cm. broad, rounded, emarginate. *Stamens* 10, unequal, shorter than the corolla, 1.3–2.5 cm. long; filaments glabrous. *Gynoecium* 3–3.5 cm. long;

ovary conoid, truncate, 4–5 mm. long, 5–7-celled, densely tomentose with a dark brown tomentum, not bristly, eglandular; style glabrous, eglandular. *Capsule* conoid, 1–1.8 cm. long, 6–9 mm. broad, tomentose, not bristly, eglandular, calyx-lobes persistent.

Forrest discovered this plant in July 1924 in the Salwin-Kiu Chiang Divide, north-west Yunnan. Later during the same month, he collected it twice on the western flank of Salwin-Kiu Chiang Divide, north-east Upper Burma. It grows on rocky slopes, in alpine meadows, and on scrub-covered cliffs, at elevations of 3,965–4,270 m. (13,000–14,000 ft.).

The species is allied to *R. chaetomallum* to which it shows a resemblance in general features, but differs in that the corolla is white, and the indumentum on the lower surface of the leaves is discontinuous, in shreds and patches. The indumentum is unistrate; the lower layer is absent; the upper layer is Dendroid with ribbon-like branches.

The plant was introduced by Forrest in 1924 (No. 25564). (This number has been wrongly recorded as *citriniflorum* ssp. *horaeum* in *The Rhododendron Handbook* 1980 page 290). In cultivation it is a small, somewhat rounded shrub about 2 feet high, and makes a fine show with its white flowers produced freely in trusses of 4–6. The species is rare in cultivation, but is well worth a place in every collection of rhododendrons.

Epithet. With snowy flowers.
Hardiness 3. April–May.

R. coelicum Balf. f. et Farrer in Notes Roy. Bot. Gard. Edin., Vol. 13 (1922) 250.
A broadly upright or bushy shrub, 92 cm.–1.83 m. (3–6 ft.) high, or rarely a small, stout tree, *branchlets eglandular* or rarely sparsely glandular with short-stalked glands, not hairy or sparsely hairy with long hairs, not bristly, those below the inflorescences 4–6 mm. in diameter; leaf-bud scales deciduous. *Leaves* obovate or oblong-obovate, lamina thick, leathery, 5.4–9.5 cm. long, 2.7–4.7 cm. broad, apex rounded, mucronate, base obtuse or rounded; upper surface dark green, shining, not glaucous, glabrous or with vestiges of hairs, midrib grooved, primary veins 8–14 on each side, impressed; *under surface covered with a thick, woolly, continuous brown, unistrate indumentum of Ramiform hairs with long, much twisted branches*, midrib raised, primary veins concealed; *petiole* 0.8–1.5 cm. long, *eglandular* or rarely glandular with short-stalked glands, glabrous or sparsely hairy with long hairs. *Inflorescence* terminal, a racemose umbel of 6–15 flowers; rhachis 5–7 mm. long, tomentose with a cinnamon or brown tomentum, eglandular; pedicel 0.8–1.5 cm. long, glandular with short-stalked glands, not hairy, not bristly. *Calyx* 5-lobed, *3–8 mm. long*, crimson or red, divided to about the middle or to the base, lobes unequal, irregular, ovate or oblong, *outside* glabrous or rarely hairy, *eglandular, margin* glabrous or hairy, *eglandular. Corolla* tubular-campanulate, fleshy, 3.4–4.5 cm. long, deep scarlet or deep crimson, 5 nectar pouches at the base; lobes 5, 1–1.2 cm. long, 2–2.4 cm. broad, rounded, emarginate. *Stamens* 10, unequal, shorter than the corolla, 1.8–3.5 cm. long; filaments glabrous. *Gynoecium* 2.8–3.7 cm. long; ovary conoid, truncate, 4–5 mm. long, 5-celled, densely glandular with short-stalked glands or rarely eglandular, brown-hairy or not hairy; style glabrous, eglandular or rarely glandular at the base. *Capsule* oblong, 1–1.4 cm. long, 5–8 mm. broad, straight, glandular with short-stalked glands, hairy or not hairy, not bristly, calyx-lobes persistent.

The discovery of this species has been wrongly credited to Farrer. It was first collected by Kingdon-Ward in June 1919 at Laktang, north-east Upper Burma. In May 1920, it was found by Farrer in the Chawchi Pass in the same region. Subsequently it was collected by Forrest on several occasions in the Salwin-Kiu Chiang Divide, north-west Yunnan. It grows in cane brakes, on cliffs, on scrub-covered rocky slopes, and on granite ridges in rhododendron forest, at elevations of 2,745–4,270 m. (9,000–14,000 ft.). Farrer records it as flopping over precipices or making a tangle in the cane brakes at 3,355 m. (11,000 ft.).

R. *coelicum* is closely allied to R. *pocophorum* which it resembles in general features, but is readily distinguished by the eglandular branchlets and petioles. It also differs usually in the smaller calyx. The indumentum on the lower surface of the leaves is unistrate. The lower layer is absent; the upper layer is Ramiform with long much twisted branches.

The species was first introduced by Forrest in 1924 (Nos. 25625, 25647). In cultivation it is a broadly upright shrub up to 5 feet high. As it has been introduced from elevations of 13,000–14,000 feet, it is hardy outdoors, and has proved to be of sturdy habit. The leaves are obovate or oblong-obovate, dark green and shiny on the upper surfaces. The plant is free-flowering, and makes a fine show with its deep crimson flowers in trusses of 6–15. The species is uncommon in cultivation, but is worth being more widely grown.

It received an Award of Merit when exhibited by Col. Lord Digby, Minterne, Dorset, in 1955.

Epithet. Heavenly.
Hardiness 3. April–May

R. haematodes Franch. in Bull. Soc. Bot. France, Vol. 33 (1886) 232.

Syn. R. *haematodes* Franch. var. *calycinum* Franch. in Bull. Soc. Bot. France, Vol. 34 (1887) 280.

R. *haematodes* Franch. var. *hypoleucum* Franch. ibid. Vol. 34 (1887) 280.

Illustration. Bot. Mag. Vol. 153 t. 9165 (1929).

A compact spreading or rounded or broadly upright shrub, 30 cm.–1.22 m. (1–4 ft.) or rarely 5–8 cm. (2–3 in.) high, or sometimes up to 1.83–3 m. (6–10 ft.) high, *branchlets densely tomentose* with a dark brown, brown or whitish tomentum, not bristly or rarely sparsely bristly, *eglandular,* those below the inflorescences 3–7 mm. in diameter; leaf-bud scales deciduous or persistent. *Leaves* oblong, oblong-obovate or obovate, lamina thick, leathery, 3.5–9.6 cm. long, 1.6–4.5 cm. broad, apex obtuse or rounded, mucronate, base obtuse or tapered; *upper surface* dark green, *shining,* slightly rugulose or *not rugulose,* glabrous or with vestiges of hairs, midrib grooved, primary veins 7–12 on each side, impressed; *under surface covered with* a *very thick woolly spongy, continuous,* dark brown, brown, cinnamon-brown or rarely pale chocolate colour, *bistrate indumentum* of hairs, *upper layer Dendroid, lower layer Rosulate,* midrib raised, primary veins concealed; *petiole* 0.6–1.4 cm. long, grooved above, *densely tomentose* with a dark brown or brown or whitish tomentum, not bristly, eglandular. *Inflorescence* terminal, a racemose umbel of 2–8 flowers; rhachis 3–5 mm. long, moderately or densely tomentose with a brown tomentum, eglandular; pedicel 1.3–2.3 cm. long, *densely tomentose* with a brown tomentum or glabrous, moderately or densely bristly or not bristly, eglandular or rarely bristly-glandular. *Calyx* 5-lobed, 0.3–1.4 cm. long, red, lobes unequal, rounded or ovate, outside glabrous or rarely hairy, eglandular, margin hairy or glabrous, eglandular. *Corolla* tubular-campanulate, fleshy, 3–5 cm. long, deep crimson or crimson or scarlet, rarely black-crimson or rose, 5 nectar pouches at the base; lobes 5–6, 1.3–1.5 cm. long, 1.6–2.3 cm. broad, rounded, emarginate. *Stamens* 10–12, unequal, shorter than the corolla, 1.5–2.7 cm. long; filaments puberulous at the base or glabrous. *Gynoecium* 2.5–3.3 cm. long; *ovary* conoid, truncate, 4–5 mm. long, 5-celled, *densely tomentose* with a brown or dark brown tomentum, eglandular or rarely glandular with short-stalked glands; style glabrous or rarely floccose at the base, eglandular. *Capsule* broadly oblong or ovoid or short stout, 0.9–2.4 cm. long, 0.5–1 cm. broad, moderately or *densely tomentose,* eglandular, calyx-lobes persistent.

This species was discovered by the Abbé Delavay in 1885 on Mount Tsang chan in the Tali range, Yunnan. It was afterwards found by Forrest and other collectors in west Yunnan. The plant grows in rocky open situations on mountain meadows, in moist stony pasture, and in *Abies* forests, at elevations of 3,355–4,000 m. (11,000–13,111 ft.).

R. haematodes is a distinct species and cannot be confused with other members of its Subseries. The characteristic features are the thick, woolly spongy, continuous indumentum of hairs covering the lower surface of the leaves, and the densely tomentose branchlets, petioles, ovaries, capsules, and usually the pedicels. The red calyx varies in length, from 3 mm. to 1.4 cm. The flower colour is deep crimson or crimson or scarlet. Forrest found a plant in west Yunnan with rose flowers; another plant which he collected in north-west Yunnan has black-crimson flowers. The indumentum on the lower surface of the leaves is bistrate; an upper layer of Dendroid hairs, and a lower layer of Rosulate hairs.

The species was first introduced by Forrest in 1910 (No. 6773). It was reintroduced by him under Nos. 15521 and 28351. Rock sent seeds on three occasions. McLaren introduced it three times. In its native home it grows 1–4 feet (rarely 2–3 inches) high or sometimes up to 6–10 feet. Two distinct growth forms are in cultivation: Form 1. A compact spreading shrub 2 feet high. Form 2. A broadly upright shrub with ascending branches, 4 feet high. The species will take some years before it flowers with freedom. It is a late-flowerer, in May and June, and it usually escapes the spring frosts. The dwarf form, 2 feet high, should be a most valuable acquisition to any rock garden. The species occasionally sets good and plentiful fertile seed. It is hardy, free-flowering, and provides an admirable display with its crimson flowers in trusses of 2–8, for which the foliage with dark green shining upper surface provides an excellent background.

The plant was given a First Class Certificate when shown by A. M. Williams, Launceston, Cornwall, in 1926.

Epithet. Blood-like.
Hardiness 3. May–June.

R. hemidartum Balf. f. ex Tagg in Notes Roy. Bot. Gard. Edin., Vol. 15 (1927) 314.
    Syn. *R. pocophorum* Balf. f. ex Tagg var. *hemidartum* (Balf. f. ex Tagg) Chamberlain in Notes Roy. Bot. Gard. Edin., Vol. 37 (1978) 334.

A somewhat compact rounded, or broadly upright shrub, 60 cm.–1.83 m. (2–6 ft.) high, *branchlets rather densely or moderately glandular* with short- or medium-stalked (rarely long-stalked) glands, glabrous or rarely hairy with long hairs, not bristly, those below the inflorescences 4–7 mm. in diameter; leaf-bud scales deciduous. *Leaves* oblong, obovate or oblong-obovate, lamina thick, leathery, 6–14 cm. long, 2.4–5.2 cm. broad, apex rounded or broadly obtuse, mucronate, base obtuse or slightly auricled; upper surface green with a glaucous bloom, matt, glabrous or with vestiges of hairs, midrib grooved, primary veins 9–14 on each side, impressed; *under surface with a thick, woolly, interrupted, in shreds and patches,* brown, *unistrate indumentum of Ramiform hairs, with long, much twisted branches,* sparsely glandular with minute short-stalked or sessile glands or eglandular, midrib raised, primary veins partly concealed; *petiole* 1–1.8 cm. long, *rather densely or moderately glandular* with short- or medium- or long-stalked glands, hairy with long hairs. *Inflorescence* terminal, a racemose umbel of 5–10 flowers; rhachis 0.6–1 cm. long, tomentose or floccose, eglandular or rarely glandular with short-stalked glands; pedicel 1–1.4 cm. long, moderately or rather densely glandular with short-stalked glands or eglandular, hairy with long hairs or not hairy. *Calyx* 5-lobed, 0.3–1.1 cm. long, crimson, divided to about ⅓ from the base or to the base, lobes unequal, oblong or rounded, outside not hairy or rarely hairy, eglandular, margin not hairy, eglandular or rarely glandular with short-stalked glands. *Corolla* tubular-campanulate, fleshy, 3.8–5.3 cm. long, deep rich crimson, crimson, scarlet or light red, without markings, 5 nectar pouches at the base; lobes 5, 1–1.5 cm. long, 1.6–2.4 cm. broad, rounded, emarginate. *Stamens* 10, unequal, shorter than the corolla, 1.8–3.8 cm. long; filaments glabrous. *Gynoecium* 3.8–5 cm. long; *ovary* conoid or oblong, truncate, 4–5 mm. long, 5-celled, *densely glandular* with short-stalked glands, not hairy, not bristly; style glabrous, eglandular. *Capsule* broadly oblong or short stout, 1–2 cm. long, 0.6–1 cm. broad, *densely glandular* with short-stalked glands, not hairy, not bristly, calyx-lobes persistent.

Forrest first collected this plant in August 1921 in the Salwin-Kiu Chiang Divide, Tsarong, east Tibet. He found it again later a few times in the same region and in south-east Tibet. In 1923 Rock collected it on several occasions in south-east Tibet. It grows in mixed rhododendron scrub on rocky slopes, in rocky alpine meadows, and in open alpine regions among rocky spurs, at elevations of 3,355–4,270 m. (11,000–14,000 ft.).

As the name suggests "half-flayed", a diagnostic feature is the thick, woolly, interrupted indumentum in patches and shreds on the lower surface of the leaves, revealing bare areas. In this respect the species is readily distinguished from its ally *R. pocophorum*. The indumentum on the lower surface of the leaves is unistrate. The lower layer is absent; the upper layer is Ramiform with long, much twisted branches.

R. hemidartum was first introduced by Forrest in 1921 (No. 20028—the Type number). It was reintroduced by him in 1922 (Nos. 21707, 22941). Rock sent seeds under two different seed numbers (Nos. 11162, 11179). In cultivation the species is a somewhat compact rounded or broadly upright shrub up to 5–6 feet high, a robust grower with thick, rigid branchlets. It is hardy, fairly fast-growing, and is an unusually attractive sight with its crimson flowers in trusses of 5–10. Occasionally it produces one or two capsules with good fertile seeds. The plant is uncommon in cultivation but is very desirable for inclusion in every collection of rhododendrons.

Epithet. Half-flayed.

Hardiness 3. April–May.

R. hillieri Davidian in Rhododendrons with Magnolias and Camellias (1974) 46–49.

A rounded shrub, 30 cm.–1.83 m. (1–6 ft.) high, branchlets rather densely or moderately bristly-hairy with branched, brown bristly hairs, eglandular, those below the inflorescences 3–4 mm. in diameter; leaf-bud scales deciduous or persistent. *Leaves* evergreen, obovate or oblong-obovate, *lamina* coriaceous, 3–6 cm. long, 1.6–3.1 cm. broad, apex rounded, base obtuse; upper surface dark green, shining, glabrous or with vestiges of hairs, midrib grooved, primary veins 8–10 on each side, deeply impressed; *under surface with a thin* or somewhat thin, *discontinuous* or continuous, brown, *unistrate indumentum* of *Dendroid hairs* with short or long, ribbon-like or narrower much twisted branches, midrib prominent, primary veins slightly raised; petiole 4–6 mm. long, grooved above, rather densely or moderately bristly-hairy with branched, brown bristly hairs, eglandular. *Inflorescence* a racemose umbel of 2–7 flowers, flower-bud scales deciduous; rhachis 2–4 mm. long, floccose, eglandular; pedicel 1–2 cm. long, densely or moderately bristly-hairy, eglandular. *Calyx* 5-lobed, crimson-rose or crimson, 2–5 mm. long, lobes unequal, ovate or triangular, outside glabrous, eglandular, margin hairy, eglandular. *Corolla* campanulate, fleshy, *2.8–4 cm. long,* bright rose-crimson, crimson-rose, light crimson, crimson or rose, 5 nectar pouches at the base; lobes 5, 1–1.3 cm. long, 1.5–2 cm. broad, rounded, emarginate. *Stamens* 10, unequal, 1.2–2.3 cm. long; filaments glabrous or rather densely puberulous at the base. *Gynoecium* 2–2.7 cm. long, shorter than the corolla; ovary conoid, 3–5 mm. long, 5–6-celled, densely hairy with branched brown hairs, eglandular; style glabrous, eglandular. *Capsule* oblong or ovoid, 0.8–1.4 cm. long, 5–6 mm. broad, moderately or sparsely hairy with branched hairs, eglandular, calyx-lobes persistent.

Forrest discovered this plant in June 1922 in the Salwin-Kiu Chiang Divide, south-east Tibet. He found it again in the same month on several occasions in that area. It grows in moorland, amongst alpine scrub, in open stony alpine meadows, and on ledges of cliffs in alpine corries, at elevations of 3,965–4,270 m. (13,000–14,000 ft.).

R. hillieri is a distinctive species of the Haematodes Subseries. In some respects, it shows a resemblance to R. chaetomallum, from which it differs markedly in that the leaves are smaller, the indumentum on the lower surface of the leaves is thin, usually discontinuous, and the flowers are smaller.

It was introduced by Forrest in 1922 (No. 21736—the Type number, and Nos. 21737, 21858). In its native home it is a small shrub, 1–3 feet high, but in cultivation it reaches 6 feet. Two colour forms are in cultivation, crimson and rose. The plant is hardy, free-flowering, and is easy to grow.

Epithet. After H. G. Hillier.

Hardiness 3. April–May.

R. mallotum Balf. f. et Ward in Notes Roy. Bot. Gard. Edin., Vol. 10 (1917) 118.

Syn. R. aemulorum Balf. f. in Notes Roy. Bot. Gard. Edin., Vol 12 (1920) 86.

Illustration. Bot. Mag. Vol. 158 t. 4919 (1935).

A broadly upright shrub or small tree, 1.53–4.58 m. (5–15 ft.) high, *branchlets densely tomentose* with a cinnamon-brown or rarely cinnamon-grey tomentum, not bristly, *eglandular*, those below the inflorescences 6–8 mm. in diameter; leaf-bud scales deciduous. *Leaves* obovate or rarely oblong-obovate, *lamina very thick*, leathery, *stiff, 7– 15.8 cm. long*, 3.5–8 cm. broad, apex rounded, truncate or notched, mucronate, base broadly obtuse or rarely rounded; *upper surface* dark green, *markedly rugulose, rough*, glabrous or with vestiges of hairs, midrib grooved, densely or moderately tomentose with a brown or grey tomentum or glabrous, primary veins 12–15 on each side, impressed; *under surface covered with a thick woolly continuous cinnamon-brown, bistrate indumentum of hairs, upper layer Dendroid with ribbon-like branches, lower layer Rosulate* continuous, midrib prominent, primary veins covered; *petiole* 1.3–3.6 cm. long, *densely tomentose* with a cinnamon-brown or whitish or dark brown tomentum, not bristly, *eglandular. Inflorescence* terminal, a *very compact* racemose umbel of *10–20 flowers; flower-bud large, globose, densely tomentose with a brown tomentum;* rhachis 0.8–1 cm. long, densely tomentose with a brown or cinnamon-brown tomentum, not bristly, eglandular; *pedicel* 0.6–1.5 cm. long, *stout, densely tomentose* with a brown or cinnamon-brown tomentum, not bristly, *eglandular. Calyx* 5-lobed, *minute 0.5 mm. long,* lobes triangular, densely tomentose with a cinnamon-brown tomentum, eglandular. *Corolla* tubular-campanulate, fleshy, 2.8–4.3 cm. long, scarlet-crimson, deep crimson or crimson, 5 nectar pouches at the base; lobes 5, 1–1.5 cm. long, 1.5–2.5 cm. broad, rounded, emarginate. *Stamens* 10, unequal, shorter than the corolla, 1.7–2.9 cm. long; filaments red, glabrous. *Gynoecium* 2–3.7 cm. long; ovary conoid, truncate, 4–7 mm. long, 5–7-celled, *densely tomentose* with a cinnamon-brown or brown tomentum, not bristly, *eglandular;* style glabrous, eglandular. *Capsule* broadly oblong or ovoid, 1.2–1.6 cm. long, 6–9 mm. broad, *densely woolly* with cinnamon-brown bristly hairs, *eglandular,* calyx-lobes persistent.

R. mallotum was discovered by Kingdon-Ward in May 1914 at the Hpimaw Pass, eastern Upper Burma. In 1919 Forrest collected it in the N'Maikha-Salwin Divide, western Yunnan, and in the same year Farrer found it at the Hpimaw Pass. In 1924 Forrest also collected it at the Hpimaw Pass. It grows on open hillsides, on rocky slopes, at the margins of thickets, in cane brakes, in rhododendron thickets, and in mixed cane and rhododendron scrub, at elevations of 3,050–3,660 m. (10,000–12,000 ft.). Kingdon-Ward records it as being a scraggy tree 10–15 feet high. According to Forrest it is a shrub of 5–8 feet, whilst Farrer describes it as a dwarfish, many-branched thin tree of 15 feet.

In 1920 R. aemulorum Balf. f. was described from specimens collected by Forrest and Farrer, and in The Species of Rhododendron the name was placed under R. mallotum in synonymy.

The most striking characters of this plant are the very thick, stiff, leathery leaves up to 15.8 cm. long, markedly rugulose, rough and dark green on the upper surface, with a thick, woolly, continuous, cinnamon-brown indumentum on the lower surface, and the very compact inflorescence of 10–20 deep crimson or crimson flowers. Other marked characteristics are the large globose flower-bud covered with brown tomentum, the densely tomentose, eglandular branchlets, petioles, pedicels, ovaries and capsules, and the minute calyx, 0.5 mm. long. The indumentum on the lower surface of the leaves is bistrate; an upper layer of Dendroid hairs with ribbon-like branches, and a lower layer of continuous Rosulate hairs.

R. mallotum was first introduced in 1919 simultaneously by Forrest from the eastern flank of the N'Maikha-Salwin Divide, west Yunnan (No. 17853), and by Farrer from the Hpimaw Pass, eastern Upper Burma (No. 815). From these gatherings and introductions at the same time by these two collectors, Isaac Bayley Balfour described R. aemulorum = "Rhododendron of the Rivals"; it is a pity that this name had to be reduced to synonymy. R. mallotum was reintroduced by Forrest in 1924 from the Hpimaw Pass (No. 25067).

In cultivation, R. mallotum is a broadly upright shrub, usually 5–10 feet or sometimes up to 15 feet high. It is undoubtedly a beautiful foliage plant, and with charming young growths. In some gardens the leaves are attacked by weevils producing small or large holes over the whole leaf surface. The large globose flower-buds, covered with a brown tomentum, are an attractive feature early in the season. The plant is an early flowerer, the blooms appearing in March–April, but are apt to be destroyed by spring frosts. The corolla with five nectar pouches at the base is a characteristic feature of the species and of the other members of its Subseries. Very often, little birds, such as, blue tits, tear the flowers into shreds in order to reach the honey in the nectar pouches. It is to be noted that during frosty weather, sometimes a ring of five circular holes appear at the base of the corolla-tube. This is caused possibly by water which accumulates in the nectar pouches, and when it freezes and expands, opens the ring of five holes. The plant is hardy in sheltered positions, and a well-grown plant is most effective with its crimson flowers produced freely in trusses of up to 20.

The species received an Award of Merit when exhibited by Col. S. R. Clarke, Borde Hill, Sussex, in 1933. It was given the same Award, as a foliage plant, when shown by the Crown Estate Commissioners, Windsor Great Park, in 1973.

Epithet. Woolly.
Hardiness 3. March–April.

R. piercei Davidian in American Rhododendron Society, Quarterly Bulletin (1976) Vol. 30 No. 4. Also Illustration, Front Cover.

    Syn. R. beanianum Cowan var. compactum Cowan in Notes Roy. Bot. Gard. Edin., Vol 21 (1953) 148.

A *compact spreading shrub*, 1.22–1.53 m. (4–5 ft.) high, *branchlets* densely hairy with short, brown, branched hairs, *not bristly, not bristly-glandular*, those below the inflorescences 6–9 mm. in diameter; leaf-bud scales deciduous. *Leaves* evergreen, oblong, oblong-oval or oblong-obovate, lamina coriaceous, 6–11 cm. long, 2.7–5.2 cm. broad, apex rounded, mucronate, base rounded or slightly cordulate; upper surface dark green, slightly rugulose, shining, glabrous, midrib grooved, densely or moderately hairy in its entire length or in the lower one-third, eglandular, primary veins 10–14 on each-side, deeply impressed; *under surface covered with a thick, woolly,* brown, *continuous, bistrate indumentum* of hairs, *upper layer a form of Dendroid* with short ribbon-like branches, *lower layer* continuous *Rosulate*, midrib prominent, somewhat glabrous or densely hairy, primary veins raised or concealed; *petiole* 1–2 cm. long, grooved above, densely hairy with short, brown branched hairs, *not bristly, not bristly-glandular* or rarely sparsely bristly-glandular. *Inflorescence* a racemose umbel of 6–8 flowers, flower-bud scales deciduous; rhachis 4–5 mm. long, hairy, eglandular; pedicel 1.2–1.5 cm. long, densely or moderately hairy with branched hairs, eglandular. *Calyx* 5-lobed, 3–6 mm. long, crimson, lobes unequal, oblong, oblong-oval or oval, glabrous, eglandular. *Corolla* tubular-campanulate, 2.8–3.6 cm. long, crimson, fleshy, 5 nectar pouches at the base; lobes 5, 1–1.3 cm. long, 1–2 cm. broad, rounded, emarginate. *Stamens* 10, unequal, 2–3 cm. long, shorter than the corolla; filaments glabrous. *Gynoecium* 3–3.4 cm. long, as long as the corolla or longer; ovary oblong or conoid, 5 mm. long, 6-celled, densely tomentose with a fawn tomentum, eglandular; style long, slender, straight, hairy at the base, eglandular. *Capsule* oblong or somewhat slender, 1.4–1.8 cm. long, 4–5 mm. broad, curved, densely hairy with long, fawn, branched hairs, eglandular, calyx-lobes persistent.

Kingdon-Ward discovered this species in fruit in December 1933 at Dri La, Zayul, Tibet, growing at an elevation of 3,660–3,965 m. (12,000–13,000 ft.).

It has long been known under the name *R. beanianum* var. *compactum. R. piercei* is a distinctive species. It is allied to *R. beanianum* from which it differs markedly in that it is a compact spreading shrub, 1.22–1.53 m. (4–5 ft.) high, the branchlets and petioles are not bristly, not bristly-glandular, the indumentum on the under surface of the leaves is bistrate, brown, and the upper surface of the leaves is slightly rugulose.

The species was introduced into cultivation by Kingdon-Ward in 1933 (No. 11040—the Type number). It is hardy, free-flowering, and it often produces a few capsules containing fertile seeds in plenty. An exceptionally fine sight in the woodland garden in the Royal Botanic Garden, Edinburgh was a superb plant of *R. piercei* and was undoubtedly the finest specimen of this species in general cultivation. It was a compact spreading shrub, 5 feet high and 16 feet across, and was of exquisite beauty with its crimson flowers in trusses of 6–8, for which the dark green shining leaves provided a charming contrast. Unfortunately it has now been lost to cultivation. The species should be a most valuable acquisition to every collection of rhododendrons.

Epithet. After Mr. & Mrs. Lawrence J. Pierce, Seattle, Washington, U.S.A., rhododendron growers.

Hardiness 3. March–May.

R. pocophorum Balf. f. ex Tagg in Notes Roy. Bot. Gard. Edin., Vol. 15 (1927) 316.

A somewhat rounded compact, or broadly upright somewhat lax shrub, 92 cm.–3 m. (3–10 ft) high, *branchlets rather densely glandular* with short- or medium-stalked (rarely long-stalked) glands, not tomentose, not bristly, those below the inflorescences 4–7 mm. in diameter; leaf-bud scales deciduous. *Leaves* oblong-obovate, obovate or oblong, lamina thick, leathery, 6–16 cm. long, 2.4–6.8 cm. broad, apex rounded, mucronate, base obtuse or sometimes rounded; upper surface pale or dark green, glaucous with a wax-like bloom or not glaucous, glabrous or with vestiges of hairs, midrib grooved, primary veins 8–14 on each side, impressed; *under surface covered with a thick woolly, continuous* brown, dark brown or cinnamon-coloured, *unistrate indumentum of Ramiform hairs, with long much twisted branches,* midrib raised, primary veins concealed; *petiole* 0.8–2.6 cm. long, *rather densely or moderately glandular* with short- or medium- or long-stalked glands, hairy with long branched or unbranched hairs or glabrous. *Inflorescence* terminal, a racemose umbel of 6–20 flowers; rhachis 0.6–1 cm. long, tomentose with a cinnamon or dark brown tomentum, glandular with short-stalked glands or eglandular; *pedicel* 1–2 cm. long, *rather densely* or rarely moderately *glandular* with short- or rarely medium-stalked glands, not hairy, not bristly. *Calyx* 5-lobed, *0.3–1.4 cm. long,* crimson, divided to about the middle or to the base, lobes unequal, irregular, ovate or rounded, outside glabrous or rarely hairy, eglandular or rarely glandular with short-stalked glands, margin glabrous or rarely hairy, glandular with short-stalked glands or sometimes eglandular. *Corolla* tubular-campanulate, fleshy, 3.6–5 cm. long, deep crimson, crimson, crimson-scarlet or red, 5 nectar pouches at the base; lobes 5, 1–1.5 cm. long, 2–2.3 cm. broad, rounded, emarginate. *Stamens* 10, unequal, shorter than the corolla, 2–4 cm.

long; filaments glabrous. *Gynoecium* 3–4.1 cm. long; *ovary* oblong or conoid, truncate, 4–7 mm. long, 5-celled, *densely glandular* with short-stalked glands, not hairy, not bristly; style glabrous, eglandular or rarely glandular at the base with short-stalked glands. *Capsule* broadly oblong or short stout, 1–2 cm. long, 6–9 mm. broad, *densely* or rarely moderately *glandular* with short-stalked glands, not tomentose or rarely tomentose, not bristly, calyx-lobes persistent or rarely deciduous.

This plant was first collected by Forrest in September 1919 in the Salwin-Kiu Chiang Divide, Tsarong, south-east Tibet. It was afterwards found by him and by Rock in other localities in the same region and in east Tibet. Kingdon-Ward collected it in north-east Upper Burma in 1922, and in Assam in 1928. It grows on rocky slopes, in rhododendron thickets, in mixed thickets, in bamboo thickets, in cane brakes, in alpine scrub on rocky moorland, among limestone crags, and in fir forest, at elevations of 3,660–4,575 m. (12,000–15,000 ft.).

R. pocophorum is closely related to *R. coelicum* from which it is readily distinguished by the rather densely glandular branchlets and petioles. It also differs usually in the larger calyx. The indumentum on the lower surface of the leaves is unistrate. The lower layer is absent; the upper layer is Ramiform with long, much twisted branches.

The species was first introduced by Forrest in 1921 (Nos.19977, 19983, 20019). It was reintroduced by him under eight different seed numbers including No. 21713—the Type number. Rock sent seeds on five occasions. Kingdon-Ward introduced it from north-east Upper Burma (No. 5484) and from Assam (No. 8289). Two distinct forms are in cultivation. Form 1. A somewhat rounded, compact shrub 5–6 feet high, with large leaves, and large deep crimson flowers. Form 2. A broadly upright shrub, somewhat lax and spreading, 4–5 feet high, with smaller leaves, and smaller crimson-scarlet flowers. The species has beautiful foliage, dark green shining on the upper surface, covered on the lower surface with a thick, woolly, dark brown or brown indumentum. It is free-flowering, and makes a wonderful sight with its large, deep crimson flowers in trusses of 6–20. The flowers appear in March–April, and are liable to be destroyed by frosts. The species is hardy, but to be able to grow it satisfactorily along the east coast, a sheltered position should be provided. The plant is uncommon in cultivation, but is worthy of being widely grown.

A clone 'Cecil Nice' (Kingdon-Ward No. 8289) was given an Award of Merit when shown by the National Trust and Countess of Rosse, Nymans Garden, in 1971.

Epithet. Wool-bearing.
Hardiness 3. March–April.

NERIIFLORUM SUBSERIES

General characters: shrubs or rarely small trees, 30 cm.–6 m. (1–20 ft.) high, branchlets moderately or rather densely tomentose or glabrous, not bristly or sometimes bristly, eglandular or sometimes setulose-glandular or rarely setose-glandular. Leaves evergreen, oblong, oblong-lanceolate, lanceolate, oblanceolate or rarely oblong-elliptic, lamina 3–14.5 cm. long, 0.8–4.5 cm. broad; *under surface glabrous or with a thick* or rarely thin, *woolly, continuous or interrupted,* yellowish-fawn, fawn, whitish, brown or cinnamon-brown indumentum of Ramiform hairs (except in *R. euchroum, Foliaceous form*), papillate or sometimes epapillate; petiole tomentose or glabrous, not bristly or sometimes bristly, eglandular or sometimes setulose-glandular or rarely setose-glandular. Inflorescence a racemose umbel of 3–12 flowers; pedicel 0.5–2 cm.

long, moderately or densely tomentose or floccose or sometimes glabrous, moderately or rather densely glandular or eglandular. Calyx 5-lobed or sometimes an undulate rim, 0.1–1.8 cm. long. Corolla tubular-campanulate or rarely campanulate, fleshy, 2.5–4.5 cm. long, deep crimson, crimson, scarlet, deep rose, tawny-orange or yellow, 5 nectar pouches at the base; lobes 5. Stamens 10. *Ovary oblong, narrow, tapered to the base of the style or sometimes conoid truncate,* 0.3–1 cm. long, 5- or rarely 6-celled, densely tomentose or rarely glabrous, densely or moderately glandular or eglandular. Capsule slender or rarely oblong, 1–3 cm. long, 3–6 mm. broad, curved or sometimes straight, moderately or rather densely tomentose or sometimes glabrous, moderately or rather densely glandular or eglandular.

KEY TO THE SPECIES

A. Under surface of the leaves not hairy (except sometimes midrib, floccose or
    glandular).
    B. Branchlets, petioles, pedicels, calyx and ovaries not glandular, not bristly.
        C. Under surface of the leaves covered with waxy papillae; corolla deep
            crimson, crimson, scarlet, carmine or deep rose .... *neriiflorum*
        C. Under surface of the leaves without waxy papillae; corolla deep rose or
            white heavily flushed rose or pink .... *dimitrum*
    B. Branchlets, petioles, pedicels, calyx and ovaries usually glandular with
        medium- or long-stalked glands, and often bristly, or densely setose and
        densely setose-glandular.
        D. Branchlets, petioles and ovaries not bristly, not glandular or setulose-
            glandular; inflorescence 4–8-flowered; corolla crimson, scarlet,
            carmine, salmon-rose, tawny-orange or straw-yellow.
            E. Branchlets and petioles not setulose-glandular; pedicel, calyx and
                ovary usually glandular .... *phaedropum*
            E. Branchlets and petioles setulose-glandular; pedicel, calyx and
                ovary eglandular.............. *floccigerum* var. *appropinquans*
        D. Branchlets, petioles and ovaries densely setose and setose-glandular;
            inflorescence about 10-flowered; corolla reddish-purple..........
        .... *bijiangense*
A. Under surface of the leaves with a continuous or interrupted indumentum of hairs
    or rarely with a few scattered hairs.
    F. Branchlets, petioles, pedicels, and usually calyx, ovaries and capsules
        glandular with long- or medium-stalked glands.
        G. Leaf-apex acuminate; inflorescence 6–12-flowered; glands and hairs on
            the ovary strigose .... *ochraceum*
        G. Leaf-apex usually obtuse or acute; inflorescence 3–5-flowered; glands
            and hairs on the ovary not strigose.
            H. Indumentum on the under surface of the leaves unistrate (one
                layer); under surface of the leaves covered with waxy papillae;
                medium-sized plant, 92 cm.–2.44 m. (3–8 ft.) high ... *sperabile*
            H. Indumentum on the under surface of the leaves bistrate (two
                layers); under surface of the leaves without waxy papillae; small
                plant, 30–60 cm. (1–2 ft.) high .... *euchroum*
    F. Branchlets, petioles, pedicels, calyx, ovaries and capsules eglandular.
        I. Indumentum on the under surface of the leaves continuous, bistrate;
            under surface of the leaves without waxy papillae... *albertsenianum*
        I. Indumentum on the under surface of the leaves usually interrupted,
            unistrate; under surface of the leaves covered with waxy papillae.

J. Indumentum on the under surface of the leaves thick, woolly, or sometimes with a few scattered hairs; corolla deep crimson, crimson, scarlet, bright rose, reddish-pink, or lemon-yellow margined or flushed rose or bright crimson . . . . *floccigerum*
J. Indumentum on the under surface of the leaves thin; corolla deep or light crimson . . . . *sperabiloides*

DESCRIPTION OF THE SPECIES

R. albertsenianum Forrest in Notes Roy. Bot. Gard. Edin., Vol. 11 (1919) 21.

A broadly upright shrub, 1.22–2.14 m. (4–7 ft.) high, *branchlets* tomentose with a whitish tomentum, not bristly, *eglandular*, those below the inflorescences 3–4 mm. in diameter. *Leaves* oblong-lanceolate or oblong, lamina 6–10 cm. long, 1.5–3.3 cm. broad, apex obtuse, mucronate, base obtuse; upper surface dark green, glabrous or with vestiges of hairs, midrib grooved, primary veins 12–18 on each side, deeply impressed; margin moderately or slightly recurved; *under surface covered with a thick, woolly continuous*, brown, *bistrate indumentum* of hairs, *upper layer Ramiform with flattened branches, lower layer Rosulate, epapillate,* midrib raised, primary veins concealed; *petiole* 0.6–1.3 cm. long, tomentose with a whitish tomentum, not bristly, *eglandular. Inflorescence* terminal, a racemose umbel of 5–6 flowers; rhachis 5 mm. long, floccose with dark brown hairs, eglandular; *pedicel* 1–1.8 cm. long, moderately or sparsely floccose with dark brown hairs, *eglandular. Calyx* 5-lobed, 2–4 mm. long, lobes rounded or ovate, outside hairy or glabrous, *eglandular,* margin hairy, *eglandular. Corolla* campanulate, 2.8–3.5 cm. long, bright crimson-rose or scarlet-crimson, 5 nectar pouches at the base; lobes 5, 1.4–1.7 cm. long, 1.7–2.2 cm. broad, rounded, emarginate. *Stamens* 10, unequal, shorter than the corolla, 1.5–2.3 cm. long; filaments glabrous. *Gynoecium* 2.7–3.5 cm. long; *ovary* oblong or *conoid, truncate,* 5–6 mm. long, 5-celled, densely tomentose, *eglandular;* style glabrous, eglandular. *Capsule* oblong, 1–1.5 cm. long, 3–5 mm. broad, straight, tomentose, *eglandular,* calyx-lobes persistent.

This species is known from a single collection made by Forrest in July 1917 in the Mekong-Salwin Divide, north-west Yunnan, growing in open forests, at an elevation of 3,050 m. (10,000 ft.).

It shows a certain degree of resemblance to *R. sperabile* in general appearance, but differs in that the branchlets, petioles, pedicels, calyx, ovaries and capsules are eglandular, the under surfaces of the leaves are without waxy papillae, the indumentum of hairs is bistrate, and the ovary is oblong or conoid with truncate apex. It also differs in the structure of the Ramiform hairs.

R. albertsenianum was introduced by Forrest in 1917 (No. 14195—the Type number). In its native home it reaches a height of 7 feet; in cultivation it is a broadly upright shrub up to 5 feet. The plant is hardy outdoors, with scarlet-crimson flowers produced freely in trusses of 5 or 6. It is rare in cultivation, but is worth a place in every collection of rhododendrons.

Epithet. After M. O. Albertson, Chinese Maritime Customs.
Hardiness 3. April–May.

R. bijiangense T. L. Ming in Acta Bot. Yunnanica 3: t. 2 (1981) 116.

A shrub, about 1 m. (3⅓ ft.) high, *branchlets densely setose-glandular. Leaves* narrowly lanceolate, 3.5–10 cm. long, 2–2.5 cm. broad, apex apiculate; under surface green, epapillate, glabrous except for the glandular midrib and main lateral veins; *petiole* about 1 cm. long, *densely setulose-glandular. Inflorescence* about 10-flowered; rhachis about 1 cm. long; pedicel 1.5–2 cm. long, densely setulose-glandular. *Calyx* 7–8 mm. long, glandular, lobes more or less fleshy, reddish, margins glandular-ciliate. *Corolla* campanulate, about 3 cm. long, fleshy, reddish-purple. *Ovary densely setose-glandular,* more or less abruptly contracted into the glabrous style. *Capsule:—*

This plant was discovered by Yang in May 1980 at Bijiang Xian, west Yunnan, growing at an elevation of 2,900 m. (9,508 ft.).

R. bijiangense is a distinctive species. The diagnostic features are the densely setose-glandular branchlets, petioles and ovaries. In these respects, the species is readily distinguished from its near ally *R. phaedropum* and from all the other members of its Subseries. Other notable features are the 10-flowered inflorescence, and the ovary abruptly contracted into the style.

The plant has not been introduced into cultivation.

Epithet. From Bijiang.

Not in cultivation.

R. dimitrum Balf. f. et Forrest in Notes Roy. Bot. Gard. Edin., Vol. 11 (1919) 50.

A broadly upright shrub, 1.22–2.75 m. (4–9 ft.) high, branchlets moderately or sparsely floccose, eglandular, those below the inflorescences 2–5 mm. in diameter. *Leaves* oblong, lamina leathery, 4–10 cm. long, 1.5–3.2 cm. broad, apex acute or obtuse, base obtuse; upper surface pale green, matt, glabrous, eglandular, midrib grooved, primary veins 12–14 on each side, deeply impressed; margin slightly recurved; *under surface* paler, matt, *glabrous,* not punctulate, *epapillate,* midrib prominent, primary veins raised; petiole 0.8–1.6 cm. long, grooved above, moderately or sparsely floccose or glabrous, eglandular. *Inflorescence* a racemose umbel of 8–12 flowers; rhachis 0.8–1.2 cm. long, pubescent, eglandular; pedicel 0.9–1.6 cm. long, densely or moderately hairy with short hairs, eglandular. *Calyx* 5-lobed, *0.6–1.5 cm. long,* pink, cup-shaped, divided to the base or to about the middle, lobes unequal, ovate, rounded, irregular, oblong or triangular, outside glabrous or floccose at the base, eglandular, margin floccose or glabrous, eglandular. *Corolla* tubular-campanulate, 3.2–4 cm. long, *deep rose, white heavily flushed rose, or pink,* with or without crimson spots, 5 nectar pouches at the base, outside glandular; lobes 5, 1–1.5 cm. long, 1.4–1.8 cm. broad, rounded, emarginate. *Stamens* 10, unequal, 2–3.2 cm. long; filaments puberulous at the base. *Gynoecium* 3–3.5 cm. long; *ovary narrow, slender, tapered to the base of the style or truncate,* 5–6 mm. long, densely floccose, eglandular; style floccose at the base or in the lower half or two-thirds its length or up to the tip. *Capsule:—*

Forrest first found this plant in May 1917 on the western flank of the Tali Range, mid-west Yunnan. He collected it again later in July of that year in the same region. In 1932 McLaren's collectors found it also on the Tali Range. It grows in open thickets and pine forests, at elevations of 3,050–3,355 m. (10,000–11,000 ft.).

In *The Species of Rhododendron, R. dimitrum* has been placed in the Irroratum Series. It is an aberrant species in that Series. A distinctive feature is the large calyx, 0.6–1.5 cm. long, divided to the base or to about the middle. In this respect, the species differs markedly from the species of the Irroratum Series where the calyx is minute 1–2 mm. or rarely 4–5 mm. long.

This species was described by Isaac Bayley Balfour and Forrest. In the original description, they correctly point out that "*R. neriiflorum* Franch. is its nearest ally". *R. dimitrum* is very similar to *R. neriiflorum* in general features, particularly in the large calyx, but differs in that the lower surface of the leaves is epapillate, and the flowers are deep rose, white heavily flushed rose, or pink; in *R. neriiflorum* the lower surface of the leaves is papillate, and the flowers are deep crimson, crimson, scarlet, carmine or deep rose. These distinctions are not in favour of including *R. dimitrum* in the Irroratum Series; it will now be transferred to the Neriiflorum Subseries, Neriiflorum Series.

R. dimitrum was introduced by Forrest in 1917 (No. 15575). In its native home it grows up to 9 feet high; in cultivation it is a broadly upright shrub up to 5 feet. It is hardy outdoors, with white flushed rose flowers produced freely in trusses of 8–12. The plant is rare in cultivation but is most desirable for inclusion in every collection of rhododendrons.

Epithet. With double cap, alluding to very large calyx.

Hardiness 3. April–May.

R. euchroum Balf. f. et Ward in Notes Roy. Bot. Gard. Edin., Vol. 9 (1916) 288.

A *small spreading procumbent shrub, 30–60 cm. (1–2 ft.) high,* branchlets moderately or rather densely setulose or not setulose, setulose-glandular or not setulose-glandular, tomentose with a whitish tomentum, those below the inflorescences 2–4 mm. in diameter. *Leaves* lanceolate, oblanceolate or oblong, lamina 4–7.5 cm. long, 1–2.5 cm. broad, apex acute, obtuse or acuminate, mucronate, base tapered or obtuse; upper surface green, glabrous or with vestiges of hairs, midrib grooved, primary veins 7–12 on each side, deeply impressed; *under surface covered with a thick, woolly, continuous,* brown, *bistrate indumentum* of hairs, *upper layer Foliaceous form with very short flattened branches, lower layer Rosulate, epapillate,* midrib raised, primary veins concealed; petiole 0.6–1.5 cm. long, setulose or not setulose, setulose-glandular or not setulose-glandular, floccose. *Inflorescence* terminal, a racemose umbel of 4–5 flowers; rhachis 3–5 mm. long, hairy with dark brown hairs, glandular with short-stalked glands or eglandular; pedicel 1–1.1 cm. long, moderately or rather densely floccose, glandular with short-stalked glands. *Calyx* 5-lobed, minute, 1 mm. long, lobes rounded, ovate or oblong, outside and margin hairy, glandular with long-stalked glands. *Corolla* tubular-campanulate, fleshy, 2.6–3 cm. long, *bright brick-red,* 5 nectar pouches at the base; lobes 5, 0.8–1.2 cm. long, 0.8–1.4 cm. broad, rounded, emarginate. *Stamens* 10, unequal, shorter than the corolla, 1.8–2.5 cm. long; filaments puberulous at the base. *Gynoecium* 2.6–2.8 cm. long; *ovary oblong, narrow, tapered to the base of the style,* 5 mm. long, 5-celled, densely tomentose, glandular with long-stalked glands, not bristly; style hairy at the base or glabrous, glandular at the base with long-stalked glands or eglandular. *Capsule* slender, 1.4 cm. long, 4 mm. broad, curved, floccose, glandular with long-stalked glands, calyx-lobes persistent.

Kingdon-Ward discovered this plant in July 1914 on the ridge of Naung-Chaung, Nwai Divide, East Upper Burma. He found it again in June 1919 in the same region. It grows in damp shady situations under bamboos and conifers, at elevations of 3,050–3,355 m. (10,000–11,000 ft.). Kingdon-Ward records it as being a dwarf, spreading procumbent shrub growing on granite ridges or forming loose thickets a foot high.

R. euchroum is closely allied to *R. sperabile* which it resembles in general features, but differs in that it is a dwarf shrub 1–2 feet high, the lower surface of the leaves is epapillate, and the indumentum is bistrate. Moreover, it differs markedly in the Foliaceous form of hairs.

The plant was introduced by Kingdon-Ward in 1919 (No. 3267). In cultivation it is a dwarf shrub 1½ feet high with bright red flowers in trusses of 4 or 5. The plant has been rare, and has not been seen for a long time. It is now possibly lost to cultivation.

Epithet. With a good colour.

Not in cultivation.

R. floccigerum Franch. in Journ. de Bot. Vol. 12 (1898) 259.

Illustration. Bot. Mag. Vol. 155 t. 9290 (1932).

A rounded, somewhat compact or lax shrub, 60 cm.–2.44 m. (2–8 ft.) high, *branchlets* moderately or densely (or rarely sparsely) floccose with branched, brown or sometimes whitish hairs, not bristly, *eglandular,* those below the inflorescences 2–4 mm. in diameter. *Leaves* lanceolate or oblong, lamina 4–12 cm. long, 0.9–2.8 cm. broad, apex obtuse or acute, mucronate, base tapered, obtuse or rarely rounded; upper surface dark green, glabrous or with vestiges of hairs, midrib grooved, primary veins 10–18 on each side, deeply impressed; *under surface with a thick, woolly, interrupted* or rarely continuous or sometimes with a few hairs, cinnamon-brown or brown or pale brown *unistrate indumentum of Ramiform hairs with medium length ribbon-like branches,* covered with waxy papillae, midrib raised, primary veins partly exposed or exposed (or rarely concealed); *petiole* 0.5–1.7 cm. long, floccose with brown or whitish hairs, not bristly, *eglandular.* *Inflorescence* terminal, a racemose umbel of 4–8 flowers; rhachis 2–7 mm. long, floccose with cinnamon-brown or brown hairs, eglandular; *pedicel* 0.6–1.7 cm. long, moderately or densely floccose with dark brown or brown hairs, *eglandular* or rarely rather densely glandular with medium-stalked glands. *Calyx* 5-lobed or with 5 undulate lobes, 0.1–1.1 cm. long, lobes unequal, rounded, ovate or irregular, *outside* hairy or glabrous, *eglandular, margin* hairy or rarely glabrous, *eglandular. Corolla* tubular-campanulate, fleshy, 2.5–4.3 cm. long, *deep crimson, crimson, scarlet, carmine, bright rose, reddish-pink, lemon-yellow margined or flushed rose or bright crimson, or yellow flushed pink,* without a blotch or rarely with a deep crimson blotch at the base, 5 nectar pouches at the base; lobes 5, 1–1.5 cm. long, 1–2.1 cm. broad, rounded, emarginate. *Stamens* 10, unequal, shorter than the corolla, 1.4–3.1 cm. long; filaments glabrous or rarely puberulous at the base. *Gynoecium* 2–3.6 cm. long; *ovary* oblong, *narrow, tapered to the base of the style or conoid truncate,* 4–8 mm. long, 5–6-celled, densely tomentose, *eglandular;* style tomentose at the base or in the lower one-third or rarely glabrous. *Capsule* slender, 1.3–3 cm. long, 3–4 mm. broad, slightly or moderately curved, rather densely or moderately tomentose with brown or cinnamon-brown tomentum, *eglandular,* calyx-lobes persistent or deciduous.

R. floccigerum was discovered by the Abbé Soulié in July 1903 in the Mekong-Salwin Divide, near Tseku, north-west Yunnan. Subsequently it was found by other collectors in the same region and in south-east Tibet. It grows in rhododendron thickets, in mixed rhododendron and cane scrub, on open rocky slopes and on ledges of cliffs, in cane brakes and mixed scrub, on boulders, in pine and spruce forests, at elevations of 2,300–4,270 m. (7,541–14,000 ft.).

The species is variable in general features due to the various environmental conditions in which it is found. It grows from 2 to 8 feet high; the leaves (laminae) are 4–12 cm. long, and 9 mm.–2.8 cm. broad; the corolla varies from deep crimson to bright rose or lemon-yellow margined or flushed rose or yellow flushed pink.

It is usually easily recognised by the thick, woolly, interrupted indumentum on the lower surface of the leaves, revealing large or small bare areas of the epidermis. In this respect it is readily distinguished from all other species of its Subseries. The indumentum is unistrate; the hairs are Ramiform with medium length ribbon-like branches. It will be noted that the ovary is oblong narrow, tapered to the base of the style, or conoid truncate at the apex.

R. floccigerum was first introduced by Forrest in 1914 (Nos. 12893, 13299). It was reintroduced by him under 19 different seed numbers. Rock sent seeds on 17 occasions. Yü introduced it under three seed numbers. In cultivation it is a rounded, somewhat compact or lax shrub, usually up to 5 feet high. Several forms are in cultivation varying in leaf size and in flower colour, namely, crimson, scarlet, rose, reddish-pink, yellowish-pink, lemon-yellow flushed rose, and yellow flushed pink. The species has the merit of reaching the flowering size at an early age. The plant is hardy, and the tubular-campanulate flowers are produced freely in trusses of 4–8. Occasionally it produces slender capsules containing fertile seed in plenty.

Epithet. Bearing flecks of wool.

Hardiness 3. March–May.

R. floccigerum Franch. var. **appropinquans** Tagg et Forrest in Notes Roy. Bot. Gard. Edin., Vol. 15 (1927) 312.

Syn. *R. floccigerum* Franch. subsp. *appropinquans* (Tagg et Forrest) Chamberlain in Notes Roy. Bot. Gard. Edin., Vol. 37 (1979) 333.

This plant was first collected by Forrest in July 1922 in the Chienchuan-Mekong Divide, north-west Yunnan. It was found by him again in 1923 in the same area. Rock also collected it in the same region in 1923. It grows on the margins of mixed thickets and of open mixed forests, at elevations of 3,050–3,355 m. (10,000–11,000 ft.).

The variety differs from the species in that the under surface of the leaves is glabrous except the floccose midrib, and the branchlets and petioles are setulose-glandular. It bears a certain degree of resemblance to *R. phaedropum*, but is readily distinguished by the setulose-glandular branchlets and petioles, and by the eglandular pedicels, calyx and ovaries.

The plant was introduced by Forrest in 1922 (No. 21531). In its native home it grows 5–10 feet high; in cultivation it is a rounded shrub up to 5 feet. It is hardy, free-flowering, and is easy to cultivate.

It received an Award of Merit when exhibited by Col. Lord Digby, Minterne, Dorset, in 1957.

Epithet of the variety. Nearly glabrous.
Hardiness 3. March–May.

R. neriiflorum Franch. in Bull. Soc. Bot. France, Vol. 33 (1886) 230.

Illustration. Bot. Mag. Vol. 143 t. 8727 (1917).

A rounded, compact or somewhat lax shrub, 60 cm.–3 m. (2–10 ft.) high, *branchlets* tomentose with a thin fawn or white tomentum or glabrous, *not bristly, eglandular*, those below the inflorescences 3–4 mm. in diameter. *Leaves oblong*, rarely oblong-oval, oblong-lanceolate or lanceolate, lamina 3–12.3 cm. long, 1.3–3.9 cm. broad, apex rounded or obtuse or rarely acute, mucronate, base obtuse, sometimes tapered or rounded; upper surface dark green, glabrous or with vestiges of hairs, midrib grooved, primary veins 10–18 on each side, deeply impressed; *under surface glabrous, white, covered with waxy papillae*, not alveolate or alveolate with large or small alveoli, midrib raised, glabrous or floccose; *petiole* 0.8–2.3 cm. long, tomentose with a thin fawn or white tomentum or glabrous, *not bristly, eglandular*. *Inflorescence* terminal, a racemose umbel of 4–12 (rarely 1–2) flowers; rhachis 0.2–1.2 cm. long, hairy with dark brown or brown hairs, eglandular; *pedicel* 0.5–1.7 cm. long, moderately or densely tomentose with a thin brown or fawn tomentum, *not bristly, eglandular. Calyx* 5-lobed, divided to about the middle or to the base or sometimes an undulate rim, 0.1–1.8 cm. long, fleshy, crimson, lobes unequal, ovate, rounded, oblong or irregular, *outside and margin* hairy or glabrous, *not bristly, eglandular. Corolla* tubular-campanulate, fleshy, 2.8–4.5 cm. long, deep crimson, crimson, scarlet, carmine or deep rose, 5 nectar pouches at the base; lobes 5, 1–1.5 cm. long, 1.3–2 cm. broad, rounded, emarginate. *Stamens* 10, unequal, shorter than the corolla, 1.5–4.3 cm. long; filaments white to deep crimson at the base, glabrous or rarely puberulous at the base. *Gynoecium* 2–4.5 cm. long; *ovary oblong, narrow, tapered to the base of the style*, 0.5–1 cm. long, 5-celled, densely tomentose with a fawn, dark brown or brown tomentum, rarely glabrous, *not bristly, eglandular* or rarely glandular with short-stalked glands; style tomentose at the base or sometimes glabrous, eglandular. *Capsule* slender, 1.3–2.8 cm. long, 3–4 mm. broad, curved, moderately or rather densely tomentose with a brown tomentum, eglandular, calyx-lobes deciduous or persistent.

This well known species was discovered by the Abbé Delavay in March 1883 on Mount Tsang chan, above Tali, mid-west Yunnan. It was afterwards found by other collectors in mid-west and west Yunnan, south Tibet and North Burma. The plant grows in rocky situations, on rocky slopes and hillsides, on cliffs, on boulders, in open rocky meadows, in open situations in pine forests, amongst scrub, in rhododendron thickets, in dense mixed jungle, and in thick mixed forest, at elevations of 2,745–3,660 m. (9,000–12,000 ft.).

The characteristic features of the plant are usually the oblong leaves, rounded at both ends, upper surface dark green, under surface glabrous, glaucous-white, covered with an immense number of waxy papillae. The leaves (laminae) vary considerably in size, from 3 to 12.3 cm. long. Forrest found a plant in the Shweli-Salwin Divide, 2–3 feet high with very small leaves (laminae) 3 to 4 cm. long.

R. neriiflorum was first introduced by Forrest in 1910 (No. 6780). It was reintroduced by him under 10 different seed numbers. Rock sent seeds on three occasions in 1922. Kingdon-Ward introduced it three times, in 1922, 1931 and 1953. In cultivation it is a rounded, compact or somewhat lax, or bushy shrub, usually up to 5 or 6 feet high. The leaves are usually oblong, but there is a very distinct form with broad oblong-oval leaves up to 3.9 cm. in width. The flowers are deep crimson, crimson or scarlet; there is a form with deep rose flowers but is uncommon in gardens. A pure white form of unknown origin appeared in a garden in Argyllshire, but unfortunately it is now lost to cultivation. The young growths vary in colour; very often they are creamy-white. A plant introduced by Ludlow and Sherriff, with scarlet flowers, has distinctive brown young growths. The species has the advantage of flowering at a young age, when 1 or 1½ feet high. It is an excellent plant for gardens. The crimson or scarlet flowers are produced very freely, the dark green leaves providing a charming contrast. The plant seeds itself freely in some gardens along the west coast. It often produces a few slender capsules containing good fertile seeds.

Epithet. With flowers like *Nerium oleander*.
Hardiness 3. April–May.

R. neriiflorum Franch. var. **agetum** (Balf. f. et Forrest) Davidian, comb. nov.
Syn. *R. agetum* Balf. f. et Forrest in Notes Roy. Bot. Gard. Edin., Vol. 13 (1920) 29.
R. neriiflorum Franch. subsp. *agetum* (Balf. f. et Forrest) Tagg in The Sp. of Rhod. (1930) 533.

Forrest first collected this plant in May 1919 on the eastern flank of the N'Maikha-Salwin Divide, western Yunnan. He found it again later on several occasions in the same region. In May 1931 Kingdon-Ward collected it in the Adung Valley on the Burma-Tibet Frontier. It grows in thickets, cane brakes, open situations at the base of cliffs, on scrub-clad screes and ledges of exposed cliffs, and in forests, at elevations of 2,440–3,660 m. (8,000–12,000 ft.).

The variety differs from the species in that the leaves are small, narrowly oblong or lanceolate, lamina 3.1–7 cm. (usually up to 6 cm.) long, and 1–2 cm. (usually up to 1.5 cm.) broad.

The plant was first introduced by Forrest in 1919 (No. 17749). It was reintroduced by Kingdon-Ward in 1931 (No. 9506). In cultivation it is a rounded, spreading shrub up to 6 feet high. The plant is hardy, free-flowering, and is easy to cultivate. It is uncommon in cultivation, but is worth being more widely grown.

Epithet of the variety. Wondrous.
Hardiness 3. April–May.

R. neriiflorum Franch. var. **euchaites** (Balf. f. et Forrest) Davidian, comb. nov.
Syn. *R. euchaites* Balf. f. et Forrest in Notes Roy. Bot. Gard. Edin., Vol. 13 (1920) 43.
R. neriiflorum Franch. subsp. *euchaites* (Balf. f. et Forrest) Tagg in The Sp. of Rhod. (1930) 533.
R. phoenicodum Balf. f. et Farrer in Notes Roy. Bot. Gard. Edin., Vol. 13 (1922) 285.

R. neriiflorum Franch. subsp. *phoenicodum* (Balf. f. et Farrer) Tagg in The Sp. of Rhod. (1930) 533.

R. neriiflorum Franch. subsp. *neriiflorum Euchaites Group* R.H.S. in Rhod. Handb. (1980) p.50.

Illustration. Bot. Mag. Vol. 161 t. 9521 (1938), figured as *R. phoenicodum.*

This plant was first collected by Forrest in August 1912 on the western flank of the Shweli-Salwin Divide, west Yunnan. It was afterwards found by him and by other collectors in west and mid-west Yunnan, north-east Upper Burma, and south-east Tibet. It grows in rhododendron forest, in rhododendron and holly forest, in moss forest, in open thickets amongst rocks, in rocky shady situations, and on rocky slopes amongst scrub, at elevations of 2,440–3,355 m. (8,000–11,000 ft.). Kingdon-Ward records it as being a small tree, very common in forest at Laktang, north-east Upper Burma.

This variety differs from *R. neriiflorum* in that it is a tall upright shrub or tree, usually 2.44–6.10 m. (8–20 ft.) high.

The plant was first introduced by Forrest in 1912 (No. 8939). It was reintroduced by him under four different seed numbers. Kingdon-Ward sent seed in 1919 (No. 3040). It was introduced by McLaren (C44), and by Ludlow and Sherriff (No. 1352). In cultivation it is an upright shrub up to 15 feet high. It is hardy, a vigorous grower, with crimson flowers produced freely in trusses of 5–12. Beautiful examples of the plant are to be seen in gardens along the west coast.

It was given an Award of Merit when shown by Lady Aberconway and the Hon. H. D. McLaren, Bodnant, in 1929.

Epithet. With beautiful hairs.

Hardiness 3. April–May.

R. ochraceum Rehd. et Wils. in Plantae Wilsonianae, Vol. 1 (1913) 534.

A shrub or small tree, up to 3 m. (10 ft.) high, *branchlets setulose-glandular,* not bristly, tomentose with a whitish tomentum or not tomentose, those below the inflorescences 2–4 mm. in diameter. *Leaves* oblanceolate or lanceolate, lamina 4–9.5 cm. long, 0.9–2.5 cm. broad, *apex acuminate,* mucronate, base tapered, obtuse or rounded; upper surface matt, somewhat rugulose, glabrous or with vestiges of hairs, midrib grooved, hairy or with vestiges of hairs, glandular with medium- or long-stalked glands or eglandular, primary veins 12–16 on each side, deeply impressed; margin recurved; *under surface with somewhat thick, woolly, continuous, brown, unistrate indumentum of Ramiform hairs with many medium length very narrow branches,* waxy papillae poorly developed or absent, midrib raised, primary veins concealed; *petiole* 0.9–2 cm. long, *setulose-glandular,* not bristly, tomentose with a whitish tomentum or not tomentose. *Inflorescence* terminal, a racemose umbel of *6–12 flowers;* rhachis 0.5–1.4 cm. long, moderately or densely hairy with fawn or brown hairs, eglandular; *pedicel* 0.6–1.5 cm. long, tomentose with brown or fawn tomentum or glabrous, *moderately or rather densely glandular* with long- and medium-stalked glands *or setulose-glandular. Calyx* 5-lobed, 1–5 mm. long, lobes triangular or rounded, *outside* hairy or glabrous, *moderately or rather densely glandular* with medium- or long-stalked glands, *margin* hairy or glabrous, *glandular* with medium- or long-stalked glands. *Corolla* broadly campanulate or tubular-campanulate, 2.5–4 cm. long, crimson, unspotted, *5 nectar pouches at the base;* lobes 5, 0.8–1 cm. long, 1.3–1.6 cm. broad, rounded, emarginate. *Stamens* 10–12, unequal, shorter than the corolla, 1.5–2.6 cm. long; filaments glabrous. *Gynoecium* 2–3.4 cm. long; *ovary conoid truncate, or oblong narrow tapered to the base of the style,* 3–5 mm. long, *densely glandular with long-stalked strigose glands, hairy with strigose hairs* or glabrous; style glabrous, eglandular. *Capsule* slender, 1.8–2.5 cm. long, 5–6 mm. broad, straight or slightly curved, not hairy, sparsely or moderately *glandular* with medium-stalked glands, calyx-lobes persistent.

This species was discovered by Wilson in June 1908 at Wa-shan, western Sichuan. It was later found by other collectors in the same region and in north-west Yunnan. The plant grows in thickets, in woods, and in mixed forests, at elevations of 1,900–3,000 m. (6,230–9,836 ft.).

R. *ochraceum* has been placed in the Maculiferum Subseries, Barbatum Series. It is an aberrant species in this Subseries with which it has very little in common. The main features of this plant are the lanceolate or oblanceolate leaves covered on the under surfaces with a thick, woolly, continuous, unistrate indumentum of Ramiform hairs, and the tubular-campanulate crimson corolla with 5 nectar pouches at the base. In these and other respects, *R. ochraceum* is very similar to *R. sperabile* and allies in the Neriiflorum Subseries, Neriiflorum Series, to which it will now be transferred. It differs from *R. sperabile* in that the leaf-apex is acuminate, the waxy papillae on the under surfaces of the leaves are poorly developed or are absent, the inflorescence is 6–12-flowered, and the glands and hairs on the ovary are strigose.

The plant has not been introduced into cultivation.

Epithet. Yellowish.

Not in cultivation.

R. phaedropum Balf. f. et Farrer in Notes Roy. Bot. Gard. Edin., Vol. 13 (1922) 283.
    Syn. *R. neriiflorum* Franch. subsp. *phaedropum* (Balf. f. et Farrer) Tagg in The Sp. of Rhod. (1930) 533.

A rounded or compact bushy or broadly upright shrub or tree, 92 cm.–6 m. (3–20 ft.), rarely 60 cm. (2 ft.) high, branchlets tomentose with a thin fawn tomentum or densely or moderately floccose with brown hairs or glabrous, eglandular or moderately or sparsely glandular with long-stalked glands, not bristly, those below the inflorescences 2–5 mm. in diameter. *Leaves* lanceolate, oblong or oblong-lanceolate, lamina 4–14.3 cm. long, 0.8–4.5 cm. broad, apex acute, obtuse or rounded, mucronate, base obtuse, tapered or rounded; upper surface pale or dark green, glabrous or with vestiges of hairs, midrib grooved, primary veins 12–20 on each side, deeply impressed; *under surface glabrous, white, covered with waxy papillae*, midrib raised, glabrous or floccose; petiole 0.7–2.2 cm. long, tomentose with a thin fawn or white tomentum or rarely floccose or glabrous, eglandular or sometimes sparsely glandular with long-stalked glands, not bristly. *Inflorescence* terminal, a racemose umbel of 4–8 flowers; rhachis 4–8 mm. long, hairy with fawn or dark brown hairs, eglandular; *pedicel* 0.8–2 cm. long, moderately or rather densely tomentose with a thin brown tomentum or rarely rather densely floccose or glabrous, *rather densely or moderately glandular* with long- or medium-stalked glands or eglandular, not bristly. *Calyx* 5-lobed or rarely an undulate rim, 1–3 mm. long, lobes ovate, rounded or triangular, *outside* hairy or not hairy, *glandular* with medium- or long-stalked glands or eglandular, *margin* hairy or not hairy, *glandular* with long-stalked glands or eglandular. *Corolla* tubular-campanulate, fleshy, 2.6–4.5 cm. long, *crimson, scarlet, salmon-rose, tawny-orange or straw-yellow*, 5 nectar pouches at the base; lobes 5, 0.8–1.3 cm. long, 1.2–1.8 cm. broad, rounded, emarginate. *Stamens* 10, unequal, shorter than the corolla, 1.6–3.5 cm. long; filaments glabrous. *Gynoecium* 2–4 cm. long; ovary oblong, *narrow, tapered to the base of the style*, 4–9 mm. long, 5-celled, densely or rarely moderately tomentose with a brown tomentum or not tomentose, *moderately or densely glandular* with short- or long-stalked glands or eglandular, not bristly or rarely densely bristly; style tomentose at the base or glabrous, eglandular or rarely glandular at the base with medium-stalked glands. *Capsule* slender, 1.8–3 cm. long, 4 mm. broad, curved, rather densely or moderately tomentose with a brown tomentum, eglandular, calyx-lobes persistent.

This plant was discovered by Farrer in May 1920 growing as a large tree of 15 feet in alpine woodland at Nyitadi, north-east Upper Burma. Subsequently it was found by him and by other collectors in the same region and in south Tibet, Burma-Tibet Frontier, Assam, and in Bhutan. It grows in alpine woodland, in dense *Abies* and rhododendron forest, among rocks, and in thickets on cliffs, at elevations of 2,288–3,660 m.

(7,500–12,000 ft.). According to Kingdon-Ward it forms a small tree, and is abundant in mixed forest at Tara Tru Pass, north-east Upper Burma.

It bears a resemblance to *R. neriiflorum* in general features but differs in that the branchlets, pedicels, calyx and ovaries are usually moderately or densely glandular with long- or medium-stalked glands, and the corolla varies a great deal from straw-yellow, salmon-rose to crimson.

The plant was first introduced by Kingdon-Ward in 1922 (No. 5483). It was reintroduced by him under four different seed numbers (6854, 8521, 9483, 9561). Ludlow, Sherriff and Hicks sent seeds in 1949 (No. 21290). Two distinct forms are in cultivation. Form 1. A plant with small, very narrow lanceolate leaves, laminae 4–6.8 cm. long, 1–1.5 cm. broad (Kingdon-Ward No. 5483). Form 2. A plant with large, broad oblong or oblanceolate leaves, laminae 10.5–12.5 cm. long, 3.5–4 cm. broad (Kingdon-Ward No. 6854). Four colour forms are grown in gardens, namely, crimson, scarlet, tawny-orange, and straw-yellow. The plant is hardy, but to be able to grow it successfully, particularly along the east coast and in gardens inland, a sheltered position should be provided. It is fairly fast-growing, and makes a fine show with its flowers produced freely in trusses of 4–8.

Epithet. Of bright appearance.
Hardiness. 3. March–May.

R. sperabile Balf. f et Farrer in Notes Roy. Bot. Gard. Edin., Vol. 13 (1922) 297.
Illustration. Bot. Mag. Vol. 156 t. 9301 (1933).

A somewhat compact or bushy or lax shrub, 92 cm.–2.44 m. (3–8 ft.) high, *branchlets* moderately or rarely sparsely *setulose-glandular*, not bristly, moderately or rather densely tomentose with a whitish or fawn tomentum, those below the inflorescences 2–4 mm. in diameter. *Leaves* lanceolate, oblong-lanceolate or sometimes oblong, lamina 3.8–10.5 cm. long, 1–3.3 cm. broad, apex acute or obtuse, mucronate, base obtuse, tapered or rarely rounded; upper surface dark green, semi-bullate, glabrous or with vestiges of hairs, midrib grooved, hairy towards the base or glabrous, setulose-glandular towards the base or not setulose-glandular, primary veins 10–18 on each side, deeply impressed; margin recurved or sometimes flat; *under surface covered with a thick, woolly, continuous,* yellowish-fawn, fawn, brown or pale cinnamon, *unistrate indumentum of Ramiform hairs with many long filamentous very narrow branches,* covered with waxy papillae, midrib raised, primary veins concealed; *petiole* 0.5–1.7 cm. long, moderately or sometimes sparsely *setulose-glandular* or rarely not setulose-glandular, not bristly, rather densely or moderately tomentose with a fawn or whitish tomentum. *Inflorescence* terminal, a racemose umbel of 3–5 flowers; rhachis 3–5 mm. long, tomentose with a brown tomentum or glabrous, glandular with short-stalked glands or eglandular; *pedicel* 0.6–1.8 cm. long, hairy or rarely densely tomentose, *moderately or rather densely glandular with long-stalked glands* or rarely eglandular. *Calyx* 5-lobed or with 5 undulate lobes, 1–2 mm. long, lobes triangular or rounded, *outside* moderately or sparsely hairy or sometimes not hairy, *glandular with medium- or long-stalked glands* or sometimes eglandular, *margin* moderately or sparsely hairy, *glandular with medium- or long-stalked glands* or sometimes eglandular. *Corolla* tubular-campanulate, fleshy, 2.6–4.5 cm. long, scarlet, crimson or deep crimson, 5 nectar pouches at the base; lobes 5, 0.8–1.3 cm. long, 1.2–1.8 cm. broad, rounded, emarginate. *Stamens* 10, unequal, shorter than the corolla, 1.5–3.6 cm. long; filaments glabrous. *Gynoecium* 2.7–4 cm. long; *ovary oblong, narrow, tapered to the base of the style,* 5–6 mm. long, 5-celled, moderately or rather densely tomentose, *densely or moderately glandular with long- or medium-stalked glands* or rarely eglandular, not bristly; style hairy at the base or rather densely hairy on the lower half or glabrous, glandular with long-stalked glands at the base or eglandular. *Capsule* slender or oblong, 1–1.7 cm. long, 3–5 mm. broad, slightly or moderately curved or straight, hairy, *moderately or rather densely glandular with medium- or long stalked* glands, calyx-lobes persistent.

Farrer discovered this plant in May 1919 in a ravine below the Hpimaw Pass, north-east Upper Burma. In 1925 Forrest collected it in the same region. It grows amongst scrub on rocky slopes and meadows, on ledges of cliffs and humus-covered boulders, and in thickets, at elevations of 3,050–3,660 m. (10,000–12,000 ft.).

The main features of this species are the lanceolate, oblong-lanceolate or sometimes oblong leaves, with a thick, woolly, continuous indumentum covering the lower surface of the leaves, the setulose-glandular branchlets and petioles, and the moderately or rather densely glandular pedicels, calyx, ovaries and capsules, with long- or medium-stalked glands. It is closely related to R. euchroum. The distinctions between them are discussed under the latter.

R. sperabile was first introduced by Farrer in 1919 (No. 888—the Type number). It was reintroduced by Forrest under six different seed numbers. The plant flowered for the first time at Exbury in 1926. In its native home it grows up to 8 feet high; in cultivation it is somewhat compact or lax, usually 3–5 feet in height. It is a pleasing shrub with crimson or scarlet flowers produced freely in trusses of 3–5. As it has been introduced from elevations of 10,000–12,000 feet, it is hardy outdoors. Along the east coast and in gardens inland, some forms are susceptible to bark-splitting and injury by late spring frosts.

The species received an Award of Merit when exhibited by L. de Rothschild, Exbury, in 1925 (Farrer No. 888 with scarlet flowers).

Epithet. To be hoped for.
Hardiness 3. April–May.

R. sperabile Balf. f. et Farrer var. **weihsiense** Tagg et Forrest in Notes Roy. Bot. Gard. Edin., Vol. 15 (1927) 319.

This plant was first collected by Forrest in May 1924 in the Mekong-Salwin Divide, north-west Yunnan. It was afterwards found by him in the same region and in north-east Upper Burma. Rock, and McLaren's collectors also found it in north-west Yunnan. It grows on cliffs and rocky slopes, and amongst scrub in side valleys, at elevations of 3,230–4,270 m. (10,590–14,000 ft.).

The variety differs from the species in that the indumentum on the lower surface of the leaves is less dense, white or rarely pale fawn. Moreover, often the leaves (laminae) are larger up to 14.7 cm. long and 5 cm. broad, the petiole up to 2.7 cm. long, the inflorescence up to 7-flowered or rarely 16-flowered, the calyx up to 4 mm. long, the stamens up to 4.2 cm., and the capsule up to 2.3 cm. long.

The plant was first introduced by Forrest in 1924 (No. 25447—the Type number). It was reintroduced by him on four other occasions. Rock sent seeds under four different seed numbers. McLaren introduced it under number D7. Two distinct forms are in cultivation. Form 1. A somewhat compact, broadly upright shrub 5 feet high, with scarlet flowers. Form 2. A lax shrub, 5–6 feet high with larger leaves up to 5 inches long, and crimson flowers. Both forms are charming plants and seldom fail to display the beauty of their flowers produced with freedom. The variety is hardy, and is successfully grown along the east coast in well-sheltered positions in gardens.

Epithet of the variety. From Weihsi, China.
Hardiness 3. April–May.

R. sperabiloides Tagg et Forrest in Notes Roy. Bot. Gard. Edin., Vol. 15 (1927) 319.

A rounded or broadly upright shrub, 60 cm.–1.22 m. (2–4 ft.) high, branchlets tomentose with a whitish tomentum, not bristly, eglandular, those below the inflorescences 2–4 mm. in diameter. *Leaves* oblanceolate, lanceolate, oblong or oblong-elliptic, lamina 3–7.7 cm. long, 1.4–2.6 cm. broad, apex obtuse, mucronate, base obtuse or tapered; upper surface green, glabrous or with vestiges of hairs, midrib grooved, primary veins 10–14 on each side, deeply impressed; *under surface with a thin, interrupted, whitish or fawn, unistrate indumentum of Ramiform hairs with medium or some-*

what short ribbon-like branches, and medium or short stem, covered with waxy papillae, midrib raised, primary veins exposed or partly exposed; petiole 0.6–1.3 cm. long, tomentose with a whitish tomentum, not bristly, eglandular. *Inflorescence* terminal, a racemose umbel of 4–11 flowers; rhachis 2–5 mm. long, floccose with dark brown or brown hairs, eglandular; pedicel 1–2 cm. long, moderately or rather densely floccose with brown hairs, eglandular. *Calyx* 5-lobed, 2–8 mm. long, crimson, lobes unequal, rounded or irregular, outside glabrous or rarely hairy, eglandular, margin hairy or glabrous, eglandular. *Corolla* tubular-campanulate, fleshy, 2.5–3.8 cm. long, *deep to light crimson,* 5 nectar pouches at the base; lobes 5, 0.8–1.5 cm. long, 1–2 cm. broad, rounded, emarginate. *Stamens* 10, unequal, shorter than the corolla, 1.4–2.5 cm. long; filaments puberulous at the base or glabrous. *Gynoecium* 2.3–3.5 cm. long; *ovary* oblong, *narrow, tapered to the base of the style or conoid truncate,* 4–6 mm. long, 5-celled, densely tomentose, eglandular; style glabrous or tomentose at the base, eglandular. *Capsule* slender, 1–2 cm. long, 3–4 mm. broad, slightly or moderately curved, rather densely hairy, eglandular, calyx-lobes deciduous or persistent.

Forrest discovered this plant in fruit in July 1921 in the Salwin-Kiu Chiang Divide, east Tibet. He found it again later in the same region and in south-east Tibet. It grows in alpine scrub, and amongst rhododendron scrub on rocky slopes, at elevations of 3,660–3,965 m. (12,000–13,000 ft.).

R. sperabiloides is very similar to *R. albertsenianum* in general characters, particularly in the eglandular branchlets, petioles, pedicels, calyx, and ovaries. The main distinctions between them are that in *R. sperabiloides* the indumentum on the lower surface of the leaves is thin, interrupted (discontinuous) with large or small bare areas, unistrate (the lower layer is absent), and moreover, the lower surface is covered with waxy papillae; whereas in *R. albertsenianum* the indumentum on the lower surface of the leaves is thick, woolly, continuous, bistrate, and the waxy papillae are absent.

R. sperabiloides was first introduced by Forrest in 1921 (Nos. 20003, 20825). It was reintroduced by him in 1922 (No. 21824—the Type number, and No. 22900). In cultivation it is a rounded or broadly upright shrub, 3–4 feet high. The crimson flowers are produced freely in trusses of 4–8. The plant is hardy, but along the east coast it requires some protection from wind for the best results to be obtained. It is uncommon in cultivation.

The species was given an Award of Merit when shown by L. de Rothschild, Exbury, in 1933.

Epithet. Like *R. sperabile.*
Hardiness 3. April–May.

SANGUINEUM SUBSERIES

General characters: small or medium-sized shrubs, 30 cm.–2.44 m. (1–8 ft.) or sometimes 8–15 cm. (3–6 in.) high, branchlets tomentose or floccose or sometimes glabrous. Leaves evergreen, oblanceolate, obovate, oblong-obovate, oblong, oblong-lanceolate, rarely oval, elliptic or lanceolate, lamina 2–11.5 cm. long, 0.6–4.5 cm. broad, base tapered or obtuse, often decurrent on the petiole; *under surface with* a *thin usually plastered Rosulate hairs or sometimes with a thick woolly, continuous indumentum of Ramiform hairs or with a thin veil of hairs* or with scattered hairs *or glabrous;* petiole 0.1–2 cm. long, margins often narrowly winged or ridged by the decurrent base of the lamina, tomentose or floccose or sometimes glabrous. Inflorescence terminal, a racemose umbel of 2–8 flowers; pedicel 0.6–3.6 cm. long, moderately or rather densely hairy or sometimes glabrous, eglandular, sometimes glandular or setulose-glandular. Calyx 5-lobed, 0.1–2.5 cm. long. Corolla tubular-campanulate or campanulate, thin or fleshy, 2–5 cm. long, rose, pink, white, yellow, orange, scarlet, rose-crimson, crimson, deep crimson or black-crimson, 5 nectar pouches at the base; lobes 5. Stamens 10. *Ovary conoid or ovoid or sometimes oblong, truncate, 2–7 mm. long, 5–9-celled, densely or sometimes moderately hairy or rarely glabrous, eglandular or moderately or densely glandular. Capsule oblong or conoid, rarely ovoid or short stout, 0.6–2.3 cm. long, 0.3–1 cm. broad, densely or moderately hairy or rarely glabrous, eglandular or glandular.*

KEY TO THE SPECIES

1. Under surface of the leaves glabrous or sparsely hairy or with a thin veil of hairs or rarely with small or large shreds and patches of hairs.
    2. Leaf-bud scales persistent; branchlets and petioles esetulose, eglandular or rarely glandular . . . . *aperantum*
    2. Leaf-bud scales deciduous; branchlets and petioles setulose or esetulose, setulose-glandular or not setulose-glandular.
        3. Under surface of the leaves glabrous or sparsely hairy.
            4. Corolla deep crimson, crimson, carmine or light to dark purplish-crimson . . . . *temenium*
            4. Corolla yellow, yellow flushed rose, white flushed rose, deep rose, purplish, orange-red or white.
                5. Corolla with numerous crimson spots on the posterior side; pedicels glabrous; ovary usually glabrous and eglandular. . . . . *parmulatum*
                5. Corolla without spots; pedicels rather densely or moderately hairy; ovary usually densely hairy, glandular or eglandular.
                    6. Corolla yellow or creamy-yellow . . . . *fulvastrum*
                    (part)
                    6. Corolla white, white flushed rose, deep rose, purplish, orange-red or pale yellow faintly flushed rose.
                        7. Corolla white . . . . *glaphyrum* var. *dealbatum*
                        7. Corolla white flushed rose, deep rose, purplish, orange-red or pale yellow faintly flushed rose.
                            8. Ovary, calyx margin and usually pedicels eglandular; branchlets and petioles often not setulose. . . . . *glaphyrum*
                            8. Ovary, calyx margin and pedicels glandular;. branchlets and petioles setulose . . . .
                            . . . . *trichomiscum*
                            (part)
        3. Under surface of the leaves with a thin veil of hairs.
            9. Corolla pale lemon-yellow, creamy-yellow, yellow or rarely yellow tinged pink. . . . . *fulvastrum*
            (part)
            9. Corolla rose-crimson, crimson, rose, white, white flushed rose, pink or orange-red.
                10. Ovary, calyx margin, and usually pedicels glandular.
                    11. Branchlets and petioles not setulose; calyx 2–8 mm. long. . . . . *eudoxum*
                    11. Branchlets and petioles setulose; calyx 1–2 mm. long. . .
                    . . . . *trichomiscum*
                    (part)

10. Ovary, calyx margin, and pedicels eglandular.
 12. Leaves (laminae) usually 7–8.5 cm. long; corolla 3.5–4 cm. long; calyx 1–2 mm. long........ *brunneifolium*
 12. Leaves (laminae) 3–6.5 cm. long; corolla 2.3–3.5 cm. long; calyx 1 mm.–1 cm. long .... *mesopolium*
1. Under surface of the leaves covered with a continuous indumentum of hairs.
 13. Corolla black-crimson, dark crimson, black-carmine, nearly black, deep crimson, crimson, scarlet or carmine.
  14. Corolla black-crimson, dark crimson, black-carmine or nearly black.
   15. Branchlets, petioles, calyx outside and capsules eglandular; pedicels and ovaries hairy, eglandular (except *R. haemaleum* var. *atrorubrum* densely glandular); leaf-bud scales usually deciduous .... *haemaleum*
   15. Branchlets, petioles, calyx outside and capsules setulose-glandular; pedicels and ovaries not hairy, glandular; leaf-bud scales more or less persistent .... *didymum*
  14. Corolla crimson, deep crimson, scarlet or carmine.
   16. Leaf-bud scales persistent.
    17. Indumentum on the under surface of the leaves thick, woolly, *bistrate;* calyx usually 6 mm.–2 cm. long; upper surface of the leaves semi-bullate .... *horaeum* (part)
    17. Indumentum on the under surface of the leaves thin, plastered, *unistrate;* calyx 1–3 mm. long; upper surface of the leaves not bullate.......... *sanguineum* var. *sanguineoides*
   16. Leaf-bud scales deciduous.
    18. Calyx not cup-shaped, not saucer-shaped, usually small 1–4 mm. long.
     19. Indumentum on the under surface of the leaves thin usually plastered, or semi-woolly, *unistrate;* upper surface of the leaves not bullate.
      20. Indumentum on the under surface of the leaves thin usually plastered, hairs *Rosulate;* leaves obovate, oblong-obovate or oblong........... .... *sanguineum* (part)
      20. Indumentum on the under surface of the leaves semi-woolly, not plastered, hairs *Ramiform* with long, flat ribbon-like branches; leaves oblong or oblong-lanceolate .... *gymnocarpum*
     19. Indumentum on the under surface of the leaves thick woolly, *bistrate;* upper surface of the leaves semi-bullate..................... *horaeum* var. *rubens*
    18. Calyx cup-shaped or saucer-shaped, large, 4 mm.–2 cm. long.
     21. Pedicel and ovary eglandular............. *apodectum* (part)
     21. Pedicel and ovary moderately or densely setulose-glandular.
      22. Usually a large plant, 92 cm.–1.53 m. (3–5 ft.) high; leaves usually obovate or oblong-obovate..... .... *scyphocalyx* (part)
      22. Usually a small plant, 15–60 cm. (6 in.–2 ft.) high; leaves usually oblanceolate .... *herpesticum* (part)

13. Corolla yellow, orange, orange flushed crimson, rose-orange, rose, rose-crimson, white or pink.

    23. Calyx usually cup-shaped or saucer-shaped; corolla usually orange, or orange flushed crimson, or rose-orange, very fleshy.

        24. Leaf-bud scales persistent; indumentum on the under surface of the leaves thick, woolly, *bistrate;* upper surface of the leaves semi-bullate .... *horaeum*
                    (part)

        24. Leaf-bud scales deciduous; indumentum on the under surface of the leaves thin, plastered, *unistrate* (except in *R. apodectum* often somewhat thick woolly); upper surface of the leaves not bullate.

           25. Pedicel and ovary eglandular.

               26. Leaf-base tapered or obtuse; indumentum on the under surface of the leaves thin, plastered; leaves usually oblong, oblanceolate or obovate........ *dichroanthum*

               26. Leaf-base usually rounded; indumentum on the under surface of the leaves often somewhat thick, woolly; leaves usually oval, elliptic or obovate.... *apodectum*
                        (part)

           25. Pedicel and ovary moderately or densely setulose-glandular.

               27. Usually a large plant, 92 cm.–1.53 m. (3–5 ft.) high; leaves usually obovate or oblong-obovate ....
                     .... *scyphocalyx*
                        (part)

               27. Usually a small plant, 15–60 cm. (6 in.–2 ft.) high; leaves usually oblanceolate.................. *herpesticum*
                        (part)

    23. Calyx not cup-shaped, not saucer-shaped (except sometimes in *R. citriniflorum*); corolla yellow, lemon-yellow, yellow margined or flushed rose, rose, pink, rose-crimson or white, usually thin.

        28. Corolla yellow, lemon-yellow, or yellowish margined or flushed deep rose.

           29. Corolla yellow or lemon-yellow.

               30. Pedicels, ovaries, and calyx margin usually glandular; indumentum on the under surface of the leaves usually *thick, woolly, bistrate* .... *citriniflorum*
                        (part)

               30. Pedicels, ovaries, and calyx margin eglandular; indumentum on the under surface of the leaves thin, *plastered, unistrate.*..................... *himertum*

          29. Corolla yellowish, margined or flushed deep rose.

               31. Indumentum on the under surface of the leaves usually thick woolly, *bistrate;* calyx-lobes not deflexed......
                     .... *citriniflorum*
                        (part)

               31. Indumentum on the under surface of the leaves thin, often plastered, *unistrate;* calyx-lobes usually deflexed............................. *cloiophorum*
                        (part)

        28. Corolla deep rose, rose, pink, white, white flushed rose, rose-crimson, or rarely orange-red.

          32. Leaf apex usually obtuse or rounded; style long, slightly shorter than the corolla or about as long; indumentum on the under surface of the leaves often plastered, hairs

Rosulate; leaves oblong-obovate, obovate, oblong or sometimes oblanceolate.

33. Calyx-lobes deflexed; calyx 1 mm.–1 cm. long . . . . . .
. . . . *cloiophorum*
(part)

33. Calyx-lobes not deflexed; calyx usually 1–4 mm. long . .
. . . . *sanguineum*
(part)
and var. *didymoides*

32. Leaf apex acute; style short, one-third or one-half the length of the corolla; indumentum on the under surface of the leaves thin, not plastered, hairs *Ramiform* with long, flat, ribbon-like branches; leaves lanceolate or oblanceolate . . . .
. . . . *microgynum*

DESCRIPTION OF THE SPECIES

R. aperantum Balf. f. et Ward in Notes Roy. Bot. Gard. Edin., Vol. 13 (1922) 231.
Illustration. Bot. Mag. Vol. 160 t. 9507 (1938).

A compact rounded, or a low spreading shrub, 8–60 cm. (3 in.–2 ft.) high, sometimes 92 cm. (3 ft.) or rarely 1.53–1.83 m. (5–6 ft.) high, with *short annual growth; branchlets* tomentose with a whitish or fawn tomentum or glabrous, *eglandular* or rarely glandular with medium-stalked glands, those below the inflorescences 3–5 mm. in diameter; *leaf-bud scales persistent. Leaves almost sessile in close whorls at the ends of the branchlets, oblanceolate, obovate* or rarely oval, lamina leathery, 2–6.4 cm. long, 1–2.8 cm. broad, apex rounded or broadly obtuse or rarely acute, mucronate, *base* tapered or obtuse, *decurrent on the petiole;* upper surface dark green, somewhat rugulose, glabrous or with vestiges of hairs, midrib grooved, primary veins 8–12 on each side, deeply impressed; margin recurved; *under surface white* or whitish, *covered with waxy papillae, glabrous* or sparsely floccose with whitish hairs, midrib raised, floccose or glabrous, primary veins slightly raised; *petiole 2–6 mm.* (rarely up to 1 cm.) *long, margins winged* by the decurrent base of the lamina, moderately or sparsely tomentose with a fawn or white tomentum or glabrous, *eglandular. Inflorescence* terminal, a racemose umbel of 2–6 flowers; rhachis 2–5 mm. long, floccose with dark brown hairs, eglandular; pedicel 1–3 cm. long, moderately or rather densely hairy with long, branched, dark brown or brown hairs, eglandular or rarely glandular with long-stalked glands. *Calyx* 5-lobed, 0.2–1 cm. long, cupular or not cupular, lobes unequal, rounded, ovate, oblong or irregular, outside glabrous, eglandular, margin hairy or rarely glabrous, eglandular or rarely glandular with short-stalked glands. *Corolla* tubular-campanulate, 2.8–4.8 cm. long, deep crimson, crimson, rose-crimson, rose, pink, yellow, orange, creamy-white, white, and white flushed rose, 5 nectar pouches at the base; lobes 5, 0.8–1.4 cm. long, 1.2–2.5 cm. broad, rounded, emarginate. *Stamens* 10, unequal, shorter than the corolla, 1.3–3 cm. long; filaments glabrous. *Gynoecium* 2.4–3.7 cm. long; ovary conoid or sometimes ovoid, truncate, 3–5 mm. long, 6–8-celled, densely hairy with long hairs, eglandular or rarely glandular with medium-stalked glands; style glabrous or rarely tomentose at the base, eglandular. *Capsule* oblong or conoid, 0.8–2 cm. long, 5–8 mm. broad, straight, densely or moderately or sometimes sparsely hairy with dark brown or brown hairs, eglandular or rarely glandular with medium- or long-stalked glands, calyx-lobes persistent.

R. aperantum was discovered by Kingdon-Ward in July 1919 on the western spur of Imaw Bum, north-east Upper Burma. Subsequently it was found by other collectors in

3. **R. aperantum.**

nat. size.

a. leaf (upper surface). b. leaf (lower surface). c. stamen.
d. calyx. e. ovary, style. f. flower. g. capsule. h. petals.

the same region and in north-west Yunnan. It grows on rocky slopes, in stony alpine meadows, on cliffs and screes, and on humus-covered boulders, at elevations of 3,050–4,460 m. (10,000–14,623 ft.). Kingdon-Ward records it as forming thick, matted carpets on granite rocks on precipitous moss-covered slopes on Imaw Bum. According to Farrer, it covers the open high alpine slopes for miles, in the Chawchi Pass. In his field note, Forrest describes it as forming tangled masses on open alpine meadows in north-east Upper Burma.

The diagnostic features of the species are the almost sessile oblanceolate or obovate leaves, arranged in close whorls at the ends of the branchlets, the short annual growth, the lower surface of the leaves glabrous, white, covered with waxy papillae, and the leaf base decurrent on the petiole which is winged at the margins. Another striking character is the large persistent leaf-bud scales on the branchlets.

R. aperantum was first introduced by Kingdon-Ward in 1919 (No. 3301). It was reintroduced by Forrest under 24 different seed numbers. Rock sent seeds on three occasions. In its native home it grows from 3 inches up to 2 feet high, or sometimes up to 3 feet. Rock found a plant 5–6 feet high growing in alpine region above fir forest in northwest Yunnan. Two distinct growth forms are in cultivation. Form 1. A dwarf low spreading shrublet, 4 or 5 inches high. There was a beautiful specimen growing in the rock garden, Royal Botanic Garden, Edinburgh, 4 inches high and 4–6 inches across, with crimson flowers which appeared freely in April–May. This plant has now been lost to cultivation. Form 2. A compact rounded shrub, 2 feet high and as much across. Several colour forms are grown in gardens, namely, crimson, rose-crimson, rose, pink, yellow, creamy-white, and white flushed rose. A characteristic feature is the short annual growth surrounded with long persistent leaf-bud scales. The species is a slow grower and takes several years to bloom. It is a shy flowerer, but a dwarf form a few inches high and another larger compact form 2 feet high are free-flowering and provide an admirable display with crimson flowers in trusses of 2–6.

A form with crimson flowers received an Award of Merit when exhibited by the Marquess of Headfort, Kells, Eire, in 1931.

Epithet. Boundless.
Hardiness 3 April–May.

R. aperantum Balf f. et Ward var. **subpilosum** Cowan in Notes Roy. Bot. Gard. Edin., Vol. 20 (1940) 84.

This plant was first collected by Forrest in July 1924 on the western flank of the Salwin-Kiu Chiang Divide, north-east Upper Burma. It was found by him again later in the same year in north-west Yunnan. It grows in open rocky alpine meadows at an elevation of 3,965 m. (13,000 ft.).

The variety differs from the species in that the under surface of the leaves has a somewhat thick, discontinuous, unistrate indumentum of branched hairs in small or large shreds and patches.

The plant was introduced by Forrest in 1924 from north-west Yunnan (No. 25563 = 25878). In its native home it is a shrub of 1½ feet with white flowers. It is rare in cultivation, and has not been seen for a long time.

Epithet of the variety. Under surface pilose.
Hardiness 3. April–May.

R. apodectum Balf. f. et W. W. Sm. in Notes Roy. Bot. Gard. Edin., Vol. 10 (1917) 83.
    Syn *R. jangtzowense* Balf. f. et Forrest in Notes Roy. Bot. Gard. Edin., Vol. 13 (1922) 271.
        R. liratum Balf f. et Forrest in Notes Roy. Bot. Gard. Edin., Vol. 13 (1922) 274.
        R. dichroanthum Diels subsp. *apodectum* (Balf. f. et W. W. Sm.) Cowan in Notes Roy. Bot. Gard. Edin., Vol. 20 (1940) 86.
Illustration. Bot. Mag. Vol. 149 t. 9014 (1923).

A broadly upright or rounded, somewhat compact shrub, 30 cm.–2.44 m. (1–8 ft.) high, branchlets tomentose with a thin, white tomentum, eglandular, those below the inflorescences 2–5 mm. in diameter; leaf-bud scales deciduous. *Leaves oval, obovate, oblong-obovate,* elliptic, oblong-lanceolate, oblanceolate or oblong, lamina leathery, 3.5–8.5 cm. long, 2–3.8 cm. broad, apex rounded or obtuse, mucronate, *base rounded* or obtuse, not decurrent; *upper surface* dark or pale green, *with or without longitudinal ribbing,* glabrous or with vestiges of hairs, midrib grooved, primary veins 10–12 on each side, impressed; margin moderately or slightly recurved; *under surface covered with a somewhat thick somewhat woolly* or sometimes thin plastered, continuous, fawn, dark brown, or sometimes whitish, *unistrate indumentum of Rosulate hairs* with short arms, midrib raised, glabrous or tomentose, primary veins concealed; petiole 0.5–1.4 cm. long, margins not winged, not ridged, tomentose with a thin, white tomentum, eglandular. *Inflorescence* terminal, a racemose umbel of 2–5 flowers; rhachis 2–5 mm. long, hairy with brown hairs, eglandular; *pedicel* 1–2.5 cm. long, moderately or rather densely tomentose with fawn or brown tomentum, *eglandular. Calyx* 5-lobed, 0.4–2 cm. long, *cup-shaped,* divided to the base or to about the middle, fleshy, lobes unequal, upright, ovate, rounded or irregular, outside glabrous, eglandular, margin hairy, eglandular. *Corolla* tubular-campanulate, fleshy, 2–4.3 cm. long, deep crimson, crimson, or deep rose flushed orange, or pale or deep orange flushed rose, or bright cherry-scarlet, or deep crimson flushed orange, 5 nectar pouches at the base; lobes 5, 0.8–1.2 cm. long, 1.2–1.5 cm. broad, rounded, emarginate. *Stamens* 10, unequal, shorter than the corolla, 1.5–3 cm. long; filaments puberulous at the base or rarely glabrous. *Gynoecium* 2.3–3 cm. long; *ovary* conoid or rarely oblong, truncate, 4–7 mm. long, 5–7-celled, densely tomentose with long or short hairs, *eglandular;* style glabrous, eglandular. *Capsule* oblong, 1–1.8 cm. long, 4–7 mm. broad, straight or rarely slightly curved, moderately or densely hairy with short hairs, *eglandular,* calyx-lobes deciduous or persistent.

R. apodectum was first collected by Forrest in August 1912 on the western flank of the Shweli-Salwin Divide, west Yunnan. It was afterwards found by him in the same region and in mid-west Yunnan. In 1953 Kingdon-Ward collected it in North Triangle, North Burma. It grows at the margins of rhododendron forest, in open scrub, amongst rocks, on stony slopes, on cliffs and bouldery slopes, and at the margins of cane brakes and thickets, at elevations of 3,050–3,660 m. (10,000–12,000 ft.).

The species is related to *R. dichroanthum* which it resembles in the large cup-shaped calyx divided to the base or to about the middle, in the eglandular characters, and in the unistrate indumentum, the hairs being Rosulate with short arms, but differs in that the indumentum on the lower surface of the leaves is usually somewhat thick, woolly, the leaf-base is often rounded, and the leaves are usually oval, obovate or oblong-obovate.

R. apodectum was first introduced by Forrest in 1912 (No. 8987—the Type number). It was reintroduced by him from Yunnan under 12 different seed numbers. Kingdon-Ward sent seeds in 1953 from North Burma (No. 20923). In its native home it grows from 1 to 8 feet high. Several forms are in cultivation, including, Form 1. A small rounded, somewhat compact shrub, 2 feet high, with crimson flowers; this form is rare, but should be a most valuable acquisition to the rock garden. Form 2. A broadly upright shrub, up to 4 or 5 feet high with orange flushed rose flowers. The species is hardy outdoors, a fairly vigorous grower with rigid branchlets. A characteristic feature in some forms is the unusual longitudinal ribbing of the leaf lamina.

Epithet. Acceptable.
Hardiness 3. May–June.

R. brunneifolium Balf. f. et Forrest in Notes Roy. Bot. Gard. Edin., Vol. 13 (1920) 33.

Syn. *R. eudoxum* Balf f. et Forrest subsp. *brunneifolium* (Balf. f. et Forrest) Tagg in The Sp. of Rhod. (1930) 549.

R. eudoxum Balf f. et Forrest var. *brunneifolium* (Balf. f. et Forrest) Chamberlain in Notes Roy. Bot. Gard. Edin., Vol. 37 (1979) 333.

A broadly upright shrub, 92 cm.–1.22 m. (3–4 ft.) high, branchlets floccose or glabrous, not bristly, not setulose-glandular or sparsely setulose-glandular, those below the inflorescences 2–4 mm. in diameter; leaf-bud scales deciduous. *Leaves* oblong, oblong-elliptic or oblong-obovate, lamina leathery, 5.3–8.5 cm. long, 2.3–3.2 cm. broad, apex rounded, mucronate, base obtuse, decurrent or not decurrent on the petiole; upper surface dark green, glabrous or with vestiges of hairs, midrib grooved, primary veins 10–12 on each side, impressed; margin flat or slightly recurved; *under surface with a thin veil of white or fawn Rosulate hairs* with short arms, midrib prominent, glabrous or tomentose with a thin tomentum, primary veins slightly raised, exposed or partly concealed; petiole 0.9–1.6 cm. long, margins narrowly winged or ridged by the decurrent base of the lamina or not winged not ridged, glabrous or floccose, not bristly, eglandular or sparsely glandular with medium-stalked glands. *Inflorescence* terminal, a racemose umbel of 3–4 flowers; rhachis 3–4 mm. long, glabrous or hairy with dark brown hairs, eglandular; *pedicel 2–3 cm. long,* hairy, *eglandular. Calyx* 5-lobed, *1–2 mm. long,* divided to the base or to about the middle, lobes unequal, upright, ovate or trian-gular, *outside and margin* hairy, *eglandular. Corolla* tubular-campanulate, *3.5–4 cm. long, rose-crimson,* without markings, 5 nectar pouches at the base; lobes 5, 1.2–1.4 cm. long, 1.5–2 cm. broad, rounded, emarginate. *Stamens* 10, unequal, shorter than the corolla, 1.8–2.6 cm. long; filaments puberulous at the base. *Gynoecium* 3.5–4 cm. long; *ovary* oblong narrow or conoid, truncate, 4–5 mm. long, densely hairy with branched or unbranched hairs, *eglandular;* style glabrous, eglandular. *Capsule* slender, 1.3–1.8 cm. long, 3–4 mm. broad, slightly curved or straight, hairy, eglandular, calyx-lobes persis-tent or deciduous.

Forrest discovered this plant in July 1919 in the Salwin-Kiu Chiang Divide, Tsarong, south-east Tibet, growing in cane brakes and margins of thickets. In 1923 Rock found it on the mountains of Londjre, Mekong-Salwin watershed, north-west Yunnan.

R. brunneifolium is closely allied to *R. eudoxum* which it resembles in general features, but is readily distinguished by the eglandular ovary, calyx and pedicel, by the very small calyx 1–2 mm. long, and usually by the larger corolla and longer pedicel.

The species was introduced by Rock in 1923 (No. 10932). In cultivation it is a broadly upright shrub 3–4 feet high, with fairly large leaves, laminae up to 8.5 cm. long. It is quite hardy, free-flowering with rose-crimson flowers in trusses of 3–4. The plant is rare in cultivation.

Epithet. With brown leaves.
Hardiness 3. April–May.

R. citriniflorum Balf. f. et Forrest in Notes Roy. Bot. Gard. Edin., Vol. 11 (1919) 35.

Syn. *R. chlanidotum* Balf. f. et Forrest in Notes Roy. Bot. Gard. Edin., Vol. 13 (1920) 38.

R. citriniflorum Balf. f. et Forrest subsp. *aureolum* Cowan, ibid. Vol. 20 (1940) 75.

R. sanguineum Franch. subsp. *aizoides* Cowan, ibid. Vol. 20 (1940) 73.

R. sanguineum Franch. subsp. *melleum* Cowan, ibid. Vol. 20 (1940) 73.

A broadly upright or rounded compact shrub, 30 cm.–1.53 m. (1–5 ft.) high, branchlets tomentose with a thin, whitish tomentum, esetulose or rarely setulose, eglandular or rarely setulose-glandular, those below the inflorescences 3–5 mm. in diameter; leaf-bud scales deciduous or more or less persistent. *Leaves* obovate, oblong-obovate, oblong or oblong-lanceolate, lamina leathery, 2.8–8.5 cm. long, 1.2–2.8 cm.

broad, apex obtuse or rounded, mucronate, *base* obtuse or rarely tapered, *decurrent on the petiole;* upper surface dark or pale green, glabrous or with vestiges of hairs, midrib grooved, primary veins 8–12 on each side, deeply impressed; margin moderately or slightly recurved; *under surface covered with a thick woolly* (or rarely thin plastered), *continuous,* dark brown, brown, fawn or whitish, *bistrate indumentum of hairs, upper layer Ramiform* with medium length, curled branches and short stem, *lower layer Rosulate,* midrib raised, tomentose with a thin tomentum or glabrous, primary veins slightly raised, concealed or partly exposed; petiole 0.4–1.2 cm. long, margins narrowly winged or ridged by the decurrent base of the lamina, moderately or sparsely tomentose with a thin, whitish, dark brown or fawn tomentum, esetulose, eglandular or rarely setulose-glandular. *Inflorescence* terminal, a racemose umbel of 3–6 or sometimes up to 10 flowers; rhachis 2–5 mm. long, hairy with dark brown hairs, eglandular; pedicel 1.2–3 cm. long, densely or moderately hairy with long or short brown hairs or not hairy, moderately or rather densely glandular with long-stalked glands or eglandular. *Calyx* 5-lobed, 0.2–1.4 cm. long, cupular or not cupular, divided to about the middle or to the base, lobes unequal, rounded, ovate, triangular or irregular, outside and margin hairy or glabrous, glandular with long- or medium-stalked glands or eglandular. *Corolla* campanulate or tubular-campanulate, 2.3–4.5 cm. long, *bright lemon-yellow, yellow, yellow margined rose or yellowish flushed rose,* 5 nectar pouches at the base; lobes 5, 0.8–1.5 cm. long, 1–2.5 cm. broad, rounded, emarginate. *Stamens* 10, unequal, shorter than the corolla, 1.4–2.5 cm. long; filaments puberulous at the base or sometimes glabrous. *Gynoecium* 2–3.1 cm. long; ovary ovoid or conoid, truncate, 4–6 mm. long, 5–7-celled, densely hairy with long hairs or sometimes not hairy, moderately or sometimes densely glandular with long-stalked glands or eglandular; style glabrous, eglandular. *Capsule* ovoid, conoid or oblong, 0.8–1.5 cm. long, 5–9 mm. broad, moderately or rather densely hairy with brown or dark brown hairs or rarely not hairy, moderately or rarely rather densely glandular with long-stalked glands or eglandular, calyx-lobes persistent or deciduous.

R. citriniflorum was first collected by Forrest in July 1917 in the Mekong-Salwin Divide, north-west Yunnan. Subsequently it was found by him and by Rock in the same region and in south-east Tibet. It grows on rocks, cliffs, boulders, on alpine ridges and spurs, on rocky slopes, in stony moorland, in alpine meadows, in rhododendron thickets, and in cane brakes, at elevations of 3,965–4,575 m. (13,000–15,000 ft.).

In the *Notes Roy. Bot. Gard. Edin.,* Vol. 20 (1940), Cowan described three new sub-species, namely, *R. citriniflorum* Balf. f. et Forrest subsp. *aureolum* Cowan from a specimen (No. 14503) collected by Forrest in July 1917 in south-east Tibet, *R. sanguineum* Franch. subsp. *aizoides* Cowan from a specimen (No. 10108) collected by Rock in the same region, and *R. sanguineum* Franch. subsp. *melleum* Cowan from a specimen (No. 16727) collected by Forrest in 1918 also in the same region. When these specimens are examined, it will be seen that in leaf shape and size, in the indumentum on the lower surface of the leaves, in flower colour, and in all other morphological details, they are identical with *R. citriniflorum* under which they will now appear in synonymy.

R. citriniflorum bears a strong resemblance to *R. fulvastrum* in general appearance, but is readily distinguished by the thick, woolly, continuous, bistrate indumentum on the lower surface of the leaves. The bistrate indumentum consists of an upper layer of branched Ramiform hairs with medium length curled branches and short stem, and a lower layer of Rosulate hairs.

The species was first introduced by Forrest in 1917 (No. 14271—the Type number). It was reintroduced by him on 8 other occasions. Rock sent seeds under 8 different seed numbers. In its native home it grows 1–5 feet high. Two distinct growth forms are in cultivation. Form 1. A broadly upright shrub, 1–2 feet high. Form 2. A rounded compact shrub 2 feet high and as much across well-filled with foliage. Three colour forms are grown in gardens, yellow, pale lemon-yellow, and yellow margined or flushed rose. The

species varies in freedom of flowering. Some plants are shy flowerers and hardly produce more than a few trusses every year. A few other plants are of great beauty with
trusses of 3–10 flowers produced freely. The species is hardy outdoors, a robust grower,
and is easy to cultivate.

Epithet. With lemon-yellow flowers.
Hardiness 3. April–May.

R. cloiophorum Balf. f. et Forrest in Notes Roy. Bot. Gard. Edin., Vol. 11 (1919) 37.
    Syn. *R. asmenistum* Balf. f. et Forrest in Notes Roy. Bot. Gard. Edin., Vol 13 (1920)
        29.
        R. cloiophorum Balf. f. et Forrest subsp. *asmenistum* (Balf. f. et Forrest) Tagg in
          The Sp. of Rhod. (1930) 545.
        R. sanguineum Franch. subsp. *cloiophorum* (Balf. f. et Forrest) Cowan in Notes
          Roy. Bot. Gard. Edin., Vol. 20 (1940) 71.
        R. sanguineum Franch. var. *cloiophorum* (Balf. f. et Forrest) Chamberlain, ibid.
          Vol. 37 (1979) 334.

A broadly upright shrub, 30 cm.–1.53 m. (1–5 ft.) high, *branchlets* moderately or
rarely sparsely tomentose with a thin, whitish or fawn tomentum, *esetulose, eglandular,*
those below the inflorescences 3–5 mm. in diameter; leaf-bud scales deciduous. *Leaves*
oblong-obovate, obovate or oblanceolate, lamina leathery, 2.8–7.5 cm. long, 1.3–2.6 cm.
broad, apex obtuse or rounded, mucronate, *base* tapered or obtuse, *decurrent on the
petiole;* upper surface dark green, glabrous or with vestiges of hairs, midrib grooved,
primary veins 8–12 on each side, deeply impressed; margin moderately or slightly
recurved; *under surface covered with a thin, plastered* (or rarely not plastered), *continuous,*
white, whitish or fawn, *unistrate indumentum of Rosulate hairs with short or long arms,*
midrib raised, glabrous or tomentose, primary veins slightly raised, concealed or partly
exposed; *petiole* 3–8 mm. long, margins narrowly winged by the decurrent base of the
lamina, tomentose with a thin, whitish or fawn tomentum, *esetulose, eglandular. Inflorescence* terminal, a racemose umbel of 2–6 flowers; rhachis 3–5 mm. long, hairy with dark
brown hairs, eglandular; pedicel 1–2.8 cm. long, rather densely or moderately hairy
with long or short brown hairs, eglandular. *Calyx* 5-lobed, *0.1–1 cm. long,* not cupular,
divided to the base or rarely to about the middle, *lobes* unequal, *deflexed* or sometimes
upright, ovate, rounded or triangular, outside glabrous or sometimes hairy, eglandular,
margin hairy, eglandular. *Corolla* tubular-campanulate or campanulate, thin, 2.5–3.7 cm.
long, rose, yellowish towards the base, or yellowish, flushed rose or deep rose, or rose,
or rose-crimson, or white, tinged and margined rose, or orange-red, 5 nectar pouches at
the base; lobes 5, 1–1.2 cm. long, 1.3–2 cm. broad, rounded, emarginate. *Stamens* 10,
unequal, shorter than the corolla, 1.3–2.6 cm. long; filaments glabrous or puberulous at
the base. *Gynoecium* 2.1–3.2 cm. long; ovary conoid or ovoid, truncate, 3–6 mm. long, 8-
celled, densely tomentose with long hairs, eglandular; style glabrous, eglandular.
Capsule oblong or conoid, 1–1.5 cm. long, 5–6 mm. broad, straight, densely hairy with
long hairs, eglandular, calyx-lobes deciduous or persistent.

This species was first collected by Forrest in July 1917 in the Mekong-Salwin Divide,
north-west Yunnan. It was later found by him and by Rock in the same region and in
south-east Tibet. The plant grows on open rocky slopes and cliffs, amongst boulders, in
rhododendron scrub, in open cane scrub, and in open pasture, at elevations of 3,355–
4,270 m. (11,000–14,000 ft.).

R. cloiophorum is closely allied to *R. himertum* which it resembles in general features,
but differs markedly in that the corolla is rose, yellowish flushed rose, rose-crimson,
white tinged rose, or orange-red, and the calyx-lobes are usually deflexed. It is to be
noted that the indumentum on the lower surface of the leaves is thin, usually plastered,
continuous, unistrate Rosulate hairs with short or long arms.

The plant was first introduced by Forrest in 1917 (No. 14269—the Type number). It was reintroduced by him under seed Nos. 19169, 21739, 25521. Rock sent seeds on three occasions, Nos. 10899, 22064, 22202. In cultivation it is a broadly upright shrub, 4–5 feet high with somewhat rigid branchlets, and attracts attention with its rose or rose-crimson flowers in trusses of 2–6. The plant is hardy, but is rare in cultivation.

Epithet. Wearing a collar.

Hardiness 3. April–May.

R. cloiophorum Balf. f. et Forrest var. **leucopetalum** (Balf. f. et Forrest) Davidian, comb. nov.

Syn. *R leucopetalum* Balf. f. et Forrest in Notes Roy. Bot. Gard. Edin., Vol. 11 (1919) 86.

R. cloiophorum Balf. f. et Forrest subsp. *leucopetalum* (Balf. f. et Forrest) Tagg in The Sp. of Rhod. (1930) 545.

R. sanguineum Franch. subsp. *leucopetalum* (Balf. f. et Forrest) Cowan in Notes Roy. Bot. Gard. Edin., Vol. 20 (1940) 73.

The only collection of this plant was made by Forrest in July 1917 in the Mekong-Salwin Divide, north-west Yunnan. It was found on open rocky slopes and ledges of cliffs, at elevations of 3,660–3,965 m. (12,000–13,000 ft.).

The variety differs from the species in the pure white flowers, and in the setulose and setulose-glandular branchlets and petioles.

It was introduced by Forrest in 1917 (No. 14270—the Type number). In cultivation it is a broadly upright shrub, 3–4 feet high. It is hardy, with pure white flowers produced freely in trusses of 2–6. The plant is rare in cultivation.

Epithet of the variety. With white petals.

Hardiness 3. April–May.

R. cloiophorum Balf. f. et Forrest var. **mannophorum** (Balf. f. et Forrest) Davidian, comb. nov.

Syn. *R. mannophorum* Balf. f. et Forrest in Notes Roy. Bot. Gard. Edin., Vol. 13 (1920) 51.

R. cloiophorum Balf. f. et Forrest subsp. *mannophorum* (Balf. f. et Forrest) Tagg in The Sp. of Rhod. (1930) 545.

R. torquatum Balf. f. et Farrer in Notes Roy. Bot. Gard Edin., Vol. 13 (1922) 303.

This plant was first collected by Forrest in July 1919 growing on the ledges of cliffs, in the Salwin-Kiu Chiang Divide, Tsarong, south-east Tibet. In July 1920 it was found by Farrer in the Maguchi Pass, north-east Upper Burma, and is recorded as being a broad spreading bush of 2–4 feet, abundant in the upper alpine region of the same Pass. It grows at elevations of 3,355–3,660 m. (11,000–12,000 ft.).

R. torquatum Balf. f. et Farrer which was described from a plant (No. 1775) collected by Farrer in north-east Upper Burma, is identical with *R. cloiophorum* var. *mannophorum* in every morphological detail.

The variety is distinguished from the species by the moderately or densely glandular pedicel, calyx and ovary, with medium-stalked glands.

There is no record of the plant in cultivation.

Epithet of the variety. Bearing a collar.

Not in cultivation.

R. cloiophorum Balf. f. et Forrest var. **roseotinctum** (Balf. f. et Forrest) Davidian, comb. nov.

Syn. *R. roseotinctum* Balf. f. et Forrest in Notes Roy. Bot. Gard. Edin., Vol. 11 (1919) 124.

R. cloiophorum Balf. f. et Forrest subsp. *roseotinctum* (Balf. f. et Forrest) Tagg in The Sp. of Rhod. (1930) 545.

This plant was first found by Forrest in July 1917 in the Mekong-Salwin Divide, north-west Yunnan. It was afterwards collected by him and by Rock in the same region and in south-east Tibet. The plant grows in open pasture, amongst boulders, in open cane scrub, in rhododendron scrub, on cliffs and rocky slopes, at elevations of 3,355–4,270 m. (11,000–14,000 ft.).

This variety differs from the species usually in the smaller campanulate flowers, often in the dwarf compact habit of growth, and in the moderately or densely glandular pedicel, calyx margin, ovary, and capsule.

The plant was first introduced by Forrest in July 1917 (No. 14268). It was reintroduced by him under five different seed numbers. Rock sent seeds under Nos. 10953, 23636. In cultivation it is a small compact shrub, 1–2 feet high with rose flowers in trusses of 3–5. It is rare in cultivation but should be a valuable acquisition to every garden.

Epithet. Tinged with rose.
Hardiness 3. April–May.

R. dichroanthum Diels in Notes Roy. Bot. Gard. Edin., Vol. 5 (1912) 212.
Illustration. Bot. Mag. Vol. 145 t. 8815 (1919).

A broadly upright or somewhat rounded shrub, 60 cm.–2.44 m. (2–8 ft.) high, branchlets tomentose with a thin, white tomentum, eglandular, those below the inflorescences 3–5 mm. in diameter; leaf-bud scales deciduous. *Leaves oblong, oblanceolate, obovate* or oblong-obovate, lamina leathery, 4–10 cm. long, 1.3–4 cm. broad, apex broadly obtuse or rounded, mucronate, *base tapered or obtuse*, not decurrent; upper surface dark green, glabrous or with vestiges of hairs, midrib grooved, primary veins 10–14 on each side, impressed; margin slightly recurved; *under surface covered with a thin, plastered, continuous, white or sometimes fawn, unistrate indumentum of Rosulate hairs* with short arms, midrib prominent, glabrous or tomentose with a thin tomentum, primary veins slightly raised, concealed or partly exposed; petiole 0.5–1.5 cm. long, not winged, not ridged, tomentose with a thin, white tomentum, eglandular. *Inflorescence* terminal, a racemose umbel of 3–8 flowers; rhachis 3–5 mm. long, hairy with brown hairs, eglandular; pedicel 1.1–2.8 cm. long, moderately or rather densely hairy with short brown hairs, eglandular. *Calyx* 4- or 5-lobed, 0.4–2.5 cm. long, *cup-shaped, divided to the base or to about the middle,* fleshy, lobes unequal, upright, ovate, rounded or triangular, outside glabrous or rarely hairy, eglandular, margin hairy, eglandular. *Corolla* tubular-campanulate, fleshy, 3.2–4.5 cm. long, *yellowish-rose, orange, yellowish-white flushed rose, orange-red, rosy-red or pinkish-red,* 5 nectar pouches at the base; lobes 5, 1–1.5 cm. long, 1–2 cm. broad, rounded, emarginate. *Stamens* 10, unequal, shorter than the corolla, 2–3 cm. long; filaments puberulous at the base or rarely glabrous. *Gynoecium* 2.8–3.8 cm. long; ovary oblong or conoid, truncate, 4–7 mm. long, 7–8-celled, densely tomentose with long or rarely short hairs, eglandular; style glabrous or rarely hairy at the base, eglandular. *Capsule* oblong, 1.2–1.6 cm. long, 4–6 mm. broad, straight, densely hairy with long hairs, eglandular; calyx-lobes persistent.

This distinct species was discovered by Forrest in July 1906 on the eastern flank of the Tali range, west Yunnan. Subsequently it was collected by him and by McLaren's collectors in the same region. It grows in moist, rocky, shady situations in side valleys, in dry, open, rocky meadows, amongst scrub, on ledges of cliffs, and on the margins of bamboo brakes, at elevations of 2,745–3,660 m. (9,000–12,000 ft.).

A diagnostic feature of the species is the thin, white or sometimes fawn, plastered indumentum on the lower surface of the leaves. Other characteristics are the oblong, oblanceolate or obovate leaves, usually with tapered base, the cup-shaped calyx divided to the base or to about the middle, 4 mm.–2.5 cm. long, and the yellowish-rose, orange, rosy-red or pinkish-red flowers. The species is allied to *R. apodectum*. The relationship between them is discussed under the latter. It will be observed that the indumentum on the lower surface of the leaves is unistrate; the hairs are Rosulate with short arms.

R. dichroanthum was first introduced by Forrest in 1910 (Nos. 6761, 6781). It was reintroduced by him in 1913 (No. 11597), and in 1930–31 (No. 28290). In its native home it grows from 2 to 8 feet high; in cultivation it is a broadly upright or somewhat rounded shrub, and reaches a height of 6 feet. A few forms are in cultivation, including: Form 1. A plant with oblanceolate leaves, white indumentum, and rosy-red flowers. Form 2. A plant with oblong leaves, markedly shining fawn indumentum, and pinkish-red flowers. The species is hardy, blooms freely, and has the merit of flowering at a fairly young age.

It was given an Award of Merit when shown by Lady Aberconway and the Hon. H. D. McLaren, Bodnant, in 1923.

Epithet. With flowers of two colours.

Hardiness 3. May–June.

R. didymum Balf. f. et Forrest in Notes Roy. Bot. Gard. Edin., Vol. 13 (1922) 256.

Syn. *R. sanguineum* Franch. subsp. *didymum* (Balf. f. et Forrest) Cowan in Notes Roy. Bot. Gard. Edin., Vol. 20 (1940) 70.

Illustration. Bot. Mag. Vol. 154 t. 9217 (1928).

A broadly upright shrub, 30–92 cm. (1–3 ft.) high, *branchlets* tomentose with a thin, white tomentum, esetulose, *setulose-glandular*, those below the inflorescences 2–4 mm. in diameter; *leaf-bud scales more or less persistent. Leaves* obovate or oblong-obovate, *lamina rigid,* 2–6 cm. long, apex rounded or broadly obtuse, mucronate, base obtuse or tapered, moderately or slightly decurrent on the petiole; upper surface dark green, rugulose, glabrous or with vestiges of hairs, midrib grooved, primary veins 6–10 on each side, impressed; margin recurved; *under surface covered with a thin or somewhat thick,* continuous, white or fawn, *unistrate indumentum* of Rosulate hairs with short arms, *or bistrate, upper layer a form of Ramiform with curled branches and short stem, lower layer Rosulate,* midrib raised, tomentose with a thin tomentum, primary veins slightly raised, concealed or partly exposed; *petiole* 0.3–1.5 cm. long, margins narrowly winged or ridged by the decurrent base of the lamina, tomentose with a thin, white tomentum, esetulose, *setulose-glandular* or rarely not setulose-glandular. *Inflorescence* terminal, a racemose umbel of 3–6 flowers; *rhachis* 0.4–1 cm. long, not hairy, *setulose-glandular; pedicel* 1.3–3.4 cm. long, not hairy, *rather densely setulose-glandular. Calyx* 5-lobed, 1–2 mm. long, divided to the base or to about the middle, lobes unequal, ovate or rounded, *outside* not hairy, *rather densely or moderately setulose-glandular, margin* not hairy, *setulose-glandular. Corolla* tubular-campanulate, fleshy, 2.3–3 cm. long, *black-crimson or dark crimson,* 5 nectar pouches at the base; lobes 5, 0.8–1.3 cm. long, 0.8–1.5 cm. broad, rounded, emarginate. *Stamens* 10, unequal, shorter than the corolla, 1.1–2.6 cm. long; filaments glabrous. *Gynoecium* 1.7–2.8 cm. long; *ovary* conoid, truncate, 3–4 mm. long, 5–6-celled, not hairy or rarely sparsely hairy, *densely glandular* with medium-stalked glands; style glabrous, eglandular. *Capsule* oblong, 0.6–1 cm. long, 3–5 mm. broad, straight, not hairy or rarely hairy, *rather densely or moderately glandular* with long-stalked glands, calyx-lobes persistent.

R. didymum was first collected by Forrest in September 1921 in the Salwin-Kiu Chiang Divide, eastern Tibet. It was later found by him, by Rock and by Ludlow, Sherriff and Elliot in the same region and in south-east Tibet, also on the Yunnan-Tibet border. It grows on moist stony alpine meadows and slopes, amongst boulders, and in rocky moorland, at elevations of 4,270–4,575 m. (14,000–15,000 ft.).

The species is easily recognised by the small, rigid, obovate or oblong-obovate leaves, laminae 2–6 cm. long, by the more or less persistent leaf-bud scales, by the setulose-glandular branchlets, petioles, rhachis of the inflorescence, pedicels and calyx, by the densely glandular ovaries and capsules, and by the black-crimson or dark crimson flowers. It is related to *R. haemaleum*, but the latter is eglandular, with deciduous leaf-bud scales, and usually with larger leaves. It is to be noted that in *R. didymum* the indumentum on the under surface of the leaves is unistrate, the hairs are Rosulate with short arms; or bistrate, those of the upper layer are a form of Ramiform with curled branches, and short stem, the lower layer Rosulate.

R. didymum was first introduced by Forrest in 1921 (No. 20220—the Type number, and No. 20239). It was reintroduced by him in 1922 (No. 21750). Rock sent seeds on 10 occasions. In cultivation it is a small shrub, 1–2 feet or sometimes 3 feet high. The black-crimson or dark crimson flowers are a characteristic feature. The species has the advantage of flowering when quite young. An additional asset is that it flowers late in the season, the blooms appearing in June–July. Occasionally it sets good, fertile seed in plenty. The small forms up to 2 feet high are well-suited for the rock garden. The species is hardy in a sheltered position, and is most effective when laden with dark crimson flowers in trusses of 3–6. In the Royal Botanic Garden, Edinburgh it was successfully grown outdoors, but unfortunately the plant was recently lost to cultivation.

Epithet. Two-fold.
Hardiness 3. June–July.

R. eudoxum Balf. f. et Forrest in Notes Roy. Bot. Gard. Edin., Vol. 11 (1919) 62.

A rounded somewhat compact shrub, 30 cm.–1.83 m. (1–6 ft.) high, *branchlets* floccose or sometimes glabrous, not bristly, *glandular* with medium-stalked glands or eglandular, those below the inflorescences 2–4 mm. in diameter; leaf-bud scales deciduous. *Leaves* oblong, obovate, oblong-elliptic or oblong-lanceolate, lamina thinly leathery, 3–9 cm. long, 1.5–3.3 cm. broad, apex rounded, obtuse or rarely acute, mucronate, base obtuse, decurrent or not decurrent on the petiole; upper surface dark green, glabrous or with vestiges of hairs, midrib grooved, primary veins 10–12 on each side, impressed; margin slightly recurved or flat; *under surface with a thin veil* of white or fawn *unistrate Rosulate hairs* with short arms, midrib prominent, tomentose with a thin tomentum or glabrous, primary veins slightly raised, exposed or partly concealed; *petiole* 0.5–2 cm. long, margins narrowly winged or ridged by the decurrent base of the lamina or not winged, not ridged, floccose, not bristly, eglandular or *glandular* with medium-stalked glands. *Inflorescence* terminal, a racemose umbel of 3–6 or sometimes up to 10 flowers; rhachis 2–8 mm. long, hairy with dark brown hairs, eglandular; *pedicel* 1–2.3 cm. long, moderately or rarely rather densely hairy or sometimes glabrous, *moderately or rather densely glandular* with medium-stalked glands or eglandular. *Calyx* 5-lobed, 2–8 mm. long, not cupular, divided to the base or rarely to about the middle, the base fleshy, lobes unequal, upright or rarely deflexed, ovate, rounded or triangular, *outside* glabrous, *glandular* with medium-stalked glands or eglandular, *margin* hairy or glabrous, *glandular* with medium-stalked glands or rarely eglandular. *Corolla* campanulate or tubular-campanulate, 2.4–4 cm. long, crimson-rose or rose or magenta-rose or creamy-white faintly flushed rose, or white flushed rose, or dark red, 5 nectar pouches at the base; lobes 5, 0.8–1.5 cm. long, 1–2.3 cm. broad, rounded, emarginate. *Stamens* 10, unequal, shorter than the corolla, 1.1–3 cm. long; filaments puberulous at the base or rarely glabrous. *Gynoecium* 2.4–3.6 cm. long; *ovary* oblong narrow or conoid, truncate, 3–5 mm. long, 6-celled, *moderately or densely hairy* with branched or unbranched hairs or rarely not hairy, *moderately or rather densely* or sparsely *glandular* with medium-stalked glands; style glabrous, eglandular. *Capsule* slender or oblong, 1–2.3 cm. long, 3–8 mm. broad, slightly curved or straight, moderately or rather densely hairy, setulose-glandular or not setulose-glandular, calyx-lobes deciduous or persistent.

Forrest discovered this species in July 1917 in the Mekong-Salwin Divide, north-west Yunnan. He found it again later in the same region and in south-east Tibet. Rock, and Yü collected it in north-west Yunnan. In 1950 Kingdon-Ward found it in Tha Chu Valley, Assam. It grows in open rhododendron thickets, on ledges of cliffs, in open rocky pasture, on rocky slopes, in rhododendron and mixed scrub, and in cane scrub, at elevations of 3,355–4,270 m. (11,000–14,000 ft.).

R. eudoxum is closely allied to *R. mesopolium* from which it is distinguished usually by the glandular branchlets, petioles, calyx, and ovaries. The indumentum on the under surface of the leaves consists of a thin veil of hairs, discontinuous, and the calyx varies from 2 to 8 mm. long.

The species was first introduced by Forrest in 1917 (No. 14245—the Type number, and No. 14774). It was reintroduced by him on five other occasions. In 1950 Kingdon-Ward sent seeds from Assam (No. 19589). In its native home it grows 1–6 feet high; in cultivation it is a rounded somewhat compact shrub up to 4–6 feet. The plant is hardy, free-flowering, and makes a fine show with a distinct shade of crimson-rose flowers in trusses of 3–6.

It received an Award of Merit when exhibited by E. H. M. and P. A. Cox, Glendoick, Perth, in 1960.

Epithet. Of good report.

Hardiness 3. April–May.

R. fulvastrum Balf. f. et Forrest in Notes Roy. Bot. Gard. Edin., Vol. 13 (1920) 45.

Syn. *R. temenium* Balf. f. et Forrest subsp. *chrysanthemum* Cowan in Notes Roy. Bot. Gard. Edin., Vol. 20 (1940) 82.

R. temenium Balf. f. et Forrest var. *gilvum* (Cowan) Chamberlain *Chrysanthemum Group* R.H.S. in Rhod. Handb. (1980) p. 53.

A broadly upright or compact rounded shrub, 60 cm.–1.53 m. (2–5 ft.) high, branchlets tomentose with a thin, white or fawn tomentum, esetulose or setulose, glandular with short-stalked glands or setulose-glandular or eglandular, those below the inflorescences 3–5 mm. in diameter; leaf-bud scales deciduous. *Leaves* oblong, oblong-obovate or oblong-lanceolate, lamina leathery, 2.8–7.5 cm. long, 1–2.8 cm. broad, apex obtuse, rounded or acute, mucronate, base obtuse, decurrent on the petiole or rarely not decurrent; upper surface dark or pale green, glabrous or with vestiges of hairs, midrib grooved, primary veins 8–14 on each side, deeply impressed; margin moderately or slightly recurved; *under surface with closely or widely scattered fawn hairs or with a thin veil of unistrate hairs or rarely glabrous*, covered with waxy papillae, midrib raised, glabrous or tomentose with a thin tomentum, primary veins slightly raised, exposed or partly concealed; petiole 3–8 mm. long, margins narrowly winged or ridged by the decurrent base of the lamina (rarely not winged, not ridged), tomentose with a thin, whitish or fawn tomentum, esetulose or sometimes sparsely setulose, eglandular or rarely setulose-glandular. *Inflorescence* terminal, a racemose umbel of 2–4 flowers; rhachis 2–5 mm. long, hairy with dark brown hairs, eglandular; pedicel 1–2 cm. long, hairy with long or medium brown hairs or rarely not hairy, sparsely glandular with short-stalked glands or rarely rather densely setulose-glandular or eglandular. *Calyx* 5-lobed, 2–4 mm. long, divided to the base or to about the middle, lobes unequal, rounded or ovate, outside glabrous or rarely hairy, eglandular, margin hairy or rarely glabrous, eglandular or rarely glandular with short-stalked glands. Corolla campanulate, 2.5–3.7 cm. long, *pale lemon-yellow, creamy-yellow, yellow, or rarely yellow tinged pink*, without markings, 5 nectar pouches at the base; lobes 5, 0.9–1.2 cm. long, 1.3–2 cm. broad, rounded, emarginate. *Stamens* 10, unequal, shorter than the corolla, 1.4–2.6 cm. long; filaments glabrous or puberulous at the base. *Gynoecium* 2.1–3 cm. long; ovary conoid or ovoid, truncate, 3–5 mm. long, 6–7-celled, densely hairy with long hairs, eglandular or rarely glandular with medium-stalked glands; style glabrous or rarely hairy at the base, eglandular. *Capsule* oblong, 1.3–1.8 cm. long, 4–5 mm. broad, straight, hairy with brown hairs, eglandular, calyx-lobes persistent.

This plant was discovered by Forrest in July 1919 in the Salwin-Kiu Chiang Divide, south-east Tibet. It was afterwards found by Rock in north-west Yunnan. It grows on rocky slopes and ledges of cliffs in ravines, and in open meadows amongst rocks on the margins of conifer forests, at elevations of 3,660–4,118 m. (12,000–13,500 ft.).

A distinctive feature of *R. fulvastrum* is that the lower surface of the leaves has closely or widely scattered hairs or a thin veil of hairs or is rarely glabrous. In this respect it is readily distinguished from its nearest ally *R. himertum* where the indumentum is thin, plastered and continuous.

The plant was first introduced by Rock in 1932 from north-west Yunnan (Nos. 22271, 22298), and again later from the same region under four different seed numbers (Nos. 22272, 22290, 22292, 23640). In cultivation it is a broadly upright or compact rounded shrub, 2–3 feet high with pale lemon-yellow or creamy-yellow or yellow flowers in trusses of 2–4. It is hardy in a sheltered position, free-flowering, but is rare in cultivation.

A clone 'Cruachan' received an Award of Merit in 1958 and a First Class Certificate in 1964 when exhibited as *R. chrysanthemum* by Mrs. K. L. Kenneth, Ardrishaig, Argyllshire.

Epithet. Somewhat tawny.
Hardiness 3. April–May.

R. fulvastrum Balf. f. et Forrest var. **gilvum** (Cowan) Davidian, comb. nov.
 Syn. *R. temenium* Balf. f. et Forrest subsp. *gilvum* Cowan in Notes Roy. Bot. Gard. Edin., Vol. 20 (1940) 82.
  R. temenium Balf. f. et Forrest var. *gilvum* (Cowan) Chamberlain, ibid. Vol. 37 (1979) 334.

Forrest first collected this plant in June 1922 in the Salwin-Kiu Chiang Divide, Tsarong, south-east Tibet. In 1923 Rock found it in north-west Yunnan, and in 1932 he collected it in the province of Tsarong, south-east Tibet. It grows on open rocky slopes in ravines, on ledges of cliffs, in moss forest, and in alpine region, at elevations of 3,965–4,118 m. (13,000–13,500 ft.).

The variety differs from the species in that the under surface of the leaves is glabrous. It also differs usually in the setulose branchlets, and usually in the glandular calyx margin and ovaries.

The plant was first introduced by Forrest in 1922 (No. 21914—the Type number). It was reintroduced by him in the same year (No. 22701). In cultivation it is a broadly upright or somewhat rounded shrub, 3–4 feet high. As it comes from high elevations it is hardy outdoors, and makes a fine show with its pale yellow or yellow flowers in trusses of 2–4. The plant is rare in cultivation.

Epithet of the variety. Yellowish.
Hardiness 3. April–May.

R. glaphyrum Balf. f. et Forrest in Notes Roy. Bot. Gard. Edin., Vol. 13 (1920) 45.
 Syn. *R. eudoxum* Balf. f. et Forrest subsp. *glaphyrum* (Balf. f. et Forrest) Tagg in The Sp. of Rhod., (1930) 549.
  R. temenium Balf. f. et Forrest subsp. *glaphyrum* (Balf. f. et Forrest) Cowan in Notes Roy. Bot. Gard. Edin., Vol. 20 (1940) 82.

A rounded compact shrub, 30–92 cm. (1–3 ft.) or rarely up to 1.53 m. (5 ft.) high, branchlets floccose, not setulose or sometimes setulose, setulose-glandular or not setulose-glandular, those below the inflorescences 2–4 mm. in diameter; leaf-bud scales deciduous. *Leaves* oblong or obovate, rarely elliptic, oblong-lanceolate or oblong-obovate, lamina 3–6.8 cm. long, 1.4–3.3 cm. broad, apex rounded or obtuse, mucronate, base rounded or obtuse, decurrent on the petiole; upper surface olive-green or dark green, glabrous or with vestiges of hairs, midrib grooved, primary veins 8–12 on each side, impressed; margin slightly recurved or flat; *under surface glabrous* or sometimes sparsely hairy on the primary veins, hairs white, short broad filaments, waxy papillae poorly developed, midrib prominent, floccose or sometimes glabrous, primary veins slightly raised; petiole 1–5 mm. long, margins narrowly winged or ridged by the decurrent base of the lamina, floccose, not setulose or sometimes setulose, not setulose-glandular or rarely setulose-glandular. *Inflorescence* terminal, a racemose umbel of 2–5 or sometimes up to 11 flowers; rhachis 2–5 mm. long, hairy with branched hairs, *eglandular* or rarely sparsely glandular with medium-stalked glands. *Calyx* 5-lobed, 2–6 mm. long, not cupular, divided to the base or to about the middle, lobes unequal, deflexed or upright, ovate, rounded or irregular, *outside* glabrous, *eglandular, margin* hairy, *eglandular. Corolla* campanulate or rarely tubular-campanulate, 2.6–4 cm. long, *white flushed rose, or deep rose, or pale yellow faintly flushed rose or margins, or pale yellow flushed very faintly rose,* 5 nectar pouches at the base; lobes 5, 1–1.3 cm. long, 1.1–2.4 cm. broad, rounded, emarginate. *Stamens* 10, unequal, shorter than the corolla, 1–2.9 cm. long; filaments glabrous. *Gynoecium* 1.7–3.2 cm. long; *ovary* conoid or rarely oblong, truncate, 3–5 mm. long, 6-celled, densely hairy, *eglandular;* style glabrous, eglandular. *Capsule* oblong or rarely short stout, 1–1.5 cm. long, 0.4–1 cm. broad, straight, rather densely or moderately hairy, *eglandular,* calyx-lobes persistent.

This plant was first collected by Forrest in July 1919 in the Salwin-Kiu Chiang Divide, Tsarong, south-east Tibet. Subsequently it was found by him, and by Rock in the same region and in east Tibet. Yü collected it in north-west Yunnan. It grows at the margins of rhododendron thickets, on cliffs, on rocky slopes, in rocky scrubby moorland, in stony meadows, in mixed scrub, and on screes, at elevations of 3,965–4,575 m. (13,000–15,000 ft.).

A diagnostic feature is the glabrous lower surface of the leaves. The plant is very closely related to *R. temenium* but is distinguished by the white flushed rose, or deep rose, or pale yellow faintly flushed rose flowers; in *R. temenium* the flowers are deep crimson, crimson or carmine.

The plant was first introduced by Forrest in 1921–22 (No. 19960). During the same period, it was reintroduced by him under seven different seed numbers. In cultivation it is a rounded compact shrub 2–3 feet high. It is hardy, blooms freely, but requires a sunny aspect with some protection from wind, for the best results to be obtained. It often produces a second flush of flowers in October or November. The plant is rare in cultivation but should be a valuable acquisition to every collection of rhododendrons.

Epithet. Polished.
Hardiness 3. April–May.

R. glaphyrum Balf. f. et Forrest var. **dealbatum** (Cowan) Davidian, comb. nov.
  Syn. *R. temenium* Balf. f. et Forrest subsp. *dealbatum* Cowan in Notes Roy. Bot. Gard. Edin., Vol. 20 (1940) 83.
  R. temenium Balf. f. et Forrest var. *dealbatum* (Cowan) Chamberlain in Notes Roy. Bot. Gard. Edin., Vol. 37 (1979) 334.
  R. temenium Balf. f. et Forrest subsp. *albipetalum* Cowan in Notes Roy. Bot. Gard. Edin., Vol. 20 (1940) 83.

Forrest discovered this plant in July 1921 in the Salwin-Kiu Chiang Divide, Tsarong, south-east Tibet. In 1932 Rock collected it in the same region. It grows in rocky moorland, in forests and alpine region, at elevations of 3,965–4,270 m. (13,000–14,000 ft.).

The variety differs from the species in that the flowers are white, the branchlets are not setulose-glandular, and often the ovaries and capsules are glandular with medium-stalked glands.

The plant was introduced by Rock in 1932 (No. 22295). In cultivation it is a somewhat compact rounded shrub, 2–2½ feet high and almost as much across. It is a somewhat slow grower, and takes some years to produce the flowers. The plant is hardy in a sheltered position, with white, unspotted flowers in trusses of 2–3 or more. It is rare in cultivation.

Epithet of the variety. White powder.

Hardiness 3. April–May.

R. gymnocarpum Balf. f. ex Tagg in Notes Roy. Bot. Gard. Edin., Vol. 15 (1927) 313.
      Syn. *R. microgynum* Balf. f. et Forrest *Gymnocarpum Group* R.H.S. in Rhod. Handb. (1980) p.50.

A rounded compact, or broadly upright shrub, 60 cm.–1.53 m. (2–5 ft.) high, branchlets tomentose with a thin, white or fawn tomentum, setulose or not setulose, eglandular or sparsely glandular with short-stalked glands, those below the inflorescences 3–6 mm. in diameter; leaf-bud scales deciduous. *Leaves oblong or oblong-lanceolate,* lamina leathery, 4–11.5 cm. long, 1.5–3.7 cm. broad, apex obtuse, mucronate, base obtuse or tapered, not decurrent or slightly decurrent on the petiole; upper surface dark green, slightly rugulose, glabrous or with vestiges of hairs, midrib grooved, primary veins 10–15 on each side, impressed; margin recurved; *under surface covered with a semi-woolly* medium thick, *continuous,* fawn or brown, *unistrate indumentum of a form of Ramiform hairs with long, flat ribbon-like uncurled branches, with short stem,* minutely glandular or eglandular, midrib prominent, hairy, primary veins concealed; petiole 0.5–1.6 cm. long, tomentose with a thin, white or fawn tomentum, not setulose, eglandular. *Inflorescence* terminal, a racemose umbel of 3–6 flowers; rhachis 2–9 mm. long, hairy with dark brown hairs, eglandular; pedicel 1.4–3.4 cm. long, hairy, moderately or sparsely glandular with minute short-stalked glands or eglandular. *Calyx* 5-lobed, 1–3 mm. long, divided to the base, lobes triangular, ovate or rounded, outside glabrous, eglandular, margin hairy, eglandular. *Corolla* campanulate, fleshy, 3–4 cm. long, *deep claret-crimson or deep crimson* with deeper markings on the posterior side, 5 nectar pouches at the base; lobes 5, 1–1.5 cm. long, 1.4–2 cm. broad, rounded, emarginate. *Stamens* 10, unequal, shorter than the corolla, 1.5–3 cm. long; filaments puberulous at the base or up to one-half their length. *Gynoecium* 2.2–4 cm. long; *ovary* conoid or oblong, *truncate,* 4–5 mm. long, 6-celled, sparsely to densely hairy, eglandular or sparsely to densely glandular with medium-stalked glands; style glabrous, eglandular. *Capsule* oblong, 1.2–1.4 cm. long, 4–5 mm. broad, straight, hairy, sparsely or moderately glandular with long-stalked glands, calyx-lobes persistent.

Forrest discovered this species in July 1918 on Ka-gwr-pw, in the Mekong-Salwin Divide, Tsarong, south-east Tibet. He found it again later in October of the same year on the mountains north-east of Chungtien, Yunnan. It grows in cane brakes, amongst rocks, and in open pine forest, at elevations of 3,660–4,270 m. (12,000–14,000 ft.).

R. gymnocarpum is an aberrant species in the Roxieanum Subseries, Taliense Series. It has little in common with the species of this Series. In its lax inflorescence of 3–6 flowers, particularly in the shape, size and deep claret-crimson or deep crimson flowers, and in the truncate ovary, it shows a marked similarity to the species of the Sanguineum Subseries, Neriiflorum Series in which it will now be placed.

It is allied to *R. sanguineum* and *R. microgynum.* It is distinguished from the former by the semi-woolly, medium thick indumentum on the lower surface of the leaves, by the Ramiform hairs of the leaf-indumentum with long, flat ribbon-like branches and short stem, and often by the oblong-lanceolate leaves; from the latter by the deep claret-crimson or deep crimson flowers, usually by the larger corolla, by the longer style, and by the obtuse leaf-apex.

R. gymnocarpum was introduced by Forrest in 1918 (No. 16687—the Type number). In cultivation it is a rounded compact or broadly upright shrub, 3–5 feet high, well-filled with dark green foliage. It is hardy, a vigorous grower, and is most attractive with its deep crimson flowers produced freely in trusses of 3–6. One of its chief merits is that it flowers at a fairly young age. It often produces a few capsules containing good fertile seeds in plenty.

The plant was given an Award of Merit when shown by L. de Rothschild, Exbury, in 1940.

Epithet. With naked fruit.

Hardiness 3. April–May.

R. haemaleum Balf. f. et Forrest in Notes Roy. Bot. Gard. Edin., Vol. 11 (1919) 71.

Syn. *R. sanguineum* Franch. subsp. *haemaleum* (Balf. f. et Forrest) Cowan in Notes Roy. Bot. Gard. Edin., Vol. 20 (1940) 69.

R. sanguineum Franch. var. *haemaleum* (Balf. f. et Forrest) Chamberlain, ibid. Vol. 37 (1979) 334.

Illustration. Bot. Mag. Vol. 155 t. 9263 (1932), figured as *R. sanguineum*.

A broadly upright or rounded shrub, 30 cm.–1.83 m. (1–6 ft.) or rarely up to 2.44 m. (8 ft.) high, *branchlets* tomentose with a thin, white tomentum, not setulose or sometimes setulose, *eglandular,* those below the inflorescences 2–5 mm. in diameter; leaf-bud scales deciduous. *Leaves* oblanceolate, oblong, obovate, oblong-obovate or sometimes nearly orbicular, lamina 2.6–9.5 cm. long, 1.3–3.8 cm. broad, apex rounded or obtuse, mucronate, base tapered or obtuse, slightly or moderately decurrent on the petiole; upper surface dark green, glabrous or with vestiges of hairs, midrib grooved, primary veins 8–14 on each side, impressed; margin slightly recurved or flat; *under surface covered with a thin,* plastered or not plastered, *continuous,* white, fawn, brown or sometimes dark brown, *unistrate indumentum of Rosulate hairs* with short arms, midrib prominent, glabrous or tomentose with a thin tomentum, primary veins slightly raised, concealed or partly exposed; *petiole* 0.3–1.4 cm. long, margins narrowly winged or ridged by the decurrent base of the lamina, tomentose with a thin, white or rarely brown tomentum, not setulose or rarely setulose, *eglandular. Inflorescence* terminal, a racemose umbel of 2–6 flowers; rhachis 2–5 mm. long, hairy with dark brown or brown hairs, eglandular; *pedicel* 1–2.8 cm. long, *moderately or rather densely hairy* with branched or unbranched hairs, *eglandular,* or rarely rather densely or moderately glandular with long-stalked glands. *Calyx* 5-lobed, 1–9 mm. long, not cupular, divided to the base or sometimes to about the middle, the base fleshy, coloured like the corolla, lobes unequal, upright or deflexed, ovate, rounded or irregular, *outside* glabrous or rarely hairy, *eglandular, margin* hairy, *eglandular* or rarely glandular with medium-stalked glands. *Corolla* tubular-campanulate or sometimes campanulate, fleshy, 2.3–4 cm. long, *black-crimson, black-carmine, dark carmine or nearly black,* 5 nectar pouches at the base; lobes 5, 0.8–1.3 cm. long, 1.1–1.6 cm. broad, rounded, emarginate. *Stamens* 10, unequal, shorter than the corolla, 1–2.7 cm. long; filaments puberulous at the base or glabrous. *Gynoecium* 1.5–3.7 cm. long; *ovary* conoid or rarely ovoid, truncate, 3–6 mm. long, 6–7-celled, *densely hairy* with branched or unbranched hairs, *eglandular;* style glabrous or rarely hairy at the base, eglandular. *Capsule* oblong or short stout, 0.9–2 cm. long, 4–8 mm. broad, straight, moderately or rather densely hairy, *eglandular,* calyx-lobes persistent or deciduous.

This plant was discovered by Forrest in August 1904 in the Mekong-Salwin Divide, north-west of Tsekou, south-east Tibet. It was afterwards found by him and by other collectors in the same region, and in north-west Yunnan, also in Assam. It grows in open rocky situations, in open rocky moorland, in rhododendron scrub and in mixed scrub, in thickets, in open alpine meadows, on cliffs and rocky slopes, and in cane brakes, at elevations of 3,050–4,423 m. (10,000–14,500 ft.). Kingdon-Ward records it as being abundant all through the upper *Abies* forest along a ridge in Assam.

R. haemaleum bears a strong resemblance to *R. sanguineum* in general features, but differs markedly in its black-crimson, black-carmine, dark carmine and nearly black flowers.

The plant was first introduced by Forrest in 1917–19 (Nos. 14166, 16736, 18934). It was reintroduced by him on four other occasions. Rock sent seeds under five different seed numbers. In its native home it grows from 1 to 6 feet or rarely 8 feet high; in cultivation it is a broadly upright or rounded shrub up to 4 or 5 feet high with dark green foliage. Three flower colour forms are in cultivation: black-crimson, dark carmine, and nearly black. The plant is hardy, a fairly robust grower, and is easy to cultivate. Occasionally it produces good and plentiful fertile seed.

It received an Award of Merit when exhibited by the Countess of Rosse and National Trust, Nymans, in 1973.

Epithet. Blood-red.
Hardiness 3. April–May.

R. haemaleum Balf. f. et Forrest var. **atrorubrum** (Cowan) Davidian, comb. nov.
> Syn. *R. sanguineum* Franch. subsp. *atrorubrum* Cowan in Notes Roy. Bot. Gard. Edin., Vol. 20 (1940) 69.

Forrest first collected this plant in 1919 in Tsarong, south-east Tibet. In 1923–24 it was found by Rock in north-west Yunnan. It grows on rocky slopes and in rhododendron scrub.

The variety differs from the species in that the pedicel and ovary are densely glandular, and the calyx margin is often glandular.

The plant is in cultivation, possibly introduced by Rock in 1948–49. It grows up to about 2 feet high with dark carmine flowers in trusses of 3–5. The plant is rare in cultivation but is worthy of being widely grown.

Epithet. Dark red.
Hardiness 3. April–May.

R. haemaleum Balf. f. et Forrest var. **mesaeum** (Balf. f. ex Cowan) Davidian, comb. nov.
> Syn. *R. sanguineum* Franch. subsp. *mesaeum* Balf. f. ex Cowan in Notes Roy. Bot. Gard. Edin., Vol. 20 (1940) 70.

This plant was first collected by Forrest in August 1921 in the Salwin-Kiu Chiang Divide, Tsarong, eastern Tibet. It was later found by him and by Rock in the same region and in south-eastern Tibet. It grows on rocky moist slopes, in open rocky moorland, in stony alpine meadows, on cliffs, in rhododendron scrub, and in ravines amongst scrub, at elevations of 3,660–4,575 m. (12,000–15,000 ft.).

The variety differs from the species in that the leaf-bud scales are persistent or sometimes more or less persistent, the leaves (laminae) are usually smaller 2–4 cm. long, 1–1.4 cm. broad, and the corolla is usually smaller 2–2.6 cm. long.

The plant was first introduced by Forrest in August 1921 (No. 19958—the Type number). It was reintroduced by him under three different seed numbers. Rock sent seeds on four occasions. In its native home it grows from 9 inches up to 5 feet high; in cultivation it grows up to 2 feet. The persistent leaf-bud scales and small flowers are characteristic features. The plant is hardy, easy to grow, but is uncommon in cultivation.

Epithet of the variety. Middle.
Hardiness 3. April–May.

R. herpesticum Balf. f. et Ward in Notes Roy. Bot. Gard. Edin., Vol. 10 (1917) 114.
> Syn. *R. dichroanthum* Diels subsp. *herpesticum* (Balf. f. et Ward) Cowan in Notes Roy. Bot. Gard. Edin., Vol. 20 (1940) 87.
> *R. dichroanthum* Diels subsp. *scyphocalyx* Balf. f. et Forrest *Herpesticum Group* R.H.S. Rhod. Handb. (1980) p.47.

A broadly upright shrub, *15–60 cm. (6 in.–2 ft.) high*, branchlets tomentose with a thin, white or fawn tomentum or rarely glabrous, not bristly or sometimes bristly, bristly-glandular or not bristly-glandular, those below the inflorescences 2–5 mm. in diameter; leaf-bud scales deciduous or rarely persistent. *Leaves oblanceolate*, oblong-obovate or sometimes obovate, lamina leathery, 3–7 cm. long, 1.4–3 cm. broad, apex rounded, mucronate, base tapered or obtuse, not auricled or slightly auricled, decurrent on the petiole; upper surface green, glabrous or with vestiges of hairs, midrib grooved, primary veins 10–12 on each side, impressed; margin slightly recurved; *under surface covered with a thin, plastered, continuous*, fawn or white, *unistrate indumentum of Rosulate hairs* with short arms, midrib prominent, glabrous or tomentose with a thin tomentum, primary veins slightly raised or not raised, concealed or partly exposed; petiole 0.4–1 cm. long, margins narrowly winged or ridged by the decurrent base of the lamina, tomentose with a thin, white or fawn tomentum or rarely glabrous, not bristly, eglandular. *Inflorescence* terminal, a racemose umbel of 2–5 flowers; rhachis 2–5 mm. long, hairy with dark brown hairs, eglandular; *pedicel* 1.5–3.2 cm. long, moderately or sometimes sparsely hairy with branched hairs, *moderately or rather densely* (or rarely sparsely) *setulose-glandular. Calyx* 5-lobed, 0.4–1 cm. long, cup-shaped, divided to about the middle or not divided, (the base fleshy), lobes unequal, upright, ovate, rounded or irregular, outside glabrous or hairy, setulose-glandular at the base or not setulose-glandular, margin hairy or sometimes glabrous, glandular with medium-stalked glands or sometimes eglandular. *Corolla* tubular-campanulate, fleshy, 2.5–4.3 cm. long, *orange or deep crimson; or orange flushed rose or crimson; or yellow flushed rose or crimson,* 5 nectar pouches at the base; lobes 5, 1–1.2 cm. long, 1.3–2 cm. broad, rounded, emarginate. *Stamens* 10, unequal, shorter than the corolla, 1.2–2.8 cm. long; filaments puberulous at the base. *Gynoecium* 2.1–3.4 cm. long; *ovary* conoid or ovoid, truncate, 4–6 mm. long, 5–8-celled, densely or moderately hairy with short or long hairs or rarely not hairy, *moderately or densely setulose-glandular* or rarely not setulose-glandular; style glabrous, eglandular. *Capsule* oblong or short stout, 1–2 cm. long, 4–9 mm. broad, straight, hairy with long or short hairs, *setulose-glandular* or rarely not setulose-glandular, calyx-lobes persistent or rarely deciduous.

Kingdon-Ward discovered this plant in July 1914 in the Nwai Divide, eastern Upper Burma. Subsequently it was collected by him, by Forrest, and by Farrer in the same region and in north-east Upper Burma. Forrest found it in north-west Yunnan. It grows amongst bamboos, in stony alpine meadows, on ledges of cliffs, on boulders, on screes, amongst rhododendron scrub, in thickets, and in stony moorland, at elevations of 3,660–4,270 m. (12,000–14,000 ft.). Kingdon-Ward records it as forming tangled growths covering a good deal of ground and rising to a height of about a foot, at 12,000–13,000 feet in eastern Upper Burma.

R. herpesticum is very closely allied to R. scyphocalyx which it resembles in general appearance, but differs usually in the smaller habit of growth and in the shape of the leaves, and often in the smaller flowers. The flower colour is variable; it is orange, deep crimson, or yellow flushed rose or crimson.

The plant was first introduced by Forrest in 1924–25 (No. 24616). It was reintroduced by him on several occasions. In cultivation it grows up to 2 feet high. The plant is hardy, free-flowering, and is easy to grow. The deep crimson flowering form is rare in cultivation.

Epithet. Spreading.
Hardiness 3. May–June.

R. himertum Balf. f. et Forrest in Notes Roy. Bot. Gard. Edin., Vol. 13 (1920) 48.

Syn. *R. poliopeplum* Balf. f. et Forrest in Notes Roy. Bot. Gard. Edin. Vol. 13 (1920) 56.

R. sanguineum Franch. subsp. *himertum* (Balf. f. et Forrest) Cowan in Notes Roy. Bot. Gard. Edin., Vol. 20 (1940) 72.

R. sanguineum Franch. var. *himertum* (Balf. f. et Forrest) Chamberlain, ibid. Vol. 37 (1979) 334.

A broadly upright or compact rounded shrub, 45–92 cm. (1½–3 ft.) high, *branchlets tomentose* with a thin, whitish or fawn tomentum, esetulose, *eglandular*, those below the inflorescences 3–5 mm. in diameter; leaf-bud scales deciduous or rarely more or less persistent. *Leaves* oblong-obovate, oblong or obovate, lamina leathery, 3–6.7 cm. long, 1–2.3 cm. broad, apex obtuse, rounded or rarely acute, mucronate, base obtuse or rarely tapered, decurrent on the petiole; upper surface dark or pale green, glabrous or with vestiges of hairs, midrib grooved, primary veins 8–10 on each side, deeply impressed; margin moderately or slightly recurved; *under surface covered with a thin plastered* (or rarely not plastered), *continuous,* white or whitish or fawn *unistrate indumentum of Rosulate hairs with long or short arms,* midrib raised, glabrous or rarely tomentose, primary veins slightly raised, concealed or partly exposed; *petiole* 0.4–1 cm. long, margins narrowly winged or ridged by the decurrent base of the lamina or not winged not ridged, tomentose with a thin, whitish or fawn tomentum, esetulose, *eglandular. Inflorescence* terminal, a racemose umbel of 3–7 flowers; rhachis 3–5 mm. long, hairy with dark brown hairs, eglandular; *pedicel* 1–2.9 cm. long, moderately or rather densely hairy with long brown hairs, *eglandular. Calyx* 5-lobed, 1–6 mm. long, cupular or not cupular, divided to the base or to about the middle, lobes unequal, rounded, ovate or irregular, *outside* moderately or sparsely hairy, *eglandular, margin* hairy, *eglandular. Corolla* campanulate or tubular-campanulate, 2.5–3.6 cm. long, *yellow, lemon-yellow or bright yellow,* 5 nectar pouches at the base; lobes 5, 1–1.2 cm. long, 1.1–1.7 cm. broad, rounded, emarginate. *Stamens* 10, unequal, shorter than the corolla, 1.4–2 cm. long; filaments glabrous or sometimes puberulous at the base. *Gynoecium* 2–2.8 cm. long; *ovary* conoid or ovoid, truncate, 3–5 mm. long, 6–8-celled, densely hairy with long hairs, *eglandular* or rarely sparsely glandular with medium-stalked glands; style glabrous, eglandular. *Capsule* oblong, conoid or ovoid, 0.6–1.5 cm. long, 4–6 mm. broad, moderately or rather densely hairy with brown hairs, glandular with medium-stalked glands or eglandular, calyx-lobes persistent.

Forrest discovered this plant in July 1918 in Tsarong, south-east Tibet. He found it again in 1919 in the Salwin-Kiu Chiang Divide, in the same region. Rock collected it later in north-west Yunnan and south-east Tibet. It grows in open meadows, on rocky slopes, and on ledges of cliffs, at elevations of 3,660–3,965 m. (12,000–13,000 ft.).

R. himertum is closely allied to *R. citriniflorum* which it resembles in leaf shape and size, and in flower size and colour, but differs markedly in that the indumentum on the lower surface of the leaves is thin, plastered, unistrate consisting of Rosulate hairs with long or short arms; moreover, the pedicel, calyx and ovary are not glandular. In *R. citriniflorum,* the indumentum is thick, woolly, bistrate consisting of an upper layer of Ramiform hairs with curled branches and short stem and a lower layer of Rosulate hairs; moreover, the pedicel, calyx and ovary are usually glandular with long-stalked glands.

The plant was first introduced by Forrest in 1918 (No. 16728). It was later introduced by him under No. 21782. In cultivation it is a broadly upright or compact rounded shrub 2–3 feet high with yellow or lemon-yellow flowers in trusses of 3–7. The plant is hardy, but is rare in cultivation.

Epithet. Lovely.
Hardiness 3. April–May.

R. horaeum Balf. f. et Forrest in Notes Roy. Bot. Gard. Edin., Vol. 13 (1922) 264.
    Syn. *R. citriniflorum* Balf. f. et Forrest subsp. *horaeum* (Balf. f. et Forrest) Cowan in Notes Roy. Bot. Gard. Edin., Vol. 20 (1940) 76.
        R. citriniflorum Balf f. et Forrest var. *horaeum* (Balf. f. et Forrest) Chamberlain, ibid. Vol. 37 (1979) 332.

A broadly upright or compact rounded shrub, sometimes prostrate or semi-prostrate, 15 cm.–1.53 m. (6 in.–5 ft.) high, branchlets tomentose with a thin, white tomentum, not setulose or rarely setulose, not setulose-glandular or rarely setulose-

4. **R. horaeum.** nat. size.
 a. capsule. b. flower. c. stamen.
 d. ovary, style. e. section. f. leaf (lower surface).

glandular, those below the inflorescences 2–6 mm. in diameter; *leaf-bud scales persistent or rarely deciduous*. *Leaves* obovate, oblong-obovate or rarely oblong-lanceolate, lamina leathery, 2.3–6 cm. long, 1.2–2.4 cm. broad, apex rounded or rarely obtuse, mucronate, base obtuse or tapered or rarely rounded, decurrent on the petiole; *upper surface* dark green, *semi-bullate*, glabrous or with vestiges of hairs, midrib grooved, primary veins 8–10 on each side, impressed; margin slightly recurved; *under surface covered with a thick* or rarely thin, *woolly continuous*, brown, dark brown, whitish-brown or fawn, *bistrate indumentum of hairs, upper layer a form of Ramiform with curled branches and short stem, lower layer Rosulate* with short arms, midrib raised, glabrous or tomentose with a thin tomentum, primary veins slightly raised, concealed or partly exposed; petiole 0.4–1.3 cm. long, margins narrowly winged by the decurrent base of the lamina, tomentose with a thin, white tomentum, esetulose, eglandular. *Inflorescence* terminal, a racemose umbel of 2–4 flowers; rhachis 2–5 mm. long, hairy with dark brown hairs, eglandular; pedicel 1–2.5 cm. long, moderately or densely hairy or rarely not hairy, not setulose or setulose, not setulose-glandular or moderately or rarely rather densely setulose-glandular. *Calyx* 5-lobed, *0.2–2 cm. long*, cupular or sometimes not cupular, divided to about the middle or to the base, the base fleshy, coloured like the corolla, lobes unequal, irregular, ovate or rounded, persistent or rarely deciduous, outside glabrous, eglandular, margin hairy, eglandular. *Corolla* tubular-campanulate, fleshy, 2.6–3.8 m. long, *deep crimson, rose-crimson, carmine, deep yellowish-crimson, orange-crimson, yellow heavily margined crimson, or pale rose margined deeper,* 5 nectar pouches at the base; lobes 5, 0.8–1.3 cm. long, 1–2.2 cm. broad, rounded, emarginate. *Stamens* 10, unequal, shorter than the corolla, 1.1–2.5 cm. long; filaments puberulous at the base or rarely glabrous. *Gynoecium* 2–3 cm. long; *ovary* conoid, rarely ovoid or oblong, truncate, 4–5 mm. or rarely 7 mm. long, densely tomentose with branched or unbranched hairs, *eglandular*; style glabrous, eglandular. *Capsule* conoid or oblong, 0.8–1.4 cm. long, 5–8 mm. broad, rather densely or moderately tomentose, *eglandular*, calyx-lobes persistent or deciduous.

This species was discovered by Forrest in September 1921 in the Salwin-Kiu Chiang Divide, Tsarong, eastern Tibet. It was afterwards found by him and by Rock in south-eastern Tibet. Yü collected it in north-west Yunnan. The plant grows on cliffs and rocky slopes, in alpine scrub, in rocky moorland, and on boulders, at elevations of 3,965–4,575 m. (13,000–15,000 ft.). Yü records it as being common around the lake Tsukuai, Salwin-Kiu Chiang Divide, Yunnan.

R. horaeum is a distinct species and cannot be confused with other species of its Subseries. The diagnostic features are the persistent leaf-bud scales, the deep crimson, rose-crimson, carmine or orange-crimson flowers, and the eglandular ovary. In these respects it is readily distinguished from its ally *R. citriniflorum*. Other striking characters are the thick, woolly continuous, dark brown, brown or whitish-brown, bistrate indumentum of hairs, upper layer a form of Ramiform with curled branches and short stem, lower layer Rosulate, and the cup-shaped calyx usually 6 mm.–2 cm. long, divided to about the middle or to the base.

The species was first introduced by Forrest in 1921–22 (No. 21754). It was reintroduced by him on three occasions. Rock sent seeds under four different seed numbers. In its native home it grows up to 3 feet in height, sometimes prostrate or semi-prostrate 6 inches high; in cultivation it is a broadly upright or compact rounded shrub up to 2–5 feet. Two colour forms are found in gardens, namely, deep crimson and orange-crimson. As the plant comes from high elevations, it is hardy, a robust grower, and is easy to cultivate. The species is a late-flowerer, prolonging the flowering season into May or June. It is uncommon in cultivation, but is very desirable for inclusion in every collection of rhododendrons.

Epithet. Beautiful.
Hardiness 3. May–June.

R. horaeum Balf. f. et Forrest var. **rubens** (Cowan) Davidian, comb. nov.

Syn *R. citriniflorum* Balf. f. et Forrest subsp. *rubens* Cowan in Notes Roy. Bot. Gard. Edin., Vol. 20 (1940) 76.

This plant was first collected by Rock in May–June 1932 on the mountains west of Ka-gwr-pw, Doker-la and Yundshi, south-east Tibet, growing in alpine region at an elevation of 4,118 m. (13,500 ft.).

The variety differs from the species in the deciduous leaf-bud scales, in the densely setulose-glandular ovary, in the moderately setulose-glandular calyx margin, and usually in the small calyx 2 mm. long.

It was introduced by Rock in 1932 (No. 23245—the Type number = 23669). In cultivation it is 2–3 feet high, with a small calyx 2 mm. long, and red or crimson flowers. The plant is hardy, but is rare in cultivation.

Epithet of the variety. Reddish.

Hardiness 3. May–June.

R. mesopolium Balf. f. et Forrest in Notes Roy. Bot. Gard. Edin., Vol. 13 (1920) 51.

Syn. *R. epipastum* Balf. f. et Forrest in Notes Roy. Bot. Gard. Edin., Vol. 13 (1922) 258.

R. asteium Balf. f. et Forrest in Notes Roy. Bot. Gard. Edin., Vol. 13 (1922) 235.

R. eudoxum Balf. f. et Forrest subsp. *asteium* (Balf. f. et Forrest) Tagg in The Sp. of Rhod. (1930) 549.

R. eudoxum Balf. f. et Forrest subsp. *epipastum* (Balf. f. et Forrest) Tagg in The Sp. of Rhod. (1930) 549.

R. eudoxum Balf. f. et Forrest subsp. *mesopolium* (Balf. f. et Forrest) Tagg in The Sp. of Rhod. (1930) 549.

R. fulvastrum Balf. f. et Forrest subsp. *mesopolium* (Balf. f. et Forrest) Cowan in Notes Roy. Bot. Gard. Edin., Vol. 20 (1940) 79.

R. eudoxum Balf. f. et Forrest var. *mesopolium* (Balf. f. et Forrest) Chamberlain ibid. Vol. 37 (1979) 333.

A rounded somewhat compact shrub, 45 cm.–1.53 m. (1½–5 ft.) high, *branchlets* floccose or tomentose with a thin white tomentum or glabrous, not bristly, *eglandular*, those below the inflorescences 2–4 mm. in diameter; leaf-bud scales deciduous. *Leaves* oblong, oblong-obovate or obovate, lamina 3–6.5 cm. long, 1.2–2.8 cm. broad, apex rounded or broadly obtuse, mucronate, base obtuse, decurrent on the petiole; upper surface dark green, glabrous or with vestiges of hairs, midrib grooved, primary veins 9–12 on each side, impressed; margin slightly recurved or flat; *under surface with a thin veil of* white or fawn *unistrate, Rosulate hairs* with short arms or *somewhat Ramiform*, midrib prominent, glabrous or tomentose with a thin tomentum, primary veins slightly raised, exposed or partly concealed; *petiole* 3–8 mm. long, margins narrowly winged or ridged by the decurrent base of the lamina, tomentose with a thin tomentum or floccose, not bristly, *eglandular*. *Inflorescence* terminal, a racemose umbel of 2–4 or sometimes up to 10 flowers; rhachis 2–4 mm. long, hairy with dark brown hairs, eglandular; *pedicel* 1–2.3 cm. long, moderately or rather densely hairy with branched or unbranched hairs, *eglandular*. *Calyx* 5-lobed, 0.1–1 cm. long, not cupular, divided to the base or to about the middle, the base fleshy, lobes unequal, deflexed or upright, ovate, rounded or irregular, *outside* glabrous, *eglandular, margin* hairy or sometimes glabrous, *eglandular*. *Corolla* tubular-campanulate or campanulate, 2.3–3.5 cm. long, *pale rose or rose, or rose margined and lined a deeper shade, or bright pink, or white,* or rarely crimson, 5 nectar pouches at the base; lobes 5, 0.8–1.2 cm. long, 1.1–1.8 cm. broad, rounded, emarginate. *Stamens* 10, unequal, shorter than the corolla, 1.1–2.4 cm. long; filaments puberulous at the base or glabrous. *Gynoecium* 2–3 cm. long; *ovary* conoid, truncate, 3–5 mm. long, 6–8-celled, densely hairy with branched or unbranched hairs, *eglandular* or rarely sparsely glandular with medium-stalked glands; style glabrous, eglandular. *Capsule* oblong, 1–

1.6 cm. long, 6–8 mm. broad, straight, moderately or rather densely hairy, *eglandular*, calyx-lobes persistent or deciduous.

R. mesopolium was first collected by Forrest in July–August 1918 on Doker-la, Tsarong, south-east Tibet. It was afterwards found by him and by Rock in the same region and in north-west Yunnan. It grows in open, dry, bouldery pasture, on open cliffs, and on rocky slopes, at elevations of 3,660–4,270 m. (12,000–14,000 ft.).

In 1922 two other species, *R. asteium* Balf. f. et Forrest and *R. epipastum* Balf f. et Forrest were described from specimens collected by Forrest in south-east Tibet. They are identical with *R. mesopolium* in every respect.

R. mesopolium is closely related to *R. eudoxum* but differs in the eglandular branchlets, petioles, pedicels, calyx and ovaries, and often in the smaller rose flowers. A marked feature is the thin veil of hairs on the lower surface of the leaves.

The plant was first introduced by Forrest in 1918 (No. 16751—the Type number). It was reintroduced by him under four different seed numbers. In cultivation it is a rounded, somewhat compact shrub 3–5 feet high. It is hardy, blooms freely with trusses of 2–10 flowers. The plant is rare in cultivation.

Epithet. Grey in middle.
Hardiness 3. April–May.

R. microgynum Balf. f. et Forrest in Notes Roy. Bot. Gard. Edin., Vol. 11 (1919) 99.

A broadly upright or rounded compact shrub, 92 cm.–1.22 m. (3–4 ft.) high, branchlets tomentose with a thin, white or fawn tomentum, not setulose, sparsely glandular with short-stalked glands, those below the inflorescences 4–5 mm. in diameter; leaf-bud scales deciduous. *Leaves lanceolate or oblanceolate,* lamina leathery, 4–9 cm. long, 1.5–2.5 cm. broad, *apex acute,* mucronate, base tapered or obtuse, not decurrent; upper surface dark green, glabrous or with vestiges of hairs, midrib grooved, primary veins 12–15 on each side, impressed; margin recurved; *under surface covered with a thin, continuous, brown, unistrate indumentum of Ramiform hairs with long, flat, ribbon-like, uncurled branches, with short stem,* midrib prominent, hairy, primary veins slightly raised, concealed; petiole 0.5–1 cm. long, tomentose with a thin, white or fawn tomentum, not setulose, eglandular. *Inflorescence* terminal, a racemose umbel of 5–6 flowers; rhachis 4–5 mm. long, hairy with brown hairs, eglandular; pedicel 0.9–1.3 cm. long, hairy, moderately or sparsely glandular with minute, short-stalked glands. *Calyx* 5-lobed, 1–2 mm. long, lobes triangular or rounded, outside hairy or glabrous, sparsely glandular with short-stalked glands or eglandular, margin hairy, eglandular. *Corolla* broadly campanulate, fleshy, *2.2–3 cm. long, dull soft rose with faint crimson markings,* 5 nectar pouches at the base; lobes 5, 2.2–3 cm. long, 1.4–2 cm. broad, rounded, emarginate. *Stamens* 10, unequal, shorter than the corolla, 0.9–2.1 cm. long; filaments puberulous at the base. *Gynoecium* 0.8–1.5 cm. long; *ovary* conoid, truncate, *2–3 mm. long,* sparsely hairy or glabrous, moderately or rather densely glandular with short-stalked glands; *style short, one-third or one-half the length of the corolla,* glabrous, eglandular. *Capsule* conoid or oblong, 1–1.2 cm. long, 3–4 mm. broad, hairy or glabrous, glandular with short-stalked glands, calyx-lobes persistent.

This species is known from a single collection made in July 1917 by Forrest, on Ka-gwr-pw, Tsarong, south-east Tibet. It is found in open situations on rocky slopes, at an elevation of 3,660 m. (12,000 ft.).

R. microgynum is an aberrant species in the Roxieanum Subseries, Taliense Series, from which it differs markedly in the lax inflorescence of 5–6 flowers, in the indumental characters on the lower surface of the leaves, in the deciduous leaf-bud scales, and usually in the rose flowers; in these and other respects it agrees with the Sanguineum Subseries, Neriiflorum Series to which it is now transferred.

The species is related to *R. gymnocarpum* with which it has been confused. The main distinctions between them are that in *R. microgynum* the corolla is soft rose with faint crimson markings, small 2.2–3 cm. long, the style is short, one third or one-half the length of the corolla, and the leaves are lanceolate or oblanceolate with acute apex; whereas in *R. gymnocarpum* the corolla is deep claret-crimson with deeper markings on the posterior side, or deep crimson, usually larger 3–4 cm. long, the style is slightly shorter or about as long as the corolla, and the leaves are oblong or oblong-lanceolate with obtuse apex.

R. microgynum was introduced by Forrest in 1917 (No. 14242—the Type number). In cultivation it is a broadly upright or rounded compact shrub 3–4 feet high with rose flowers produced freely in trusses of 5–6. The plant is rare in cultivation, but is worth being more widely grown. Some plants in cultivation which have been labelled *R. microgynum*, are in fact, *R. gymnocarpum*.

Epithet. With small ovary.

Hardiness 3. April–May.

R. parmulatum Cowan in Notes Roy. Bot. Gard. Edin., Vol. 19 (1936) 182.

Illustration. Bot. Mag. Vol. 163 t. 9624 (1941).

A broadly upright or rounded shrub, 60 cm.–1.22 m. (2–4 ft.) high, *branchlets floccose or glabrous, not setulose or rarely sparsely setulose, eglandular* or rarely glandular with short-stalked glands, those below the inflorescences 2–4 mm. in diameter; leaf-bud scales deciduous. *Leaves oblong-oval, oblong or oblong-obovate,* lamina leathery, 3.5–8.6 cm. long, 1.5–4.5 cm. broad, apex rounded or broadly obtuse, mucronate, base rounded or obtuse, not auricled or slightly auricled, not decurrent or slightly decurrent on the petiole; upper surface green, glabrous or with vestiges of hairs, midrib grooved, primary veins 10–14 on each side, impressed; margin slightly recurved; *under surface glabrous or hairy on the lateral veins,* hairs white, *unistrate Rosulate* with short arms, covered with waxy papillae, midrib prominent, moderately or sparsely floccose, primary veins slightly raised; *petiole 2–8 mm. long, not winged, floccose or glabrous, esetulose, eglandular. Inflorescence terminal, a racemose umbel of 3–5 flowers;* rhachis 3–6 mm. long, glabrous or rarely sparsely floccose, eglandular; *pedicel 0.6–2.3 cm. long, glabrous, eglandular. Calyx 5-lobed, 3–7 mm. long, cup-shaped or disc-like,* divided to about the middle or to the base, fleshy, lobes unequal, ovate or rounded, outside and margin glabrous, eglandular. *Corolla* tubular-campanulate, *3.3–5 cm. long, white, pale yellow, pale creamy-yellow, whitish-pink, or white flushed crimson, with numerous crimson spots on the posterior side,* 5 nectar pouches at the base; lobes 5, 0.8–2 cm. long, 1.3–2.5 cm. broad, rounded, emarginate. *Stamens* 10, unequal, shorter than the corolla, 1.6–3.7 cm. long; filaments glabrous or puberulous at the base. *Gynoecium 2.8–4.7 cm. long; ovary* oblong or rarely conoid, truncate, 4–7 mm. long, sparsely or rarely moderately hairy or *glabrous, eglandular* or rarely sparsely glandular with medium-stalked glands; style glabrous, eglandular. *Capsule* oblong or conoid, 1–1.6 cm. long, 0.4–1 cm. broad, sparsely hairy or glabrous, *eglandular,* calyx-lobes persistent.

R. parmulatum was discovered by Kingdon-Ward in June 1924 at Doshong La, southeast Tibet. It was afterwards found by Ludlow, Sherriff and with Elliot in the same locality, and at Pemakochung, Tsangpo Gorge, same region. It grows on steep rocky slopes and on cliffs, at elevations of 3,355–4,270 m. (11,000–14,000 ft.). According to Kingdon-Ward it is fairly abundant at Doshong La at 11,000–12,000 feet.

The main features of this plant are the large, white, pale yellow to white flushed crimson corolla with numerous crimson spots on the posterior side, the cup-shaped or disc-like calyx, usually the glabrous or sparsely hairy ovary, and the oblong to oblong-oval leaves, glabrous on the lower surface or hairy on the lateral veins, covered below with waxy papillae. The species is related to *R. glaphyrum* but differs in that the corolla has numerous crimson spots on the posterior side, the pedicel is glabrous, the ovary is usually glabrous or sparsely hairy, and the calyx is cup-shaped or disc-like with glabrous margin.

R. parmulatum was first introduced by Kingdon-Ward in 1924 (No. 5875—the Type number). It was reintroduced by him in the same year. It flowered for the first time in April 1936 in Col. Stevenson Clarke's garden at Borde Hill, Haywards Heath, Sussex, and in the Royal Botanic Garden, Edinburgh. In cultivation it grows up to 3 or 4 feet high, and has three colour forms, namely, white, pale yellow, and white flushed crimson, with numerous crimson spots on the posterior side. The species is hardy, and provides a fine display with its large flowers in trusses of 3–5.

It was given an Award of Merit when shown by Maj.-Gen. E. G. W. Harrison, Tremeer, Cornwall, in 1977.

Epithet. With a small round shield.
Hardiness 3. April–May.

R. sanguineum Franch. in Journ. de Bot. Vol. 12 (1898) 295.

A rounded shrub, 30 cm.–1.22 m. (1–4 ft.) or rarely up to 2.44 m. (8 ft.) high, *branchlets* tomentose with a thin, white tomentum, not setulose or rarely setulose, *eglandular*, those below the inflorescences 2–4 mm. in diameter; *leaf-bud scales deciduous. Leaves obovate, oblong-obovate or oblong,* lamina 2.4–10.5 cm. long, 1–3.5 cm. broad, apex rounded or obtuse, mucronate, base obtuse or tapered, moderately or slightly decurrent on the petiole; upper surface dark green, glabrous or with vestiges of hairs, midrib grooved, primary veins 8–12 on each side, impressed; margin flat or slightly or moderately recurved; *under surface covered with a thin plastered* or rarely not plastered, fawn, white, brown or sometimes dark brown, *continuous, unistrate indumentum of Rosulate hairs* with short or rarely long arms, waxy papillae poorly developed, midrib prominent, glabrous or tomentose with a thin tomentum, primary veins slightly raised, concealed or partly exposed; *petiole* 0.3–1 cm. long, margins narrowly winged or ridged by the decurrent base of the lamina, tomentose with a thin, white tomentum, not setulose, *eglandular. Inflorescence* terminal, a racemose umbel of 3–5 flowers; *rhachis* 2–5 mm. long, hairy with dark brown hairs, eglandular; *pedicel* 1–3.6 cm. long, *rather densely or moderately hairy, eglandular* or rarely glandular with long-stalked glands. *Calyx* 5-lobed, 1–4 mm. or rarely up to 7 mm. long, not cupular, divided to the base, the base fleshy, coloured like the corolla, lobes unequal, upright or deflexed, rounded, ovate, triangular or irregular, *outside* glabrous or hairy, *eglandular* or rarely glandular with long-stalked glands, *margin* hairy, *eglandular* or rarely glandular with medium-stalked glands. *Corolla* tubular-campanulate or campanulate, fleshy, 2.4–4 cm. long, *deep crimson, crimson, rose-crimson, carmine or scarlet,* 5 nectar pouches at the base; lobes 5, 0.8–1.9 cm. long, 1.2–2 cm. broad, rounded, emarginate. *Stamens* 10, unequal, shorter than the corolla, 1–2.7 cm. long; filaments glabrous or puberulous at the base. *Gynoecium* 2.1–3.2 cm. long; *ovary* conoid or rarely ovoid, truncate, 3–5 mm. long, 6–9-celled, densely hairy with branched or unbranched hairs, *eglandular;* style glabrous, eglandular. *Capsule* oblong, 0.7–2.2 cm. long, 4–8 mm. broad, straight, moderately or rather densely hairy, *eglandular;* calyx-lobes persistent or deciduous.

This species was discovered by the Abbé Soulié in June 1895 at Sela, near Tsekou, Mekong-Salwin Divide, south-east Tibet. Subsequently it was found by the Abbé Monbeig, Forrest, Kingdon-Ward, Rock, and Yü in other localities in the same region and in north-west Yunnan. It grows in open rocky situations, in open rhododendron scrub, in open pasture, on the margins of rhododendron and pine forests, in open moorland, on cliffs, in thickets, on boulders, and on granite screes, at elevations of 3,355–4,423 m. (11,000–14,500 ft.).

The characteristic features of this plant are the obovate, oblong-obovate or oblong leaves, with a thin, usually plastered continuous, fawn, white to dark brown unistrate indumentum of Rosulate hairs, and the deep crimson, crimson, rose-crimson, carmine or scarlet fleshy corolla with 5 nectar pouches at the base. It is an eglandular species. The plant is allied to *R. haemaleum* but is readily distinguished by the flower colour.

R. sanguineum was first introduced by Forrest in 1917 (No. 14012). It was reintroduced by him on two other occasions. Kingdon-Ward sent seeds in 1922 (No. 5416). Rock introduced it under seven different seed numbers. In cultivation it is a rounded shrub 2–5 feet high and as much across. Two colour forms are grown in gardens, crimson and scarlet. The plant is hardy and is not particular as to position in the garden. One of its chief merits is that it flowers when fairly young. The species is uncommon in cultivation.

Epithet. Blood red.

Hardiness 3. March–May.

R. sanguineum Franch. var. **consanguineum** (Cowan) Davidian, comb. nov.
> Syn. *R. sanguineum* Franch. subsp. *consanguineum* Cowan in Notes Roy. Bot. Gard.
> Edin., Vol. 20 (1940) 68.

This plant was first collected by Rock in 1923 on the mountains of Londjre, Mekong-Salwin watershed, north-west Yunnan. It was later found by him in the same region and in south-east Tibet. In 1924 Forrest collected it in the Mekong-Yangtze Divide, east of Awa, north-west Yunnan. It grows on rocky slopes and meadows, and in alpine region, at an elevation of 4,270 m. (14,000 ft.).

The variety differs from the species in that the pedicel, calyx, ovary, and capsule are moderately or rather densely glandular with medium- or long-stalked glands, and moreover, the pedicel is not hairy.

The plant was first introduced by Rock in 1923 (No. 10904) It was reintroduced by Forrest in 1924 (No. 25507—the Type number), and by Kingdon-Ward in 1926 (No. 6831). In cultivation it is a compact rounded shrub 2–3 feet high and as much across, well-filled with dark green foliage. The flowers are crimson or carmine, and are produced in trusses of 3–5. The plant is hardy but is rare in cultivation.

Epithet of the variety. Very blood red.

Hardiness 3. April–May.

R. sanguineum Franch. var. **didymoides** Tagg et Forrest in Notes Roy. Bot. Gard. Edin.,
> Vol. 16 (1931) 208; Tagg in The Sp. of Rhod. (1930) 555.
> Syn. *R. sanguineum* Franch. subsp. *didymoides* (Tagg et Forrest) Cowan in Notes
> Roy. Bot. Gard. Edin., Vol. 20 (1940) 72.

This variety was first collected by Forrest in July 1921 in the Salwin-Kiu Chiang Divide, Tsarong, south-east Tibet. It was afterwards found by him and by Rock in the same region and in eastern Tibet. It grows in rhododendron and cane thickets, on cliffs and rocky slopes amongst rhododendron scrub, and in stony alpine meadows, at elevations of 3,965–4,423 m. (13,000–14,500 ft.).

The variety differs from the species in that the flowers are rose, or yellow flushed and margined crimson, or orange-red, or rarely red, the corolla ia small usually 2–2.6 cm. long, and the leaves are small, laminae usually 1.8–4 cm. long. Moreover, the leaf-bud scales are persistent, and the ovary and capsule are often densely or moderately glandular with medium- or long-stalked glands.

The plant was first introduced by Forrest in 1921 (No. 19982—the Type number). It was reintroduced by him on three other occasions. In cultivation it is a rounded or a broadly upright shrub up to 2–3 feet high with small leaves and small flowers. The plant is hardy, easy to grow, but is rare in cultivation.

Epithet of the variety. Resembling *R. didymum*.

Hardiness 3. April–May.

R. sanguineum Franch. var. **sanguineoides** (Cowan) Davidian, comb. nov.
Syn. *R. sanguineum* Franch. subsp. *sanguineoides* Cowan in Notes Roy. Bot. Gard. Edin., Vol. 20 (1940) 69.

Rock first collected this plant in May–June 1932 on the northern slopes of Mt. Kenichunpo, north of Sikitung, Upper Salwin River, Tsarong, south-east Tibet. He found it again later on several occasions in the same region. It grows on alpine ridges and spurs, and in rhododendron scrub, at elevations of 3,965–4,423 m. (13,000–14,500 ft.).

The variety is readily distinguished from the species by the persistent leaf-bud scales. The flowers are red in trusses of 2–3.

The plant was introduced by Rock in 1932 (No. 22203—the Type number). In its native home it grows 1–6 feet high; in cultivation it is a rounded shrub, 2–3 feet high with red flowers produced with freedom. The plant is hardy, a fairly robust grower, but is rare in cultivation.

Epithet. Resembling *R. sanguineum*.
Hardiness 3. April–May.

R. scyphocalyx Balf. f. et Forrest in Notes Roy. Bot. Gard. Edin., Vol. 13 (1922) 291.
Syn. *R. dichroanthum* Diels subsp. *scyphocalyx* (Balf. f. et Forrest) Cowan in Notes Roy. Bot. Gard. Edin., Vol. 20 (1940) 88.

A broadly upright or somewhat rounded shrub, 92 cm.–1.53 m. (3–5 ft.) high, branchlets tomentose with a thin, white or rarely fawn tomentum, eglandular or setulose-glandular, those below the inflorescences 3–5 mm. in diameter; leaf-bud scales deciduous. *Leaves* obovate or oblong-obovate, lamina leathery, 3.5–9.5 cm. long, 2–4 cm. broad, apex rounded or rarely obtuse, mucronate, base obtuse, slightly auricled or not auricled, decurrent on the petiole; upper surface dark or pale green, glabrous or with vestiges of hairs, midrib grooved, primary veins 10–14 on each side, impressed; margin slightly recurved; *under surface covered with a thin, plastered, continuous, white or fawn, unistrate indumentum of Rosulate hairs* with short arms, midrib prominent, tomentose with a thin tomentum or glabrous, primary veins not raised or slightly raised, concealed or partly exposed; petiole 0.4–1.2 cm. long, margins narrowly winged or ridged by the decurrent base of the lamina, tomentose with a thin, white tomentum or rarely glabrous, eglandular or rarely setulose-glandular. *Inflorescence* terminal, a racemose umbel of 3–5 flowers; rhachis 3–5 mm. long, hairy with dark brown hairs, eglandular; *pedicel* 1.4–2.8 cm. long, hairy with branched or rarely unbranched hairs, rather densely or rarely moderately *setulose-glandular* or rarely eglandular. *Calyx* 5-lobed, *0.4–1 cm. long, cup-shaped.* divided to about the middle, the base fleshy, lobes unequal, upright, ovate or rounded, outside glabrous or rarely hairy at the base, *setulose-glandular at the base* or rarely eglandular, margin hairy or glabrous, eglandular or glandular with short- or medium-stalked glands. *Corolla* tubular-campanulate, fleshy, 2.5–4.3 cm. long, *yellowish-crimson, rose-orange, coppery-yellow, orange, deep crimson or orange flushed crimson,* 5 nectar pouches at the base; lobes 5, 1–1.5 cm. long, 1.1–2 cm. broad, rounded, emarginate. *Stamens* 10, unequal, shorter than the corolla, 1.3–3 cm. long; filaments puberulous at the base or rarely glabrous. *Gynoecium* 2.5–3.5 cm. long; *ovary* conoid or ovoid, truncate, 4–6 mm. long, 6–8-celled, densely or moderately hairy with long hairs, *moderately or densely setulose-glandular;* style glabrous, eglandular. *Capsule* oblong or short stout, 1–1.8 cm. long, 4–8 mm. broad, straight or slightly curved, moderately or densely hairy with long or short hairs, moderately or rarely rather densely *setulose-glandular,* calyx-lobes persistent.

R. scyphocalyx was first collected by Forrest in May 1919 on the western flank of the N'Maikha-Salwin Divide, north-east Upper Burma. It was afterwards found by him in the same region, and in mid-west Yunnan. Farrer collected it in north-east Upper Burma. It grows in bamboo and mixed scrub, on open rocky slopes, in open cane brakes, amongst boulders, on cliffs, on humus-covered boulders, on screes, in alpine meadows, and on rocky grassy slopes, at elevations of 3,050–4,270 m. (10,000–14,000 ft.). According to Farrer it is very abundant over all the high alpine region, at Hpimaw Pass, north-east Upper Burma.

As the name suggests, a characteristic feature of *R. scyphocalyx* is the cup-shaped calyx, divided to about the middle, 4 mm.–1 cm. long. Other well-marked characters are the rather densely or moderately setulose-glandular pedicels, calyx, ovaries and capsules, and the thin, plastered, continuous white or fawn, unistrate indumentum of Rosulate hairs on the lower surface of the leaves. The species shows a strong resemblance to *R. herpesticum.* The distinctions between them are discussed under the latter.

The plant was first introduced by Farrer in 1919 (No. 1024). It was reintroduced by Forrest on many occasions. In cultivation it is a broadly upright or a somewhat rounded shrub up to 4 or 5 feet high. Several colour forms are grown in gardens, namely, yellowish-crimson, rose-orange, coppery-yellow, orange, deep crimson, or orange flushed crimson. The deep crimson form is rare in cultivation. The species has the advantage of flowering when quite young. Occasionally it produces a few capsules containing good fertile seeds. It is hardy, free-flowering, and is not particular as to position in the garden.

Epithet. Cup-shaped calyx.
Hardiness 3. May–June.

R. scyphocalyx Balf. f. et Forrest var. **septendrionale** Tagg ex Davidian, var. nov. See page 344.

Syn. *R. dichroanthum* Diels subsp. *septendrionale* Tagg ex Cowan in Notes Roy. Bot. Gard. Edin., Vol. 20 (1940) 87.

Forrest first collected this plant in July 1924 on the western flank of the Salwin-Kiu Chiang Divide, north-east Upper Burma. He found it again later on several occasions in north-west Yunnan. It grows in alpine meadows and moorland, on ledges of cliffs, on boulders in ravines, in open thickets, and amongst alpine scrub, at elevations of 3,660–4,270 m. (12,000–14,000 ft.).

The variety differs from the species in that the ovary, calyx and usually the pedicel are not setulose-glandular, and the leaves are oblanceolate. Moreover, in cultivation it flowers in May–July, usually a few weeks after *R. scyphocalyx* has opened its flowers.

The plant was introduced by Forrest in 1924 from north-west Yunnan (Nos. 25577, 25579). In its native home it grows from 1½ to 4 feet high; in cultivation it is a broadly upright shrub and reaches a height of 5 feet. It is hardy with tubular-campanulate flowers, yellow flushed rose at the base or lemon-yellow, produced freely in trusses of 2–3. The plant is rare in cultivation.

Epithet of the variety. Northern.
Hardiness 3. May–July.

R. temenium Balf. f. et Forrest in Notes Roy. Bot. Gard. Edin., Vol. 11 (1919) 146.

Syn. *R. eudoxum* Balf. f. et Forrest subsp. *temenium* (Balf. f. et Forrest) Tagg in The Sp. of Rhod. (1930) 549.
R. pothinum Balf. f. et Forrest in Notes Roy. Bot. Gard. Edin., Vol. 12 (1920) 147.
R. eudoxum Balf. f. et Forrest subsp. *pothinum* (Balf. f. et Forrest) Tagg in The Sp. of Rhod. (1930) 549.
R. trichophlebium Balf. f. et Forrest in Notes Roy. Bot. Gard. Edin., Vol. 13 (1920) 62.
R. fulvastrum Balf. f. et Forrest subsp. *trichophlebium* (Balf. f. et Forrest) Cowan, ibid. Vol. 20 (1940) 79.

A rounded compact shrub, 30 cm.–1.22 m. (1–4 ft.) high, branchlets floccose or rarely tomentose with a thin white tomentum or glabrous, setulose or sometimes not setulose, not setulose-glandular or rarely setulose-glandular, those below the inflorescences 2–4 mm. in diameter; leaf-bud scales deciduous. *Leaves* oblong, obovate, oblong-obovate or oblong-lanceolate, lamina 2–7.5 cm. long, 0.6–2.5 cm. broad, apex rounded or obtuse, mucronate, base obtuse or rounded, decurrent on the petiole; upper surface dark green, glabrous or with vestiges of hairs, midrib grooved, floccose or glabrous, setulose one-half its length or at the base or not setulose, primary veins 6–12 on each side, impressed; margin slightly recurved or flat; *under surface glabrous* or sometimes hairy on the lateral veins, hairs white Rosulate with short arms, midrib prominent, floccose or glabrous, primary veins slightly raised; petiole 1–6 mm. long, margins narrowly winged by the decurrent base of the lamina, floccose or rarely tomentose with a thin white tomentum, setulose or sometimes not setulose, not setulose-glandular or rarely setulose-glandular. *Inflorescence* terminal, a racemose umbel of 3–10 flowers; rhachis 2–6 mm. long, hairy with dark brown hairs or rarely glabrous, eglandular; *pedicel* 0.9–1.8 cm. long, moderately or rather densely hairy with branched or unbranched hairs or rarely glabrous, *eglandular* (rarely glandular with medium-stalked glands or setulose-glandular). *Calyx* 5-lobed, 1–7 mm. long, not cupular, divided to the base or to about the middle, the base fleshy, lobes unequal, deflexed or upright, ovate, rounded, oblong or rarely triangular, *outside* glabrous, *eglandular, margin* hairy or glabrous, *eglandular* or rarely glandular with medium- or short-stalked glands. *Corolla* tubular-campanulate or campanulate, fleshy, 2–4.3 cm. long, *deep crimson, crimson, carmine, light to dark purplish-crimson or purplish-red,* 5 nectar pouches at the base; lobes 5, 0.8–1.6 cm. long, 1–2.3 cm. broad, rounded, emarginate. *Stamens* 10, unequal, shorter than the corolla, 1.2–3 cm. long; filaments glabrous or rarely puberulous at the base. *Gynoecium* 1.8–3.3 cm. long; ovary conoid or rarely ovoid, truncate, 2–5 mm. long, 5–6-celled, densely hairy with branched or unbranched hairs or rarely glabrous, sparsely or rarely densely glandular with medium-stalked glands or eglandular; style glabrous, eglandular. *Capsule* oblong or rarely short stout, 1–1.9 cm. long, 4–8 mm. broad, straight, moderately or sparsely hairy, sparsely glandular with medium-stalked glands or eglandular, calyx-lobes persistent.

This plant was discovered by Forrest in July 1917 on Ka-gwr-pw, Mekong-Salwin Divide, Tsarong, south-east Tibet. It was later collected by him, and by Rock, Kingdon-Ward and Yü in the same region and in east Tibet, also in north-west Yunnan. It grows in open moorland, in open rocky meadows, amongst dense rhododendron thickets, in cane scrub, in cane brakes, on cliffs, and in alpine rocky region, at elevations of 3,400–4,423 m. (11,148–14,500 ft.). Yü records it as being common in the Salwin-Kiu Chiang Divide, north-west Yunnan.

In 1920 two other species which were described as *R. pothinum* Balf. f. et Forrest and *R. trichophlebium* Balf. f. et Forrest, are identical with *R. temenium* in all morphological characters.

R. temenium is easily recognised by the oblong to obovate leaves glabrous on the lower surfaces, and by the deep crimson, crimson or carmine flowers. It is very closely related to *R. glaphyrum* but is readily distinguished by the flower colour; in the latter it is white flushed rose or deep rose or pale yellow faintly flushed rose.

The plant was first introduced by Forrest in 1917 (No. 14364—the Type number, and No. 14365). It was reintroduced by him under three different seed numbers. Rock sent seeds on six occasions. In 1924 Kingdon-Ward introduced it under No. 5878. It is one of the most charming members of the Sanguineum Subseries. In cultivation it is a rounded compact shrub 2–3 feet high and as much across, well-filled with dark green leaves which provide an excellent background to the crimson flowers. The plant is hardy, free-flowering, and should be a most valuable acquisition to every collection of rhododendrons.

Epithet. From a sacred place near Doker La, Tsarong, in E. Tibet.
Hardiness 3. April–May.

R. trichomiscum Balf. f. et Forrest in Notes Roy. Bot. Gard. Edin., Vol. 12 (1920) 169.
   Syn. *R. eudoxum* Balf. f. et Forrest subsp. *trichomiscum* (Balf. f. et Forrest) Tagg in
     The Sp. of Rhod. (1930) 549.
      R. fulvastrum Balf. f. et Forrest subsp. *trichomiscum* (Balf. f. et Forrest) Cowan
       in Notes Roy. Bot. Gard. Edin., Vol. 20 (1940) 79.
      R. temenium Balf. f. et Forrest subsp. *rhodanthum* Cowan, ibid. Vol. 20 (1940)
       81.

A compact spreading or somewhat rounded shrub, 60 cm.–1.22 m. (2–4 ft.) high, *branchlets* glabrous or tomentose with a thin white tomentum, *setulose*, not setulose-glandular or sparsely setulose-glandular, those below the inflorescences 2–4 mm. in diameter; leaf-bud scales deciduous. *Leaves* oblong or lanceolate, lamina 3.2–6.5 cm. long, 1.2–2 cm. broad, apex rounded or obtuse, mucronate, base obtuse or tapered, decurrent on the petiole; upper surface green, glabrous or with vestiges of hairs, midrib grooved, floccose or glabrous, not setulose or setulose one-half its length or at the base, primary veins 6–12 on each side, impressed; margin slightly or moderately recurved or flat; *under surface with closely or widely scattered hairs or a thin veil of* white or fawn *unistrate Rosulate hairs* with short arms, midrib prominent, floccose or glabrous, setulose at the base or not setulose, primary veins slightly raised, exposed or partly concealed; *petiole* 1–5 mm. long, floccose or tomentose with a thin white tomentum or glabrous, *setulose,* not setulose-glandular or sparsely setulose-glandular. *Inflorescence* terminal, a racemose umbel of 2–4 flowers; rhachis 2–4 mm. long, hairy with dark brown hairs, eglandular; *pedicel* 1.5–1.7 cm. long, moderately or rather densely hairy with unbranched hairs, *moderately or sparsely or rather densely glandular* with medium- or long-stalked glands. *Calyx* 5-lobed, 1–2 mm. long, divided to the base or to about the middle, the base fleshy, lobes unequal, upright or deflexed, ovate, rounded or triangular, outside glabrous, eglandular, *margin* hairy, *moderately or sparsely glandular* with medium-stalked glands. *Corolla* tubular-campanulate, 2.5–3.8 cm. long, pale rose-pink or pur-plish or orange-red, without markings, 5 nectar pouches at the base; lobes 5, 0.8–1.3 cm. long, 1.3–2 cm. broad, rounded, emarginate. *Stamens* 10, unequal, shorter than the corolla, 1.4–2.3 cm. long; filaments glabrous or puberulous at the base. *Gynoecium* 2.2–2.8 cm. long; *ovary* conoid, truncate, 3–4 mm. long, moderately or sparsely hairy or not hairy, *densely or moderately glandular* with medium-stalked glands; style glabrous, eglandular. *Capsule* oblong, 1–1.2 cm. long, 4–8 mm. broad, straight, hairy or not hairy, *glandular* with medium-stalked glands, calyx-lobes persistent.

R. trichomiscum was first collected by Forrest in July 1918 on Ka-gwr-pw, Mekong-Salwin Divide, Tsarong, south-east Tibet. It was afterwards found by Rock in various localities in north-west Yunnan. The plant grows in cane brakes and rhododendron thickets, at elevations of 4,118–4,270 m. (13,500–14,000 ft.).

A diagnostic feature of the species is the setulose branchlets and petioles; other well-marked characters are the moderately or rather densely glandular pedicels, calyx margin, ovaries and capsules. In all these respects it usually differs from its ally *R. glaphyrum.* It also differs in that the lower surface of the leaves is hairy with closely or widely scattered hairs or with a thin veil of hairs.

R. trichomiscum was first introduced by Rock in 1932 (No. 22235). It was also possibly introduced by Forrest. In cultivation it is a compact spreading or somewhat rounded shrub, 2 feet high and as much across or wider, with pale rose-pink flowers in trusses of 2–4. It is hardy, but is rare in cultivation.

Epithet. With bristly twigs.
Hardiness 3. April–May.

Forest on alpine slopes on the Tali Range, Yunnan. Photo J. F. Rock.

PARISHII SERIES

General characters: shrubs or trees, 1.22–12.20 m. (4–40 ft.) high, *branchlets* glabrous or moderately or rather densely *hairy* usually *with Stellate hairs,* eglandular or setulose-glandular or glandular with medium- or short-stalked glands. Leaves oblong, oblong-obovate, oblong-oval, oblong-elliptic, elliptic, obovate, oblong-lanceolate, oblanceolate or lanceolate, lamina 6–28 cm. long, 1.7–11 cm. broad; *upper surface* glabrous or sometimes hairy *with Stellate hairs (in young leaves* moderately or rarely densely *hairy with Stellate hairs); under surface glabrous or* moderately or densely *hairy with* a discontinuous or sometimes continuous *indumentum of Stellate hairs (in young leaves densely or moderately hairy with Stellate hairs or rarely glabrous); petiole* glabrous or rather densely or sparsely *hairy with Stellate hairs,* eglandular or setulose-glandular. Inflorescence a racemose umbel of 5–16 flowers; *pedicel* 0.6–3.2 cm. long, moderately or densely *hairy* usually *with Stellate hairs* or glabrous, moderately or rather densely setulose-glandular or eglandular, or moderately or rather densely glandular with short-stalked glands. Calyx 0.5–5 mm. or sometimes 0.9–2 cm. long. Corolla tubular-campanulate or sometimes campanulate, 2.5–6 cm. long, deep crimson, crimson, scarlet, rose-crimson, deep rose, or sometimes white, pink or red-purple. Stamens 10. *Ovary* conoid or oblong, 3–9 mm. long, 5–6- or sometimes 7–10-celled, densely or sometimes moderately *tomentose with Stellate hairs,* moderately or sparsely or rarely densely glandular with long- or short-stalked glands or eglandular; *style hairy* throughout to the tip or on the lower half or at the base usually *with Stellate hairs* or rarely glabrous, glandular throughout to the tip or at the base with short- or long-stalked glands or eglandular. *Capsule* oblong or sometimes slender, 1.2–4 cm. long, 0.3–1 cm. broad, moderately or rather densely *hairy with Stellate hairs,* glanduluar with long- or short-stalked glands or eglandular.

Distribution. North-east and east Upper Burma, Lower Burma, mid-west, west and north-west Yunnan, west Sichuan, south-east Tibet, and Assam.

The diagnostic feature of this Series is the Stellate type of hair on the branchlets, leaves (laminae), petioles, pedicels, calyx, ovaries and capsules. In this respect the Series is readily distinguished from all the other Series. Another distinctive characteristic is the setulose-glandular feature of the species (except *R. schistocalyx*).

KEY TO THE SPECIES

A. Calyx large, 9 mm.–2 cm. long, split on one side almost to the base, lobes unequal; plant eglandular. . . . . *schistocalyx*

A. Calyx small, 0.5–5 mm. long, not split on one side, lobes usually equal; plant glandular.

   B. Corolla white, pink or red-purple.

      C. Stem and branches usually with smooth brown flaking bark; corolla white or sometimes pink or red-purple. . . . . *cookeanum*

      C. Stem and branches with rough bark; corolla purple . . . . . . *sikangense*

   B. Corolla deep crimson, crimson, crimson-scarlet, scarlet, crimson-rose or deep rose.

      D. Leaves oblong-oval, oblong-obovate, oblong-elliptic, oblong to lanceolate, lamina usually 2½–4 times as long as broad, usually 9–28 cm. long; corolla deep crimson, crimson, scarlet-crimson, scarlet, crimson-rose, or deep rose, without darker bands along the petals.

         E. Corolla 2.8–3.8 cm. long; leaves oblong-lanceolate, lanceolate or oblanceolate, 1.7–4 cm. broad. . . . . *venator*

         E. Corolla usually 3.8–5.5 cm. long; leaves oblong-oval, oblong-obovate, oblong-elliptic to lanceolate, 3.5–10 cm. broad.

            F. Under surface of the adult leaves usually moderately or densely hairy with a discontinuous indumentum of Stellate hairs, setulose-glandular or eglandular; pedicel moderately or rather densely setulose-glandular.

               G. Style usually hairy throughout to the tip or on the lower half with Stellate hairs, often glandular throughout to the tip; pedicel 1.5–3 cm. long; calyx 2–5 mm. long. . . . . *kyawii*

               G. Style hairy only at the base with Stellate hairs, glandular at the base or eglandular; pedicel 1.3–1.8 cm. long; calyx 2 mm. long . . . . *agapetum*

            F. Under surface of the adult leaves usually glabrous, eglandular; pedicel eglandular or moderately or rather densely glandular with short-stalked glands.

               H. Calyx outside rather densely or moderately hairy with Stellate hairs (or rarely glabrous); stamens (filaments) puberulous on the lower half or at the base; pedicel moderately or rather densely hairy with Stellate hairs, often eglandular; ovary eglandular; corolla 2.5–5 cm. long. From western Yunnan and north-east Burma. . . . . *facetum*

               H. Calyx outside not hairy; stamens (filaments) glabrous; pedicel not hairy, rather densely or moderately glandular with short-stalked glands; ovary moderately or densely glandular with short-stalked glands; corolla 4.5–5.5 cm. long. From Assam . . . . *elliottii*

      D. Leaves elliptic or obovate, lamina twice or hardly twice as long as broad, 6–12.3 cm. long; corolla deep red, with darker bands along the petals. . . . . *parishii*

DESCRIPTION OF THE SPECIES

R. agapetum Balf. f. et Ward in Notes Roy. Bot. Gard. Edin., Vol. 9 (1916) 212.

A broadly upright or rounded shrub or tree, 1.83–10.68 m. (6–35 ft.) high, branchlets *hairy with Stellate hairs* or glabrous, setulose-glandular or eglandular, those below the inflorescences 5–8 mm. in diameter. *Leaves* oblong, oblong-obovate or oblong-oval, lamina leathery, 10–22.8 cm. long, 4.5–8.3 cm. broad, apex obtuse or rounded, base obtuse or rounded; upper surface dark green, glabrous or rarely hairy with *Stellate* hairs (in young leaves hairy with *Stellate* hairs), eglandular, midrib grooved, glabrous or hairy with *Stellate* hairs, setulose-glandular or eglandular, primary veins 15–20 on each side, deeply impressed; margin slightly recurved or flat; *under surface paler, at first moderately or densely hairy with a discontinuous indumentum of Stellate hairs which ultimately remain or partially or almost completely fall off* leaving the under surface of the adult leaves partly or almost completely glabrous (in young leaves densely hairy with *Stellate* hairs), setulose-glandular or eglandular, midrib prominent, setulose-glandular or eglandular, primary veins raised; petiole 1.8–4 cm. long, rounded, grooved above, hairy with *Stellate* hairs or glabrous, eglandular or setulose-glandular. *Inflorescence* a racemose umbel of 9–11 flowers; rhachis 1.8–2.5 cm. long, moderately or rather densely pubescent, glandular with long- or medium-stalked glands; *pedicel 1.3–1.8 cm. long,* pubescent or glabrous, rather densely setulose-glandular. *Calyx* 5-lobed, *2 mm. long,* lobes ovate or rounded, outside glabrous, rather densely glandular with long- and medium-stalked glands, margin glabrous, moderately glandular with long- and medium-stalked glands. *Corolla* tubular-campanulate or campanulate, 3.8–5.3 cm. long, fleshy, crimson-scarlet or deep crimson, without spots, *5 nectar pouches at the base,* outside glabrous, setulose-glandular at the base or eglandular; lobes 5, 1.3–1.8 cm. long, 1.5–2 cm. broad, rounded, emarginate. *Stamens* 10, unequal, 2.5–4.5 cm. long, filaments puberulous at the base. *Gynoecium* 3.6–5 cm. long; *ovary* conoid or oblong, 5–8 mm. long, 6-celled, *densely tomentose with Stellate hairs,* glandular with long-stalked glands or eglandular; *style hairy at the base with Stellate hairs, glandular at the base with long-stalked glands* or rarely eglandular. *Capsule* oblong, 2.3–2.8 cm. long, 5–8 mm. broad, slightly curved, moderately or rather densely *hairy with Stellate hairs,* glandular with long-stalked glands, grooved, calyx-lobes persistent.

This species was discovered by Kingdon-Ward in July 1914 at Hpimaw, East Upper Burma. It was later found by him in the Taron Gorge and in Nam Tamai Valley, Upper Burma-Tibet borders. Subsequently it was collected by Forrest in East Upper Burma and in north-west Yunnan. It grows on steep limestone cliffs, in forests, and on granite ridges in forests, at elevations of 1,830–3,050 m., (6,000–10,000 ft.). According to Kingdon-Ward, it is fairly abundant in the forest in the Taron Gorge, and forms a fair-sized tree 35 feet high.

R. agapetum is closely related to *R. kyawii* but differs in that the style is hairy and glandular only at the base or eglandular, the pedicel is usually shorter, and the calyx is usually smaller.

The species was first introduced by Kingdon-Ward in 1922 (Nos. 5469, 5533). It was reintroduced by Forrest in 1924 (No. 24680), and in 1930–31 (Nos. 29926, 30375, wrongly recorded as *R. facetum* in *The Rhododendron Handbook* 1980, p. 300). In cultivation it is a broadly upright shrub up to 10 feet high. The young leaves are at first hairy with *Stellate* hairs which ultimately remain or partially fall off leaving the lower surface of the adult leaf almost completely or partly glabrous. The species is hardy outdoors in the west coast, but in the east coast it is tender and requires the protection of a greenhouse. It is rare in cultivation.

Epithet. Delightful.

Hardiness 1–3. May–June.

R. cookeanum Davidian in The Rhododendron and Camellia Year Book (1962) 105.

A broadly upright or rounded shrub or tree, 1.22–8 m. (4–26 ft.) high; *stem and branches usually with smooth, brown, flaking bark;* branchlets densely or moderately tomentose with a thin, whitish or fawn tomentum, eglandular or sometimes glandular with short-stalked glands, those below the inflorescences 4–6 mm. in diameter. *Leaves* oblong-lanceolate or oblong-elliptic, lamina leathery, 6.5–15 cm. long, 2.4–6.5 cm. broad, apex acute or shortly acuminate, base obtuse or rounded; upper surface dark green, matt, glabrous (in *young leaves* with *scattered Stellate hairs*), eglandular, midrib grooved, primary veins 14–19 on each side, deeply impressed; margin slightly recurved; *under surface* paler, matt, *glabrous (in young leaves* sparsely hairy with *Stellate hairs* or glabrous), midrib prominent, glabrous or rarely sparsely floccose, eglandular or rarely sparsely glandular with short-stalked glands, primary veins raised; petiole 1–2.8 cm. long, grooved above, sparsely or moderately tomentose with a thin, whitish or fawn tomentum or sometimes glabrous, eglandular or rarely glandular with short-stalked glands. *Inflorescence* a racemose umbel of 8–15 flowers; rhachis 1–2.5 cm. long, floccose, eglandular or rarely glandular with short-stalked glands; *pedicel* 0.8–3.2 cm. long, *densely* or rarely sparsely *hairy with Stellate hairs*, eglandular or rarely glandular with short-stalked glands. *Calyx* 5-lobed, minute, 0.5–1 mm. or rarely 2 mm. long, lobes triangular or rounded, *outside and margin densely or moderately hairy with Stellate hairs* or rarely glabrous, eglandular or rarely glandular with short-stalked glands. *Corolla* campanulate, 3–5 cm. long, fleshy, *white, pink or red-purple*, with or without a crimson blotch at the base, outside glabrous, eglandular; lobes 5, 1–2 cm. long, 1.5–2.6 cm. broad, rounded, emarginate or rarely entire. *Stamens* 10, unequal, 1.1–3.4 cm. long; filaments densely villous at the base or up to three-fourths their length. *Gynoecium* 2.4–4.2 cm. long; *ovary* oblong, 4–7 mm. long, 8–10-celled, densely or rarely moderately *tomentose with Stellate hairs*, eglandular or rarely glandular with short-stalked glands; style glabrous or floccose at the base, eglandular or rarely sparsely glandular at the base with short-stalked glands. *Capsule* slender or rarely oblong, 1.6–3.4 cm. long, 3–4 mm. or rarely 6 mm. broad, curved or sometimes straight, moderately or sparsely *tomentose with Stellate hairs*, eglandular, grooved, calyx-lobes persistent.

This plant was first collected by Rock in 1929 in Muli, south-west Sichuan. It was afterwards found by him again in the same region. The plant grows in spruce forests, among alpine rocks, and in alpine meadows, at elevations of 3,660–4,460 m. (12,000–14,623 ft.). Rock records it as being a tree 20 feet high forming forests on alpine ridges and spurs.

R. cookeanum agrees with the species of the Parishii Series in that the hairs on the young leaves, pedicels, calyx, ovaries and capsules are *Stellate*—a criterion of diagnostic importance to this Series. A characteristic feature of typical *R. cookeanum* is the smooth, brown, flaking bark of the stem and branches. In this respect and usually in its white flowers it is readily distinguished from its allies *R. facetum* and *R. sikangense* and from all the other members of its Series.

The species was first introduced under Forrest No. 8 (this number was given in the Royal Botanic Garden, Edinburgh, to one of the 100 packets of Forrest's seeds which were received unnumbered from Yunnan after his death). It first flowered about 1952 in Mr. R. B. Cooke's garden at Corbridge, Northumberland. In cultivation it is a broadly upright or rounded shrub up to 12 feet high. Unlike the species of its Series, except *R. venator*, it is hardy outdoors along the east coast, with white flowers in trusses of 8–15. It is a valuable plant in that it is a late-flowerer, the flowers appearing in May–June or sometimes in July. The species is rare in cultivation, but is well worth a place in every collection of rhododendrons.

Epithet. After R. B. Cooke, 1880–1973, rhododendron grower, Corbridge, Northumberland.

Hardiness 3. May–July.

R. elliottii Watt ex Brandis, Indian Trees (1906) 410; Lace et W. W. Sm. in Notes Roy. Bot. Gard. Edin., Vol. 8, Plate 140 (1914) 214.

Illustration. Bot. Mag. Vol. 161 t. 9546 (1939).

A rounded or broadly upright shrub or tree, 2.44–4.58 m. (8–15 ft.) high, *branchlets hairy with Stellate hairs*, setulose-glandular or eglandular, those below the inflorescences 4–5 mm. in diameter. *Leaves* oblong-lanceolate, oblong-elliptic or oblong-oval, lamina leathery, 6–15 cm. long, 2.6–6 cm. broad, apex shortly acuminate or obtuse, base obtuse or rounded; upper surface dark green, matt or shining, glabrous (in young leaves hairy with *Stellate* hairs), eglandular, midrib grooved, primary veins 10–14 on each side, deeply impressed; margin slightly recurved; *under surface* paler, somewhat shining, *glabrous* (in young leaves hairy with *Stellate* hairs), punctulate with minute red glands, midrib prominent, hairy at the base with *Stellate* hairs or glabrous, primary veins raised; petiole 1.3–3 cm. long, grooved above, sparsely hairy with *Stellate* hairs or glabrous, setulose-glandular or eglandular. *Inflorescence* a racemose umbel of 9–15 flowers; rhachis 1–1.6 cm. long, floccose, glandular with short-stalked glands; *pedicel* 0.8–1.2 cm. long, *glabrous, rather densely or moderately glandular* with short-stalked glands. *Calyx* cupular or spreading, 5-lobed, 2–4 mm. long, reddish, lobes ovate, rounded or triangular, *outside glabrous*, moderately or rather densely glandular with short-stalked glands, margin glabrous, glandular with short-stalked glands. *Corolla* tubular-campanulate, *4.5–5.5 cm. long*, fleshy, crimson, scarlet-crimson, scarlet or deep rose, with numerous darker spots, *5 nectar pouches at the base*, outside glabrous, eglandular; lobes 5, 1–1.5 cm. long, 1.5–1.8 cm. broad, rounded, emarginate. *Stamens* 10, unequal, 2–4.2 cm. long; filaments glabrous. *Gynoecium* 4–4.8 cm. long; *ovary* oblong, 6–7 mm. long, 6-celled, *densely or moderately tomentose with Stellate hairs, moderately or densely glandular* with short-stalked glands; *style* sparsely hairy throughout to the tip or on the lower half with *Stellate* hairs, *glandular throughout to the tip* with short-stalked glands. *Capsule* oblong, 1.5–2 cm. long, 5–6 mm. broad, slightly curved, *hairy with Stellate hairs*, eglandular or slightly glandular, grooved, calyx-lobes persistent.

R. elliottii was discovered by Sir George Watt in January 1882 on Mount Japvo in the Naga Hills, Assam. It was collected by him again later in March and May of the same year in that region. In December 1927 Kingdon-Ward found it also on Mount Japvo growing with *R. macabeanum* and *R. manipurense*; he found it again in the same area in 1949. It grows in forests at elevations of 2,440–2,745 m. (8,000–9,000 ft.). The species was given a short description by Brandis in 1906, but later in 1914 Lace and W. W. Smith described it in some detail.

R. elliottii is closely allied to *R. facetum* which it resembles in general features, but differs in that the outside of the calyx and the pedicel are not hairy, but rather densely or moderately glandular with short-stalked glands, the ovary is moderately or densely glandular with short-stalked glands, the stamens are glabrous, and the corolla is often larger. Moreover, *R. elliottii* is found in Assam, whereas *R. facetum* comes from northeast Burma and western Yunnan.

The species was first introduced by Kingdon-Ward in 1927 (No. 7725). It was reintroduced by him in 1949 (No. 19083). In its native home it is a small or medium-sized tree, but in cultivation it is a rounded or broadly upright shrub up to 8–10 feet high. As it comes from relatively low elevations of 8,000–9,000 feet, it is hardy outdoors only in well-sheltered gardens along the west coast, but along the east coast it is tender and should be grown in a greenhouse. The plant is a late-flowerer, prolonging the flowering season into May, June, July. It is free-flowering and provides an admirable display with its large crimson flowers in trusses of 9–15. The new growth is late in the season, and is liable to be damaged by autumn frosts. A superb example of this species 12 feet high existed in the Rhododendron glasshouse, Royal Botanic Garden, Edinburgh; unfortunately in 1965 it was lost to cultivation. See page 329.

The species received an Award of Merit when exhibited by J. J. Crossfield, Embley

Park, Romsey, in 1934 (Kingdon-Ward No. 7725), and a First Class Certificate when shown by Admiral A. W. Heneage-Vivian, Clyne Castle, Swansea, in 1937 (Kingdon-Ward No. 7725).

Epithet. After Mr. Elliott, a friend of its discoverer, Sir George Watt.
Hardiness 1–3. May–July.

R. facetum Balf. f. et Ward in Notes Roy. Bot. Gard. Edin., Vol. 10 (1917) 104.

Syn *R. eriogynum* Balf. f. et W. W. Sm. in Notes Roy. Bot. Gard. Edin., Vol. 10 (1917) 101.

Illustration. Bot. Mag. Vol. 157 t. 9337 (1934), figured as *R. eriogynum* Balf. f. et W. W. Sm.

A rounded or broadly upright shrub or tree, 1.53–12.20 m. (5–40 ft.) high, branchlets glabrous or hairy with *Stellate* hairs, eglandular or glandular with medium- or short-stalked glands, those below the inflorescences 3–6 mm. in diameter. *Leaves* oblong-elliptic, oblong-obovate, oblong-lanceolate or oblanceolate, lamina leathery, 9–25 cm. long, 3–7.8 cm. broad, apex acute, obtuse or rounded, base obtuse, tapered, rounded or truncate; upper surface dark green, matt, glabrous (in young leaves densely or moderately mealy (= hairy) with *Stellate* hairs), eglandular, midrib grooved, primary veins 12–20 on each side, deeply impressed; margin flat or slightly recurved; *under surface* paler, somewhat shining, *glabrous or sometimes with a few small patches of Stellate hairs (in young leaves densely or moderately mealy (= hairy) with Stellate hairs)*, punctulate with minute, red glands, midrib prominent, glabrous or rarely hairy at the base with *Stellate* hairs, eglandular, primary veins raised; petiole 1.5–3.4 cm. long, grooved above, glabrous or hairy with *Stellate* hairs, eglandular or rarely glandular with medium-stalked glands. *Inflorescence* a racemose umbel of 8–16 flowers; *rhachis* 1–2.3 cm. long, *hairy with Stellate hairs*, or rather densely or moderately floccose or pubescent, eglandular or rarely glandular with short-stalked glands; *pedicel* 0.6–2 cm. long, *moderately or rather densely hairy with Stellate hairs* or rarely glabrous, *eglandular* or sometimes moderately or rather densely glandular with short-stalked glands. *Calyx* 5-lobed, 2–5 mm. long, reddish, lobes unequal, ovate, triangular or rounded, *outside rather densely or moderately hairy, hairs Stellate* or rarely not *Stellate,* or rarely glabrous, eglandular or glandular with short-stalked glands, *margin hairy with Stellate hairs* or rarely ciliate, or rarely glabrous, eglandular or glandular with short-stalked glands. *Corolla* tubular-campanulate, *2.5–5 cm. long,* fleshy, crimson, deep crimson, scarlet-crimson, scarlet, crimson-rose or deep rose, without or rarely with a blotch, and with or without darker spots, *5 nectar pouches at the base,* deep purple within, outside glabrous or sometimes sparsely or moderately hairy at the base with *Stellate* hairs, eglandular or rarely glandular at the base with medium-stalked glands; lobes 5, 1–1.6 cm. long, 1.2–2.3 cm. broad, rounded, emarginate. *Stamens* 10, unequal, 1.4–3.8 cm. long; *filaments puberulous on the lower half or at the base.* Gynoecium 2.1–4.5 cm. long; *ovary* conoid or oblong, 4–9 mm. long, 6-celled or rarely 7- or 8-celled, *densely tomentose with Stellate hairs, eglandular; style moderately or densely hairy throughout to the tip or on the lower two-thirds of its length with Stellate hairs,* glandular at the upper end or on the upper half or throughout to the tip with short- or medium-stalked glands, or rarely eglandular. *Capsule* oblong or oblong-oval, 1.2–3.4 cm. long, 4–9 mm. broad, slightly curved or straight, *moderately or rather densely hairy with Stellate hairs,* eglandular or rarely glandular with short-stalked glands, grooved, calyx-lobes persistent.

This species was first collected by Kingdon-Ward in June 1914 at Fengshui-ling Camp, east Upper Burma. Subsequently it was found by him and other collectors in east and north-east Upper Burma, mid-west and west Yunnan. It grows in thickets, in pine, rhododendron, fir, and mixed forests, in open deciduous forests, and amongst scrub on open stony slopes, at elevations of 2,300–3,660 m. (7,541–12,000 ft.). Kingdon-Ward records it as being a big tree of 40 feet in the lower forest, a fine sight at Laktang, north-east Upper Burma at 2,440 m. (8,000 ft.).

R. *eriogynum* Balf. f. et W. W. Sm., first collected by Forrest in July 1914 and which was described in 1917 is identical with R. *facetum* under which it will now appear in synonymy.

R. *facetum* is closely related to R. *elliottii*. The distinctions between them are discussed under the latter. It is also related to R. *kyawii*, but is a much less glandular species, and the under surface of the adult leaves is usually glabrous.

The species was first introduced by Forrest in July 1917 (No. 13508—the Type number of R. *eriogynum*). It was reintroduced by him under 15 different seed numbers. Farrer sent seeds in 1919 (No. 1022). The species was introduced by Rock (No. 7468) and by Yü (No. 21000). In cultivation it is a rounded or broadly upright shrub up to 15 feet high. It flowered for the first time in 1926 in Mr. G. H. Johnstone's garden at Trewithen, Cornwall. Two distinct forms are in cultivation: Form 1. A medium-sized shrub, 1.53 m. (5 ft.) high with oblong-obovate leaves, (laminae) 12–14 cm. long, corolla 4 cm. long, introduced by Forrest. Form 2. A large shrub 3 m. (10 ft.) high with oblanceolate leaves, (laminae) 22–25 cm. long, corolla large 5 cm. long, introduced by Farrer. The species is hardy outdoors along the west coast, but along the east coast it is tender and requires the protection of a greenhouse. It flowers late in the season, in June and July, and the late growth is apt to be destroyed by autumn frosts. The tubular-campanulate flowers are produced freely in trusses of 8–16. Beautiful plants of the two distinct forms were to be seen in the Rhododendron glasshouse, Royal Botanic Garden, Edinburgh, but in 1965 both plants ceased to exist. See page 331.

The species was given an Award of Merit when shown by T. H. Lowinsky, Sunninghill, in 1924, and again the same Award when exhibited by Admiral A. W. Heneage-Vivian, Clyne Castle, Swansea, in 1938.

Epithet. Elegant.

Hardiness 1–3. June–July.

R. kyawii Lace et W. W. Sm. in Notes Roy. Bot. Gard. Edin., Vol. 8 (1914) 216.

Syn. R. *prophantum* Balf. f. et Forrest in Notes Roy. Bot. Gard. Edin., Vol. 13 (1920) 58.

Illustration. Bot. Mag. Vol. 155 t. 9271 (1932).

A rounded or broadly upright spreading shrub or tree, 3–7.63 m. (10–25 ft.) high, branchlets at first moderately or rather densely hairy with *Stellate* hairs, setulose-glandular, finally glabrous, eglandular, those below the inflorescences 5–8 mm. in diameter. *Leaves* oblong, oblong-obovate, oblong-oval or rarely oblong-lanceolate, lamina leathery, 14–28 cm. long, 3–11 cm. broad, apex rounded, obtuse or rarely acute, base obtuse or rounded; *upper surface* dark green, at first sparsely hairy with *Stellate* hairs later glabrous (*in young leaves hairy with Stellate hairs*), eglandular, midrib grooved, setulose-glandular or eglandular, primary veins 15–20 on each side, deeply impressed; margin slightly recurved or flat; *under surface* paler, *at first moderately or rather densely sprinkled (discontinuous) with* an indumentum of *Stellate hairs which ultimately remain or partially or completely fall off* leaving the under surface of the adult leaf partly or completely glabrous (in young leaves rather densely sprinkled with *Stellate* hairs), *at first setulose-glandular* later the glands remain or fall off, midrib prominent, setulose-glandular later eglandular, primary veins raised; petiole 2–6 cm. long, rounded, grooved above, at first moderately or densely hairy with *Stellate* hairs, setulose-glandular, later both hairs and glands remain or fall off. *Inflorescence* a racemose umbel of 12–16 flowers; rhachis 2–5 cm. long, moderately or rather densely hairy, hairs *Stellate* or *not Stellate*, setulose-glandular or eglandular; *pedicel* 1.5–3 cm. long, moderately or rather densely hairy, hairs *Stellate* or *not Stellate*, or glabrous, not pubescent or pubescent, *moderately or rather densely setulose-glandular. Calyx* 5-lobed, 2–5 mm. *long*, lobes triangular, ovate, rounded or irregular, *outside* floccose or glabrous, *moderately or rather densely glandular* with long- or medium-stalked glands, *margin* floccose or glabrous, *glandular* with long- or medium-stalked glands, *Corolla* tubular-campanulate,

4.5–6 cm. long, fleshy, deep crimson, crimson or crimson-scarlet, without spots, *5 nectar pouches at the base*, dark crimson within, *outside moderately or sparsely hairy, hairs Stellate* or rarely not *Stellate*, setulose-glandular or not setulose-glandular; lobes 5, 1.5–2 cm. long, 1.5–2.8 cm. broad, rounded, emarginate. *Stamens* 10, unequal, 2.8–4.5 cm. long; filaments puberulous at the base. *Gynoecium* 4–5.5 cm. long; *ovary* conoid or oblong, 6–8 mm. long, 5–6-celled, *densely tomentose with Stellate hairs*, moderately or sparsely glandular with long- or medium-stalked glands or eglandular; *style hairy throughout to the tip or on the lower half* or at the base *with Stellate hairs* or rarely glabrous, *glandular throughout to the tip* or at the base with short- or long-stalked glands or sometimes eglandular. *Capsule* oblong, 2.3–4 cm. long, 0.6–1 cm. broad, slightly curved, *moderately or rather densely hairy with Stellate hairs*, glandular with long- or medium-stalked glands or eglandular, grooved, calyx-lobes persistent.

This species was discovered by Maung Kyaw in September 1912 near Paypat bungalow, at Myitkyna, north-east Upper Burma. It was later found by Forrest and Farrer in the same region. Forrest also collected it in north-west and mid-west Yunnan. The plant grows in mixed and rhododendron forests, in rhododendron thickets, and in mixed thickets, at elevations of 1,830–3,660 m. (6,000–12,000 ft.).

In 1920 *R. prophantum* Balf. f. et Forrest was described from a specimen collected by Forrest, and in *The Species of Rhododendron* it correctly appears under *R. kyawii* in synonymy.

R. kyawii is closely allied to *R. agapetum*. The relationship between them is discussed under the latter.

The species was first introduced by Forrest in 1919 (No. 17928—the Type number of *R. prophantum*). It was reintroduced by him under four different seed numbers. Farrer and E. H. M. Cox sent seeds in 1919 (No. 1444). In its native home it is a shrub or tree, 10–25 feet high; in cultivation it is a rounded or broadly upright spreading shrub up to 12 feet in height. At first the lower surface of the leaves is rather densely sprinkled with Stellate hairs mixed with fewer setulose-glands both of which ultimately remain or partially or completely fall off under the adult leaves. As the species has been introduced from elevations of 9,000–12,000 feet, its hardiness varies in cultivation. It is successfully grown outdoors along the west coast, but along the east coast it needs a cool greenhouse. Like its allies it is a late-flowerer, the flowers appearing in June–July. It is a charming plant and is most effective with its deep crimson flowers in trusses of 12–16. An admirable plant which was grown in the Rhododendron glasshouse, Royal Botanic Garden, Edinburgh, was also one of the casualties. See page 329.

Epithet. After Maung Kyaw, a Burmese plant collector.
Hardiness 1–3. June–July.

R. parishii C. B. Clarke in Hook. Fl. Brit. Ind. Vol. 3 (1882) 475; descript. ampl. Lace in Notes Roy. Bot. Gard. Edin., Vol. 8 (1914) 214.

A shrub or tree, 6–8 m. (20–26 ft) high, *branchlets hairy with Stellate hairs* or glabrous, eglandular or sparsely glandular with medium-stalked glands, those below the inflorescences 5–9 mm. in diameter. *Leaves elliptic or obovate*, lamina leathery, 6–12.3 cm. long, *3.4–6.5 cm. broad*, apex shortly acuminate or obtuse, base obtuse; upper surface dark green, matt, glabrous (in young leaves hairy with brown, *Stellate* hairs), eglandular, midrib grooved, densely hairy on the lower half with *Stellate* hairs or glabrous, primary veins 10–14 on each side, deeply impressed; margin slightly recurved or flat; *under surface* paler, somewhat shining, *glabrous (in young leaves mealy (= hairy) with brown Stellate hairs)*, not punctulate or punctulate with minute red glands, midrib prominent, hairy with *Stellate* hairs or glabrous, primary veins raised; *petiole* 1.2–2.5 cm. long, grooved above, *rather densely or moderately hairy with Stellate hairs*, eglandular. *Inflorescence* a racemose umbel of 8–12 flowers; rhachis 1.5–2 cm. long, rather densely pubescent, glandular with short-stalked glands; pedicel 1–1.5 cm. long, glabrous or sparsely tomentose, rather densely or moderately glandular with short-stalked glands. *Calyx* 5-lobed, minute, 1–2 mm. long, reddish, lobes ovate, outside glabrous, glandular with short-stalked glands, margin eciliate or sparsely ciliate, glandular with short-stalked glands. *Corolla* tubular-campanulate or campanulate, *3–3.5 cm. long*, fleshy, *deep red, with darker bands along the petals, 5 nectar pouches at the base*, outside glabrous, eglandular; lobes 5, 1–1.3 cm. long, 1.2–1.5 cm. broad, rounded, emarginate. *Stamens* 10, unequal, 1.8–2.5 cm. long; filaments glabrous. *Gynoecium* 3–3.5 cm. long; *ovary* conoid or ovoid, 5 mm. long, 6-celled, *densely tomentose with Stellate hairs*, eglandular or sparsely glandular with short-stalked glands; *style* hairy on the lower two-thirds of its length or at the base with *Stellate* hairs, *glandular throughout to the tip* with medium- and short-stalked glands. *Capsule* oblong, 2.3–2.8 cm. long, 0.8–1 cm. broad, straight or slightly curved, *hairy with Stellate hairs*, eglandular, grooved, calyx-lobes persistent.

R. parishii was described by C. B. Clarke in 1882 from a specimen collected by the Rev. C. S. Parish at the southern end of the Dawna Range, south-east of the port of Moulmein, Lower Burma. In January 1912 it was found in flower and fruit in the type locality by J. H. Lace, Chief Conservator of Forests, Burma; from this specimen the species was more amply described in 1914 by Lace. It grows at elevations of 1,830–1,891 m. (6,000–6,200 ft.).

The species is closely related to *R. elliottii* from which it differs in that the leaves are elliptic or obovate, relatively broad, the lamina being twice or hardly twice as long as broad, the corolla is shorter 3–3.5 cm. long, deep red with darker bands along the petals, and the ovary is eglandular or sparsely glandular.

R. parishii was introduced possibly by Lace. The plant is now possibly lost to cultivation.

Epithet. After Rev. C. S. Parish, 1822–1897, chaplain at Moulmein.

Not in cultivation.

R. schistocalyx Balf. f. et Forrest in Notes Roy. Bot. Gard. Edin., Vol. 13 (1920) 58.

A broadly upright or rounded shrub, 1.83–6 m. (6–20 ft.) high, *branchlets* moderately or sparsely *hairy with Stellate hairs, eglandular*, those below the inflorescences 3–4 mm. in diameter. *Leaves* oblanceolate or oblong, lamina leathery, 10–15.5 cm. long, 2.3–5 cm. broad, apex rounded or obtuse, base tapered, obtuse or rounded; upper surface dark green, matt, glabrous (in young leaves hairy with *Stellate* hairs), eglandular, midrib grooved, primary veins 12–20 on each side, deeply impressed; margin flat or slightly recurved; *under surface paler, matt, glabrous (in young leaves hairy with Stellate hairs)*, eglandular, midrib prominent, moderately or sparsely hairy at the base with *Stellate* hairs, primary veins raised; *petiole* 1–2.5 cm. long, grooved above, moderately or sparsely *hairy with Stellate hairs, eglandular*. *Inflorescence* a racemose umbel of 8–10 flowers; *rhachis* 0.8–1 cm. long, pubescent or floccose, *eglandular; pedicel* 1–1.5 cm. long, *densely hairy, hairs Stellate* or rarely not *Stellate, eglandular*. *Calyx* 5-lobed, *large, 0.9–2 cm. long, reddish, split on one side almost to the base, lobes unequal*, ovate, rounded, triangular or irregular, outside glabrous or rarely floccose at the base, eglandular, margin ciliate or eciliate, eglandular. *Corolla* tubular-campanulate, 4–5 cm. long, *rose-crimson or crimson, 5 nectar pouches at the base*, dark crimson within, outside glabrous, eglandular; lobes 5, 1–1.6 cm. long, 1.5–2.3 cm. broad, rounded, emarginate. *Stamens* 10, unequal, 2.5–3.8 cm. long; filaments puberulous at the base or rarely glabrous. *Gynoecium* 3.2–4 cm. long; *ovary* conoid or oblong, 5–7 mm. long, 6-celled, *densely tomentose with Stellate hairs, eglandular; style* rather densely or moderately hairy on the lower half or lower third with *Stellate* hairs or rarely glabrous, *eglandular. Capsule* oblong, 1.5 cm. long, 5 mm. broad, slightly curved, *hairy with Stellate hairs, eglandular*, grooved, calyx-lobes persistent.

Forrest discovered this plant in May 1917 in the Shweli-Salwin Divide, western Yunnan. He found it again later in the same region in July 1918 and in April 1931. It grows in thickets and in open pine forests at elevations of 2,745–3,355 m. (9,000–11,000 ft.).

A diagnostic feature of this species is the large, reddish, unequal calyx 9 mm.–2 cm. long, split on one side almost to the base. In this respect it is readily distinguished from its near ally *R. facetum* and from all the other members of its Series; it further differs in that it is an eglandular species. In its large calyx, it resembles *R. diphrocalyx*, Glischrum Subseries, Barbatum Series, and *R. catacosmum*, Haematodes Subseries, Neriiflorum Series, but differs markedly in the *Stellate* hairs on the various parts of the plant.

R. schistocalyx was first introduced by Forrest in 1917 (No. 15651). It was reintroduced by him in 1918 (No. 17637—the Type number). In its native home it grows 6–20 feet high; in cultivation it is a broadly upright or rounded shrub up to 8 feet. As it has been introduced from elevations of 10,000–11,000 feet, the plant is hardy outdoors along the west coast, but nevertheless along the east coast it should be given a well-sheltered position. The species was successfully grown in a few gardens; it is now rare in cultivation.

Epithet. With split calyx.
Hardiness 2–3. April–May.

R. sikangense Fang, Acta Phytotax. Sinica 2: 81 t. 7 (1952).

A shrub or small tree, 3–5 m. (10–16 ft.) high; *stem and branches with rough bark; branchlets at first whitish-floccose, later glabrous*, those below the inflorescences 6 mm. in diameter. *Leaves* lanceolate or oblong-lanceolate, lamina coriaceous, 8–10 cm. long, 2.5–3 cm. broad, apex shortly acuminate or acute, base obtuse or almost rounded; upper surface dark green, glabrous, midrib grooved, primary veins 10–12 on each side, deeply impressed; under surface pale green, glabrous, midrib prominent, slightly floccose, lateral veins raised; *petiole* 1–1.5 cm. long, grooved above, *red-brown tomentose when young with Stellate hairs. Inflorescence* a racemose umbel of about 10 flowers; rhachis 2 cm. long, red-brown tomentose; *pedicel* 1.5–2 cm. long, *white-tomentose with Stellate hairs. Calyx* 5-lobed, 2 mm. long, lobes triangular or rounded, *outside hairy with Stellate hairs. Corolla* campanulate, 4 cm. long, *purple, with a red blotch at the base, and with purple spots* in the upper part; lobes 5, 1.5 cm. long, 2 cm. broad, rounded. *Stamens* 10, unequal, 1.5–3 cm. long; filaments puberulous at the base. *Gynoecium* 3.5 cm. long; *ovary* ovoid, 5 mm. long, 5–6-celled, densely tomentose *with* red-brown *Stellate hairs;* style glabrous. *Capsule* cylindric, up to 2 cm. long, *hairy with* red-brown *Stellate hairs.*

This species was first collected by W. K. Hu and C. Ho in June 1951 at Erlang Shan, west Sichuan. It was found by them again later during the following month in the same area. The plant grows on slopes and in forests.

R. sikangense agrees with the species of the Parishii Series in its *Stellate* hairs. It is related to *R. cookeanum;* the distinctions between them are discussed under the latter.

Epithet. From Sikang.
Hardiness 3. May–July.

R. venator Tagg in Notes Roy. Bot. Gard. Edin., Vol. 18 (1934) 219.

A bushy lax, or straggly shrub, 1.53–3 m. (5–10 ft.) high, *branchlets* moderately or rather densely *hairy with Stellate hairs*, eglandular or sparsely or moderately setulose-glandular, those below the inflorescences 2–5 mm. in diameter. *Leaves oblong-lanceolate, lanceolate or oblanceolate*, lamina leathery, somewhat revolute, 6–14 cm. long, 1.7–4 cm. broad, apex acute, acuminate or obtuse, base obtuse or rounded; *upper surface* dark green, *somewhat rugulose*, matt or somewhat shining, glabrous or moderately or sparsely *hairy with Stellate hairs* (in young leaves hairy with *Stellate* hairs), eglandular, midrib grooved, primary veins 12–19 on each side, deeply impressed, margin slightly recurved; *under surface* whitish, matt, *with widely or closely scattered white Stellate hairs* (in young leaves hairy with white *Stellate* hairs), eglandular, papillate, *midrib* prominent, *hairy with Stellate hairs,* primary veins somewhat markedly raised; *petiole* 0.9–1.6 cm. long, grooved above, moderately or rather densely *hairy with Stellate hairs,* sparsely or moderately setulose-glandular or rarely eglandular. *Inflorescence* a racemose umbel of 5–10 flowers; rhachis 0.6–1 cm. long, densely tomentose with a brown or cinnamon tomentum, eglandular; *pedicel* 0.8–2.3 cm. long, moderately or densely *hairy with Stellate hairs,* moderately or sparsely setulose-glandular or rarely eglandular. *Calyx* 5-lobed, 1–2 mm. long, lobes ovate, triangular or rounded, outside moderately or densely *hairy with Stellate hairs,* eglandular, margin glabrous or floccose, setulose-glandular. *Corolla* tubular-campanulate, *2.8–3.8 cm. long,* fleshy, scarlet or deep crimson, *5 nectar pouches at the base,* dark crimson within, outside glabrous, eglandular; lobes 5, 1–1.4 cm. long, 1–1.6 cm. broad, rounded, emarginate. *Stamens* 10, unequal, 1.5–3.5 cm. long; filaments glabrous. *Gynoecium* 2.5–4.2 cm. long; *ovary* conoid or oblong, 3–7 mm. long, 5–6-celled, densely tomentose *with Stellate hairs,* eglandular or sometimes setulose-glandular at the base; style moderately or rarely sparsely hairy at the base with *Stellate* hairs or rarely glabrous, eglandular or rarely setulose-glandular at the base. *Capsule* oblong or slender, 1.5–2.3 cm. long, 3–4 mm. broad, slightly curved, moderately or rather densely *hairy with Stellate hairs,* eglandular, grooved, calyx-lobes persistent.

R. venator was discovered by Kingdon-Ward in November 1924 in the Tsangpo Gorge, near Pemakochung, south-east Tibet, forming tangled thickets in swampy ground both in the forest and outside, at elevations of 2,135–2,440 m. (7,000–8,000 ft.). Kingdon-Ward records it as being of a bushy habit, 8–10 feet high, the branches more or less ascending, abundant throughout the Gorge. In April 1947, Ludlow, Sherriff and Elliot collected it between Senge Dzong and Pemakochung, Tsangpo Gorge, growing as a straggly shrub on rock faces or in swamps at 2,593 m. (8,500 ft.). The species was described by Tagg in 1934; the details of the truss and flowers were taken from plants raised in cultivation under Kingdon-Ward's No. 6285.

R. venator agrees with the species of the Parishii Series in the *Stellate* type of hair on the branchlets, petioles, leaves (laminae), pedicels, calyx, ovaries and capsules; it also shows a strong resemblance in its setulose-glandular features, in the tubular-campanulate scarlet corolla with 5 nectar pouches at the base, and often in the oblong-lanceolate, lanceolate or oblanceolate leaves. It differs from the Parishii Series in its relatively small and narrow leaves and often in the smaller corolla.

The species was introduced by Kingdon-Ward in 1924 (No. 6285—the Type number). In cultivation it is a bushy lax, or straggly shrub, usually up to 5 feet high. Although it comes from elevations as low as 7,000–8,000 feet, it is hardy outdoors, and is easy to grow. The scarlet flowers in trusses of 5–10 are produced freely in May–June.

R. venator received an Award of Merit when exhibited by the Hon. H. D. McLaren, Bodnant, in 1933 (Kingdon-Ward No. 6285).

Epithet. Hunter, alluding to the scarlet colour of the flowers.

Hardiness 3. May–June.

PONTICUM SERIES

General characters: shrubs or sometimes trees, 1–6.10 m. (3⅓–20 ft.) high or rarely small, prostrate or semi-prostrate shrubs 10–30 cm. (6–12 in.) high. Leaves oblong, obovate, oblong-obovate, lanceolate, oblong-lanceolate, elliptic or oval, lamina 5–25.5 cm. or rarely 2.3 cm. long, 0.8–7.5 cm. broad; under surface glabrous or covered with a continuous, thin unistrate, or thick woolly or felty bistrate indumentum of hairs. *Inflorescence a candelabroid umbel* of 3–30 flowers; *pedicel 1.8–6 cm. long, elongating in fruit,* eglandular or rather densely or moderately or sparsely glandular with short- or rarely long-stalked glands. Calyx 5– or rarely 6–7-lobed or rarely an undulate rim, 0.5–1.3 cm. long. Corolla widely funnel-shaped or funnel-campanulate or campanulate, 2–5 cm. long, yellow, pale cream, white, pink, rose, purple, lilac-purple, mauve or deep mauve, with or without spots. Stamens 10, rarely 8 or up to 14. Ovary ovoid, conoid or oblong, 2–7 mm. long, 5– or sometimes 6–7-celled, densely tomentose with rusty, brown or whitish hairs or glabrous, eglandular or densely glandular with short- or long-stalked glands. Capsule oblong or oblong-oval or rarely slender, moderately or densely tomentose with rusty, brown or rarely whitish tomentum or glabrous, eglandular or moderately or densely glandular with short- or long-stalked glands.

Distribution. Eastern Sichuan, western Hupeh, west Siberia, Mongolia, Manchuria, Kamtschatka, Alaska, Sakhalin Island, Kurile Islands, Korea, Japan, USSR, Taiwan (Formosa), Turkey, Caucasus, Lebanon, south-east Bulgaria, Portugal, Spain, U.S.A., eastern Canada, and Nova Scotia.

The diagnostic features of this Series are the candelabroid inflorescence often with a long rhachis, the long unequal pedicels elongating in fruit, and very often the widely funnel-shaped corolla. In most species, the lower surface of the leaves is covered with a thin unistrate or a thick woolly or felty bistrate indumentum of hairs; in a few species the lower surface is glabrous. The species fall into the following categories with regard to hair structure: 1. Radiate. 2. Dendroid. 3. Ramiform.

KEY TO THE SPECIES

A. Under surface of the leaves glabrous.
    B. Small, usually prostrate or semi-prostrate shrubs, 10–60 cm. or sometimes up to 1 m. high; corolla yellow; leaf-bud scales persistent or deciduous.
        C. Leaves (laminae) 2.3–8 cm. or sometimes 9.5 cm. long; leaf-bud scales persistent; dwarf shrub 10–60 cm. (4in.–2ft.) high; annual growth short . . . . *aureum*
        C. Leaves (laminae) 7.5–13.5 cm. long; leaf-bud scales usually deciduous; dwarf or small shrub up to 1 m. (3⅓ ft.) high; annual growth long . . . . .
        . . . . *hypopitys*
    B. Medium-sized or large shrubs, 50 cm.–6.10 m. high; corolla white, pink, rose, purple, mauve, deep mauve, pale violet-purple, or rarely yellow; leaf-bud scales usually deciduous.
        D. Style longer than the stamens; gynoecium 2.5–5 cm. long; corolla white, pink, rose, purple, mauve, deep mauve, pale violet-purple or rarely yellow.
            E. Leaf base rounded or broadly obtuse, broadest at the middle; leaves oblong-oval, oval, elliptic or oblong-elliptic; pedicel moderately or rather densely floccose. (From the U.S.A.) . . . . . *catawbiense*
            E. Leaf base tapered, cuneate or obtuse, broadest above or at the middle; leaves lanceolate, oblong-lanceolate, oblong, oblong-obovate or elliptic; pedicel glabrous or floccose.
                F. Style floccose and glandular with short-stalked glands on lower third or floccose at the base; corolla campanulate or funnel-campanulate, white; ovary usually densely glandular with short-stalked glands. From Taiwan (Formosa) . . . . .
                . . . . *hyperythrum*
                F. Style glabrous, eglandular; corolla widely funnel-shaped, pink, rose, purple, mauve, deep mauve, pale violet-purple or rarely white; ovary eglandular (except in *R. maximum*, densely glandular with short-stalked glands). From U.S.A., Turkey, Caucasus, Spain, and Portugal.
                    G. Calyx large 3–7 mm. long; branchlets and calyx outside and margin moderately or rather densely glandular with short-stalked glands; gynoecium shorter than the corolla . . . . *maximum*
                    (part)
                    G. Calyx minute or small 0.5–2 mm. long; branchlets and calyx outside and margin eglandular; gynoecium usually as long as the corolla or longer.
                        H. Ovary not hairy. From Turkey, Caucasus, Lebanon, Bulgaria, Portugal, and Spain . . . . *ponticum*
                        H. Ovary densely hairy with long hairs. From U.S.A.. . . . . *macrophyllum*
        D. Style shorter than the stamens; gynoecium 1.3–1.5 cm. long; corolla white or yellowish, flushed pink along the middle of the petals . . .
        . . . . *fauriei*
A. Under surface of the leaves covered with a thin, or thick woolly, continuous indumentum of hairs.
    I. Under surface of the leaves covered with a thin, unistrate, continuous indumentum of hairs, or sometimes a thin film of hairs.

J. Branchlets, petioles, rhachis of the inflorescence, pedicels, calyx, ovaries, and capsules eglandular; calyx 1–2 mm. long; leaf apex obtuse or rounded.

    K. Style shorter than the stamens; gynoecium 1.3–1.8 cm. long; leaf-bud scales and flower-bud scales deciduous; corolla white, white flushed pink, or creamy-white flushed pink along the middle of the petals, with green spots. From Japan....... *brachycarpum*

    K. Style longer than the stamens; gynoecium 2.3–3.5 cm. long; leaf-bud scales and flower-bud scales persistent; corolla pale cream, white flushed lemon-yellow, very pale lemon flushed pink, or pale lemon, with or without green spots. From N.E. Turkey, and USSR (Caucasus) .... *caucasicum*

J. Branchlets, usually petioles, rhachis of the inflorescence, pedicels, calyx, ovaries, and capsules moderately or rather densely glandular with short-stalked glands; calyx 3–7 mm. long; leaf apex acute.... *maximum* (part)

I. Under surface of the leaves covered with a thick, woolly or felty, bistrate, continuous indumentum of hairs.

    L. Pedicels, ovaries, calyx, and usually branchlets and petioles not glandular.

        M. Leaf-bud scales persistent; leaves lanceolate or narrowly lanceolate, 0.8–2.5 cm. broad; calyx 1–7 mm. long .... *makinoi*

        M. Leaf-bud scales usually deciduous; leaves usually oblong-obovate, oblong, oblanceolate or oblong-lanceolate, usually 2–8 cm. broad; calyx 1–2 mm. long.

            N. Very compact rounded or broadly upright shrub; indumentum on the under surface of the leaves woolly, thick; corolla pale pink, eventually pure white or very pale pink, 5-lobed; stamens 10; ovary 5-celled............... *yakushimanum*

            N. Usually broadly upright shrub; indumentum on the under surface of the leaves felty, thick or somewhat thin; corolla whitish-pink, rose or deep rose, 5–7-lobed; stamens 10–14; ovary 5–8-celled

                O. Corolla 5-lobed; stamens 10; ovary 5-celled .... *degronianum*

                O. Corolla 6–7-lobed; stamens 14; ovary 7–8-celled..... .... *degronianum* var. *heptamerum*

L. Pedicels, ovaries (except in *R. smirnowii*), and usually calyx, branchlets and petioles rather densely or moderately glandular with long- or short-stalked glands.

    P. Ovary densely tomentose; calyx 1–2 mm. long; capsule densely hairy with whitish silky hairs .... *smirnowii*

    P. Ovary not tomentose or sometimes minutely puberulous; calyx 3mm.–1.3 cm. long; capsule not hairy or sometimes puberulous.

        Q. Leaf apex rounded, often apiculate (abruptly acute); inflorescence 12–30-flowered; gynoecium 2.3–3 cm. long, shorter than the stamens; corolla-tube pubescent and usually glandular with long- or short-stalked glands outside. From Turkey and USSR (Georgia)................. *ungernii*

        Q. Leaf apex acute or acuminate; inflorescence 4–8-flowered; gynoecium 4.2–4.5 cm. long, longer than the stamens; corolla-tube glabrous, eglandular outside. From east Sichuan and Hupeh....................... *adenopodum*

DESCRIPTION OF THE SPECIES

R. adenopodum Franch. in Journ. de Bot., Vol. 9 (1895) 391.

A rounded, somewhat lax and often spreading shrub, 1.22–3 m. (4–10 ft.) high, branchlets densely or moderately tomentose with a thin, whitish or fawn tomentum, glandular with short-stalked glands or eglandular, those below the inflorescences 3–5 mm. in diameter; leaf-bud scales deciduous or persistent. *Leaves oblanceolate or lanceolate,* lamina coriaceous, 7.5–20 cm. long, 2–4.6 cm. broad, broadest above the middle or at the middle, apex acute or acuminate, base tapered or cuneate; upper surface dark green, matt, flat, glabrous or with vestiges of hairs (in young leaves densely tomentose with fawn tomentum), midrib grooved, glabrous, primary veins 12–16 on each side, deeply impressed; margin flat or slightly recurved; *under surface covered with a somewhat thick, felty or woolly,* whitish or fawn or brown, *continuous bistrate indumentum of hairs, upper layer Ramiform with long narrow stem, and very long, narrow filamentous branches,* and a *lower layer* of small or large *Rosulate hairs,* with widely scattered short-stalked glands, midrib prominent, glabrous or hairy, primary veins concealed; petiole 1.5–3.2 cm. long, grooved or not grooved above, densely or moderately tomentose with a thin, whitish or fawn tomentum, glandular with short-stalked glands or eglandular. *Inflorescence a candelabroid umbel of 4–8 flowers,* flower-bud scales persistent or semi-persistent; rhachis 1.2–3 cm. or rarely up to 5 cm. long, densely or moderately floccose (hairs whitish or fawn), eglandular; *pedicel 3–4 cm. long,* glabrous or hairy, *rather densely or moderately glandular* with long- or rarely short-stalked glands. *Calyx* 5-lobed, 0.3–1.3 cm. long, lobes ovate, oblong or lanceolate, outside glabrous, eglandular or glandular with short-stalked glands, margin glabrous or hairy, glandular with short-stalked glands or eglandular. *Corolla* funnel-campanulate, 3.6–5 cm. long, *pale rose,* with or without deeper spots, outside glabrous or rarely pubescent at the base of the tube, eglandular, inside rather densely pubescent at the base of the tube; lobes 5, as long as the tube or shorter, 1.5–2 cm. long, 1.8–2.8 cm. broad, rounded, emarginate. *Stamens* 10 or rarely 8, unequal, 2–3.7 cm. long, shorter than the corolla; filaments densely pubescent towards the base. *Gynoecium* 4.2–4.5 cm. long, as long as the corolla or longer; *ovary* conoid, 4–5 mm. long, 5–6-celled, minutely puberulous or glabrous, *densely glandular* with long-stalked glands; style slender, glabrous, eglandular. *Capsule* oblong, 1.5 cm. long, 6–7 mm. broad, straight, ridged, puberulous or glabrous, *glandular* with long-stalked glands, calyx-lobes persistent.

This species was discovered by the French missionary, the Abbé Farges near Tchenkeou-tin, eastern Sichuan, and was described by Franchet in 1895. It was later found by Wilson in western Hupeh when collecting for Messrs. Veitch & Sons. Wilson records it as being rare in western Hupeh where it grows in woods at elevations of 1,525–2,135 m. (5,000–7,000 ft.).

R. adenopodum is a typical species of the Ponticum Series on account of the candelabroid inflorescence of up to 8 flowers. The indumentum on the lower surface of the leaves is somewhat thick, felty or woolly, continuous, bistrate, an upper layer of Ramiform hairs with long very narrow filamentous branches, and a lower layer of Rosulate hairs. The species is related to *R. degronianum* but differs in that the pedicel, ovary and capsule are densely or moderately glandular with long-stalked glands, the calyx is larger 3 mm.–1.3 cm. long, and the ovary and capsule are minutely puberulous or glabrous. It further differs somewhat in the structure of the hairs. The species is also allied to *R. smirnowii* but is distinguished by well-marked characters.

The species was first introduced by Wilson in 1900 (No. 505). In 1901 the Abbé Farges sent seeds to M. Maurice de Vilmorin, and it first flowered in a greenhouse at Les Barres in 1909. In cultivation it is a rounded shrub, somewhat lax and often spreading, up to about 8 feet high. A distinctive feature is the oblanceolate or lanceolate leaves up to 8 inches long. Another marked characteristic is the candelabroid inflorescence with long unequal pedicels. Although it comes from elevations as low as 5,000–7,000 feet, it is hardy outdoors in a sheltered position. It blooms freely, with funnel-campanulate rose flowers.

It received an Award of Merit when exhibited by G. W. E. Loder, Wakehurst Place, Sussex, in 1926.

Epithet. With glandular pedicel.

Hardiness 3. April–May.

R. aureum Georgi, Reise Russ. Reich. I (1775) 214.

Syn. *R. chrysanthum* Pallas, Reise Vol. III (1776) 729.

R. officinale Salisbury, Parad. Lond. t. 80 (1807).

A *small, prostrate or semi-prostrate or compact spreading shrub, 10–60 cm. (4 in.–2 ft.) high; annual growth short,* branchlets rather densely minutely puberulous or glabrous, eglandular, those below the inflorescences 3–4 mm. in diameter; *leaf-bud scales persistent. Leaves* obovate, oblanceolate, ovate or oblong-elliptic, lamina coriaceous, 2.3–9.5 cm. long, 0.8–4 cm. broad, apex rounded or obtuse, base cuneate or obtuse; upper surface dark green or olive-green, slightly rugulose, glabrous, midrib grooved, primary veins 6–15 on each side, deeply impressed; margin recurved or flat; *under surface* pale green, *glabrous, under magnification punctulate with minute hairs,* midrib prominent, glabrous or hairy, primary veins raised; petiole 0.5–2 cm. long, grooved above, rather densely puberulous or hairy, eglandular. *Inflorescence a candelabroid umbel of 3–8 flowers,* flower-bud scales persistent; rhachis 0.5–1 cm. long, densely or moderately pubescent, eglandular; pedicel 2.5–4.8 cm. long, rather densely hairy, eglandular. *Calyx* an undulate rim or 5-lobed, minute, 0.5–1 mm. long, lobes ovate or triangular, outside and margin hairy, eglandular. *Corolla widely funnel-shaped,* 2–3 cm. long, *yellow,* with or without purplish spots, outside glabrous, eglandular, inside puberulous at the base of the tube; lobes 5, as long as the tube or longer, 1–1.5 cm. long, 0.8–1.5 cm. broad, rounded, emarginate. *Stamens* 10, unequal, 1–2.3 cm. long, shorter than the corolla; filaments puberulous towards the base. *Gynoecium* 2.5–3 cm. long, as long as the corolla or longer; ovary ovoid, 2–4 mm. long, 5-celled, densely hairy with rusty or brown hairs, eglandular; style slender, glabrous, eglandular. *Capsule* oblong or oblong-oval, 0.6–1.1 cm. long, 3–6 mm. broad, straight, ridged, hairy with rusty hairs, eglandular, calyx-lobes persistent.

R. aureum was described by Georgi in 1775. It has a wide area of distribution extending from the Altai mountains in west Siberia to the mountains of Mongolia and Manchuria, Kamtschatka, Sakhalin Island, Kurile Islands, Korea, and Japan.

The plant has been known for some time as *R. chrysanthum* Pallas. The nomenclature was clarified by E. D. Merrill in *Brittonia,* Vol. 4 (1941) 148.

The species varies considerably in some features. It is a small, prostrate or semi-prostrate or somewhat compact spreading shrub, 4 in.–2 ft. high; the leaves are ovate, obovate or oblanceolate, laminae 2.3–9.5 cm. long, 8 mm.–4 cm. broad. The plant shows a strong resemblance to *R. hypopitys* from Siberia but is distinguished mainly by the dwarf habit of growth, by the short annual growths, by the short internodes, and by the persistent leaf-bud scales. It is also related to *R. caucasicum* from the Caucasus, but differs in that it is a dwarf prostrate or semi-prostrate shrub, and the lower surface of the leaves is glabrous, although under magnification it is punctulate with minute hairs; in *R. caucasicum* the lower surface of the leaves is covered with a thin continuous indumentum of hairs.

R. aureum was first introduced from Russia in 1796. Two distinct forms are in cultivation: Form 1. A semi-prostrate, somewhat compact spreading shrub, about 2 feet high and up to 1½–2 feet across, with large leaves (laminae) up to 9.5 cm. long and 4 cm. broad, and large flowers 3 cm. long, sometimes known as the "Siberian form". Form 2. A prostrate spreading shrub, up to 4–6 inches high with small leaves (laminae) up to 3 cm. long and 2 cm. broad, and small flowers 2 cm. long, sometimes known as the "Japanese form". The species is a slow grower. The short annual growths with persistent leaf-bud scales are a characteristic feature. When raised from seed the species flowers in 10–12 years or more. It varies in freedom of flowering. Some forms flower freely; other forms are shy flowerers and hardly produce more than a few flowers a year. The large compact form often produces good fertile seeds in plenty. The species is hardy but is uncommon in cultivation.

Epithet. Golden.

Hardiness 3. April–May.

R. × nikomontanum (Komatsu) Nakai in Tokyo Bot. Mag. XXXI (1917) 242—*R. aureum* × *R. brachycarpum*.

> Syn.*R. chrysanthum* Pallas var. *nikomontanum* Komatsu in Matsumura Icon. Pl. Koisikav. III t. 195 (1917).

R. brachycarpum D. Don ex G. Don, Gen. Hist. Dichlamydeous Plants, Vol. 3 (1834) 843.

> Syn. *R. brachycarpum* D. Don ex G. Don var. *roseum* Koidzumi in Tokyo Bot. Mag. XXX (1916) 77.
>
> *R. fauriei* Franch. var. *rufescens* Nakai, Trees Shrubs Japan, ed. 2, I (1927) 56.

Illustration. Bot. Mag. Vol. 129 t. 7881 (1903).

A rounded somewhat compact, occasionally lax shrub, 1.22–3 m. (4–10 ft.) high, branchlets tomentose with a thin, brown or fawn tomentum or glabrous, eglandular, those below the inflorescences 5–7 mm. in diameter; leaf-bud scales deciduous. *Leaves* oblong-elliptic, oblong or oblong-obovate, lamina coriaceous, 7–15 cm. long, 2.6–7 cm. broad, apex rounded or obtuse, base rounded, obtuse or cuneate; upper surface dark green or bright green, not rugulose, glabrous, midrib grooved, yellow, primary veins 12–16 on each side, deeply impressed; margin recurved or flat; *under surface covered with a thin,* brown or fawn, *continuous unistrate indumentum of Radiate hairs,* midrib prominent, glabrous or somewhat tomentose, primary veins slightly raised; petiole 1.3–2 cm. long, yellow, grooved and flattish above, rounded below, glabrous or with vestiges of hairs, eglandular. *Inflorescence a candelabroid umbel of 8–21 flowers,* flower-bud scales deciduous; rhachis 2–5 cm. long, rather densely or moderately puberulous, eglandular; pedicel 2–4.8 cm. long, moderately or rather densely hairy, eglandular. *Calyx* 5-lobed, minute, 1 mm. long, lobes ovate or triangular, outside and margin moderately or densely hairy, eglandular. *Corolla* widely funnel-shaped, 2.5–3 cm. long, *white, white flushed pink, or creamy-white flushed pink along the middle of the petals,* with green spots, outside glabrous, eglandular, inside rather densely hairy at the base of the tube; lobes 5, as long as the tube, 1.2–1.5 cm. long, 1.2–2 cm. broad, rounded, emarginate. *Stamens* 10, unequal, 1–2.6 cm. long, shorter than the corolla; filaments densely hairy on lower third or half. *Gynoecium* 1.3–1.8 cm. long, shorter than the corolla, shorter than the tall 3 or 4 stamens; ovary ovoid or conoid, 3–5 mm. long, 5-celled, densely tomentose with dark brown or brown tomentum, eglandular; style slender, glabrous, eglandular. *Capsule* oblong, 1.4–2 cm. long, 4–5 mm. broad, straight or slightly curved, ridged, rather densely or moderately tomentose with brown tomentum, eglandular, calyx-lobes persistent.

R. brachycarpum is widely distributed in the mountain regions of North and Central Japan, descending to near sea-level in Hokkaido, and extends south to the Kuriles, and to mid and south Korea. It often covers vast tracts in Japan above the forest region at 1,700–2,300 m. (5,574–7,541 ft.).

A diagnostic feature of the species is the thin continuous indumentum on the lower surface of the leaves. The indumentum is unistrate consisting of Radiate hairs. In these respects the species is readily distinguished from *R. fauriei* where the leaves are glabrous on the lower surface.

R. brachycarpum was introduced towards the end of the last century. In cultivation it is a rounded somewhat compact, occasionally lax shrub, up to about 6 feet high and as much across. It is a late flowerer, prolonging the flowering season into June and July. The plant is hardy, free-flowering with trusses of 8–21 widely funnel-shaped flowers. It often sets good and plentiful fertile seeds.

Epithet. With short fruit.

Hardiness 3. June–July.

R. brachycarpum D. Don ex G. Don var. **tigerstedtii** (Nitzelius) Davidian, comb. nov.
> Syn. *R. brachycarpum* D. Don ex G. Don subsp. *tigerstedtii* Nitzelius in Deutsche Baumshule, (July 1970), pp. 207–212.

This plant is a native of Korea, and is found in fir forest, on cliffs, and in woods. It is recorded as being common at 200–900 m. (656–2,951 ft.).

The variety differs from the species in that the leaves are longer, 15–25 cm. in length, and the flowers are broader, 7cm. in breadth.

The plant was introduced by Dr. Tigerstedt to his famous Mustila Arboretum in southern Finland from Kongosan in central Korea. In cultivation it is a somewhat rounded or broadly upright shrub up to 6 feet or more in height. It is hardy with white flowers spotted green.

Epithet. After Dr. Tigerstedt, the former owner of the Mustila Arboretum in south Finland.

Hardiness 3. June–July.

R. catawbiense Michaux in Fl. Bor. Amer., Vol. 1 (1803) 258.
> Illustration. Bot. Mag. Vol. 40 t. 1671 (1814).

A spreading or rounded shrub, 92 cm.–3 m. (3–10 ft.) or rarely 6 m. (20 ft.) high, branchlets moderately or sparsely floccose, eglandular, those below the inflorescences 4–6 mm. in diameter; leaf-bud scales deciduous. *Leaves oblong-oval, oval, elliptic or oblong-elliptic,* lamina coriaceous, 6.5–15 cm. long, 2.6–6.3 cm. broad, broadest at the middle, apex broadly obtuse, *base rounded or obtuse;* upper surface dark green or olive-green, shining, flat, glabrous, midrib slightly grooved, glabrous, primary veins 14–16 on each side, slightly impressed; margin flat; *under surface* pale whitish-green, *glabrous,* under magnification punctulate with minute hairs, midrib prominent, glabrous or hairy, primary veins slightly raised; petiole 1.6–4 cm. long, grooved above, sparsely or moderately floccose, eglandular. *Inflorescence a candelabroid umbel of 8–20 flowers,* flower-bud scales deciduous; rhachis 1.6–4 cm. long, rather densely or moderately minutely puberulous or floccose or glabrous, eglandular; *pedicel* 2–5 cm. long, *moderately or rather densely floccose,* eglandular or sometimes glandular with short-stalked glands. *Calyx* 5-lobed, 1 mm. or rarely 2–3 mm. long, lobes triangular or ovate or rarely lanceolate, outside glabrous, eglandular, margin floccose or glabrous, eglandular. *Corolla* funnel-campanulate, 3.5–4.3 cm. long, *rose, lilac-purple, pink or white, with olive-green spots,* outside glabrous, eglandular, inside rather densely or moderately pubescent at the base of the tube; lobes 5, as long as the tube or longer, 1.5–2.5 cm. long, 1.8–2.6 cm. broad, rounded, emarginate. *Stamens* 10, unequal, 1.6–4 cm. long, shorter than the corolla; filaments densely pubescent towards the base. *Gynoecium* 3.5–4.7 cm. long, as long as the corolla or longer; ovary oblong or conoid, 3–5 mm. long, 5-celled, densely tomentose with rusty tomentum or rarely glabrous, eglandular or rarely densely glandular with short-stalked glands; style slender, glabrous, eglandular. *Capsule* oblong, 1.4–2.3 cm. long, 3–5 mm. broad, straight or slightly curved, ridged, hairy with rusty hairs, eglandular or rarely densely glandular with short-stalked glands, calyx-lobes persistent.

R. catawbiense is a native of the United States of America. It grows on the slopes and summits of mountains in North Carolina and Virginia, at elevations of 1,200–1,983 m. (3,934–6,500 ft.). It is recorded as forming dense thickets at the higher elevations.

The species is allied to *R. macrophyllum,* but is distinguished usually by the oblong-oval or oval leaves with rounded base, and by the moderately or rather densely floccose pedicels. It is also related to *R. maximum,* but is distinguished by well-marked characters.

R. catawbiense was first introduced by John Fraser in 1809 from near the source of the Catawba river, North Carolina, and it flowered for the first time in 1813. It is a spreading or rounded shrub, and in its native home it grows up to 6 feet or rarely 20 feet high. In cultivation it is only 4–5 feet, rarely 10–12 feet in height. The plant is very hardy and provides a fine display with its rose or white flowers produced freely in trusses of 8–20. Moreover, it has the advantage of flowering late in the season, the blooms appearing in May–June. The species is rare in cultivation, but should be a valuable acquisition to every collection of rhododendrons.

It is to be noted that a form with white flowers found by Powell Glass in Virginia has been known as *R. catawbiense* var. *album.* A dwarf form up to 3 feet high on Mt. Mitchell has been named as var. *compactum.* Large-flowered and large-leaved plants from eastern North Carolina have been known as forma *insularis* Coker (in *J. Elisha Mitchell Sci. Soc.* 34:76 et sec., t. 19 (1919)).

Epithet. After the Catawba river, North Carolina, U.S.A.
Hardiness 3. May–June.

R. caucasicum Pallas in Fl. Rossica, Vol. 1 t. 31 (1784) 46.
Illustration. Bot. Mag. Vol. 28 t. 1145 (1808), as *R. caucaseum.* Inadequate.

A compact spreading shrub, 30 cm.–1 m. (1–3½ ft.) high, branchlets moderately or rather densely tomentose with a thin, whitish or fawn tomentum, eglandular, those below the inflorescences 4–7 mm. in diameter; *leaf-bud scales persistent. Leaves* oblong, oblong-obovate or obovate, lamina coriaceous, 4–14 cm. long, 1.5–4.5 cm. broad, apex obtuse or rounded, base obtuse or cuneate, slightly decurrent on petiole; upper surface dark green, slightly rugulose, glabrous, midrib grooved, primary veins 10–16 on each side, deeply impressed; margin recurved or flat; *under surface covered with a thin,* fawn, brown or yellowish, *continuous, unistrate indumentum of Radiate or somewhat Long-rayed hairs,* midrib prominent, glabrous or somewhat hairy, primary veins slightly raised; petiole 1–1.5 cm. long, grooved above, margins slightly winged or not winged, moderately or rather densely tomentose with a thin, whitish or fawn tomentum, eglandular. *Inflorescence a candelabroid umbel of 3–14 flowers, flower-bud scales persistent;* rhachis 0.5–1 cm. long, densely hairy with rusty or dark brown hairs, eglandular; *pedicel* 3–6 cm. long, *rather densely hairy* with rusty, brown or fawn hairs, eglandular. *Calyx* an undulate rim or 5-lobed, 1–2 mm. long, lobes ovate or triangular, outside and margin densely or moderately hairy, eglandular. *Corolla* widely funnel-shaped or funnel-campanulate, 2.3–3.5 cm. long, *pale cream, white flushed lemon-yellow, very pale lemon flushed pink, or pale lemon,* with or without green spots, outside glabrous, eglandular, inside rather densely or moderately pubescent at the base of the tube; lobes 5, as long as the tube or longer, 1–2 cm. long, 1.3–2.1 cm. broad, rounded, emarginate. *Stamens* 10, unequal, 1.7–2.8 cm. long, shorter than the corolla; filaments densely or moderately pubescent towards the base. *Gynoecium* 2.3–3.5 cm. long, as long as the corolla or longer; *ovary* ovoid or conoid, 4–7 mm. long, 5-celled, *densely tomentose* with rusty or brown tomentum, eglandular; style slender, glabrous, eglandular. *Capsule* oblong, 1.2–1.8 cm. long, 6–7 mm. broad, straight or slightly curved, ridged, rather densely or moderately tomentose with rusty or brown tomentum, eglandular, calyx-lobes persistent.

R. caucasicum is a native of north-east Turkey, the Caucasus and the adjacent parts of the USSR. It grows above the forests, on mountain slopes, on granite ledges, often

5. R. caucasicum.
nat. size.
a. capsules. b. flower.
c. stamen. d. ovary, style.

forming dense thickets covering large areas, at elevations of 1,830–3,000 m. (6,000–9,836 ft.).

The species shows a resemblance to *R. aureum* and *R. hypopitys* in some features, but differs markedly from both in that the lower surface of the leaves is covered with a thin continuous indumentum of unistrate Radiate or somewhat Long-rayed hairs. In the latter two species the lower surface of the leaves is glabrous.

R. caucasicum was first introduced in 1803. It was very rare until about the middle of the present century. In 1952 Peter Davis reintroduced it from the Caucasus, and in 1962 Cox and Hutchison brought seeds from north-east Turkey. In cultivation it is a compact spreading shrub up to 2–3 feet high and as much or more across. Although a slow grower, it flowers when quite young. The species is hardy, free-flowering, with pale cream, widely funnel-shaped flowers in candelabroid trusses of up to 14. It often produces a large number of fairly large capsules containing fertile seeds in plenty. When raised from open-pollinated seeds, the vast majority of the seedlings come true to type. The plant is uncommon in cultivation, but is worth being more widely grown.

Epithet. From the Caucasus.
Hardiness 3. April–May.

R. degronianum Carrière in Revue Horticole, Vol. 40, 368 (1869).

Syn. *R. metternichii*, nom. illegit f. *pentamerum* Maxim.

R. japonicum (Bl.) Schneid. var. *pentamerum* Hutch. in Bot. Mag. Vol. 137, t. 8403 (1911).

Illustration. Bot. Mag. Vol. 137, t. 8403 (1911), as *R. japonicum* var. *pentamerum* Hutch.

A somewhat compact rounded, or broadly upright shrub, 92 cm.–2 m. (3–6 ft.) high, branchlets moderately or densely tomentose with a thin, whitish tomentum, glandular with minute short-stalked glands or eglandular, those below the inflorescences 4–7 mm. in diameter, leaf-bud scales deciduous. *Leaves* oblong, oblong-elliptic, obovate or oblong-lanceolate, lamina coriaceous, 8–18 cm. long, 2.2–4.6 cm. broad, broadest at the middle or above the middle, apex obtuse or acute, base obtuse or tapered; upper surface dark green or olive-green, shining, convex or flat, glabrous, midrib grooved, primary veins 12–16 on each side, deeply impresed; margin recurved or flat; *under surface covered with a thick or somewhat thin, felty, fawn or brown, continuous, bistrate indumentum of hairs, upper layer Dendroid with short, medium or long stem, and long very narrow filamentous branches, lower layer* with small and large Rosulate hairs, eglandular, midrib prominent, reddish-purple or green, glabrous or hairy, primary veins concealed; petiole 1.8–3.2 cm. long, grooved above, moderately or densely tomentose with whitish tomentum, glandular with minute short-stalked glands or eglandular. *Inflorescence a candelabroid umbel of 6–15 flowers*, flower-bud scales deciduous or semi-persistent; rhachis 0.8–2 cm. long, densely or moderately floccose, eglandular; pedicel 2.5–4 cm. long, moderately or rather densely floccose, eglandular. *Calyx 5-lobed*, 1–2 mm. long, lobes ovate or triangular, outside and margin floccose, eglandular. *Corolla* campanulate, 2.8–4.3 cm. long, pink, rose, deep rose, reddish or rarely white, with or without deeper spots, with or without deep pink lines along the middle of the petals, outside glabrous, eglandular, inside rather densely or moderately pubescent at the base of the tube; *lobes 5*, as long as the tube or shorter, 1–1.6 cm. long, 1.2–2.3 cm. broad, rounded, emarginate. *Stamens 10*, unequal, 1.4–3.6 cm. long, shorter than the corolla; filaments rather densely puberulous towards the base. *Gynoecium* 3.4–4.2 cm. long, as long as the corolla or longer; ovary conoid or oblong, 4–5 mm. long, 5-celled, densely tomentose with rusty or brown tomentum, eglandular; style glabrous, eglandular. *Capsule* oblong, 1.4–2 cm. long, 5–7 mm. broad, straight or slightly curved, ridged, densely tomentose with rusty or brown tomentum, eglandular, calyx-lobes persistent.

R. metternichii nom. illegit is now known as *R. degronianum*. This change of name is regrettable but is strictly in accordance with the *International Code of Botanical Nomenclature.*

R. degronianum is a native of central and southern Japan, and grows in woods, also forms thickets, at elevations of up to 1,830 m. (6,000 ft.). The diagnostic features of the species are the 5-lobed corolla, the 10 stamens, and the 5-celled ovary. It should be noted that the oblong, obovate or oblong-lanceolate leaves are covered on the lower surface with a thick or somewhat thin, felty continuous indumentum of bistrate hairs, upper layer Dendroid with long very narrow filamentous branches, lower layer with small and large Rosulate hairs. Moreover, the calyx is 5-lobed; the branchlets and petioles are glandular with minute short-stalked glands or eglandular.

The species was first introduced from Tokyo in 1894. In cultivation it is a somewhat compact rounded, or broadly upright shrub, 3–6 feet high, rarely a low spreading bush. The plant is free-flowering and makes a fine show with its pink, rose, reddish or rarely white flowers in trusses of 6–15; it is hardy and easy to grow.

Epithet. After M. Degron, Director of the French Posts in Yokohama in 1869.

Hardiness 3. April–May.

R. degronianum Carr. var. heptamerum (Maxim.) Sealy, comb. nov.

Syn. *R. metternichii* Sieb. et Zucc., nom. illegit.

Hymenanthes japonica Blume, Bijdre (1826) 862.

R. metternichii Siebold et Zuccarini var. *heptamerum* Maxim, Rhododendrons As. (1870) 21.

R. hymenanthes Makino var. *heptamerum* (Maxim.) Makino.

R. japonicum (Blume) Schneider (1912), not (A. Gr.) Suringar (1908).

R. metternichii Sieb. et Zucc. var. *micranthum* Nakai in Tokio Bot. Mag. Vol. 38 (1924) 27.

The variety differs from the species in that the corolla is 7- or sometimes 6-lobed, the stamens are 14 in number, and the ovary is 7–8-celled.

The plant is recorded as having been first introduced in 1870, or possibly in 1862 when Fortune may have sent it from Japan to Standish's nursery. In its native home it grows up to 13 feet high; in cultivation it is a somewhat compact rounded or broadly upright shrub up to about 6 feet, well-filled with foliage.

R. degronianum varies considerably in leaf-shape and size, and in flower colour. It includes the varieties known as var. *hondoense* and var. *kyomaruense* which are possibly geographical variants of *R. degronianum.* Other variants include 'Metternianum', 'Sadoense' and 'Wada's Form'.

It may be remarked that T. Nitzelius who examined a large number of plants in their natural habitat in the course of his field-studies in Japan, concludes that there is no other difference between the 5-lobed and 7-lobed plants, and he does not accept them as even varietally distinct (*Acta Hort. Gotoburg.,* Vol. 24 (1961) pp. 159–67).

An Award of Merit was given to a clone 'Ho Emma' when shown by R. N. S. Clarke, Borde Hill, Sussex, in 1976.

Epithet of the variety. 7-lobed.

Hardiness 3. April–May.

R. fauriei Franch. in Bull. Soc. Philom. Paris, Ser. 7, Vol. 10 (1886) 143.

Syn. *R. brachycarpum* D. Don ex G. Don subsp. *fauriei* (Franch.) Chamberlain in Notes Roy. Bot. Gard. Edin., Vol. 37 (1979) 335.

A rounded compact shrub, 92 cm.–3 m. (3–10 ft.) high, branchlets tomentose with a thin, whitish tomentum, eglandular, those below the inflorescences 4–7 mm. in diameter; leaf-bud scales deciduous. *Leaves* oblong-obovate, oblong-elliptic or oblong-lanceolate, lamina coriaceous, 6.6–10.3 cm. long, 3–4.5 cm. broad, apex rounded or obtuse, base rounded or obtuse; upper surface dark green or bright green, not rugulose, glabrous, midrib grooved, yellow, primary veins 12–15 on each side, deeply impressed; margin flat or recurved; *under surface* pale green, *glabrous,* under magnification not punctulate or punctulate with minute hairs, midrib prominent, glabrous, primary veins slightly raised; petiole 1–1.6 cm. long, yellow, grooved and flattish above, rounded below, glabrous or sparsely floccose, eglandular. *Inflorescence a candelabroid umbel of 12–20 flowers,* flower-bud scales deciduous; rhachis 1.3–2 cm. long, rather densely puberulous, eglandular; pedicel 2–2.7 cm. long, moderately or rather densely hairy, eglandular. *Calyx* 5-lobed, minute, 1 mm. long, lobes ovate or triangular, outside and margin moderately or rather densely hairy, eglandular. *Corolla* widely funnel-shaped, 2.1–2.5 cm. long, *white or yellowish, flushed pink along the middle of the petals, with green spots,* outside glabrous, eglandular, inside rather densely hairy at the base of the tube; lobes 5, as long as the tube, 0.8–1 cm. long, 1–1.5 cm. broad, rounded, emarginate. *Stamens* 10, unequal, 1–1.7 cm. long, shorter than the corolla; filaments densely hairy on lower third or half. *Gynoecium* 1.3–1.5 cm. long, shorter than the tall 3 or 4 stamens; ovary conoid or ovoid, 3–5 mm. long, 5-celled, densely tomentose with dark brown or brown tomentum, eglandular; style slender, glabrous, eglandular. *Capsule* oblong, 0.9–1.3 cm. long, 4–5 mm. broad, straight or slightly curved, ridged, rather densely or moderately tomentose with brown tomentum, eglandular, calyx-lobes persistent.

This plant was first collected by the Abbé Faurie in May–June 1886 on Mount Shichinohe, in the province of Aomori, North Japan.

It is very similar to *R. brachycarpum* in general features, but differs in that the lower surface of the leaves is glabrous; in *R. brachycarpum* the lower surface is covered with a thin continuous indumentum of unistrate Radiate hairs.

R. fauriei has been in cultivation for a long time. The date of its introduction into cultivation in Europe is unknown. The plant which flowered in the Royal Botanic Garden, Edinburgh came from Reuthe in 1916. In cultivation it is a rounded compact shrub up to 3–4 feet high usually well-filled with dark green foliage. It varies greatly in its freedom of flowering; some plants bloom freely, whilst others are shy flowerers. It is very hardy, and is easy to grow.

Epithet. After Père L. F. Faurie, French Foreign Missions, China.
Hardiness 3. June–July.

R. hyperythrum Hayata in Icones Plant. Formosan, Vol. 3 (1913) 133.
     Syn. *R. rubropunctatum* Hayata, ibid. Vol. 3 (1913) 141, non Léveillé et Van. (1911).
Illustration. Bot. Mag. n.s. Vol. 167 t. 109 (1950).
A compact, rounded or spreading shrub, 92 cm.–2.44 m. (3–8 ft.) high, branchlets glabrous or floccose, eglandular or glandular with short-stalked glands, those below the inflorescences 5–6 mm. in diameter; leaf-bud scales persistent or deciduous. *Leaves* oblong, lanceolate, oblong-lanceolate or elliptic-lanceolate, lamina coriaceous, 6.8–11.5 cm. long, 1.6–5 cm. broad, apex acute or shortly acuminate, base obtuse or tapered; upper surface dark green, not rugulose, glabrous, midrib grooved, primary veins 10–15 on each side, deeply impressed; *usually revolute,* margin recurved; *under surface* pale green, *glabrous, under magnification with reddish or brownish or fawn punctulations,* midrib prominent, glabrous or hairy with short hairs, primary veins slightly raised; petiole 1.5–2.5 cm. long, grooved above, glabrous or floccose, eglandular or glandular with short-stalked glands. *Inflorescence a candelabroid umbel of 7–12 flowers,* flower-bud scales deciduous; rhachis 1.5–2 cm. long, floccose, eglandular or glandular with short-stalked glands; pedicel ascending, spreading, 2–5 cm. long, floccose, moderately or sparsely glandular with short-stalked glands. *Calyx* 5-lobed, 1–3 mm. long, lobes triangular, ovate or oblong, outside glabrous, moderately or sparsely glandular with short-stalked glands, margin glabrous or sparsely hairy, glandular with short-stalked glands. *Corolla* campanulate or funnel-campanulate, 3–5 cm. long, *white or pink,* with or without purple spots, outside glabrous, eglandular, inside glabrous; lobes 5, as long as the tube, 1.5–2.3 cm. long, 1.6–2.6 cm. broad, rounded, slightly emarginate or not emarginate. *Stamens* 10

or rarely 10–12, unequal, 2.5–4 cm. long, shorter than the corolla; filaments densely puberulous towards the base. *Gynoecium* 3–5 cm. long, as long as the corolla or longer; ovary conoid, 4–6 mm. long, 5-celled, densely glandular with short-stalked glands or densely tomentose or densely glandular with short-stalked glands and tomentose; style slender, floccose and glandular with short-stalked glands on lower third, or sparsely or moderately floccose at the base, stigma lobulate. *Capsule* oblong, 1.2–1.5 cm. long, 4–6 mm. broad, straight or slightly curved, ridged, hairy or glandular with short-stalked glands, or glandular with short-stalked glands and hairy, calyx-lobes persistent.

This species was described by Hayata in 1913 from a specimen collected on Mt. Shichisei, Taiwan (Formosa). It is said to be local at elevations of 900–1,220 m. (2,951–4,000 ft.).

R. hyperythrum is a distinctive plant, and is one of the finest of its Series. A characteristic feature is the lower surface of the leaves which appears glabrous, but under magnification it is dotted with reddish or brownish or fawn punctulations.

The species has been associated with *R. morii* in the Maculiferum Subseries, Barbatum Series. Tagg placed it in the Ponticum Series in *The Species of Rhododendron* 1930, possibly on account of the candelabroid inflorescence which is the main diagnostic feature of this Series. Meanwhile, it will be allowed to stand in its present Series.

R. rubropunctatum Hayata is identical with *R. hyperythrum* under which it appears in synonymy.

R. hyperythrum was first introduced by Lionel de Rothschild in the 1930s. In cultivation it is usually a compact, rounded or spreading shrub up to 6 feet high and as much or more across. A characteristic feature of the species is the revolute leaf with recurved margins, although in its native home this is not persistent in all seasons of the year. In cultivation the flowers are pure white, sometimes with purple spots; both white and pink forms occur in Taiwan. It is free-flowering and provides an admirable display with its funnel-campanulate flowers in trusses of 7–12. The plant is hardy, but to grow it satisfactorily, a sheltered position should be provided. It is uncommon in cultivation, but is worthy of being widely grown.

A clone 'Omo' received an Award of Merit when exhibited by Capt. C. Ingram, Benenden, Kent, in 1976.

Epithet. Reddish below.

Hardiness 3. April–May.

R. hypopitys Pojarkova in Fl. USSR Vol. 18 t. 1 (1952) 721.
    Syn. *R. aureum* Georgi var. *hypopitys* (Pojarkova) Chamberlain in Notes Roy. Bot.
        Gard. Edin., Vol. 37 (1979) 335.

A shrub, *about 1 m. (3⅓ ft.) high; annual growth long, branchlets long with long internodes,* minutely puberulous, eglandular, those below the inflorescences 4–8 mm. in diameter; *leaf-bud scales* persistent or deciduous. *Leaves* oblong, elliptic or oblong-elliptic, *lamina* coriaceous, *7.5–13.5 cm. (rarely 6 cm.) long, 2.8–7 cm. (rarely 2 cm.) broad,* apex rounded or shortly acute, base cuneate; upper surface dark green, slightly rugulose, glabrous, midrib grooved, primary veins 9–15 on each side, deeply impressed; margin slightly recurved or flat; *under surface* pale green, *glabrous,* midrib prominent, glabrous, primary veins raised; petiole 1–2 cm. long, grooved above, minutely puberulous, eglandular. *Inflorescence* terminal, *a candelabroid umbel of 3–8 flowers,* flower-bud scales somewhat persistent; rhachis 1–2 cm. long, rather densely or moderately pubescent, eglandular; pedicel 4–6 cm. (rarely 3 cm.) long, hairy with dark brown hairs, eglandular. *Calyx* 5-lobed, minute, 0.5–1 mm. long, lobes ovate or triangular, outside and margin with dark brown hairs, eglandular. *Corolla* widely funnel-shaped, 2.3–3 cm. long, *yellow,* outside glabrous, eglandular; lobes 5, 1–1.5 cm. long, 0.9–1.5 cm. broad, rounded. *Stamens* 10, unequal, 1.4–2.3 cm. long, shorter than the corolla; filaments puberulous towards the base. *Gynoecium* 3–3.2 cm. long, as long as the corolla or longer; ovary oblong or conoid, 3–4 mm. long, 5-celled, densely hairy with rusty hairs, eglandular; style slender, glabrous, eglandular. *Capsule* oblong, 1.3–1.7 cm. long, 3–6 mm. broad, straight or slightly curved, ridged, hairy with rusty hairs, eglandular, calyx persistent, pedicel elongating 6–8 cm. long.

R. hypopitys was described by Pojarkova in 1952. It is a native of eastern USSR, around the shores of Rivers Amur and Tuta, Sichote-Alinj. The plant grows in *Abies* and *Picea*, rarely in *Larix*, woods.

It bears a resemblance to *R. aureum* in general appearance, but is readily distinguished by the height of growth 1 m. (3⅓ ft.) high, by the long annual growth, by the long branchlets with long internodes, usually by the deciduous leaf-bud scales, and by the large leaves, laminae up to 13.5 cm. long, and up to 7 cm. broad.

There is no record of its occurrence in cultivation.

Epithet. Growing under pines.

Not in cultivation.

R. macrophyllum D. Don ex G. Don. Gen. Hist. Dichlamydeous Plants, Vol. 3 (1834) 843.

Syn. *R. californicum* W. Hooker in Bot. Mag. Vol. 81 t. 4863 (1855).

Illustration. Bot. Mag. Vol. 81 t. 4863 (1855), as *R. californicum*.

A broadly upright or somewhat rounded shrub, 1.83–3.66 m. (6–12 ft.) or sometimes 9 m. (30 ft.) high, branchlets glabrous, eglandular or rarely glandular with short-stalked glands, those below the inflorescences 3–5 mm. in diameter; leaf-bud scales deciduous. *Leaves elliptic, oblong-elliptic, oblong-obovate or oblong-lanceolate*, lamina 6.5–17 cm. long, 3–6 cm. broad, broadest at the middle or above the middle, apex obtuse or abruptly acute, base obtuse or cuneate; upper surface dark green, matt, flat, glabrous, midrib grooved, primary veins 12–18 on each side, deeply impressed; margin flat or slightly recurved; *under surface* pale green, *glabrous*, under magnification not punctulate, midrib prominent, glabrous or rarely hairy, eglandular or rarely glandular with short-stalked glands, primary veins slightly raised; petiole 1–2.3 cm. long, grooved above, glabrous or rarely hairy, eglandular or rarely glandular with short-stalked glands. *Inflorescence a candelabroid umbel of 9–20 flowers*, flower-bud scales persistent or deciduous; rhachis 1.5–2.5 cm. long, densely hairy or rather densely puberulous or glabrous, eglandular; *pedicel* 1.8–5 cm. long, *glabrous or minutely puberulous*, eglandular or rarely glandular with minute, short-stalked glands. *Calyx* 5-lobed, minute, 1 mm. long, lobes ovate or triangular, outside glabrous, eglandular, margin glandular with minute, short-stalked glands or hairy, or eglandular glabrous. *Corolla* widely funnel-shaped, 2.8–4 cm. long, *pink, rose or rose-purple, with reddish-brown or yellowish spots*, outside glabrous, eglandular, inside moderately or rather densely pubescent at the base of the tube; lobes 5, as long as the tube or longer, 1–2.3 cm. long, 1.2–2.3 cm. broad, oblong-oval or rounded, emarginate or not emarginate. *Stamens* 10, unequal, 1–3.2 cm. long, shorter than the corolla; filaments densely pubescent towards the base. *Gynoecium* 2.5–4 cm. long, shorter or longer than the corolla; *ovary* conoid or ovoid, 2–5 mm. long, 5-celled, *densely* or rarely moderately *hairy* with long hairs, eglandular; style slender, glabrous, eglandular. *Capsule* oblong, 1.8–2.5 cm. long, 5–9 mm. broad, straight or slightly curved, ridged, *rather densely or moderately hairy* with long hairs, eglandular, calyx-lobes persistent.

R. macrophyllum is a native of the United States of America, and is distributed from California north to British Columbia, at elevations of sea level up to 1,200 m. (3,934 ft.). It has been regarded as the western counterpart of the eastern *R. catawbiense*.

The species is very closely allied to *R. catawbiense* to which it shows a strong resemblance in general features. The main distinctions between them are that in

R. macrophyllum the leaves are elliptic, oblong-elliptic to oblong-lanceolate, broadest at the middle or above the middle, apex obtuse or abruptly acute, base obtuse or cuneate, and the pedicels are glabrous or minutely puberulous; whereas in *R. catawbiense* the leaves are oval, oblong-oval, elliptic or oblong-elliptic, broadest at the middle, apex broadly obtuse, base rounded or obtuse, and the pedicels are moderately or rather densely floccose. *R. macrophyllum* is also closely related to *R. ponticum* but differs in the densely hairy ovary and capsule, and often in the colour of the flowers; it also differs in its geographical distribution.

    R. macrophyllum was first introduced by W. Lobb in 1850 from California. In its native home it grows up to 12 feet or sometimes up to 30 feet high; in cultivation it is broadly upright or occasionally somewhat rounded, up to 12 feet. The plant is hardy in the open along the west coast; in the east coast it succeeds admirably in the Royal Botanic Garden, Edinburgh, but in one or two very cold gardens it has proved to be somewhat difficult. It is a late flowerer, the flowers appearing in May–June. The plant is a robust grower, and provides a mass of colour with its pink or rose flowers in trusses of 9–20. It is now uncommon in cultivation.

    A form with white flowers is known as **R. macrophyllum** D. Don ex G. Don forma **album** Rehder in Journ. Arn. Arb. Vol. 28 (1947) 254.

    Epithet. With big leaves.

    Hardiness 3. May–June.

R. makinoi Tagg in Nakai & Koidzumi, Trees and Shrubs, Japan, Vol. I (1927) 61.

    Syn. *R. metternichii* Siebold & Zuccarini var. *pentamerum* Maximovicz forma *angustifolium* Makino in Tokyo Bot. Mag. Vol. 10 (1896) 211.

        R. stenophyllum Makino in Tokyo Bot. Mag. Vol. 24 (1910) 99, non Hook. f. (1878).

        R. yakushimanum Nakai subsp. *makinoi* (Tagg) Chamberlain in Notes Roy. Bot. Gard. Edin. Vol. 37 (1979) 336.

    A compact rounded or broadly upright shrub, 92 cm.–2.44 m. (3–8 ft.) high; *branchlets densely* brown *woolly,* eglandular, those below the inflorescences 5–7 mm. in diameter; *leaf-bud scales persistent. Leaves lanceolate or narrowly lanceolate,* lamina coriaceous, 5–17 cm. long, *0.8–2.5 cm. broad,* apex acute, curved, base tapered; upper surface dark green or bright green, reticulate, glabrous (in young leaves densely or moderately whitish woolly), midrib grooved, woolly or glabrous, primary veins 12–15 on each side, deeply impressed; margin recurved or somewhat recurved; *under surface covered with a thick, woolly,* brown or dark brown, *continuous bistrate indumentum of hairs, upper layer Ramiform with long stem, and long filamentous branches, lower layer* with small or large *Rosulate hairs,* midrib prominent, densely woolly or glabrous, primary veins concealed; *petiole* 0.6–2 cm. long, slightly grooved or not grooved above, *densely* brown *woolly,* eglandular. *Inflorescence a candelabroid umbel of 5–8 flowers,* flower-bud scales persistent; rhachis 2–3 mm. long, densely woolly with brown or rusty wool, eglandular; *pedicel* 1.8–3 cm. long, *densely hairy* with rusty or brown hairs, eglandular. *Calyx* 5-lobed, 1–7 mm. long, lobes triangular or ovate or oblong, *outside and margin densely or moderately hairy* with rusty or brown hairs, eglandular. *Corolla* funnel-campanulate, 3–4 cm. long, *pink or rose,* with or without crimson spots, outside glabrous, eglandular, inside rather densely or moderately pubescent at the base of the tube or glabrous; lobes 5, as long as the tube, 1.3–2 cm. long, 1.5–2.1 cm. broad, rounded, emarginate. *Stamens* 10, unequal, 1.6–3.3 cm. long, shorter than the corolla; filaments rather densely puberulous towards the base. *Gynoecium* 3–3.5 cm. long, as long as the corolla or longer; *ovary* conoid, 4–5 mm. long, 5-celled, *densely* brown *woolly,* eglandular; style slender, glabrous, eglandular. *Capsule* oblong-oval, 1–1.3 cm. long, 0.8–1 cm. broad, straight, brown *woolly,* eglandular, calyx-lobes persistent.

    The distribution of *R. makinoi* is restricted to a small area in central Honshu, Japan. It

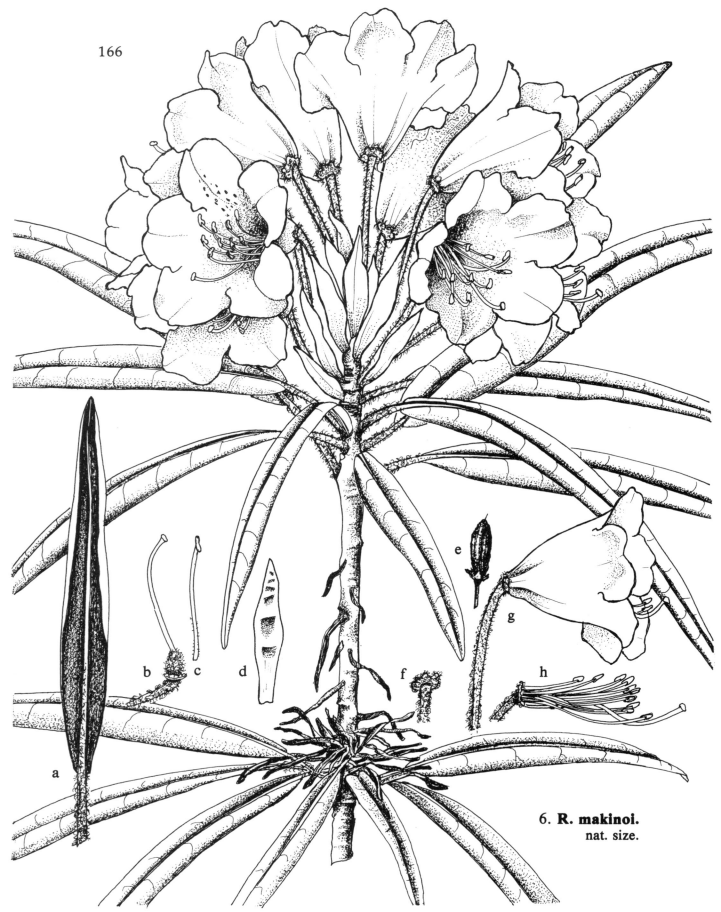

6. **R. makinoi.**
nat. size.

a. leaf (lower surface). b. ovary, style. c. stamen.
d. flower-bud scale. e. capsule. f. calyx. g. flower. h. section.

is said to grow on the mountains, in forests, and on rocks, at elevations of about 458–549 m. (1,500–1,800 ft.).

The species is easily recognised by the markedly narrow lanceolate or lanceolate leaves, covered on the lower surface with a thick, woolly, continuous indumentum of hairs, by the persistent leaf-bud scales, and by the densely woolly branchlets and petioles. The indumentum is bistrate consisting of an upper layer of Ramiform hairs with a long stem and long filamentous branches, and a lower layer of Rosulate hairs. The plant is related to *R. degronianum,* but is distinguished by well-marked characteristics.

It may be of interest to note that prior to the year 1925, several plants in cultivation at the Royal Botanic Garden, Edinburgh, were under the name *R. metternichii* var. *pentamerum.* These were very distinct from *R. metternichii* and also very different from the plants now known as *R. degronianum* (*R. metternichii* var. *pentamerum*). It is recorded that these plants were received from the Yokohama Nursery Co. under the name *R. metternichii.* When Professor Nakai visited Edinburgh, he identified these plants as *R. stenophyllum,* described by Makino in the *Botanical Magazine,* Tokyo, XXIV (1910) 99. As the specific name *"stenophyllum"* had previously been used by Sir Joseph Hooker for a rhododendron from Borneo, Professor Nakai suggested that the name would be *R. makinoi.* Accordingly, in 1927, Tagg described the species as *R. makinoi.*

In cultivation *R. makinoi* is a compact rounded or sometimes a broadly upright shrub up to 5 or 6 feet high. It is very hardy, and blooms freely with pink or rose flowers in candelabroid trusses of 5–8. It is a late flowerer, prolonging the flowering season into May or June. The young growths covered with a white tomentum are an attractive feature in August or September. Occasionally the plant produces oblong-oval capsules covered with brown wool, containing plentiful fertile seeds.

Epithet. After T. Makino, a Japanese botanist.

Hardiness 3. May–June.

R. maximum Linn. Sp. Pl. (1753) 392.

Syn. *R. procerum* Salisbury, Prodr. (1796) 287, nomen nudum.

R. maximum Linn. var. *purpureum* Pursh and var. *album* Pursh, Fl. Amer. Sept. 1 (1814) 297.

R. purpureum (Pursh) G. Don, Gen. Syst. Vol. 3 (1834) 843.

R. purshii G. Don, ibid. Vol. 3 (1834) 843.

R. ashleyi Coker, J. Elisha Mitchell Sci. Soc. 51: 189, t. 53 (1935) 54.

Illustration. Bot. Mag. Vol. 24 t. 951 (1806).

A compact rounded or spreading, or broadly upright shrub, 1.22–3.66 m. (4–12 ft.) or sometimes a tree up to 12.20 m. (40 ft.) high, *branchlets* floccose, *moderately or rather densely glandular* with short-stalked glands or rarely eglandular, those below the inflorescences 4–7 mm. in diameter, leaf-bud scales deciduous. *Leaves* lanceolate or oblong-obovate, lamina coriaceous, 9–20 cm. long, 2.5–7 cm. broad, broadest above the middle, apex acute, base cuneate, tapered, obtuse or rounded; upper surface dark green, somewhat matt, flat, glabrous or with vestiges of hairs, midrib grooved, primary veins 12–16 on each side, slightly impressed; margin flat; *under surface with a thin film of hairs, or covered with a thin* whitish, fawn or brown, *continuous, unistrate indumentum of* small or large *Rosulate hairs, or glabrous,* under magnification punctulate with minute hairs, midrib prominent, glabrous or tomentose, glandular with short-stalked glands or eglandular, primary veins slightly raised, somewhat glabrous or concealed; *petiole* 1.6–4 cm. long, grooved or not grooved above, floccose, *glandular* with short-stalked glands or sometimes eglandular. *Inflorescence a candelabroid umbel of 12–30 flowers,* flower-bud scales persistent or deciduous; *rhachis* 1.2–5.6 cm. long, floccose or glabrous, *glandular* with short-stalked glands; *pedicel* 2–5 cm. long, glabrous or hairy, *rather densely glandular* with short-stalked glands. *Calyx 5-lobed, 3–7 mm. long,* lobes ovate, oval or rounded, *outside* puberulous or glabrous, *moderately or sparsely glandular* with short-stalked glands or rarely eglandular, *margin* glabrous or hairy, *moderately or rather densely glandular* with short-stalked glands or rarely eglandular. *Corolla* campanulate, 2.3–3.1 cm. long, white, white tinged pink, pink, light rose, rose, or purplish, with green or yellowish-green spots on the posterior lobe, outside glabrous or pubescent towards the base of the tube, glandular with short-stalked glands towards the base of the tube or sometimes eglandular, inside rather densely or moderately pubescent at the base of the tube; lobes 5, as long as the tube or longer, 1–1.8 cm. long, 0.9–1.8 cm. broad, oblong-oval or rounded, emarginate or not emarginate. *Stamens* 10 or rarely 8–12, unequal, shorter than the corolla; filaments densely pubescent towards the base. *Gynoecium* 1.6–2.5 cm. long, *shorter than the corolla,* as long as the longer 2 or 3 stamens or shorter; *ovary* conoid or ovoid, 3–5 mm. long, 5-celled, glabrous or hairy, *densely glandular* with short-stalked glands; style slender, glabrous, eglandular. *Capsule* oblong or oblong-oval, 1–1.6 cm. long, 4–6 mm. broad, straight or slightly curved, ridged, glabrous, *moderately or rather densely glandular* with short-stalked glands, calyx-lobes persistent.

This species is a native of eastern North America. Its distribution extends from Ontario, Quebec, Nova Scotia southward through New England along the Appalachian Mountains to Georgia. It grows from nearly sea level up to about 915 m. (3,000 ft.), and forms dense thickets in central and southern areas.

A distinctive feature of *R. maximum* is the lower surface of the leaves with a thin film of hairs, or covered with a thin continuous indumentum of unistrate Rosulate hairs; sometimes the lower surface appears glabrous, but under magnification it is punctulate with minute hairs. Another marked character is the moderately or rather densely glandular branchlets, petioles, rhachis, pedicels, calyx, ovaries and capsules, with short-stalked glands. Other characteristics are the inflorescence of 12–30 flowers, the comparatively large calyx 3–7 mm. long, and the gynoecium shorter than the corolla. The species is allied to *R. macrophyllum* but differs in distinctive features.

R. maximum was first introduced by Peter Collinson in 1736. In its native home it is a shrub up to 12 feet or sometimes a tree up to 40 feet high. In cultivation it is compact rounded or spreading, up to 5–6 feet high and as much across. The pink, rose, or white flowers are produced freely in candelabroid trusses of 12–30. Along the west coast the species is hardy and is successfully grown outdoors; along the east coast it is fairly hardy, somewhat a slow grower, and requires a well-sheltered position in the garden. The plant is rare in cultivation.

A form with smaller leaves than those of the species, with deeply waved margins and globular flower-buds, is known as *R. maximum* Linn. var. *leachii* Harkness.

A clone 'Summer Time' was given an Award of Merit when shown by the Crown Estate Commissioners, Windsor, in 1974.

Epithet. Largest.
Hardiness 3. July.

R. ponticum Linn. Sp. Pl. ed. 2 (1762) 562.
   Syn. *R. lancifolium* Moench, Meth. (1794) 45, nomen illegit.
      R. speciosum Salisbury, Prodr. (1796) 287, nomen illegit.
      R. baeticum Boissier & Reuter in Boissier, Diagn. Ser. 2, 3: (1856) 118.
      R. ponticum Linn. var. *brachycarpum* Boissier, Fl. Or. 3: (1875) 972.
      R. ponticum Linn. subsp. *baeticum* (Boissier & Reuter) Handel-Mazzetti, Ann. Naturhist. Mus. Wien 23: (1909) 53.
   Illustration. Bot. Mag. Vol. 17 t. 650 (1803).
A lax or broadly upright or compact shrub, 1–4.60 m. (3⅓–15 ft.) or a tree up to 7.63 m. (25 ft.) high, *branchlets glabrous,* eglandular or sometimes glandular with short-stalked glands, those below the inflorescences 3–6 mm. in diameter, leaf-bud scales deciduous. *Leaves lanceolate, oblong-lanceolate, oblanceolate, oblong* or *oblong-obovate,* lamina coriaceous, 6.5–21 cm. long, 2.1–6 cm. broad, broadest at the middle or above

the middle, apex acute or obtuse, base tapered, cuneate or obtuse; upper surface dark green, shining, flat, glabrous, midrib grooved, primary veins 12–18 on each side, deeply impressed; margin flat or slightly recurved; *under surface* pale green, *glabrous,* under magnification not punctulate or rarely punctulate with minute hairs, eglandular, midrib prominent, glabrous, eglandular, primary veins raised; *petiole* 1–2 cm. long, grooved above, *glabrous,* eglandular or sometimes glandular with short-stalked glands. *Inflorescence a candelabroid umbel of 6–19 flowers,* flower-bud scales deciduous or persistent; rhachis 1–4 cm. long, rather densely or moderately hairy or glabrous, eglandular or rarely glandular with short-stalked glands; pedicel 2–4.5 cm. long, glabrous or minutely puberulous or hairy, eglandular or glandular with short-stalked glands. *Calyx* 5-lobed, 1–2 mm. long, lobes triangular or ovate or rarely lanceolate, *outside and margin glabrous,* eglandular or rarely glandular with short-stalked glands. *Corolla widely funnel-shaped,* 3–5 cm. long, *deep mauve, mauve, lavender, purple, rosy-purple, lilac-purple, pinkish-purple or pink,* with greenish-yellow or brownish spots, outside glabrous, eglandular, inside pubescent at the base of the tube; lobes 5, longer than the tube, 1.5–2.5 cm. long, 1–2.6 cm. broad, rounded or oblong-oval, emarginate. *Stamens* 10, unequal, 2.2–4.2 cm. long, shorter than the corolla; filaments densely pubescent towards the base. *Gynoecium* 3–5 cm. long, as long as the corolla or longer; *ovary* oblong or conoid, 3–6 mm. long, 5-celled, *glabrous* or rarely hairy, eglandular or rarely glandular with short-stalked glands; style glabrous, eglandular. *Capsule* oblong or slender or oblong-oval, 1.2–2.8 cm. long, 3–6 mm. broad, straight or slightly curved, ridged, *glabrous,* eglandular, calyx-lobes persistent.

This well-known rhododendron was described by Linnaeus in 1762. It is distributed in the Pontic ranges of North Anatolia, Turkey in the region of the Black Sea, in the Caucasus and Lebanon, on the mountains of north-west European Turkey, and the bordering areas of south-east Bulgaria. It also occurs in several localities in Portugal and Spain. It grows in *Abies,* pine, mixed deciduous, alder with laurel, beech-*Carpinus, Carpinus,* and spruce forests, and in scrub, also forms thickets, at elevations of sea-level up to 1,800 m. (5,902 ft.). It is recorded as being abundant in open woodland in Turkey at elevations of 1,200–1,700 m. (3,934–5,574 ft.).

The Iberian form has been known as *R. baeticum.* When the herbarium specimens and plants in cultivation under this name are examined, it will be seen that in habit and height of growth, in leaf shape and size, in flower shape, size and colour, and in all morphological details, *R. baeticum* is identical with *R. ponticum* under which it is now placed in synonymy. Similarly the Lebanon form named *R. ponticum* var. *brachycarpum* is synonymous with *R. ponticum.*

R. ponticum varies considerably in habit and height of growth, it may be a lax or broadly upright or a compact shrub up to 4.60 m. (15 ft.) or a tree up to 7.63 m. (25 ft.) high; and in the size of the leaves 6.5–21 cm. (2½–8½ in.) long. Characteristic features of the species are the lanceolate, oblanceolate to oblong leaves, the glabrous branchlets, petioles, lower surface of the leaves, calyx, ovaries and capsules, and the widely funnel-shaped deep mauve to pink flowers.

The species was first introduced in 1763 from Gibraltar. Fossil evidence indicates that in a comparatively recent geological era, *R. ponticum* occurred in Northern Ireland and may have been a member of the British flora. The plant was originally cultivated as an ornamental, but in the course of years it naturalized itself in the countryside in many parts of the British Isles, spreading by seed and by layers. It has established itself firmly and is invading so much valuable land, being very difficult to eradicate, that it has become a problem to foresters and conservationists. However, the species is a late-flowerer and provides an attractive sight when covered with masses of flowers in woods and on hillsides in June and July. It may be noted that a good proportion of the plants growing in the countryside are pure *R. ponticum,* although a large number must be regarded as *R. ponticum* hybrids, mainly *R. ponticum* crossed with *R. catawbiense,*

R. maximum, and other hardy hybrids.

In cultivation *R. ponticum* makes an effective windbreak, and a fast-growing hedge. It is used as an understock on which other rhododendrons are grafted, although the species is reputed for its sucker-growths.

Epithet. From the Pontus, Asia Minor.

Hardiness 4. June–July.

R. ponticum Linn. forma **album** (Sweet) Zab.

Syn. *R. ponticum* Linn. var. *album* Sweet.

Illustration. Rhododendron and Camellia Year Book, Fig. 14 (1963) 65.

The forma differs from the species in its pure white flowers. It is rare in cultivation.

Epithet. White.

Hardiness 4. June–July.

The following forms appeared either as "sports" or hybrids in cultivation:

R. 'Aucubifolium'. Leaves variegated, with yellow spots.

R. 'Cheiranthifolium'. Leaves narrow, with very wavy margins, flowers purple.

R. 'Folius Purpureus'. Leaves bronzy-purple. It received a First Class Certificate when exhibited by the nurseryman William Paul, in 1895.

R. 'Lancifolium' Moench. nomen illegit. Leaves small, narrow, flat, not wavy. Flowers in small trusses, white in the centre, tinged purple towards the margin.

R. 'Variegatum'. Leaves small and narrower than in the species, edged creamy-white.

R. × Sochadzea Char et Davlianidze, Zam. Sist. Geogr. Rast. 27: (1967) 84. *R. ponticum* × *R. caucasicum.*

Syn. *R. ponticum* Linn. subsp. *artvinense,* nomen nudum.

This is a natural hybrid found in Georgia USSR, in Turkey and the Caucasus at elevations of 1,700–2,400 m. (5,574–7,868 ft.).

R. smirnowii Trautvetter, Gartenflora (1885) 335.

Illustration. Bot. Mag. Vol. 122 t. 7495 (1896).

A broadly upright or somewhat lax or compact shrub, or tree, 50 cm.–6.10 m. (1½–20 ft.) high, *branchlets densely woolly* with whitish or fawn wool, rather densely or moderately glandular with minute, short-stalked glands, those below the inflorescences 4–8 mm. in diameter, leaf-bud scales persistent or semi-persistent. *Leaves* oblong-obovate or oblanceolate, lamina coriaceous, 6.5–16 cm. long, 1.8–4.2 cm. broad, broadest above the middle, apex rounded, obtuse or abruptly acute, not mucronate, base tapered or cuneate; upper surface dark green or olive-green, shining, slightly rugulose, convex or flat, glabrous (in young leaves densely whitish woolly), midrib grooved, woolly or glabrous, primary veins 10–14 on each side, deeply impressed; margin recurved or flat; *under surface covered with a thick, woolly, fawn or brown, continuous bistrate indumentum of hairs, upper layer Ramiform with long narrow stem, and long very narrow filamentous branches, lower layer* with small and large *Rosulate* hairs, eglandular, midrib prominent, densely woolly, primary veins concealed; *petiole* 1–3 cm. long, grooved above, *densely woolly* with whitish or fawn wool, rather densely or moderately glandular with minute, short-stalked glands. *Inflorescence a candelabroid umbel of 6–12 flowers,* flower-bud scales persistent or semi-persistent; rhachis 0.5–1.6 cm. long, moderately or rather densely floccose, glandular with minute, short-stalked glands or eglandular; pedicel 2.6–6 cm. long, rather densely or sparsely floccose, rather densely or moderately glandular with short-stalked glands. *Calyx* 5-lobed, *1–2 mm. long,* lobes triangular or ovate, outside floccose or glabrous, glandular with short-stalked glands, margin floccose or glabrous, glandular with short-stalked glands or eglandular. *Corolla* funnel-campanulate, 3.1–4.8 cm. long, pink, deep pink, rose-red or rose-purple, with or without yellow or brownish or greenish spots, outside glabrous, eglandular, inside rather densely or moderately pubescent at the base of the tube; lobes 5, as long as the tube or longer, 1.4–2.5 cm. long, 1.5–2.8 cm. broad, rounded, emarginate. *Stamens* 10, unequal, 2–4 cm. long, shorter than the corolla; filaments rather densely puberulous towards the base. *Gynoecium* 3.1–4.3 cm. long, as long as the corolla or longer, longer than the stamens; *ovary* conoid or rarely oblong, 4–6 mm. long, 5-celled, *densely tomentose* with whitish tomentum, eglandular; style slender, glabrous, eglandular. *Capsule* oblong, 1–1.6 cm. long, 5–7 mm. broad, straight or slightly curved, ridged, *densely hairy* with whitish hairs, eglandular, calyx-lobes persistent.

R. smirnowii is a native of N.E. Turkey, Caucasus, and the USSR (Georgia). It was discovered by Baron Ungern-Sternberg in 1885 around Artvin in north-east Turkey. The plant grows on igneous slopes, in *Picea* forest, in *Picea*-rhododendron forest, in mixed rhododendron scrub, and in exposed situations, at elevations of 800–2,800 m. (2,623–9,180 ft.).

The main characters of this species are the thick, woolly, continuous indumentum of hairs, at first white, later fawn or brown, covering the lower surface of the leaves, the densely woolly branchlets and petioles, and the densely tomentose ovaries and capsules. The indumentum is bistrate, consisting of an upper layer of Ramiform hairs with long narrow stem, and long very narrow filamentous branches, and a lower layer of Rosulate hairs.

R. smirnowii is related to *R. ungernii*. The main distinctions between them are that in *R. smirnowii* the calyx is small 1–2 mm. long, the ovary and capsule are densely tomentose with whitish tomentum, not glandular, the corolla is not hairy, not glandular outside, the gynoecium is as long as the corolla or longer, and the leaves (laminae) are up to 16 cm. long and up to 4.2 cm. broad; whereas in *R. ungernii* the calyx is larger 4–8 mm. long, the ovary and capsule are not hairy (ovary rarely hairy), densely glandular with long- or short-stalked glands, the corolla is pubescent and glandular with long- or short-stalked glands on the tube outside (rarely eglandular), the gynoecium is shorter than the corolla, and the leaves (laminae) are up to 25.5 cm. long, and up to 7.5 cm. broad.

R. smirnowii was first introduced to Kew in 1886 by way of St. Petersburg. It flowered for the first time when only a foot high in May 1894. In its native home it is a shrub or tree 1½–20 feet high; in cultivation it is a broadly upright or somewhat lax shrub up to 12 feet in height. It is very hardy, a robust grower, with pink or rose-purple flowers produced freely in candelabroid trusses of 6–12. The plant is a late-flowerer, the flowers appearing in May–June. It is uncommon in cultivation.

Epithet. After M. Smirnow, a friend of its discoverer, Baron Ungern-Sternberg.
Hardiness 3–4. May–June.

R. ungernii Trautvetter, Gartenflora (1885) 335.
Illustration. Bot. Mag. Vol. 136 t. 8332 (1910).
A broadly upright or somewhat rounded shrub, or tree, 1–6 m. (3⅓–20 ft.) high, *branchlets* rather densely or sparsely tomentose with whitish tomentum, *moderately or sparsely glandular* with short- or long-stalked glands, those below the inflorescences 5–8 mm. in diameter, leaf-bud scales deciduous. *Leaves* oblong-oblanceolate, oblong-obovate or oblanceolate, *lamina* coriaceous, *9–25.5 cm. long, 2.8–7.5 cm. broad*, broadest above the middle, *apex* rounded, *apiculate* or sometimes not apiculate, mucronate, base tapered, cuneate or obtuse; upper surface dark green, shining or matt, slightly rugulose, convex or flat, glabrous (in young leaves hairy), midrib grooved, glabrous, primary veins 12–18 on each side, deeply impressed; margin recurved or flat; *under surface covered with a thick, woolly, whitish or fawn, continuous, bistrate indumentum of hairs, upper layer Ramiform with long or medium narrow stem, and long very narrow or short broad filamentous branches,* and a *lower layer of* small and large *Rosulate hairs*, sparsely glandular with long-stalked glands, midrib prominent, hairy or glabrous, primary veins raised or

concealed; petiole 1–3 cm. long, grooved above, glabrous or tomentose with whitish tomentum, eglandular or moderately or sparsely glandular with long-stalked glands. *Inflorescence a candelabroid umbel of 12–30 flowers*, flower-bud scales deciduous or persistent; *rhachis* 2.5–5 cm. long, floccose or glabrous, *moderately or rather densely glandular* with long- or short-stalked glands; *pedicel* 2–4.5 cm. long, sparsely or moderately floccose or glabrous, *moderately or rather densely glandular* with long- or short-stalked glands. *Calyx* 5-lobed, 4–8 mm. long, lobes unequal, lanceolate or oblong, *outside* glabrous, *rather densely or moderately glandular* with short-stalked glands, *margin* glabrous or rarely floccose, *glandular* with short-stalked glands or eglandular. *Corolla* funnel-campanulate, 3–4.5 cm. long, pale rose, pink or white, with or without pale green spots, *outside pubescent on the tube, glandular* with long- or short-stalked glands *on the tube* or rarely eglandular, inside rather densely or moderately pubescent at the base of the tube; lobes 5, as long as the tube or shorter, 1–1.5 cm. long, 1.3–2 cm. broad, rounded, emarginate. *Stamens* 10 or rarely 12, unequal, 2–3.2 cm. long, shorter than the corolla; filaments densely pubescent towards the base. *Gynoecium* 2.3–3 cm. long, *shorter than the corolla*, as long as the longer 2 or 3 *stamens or shorter; ovary* conoid or oblong, 5–6 mm. long, 5-celled, glabrous or rarely hairy, *densely glandular* with long- or short-stalked glands; style slender, glabrous, eglandular. *Capsule* oblong, 0.8–1.7 cm. long, 4–6 mm. broad, straight or slightly curved, ridged, glabrous, *densely glandular* with long-stalked glands, calyx-lobes persistent.

This species was discovered by Baron Ungern-Sternberg in 1885 in the Artvin region, north-east Turkey. It also occurs in adjacent USSR (Georgia). The plant grows in *Picea* forest on igneous slopes, in *Abies* and *Picea* forest, in *Picea*-beech forest, in mixed rhododendron scrub, and forms thickets 6–8 feet high, at elevations of 850–2,000 m. (2,787–6,557 ft.). It is recorded as being abundant in the forest up to the tree line at 6,557 feet at Artvin.

The distinctive features of *R. ungernii* are the large leaves, laminae up to 25.5 cm. long and up to 7.5 cm. broad, usually abruptly acute at the apex, mucronate, the thick, woolly, continuous indumentum of whitish or fawn hairs covering the lower surface of the leaves, the densely glandular ovary and capsule, and the corolla-tube pubescent and glandular outside. The indumentum is bistrate and consists of an upper layer of Ramiform hairs with long or medium narrow stem, and long very narrow or short broad filamentous branches, and a lower layer of Rosulate hairs. The species is allied to *R. smirnowii*; the distinctions between them are discussed under the latter.

R. ungernii was first introduced in 1886 from St. Petersburg. In its native home it is a shrub or a tree up to 20 feet high; in cultivation it is a broadly upright or somewhat rounded, small or medium-sized shrub, usually 3–6 feet in height. Along the west coast and south it succeeds well; along the east coast, to be able to grow it satisfactorily a well-sheltered position in the garden is essential. In a few very cold gardens with heavy frosts, it tends to be difficult. The species is free-flowering with pink or white flowers in large candelabroid trusses of 12–30. It has the advantage of flowering late in the season, in June and July.

The plant was given an Award of Merit when shown by Lord Aberconway and National Trust, Bodnant, in 1973.

Epithet. After Baron F. von Ungern-Sternberg, 1800–1868, Professor at Dorpat. Hardiness 3. June–July.

R. yakushimanum Nakai in Tokyo Bot. Mag. Vol. 35 (1921) 135.
  Syn. *R. metternichii* Sieb. et Zucc. var. *yakushimanum* (Nakai) Ohwi, Bull. Natl. Sci.
    Mus. 33: 1953 (81).
    R. metternichii Sieb. et Zucc. subsp. *yakushimanum* (Nakai) Sugimoto, New
    Key Jap. Trees, (1961) 470.

R. *degronianum* Carrière var. *yakushimanum* (Nakai) Kitamura, Acta
Phytotax. Geobot. 25: (1972) 38.

A *very compact* or lax shrub, 30 cm.–2.5 m. (1–8 ft.) high, *branchlets* densely or moderately *whitish woolly*, eglandular, those below the inflorescences 5–7 mm. in diameter,
leaf-bud scales deciduous or persistent. *Leaves* lanceolate, oblanceolate or oblong-
obovate, (rarely broadly elliptic), lamina coriaceous, 5–10 cm. long, 3–8 cm. broad, apex
obtuse, base obtuse or cuneate; upper surface dark green, slightly rugulose, markedly
convex or flat, glabrous (*in young leaves densely whitish woolly*), midrib grooved, hairy or
glabrous, primary veins 10–15 on each side, deeply impressed; margin recurved or flat;
*under surface covered with a thick, woolly, fawn, continuous, bistrate indumentum of hairs,
upper layer Ramiform* with long stem, and long filamentous branches, *lower layer with*
small and large *Rosulate hairs*, midrib prominent, densely woolly, primary veins
concealed; *petiole* 1–2 cm. long, grooved above, *densely whitish woolly*, eglandular.
Inflorescence a candelabroid umbel of 8–12 flowers, flower-bud scales persistent; rhachis 4–8
mm. long, densely brown woolly, eglandular; pedicel 1.2–2.8 cm. long, densely brown
hairy, eglandular. *Calyx* 5-lobed, minute, 1 mm. long, lobes triangular or ovate, outside
and margin densely brown hairy, eglandular. *Corolla* campanulate, 3.2–3.6 cm. long,
flower-buds rich pink, fading to pale pink, finally *corolla pure white* when opened *or very
pale pink*, outside glabrous, eglandular, inside rather densely pubescent at the base of
the tube; lobes 5, as long as the tube or shorter, 1–1.4 cm. long, 1.5–2.2 cm. broad,
rounded, emarginate. *Stamens* 10, unequal, 1.5–2.3 cm. long, shorter than the corolla;
filaments rather densely puberulous towards the base or glabrous. *Gynoecium* 2.4–3.2
cm. long, as long as the corolla or shorter; ovary conoid, 5 mm. long, 5-celled, densely
brown woolly, eglandular; style slender, glabrous, eglandular. *Capsule* oblong, 1–1.2
cm. long, 6–7 mm. broad, straight, ridged, densely brown woolly, eglandular, calyx-
lobes persistent.

R. *yakushimanum*, as the name implies, is a native of Yakushima, a small mountainous island in the south of Kyushu one of the main islands of Japan. The species was
described by Nakai in 1921.

It is very variable in habit and height of growth, and in leaf shape and size. Dr. A. F.
Serbin who collected on the island in 1960, gives a good account of this plant and its
habitats (American Rhododendron Society's *Quarterly Bulletin*, Vol. 14 (1960) pp. 9–14).
It would be of interest to record some of his observations. He states that "at the lowest
part of the windless side of the summit at approximately 1,500 m. (4,918 ft.), there are
two varieties of R. *yakushimanum*. The first variety known as *planum* grows to a height of
4–5 feet or even 6–8 feet with a lax habit of growth, and leaves 3–4 inches long, moderately pointed, flat, not convex." Serbin notes that it resembles the plant known as
R. *degronianum*.

"The second variety encountered also on the windless side, on the exposed por-
tions of the summit, is a true dwarf, 15–18 inches high, rarely reaching a height of more
than 2½ feet, known as *parvum* (round-leaved variety). It is much more dense in growth
than *planum*, with small leaves 1½–2½ inches in length with a tendency to rounded
margins with slight convexity, and is the rarest of all forms of this species.

"However, on the wind-swept side of the mountain summit, approximately 800 to
1,000 feet above the timber line, and up to the summit of Miyanoura Peak, 6,400 feet, a
third variety, *convexum*, is found growing, being the finest of the three varieties. It grows
up to a height of 3 feet, compact, densely filled with foliage, leaves 3½ inches long,
convex, curled almost into a complete circle. The plant is completely exposed to wind
and sun throughout most of the year, being under snow for five months of the year."
Serbin notes that the plants sent to Exbury were selected possibly from this choice
group.

R. *yakushimanum* was first introduced in 1934 by Lionel de Rothschild. He received
two 10 inch plants from K. Wada's Hakoneya Nurseries, Numazuchi, Japan. According

to Francis Hanger (who was then employed at Exbury), one plant had only four leaves when received. One of these plants was ultimately moved to the Royal Horticultural Society's Garden at Wisley.

Although the species is a slow grower, it has the merit of flowering at a fairly young age. The leaves are convex, with recurved margins, and are covered on the lower surface with a beautiful thick, woolly, fawn indumentum. An additional asset is the charming young growth densely covered with white wool. The plant is hardy and provides an admirable display when covered with bell-shaped flowers in trusses of 8–12. The flower-buds are rich pink, fading to pale pink, finally the corolla is pure white when opened; in some other forms the corolla remains very pale pink.

A clone 'Koichiro Wada' received a First Class Certificate when exhibited by the Royal Horticultural Society, Wisley, in 1947.

Epithet. From Yakushima Island, Japan.

Hardiness 3. May.

SHERRIFFII SERIES

General characters: shrubs or trees, 1.53–6 m. (5–20 ft.) high, branchlets floccose or glabrous, eglandular or sparsely glandular. *Leaves* oval, obovate, elliptic or oblong, lamina 3.3–6 cm. long, 1.5–4 cm. broad; *under surface covered with a thick woolly, unistrate, continuous indumentum of hairs;* petiole floccose or glabrous, eglandular or glandular. *Inflorescence a lax racemose umbel of 3–6 flowers;* pedicels glabrous or sparsely hairy. Calyx 5-lobed, irregular, 2 mm.–1.4 cm. long, crimson or carmine, glabrous. *Corolla* campanulate or tubular-campanulate, 2.8–4 cm. long, *deep crimson or rich deep carmine,* with 5 dark nectar pouches at the base, lobes 5. Stamens 10, filaments glabrous. *Ovary* slender, oblong or oblong-conoid, *glabrous,* 5-celled. Capsule narrowly elongate-cylindric or oblong, 1.3–1.4 cm. long, 3–7 mm. broad, straight, glabrous.

Distribution. South Tibet.

This Series consists of two species. It is allied to the Fulgens Series but differs markedly in that the inflorescence is lax, 3–6-flowered.

KEY TO THE SPECIES

A. Corolla 2.8–3 cm. long; indumentum on the under surface of the leaves brown or fawn, the hairs Fasciculate with fairly long stem and long, narrow ribbon-like branches; calyx 2 mm.–1.4 cm. long; pedicels 5–6 mm. long . . . . *miniatum*

A. Corolla 3.5–4 cm. long; indumentum on the under surface of the leaves cinnamon-brown, the hairs Long-rayed with short, broad ribbon-like arms; calyx 3–5 mm. long; pedicels 8 mm.–2 cm. long. . . . . *sherriffii*

DESCRIPTION OF THE SPECIES

R. miniatum Cowan in Notes Roy. Bot. Gard. Edin., Vol. 19 (1937) 229.

A shrub or small tree, 1.53–4.58 (5–15 ft.) high, branchlets floccose, eglandular, those below the inflorescences 3 mm. in diameter. *Leaves* oblong-ovate, oval, elliptic, obovate or oblong, lamina 3.3–5.5 cm. long, 1.5–3 cm. broad, apex obtuse or rounded, mucronate, base cordulate or rounded; upper surface glabrous, opaque, midrib grooved, moderately or sparsely hairy, primary veins 6–10 on each side, deeply impressed; margin slightly recurved; *under surface covered with a thick woolly, brown or fawn, continuous, unistrate indumentum of Fasciculate hairs with fairly long stem and long, narrow ribbon-like branches,* midrib prominent, glabrescent or obscured; petiole 6–9 mm. long, grooved above, floccose, eglandular. *Inflorescence* a racemose umbel of 4–6 flowers; rhachis about 5 mm. long, tomentose; pedicel 5–6 mm. long, glabrous or sparsely hairy. *Calyx* 5-lobed, irregular, small or large, *2 mm.–1.4 cm. long,* lobes unequal, fleshy, crimson, glabrous. *Corolla* campanulate or tubular-campanulate, *2.8–3 cm. long,* fleshy, *deep crimson* or very deep rose; lobes 5, 1–1.2 cm. long, 1.2–1.6 cm. broad, rounded, emarginate. *Stamens* 10, unequal, 1–2.5 cm. long; filaments glabrous, anthers dark brown. *Gynoecium* 2.8–3 cm. long; ovary slender or oblong, 4–5 mm. long, furrowed, glabrous, eglandular, 5-celled; style slender, straight, rose or white. *Capsule* narrowly elongate-cylindric, 1.4 cm. long, 3 mm. broad, straight, grooved, glabrous.

Ludlow and Sherriff discovered this plant in May 1936 at Podzo Sumdo, Tsari Chu, south Tibet. They found it again a few days later at Tsari Chu, Migyitun, in the same region. It grows in rhododendron and fir forest, and beside cliffs near rhododendrons, at elevations of 3,173–3,660 m. (10,500–12,000 ft.).

R. miniatum is closely allied to *R. sherriffii.* There is a strong similarity between them in habit and height of growth, in the size and somewhat in the shape of the leaves, in the thick woolly, unistrate, continuous indumentum on the lower surface of the leaves, in the lax 3–6-flowered inflorescence, in the campanulate or tubular-campanulate crimson corolla, and in the glabrous ovary. The main distinctions between them are that in *R. miniatum* the corolla is 2.8–3 cm. long; the indumentum on the lower surface of the leaves is brown or fawn, the hairs are Fasciculate with fairly long stem and long, narrow ribbon-like branches, the calyx is 2 mm.–1.4 cm. long, and the pedicels are 5–6 mm. long; whereas in *R. sherriffii* the corolla is 3.5–4 cm. long, the indumentum on the lower surface of the leaves is cinnamon-brown, the hairs are Long-rayed with broad ribbon-like arms, the calyx is 3–5 mm. long, and the pedicels are 8 mm.–2 cm. long.

R. miniatum has not been introduced into cultivation.

Epithet. Flame-scarlet.

Not in cultivation.

R. sherriffii Cowan in Notes Roy. Bot. Gard. Edin., Vol. 19 (1937) 231.

A broadly upright shrub or tree, 1.53–6 m. (5–20 ft.) high; *stem and branches with smooth, brown flaking bark;* branchlets sparsely hairy or glabrous, sparsely glandular with short-stalked glands or eglandular, those below the inflorescences 3–4 mm. in diameter. *Leaves* oval, obovate or oblong-elliptic, lamina coriaceous, 4.5–6 cm. long, 2.5–4 cm. broad, apex rounded or broadly obtuse, mucronate, base rounded or obtuse; upper surface dark green, somewhat shining, glabrous; margin slightly recurved or flat; *under surface covered with a thick woolly cinnamon-brown, continuous, unistrate indumentum of Long-rayed hairs with short, broad ribbon-like arms,* midrib raised, glabrous or obscured; petiole 1–1.8 cm. long, grooved above, reddish-purple, glabrous, glandular with short-stalked glands or eglandular. *Inflorescence* a racemose umbel of 3–6 flowers; rhachis about 4 mm. long, glabrous; *pedicel 0.8–2 cm. long,* reddish, glabrous. *Calyx* 5-lobed, unequal, *3–5 mm. long,* carmine with a thin glaucous bloom, lobes rounded, glabrous. *Corolla* tubular-campanulate, fleshy, *3.5–4 cm. long, rich deep carmine,* with or without small deep magenta patches at the base of each petal, 5 dark nectar pouches at the base; lobes 5, 0.6–1.4 cm. long, 1.4–1.6 cm. broad, rounded, emarginate. *Stamens* 10, unequal, 2.2–3 cm. long; filaments glabrous. *Gynoecium* 3.6–4.4 cm. long; ovary oblong or oblong-conoid, about 5 mm. long, furrowed, glabrous, 5-celled; style glabrous, carmine, stigma lobulate, deep carmine or red. *Capsule* oblong-oval, 1.3 cm. long, 7 mm. broad, straight, calyx-lobes persistent.

The distribution of *R. sherriffii* is restricted to south Tibet. It was discovered by Ludlow and Sherriff in April 1936 at Chayul Chu, Lung, south Tibet. It was collected by them again later in October of that year in the same area. The plant grows in rhododendron forest above the Bamboo zone, and on steep hillside near the edge of the Fir and Larch zone, at elevations of 3,508–3,813 m. (11,500–12,500 ft.).

The diagnostic features of *R. sherriffii* are the cinnamon-brown indumentum on the lower surface of the leaves, the Long-rayed hairs with short, broad ribbon-like arms, the smooth, brown flaking bark of the stem and branches, the deep carmine corolla, and the glabrous ovary. It may be noted that the Long-rayed hair with short, broad ribbon-like arms is most distinctive, unlike that of any other known species, somewhat resembling the hair of *R. traillianum*, Lacteum Series. The species is allied to *R. miniatum;* the relationship between them is discussed under the latter.

The plant figured in the *Botanical Magazine* n.s. Vol. 172 t. 337 (1959), with lanceolate leaves, would appear to be a "rogue".

The species was introduced by Ludlow and Sherriff in 1936 (No. 2751). In its native home it is a shrub or tree, 5–20 feet high; in cultivation it is a broadly upright shrub up to 5–6 feet. A notable characteristic is the cinnamon-brown indumentum covering the lower surface of the leaves. Another attractive feature is the smooth, brown flaking bark of the stem and branches. The species is a somewhat slow grower, and requires several years before it reaches the flowering size. The deep carmine flowers are produced moderately in lax trusses of 3–6. The plant hardly sets good fertile seeds. It is hardy, but to be able to grow it satisfactorily particularly along the east coast, a sunny aspect and a well-sheltered position should be provided. It is rare in cultivation.

The species was given an Award of Merit when shown by the Crown Estate Commissioners, Windsor Great Park, in 1966.

Epithet. After Major G. Sherriff, 1898–1967, notable plant collector.

Hardiness 3. March–April.

Forest on the Lichiang Range. Photo J. F. Rock.

TALIENSE SERIES

General characters: shrubs or trees, 30 cm.–10 m. (1–33 ft.) high, branchlets densely or moderately tomentose or woolly or glabrous, moderately or rather densely glandular or eglandular. Leaves lanceolate, linear, linear-lanceolate, oblong-lanceolate, elliptic to ovate, lamina 3–19 cm. long, 0.2–8.7 cm. broad; *under surface usually covered with a thick, woolly, continuous indumentum of hairs.* Inflorescence a racemose umbel of 3–20 flowers; pedicel 0.5–5.6 cm. long, moderately or densely glandular or eglandular. Calyx 5-lobed, 0.5 mm.–1.7 cm. long, outside and margin moderately or densely glandular or eglandular. Corolla campanulate or funnel-campanulate, 1.9–5.6 cm. long, white, creamy-yellow, yellow, pink, rose, pinkish-purple or reddish-purple; lobes 5 or rarely 6–7. Stamens 10 or rarely up to 14. Ovary conoid, ovoid, oblong or sometimes slender, 3–9 mm. (or rarely 1 cm.) long, 5–9-celled, glabrous or moderately or densely tomentose, densely or moderately glandular or eglandular. Capsule oblong, conoid, oblong-oval or slender, 0.6–3.2 cm. long, 0.4–1.2 cm. broad, moderately or rather densely glandular or eglandular.

Distribution. North-west, mid-west, west, north-east Yunnan, south-west, west, south-east, east Sichuan, south-east, east Tibet, Shensi 1 species, Kansu 1 species, Upper Burma 1 species, Taiwan (Formosa) 1 species.

This is a large Series of 46 species, consisting of small, medium-sized and large shrubs, and trees. It is related to the Lacteum Series but differs in that the indumentum on the lower surface of the leaves, with some exceptions, is thick woolly with Ramiform hairs, and is usually continuous. The Series varies considerably in habit and height of growth, in leaf shape and size, and in the glandular and eglandular features. Accordingly, it is divided into four Subseries, namely, Adenogynum Subseries, Roxieanum Subseries, Taliense Subseries, and Wasonii Subseries.

KEY TO THE SUBSERIES

A. Ovary eglandular, not hairy; calyx eglandular, not hairy or rarely hairy.
    B. Large shrubs, usually 92 cm.–4.58 m. (3–15 ft.) high .... *Taliense Subseries*
    B. Dwarf or prostrate shrubs, usually 5–60 cm. (2 in.–2 ft.) high ....
        .... *R. lampropeplum* and *R. pronum*
A. Ovary densely or moderately glandular or eglandular, and/or hairy; calyx glandular or eglandular, hairy or not hairy.
    C. Calyx usually large, 3–1.7 cm. long (or sometimes 0.5–2 mm. long), moderately or rather densely glandular; ovary densely or moderately glandular .... *Adenogynum Subseries*
    C. Calyx usually small, 0.5–2 mm. long (except in *R. recurvoides* 5–8 mm. long), eglandular or glandular; ovary eglandular or densely or moderately glandular.
        D. Inflorescence lax up to 10 flowers; leaves usually oblong, oblong-obovate, elliptic, ovate or ovate-lanceolate, margins flat; leaf-bud scales deciduous; annual growth long .... *Wasonii Subseries*
        D. Inflorescence compact up to 20 flowers; leaves usually lanceolate, oblanceolate, oblong-lanceolate, linear, linear-lanceolate (or sometimes oblong), margins usually recurved; leaf-bud scales often persistent; annual growth short.................... *Roxieanum Subseries*

ADENOGYNUM SUBSERIES

General characters: shrubs or trees, 46 cm.–10 m. (1½–33 ft.) high, branchlets floccose or densely woolly or sometimes glabrous, glandular or sometimes eglandular, leaf-bud scales deciduous (except in *R. detersile* persistent, in *R. codonanthum* persistent or semi-persistent). Leaves lanceolate, oblong-lanceolate, ovate-lanceolate, oblanceolate, elliptic or obovate, lamina 3–18 cm. long, 1–7.8 cm. (or rarely 6 mm.) broad; under surface covered with a thick, woolly, usually continuous, bistrate indumentum of hairs, upper layer Ramiform, lower layer Rosulate, or sometimes unistrate with Long-rayed hairs (plastered in *R. balfourianum*, thin in *R. detonsum*, patchy in *R. codonanthum* and *R. detersile*). Inflorescence a racemose umbel of 3–20 flowers, *pedicel 1–5.6 cm. long, sparsely to densely glandular* or rarely eglandular. *Calyx* 5-lobed, 0.2–1.7 cm. (or rarely 0.5 mm.) long, *outside and margin moderately or rather densely glandular* (or rarely eglandular). Corolla funnel-campanulate or campanulate, 2.3–5.6 cm. long, white, creamy-white, rose, pink, pinkish-purple or reddish-purple; lobes 5 (or rarely 6 or 7). Stamens 10 (or rarely up to 14). *Ovary* conoid, ovoid or oblong, 3–7 mm. (or rarely 1 cm.) long, glabrous or moderately or densely hairy, *densely or moderately glandular* (or rarely eglandular); style glabrous or hairy up to one-half of its length, glandular at the base or up to two-thirds of its length or eglandular. *Capsule* oblong, oblong-oval or ovoid, 1–2.8 cm. long, 0.4–1 cm. broad, glabrous or sometimes moderately or rather densely hairy, *moderately or rather densely glandular.*

KEY TO THE SPECIES

A. Corolla white, pink, rose or reddish-purple; style eglandular or glandular at the base or up to two-thirds of its length; indumentum on the under surface of the leaves continuous or discontinuous with woolly patches.

  B. Leaf-bud scales deciduous; margins of leaves flat or slightly recurved; indumentum on the under surface of the leaves a thin veil, or plastered, or thick spongy or woolly continuous or sometimes not continuous.

  C. Indumentum on the under surface of the leaves a thin veil or scattered tufts of hairs or very thin, not continuous.

  D. Leaves oblong-lanceolate or oblong; branchlets and petioles moderately floccose; ovary not hairy; calyx 3–5 mm. long.... .... *detonsum*

  D. Leaves broadly elliptic, elliptic or oblong-elliptic; branchlets and petioles densely tomentose with a thin tomentum; ovary hairy or rarely not hairy; calyx 5 mm.–1 cm. long............. *prattii*

  C. Indumentum on the under surface of the leaves plastered or thick spongy or woolly, continuous.

  E. Branchlets and usually petioles not hairy or moderately floccose.

  F. Leaves lanceolate, oblong-lanceolate or ovate-lanceolate; indumentum on the under surface of the leaves not worn off in patches, not split all over.

  G. Indumentum on the under surface of the leaves plastered........................... *balfourianum*

  G. Indumentum on the under surface of the leaves thick, spongy or woolly, not plastered.

  H. Indumentum on the under surface of the leaves spongy with a distinct surface pellicle .... *balfourianum* var. *aganniphoides*

  H. Indumentum on the under surface of the leaves woolly (except sometimes *R. adenogynum*) usually without a surface pellicle.

  I. Calyx large, usually 2 mm.–1.5 cm. long; style usually glandular at the base or up to one-half its length; calyx outside and margin often glandular.

  J. Indumentum on the under surface of the leaves yellowish, yellowish-brown or fawn; pedicel not hairy or moderately floccose; calyx outside and margin not hairy.................. *adenogynum*

  J. Indumentum on the under surface of the leaves brown; pedicel densely or moderately floccose; calyx outside and margin often hairy.......... *mimetes* (part)

  I. Calyx small, 0.5–2 mm. long; style eglandular; calyx outside and margin often eglandular.. .... *alutaceum*

  F. Leaves elliptic, oblong-elliptic, ovate, oblong-ovate or sometimes oblong-lanceolate; indumentum on the under surface of the leaves worn off in small or large patches, or split all over.

K. Leaves elliptic, oblong-elliptic or oblong-lanceolate, base rounded or obtuse; indumentum on the under surface of the leaves with small or large patches worn off; ovary densely or rarely sparsely hairy. . . . . *mimetes* (part)

K. Leaves ovate or oblong-ovate, base cordulate; indumentum on the under surface of the leaves split all over; ovary not hairy . . . . *mimetes* var. *simulans*

E. Branchlets and petioles densely woolly (or rarely densely tomentose with a somewhat thin tomentum).

L. Woolly tomentum on the branchlets and petioles, and indumentum on the under surface of the leaves brown, whitish or brownish-yellow.

M. Calyx large, 6 mm.–1 cm. long.

N. Leaves oblong-lanceolate or lanceolate; corolla 4–4.5 cm. long; gynoecium 3.5–4 cm. long; style glandular at the base with medium-stalked glands; upper layer of the bistrate indumentum is not shed at maturity. . . . . *bureavioides* (part)

N. Leaves oblong-elliptic, elliptic, oblong-oval, obovate (or rarely oblong-lanceolate); corolla 3.8–4 cm. long; gynoecium 2.7–3 cm. long; style usually eglandular; upper layer of the bistrate indumentum is mostly shed at maturity . . . . *faberi*

M. Calyx minute, 0.5 mm. long.

O. Corolla 2.5–3 cm. long; petiole and midrib on the under surface of the leaves eglandular; pedicel and calyx glandular; indumentum on the under surface of the leaves brownish-yellow; hairs of the upper layer of the bistrate indumentum with very short stem and curly branches, lower layer with widely scattered Rosulate hairs. . . . . *circinnatum*

O. Corolla 3.2–5 cm. long; petiole and midrib on the under surface of the leaves glandular; pedicel and calyx eglandular; indumentum on the under surface of the leaves reddish-brown or brown; hairs of the upper layer of the bistrate indumentum with medium stem and non-curly branches, lower layer with compact Rosulate hairs. . . . . *nigroglandulosum*

L. Woolly tomentum on the branchlets and petioles, and indumentum on the under surface of the leaves cinnamon-coloured or rusty-red.

P. Calyx small, 1–4 mm. long; corolla small 2–3 cm. long; gynoecium 2–2.6 cm. long . . . . *cruentum*

P. Calyx large, 6 mm.–1 cm. long; corolla usually 3–5 cm. long; gynoecium usually 2.7–4.6 cm. long.

Q. Upper layer of the bistrate indumentum on the under surface of the leaves is mostly shed at maturity revealing a thin, whitish lower layer; leaves usually oblong-elliptic, elliptic, oblong-oval or obovate.

R. Corolla 3.8–4 cm. long; ovary often glabrous, conoid; calyx outside often moderately or sparsely glandular with short-stalked glands .... *faberi* (part)

R. Corolla 2.8–3.5 cm. long; ovary densely hairy with long hairs, ovoid; calyx outside eglandular .... *wuense*

Q. Upper layer of the bistrate indumentum on the under surface of the leaves is not shed; leaves oblong-lanceolate, lanceolate, oblong-elliptic or elliptic.

S. Corolla 2.6–3.3 cm. long; leaves (laminae) 1.3–3.1 cm. broad; gynoecium 2.4–3 cm. long; indumentum on the under surface of the leaves is more felty and less woolly......
.... *elegantulum*

S. Corolla 4–4.5 cm. long; leaves (laminae) 2.5–6 cm. broad; gynoecium 3–4.6 cm. long; indumentum on the under surface of the leaves thick woolly.

T. Ovary densely or moderately hairy; upper surface of the leaves slightly rugulose, somewhat matt or shining; leaves oblong-elliptic, elliptic or oblong-lanceolate; style hairy at the base or in the lower one-third of its length; woolly tomentum on branchlets and petioles, and indumentum on the under surface of the leaves cinnamon-coloured or rusty-red .... *bureavii*

T. Ovary not hairy; upper surface of the leaves not rugulose, shining; leaves oblong-lanceolate or oblanceolate; style not hairy; woolly tomentum on branchlets and petioles, and indumentum on the under surface of the leaves pale fawn, brown, rust- or cinnamon-coloured .... *bureavioides* (part)

B. Leaf-bud scales persistent; margins of the leaves markedly recurved; indumentum on the under surface of the leaves woolly, patchy, not continuous... *detersile*

A. Corolla bright yellow; style glandular throughout to the tip; indumentum on the under surface of the leaves discontinuous, with small woolly patches.......
.... *codonanthum*

DESCRIPTION OF THE SPECIES

R. adenogynum Diels in Notes Roy. Bot. Gard. Edin., Vol. 5 (1912) 216.

Syn. *R. adenophorum* Balf. f. et W. W. Sm. in Notes Roy. Bot. Gard. Edin., Vol. 9 (1916) 211.

R. adenogynum Diels *Adenophorum Group* R. H. S. in Rhod. Handb. (1980) p. 58.

Illustration. Bot. Mag. Vol. 155 t. 9253 (1931).

A broadly upright, or broadly upright and spreading shrub, or somewhat rounded, or bushy shrub, or a dwarf compact and spreading shrub, or tree, 46 cm.–5.50 m. (1½–18 ft.) high, branchlets floccose or rarely densely tomentose or sometimes glabrous, moderately or rather densely glandular with short- and medium-stalked glands or sometimes eglandular, those below the inflorescences 5–8 mm. in diameter; leaf-bud scales deciduous. *Leaves lanceolate, oblong-lanceolate* or rarely ovate-lanceolate, lamina coriaceous, 5–13.5 cm. long, 1.3–4 cm. broad, apex acute or acuminate, base rounded, cordulate or obtuse; upper surface dark green, rugulose, glabrous or with vestiges of hairs, eglandular, midrib grooved, hairy or glabrous, glandular or eglandular, primary veins 12–18 on each side, deeply impressed; *under surface covered with a thick, woolly* (sometimes with a shining pellicle), *yellowish, yellowish-brown, fawn or brown, continuous, bistrate indumentum of hairs, upper layer Ramiform,* with stem of medium length, and long narrow branches, *lower layer small Rosulate hairs,* midrib prominent, hairy or glabrous, moderately or rather densely glandular with short- and medium-stalked glands or sometimes eglandular, primary veins concealed; petiole 1–2.5 cm. long, grooved above, floccose or rarely densely tomentose or sometimes glabrous, moderately or rather densely glandular with short- and medium-stalked glands or sometimes eglandular. *Inflorescence* a racemose umbel of 4–8 or sometimes 12 flowers; rhachis 0.4–1 cm. long, floccose, glandular with short- or medium-stalked glands or sometimes eglandular; *pedicel* 1.5–4 cm. long, glabrous or floccose, *densely glandular* with medium- and long-stalked or sometimes short-stalked glands. *Calyx* 5-lobed, *0.5–1.5 cm. long,* purplish or yellowish-green, lobes unequal, oblong or oblong-oval, *outside glabrous, rather densely or moderately glandular* with short- or medium-stalked glands, *margin glabrous, rather densely glandular* with short- or medium-stalked glands. *Corolla* funnel-campanulate, 3.5–5.3 cm. long, rose, magenta-rose, reddish-purple, pink, white tinged pink or rose, white or rarely creamy-white, with or without crimson spots; lobes 5, 1.5–2.8 cm. long, 1.6–3 cm. broad, rounded, emarginate. *Stamens* 10, unequal, 1.6–3.5 cm. long, shorter than the corolla; filaments rather densely pubescent towards the base. *Gynoecium* 3–4 cm. long, shorter than the corolla, longer than the stamens; *ovary* oblong, conoid or rarely ovoid, 5–7 mm. long, 5–6-celled, glabrous, *densely glandular* with long- or short-stalked glands; *style* glabrous, *glandular* with medium-stalked glands *at the base or on the lower third of its length. Capsule* oblong or oblong-oval, 1–2.2 cm. long, 0.6–1 cm. broad, slightly curved or straight, glabrous, *moderately or rather densely glandular* with medium- or long-stalked glands, calyx-lobes persistent.

R. adenogynum was discovered by Forrest in June 1906, on the eastern flank of the Lichiang Range, north-west Yunnan. It was later found by him and other collectors in the same region, and in mid-west Yunnan, south-west Sichuan, and south-east Tibet. It grows on grassy mountain slopes, on rocks, on limestone cliffs, on open rocky slopes, in stony pasture, amongst boulders, in open alpine meadows, in rhododendron and mixed thickets, in scrub, in cane brakes, in pine and in fir forests, at elevations of 3,355–4,270 m. (11,000–14,000 ft.). Forrest records it as forming thickets in north-west Yunnan. According to Yü it is common in the same region.

In 1916 *R. adenophorum* Balf. f. et W. W. Sm. was described from a specimen No. 10429 collected by Forrest in the north-east of the Yangtze bend, mid Yunnan. It differs from *R. adenogynum* in that the branchlets, petioles, and usually the midrib on the lower

7. R. adenogynum.

nat. size.

a. leaf (lower surface). b. flower. c. calyx. d. section. e. stamen. f. ovary, style. g. capsule.

surface of the leaves are moderately or rather densely glandular. On these distinctions alone which are not always constant, *R. adenophorum* does not merit a specific status.

R. adenogynum bears a strong resemblance to *R. balfourianum* var. *aganniphoides* in general features, but is readily distinguished by indumental characters on the lower surface of the leaves.

The species was first introduced by Forrest in 1910 (No. 5868). It was reintroduced by him on 15 other occasions. Rock sent seeds in 1932, and Yü in 1937. In its native home it is a shrub or bush or tree 1½–18 feet high. Four different forms are in cultivation: Form 1. A broadly upright shrub up to 6–8 feet high, indumentum on the under surface of the leaves woolly, flower colour variable. Form 2. A broadly upright shrub up to 5–6 feet high, indumentum on the under surface of the leaves with a shining surface pellicle, flower colour variable. Form 3. A dwarf compact and spreading plant, 2 feet high and as much or more across, with large white flowers. This form is well suited for the rock garden; rare in cultivation. Form 4. A rounded, bushy shrub, 3–4 feet high, with long, narrow, convex leaves. The species is a robust grower, and is adaptable to any position in the garden. It is very hardy, free-flowering, and unlike most species in the Taliense Series, it flowers when quite young. The plant often produces large oblong or oblong-oval capsules containing good fertile seeds in plenty.

A clone 'Kirsty' was given an Award of Merit when shown as *R. adenophorum* by R. N. S. Clarke, Borde Hill, Sussex, in 1976.

Epithet. With glandular ovary.
Hardiness 3. April–May.

R. alutaceum Balf. f. et W. W. Sm. in Notes Roy. Bot. Gard. Edin., Vol. 10 (1917) 81.

A broadly upright shrub, 1.83–4.27 m. (6–14 ft.) high, branchlets tomentose with a fawn tomentum or glabrous, rather densely or moderately glandular with short-stalked glands, those below the inflorescences 5–8 mm. in diameter; leaf-bud scales deciduous. *Leaves* oblong-lanceolate or lanceolate, lamina coriaceous, 8–14 cm. long, 2–3.9 cm. broad, apex acute or acuminate, base obtuse, rounded or cordulate; upper surface dark green, slightly rugulose, glabrous or with vestiges of hairs, eglandular, midrib grooved, floccose or glabrous, eglandular, primary veins 12–18 on each side, deeply impressed; *under surface covered with a thick, woolly, fawn, brown or dark brown, continuous, bistrate indumentum of hairs, upper layer Ramiform* with long or shorter branches, *lower layer Rosulate*, without pellicle, midrib prominent, densely or moderately hairy, eglandular or glandular with short-stalked glands, primary veins concealed or slightly raised; petiole 1–2 cm. long, grooved above, moderately or densely tomentose with a fawn tomentum or glabrous, glandular with short-stalked glands or eglandular. *Inflorescence* a racemose umbel of *8–12 flowers*; rhachis 1–2.5 cm. long, sparsely or rather densely floccose, glandular with short-stalked glands or eglandular; *pedicel* 1–2.6 cm. long, floccose or glabrous, *moderately or rather densely glandular* with short- and medium-stalked glands. *Calyx* 5-lobed, 0.5–2 mm. long, lobes triangular or ovate, *outside and margin glabrous, eglandular* or glandular with short-stalked glands. *Corolla* funnel-campanulate, 3.5–4.5 cm. long, rose or deep rose, with crimson spots; lobes 5, 1.5–2 cm. long, 1.6–2.5 cm. broad, rounded, emarginate. *Stamens* 10, unequal, 1–3.2 cm. long, shorter than the corolla; filaments rather densely pubescent towards the base. *Gynoecium* 2.8–3.8 cm. long, shorter than the corolla, longer than the stamens; ovary conoid or oblong, 4–6 mm. long, 5-celled, glabrous or hairy, densely or moderately glandular with short- or medium-stalked glands; *style glabrous, eglandular. Capsule* oblong or oblong-oval, 1–1.8 cm. long, 6–8 mm. broad, slightly curved or straight, glabrous or hairy, glandular with medium-stalked glands, calyx-lobes persistent.

This species is known from a single collection made by Forrest in August 1914 in the Kari Pass, Mekong-Yangtze Divide, north-west Yunnan, growing in open thickets at an elevation of 3,660 m. (12,000 ft.).

It is closely related to *R. adenogynum* which it resembles in general appearance, but differs in that the calyx is usually smaller, 0.5–2 mm. long, the style is eglandular, and the inflorescence is many-flowered. The indumentum on the under surface of the leaves is bistrate, an upper layer of Ramiform hairs with long or shorter branches, and a lower layer of Rosulate hairs.

R. alutaceum has been in cultivation for a long time, possibly introduced by Forrest from north-west Yunnan. In its native home it grows up to 12–14 feet high; in cultivation it is a broadly upright shrub and reaches only 6 feet. It is hardy, with deep rose flowers produced freely in trusses of 8–12. The plant is rare in cultivation. An admirable plant 6 feet high which was grown in the Royal Botanic Garden, Edinburgh, has now been lost to cultivation.

Epithet. Like soft leather.

Hardiness 3. April–May.

R. balfourianum Diels in Notes Roy. Bot. Gard. Edin., Vol. 15 (1912) 214.

A broadly upright shrub, 92 cm.–4.58 m. (3–15 ft.) high, branchlets glabrous or moderately or sparsely floccose, eglandular or moderately or sparsely glandular with short-stalked glands, those below the inflorescences 5–7 mm. in diameter, leaf-bud scales deciduous. *Leaves* lanceolate, ovate-lanceolate, oblong-lanceolate or oblong, lamina coriaceous, 5–13.2 cm. long, 1.9–4.8 cm. broad, apex acute or acuminate, base obtuse, rounded or cordulate; upper surface dark green, matt, slightly rugulose, glabrous or with vestiges of hairs, midrib grooved, hairy or glabrous, eglandular, primary veins 12–16 on each side, deeply impressed; *under surface covered with a thin, plastered* (or more or less plastered), brown, fawn or silvery, *continuous, unistrate indumentum of large Rosulate hairs,* midrib prominent, hairy or glabrous, glandular with short-stalked glands or eglandular, primary veins concealed or slightly raised; petiole 1–2.3 cm. long, grooved above, hairy or glabrous, glandular with short-stalked glands or eglandular. *Inflorescence* a racemose umbel of 4–10 flowers; rhachis 4–5 mm. long, hairy or glabrous, glandular with short-stalked glands or eglandular; *pedicel* 1.3–3.4 cm. long, hairy or glabrous, *rather densely glandular* with short- and medium-stalked glands. *Calyx* 5-lobed, 3–8 mm. long, lobes rounded, ovate or oblong, *outside* glabrous, *moderately or rather densely glandular* with short-stalked glands or rarely eglandular, *margin* glabrous, *rather densely glandular* with short-stalked glands. *Corolla* funnel-campanulate, 3–4.8 cm. long, pale or deep rose, pink or white, with or without crimson spots; lobes 5, 1.3–2 cm. long, 1.8–2.5 cm. broad, rounded, emarginate. *Stamens* 10, unequal, 1.8–3 cm. long, shorter than the corolla; filaments rather densely pubescent at the base. *Gynoecium* 3–4 cm. long, shorter than the corolla, longer than the stamens; *ovary* conoid or oblong, 5–7 mm. long, 5–6-celled, glabrous, *densely glandular* with short- or medium-stalked glands; style glabrous, glandular on the lower one-third of its length or at the base with medium-stalked glands or eglandular. *Capsule* oblong, 1–2.8 cm. long, 5–8 mm. broad, straight or slightly curved, glabrous, rather densely or moderately glandular with short- or medium-stalked glands or eglandular, calyx-lobes persistent.

Forrest discovered this plant in July 1906 on the eastern flank of the Tali Range, western Yunnan. Subsequently he found it again in the same area and on the western flank of the Tali Range, also in the Yangtze-Chungtien Divide, and in the Chien chuan-Mekong Divide, north-west Yunnan. It grows in rocky mountain meadows, in open rocky slopes, in rhododendron forest and thickets, and at the margins of pine forests, at elevations of 3,355–4,270 m. (11,000–14,000 ft.).

R. balfourianum is a distinctive species. A diagnostic feature is the thin, plastered, unistrate indumentum of large Rosulate hairs on the lower surface of the leaves. In this respect it is readily distinguished from its ally *R. adenogynum* where the indumentum is thick, woolly and bistrate, upper layer Ramiform, lower layer Rosulate. It also differs from the latter in that the indumentum is often silvery and the calyx is often smaller. In

R. adenogynum, the indumentum is yellowish, yellowish-brown, fawn or brown, and the calyx is often larger.

   R. balfourianum was first introduced by Forrest in 1910 (No. 6774). It was reintroduced by him twice in 1917 (Nos. 15497, 15969). In its native home it grows 3–15 feet high; in cultivation it is a broadly upright shrub 5–6 feet in height. A characteristic feature is the silvery, plastered indumentum on the lower surface of the leaves. The plant is hardy, and makes a fine show with its rose flowers in trusses of 4–10. The species is rare in cultivation. In the Royal Botanic Garden, Edinburgh, the species was represented by a beautiful plant 5 feet high; unfortunately the plant has now been lost to cultivation.

   Epithet. After Sir Isaac Bayley Balfour, 1853–1922, former Regius Professor of Botany, Edinburgh.

   Hardiness 3. April–May.

R. balfourianum Diels var. **aganniphoides** Tagg et Forrest in Notes Roy. Bot. Gard. Edin., Vol. 15 (1927) 306.

   Illustration. Bot Mag. n.s. Vol. 177 t. 531 (1969).

   This plant was first collected by Forrest in June 1918 on the mountains around Muli, south-west Sichuan. It was afterwards found by him and by other collectors in the same region and in west Yunnan. The plant grows on open rocky slopes, on the margins of conifer forests, in spruce forest, in thickets, in mixed scrub, and among boulders, at elevations of 3,050–5,335 m. (10,000–17,492 ft.). In his field notes, Kingdon-Ward describes it as being common, but always mixed with other species, on the Yunnan-Sichuan border. Yü records it as being also common in spruce forest at Muli, south-west Sichuan.

   The variety differs from the species in that the indumentum on the under surface of the leaves is thick, spongy, bistrate, upper layer Ramiform hairs or sometimes very large Rosulate hairs, and a lower layer of Rosulate hairs with short or long arms, with a distinct pellicle or skin on the surface. It is recorded that the pellicle is formed by the hairs being glued together with a resinous material.

   The plant was first introduced by Forrest in 1918 (Nos. 16316, 16806). It was reintroduced by him in 1921 (No. 20456—the Type number), and again later under eight different seed numbers. Kingdon-Ward sent seed in 1921 (No. 4177). The plant was also introduced by Rock on 12 occasions, and by Yü under No. 14662. In its native home it is a shrub or sometimes a tree, 2–16 feet high; in cultivation it is a rounded compact shrub up to 5 or 6 feet high and as much across, well-filled with dark green foliage. A remarkable feature is the beautiful fawn or brown, spongy, continuous indumentum of hairs with a distinct pellicle on the lower surface of the leaves. The plant is a vigorous grower, and is of great beauty when covered with large funnel-campanulate pale or deep rose flowers. Worth noting is the fact that some forms often produce a second flush of flowers in October or November. The plant usually produces large oblong capsules containing plentiful good fertile seeds. It is very hardy, easy to grow, and is a valuable acquisition to every collection of rhododendrons.

   Epithet of the variety. Resembling *R. aganniphum*.

   Hardiness 3. April–May.

R. bureavii Franch. in Bull. Soc. Bot. France, Vol. 34 (1887) 281.

   A broadly upright or rounded somewhat compact shrub, or tree, 1.22–7.63 m. (4–25 ft.) high, *branchlets densely woolly with cinnamon-coloured or rusty-red wool*, moderately or sparsely glandular with long-stalked glands, those below the inflorescences 5–9 mm. in diameter, leaf-bud scales deciduous. *Leaves* oblong-elliptic, elliptic, oblong-lanceolate, rarely ovate or broadly elliptic, lamina coriaceous, 5.5–14 cm. long, 2.5–6 cm. broad, apex acuminate, base rounded or obtuse; upper surface dark green, somewhat matt or shining, slightly rugulose, glabrous, midrib grooved, woolly at the base or up to one-half its length, eglandular, primary veins 12–18 on each side, deeply impressed; *under surface covered with a thick, woolly, cinnamon-coloured or rusty-red, continuous, bistrate indumentum of hairs, upper layer Ramiform* with medium or long stem, and *very long narrow branches often jointed, lower layer with closely or widely scattered Rosulate hairs,* without pellicle, midrib raised, densely woolly, eglandular, primary veins concealed; *petiole* 1– 2.5 cm. long, thick, grooved above, *densely woolly with cinnamon-coloured or rusty-red wool,* moderately or sparsely glandular with long-stalked glands. *Inflorescence* a racemose umbel of 6–15 flowers; *rhachis* 0.5–1 cm. long, *densely or moderately woolly with cinnamon-coloured or brown wool,* glandular with short-stalked glands or eglandular; *pedicel* 1–2.8 cm. long, *densely woolly with brown or rust-coloured wool,* sparsely or moderately glandular with medium- or long-stalked glands. *Calyx* 5-lobed, 0.6–1 cm. long, lobes oblong or oblong-oval, outside hairy with brown hairs, moderately or rather densely glandular with short-stalked glands, margin glabrous or hairy with brown hairs, rather densely glandular with short-stalked glands. *Corolla* campanulate, 4–5 cm. long, rose, reddish, white, white flushed rose or creamy-white flushed rose, with crimson spots; lobes 5, 1.2–1.6 cm. long, 1.8–3 cm. broad, rounded, emarginate. *Stamens* 10, unequal, 1.4–3.4 cm. long, shorter than the corolla; filaments densely pubescent at the base. *Gynoecium* 3–4.6 cm. long, shorter than the corolla, longer than the stamens; *ovary* conoid, 4–5 mm. long, 6–8-celled, *densely or moderately hairy with rust-coloured or brown hairs,* moderately or densely glandular with long-stalked glands; style hairy at the base or on the lower one-third of its length, glandular at the base with long-stalked glands. *Capsule* ovoid or oblong-oval, 1–1.8 cm. long, 0.8–1 cm. broad, moderately or rather densely hairy with long, brown or rust-coloured hairs, glandular with long-stalked glands, calyx-lobes persistent.

R. bureavii was discovered by the Abbé Delavay in June 1886 near Lankiung, north of Tali, north-west Yunnan. It was later collected by him again, also by Forrest and Rock in other localities in the same region. Wilson, and McLaren's collectors found it in south-west Sichuan. The plant grows in rhododendron forest, in open pine forest, in fir forest, on the margins of open conifer forests, in rhododendron thickets, and in open pasture, at elevations of 3,200–4,270 m. (10,492–14,000 ft.). Rock records it as being a tree 20 feet high, forming forests at 14,000 feet above fir forest, at Sun-kwe Pass, south of Likiang, Yunnan.

The most striking character of the plant is the thick woolly, cinnamon-coloured or rusty-red indumentum of hairs covering the lower surface of the leaves. Other distinctive features are the densely, cinnamon or rusty-red woolly branchlets, petioles, rhachis of the inflorescence, pedicels and ovaries. The size of the calyx varies from 6 mm.–1 cm. in length.

R. bureavii was first introduced by Forrest in 1917 (No. 15609). Rock sent seeds on six occasions (Nos. 6296, 11382, 25435, 25436, 25439, 25442). McLaren introduced it in 1938 from Tatsienlu, south-west Sichuan (No. 23). In its native home it is a shrub or tree, 4–25 feet high. Two distinct growth forms are in cultivation: Form 1. A broadly upright shrub 9–10 feet high. Form 2. A rounded somewhat compact shrub about 4 feet high and almost as much across.

The species is an exceptionally fine foliage plant. In cultivation the cinnamon or rusty-red indumentum on the lower surface of the leaves is a noteworthy characteristic. Another prominent feature is the young foliage, bronzy-brown in colour. The plant varies in leaf shape, from oblong-lanceolate, oblong-elliptic to elliptic; there is a form with ovate or broadly elliptic leaves almost orbicular, but is rare in cultivation. It is a slow grower, and takes several years to reach the flowering size. The plant varies greatly in its freedom of flowering. Some forms are shy flowerers; a few other forms make a fine show with white or white flushed rose flowers produced freely in trusses of 6–15. The species is hardy, and although it comes from high elevations in its native home, to be able to grow it satisfactorily along the east coast and in gardens inland, it should be given a sheltered position from wind.

The species received an Award of Merit when exhibited by L. de Rothschild, Exbury, in 1939. It was given the same Award when shown, as a foliage plant, by the Royal Botanic Gardens, Wakehurst, in 1972.

Epithet. After E. Bureau, 1830–1918, a French professor.

Hardiness 3. May.

R. bureavioides Balf. f. in Notes Roy. Bot. Gard. Edin., Vol. 13 (1920) 33.

A broadly upright shrub, 1.22–3 m. (4–10 ft.) high, branchlets densely woolly with pale fawn or rust-coloured wool, sparsely glandular with long-stalked glands, those below the inflorescences 8 mm. in diameter, leaf-bud scales deciduous. *Leaves oblong-lanceolate or oblanceolate*, lamina coriaceous, 10–16.5 cm. long, 2–5.8 cm. broad, apex acuminate, base rounded, obtuse or cordulate; upper surface dark green, shining, slightly rugulose or not rugulose, glabrous or with vestiges of hairs, midrib grooved, woolly up to three-fourths its length or at the base or glabrous, eglandular, primary veins 16–18 on each side, deeply impressed; *under surface covered with a thick, woolly, pale fawn*, cinnamon-coloured or brown, *continuous, bistrate indumentum of hairs, upper layer Ramiform with medium or long stem, with very long narrow branches often jointed, lower layer* with closely scattered *Rosulate hairs*, without pellicle, midrib raised, densely or moderately woolly, eglandular or glandular with medium-stalked glands, primary veins concealed; petiole 1–3 cm. long, thick, grooved above, densely woolly with pale fawn, rust-coloured or brown wool, eglandular or glandular with medium-stalked glands. *Inflorescence* a racemose umbel of 8–15 flowers; rhachis 8 mm. long, densely woolly with pale fawn or brown wool, eglandular; pedicel 1.5–1.6 cm. long, densely or moderately woolly with pale fawn or brown wool, rather densely glandular with short-stalked glands. *Calyx* 5-lobed, 7–8 mm. long, lobes oblong, outside glabrous or sparsely hairy, rather densely glandular with short-stalked glands, margin glabrous, rather densely glandular with short- or medium-stalked glands. *Corolla* funnel-campanulate, 4–4.5 cm. long, rose, with a deep blotch at the base, and with crimson spots; lobes 5, 1.3–1.5 cm. long, 1.8–2.2 cm. broad, rounded, emarginate. *Stamens* 10, unequal, 2–3 cm. long, shorter than the corolla; filaments pubescent at the base. *Gynoecium* 3.5–4 cm. long, as long as the corolla or shorter, longer than the stamens; *ovary* conoid, 5 mm. long, *glabrous*, densely glandular with medium- or long-stalked glands; *style glabrous*, glandular at the base with medium-stalked glands. *Capsule* oblong-oval, 1.2–1.8 cm. long, 0.6–1 cm. broad, glabrous, glandular with long-stalked glands, calyx-lobes persistent.

This plant was first collected by Wilson in June 1904 at Tatsienlu, south-west Sichuan.

It is closely allied to *R. bureavii* which it resembles in general features, but differs markedly in the narrow oblong-lanceolate or oblanceolate leaves, in the ovary and style without hairs, and often in the non-rugulose upper surface of the leaves.

R. bureavioides was introduced by Wilson in 1904. In its native home it grows up to 10 feet high; in cultivation it is a broadly upright shrub up to 6 feet. A characteristic feature of some plants raised from Wilson's seed, is the pale fawn indumentum on the lower surface of the leaves and on other parts of the plant. The species is hardy, free-flowering, and has proved to be most attractive with its rose flowers in trusses of 8–15. It is uncommon in cultivation, but is worthy of a place in every collection of rhododendrons.

Epithet. Resembling *R. bureavii*.

Hardiness 3. May.

R. circinnatum Cowan et Ward in Notes Roy. Bot. Gard. Edin., Vol. 19 (1936) 179.

A tree or often a bushy shrub, 6.10–7.63 m. (20–25 ft.) high, branchlets with a thick, buff or whitish-buff tomentum, those below the inflorescences 7–8 mm. in diameter; leaf-bud scales deciduous. *Leaves* oblong or oblong-lanceolate, lamina coriaceous, 10–

14 cm. long, 2.8–4 cm. broad, apex acute or shortly acuminate, base rounded or cordulate; upper surface olive-green, matt, glabrous, midrib grooved, densely woolly with whitish wool at the base or on the lower one-third of its length; *under surface covered with a thick, woolly, brownish-yellow, continuous, indumentum of bistrate hairs, upper layer Ramiform with very short stem and narrow curly branches, lower layer with widely scattered Rosulate hairs*, without pellicle, midrib prominent, densely woolly, eglandular; *petiole* 2–3 cm. long, grooved above, densely woolly with whitish wool, *eglandular. Inflorescence* a racemose umbel of about 12 flowers; rhachis about 1 cm. long, with a dense tomentum; pedicel 2 cm. long, densely floccose, glandular with short-stalked glands. *Calyx* 5-lobed, *minute, 0.5 mm. long*, lobes triangular or ovate, outside and margin floccose, glandular with short-stalked glands. *Corolla* funnel-campanulate, *2.5–3 cm. long*, (colour not known); lobes 5, 1 cm. long, 1–1.3 cm. broad, rounded, emarginate. *Stamens* 10, unequal, 1.5–2.5 cm. long, shorter than the corolla; filaments densely pubescent at the base or on the lower one-third of their length. *Gynoecium* 2.5–3.5 cm. long, as long as the corolla or longer, longer than the stamens; ovary oblong, 1 cm. long, 6-celled, glabrous or densely hairy at the base, densely glandular with short-stalked glands; style glabrous, eglandular. *Capsule:—*

The only collection of this species was made by Kingdon-Ward in July 1935 at Bimbi La, south-east Tibet. It was found at and above the tree line, on sheltered slopes, at an elevation of 3,965–4,270 m. (13,000–14,000 ft.).

R. circinnatum bears a strong resemblance to *R. adenogynum* in its habit and height of growth, in leaf shape and size, in the thick woolly continuous indumentum of bistrate hairs, and particularly in the glandular pedicels, calyx and ovaries, but differs in that the petioles are not glandular, the corolla and usually the calyx are smaller, and the Ramiform hairs on the lower surface of the leaves have shorter narrow curly branches.

The plant has not been introduced into cultivation.

Epithet. Made round, i.e. coiled, alluding to the curled hairs.

Not in cultivation.

R. codonanthum Balf. f. et Forrest in Notes Roy. Bot. Gard. Edin., Vol. 13 (1922) 249.

A broadly upright or rounded compact shrub, 30 cm.–1.22 m. (1–4 ft.) high, branchlets sparsely or moderately hairy with brown hairs, moderately or sparsely glandular with short-stalked glands or eglandular, those below the inflorescences 3–4 mm. in diameter; leaf-bud scales persistent or semi-persistent. *Leaves lanceolate or oblanceolate, lamina* coriaceous, *3–6.8 cm. long, 0.6–2 cm. broad*, apex acute, base obtuse or tapered; upper surface dark green, matt or shining, slightly rugulose, glabrous or with vestiges of hairs, midrib grooved, glabrous, primary veins 10–12 on each side, deeply impressed; *margin recurved; under surface very sparsely hairy with a few very small patches of woolly hairs, discontinuous, or more or less glabrous, hairs unistrate Ramiform with long stem and ribbon-like branches*, midrib prominent, hairy, glandular with short-stalked glands at the base or eglandular, primary veins slightly raised; petiole 0.6–1 cm. long, grooved above, floccose, glandular with short-stalked glands or eglandular. *Inflorescence* a racemose umbel of *about 6 flowers;* rhachis 2–3 mm. long, floccose, eglandular; pedicel 1.8–2.1 cm. long, glabrous, glandular with short-stalked glands. *Calyx* 5-lobed, 2–4 mm. long, lobes rounded or ovate, outside glabrous, sparsely or moderately glandular with short-stalked glands, margin sparsely ciliate or eciliate, densely glandular with short-stalked glands. *Corolla* campanulate, 2.7–3 cm. long, *bright yellow*, with minute crimson markings; lobes 5, 0.8–1 cm. long, 1.3–1.5 cm. broad, rounded, emarginate. *Stamens* 10, unequal, 1–1.6 cm. long, shorter than the corolla; filaments rather densely pubescent at the base. *Gynoecium* 2.3–2.6 cm. long, shorter than the corolla, longer than the stamens; ovary conoid, 4 mm. long, glabrous, densely glandular with short-stalked glands; *style glandular throughout to the tip* with short-stalked glands. *Capsule:—*

Forrest discovered this species in June 1921 in the Loudre Pass, Mekong-Salwin Divide, north-west Yunnan. He found it again a month later in the Mekong-Yangtze Divide, Mekong Valley, and in September of the same year on the mountains north-east of Atuntze, also in the Mekong-Salwin Divide. It grows amongst rhododendron scrub on rocky slopes, in open scrub on rocky hillsides, on ledges of cliffs, and in rhododendron scrub in alpine moorland, at elevations of 3,660–4,270 m. (12,000–14,000 ft.).

R. codonanthum is a unique species in that the lower surface of the leaves is very sparsely hairy consisting of a few very small patches of woolly hairs, or it is more or less glabrous. In this respect it is readily distinguished from all the species of its Subseries and the species of the Taliense Series. Other distinctive features are the small and narrow lanceolate or oblanceolate leaves, 3–6.8 cm. long, 0.6–2 cm. broad, with recurved margins, and the inflorescence of about 6 campanulate bright yellow flowers with minute crimson markings.

The species has been in cultivation for a long time, introduced by Forrest possibly in 1921. In its native home it grows 1–4 feet high; in cultivation it is a rounded compact shrub, 1½ feet high and as much across, well-filled with dark green leaves. It is a very slow grower and many years are required before it produces the flowers. However, the plant is perfectly hardy, a good foliage plant, and is well-suited for the rock garden. It is rare in cultivation. There was a remarkable plant growing in the rock garden, Royal Botanic Garden, Edinburgh; it was 1½ feet high and as much across, with lanceolate leaves glabrous on the lower surface. Unfortunately this plant has now been lost to cultivation.

Epithet. With a bell-shaped flower.
Hardiness 3. April–May.

R. cruentum Lévl. in Fedde Repert., Vol. 12 (1913) 284.

A shrub 92 cm.–1.22 m. (3–4 ft.) high or a small tree, *branchlets densely woolly with cinnamon-coloured or rusty-red wool*, glandular with medium-stalked glands, those below the inflorescences 5–7 mm. in diameter; leaf-bud scales deciduous. *Leaves* elliptic-lanceolate, oblong-lanceolate, oblong-elliptic or elliptic, lamina coriaceous, *2.8–8.3 cm. long, 1.5–3.7 cm. broad*, apex acute or acuminate, base obtuse or rounded; upper surface dark green, somewhat shining, slightly rugulose, glabrous, midrib grooved, densely woolly at the base, eglandular, primary veins 8–15 on each side, deeply impressed; *under surface covered with a thick, woolly, cinnamon-coloured or rusty-red, continuous, unistrate indumentum of Ramiform hairs*, with medium stem, and *very long branches often jointed*, without pellicle, midrib raised, densely woolly, eglandular, primary veins concealed; *petiole* 0.8–2.5 cm. long, stout, grooved above, *densely woolly with cinnamon-coloured or rusty-red wool*, moderately or sparsely glandular with medium- or long-stalked glands. *Inflorescence* a racemose umbel of 5–10 flowers; rhachis 3–4 mm. long, brown woolly, eglandular; *pedicel* 1–1.5 cm. long, *densely brown woolly*, moderately or sparsely glandular with medium-stalked glands. *Calyx* 5-lobed, *1–4 mm. long*, lobes ovate or oblong, outside densely brown hairy, moderately or sparsely glandular with short-stalked glands, margin hairy or glabrous, moderately or sparsely glandular with short-stalked glands. *Corolla* funnel-campanulate, *2–3 cm. long*, white or white flushed rose, without spots; lobes 5, 0.6–1.5 cm. long, 0.8–2 cm. broad, rounded, emarginate. *Stamens* 10, unequal, 0.8–2.6 cm. long, shorter than the corolla; filaments densely pubescent at the base. *Gynoecium* 2–2.6 cm. long, shorter than the corolla, longer than the stamens; *ovary* conoid, 3–4 mm. long, *densely brown hairy*, glandular with medium-stalked glands; style hairy on the lower half, glandular with medium-stalked glands on the lower half or at the base or eglandular. *Capsule* oblong-oval, 1.3 cm. long, 6 mm. broad, hairy, glandular with medium-stalked glands, calyx-lobes persistent.

This plant was first collected by E. E. Maire in May 1911 on the plateau of Ta-hai-tse, north of Tungchwan, north-east Yunnan. It was collected by him again on the mountains of Laitowpo, south of Tungchwan. Subsequently, McLaren's collectors found it at Tatsienlu, south-west Sichuan. It grows at elevations of 3,000–3,200 m. (9,836–10,492 ft.).

R. cruentum is closely allied to R. bureavii which it resembles in the cinnamon-coloured or rusty-red indumentum on the lower surface of the leaves, but differs markedly in that the corolla, calyx and usually the leaves are much smaller, and the indumentum on the lower surface of the leaves is unistrate. Moreover, it is very often a smaller plant 3–4 feet high.

There is no record of its occurrence in cultivation.

Epithet. Blood-red.

Not in cultivation.

R. detersile Franch. in Journ. de Bot., Vol. 12 (1898) 260.

A shrub, 92 cm.–1.22 m. (3–4 ft.) high, *branchlets densely woolly* with rust-coloured wool, eglandular, those below the inflorescences 4–5 mm. in diameter; *leaf-bud scales persistent. Leaves oblong or oblanceolate,* lamina coriaceous, 3–6 cm. long, 1–2 cm. broad, apex obtuse or shortly acuminate, mucronate, base obtuse or cordulate; *upper surface shining, rugulose,* glabrous or with vestiges of hairs, midrib grooved, glabrous or hairy at the base, primary veins 10–12 on each side, deeply impressed; *margin recurved; under surface with a thick, woolly, patchy,* brown, *discontinuous, unistrate indumentum of Ramiform hairs with a long stem and very long narrow, jointed branches,* without pellicle, midrib prominent, hairy, eglandular, primary veins somewhat concealed; *petiole* 3–6 mm. long, grooved above, *densely or moderately woolly* with rust-coloured or brown wool, eglandular. *Inflorescence* a racemose umbel of 4–8 flowers; rhachis 2–3 mm. long, brown woolly, eglandular; pedicel 1–1.5 cm. long, densely or moderately brown woolly, moderately or rather densely glandular with short- and medium-stalked glands. *Calyx* 5-lobed, 3–4 mm. long, lobes oblong or oblong-oval, outside hairy or glabrous, glandular with short-stalked glands, margin glabrous, rather densely glandular with short-stalked glands. *Corolla* campanulate, 2.3–3 cm. long, reddish; lobes 5, 0.8–1 cm. long, 0.9–1.2 cm. broad, rounded, emarginate. *Stamens* 10, unequal, 1.1–2 cm. long, shorter than the corolla; filaments rather densely pubescent towards the base. *Gynoecium* 2.3–2.5 cm. long, as long as the corolla or slightly longer, longer than the stamens; *ovary* conoid, 5 mm. long, 5-celled, *densely hairy* with long hairs, *moderately or rather densely glandular* with medium-stalked glands; style glabrous, eglandular. *Capsule* oblong, 1–1.6 cm. long, 4–5 mm. broad, straight or slightly curved, glabrous or sparsely hairy, moderately or rather densely glandular with long-stalked glands, calyx-lobes persistent.

R. detersile was discovered by the French missionary R. P. Farges in eastern Sichuan, and was described by Franchet in 1898. It was afterwards found by Forrest in the Chienchuan-Mekong Divide, mid-west Yunnan. The plant grows on rocks and rocky slopes at elevations of 2,500–3,355 m. (8,197–11,000 ft.).

The diagnostic features of the plant are the thick, woolly, patchy indumentum on the lower surface of the leaves, and the persistent leaf-bud scales. Other distinctive features are the oblong or oblanceolate leaves, laminae 3–6 cm. long, 1–2 cm. broad, upper surface rugulose, margins recurved, and the densely or moderately woolly branchlets and petioles. The indumentum on the lower surface of the leaves is unistrate, the hairs are Ramiform with a long stem and very long narrow, jointed branches.

R. detersile shows a resemblance to the species of the Roxieanum Subseries in the persistent leaf-bud scales, in the small narrow leaves, and in the small corolla 2.3–3 cm. long. It also has a strong affinity with the members of the Adenogynum Subseries to which it belongs.

The plant has not been introduced into cultivation.
Epithet. Clean.
Not in cultivation.

R. detonsum Balf. f. et Forrest in Notes Roy. Bot. Gard. Edin., Vol. 11 (1919) 48.
Illustration. Bot. Mag. 157 t. 9359 (1934).

A broadly upright and spreading, or a bushy shrub, 2.44–3.66 m. (8–12 ft.) high, branchlets floccose, moderately or sparsely glandular with short-stalked glands, those below the inflorescences 4–6 mm. in diameter; leaf-bud scales deciduous. *Leaves* oblong-lanceolate or oblong, lamina coriaceous, 6.2–15.5 cm. long, 2–5 cm. broad, apex obtuse or shortly acuminate, base obtuse or rounded; upper surface dark green, somewhat shining, glabrous or with vestiges of hairs, eglandular, midrib grooved, glabrous or hairy, eglandular or glandular with short-stalked glands, primary veins 14–20 on each side, deeply impressed; *under surface with brown or fawn, closely or widely scattered tufts of hairs, or with a thin veil of hairs, or with a very thin, continuous or discontinuous, unistrate indumentum of Long-rayed hairs with long arms,* midrib prominent, glabrous or hairy, eglandular or glandular with short-stalked glands, primary veins slightly raised; petiole 1.8–3 cm. long, grooved above, floccose, moderately or sparsely glandular with short-stalked glands. *Inflorescence* a racemose umbel of 6–11 flowers; *rhachis 0.8–2.5 cm. long,* sparsely or moderately floccose, sparsely glandular with short-stalked glands or eglandular; *pedicel 2.4–5.6 cm. long,* sparsely or moderately floccose, glandular with short-stalked glands. *Calyx* 5-lobed, 3–5 mm. long, lobes ovate or oblong-ovate, outside glabrous, moderately or sparsely glandular with short-stalked glands, margin glabrous, rather densely glandular with short-stalked glands. *Corolla* funnel-campanulate, *4.5–5.2 cm. long,* rose-pink or pink, with a few crimson spots; lobes 5 or sometimes 6 or 7, 1.5–2 cm. long, 2.2–3 cm. broad, rounded, emarginate. *Stamens* 10–14, unequal, shorter than the corolla; filaments densely pubescent at the base or on the lower one-third of their length. *Gynoecium* 3.8–4.6 cm. long, shorter than the corolla, longer than the stamens; *ovary* oblong or conoid, 5–6 mm. long, 6–8-celled, glabrous, *densely glandular* with short-stalked glands; style glabrous, glandular on the lower two-thirds of its length with medium-stalked glands. *Capsule* oblong or oblong-oval, 2–2.3 cm. long, 0.9–1 cm. broad, straight or slightly curved, glabrous, moderately or rather densely glandular with short-stalked glands, calyx-lobes persistent.

Forrest discovered this plant in May 1917 on the eastern flank of the Sungkwei Divide, north-west Yunnan, growing on the margins of mixed forests at elevations of 3,050–3,355 m. (10,000–11,000 ft.).

R. xenosporum, an undescribed plant, is a natural hybrid. It appeared as a rogue, raised by Magor, from *R. adenogynum* seed under Forrest Nos. 5868, 5871.

The main features of *R. detonsum* are the large oblong-lanceolate or oblong leaves, under surface with scattered tufts of hairs, or with a thin veil of hairs, or with a very thin, continuous or discontinuous unistrate indumentum of Long-rayed hairs with long arms. Other marked characteristics are the large racemose inflorescence of 6–11 flowers, the long rhachis 8 mm.–2.5 cm. long, the long pedicels 2.4–5.6 cm. long, and the large funnel-campanulate corolla 4.5–5.2 cm. long. The species is closely related to *R. prattii,* but is distinguished by notable features.

R. detonsum was introduced by Forrest in 1917 (No. 13789—the Type number). It flowered for the first time in the Royal Botanic Garden, Edinburgh in 1930. In cultivation it is a broadly upright and spreading, or a bushy shrub, 8–12 feet high. The plant is hardy, a vigorous grower, and easy to cultivate. It has proved to be most attractive with its large rose-pink flowers produced in great profusion. The plant is uncommon in cultivation but is very desirable for inclusion in every collection of rhododendrons. There was a magnificent plant growing in the Royal Botanic Garden, Edinburgh, 8 feet high, free-flowering, with large trusses of rose-pink flowers; it has now ceased to exist.

Epithet. Shorn.

Hardiness 3. April–May.

R. elegantulum Tagg et Forrest in Notes Roy. Bot. Gard. Edin., Vol. 15 (1927) 311.

A broadly upright or somewhat compact shrub, 92 cm.–1.83 m. (3–6 ft.) high, *branchlets densely woolly with cinnamon-coloured or rusty-red wool*, sparsely glandular with long-stalked glands or eglandular, those below the inflorescences 5–7 mm. in diameter; leaf-bud scales deciduous. *Leaves* oblong-lanceolate or lanceolate, lamina coriaceous, 4–9 cm. long, *1.3–3.1 cm. broad*, apex acute, base rounded or cordulate; upper surface light green, matt, slightly rugulose, glabrous or with vestiges of hairs, midrib grooved, densely woolly in the lower half or at the base, eglandular, primary veins 12–18 on each side, deeply impressed; *under surface covered with a thick, felty somewhat woolly, cinnamon-coloured or rusty-red, continuous, unistrate indumentum of Ramiform hairs* with very short or medium stem, and *medium or long narrow branches, not jointed*, without pellicle, (*indumentum under young leaves deep pinkish-red*), midrib raised, densely or moderately woolly, eglandular, primary veins concealed; *petiole* 1–1.9 cm. long, grooved above, *densely woolly with cinnamon-coloured or rusty-red wool*, eglandular or slightly glandular with medium-stalked glands. *Inflorescence* a racemose umbel of 6–20 flowers; rhachis 0.6–1 cm. long, hairy, eglandular; pedicel 1–2 cm. long, densely floccose, glandular with short- or medium-stalked glands. *Calyx* 5-lobed, 0.5–1 cm. long, lobes oblong or oblong-oval, outside hairy, glandular with short-stalked glands, margin ciliate, rather densely glandular with short-stalked glands. *Corolla* funnel-campanulate, *2.6–3.3 cm. long, pale purplish-pink*, with darker spots; lobes 5, 1–1.4 cm. long, 1–1.6 cm. broad, rounded, emarginate. *Stamens* 10, unequal, 1.2–2.7 cm. long, shorter than the corolla; filaments rather densely pubescent at the base. *Gynoecium* 2.4–3 cm. long, as long as the corolla or shorter, longer than the stamens; *ovary* conoid, 4–5 mm. long, *glabrous, densely glandular* with short- and medium-stalked glands; *style glabrous* or slightly hairy at the base, glandular with medium-stalked glands at the base. *Capsule* oblong, 1–1.5 cm. long, 5–6 mm. broad, straight or slightly curved, glabrous, rather densely glandular with medium- and long-stalked glands, calyx-lobes persistent.

This species was discovered by Kingdon-Ward in May 1922 at Yung-ning, southwest Sichuan. Later in June of that year, Forrest found it on the mountains east of Yungning in the same region. It grows on steep sheltered slopes amongst Larch and *Abies*, and on open bouldery slopes and meadows, at elevations of 3,660–3,965 m. (12,000–13,000 ft.).

R. elegantulum is closely related to *R. bureavii* which it resembles in some features, but differs in that the leaves are usually narrower, the corolla is smaller, the ovary is glabrous, the style is usually glabrous, and the indumentum on the lower surface of the leaves is unistrate more felty and less woolly.

The species was introduced by Forrest in 1922 (No. 21292). In cultivation it is a broadly upright or somewhat compact shrub 4–6 feet high. It is a fine foliage plant, with charming felty indumentum on the lower surface of the leaves, deep pinkish-red on the under surface of the young leaves, turning to cinnamon-coloured or rusty-red under the adult leaves. The species takes some years to reach the flowering stage. It varies in its freedom of flowering. Some plants are shy flowerers; other plants bloom freely, and provide a fine display with pale purplish-pink flowers in trusses of 6–20. The plant often sets good fertile seed in plenty. It is hardy, uncommon in cultivation, but is worthy of being widely grown.

Epithet. Elegant.

Hardiness 3. May.

R. faberi Hemsley in Journ. Linn. Soc. Bot. Vol. 26 (1889) 22.

Syn. *R. faberioides* Balf. f. in Notes Roy. Bot. Gard. Edin., Vol. 13 (1920) 44.

A broadly upright shrub, 1–6 m. (3⅓–20 ft.) high, *branchlets densely woolly, or densely tomentose* with a somewhat thin tomentum, wool and tomentum rust-coloured, brown or whitish, moderately or sparsely glandular with short-stalked glands, those below the inflorescences 4–6 mm. in diameter; leaf-bud scales deciduous. *Leaves* oblong-elliptic, elliptic, oblong-lanceolate, oblong-oval or obovate, lamina coriaceous, 4.5–12 cm. long, 1.8–4.5 cm. broad, apex acute or acuminate, base rounded, cordulate or obtuse; upper surface dark green, matt, slightly rugulose, glabrous or with vestiges of hairs, midrib grooved, glabrous or woolly or floccose, primary veins 10–16 on each side, deeply impressed; *under surface covered with* a medium thickness or *thick, woolly, rust-coloured or dark brown, continuous, bistrate indumentum of hairs, upper layer Ramiform with minute stem and medium or long, narrow branches often jointed, lower layer Rosulate, without pellicle, upper layer is mostly shed at maturity revealing a thin whitish lower layer,* midrib prominent, hairy or glabrous, eglandular or glandular with short-stalked glands, primary veins slightly raised or concealed; *petiole* 0.8–2 cm. long, grooved above, *densely woolly, or densely or moderately tomentose* with a somewhat thin tomentum, wool and tomentum rust-coloured, brown or whitish, moderately or sparsely glandular with short-stalked glands or eglandular. *Inflorescence* a racemose umbel of 6–12 flowers; rhachis 0.6–1 cm. long, floccose, eglandular; *pedicel* 1.2–2.5 cm. long, glabrous or moderately or densely floccose, *rather densely or moderately glandular* with short- or long-stalked glands. *Calyx* 5-lobed, *0.6–1 cm. long,* lobes oblong, oblong-ovate, ovate, oblong-oval or oval, *outside* glabrous or floccose, *moderately or sparsely glandular* with short-stalked glands or eglandular, *margin* glabrous or ciliate, *moderately or rather densely glandular* with short-stalked glands. *Corolla* funnel-campanulate or campanulate, 3.8–4 cm. long, *white,* with or without a blotch at the base, and with or without red spots; lobes 5, 1–1.5 cm. long, 1.5–2 cm. broad, rounded, emarginate. *Stamens* 10, unequal, 1.3–2.4 cm. long, shorter than the corolla; filaments moderately puberulous or rather densely pubescent at the base. *Gynoecium* 2.7–3 cm. long, shorter than the corolla, longer than the stamens; *ovary* conoid, 4–5 mm. long, 6–7-celled, glabrous or densely hairy with long brown hairs, *densely or moderately setulose-glandular;* style glabrous or hairy at the base, eglandular or rarely glandular at the base with short-stalked glands. *Capsule* oblong, 1.2–2 cm. long, 5–7 mm. broad, straight or slightly curved, glabrous, glandular with medium- or long-stalked glands, calyx-lobes persistent.

This plant was discovered by Rev. E. Faber about 1887 on the summit of Mt. Omei, in western Sichuan, and was described by Hemsley in 1889. Subsequently it was found by Wilson, Fang, and Hu in the same area. It grows in thickets at elevations of 3,050–3,355 m. (10,000–11,000 ft.).

In 1920, the name *R. faberioides* Balf. f. was given to a plant No. 3436 collected by Wilson in western Sichuan. It was said to differ from *R. faberi* "in having the pedicels, calyx and ovary hairy as well as glandular". These characteristics, however, are shared by *R. faberi.*

The notable features of this plant are the thick woolly, rust-coloured or dark brown continuous bistrate indumentum of hairs on the lower surface of the leaves, and the densely woolly or densely tomentose branchlets and petioles. Worth noting is the fact that the upper layer of Ramiform hairs is mostly shed at maturity revealing a thin, whitish lower layer of Rosulate hairs.

R. faberi resembles *R. prattii* in some features, but is readily distinguished by the thick woolly, rust-coloured or dark brown continuous bistrate indumentum of hairs on the lower surface of the leaves, upper layer Ramiform, lower layer Rosulate; in *R. prattii* the indumentum consists of a thin veil of hairs, or a thin unistrate layer of hairs, or closely scattered tufts of hairs, the hairs being Long-rayed.

R. faberi was first introduced by Wilson in 1904. In its native home it grows 3–20 feet high. In cultivation it is a broadly upright shrub up to 8 feet, with campanulate white flowers in trusses of 6–12. It is hardy, easy to grow, but is rare in cultivation.

Epithet. After Rev. E. Faber, who collected in China during 1887–1891.

Hardiness 3. May.

R. mimetes Tagg et Forrest in Notes Roy. Bot. Gard. Edin., Vol. 15 (1927) 315.

Syn. *R. ochrocalyx* Franch. nomen nudum.

A broadly upright shrub, 92 cm.–2.14 m. (3–7 ft.) high, branchlets moderately or sparsely floccose, moderately or sparsely glandular with short-stalked glands, those below the inflorescences 4–7 mm. in diameter; leaf-bud scales deciduous. *Leaves elliptic, oblong-elliptic or oblong-lanceolate, lamina coriaceous, 5.5–11 cm. long, 2.5–5 cm. broad, apex obtuse, shortly acuminate or acute, base rounded or obtuse; upper surface dark green, shining, slightly rugulose, glabrous or with vestiges of hairs, midrib grooved, glabrous or floccose, eglandular or glandular with short-stalked glands, primary veins 12–18 on each side, deeply impressed; under surface covered with a somewhat thick, woolly, brown, continuous, bistrate indumentum of hairs, upper layer Ramiform with very short or medium stem, branches long, ribbon-like or narrow, lower layer Rosulate, upper layer is worn off in small or large patches revealing a thin whitish or fawn lower layer, without pellicle, midrib prominent, glabrous or moderately or densely hairy, glandular with short-stalked glands or eglandular, primary veins concealed or slightly raised; petiole 1–2 cm. long, grooved above, floccose, glandular with short-stalked glands or eglandular.* Inflorescence *a racemose umbel of 6–10 flowers; rhachis 0.5–1 cm. long, floccose, eglandular; pedicel 1.2–2.5 cm. long, densely or moderately floccose,* glandular with short-stalked glands or eglandular. Calyx *5-lobed, 2–7 mm. long, lobes unequal, ovate, rounded or oblong-oval, outside hairy or glabrous, glandular with short-stalked glands or eglandular, margin ciliate or eciliate, glandular with short-stalked glands or eglandular.* Corolla *funnel-campanulate, 2.8–4.8 cm. long, white, white faintly flushed and margined rose, or pinkish-purple,* with or without a red blotch at the base, and with or without crimson spots; lobes 5, 1.3–1.6 cm. long, 1.8–2.6 cm. broad, rounded, emarginate. Stamens *10, unequal, 1.5–3.2 cm. long, shorter than the corolla; filaments rather densely or moderately pubescent towards the base.* Gynoecium *2.2–3.7 cm. long, shorter than the corolla, longer than the stamens; ovary conoid, 3–6 mm. long, 6-celled, densely or sparsely hairy with long brown hairs, eglandular or sparsely or densely glandular with long- or short-stalked glands;* style glabrous or hairy at the base with long hairs, eglandular or rather densely glandular in the lower half with short- and medium-stalked glands. Capsule *oblong or oblong-oval, 1.2–1.4 cm. long, 5–7 mm. broad, straight or slightly curved, glabrous, rather densely glandular with medium-stalked glands,* calyx-lobes persistent.

Forrest discovered this plant in June 1921 on the mountains around Muli, south-west Sichuan. He found it again in June 1922 on the mountains, north-east of Muli, in the same region. It grows in thickets, on the margins of forests, and amongst rock and scrub on slopes in gullies, at elevations of 3,355–3,660 m. (11,000–12,000 ft.).

R. mimetes is closely allied to *R. faberi* which it resembles in the thick, woolly, continuous, bistrate indumentum on the lower surface of the leaves, upper layer wearing off in small or large patches. It differs in that the branchlets and petioles are moderately or sparsely floccose, the ovary is often densely hairy eglandular, and the calyx is often smaller.

The species was introduced by Forrest in 1921 (No. 20419). In its native home it grows 3–7 feet high; in cultivation it is a broadly upright shrub of 4–5 feet. It is hardy outdoors, a robust grower, with rigid branchlets. The large white faintly flushed rose flowers are produced freely in trusses of 6–10. The plant is rare in cultivation.

Epithet. Imitative.

Hardiness 3. May.

R. mimetes Tagg et Forrest var. **simulans** Tagg et Forrest in Notes Roy. Bot. Gard. Edin., Vol. 15 (1927) 316.

> Syn. *R. simulans* (Tagg et Forrest) Chamberlain in Notes Roy. Bot. Gard. Edin., Vol. 39 (1982) 343.

This plant is represented by a single gathering made by Forrest in June 1921 on the mountains around Muli, south-west Sichuan, growing in rhododendron thickets in side valleys at an elevation of 3,660 m. (12,000 ft.).

The variety differs from the species in that the leaves are ovate or oblong-ovate, the base is cordulate, the under surface is covered with a thick, spongy, continuous, bistrate indumentum of hairs, the upper surface splitting into very small patches (mottling), and the ovary is glabrous.

It was introduced by Forrest in 1921 (No. 20428—the Type number). In cultivation it is a broadly upright shrub 5 feet high, well-filled with dark green foliage. It is hardy, and makes a fine show with its large, funnel-campanulate, white or pinkish-purple flowers produced freely in trusses of 6–8. The plant is rare in cultivation.

Epithet. Resembling.
Hardiness 3. May.

R. nigroglandulosum Nitzelius in Rhododendrons with Magnolias and Camellias (1975) 26–30.

A shrub, 2–5 m. (6½–16 ft.) high, branchlets densely tomentose with fawn tomentum, *glandular with black* short-stalked *glands*, those below the inflorescences 5–6 mm. in diameter; leaf-bud scales deciduous. *Leaves* lanceolate, oblanceolate or oblong, lamina coriaceous, 12–17 cm. long, *3.2–5 cm. broad*, apex abruptly acute, mucronate, base cuneate or tapered; upper surface dark green, glabrous, eglandular, midrib grooved, glabrous, *glandular with black* short-stalked *glands*, primary veins 10–18 on each side, deeply impressed; margin flat; *under surface covered with a somewhat thick woolly*, reddish-brown or brown, continuous, *bistrate* indumentum of *hairs, upper layer Ramiform with medium stem and long narrow branches, lower layer Rosulate, midrib* prominent, hairy, *glandular with black* short-stalked *glands*, primary veins concealed; *petiole* 1.5–3 cm. long, grooved above, moderately or densely fawn floccose, moderately or sparsely *glandular with black* short-stalked *glands*. *Inflorescence* a racemose umbel of 8–10 flowers; rhachis 1–1.5 cm. long, pubescent, eglandular; *pedicel* 1–3 cm. long, rather densely floccose, *eglandular* or rarely glandular with black or dark brown short-stalked glands. *Calyx* 5-lobed, minute, *1 mm. long*, lobes triangular, *outside and margin* floccose, *eglandular*. *Corolla* campanulate, 3.2–5 cm. long, deep pink at first, later yellowish-pink, with purple spots; lobes 5, 1.6–1.8 cm. long, 1.8–2 cm. broad, rounded, emarginate. *Stamens* 10, unequal, 1.3–2.5 cm. long, shorter than the corolla; filaments puberulous towards the base. *Gynoecium* 3.4–4 cm. long, as long as the corolla or shorter, longer than the stamens; *ovary* conoid, 4–5 mm. long, *tomentose, glandular* with brown short-stalked glands; *style* glabrous, *eglandular*. *Capsule* oblong, 1.5–2 cm. long, about 8 mm. broad, glabrous or with vestiges of hairs, *glandular* with brown short-stalked glands, calyx-lobes persistent.

R. nigroglandulosum was described by Nitzelius from a cultivated plant raised at Goteborg from seed collected by H. Smith in 1934 at Kina, Tapanshan, Sikang, at an elevation of 3,500 m. (11,475 ft.).

The species shows a strong resemblance to *R. adenogynum* in general appearance, but differs in that the branchlets and petioles are densely tomentose, the glands on the branchlets, petioles and midrib on both surfaces of the leaves are black, the pedicels, calyx and styles are eglandular, and the leaves are often broader.

The plant was introduced by H. Smith in 1934 (No. 13979—the Type number). It is hardy outdoors with trusses of 8–10 yellowish-pink flowers, but is rare in cultivation.

Epithet. With black glands.
Hardiness 3. April–May.

R. prattii Franch. in Journ. de Bot. Vol. 9 (1895) 389.

    Syn. *R. leei* Fang in Acta Phytotax. Sin. Vol. 2 (1952) 82.

        R. faberi Hemsley subsp. *prattii* (Franch.) Chamberlain in Notes Roy. Bot. Gard. Edin., Vol. 36 (1978) 120.

A rounded somewhat compact shrub, or bush or tree, 1–6.40 m. (3⅓–21 ft.) high, *branchlets densely tomentose with a thin,* whitish or brown *tomentum,* sparsely or moderately glandular with short-stalked glands, those below the inflorescences 5–8 mm. in diameter; leaf-bud scales deciduous. *Leaves broadly elliptic, elliptic or oblong-elliptic,* lamina coriaceous, 7.4–18 cm. (or rarely 6.3 cm.) long, 3.4–7.8 cm. (or rarely 2.8 cm.) broad, apex acuminate, base rounded, obtuse or cordulate; upper surface dark green, shining, glabrous or with vestiges of hairs, eglandular, midrib grooved, glabrous or with vestiges of hairs, eglandular, primary veins 12–18 on each side, deeply impressed; *under surface with a thin,* fawn or brown *veil of hairs, or with a thin, continuous, unistrate indumentum of hairs, or with closely scattered tufts of hairs, the hairs Long-rayed,* midrib prominent, hairy, moderately or sparsely glandular with short-stalked glands or eglandular, primary veins slightly raised; *petiole* 1.5–3.5 cm. long, thick, grooved above, *densely tomentose with a thin,* whitish or brown *tomentum,* moderately or sparsely glandular with short-stalked glands or eglandular. *Inflorescence* a racemose umbel of 6–14 or sometimes 20 flowers; rhachis 0.8–2 cm. long, rather densely or moderately hairy, sparsely glandular with short-stalked glands or eglandular; pedicel 1.5–4.2 cm. long, rather densely or moderately hairy, sparsely or rather densely glandular with short- or medium-stalked glands. *Calyx* 5-lobed, *0.5–1 cm.* or rarely *1.5 cm. long,* lobes oblong-oval, oval or oblong, outside hairy or glabrous, glandular with short-stalked glands or rarely eglandular, margin glabrous or hairy, rather densely glandular with short-stalked glands. *Corolla* funnel-campanulate or campanulate, 3.6–5.6 cm. long, *white, with red spots;* lobes 5, 1.2–1.6 cm. long, 1.5–3 cm. broad, rounded, emarginate. *Stamens* 10, unequal, 1.3–3 cm. long, shorter than the corolla; filaments densely or moderately pubescent at the base or on the lower one-third of their length. *Gynoecium* 3–4.6 cm. long, shorter than the corolla, longer than the stamens; *ovary* conoid or ovoid, 4–6 mm. long, 5–8-celled, brown *hairy* or rarely glabrous, *densely or moderately glandular* with short- or medium-stalked glands; style glabrous, glandular with short-stalked glands at the base or on the lower one-third of its length. *Capsule* oblong, 1.6–2 cm. long, 5–7 mm. broad, straight or slightly curved, hairy or glabrous, *rather densely or moderately glandular* with medium-stalked glands, calyx-lobes persistent.

This species was first collected by Pratt and by the Abbé Soulié in 1890 near Tatsienlu, in western Sichuan, and was described by Franchet in 1895. It was afterwards found by Wilson, Fang, Rock, and McLaren's collectors in other localities near Tatsienlu. The plant grows in thickets, woodlands, forests, and at the margins of forests, at elevations of 2,600–4,500 m. (8,525–14,754 ft.).

R. prattii has been confused with *R. faberi* and they have been regarded by some as the same species. It would appear that *R. prattii* has been wrongly identified in the *Plantae Wilsonianae* (Vol. 1, p. 533), and distributed to gardens from the Coombe Wood Nursery under the name *R. faberi*. It is to be noted that Franchet described the leaves of *R. prattii* as being glabrous, and this was perhaps the reason for the confusion in gardens.

R. prattii and *R. faberi* are two very distinct species, and are easily recognised particularly in cultivation. The main distinctions between them are that in *R. prattii* the indumentum on the lower surface of the leaves consists of a thin veil of hairs, or thin continuous, or closely scattered tufts of hairs, it is fawn or brown, unistrate, and the hairs are Long-rayed; the branchlets and petioles are densely tomentose with a thin, whitish or brown tomentum; and the leaves and corolla are usually larger. In *R. faberi* the indumentum on the lower surface of the leaves is thick, woolly, continuous, rust-coloured or dark brown, bistrate, upper layer Ramiform, lower layer Rosulate, upper layer is mostly shed at maturity revealing a thin whitish lower layer; the branchlets and petioles are usually densely woolly with rust-coloured or brown wool; and the leaves and corolla are usually smaller.

R. *prattii* was introduced by Wilson in 1904. In its native home it is a shrub or tree, 3–21 feet high; in cultivation it is a rounded somewhat compact shrub up to 8–10 feet high and as much across. The plant is hardy outdoors, but as it comes from elevations of 8,525–14,754 feet, its hardiness varies to a certain extent. Along the east coast, to be able to grow it successfully, it should be given a sheltered position from wind. It is a vigorous grower, free-flowering with large campanulate white flowers with red spots. The plant often produces a few oblong capsules containing fertile seeds. In the Royal Botanic Garden, Edinburgh, the species was represented by two remarkable plants, 6–8 feet high and almost as much across, free-flowering with large trusses of white flowers. It is regrettable these plants have now been lost to cultivation.

A clone 'Percy Wood' was given an Award of Merit when shown by Major A. E. Hardy, Sandling Park, Kent, in 1967.

Epithet. After A. E. Pratt who discovered the species near Tatsienlu.
Hardiness 3. April–May.

R. wuense Balf. f. in Notes Roy. Bot. Gard. Edin., Vol. 13 (1920) 64.

A shrub, about 5.50 m. (18 ft.) high, branchlets at first with a thick, dense, rust-coloured tomentum. *Leaves* oblong-lanceolate, oblanceolate or oblong-elliptic, lamina coriaceous, up to 8.5 cm. long, up to 4 cm. broad, apex acute, base rounded, cordulate or obtuse; upper surface matt, minutely rugulose, glabrous, midrib grooved, with vestiges of hairs; *under surface with a dense, woolly, rust-coloured indumentum of hairs*, midrib raised, glandular; petiole about 1.5 cm. long, with thick, dense, rust-coloured tomentum. *Inflorescence* a racemose umbel of few flowers; rhachis about 1 cm. long, puberulous; *pedicel* about 1.5 cm. long, *densely tomentose, glandular* with medium-stalked glands. *Calyx* 5-lobed, 0.6–1 cm. long, lobes oblong or oblong-oval, *outside* glabrous, *eglandular*, margin glabrous, rather densely glandular with short-stalked glands. *Corolla* funnel-campanulate or campanulate, *2.8–3.5 cm. long*, (colour not known); lobes 5, about 1 cm. long, 1.3–2 cm. broad, rounded, emarginate. *Stamens* 10, unequal, 1.3–1.4 cm. long, much shorter than the corolla; filaments densely pubescent at the base. *Gynoecium* 2.3 cm. long, shorter than the corolla, longer than the stamens; *ovary ovoid, 3 mm. long, densely hairy with long,* dark brown *hairs, glandular* with long-stalked glands; style glabrous, glandular at the base with medium-stalked glands. *Capsule*:—

This plant is known from a single collection (No. 3960) made by Wilson, possibly in 1909, on Mt. Wu, in south-west Sichuan, and was described by Isaac Bayley Balfour in 1920.

It shows considerable resemblance to R. *faberi* particularly in the shape and size of the leaves, in the thick woolly, rust-coloured indumentum on the lower surface of the leaves, and in the size of the calyx, but differs in the smaller corolla 2.8–3.5 cm. long, in the ovoid small ovary 3 mm. long, densely hairy with long hairs, in the calyx eglandular outside, and in a few minor features. There would appear to be no significant difference between these two plants. Meanwhile, the name R. *wuense* may be allowed to stand until more adequate material is available.

The plant has not been introduced into cultivation.
Epithet. From Mt. Wu, Sichuan.
Not in cultivation.

ROXIEANUM SUBSERIES

General characters: shrubs or rarely trees, 60 cm.–4.58 m. (2–15 ft.) high, or sometimes creeping or prostrate or matted or spreading shrub 8–60 cm. (3 in.–2 ft.) high; *annual growths and internodes short* or rarely long; branchlets densely or moderately woolly or tomentose or rarely densely bristly, rarely glabrous, eglandular or rather densely or moderately glandular with short-stalked glands, rarely densely bristly-glandular, leaf-bud scales persistent or deciduous. Leaves lanceolate, oblanceolate, oblong-lanceolate, oblong, linear or linear-lanceolate, lamina 5–19 cm. or sometimes 1.3–4 cm. long, 1–4.3 cm. or sometimes 2–8 mm. broad; under surface covered with a thick woolly or sometimes thin, continuous, bistrate indumentum, upper layer Ramiform or Long-rayed hairs, in *R. bathyphyllum, R. lampropeplum* and *R. proteoides* unistrate, petiole densely or moderately woolly or tomentose or rarely glabrous, eglandular or moderately or rather densely glandular with short-stalked glands. *Inflorescence a compact* or sometimes lax *racemose umbel* of 6–20 or rarely 4 flowers; pedicel 0.6–3.2 cm. long, densely or moderately or sometimes sparsely tomentose or rarely glabrous, eglandular or moderately or densely glandular with short-stalked glands. *Calyx* 5-lobed, *0.5–1 mm.,* rarely 2 mm. *long.* Corolla campanulate or funnel-campanulate, 1.9–4.5 cm. long, white, white flushed rose, pink, rose, creamy-white, creamy-yellow or yellow, without or sometimes with a crimson blotch at the base. Stamens 10. Ovary oblong, conoid or sometimes slender or rarely ovoid, 3–6 mm. long, 5–8-celled, densely or moderately or sparsely tomentose or glabrous, densely or moderately or rarely sparsely glandular with short-stalked glands or eglandular. Capsule oblong, or sometimes conoid or ovoid, or rarely slender, moderately or sparsely hairy or glabrous, eglandular or sometimes moderately or sparsely glandular with short-stalked glands.

KEY TO THE SPECIES

A. Branchlets and petioles densely bristly and densely bristly-glandular, pedicels densely or moderately bristly-glandular; calyx large 5–8 mm. long ... *recurvoides*

A. Branchlets, petioles and pedicels not bristly, not bristly-glandular; calyx minute 0.5–1 mm. or rarely 2 mm. long.

  B. Indumentum on the under surface of the leaves thin or somewhat granular or thinly felty, the upper layer often detersile falling off in small or large patches, *hairs very Long-rayed or Long-rayed* (except in *R. russotinctum, Ramiform*); branchlets and petioles densely or moderately tomentose with a thin tomentum; margins of leaves flat or slightly recurved.

   C. Ovary, pedicel and calyx usually eglandular.

      D. Ovary densely tomentose; corolla usually with a crimson blotch at the base; leaves (laminae) up to 17.5 cm. long; indumentum on the under surface of the leaves thin, the upper layer detersile usually falling off in small patches .... *triplonaevium*

      D. Ovary usually sparsely floccose or glabrous; corolla usually without a crimson blotch at the base; leaves (laminae) usually up to 12 cm. long; indumentum on the under surface of the leaves somewhat thick, compact felty, upper layer not detersile not falling off .... *iodes*

   C. Ovary, pedicel and calyx densely or moderately glandular with short-stalked glands.

    E. Inflorescence 10–15-flowered; branchlets, petioles and midrib on the under surface of the leaves eglandular; ovary tomentose; corolla 2.9–4 cm. long; branchlets with short internodes; hairs of the indumentum on the under surface of the leaves Long-rayed with very long or long arms...................... *tritifolium*

    E. Inflorescence about 8-flowered; branchlets, petioles and midrib on the under surface of the leaves rather densely or moderately glandular with short-stalked glands; ovary not tomentose; corolla 2.4–3 cm. long; branchlets with long internodes; hairs of the indumentum on the under surface of the leaves Ramiform...
.... *russotinctum*

B. Indumentum on the under surface of the leaves thickly woolly, the upper layer not detersile not falling off, *hairs Ramiform*; branchlets and petioles densely or moderately woolly (except in *R. pronum*, glabrous); margins of leaves usually markedly recurved.

    F. Ovary densely or moderately tomentose and/or densely or moderately glandular with short-stalked glands.

        G. Pedicel, calyx and ovary densely or moderately glandular with short-stalked glands........................... *roxieanum*
                                              (part)

        G. Pedicel, calyx and ovary eglandular.

            H. Inflorescence compact usually 10–20-flowered; leaves (laminae) 2.5–12.5 cm. long, 1–3 cm. broad; corolla white, white flushed rose, creamy-white, or sometimes pink or rose.

                I. Leaves lanceolate, oblanceolate, oblong, oblong-lanceolate, oblong-elliptic or oblong-obovate, lamina 4–13 cm. long, 9 mm.–4 cm. broad; indumentum on the under surface of the leaves unistrate or bistrate; often a medium-sized shrub, 92 cm.–1.53 m. (3–5 ft.) high.

                    J. Leaves usually oblong, apex obtuse, base obtuse; indumentum on the under surface of the leaves unistrate...................... *bathyphyllum*

                    J. Leaves lanceolate, oblanceolate, oblong-lanceolate, oblong-elliptic or oblong-obovate, apex usually acute, acuminate or shortly acuminate, base tapered or obtuse; indumentum on the under surface of the leaves *bistrate*.

                        K. Calyx not hairy or moderately hairy; ovary moderately hairy; corolla white.

                            L. Leaves (laminae) usually 4.5–7.5 cm. long, 1.5–2.5 cm. broad ... *globigerum*
                                        (part)

                            L. Leaves (laminae) usually 8–13 cm. long, 2.5–4 cm. broad .... *cucullatum*

                      K. Calyx and ovary usually densely tomentose; corolla creamy-white, white, white flushed rose, pink, rose, or rarely yellow ....
                              .... *roxieanum*
                                            (part)

                I. Leaves narrowly oblong or narrowly oblanceolate, lamina 1.3–4 cm. long, usually 4–8 mm. broad; indumentum on the under surface of the leaves unistrate; usually a dwarf shrub, 8–60 cm. (3 in.–2 ft.) high.................................. *proteoides*

     H. Inflorescence lax 4–8-flowered; leaves (laminae) 2.5–5 cm. long, 6 mm.–1.7 cm. broad; corolla deep or pale rose . . . . *comisteum*

F. Ovary glabrous, eglandular.
    M. Dwarf or small shrubs, usually 8–92 cm. (3 in.–3 ft.) high; inflorescence 6–12-flowered; leaves oblong, oblong-obovate, or sometimes lanceolate or oblanceolate; pedicel moderately floccose or glabrous.
        N. Small, compact spreading or broadly upright shrub, usually 60–92 cm. (2–3 ft.) high; branchlets and petioles densely woolly; pedicel floccose; indumentum on the under surface of the leaves *unistrate*, branches of the hair not divided at intervals by septae. . . . . *lampropeplum*
        N. Dwarf, creeping or prostrate or matted or spreading shrub, 8–60 cm. (3 in.–2 ft.) high; branchlets, petioles, and pedicels usually glabrous; indumentum on the under surface of the leaves bistrate, branches of the hair divided at intervals by septae . . . . *pronum*
    M. Medium-sized shrub, 92 cm.–1.83 m. (3–6 ft.) high; inflorescence 12–15-flowered; leaves oblanceolate, lanceolate or oblong-lanceolate; pedicel densely or moderately tomentose . . . . *globigerum* (part)

DESCRIPTION OF THE SPECIES

R. bathyphyllum Balf. f. et Forrest in Notes Roy. Bot. Gard. Edin., Vol. 11 (1919) 27.

A broadly upright shrub, 92 cm.–1.53 m. (3–5 ft.) high, *branchlets with short internodes, densely woolly* with rust- or cinnamon-coloured wool, *eglandular*, those below the inflorescences 5–8 mm. in diameter; leaf-bud scales deciduous or rarely persistent. *Leaves oblong* or rarely oblong-lanceolate, lamina coriaceous, 4–7.5 cm. long, 1.3–2.5 cm. broad, apex obtuse, base obtuse; upper surface green, matt, slightly rugulose, glabrous or with vestiges of hairs, midrib grooved, glabrous or hairy at the base, primary veins 10–15 on each side, deeply impressed; margin recurved; *under surface covered with a thick, woolly, rust- or cinnamon-coloured, continuous, unistrate indumentum of Ramiform hairs with long stem and very long narrow branches,* midrib slightly raised, densely woolly, eglandular, primary veins concealed; *petiole* 0.6–1.3 cm. long, thick, 3–4 mm. broad, *densely woolly* with rust- or cinnamon-coloured wool, *eglandular*. *Inflorescence* a compact racemose umbel of 10–15 flowers, flower-bud scales persistent; rhachis 0.6–1 cm. long, densely or rarely moderately tomentose, eglandular; *pedicel* 1.1–2 cm. long, *densely or moderately tomentose* with rust-coloured or brown tomentum or rarely glabrous, *eglandular*. *Calyx* 5-lobed, minute, 0.5–1 mm. long, lobes triangular or ovate, outside glabrous, *eglandular*, margin hairy or rarely glabrous, *eglandular*. *Corolla* campanulate, 3–4 cm. long, white, white flushed rose or creamy-white flushed rose, with crimson spots; lobes 5, 1–1.2 cm. long, 1–2 cm. broad, rounded, emarginate. *Stamens* 10, unequal, 1.2–2.3 cm. long, shorter than the corolla; filaments densely pubescent on the lower half or two-thirds of their length. *Gynoecium* 2–2.8 cm. long, shorter than the corolla, longer than the stamens; *ovary* conoid, 4–5 mm. long, *densely tomentose* with cinnamon- or rust-coloured tomentum, *eglandular*; style glabrous, eglandular. *Capsule* oblong, 1.1–1.3 cm. long, 5–6 mm. broad, straight, floccose with rust- or cinnamon-coloured hairs, *eglandular*, calyx persistent.

Forrest discovered this species in August 1917 on Ka-gwr-pw, Mekong-Salwin Divide, Tsarong, south-east Tibet. He found it again later in 1918, 1919 and 1921 in other localities in the same region. It grows on rocky slopes, on cliffs, at the margins of thickets and pine forests, in rhododendron scrub, and in rocky moorland at the base of cliffs, at elevations of 3,355–4,270 m. (11,000–14,000 ft.).

A diagnostic feature of the plant is the *thick woolly, continuous,* rust- or cinnamon-coloured, *unistrate indumentum of Ramiform hairs with long stem and very long narrow branches.* Other distinctive characters are the densely woolly branchlets and petioles with rust- or cinnamon-coloured wool, and the oblong or rarely oblong-lanceolate leaves. The species is closely related to *R. lampropeplum* to which it bears a strong resemblance in general appearance, but differs in that the leaves are usually larger, the ovary is densely tomentose, the leaf-bud scales are usually deciduous, and the inflorescence is many-flowered.

The plant was first introduced by Forrest in 1917 (No. 14718—the Type number). It was reintroduced by him in 1918 (No. 16668). In cultivation it is a broadly upright shrub, 3–5 feet high, with short internodes, and fairly well-filled with foliage. It is a somewhat slow grower, and takes many years to produce the flowers. The plant is hardy, blooms freely with compact trusses of 10–15 white or white flushed rose flowers, with crimson spots. It is rare in cultivation but is worthy of being widely grown.

Epithet. Densely leafy.
Hardiness 3. April–May.

R. comisteum Balf. f. et Forrest in Notes Roy. Bot. Gard. Edin., Vol. 11 (1919) 42.
    Syn. *R. perulatum* Balf. f. et Forrest in Notes Roy. Bot. Gard. Edin., Vol. 11 (1919) 106.

A broadly upright shrub, 60 cm.–1.22 m. (1–4 ft.) high; *annual growths and internodes short;* branchlets stout, densely woolly or tomentose with fawn, brown or rust-coloured wool or tomentum, eglandular or sparsely glandular with short-stalked glands, those below the inflorescences 3–5 mm. in diameter; *leaf-bud scales persistent. Leaves oblanceolate or lanceolate, lamina* coriaceous, small, *2.5–5 cm. long, 6 mm.–1.7 cm. broad,* apex obtuse, mucronate, base tapered or cuneate; upper surface dark green, matt, not rugulose, glabrous or with vestiges of hairs, midrib grooved, glabrous or hairy at the base, primary veins 10–12 on each side, deeply impressed; margin recurved; *under surface covered with a thick* or somewhat thick, *woolly, rust-coloured or dark brown or brown, continuous, bistrate indumentum of hairs, upper layer Ramiform* with short or long stem, and *narrow curled or uncurled branches, lower layer Rosulate,* midrib raised, densely or moderately woolly, eglandular, primary veins concealed; petiole 4–7 mm. long, 1–2 mm. broad, grooved above, densely woolly or tomentose with fawn, brown or rust-coloured wool or tomentum, eglandular or glandular with short-stalked glands. *Inflorescence lax,* a racemose umbel of *4–8 flowers,* flower-bud scales deciduous or persistent; rhachis 2–4 mm. long, tomentose with rust-coloured tomentum, eglandular; *pedicel* 1.5–2.6 cm. long, *densely woolly* with brown or rust-coloured wool, eglandular or sparsely glandular with short-stalked glands. *Calyx* 5-lobed, 1–2 mm. long, lobes rounded, ovate or broadly triangular, outside and margin floccose, eglandular. *Corolla* campanulate or tubular-campanulate, 3–3.7 cm. long, *soft rose or deep soft rose or pale rose,* with or without a few crimson spots; lobes 5, 1–1.4 cm. long, 1.3–2 cm. broad, rounded, emarginate. *Stamens* 10, unequal, 1.2–2.2 cm. long, shorter than the corolla; filaments densely puberulous at the base. *Gynoecium* 1.3–2.8 cm. long, shorter than the corolla, longer than the stamens; *ovary* ovoid or conoid, 3–4 mm. long, 5–6-celled, *densely tomentose* with long brown hairs, eglandular or glandular with short-stalked glands; style glabrous, eglandular. *Capsule* oblong, 0.8–1 cm. long, 5–6 mm. broad, tomentose with long brown hairs, eglandular, calyx-lobes persistent.

This plant was first collected by Forrest in July 1917 on Ka-gwr-pw, Mekong-Salwin

Divide, Tsarong, south-east Tibet. It was collected by him again later in that year in the same region. In 1923 Rock found it on the mountains above Tseku in the Mekong-Salwin Divide. It grows on open stony slopes and ledges of cliffs, in open pasture, and on rocky slopes by streams, at elevations of 3,355–4,270 m. (11,000–14,000 ft.).

In 1919 *R. perulatum* Balf. f. et Forrest was described from a specimen (No. 14421) collected by Forrest in July 1917, on Doker-la, Mekong-Salwin Divide, Tsarong, south-east Tibet. It is very similar to *R. comisteum* in general characters, and in every morphological detail.

The main features of *R. comisteum* are the short annual growths and internodes, the persistent leaf-bud scales, the small oblanceolate or lanceolate leaves, lamina 2.5–5 cm. long, 6 mm.–1.7 cm. broad, the lower surface covered with a thick woolly, continuous, bistrate indumentum of hairs, the small lax inflorescence of 4–8 flowers, and the soft rose or deep soft rose or pale rose corolla.

The species was first introduced by Forrest in 1917 (No. 14508). It was reintroduced by him in the same year (No. 14421 as *R. perulatum*). In cultivation it is a pleasing shrub 2–3 feet high with soft rose flowers in trusses of 4–8. The plant has always been rare. It has not been seen for a long time; possibly it is now lost to cultivation.

Epithet. To be taken care of.
Hardiness 3. April–May.

R. cucullatum Hand.-Mazz. in Anz. Akad. Wiss. Wien, Nos. 4–5 (1921) 26.
> Syn. *R. porphyroblastum* Balf. f. et Forrest in Notes Roy. Bot. Gard. Edin., Vol. 13 (1922) 287.
> > *R. roxieanum* Forrest var. *cucullatum* (Hand.-Mazz.) Chamberlain in Notes Roy. Bot. Gard. Edin., Vol. 36 (1978) 119.

A compact rounded, or widely branched, or broadly upright shrub, 60 cm.–1.53 m. (2–5 ft.) or rarely 3 m. (10 ft.) high; *annual growths and internodes short; branchlets densely* or moderately *woolly*, glandular with short-stalked glands, those below the inflorescences 0.5–1 cm. in diameter; leaf-bud scales persistent or sometimes deciduous. *Leaves* oblong-lanceolate, oblanceolate, narrowly oblanceolate, lanceolate or rarely oblong-elliptic, lamina 6–13 cm. long, 2–4 cm. broad, apex acute or shortly acuminate or obtuse, slightly hooded or not hooded, base tapered or obtuse, decurrent or not decurrent on the petiole; *upper surface* dark green, shining or somewhat matt, *convex* or flat, slightly rugulose, glabrous or with vestiges of hairs, midrib grooved, glabrous or hairy, eglandular, primary veins 10–18 on each side, deeply impressed; *margin recurved* or flat, undulate or not undulate; *under surface covered with a thick, loose, woolly, rust- or cinnamon-coloured, continuous, bistrate indumentum of hairs, upper layer Ramiform with long stem and very long narrow branches, lower layer small or* large *Rosulate* hairs, midrib slightly raised, densely woolly, eglandular or glandular with short-stalked glands, primary veins concealed; *petiole short and broad*, 0.6–1.3 cm. long, 2–5 mm. broad, *densely or moderately woolly with cinnamon- or rust-coloured* or brown *wool*, eglandular or rather densely or moderately glandular with short-stalked glands. *Inflorescence* a compact racemose umbel of 10–20 flowers, flower-bud scales persistent; rhachis 0.5–1.5 cm. long, densely or moderately tomentose with cinnamon- or rust-coloured or fawn tomentum, eglandular or glandular with short-stalked glands; pedicel 1–1.6 cm. long, densely or moderately hairy or glabrous, moderately or rather densely glandular with short-stalked glands or rarely eglandular. *Calyx* 5-lobed, minute, 0.5–1 mm. long, lobes triangular or ovate, outside and margin densely or moderately hairy with brown hairs or glabrous, glandular with short-stalked glands or eglandular. *Corolla* campanulate or funnel-campanulate, 2–3 cm. long, white or white flushed rose, with or without crimson spots; lobes 5, 0.8–1.2 cm. long, 1–1.6 cm. broad, rounded, emarginate. *Stamens* 10, unequal, 1–1.9 cm. long, shorter than the corolla; filaments densely pubescent at the base or up to two-thirds of their length. *Gynoecium* 1.6–2.6 cm. long, shorter than the corolla, longer than the stamens; ovary conoid or oblong, 3–5 mm. long, 5–8-celled, hairy or glabrous, densely or moderately glandular with short-stalked glands; style glabrous, eglandular. *Capsule* oblong, 1.2–1.8 cm. long, 4–6 mm. broad, straight or slightly curved, brown-hairy or glabrous, moderately or sparsely glandular with short-stalked glands or sometimes eglandular, calyx-lobes persistent.

This plant was first collected by Handel-Mazzetti in April 1914, on Mount Lose-schan, south-west Sichuan. It was later found by Forrest and Rock in other localities in the same region and in north-west Yunnan. It grows in open thickets, on rocky slopes, on the margins of pine and rhododendron forests, in open conifer forest, and in open situations in ravines, at elevations of 3,660–4,770 m. (12,000–15,639 ft.).

In 1918 *R. porphyroblastum* Balf. f. et Forrest was described from a specimen (No. 16469) collected by Forrest in south-west Sichuan. It is identical with *R. cucullatum* under which it now appears in synonymy.

R. cucullatum is closely related to *R. roxieanum* which it resembles in some features but differs in that the leaves are usually longer with convex upper surface and markedly recurved margins, and the indumentum on the lower surface is loose woolly. It also differs somewhat in other indumental characters.

The species was first introduced by Forrest in 1918 (Nos. 16428, 16469). It was reintroduced by him in 1921 (Nos. 20425, 21022). Rock sent seeds under three different seed numbers. In its native home it grows 2–5 feet or rarely 10 feet high. In cultivation it is a compact rounded shrub, 4 feet high and as much across. It is slow-growing with short annual growths and internodes; it is also slow to reach the flowering state. A remarkable feature is the cinnamon- or rust-coloured densely woolly branchlets and petioles. A noteworthy characteristic is the thick, loose, bistrate, continuous indumentum, cinnamon- or rust-coloured, covering the lower surface of the leaves. The flowers are white with crimson spots, in compact trusses of 10–20. It may be of interest to note that very often weevils feed on the leaves of this plant causing a fair amount of damage.

Epithet. Hooded.
Hardiness 3. April–May.

R. globigerum Balf. f. et Forrest in Notes Roy. Bot. Gard. Edin., Vol. 13 (1922) 259.

A broadly upright shrub, 92 cm.–1.83 m. (3–6 ft.) high, *branchlets* with short internodes, *densely woolly* with whitish, fawn, brown or rust-coloured tomentum, eglandular or rarely glandular with short-stalked glands, those below the inflorescences 4–6 mm. in diameter; leaf-bud scales persistent or deciduous. *Leaves oblanceolate, lanceolate or oblong-lanceolate,* lamina coriaceous, 4.5–10.5 cm. long, 1.5–3 cm. broad, apex acute or shortly acuminate, base tapered or obtuse; upper surface dark green, matt or somewhat shining, slightly rugulose, glabrous or with vestiges of hairs, midrib grooved, glabrous or hairy at the base, eglandular, primary veins 10–18 on each side, deeply impressed; margin recurved; *under surface covered with a thick, woolly,* brown or rust-coloured, *continuous, bistrate indumentum of hairs, upper layer Ramiform with long stem and very long narrow branches, lower layer* small or large *Rosulate* hairs, midrib raised, densely woolly, eglandular or rarely glandular with short-stalked glands, primary veins concealed; *petiole* 0.6–2 cm. long, 2–4 mm. broad, grooved above, *densely woolly* with whitish, fawn, brown or rust-coloured wool, eglandular or rarely glandular with short-stalked glands. *Inflorescence* a compact racemose umbel of 12–15 flowers, flower-bud scales persistent; rhachis 5–8 mm. long, densely or moderately or rarely sparsely tomentose with fawn, brown or rust-coloured tomentum, eglandular; *pedicel* 1–2 cm. long, *densely or moderately tomentose* with brown or fawn tomentum, eglandular. *Calyx* 5-lobed, minute, 0.5–1 mm. long, lobes triangular or ovate, outside and margin glabrous or hairy, eglandular. *Corolla* campanulate or funnel-campanulate, 2–4 cm. long, white with crimson spots; lobes 5, 1–1.5 cm. long, 1–2 cm. broad, rounded, emarginate. *Stamens* 10, unequal, 1.3–2.3 cm. long, shorter than the corolla; filaments densely or moderately pubescent at the base or in the lower half. *Gynoecium* 1.8–3 cm. long, shorter than the corolla, longer than the stamens; *ovary* oblong or conoid, 4–5 mm. long, 5–6-celled, *moderately or sparsely tomentose* with rust-coloured or brown tomentum *or glabrous*, eglandular; style glabrous, eglandular. *Capsule* oblong, 1.3–1.8 cm. long, 5–6 mm. broad, straight or slightly curved, glabrous or with vestiges of hairs, eglandular, calyx-lobes persistent.

 R. globigerum was discovered by Forrest in June 1918 on the Muli mountains, southwest Sichuan. It was found by him again later in October 1922 in the Chienchuan-Mekong Divide, north-west Yunnan. Rock collected it in 1923 on Mount Peimashan, north-west Yunnan. It grows in thickets, on open rocky slopes, in rhododendron thickets, at the margins of rhododendron forests, in open alpine pasture, and in open situations in ravines, at elevations of 3,355–4,270 m. (11,000–14,000 ft.).

 It is related to *R. bathyphyllum* to which it shows a certain degree of resemblance, but differs in that the indumentum on the lower surface of the leaves is bistrate, the ovary is moderately tomentose or glabrous, and the leaves are oblanceolate, lanceolate or oblong-lanceolate, with acute or shortly acuminate apex.

 The species was introduced by Rock in 1923 (No. 11101). In cultivation it is a broadly upright shrub 5–6 feet high, well-filled with dark green foliage. It is perfectly hardy, fairly fast-growing, and has proved to be most attractive with its white flowers with numerous crimson spots, in trusses of 12–15. The plant is rare in cultivation but should be in every collection of rhododendrons.

 Epithet. Bearing a globe.
 Hardiness 3. April–May.

R. iodes Balf. f. et Forrest in Notes Roy. Bot. Gard. Edin., Vol. 13 (1920) 49.
 Syn. *R. alutaceum* Balf. f. et W. W. Sm. var. *iodes* (Balf. f. et Forrest) Chamberlain in Notes Roy. Bot. Gard. Edin., Vol. 39 (1982) 350.

 A compact, rounded or broadly upright shrub, or rarely a tree, 60 cm.–4.58 m. (2–15 ft.) high, branchlets with short internodes, densely tomentose with rust-coloured or brown tomentum, eglandular, those below the inflorescences 4–7 mm. in diameter; leaf-bud scales deciduous. *Leaves* lanceolate, oblanceolate or oblong-lanceolate, lamina coriaceous 5–12 cm. long, 1–3.3 cm. broad, apex acute, acuminate or obtuse, base tapered, obtuse or rounded, upper surface dark green, shining, glabrous or with vestiges of hairs, midrib grooved, floccose or glabrous, primary veins 12–20 on each side, deeply impressed; margin recurved or flat; *under surface covered with a somewhat thick, compact felty*, rust- or cinnamon-coloured or brown, (*in young leaves greenish-yellow*), *continuous, bistrate indumentum of hairs, upper layer not detersile, Long-rayed with long ribbon-like arms, lower layer Rosulate*, midrib prominent, densely or moderately tomentose, *eglandular* or rarely rather densely glandular with short-stalked glands, primary veins concealed; *petiole* 0.8–2.5 cm. long, 2–3 mm. broad, grooved above, densely or moderately tomentose with rust-coloured or brown tomentum, *eglandular* or rarely glandular with short-stalked glands. *Inflorescence* a compact racemose umbel of 8–18 flowers, flower-bud scales deciduous or persistent; rhachis 0.3–1.8 cm. long, moderately or densely pubescent, eglandular; pedicel 1–2.7 cm. long, densely or moderately floccose, *eglandular* or rarely sparsely glandular with short-stalked glands. *Calyx* 5-lobed, minute, 0.5–1 mm. long, lobes triangular or ovate, outside and margin floccose or glabrous, *eglandular* or rarely sparsely glandular with short-stalked glands. *Corolla* funnel-campanulate or campanulate, 2.5–3.5 cm. long, *white or white flushed rose, without* or rarely with *a crimson blotch* at the base, and with or rarely without crimson spots; lobes 5, 1–1.3 cm. long, 1–1.9 cm. broad, rounded, emarginate. *Stamens* 10, unequal, 1–2.3 cm. long, shorter than the corolla; filaments densely or moderately pubescent at the base. *Gynoecium* 2–3 cm. long, shorter than the corolla, longer than the stamens; *ovary* slender or oblong or conoid, 3–6 mm. long, 6–8-celled, *sparsely or moder-*

ately floccose or glabrous, eglandular or rarely rather densely or moderately glandular with short-stalked glands; style glabrous, eglandular. *Capsule* oblong or slender, 1.2–1.7 cm. long, 5–7 mm. broad, straight, with vestiges of hairs or glabrous, *eglandular*, calyx-lobes persistent.

Forrest discovered this plant in October 1917 on Ka-gwr-pw, Mekong-Salwin Divide, Tsarong, south-east Tibet. He collected it again later on many occasions in the same region and in north-west Yunnan. In 1932 Rock found it in other localities in Tsarung Border, Yunnan-south-east Tibet. It grows in open cane and rhododendron thickets, in mixed thickets, on open rocky slopes, in open meadows, in rhododendron scrub, amongst boulders, in open rocky moorland, at the margins of pine forests, in rhododendron forest, in pine and mixed forests, and in fir forest, at elevations of 3,355–4,270 m. (11,000–14,000 ft.).

The species is very closely related to *R. triplonaevium* which it resembles in habit and height of growth, in the shape of the leaves, and in the size of the corolla, but differs in that the leaves are often smaller, the indumentum on the under surface is somewhat thick, compact felty, the upper layer is not detersile, not falling off, the ovary is sparsely or moderately floccose or glabrous, and the corolla is usually without a crimson blotch at the base. A characteristic feature is the bistrate indumentum on the lower surface of the leaves, an upper layer of Long-rayed hairs with long ribbon-like arms, and a lower layer of Rosulate hairs.

R. iodes was first introduced by Forrest in 1917 (No. 15039). It was reintroduced by him in 1918 (No. 16745—the Type number, and Nos. 16779, 17447), and in 1921 (No. 19567). Rock sent seeds in 1932 (Nos. 23562, 23575). In its native home it is a shrub, usually 4–10 feet high, or rarely a tree up to 15 feet; in cultivation it is a densely branched, compact, rounded or broadly upright shrub 5 feet high. It is hardy, and gives a delightful colour display with its white flowers in compact trusses of 8–18. The plant is rare in cultivation, but is worthy of being widely cultivated.

Epithet. Rust-coloured.
Hardiness 3. April–May.

R. lampropeplum Balf. f. et Forrest in Notes Roy. Bot. Gard. Edin., Vol. 13 (1922) 272.

A compact spreading, or broadly upright shrub, 60 cm.–1.22 m. (2–4 ft.) high; *annual growths and internodes short; branchlets densely woolly* with rust- or cinnamon-coloured wool, eglandular, those below the inflorescences 4–5 mm. in diameter; *leaf-bud scales persistent. Leaves oblong or oblong-obovate,* lamina coriaceous, 2.8–5.5 cm. long, *1–2.5 cm. broad,* apex rounded or obtuse, base obtuse or rounded; upper surface green, matt or somewhat shining, slightly rugulose, glabrous or with vestiges of hairs, midrib grooved, glabrous or hairy at the base, eglandular, primary veins 8–10 on each side, deeply impressed; margin recurved; *under surface covered with a thick, woolly,* dark brown or rust-coloured or whitish, *continuous, unistrate indumentum of Ramiform hairs, lower layer absent or with closely scattered minute straight hairs,* midrib raised, densely woolly, eglandular, primary veins concealed; *petiole* 5–8 mm. long, 2–3 mm. broad, grooved above, *densely woolly* with whitish, rust- or cinnamon-coloured wool, eglandular. *Inflorescence* a compact or somewhat compact racemose umbel of 6–10 flowers; flower-bud scales persistent; rhachis 4–5 mm. long, moderately or sparsely tomentose with rust- or cinnamon-coloured tomentum, eglandular; *pedicel* 1–1.4 cm. long, *floccose,* eglandular. *Calyx* 5-lobed, minute, 0.5–1 mm. long, lobes triangular or ovate, outside glabrous, eglandular, margin glabrous or sparsely floccose, eglandular. *Corolla* funnel-campanulate or campanulate, 3–3.6 cm. long, *white faintly flushed rose, or creamy-white, with crimson spots;* lobes 5, 1–1.2 cm. long, 1.5–1.8 cm. broad, rounded, emarginate. *Stamens* 10, unequal, 1–2 cm. long, shorter than the corolla; filaments densely pubescent on the lower half or up to two-thirds of their length. *Gynoecium* 1.8–2.6 cm. long, shorter than the corolla, longer than the stamens; *ovary* conoid or oblong, 3–4 mm. long, 5–6-

celled, *glabrous*, eglandular; style glabrous or rarely sparsely puberulous at the base, eglandular. *Capsule* oblong, 1 cm. long, 4–5 mm. broad, straight, glabrous or sparsely hairy, eglandular, calyx-lobes persistent.

This plant was first collected by Forrest in June 1918 on the Muli mountains, southwest Sichuan. It was found by him again later in July of the same year on Ka-gwr-pw, Mekong-Salwin Divide, Tsarong, south-east Tibet. It grows in open rocky pastures, on cliffs, and on open bouldery slopes, at elevations of 3,660–4,270 m. (12,000–14,000 ft.).

R. lampropeplum is closely allied to *R. comisteum* which it resembles in general appearance, but is distinguished by the oblong or oblong-obovate leaves, by the glabrous ovary, usually by the unistrate indumentum on the lower surface of the leaves, usually by the white or creamy-white flowers, and somewhat by the nature of the hairs of the indumentum on the lower surface of the leaves. It is also similar to *R. proteoides* in some features, but differs usually in the shape of the leaves with broader laminae, in the glabrous ovary, in the floccose pedicels, and somewhat in the nature of the hairs of the indumentum on the lower surface of the leaves.

The species was introduced by Forrest in 1918 (No. 16509—the Type number, and No. 16609). In its native home it grows 2–4 feet high; in cultivation it is a compact spreading shrub up to 2 feet high, with persistent leaf-bud scales, and relatively small oblong or oblong-obovate leaves, covered on the lower surface with rust-coloured wool. It is a slow grower, with short annual growths, and white faintly flushed rose flowers in compact trusses of 6–10. It is a pleasing shrub, well-suited for the rock garden, but is rare in cultivation.

Epithet. Bright covering.
Hardiness 3. April–May.

R. pronum Tagg et Forrest in Notes Roy. Bot. Gard. Edin., Vol. 15 (1927) 318.

A creeping or prostrate or matted or spreading shrub, 8–60 cm. (3in.–2 ft.) high; annual growths and internodes very short; branchlets glabrous or rarely floccose, eglandular, those below the inflorescences 5–8 mm. in diameter; *leaf-bud scales persistent, numerous, closely set. Leaves* oblong, lanceolate, oblanceolate or oblong-obovate, lamina coriaceous, 3–8.8 cm. long, 1–2.8 cm. broad, apex obtuse or acute, base tapered or obtuse, slightly decurrent on the petiole; upper surface dark green or bluish-green (*in young leaves bluish-green*), matt, slightly rugulose, glabrous or with vestiges of hairs, midrib grooved, glabrous, eglandular, primary veins 8–15 on each side, deeply impressed; margin recurved; *under surface covered with a thick, spongy*, fawn, brown or rarely whitish, *continuous indumentum of bistrate hairs*, upper layer Ramiform with long stem and *very long ribbon-like branches divided at short intervals by septae, lower layer* small or large Rosulate, *with a surface pellicle*, midrib raised, densely woolly, eglandular, primary veins concealed; *petiole* 0.5–1.2 cm. long, 2–3 mm. broad, margins with or without ridges, *glabrous* or with vestiges of hairs, eglandular. *Inflorescence* a lax or somewhat compact racemose umbel of 6–12 flowers, *flower-bud scales persistent;* rhachis very short, 2–3 mm. long, glabrous, eglandular; *pedicel* 1.7–3.2 cm. long, *glabrous* or rarely floccose, eglandular. *Calyx* 5-lobed, 0.5–2 mm. long, lobes triangular or ovate, outside glabrous, eglandular, margin glabrous or slightly floccose, eglandular. *Corolla* campanulate, 3–4.5 cm. long, creamy-yellow or white or pink, with or without deep crimson or purple spots; lobes 5, 1–1.2 cm. long, 1.3–2 cm. broad, rounded, emarginate. *Stamens* 10, unequal, 1.3–2.6 cm. long, shorter than the corolla; filaments glabrous or moderately or densely pubescent at the base. *Gynoecium* 2–2.8 cm. long, shorter than the corolla, longer than the stamens; *ovary* conoid or oblong, 5–7 mm. long, 5–6-celled, *glabrous*, eglandular; style glabrous, eglandular. *Capsule* oblong, 1–1.4 cm. long, 5–6 mm. broad, straight, *glabrous*, eglandular, calyx-lobes persistent.

This species was discovered by Forrest in September 1922 in the Chienchuan-Mekong Divide, north-west Yunnan. Subsequently it was found by him and by Rock in various localities in the same region and in mid-west Yunnan. It grows on moist rocky slopes and humus covered boulders in side valleys, in peaty moorland, in peaty stony alpine moorland, on cliffs, and among rocks, at elevations of 3,660–4,600 m. (12,000–15,082 ft.).

R. pronum is a unique species in the Taliense Series. The most striking characters of this plant are its creeping or prostrate or spreading habit of growth, 3 inches to 2 feet high, the very short annual growths and internodes, and the numerous large closely set persistent leaf-bud scales. Other marked characteristics are the glabrous and eglandular branchlets, petioles, pedicels, calyx, ovaries, styles, and capsules. The indumentum on the lower surface of the leaves is thick, spongy, continuous, bistrate with a surface pellicle; a distinctive feature of the Ramiform hairs of the upper layer is that the ribbon-like branches are divided at short intervals by septae. The species shows a certain degree of resemblance to *R. lampropeplum,* but differs in distinctive features.

The species was first introduced by Rock in 1923 (No. 11306). It was reintroduced by him in 1932 (No. 25458). Forrest sent seeds in 1930 (No. 30880). In its native home it grows from 3 inches to 2 feet high; in cultivation it is a prostrate shrub one foot in height. It is a slow grower and requires many years to produce the flowers; moreover, it is a shy flowerer. The bluish-green young leaves are a charming feature and attract attention. The plant is hardy, but is rare in cultivation.

Epithet. Prostrate.
Hardiness 3. May.

R. proteoides Balf. f. et W. W. Sm. in Notes Roy. Bot. Gard. Edin., Vol. 9 (1916) 264.

A compact, rounded or spreading shrub, *30–92 cm. (1–3 ft.)* or rarely creeping 8–15 cm. (3–6 in.) *high; annual growths and internodes very short;* branchlets densely woolly with cinnamon- or rust-coloured wool, eglandular, those below the inflorescences 3–5 mm. in diameter; *leaf-bud scales persistent. Leaves close-set, narrowly oblong or narrowly oblanceolate, lamina coriaceous, short, narrow, 1.3–4 cm. long, 4–8 mm.* or rarely 1.1 or 1.2 cm. *broad,* apex obtuse or narrowly rounded, markedly recurved, base tapered or obtuse; upper surface dark green or green, matt, rugulose, glabrous or with vestiges of hairs, midrib grooved, glabrous or hairy at the base, primary veins 8–12 on each side, deeply impressed; *margin markedly recurved; under surface covered with a thick, woolly,* rust- or cinnamon-coloured, *continuous, unistrate indumentum of Ramiform hairs,* with long stem, and *long, narrow spirally twisted branches,* midrib slightly raised, densely woolly, eglandular, primary veins concealed; petiole short, thick, 2–6 mm. long, 2–3 mm. broad, grooved above, densely woolly with cinnamon- or rust-coloured wool, eglandular. *Inflorescence* a compact racemose umbel of 6–12 flowers, flower-bud scales persistent; rhachis 3–5 mm. long, densely or moderately tomentose with rust- or cinnamon-coloured tomentum, eglandular; *pedicel* 0.8–1.3 cm. long, *densely woolly* with cinnamon- or rust-coloured wool, eglandular. *Calyx* 5-lobed, minute, 0.5–1 mm. long, lobes ovate or triangular, outside hairy or glabrous, eglandular, margin hairy, eglandular. *Corolla* funnel-campanulate or campanulate, 1.9–3.8 cm. long, pale creamy-yellow, creamy-white, pale yellow, yellow or white, flushed or not flushed rose, with crimson spots; lobes 5, 0.8–1.2 cm. long, 1.2–1.8 cm. broad, rounded, emarginate. *Stamens* 10, unequal, 1.1–2.1 cm. long, shorter than the corolla; filaments densely or moderately pubescent on the lower half or up to two-thirds of their length. *Gynoecium* 1.5–2.7 cm. long, shorter than the corolla, longer than the stamens; *ovary* ovoid or conoid, 3–4 mm. long, 5-celled, *densely tomentose* with cinnamon- or rust-coloured tomentum, eglandular or sometimes sparsely glandular with short-stalked glands; style glabrous, eglandular. *Capsule* conoid or ovoid, 0.6–1 cm. long, 4–5 mm. broad, tomentose with cinnamon- or rust-coloured tomentum, eglandular, calyx-lobes persistent.

R. proteoides was discovered by Forrest in September 1914 in the Mekong-Salwin Divide, north-west Yunnan. It was afterwards found by him again in the same region and in south-east Tibet. It was also collected by Rock in various localities in north-west Yunnan, and in Yunnan-south-east Tibet border. It grows in open situations amongst and on boulders, on rocks, cliffs, rocky slopes, in rocky pastures, and in open rocky moorlands, at elevations of 3,660–4,575 m. (12,000–15,000 ft.).

The diagnostic features of the species are the dwarf habit of growth, and the very small, narrowly oblong or narrowly oblanceolate leaves, laminae 1.3–4 cm. long and usually 4–8 mm. broad. Other characteristics are the persistent leaf-bud scales, and the densely woolly or tomentose pedicel and ovary. It is the smallest leaved species in the Taliense Series. The plant is closely related to *R. lampropeplum* but differs in the shape of the leaves with narrower laminae, in the densely tomentose ovaries, and in the densely woolly pedicels. It also differs somewhat in the nature of the Ramiform hairs of the indumentum on the lower surface of the leaves, having a long stem and narrow spirally twisted branches.

R. proteoides was first introduced by Forrest in 1914 (No. 13348—the Type number). It was reintroduced by him in 1917, 1918 and 1919 under eight different seed numbers. Rock sent seeds on five occasions. In its native home it is a dwarf shrub 1–3 feet high; it is of interest to note that Forrest found creeping forms of the species, only 3–6 inches high in the Mekong-Salwin Divide. In cultivation it is a compact, rounded or spreading shrub, up to 1 foot high and up to 1½ feet across, with very short annual growths and internodes, and close-set leaves on the branchlets. It is a very slow grower and takes many years to reach the flowering stage. A plant introduced by Rock in 1948 under No. 151 flowered recently in Mr. Cecil Smith's garden at Seattle, Washington, U.S.A. The species has a neat habit of growth with beautiful dark green leaves, covered on the lower surface with thick woolly hairs. It is hardy, and is an excellent plant for the rock garden.

Epithet. Resembling a *Protea*.
Hardiness 3. April–May.

R. recurvoides Tagg et Ward in Rhod. Soc. Notes, Vol. III Part V (1929–31) 284.

A compact rounded or spreading or bushy, or broadly upright shrub, 60–92 cm. (2–3 ft.) or sometimes up to 1.53 m. (5 ft.) high; annual growths and internodes short or fairly long; *branchlets densely bristly, densely bristly-glandular*, those below the inflorescences 5–7 mm. in diameter; *leaf-bud scales persistent. Leaves* lanceolate, oblanceolate, oblong or sometimes oval, lamina coriaceous, 3–7 cm. long, 1–2.2 cm. broad, apex obtuse or acute, base tapered or obtuse; upper surface dark green, shining, rugulose, glabrous or with vestiges of hairs, eglandular, midrib grooved, bristly and bristly-glandular at the base or on the lower half, primary veins 10–12 on each side, deeply impressed; margin recurved; *under surface covered with a thick, woolly, yellowish-brown or dark brown, continuous, bistrate indumentum of hairs, upper layer Ramiform with long stem, and very long narrow branches, lower layer a form of large Long-rayed* hairs *with long very narrow arms*, midrib raised, glandular with short-stalked glands, primary veins concealed; *petiole* 0.5–2 cm. long, slightly grooved above, *densely bristly, densely bristly-glandular. Inflorescence* a racemose umbel of 4–7 flowers, flower-bud scales persistent; rhachis about 3 mm. long, hairy with long hairs, sparsely bristly-glandular; *pedicel* 1.2–1.6 cm. long, pubescent, *densely bristly-glandular* or glandular with long-stalked glands. *Calyx* 5-lobed, *large, 5–8 mm. long*, lobes unequal or equal, ovate or lanceolate, *outside and margin* glabrous, *rather densely glandular with long-stalked glands. Corolla* funnel-campanulate, 2.6–3 cm. long, rose or white or white tinged pink, with reddish spots; lobes 5, 1.5 cm. long, 1–1.5 cm. broad, rounded, emarginate. *Stamens* 10, unequal, 1.5–2.5 cm. long, shorter than the corolla; filaments villous at the base or on the lower half. *Gynoecium* 3–3.5 cm. long, as long as the corolla or longer, longer than the stamens; *ovary* conoid, 5–6 mm. long, glabrous, *densely glandular with long-stalked glands*; style glabrous, eglandular. *Capsule* oblong, 1.2–1.6 cm. long, 5 mm. broad, slightly curved, glabrous, *rather densely glandular with very long-stalked glands*, calyx-lobes persistent.

Kingdon-Ward discovered this plant in July 1926 in the valley of the Di Chu, in Upper Burma, scattered about on the sunniest of steep granite screes amongst boulders, at an elevation of 3,355 m. (11,000 ft.). It would appear to be a rare plant, because no other collector has found it in its native home.

R. recurvoides is a distinctive species, and is somewhat an aberrant member of its Subseries. A diagnostic feature is the densely bristly and bristly-glandular branchlets and petioles. In this respect it is readily distinguished from all the other species of the Roxieanum Subseries and the Taliense Series. Other remarkable characters are the persistent leaf-bud scales, and the large calyx 5–8 mm. long. The species resembles *R. roxieanum* in height and habit of growth, in leaf shape and size, in the characters of the indumentum on the lower surface of the leaves, and in the densely or moderately glandular calyx and ovary, but differs in well-marked characteristics.

The species was introduced by Kingdon-Ward in 1926 (No. 7184—the Type number). In its native home it is a small compact bushy shrub, sometimes as much as 5 feet high, but usually 2–3 feet or less. Two distinct forms are in cultivation. Form 1. A compact rounded or spreading shrub, up to 2 feet high and as much or more across, with short annual growths and internodes, well-filled with leaves. This is an excellent plant for the rock garden. Form 2. A broadly upright somewhat lax shrub, 3–4 feet high, with fairly long annual growths and internodes, and moderately filled with leaves. The species, particularly Form 1, is a slow grower and takes a long time to reach the flowering size. It is hardy, often a shy flowerer, with trusses of 4–7 white or white tinged pink flowers.

It received an Award of Merit when exhibited by Col. E. H. W. Bolitho, Trengwainton, Cornwall, in 1941.

Epithet. Resembling *R. recurvum.*
Hardiness 3. April–May.

R. roxieanum Forrest in Notes Roy. Bot. Gard. Edin., Vol. 8 (1915) 344.
  Syn. *R. aischropeplum* Balf. f. et Forrest in Notes Roy. Bot. Gard. Edin., Vol. 13 (1922) 229.
      R. coccinopeplum Balf. f. et Forrest, ibid. Vol. 13 (1922) 248.
      R. poecilodermum Balf. f. et Forrest, ibid. Vol. 13 (1922) 285.
      R. roxieoides Chamberlain, ibid. Vol. 39 (1982) 478.
  Illustration. Bot. Mag. Vol. 158 t. 9383 (1935).

A compact rounded or spreading, or broadly upright or lax upright shrub, 92 cm.–2.75 m. (3–9 ft.) or rarely a tree 4.58 m. (15 ft.) high; *annual growths and internodes short; branchlets densely or moderately woolly* with cinnamon- or rust-coloured, or sometimes fawn or brown wool, eglandular or moderately or sometimes rather densely glandular with short-stalked glands, those below the inflorescences 0.5–1 cm. in diameter; leaf-bud scales persistent or deciduous. *Leaves* lanceolate, oblanceolate or sometimes oblong-lanceolate, lamina coriaceous, 5–12 cm. long, 1–2.3 cm. broad, apex acute, acuminate, shortly acuminate or sometimes obtuse, base tapered or sometimes obtuse; upper surface dark green, shining or somewhat matt, slightly convex or flat, slightly rugulose, glabrous or with vestiges of hairs, midrib grooved, hairy or glabrous, eglandular, primary veins 8–20 on each side, deeply impressed; margin moderately or slightly recurved; *under surface covered with a thick,* somewhat compact or loose, *woolly,* rust- or cinnamon-coloured, or sometimes brown or fawn, *continuous, bistrate indumentum of hairs, upper layer Ramiform with long stem,* and *narrow very long branches, lower layer* small and large *Rosulate* hairs, midrib moderately or slightly raised, densely woolly, eglandular or rather densely or moderately glandular with short-stalked glands, primary veins concealed; *petiole* 0.2–1.3 cm. long, 2–5 mm. broad, grooved above, *densely or moderately woolly* with cinnamon- or rust-coloured, or sometimes brown or fawn wool, eglandular or moderately or rather densely glandular with short-stalked glands. *Inflorescence* a compact racemose umbel of 8–20 flowers, flower-bud scales persistent; rhachis 0.5–1.3 cm. long, densely or moderately tomentose with cinnamon- or rust-coloured or sometimes brown tomentum, eglandular or sometimes glandular with short-stalked glands; *pedicel* 0.6–1.8 cm. long, densely or moderately hairy with long, cinnamon- or rust-coloured or brown long hairs or glabrous, *moderately or densely glandular* with short-stalked glands or eglandular. *Calyx* 5-lobed, minute, 0.5–1 mm. long, lobes triangular or ovate, outside and margin densely or moderately tomentose with cinnamon- or rust-coloured or brown tomentum or glabrous, *moderately or sparsely glandular* with short-stalked glands or eglandular. *Corolla* campanulate or funnel-campanulate, 2.1–3.8 cm. long, creamy-white, white, white flushed rose, pink, rose or rarely yellow, with or without crimson spots; lobes 5, 0.6–1.2 cm. long, 1–2 cm. broad, rounded, emarginate. *Stamens* 10, unequal, 0.6–2.7 cm. long, shorter than the corolla; filaments densely pubescent at the base or up to two-thirds of their length. *Gynoecium* 1.3–2.8 cm. long, shorter or rarely longer than the corolla, longer than the stamens; *ovary* conoid, oblong or sometimes slender, 3–5 mm. or sometimes 2 mm. long, 5–6-celled, densely or moderately tomentose with rust- or cinnamon-coloured or brown tomentum or glabrous, *densely or moderately glandular* with short-stalked glands or eglandular; style glabrous or sometimes sparsely hairy at the base, eglandular or rarely glandular at the base. *Capsule* oblong, 1–2 cm. long, 4–6 mm. broad, straight or slightly curved, moderately or sparsely hairy with brown hairs or glabrous, *moderately or sparsely glandular* with short-stalked glands or eglandular.

R. roxieanum was discovered by Forrest in July 1913 on the mountains in the north-east of the Yangtze bend, north-west Yunnan. Further gatherings by him and other collectors show that the plant is widely distributed in north-west Yunnan, south-west Sichuan, and eastern Tibet. It grows in very varied habitats, on boulder-strewn slopes, among rocks, in open situations in side valleys, on ledges of cliffs, in open stony moorland, among limestone crags, in open pasture, in open thickets, in rhododendron and cane thickets, in rocky meadows, on the margins of conifer forests, in mixed forest, in open glades in pine forests, in rhododendron forest, and in fir forest, at elevations of 3,050–4,875 m. (10,000–15,984 ft.).

The species was described by Forrest in 1915. Later in 1922 two other species, *R. aischropeplum* Balf. f. et Forrest, and *R. poecilodermum* Balf. f. et Forrest, were founded on Forrest's Nos. 14061 and 14432, from north-west Yunnan and south-east Tibet respectively. Further gatherings show that these plants are identical with *R. roxieanum* in every respect, and this is confirmed by the additional evidence of plants in cultivation.

In 1982, *R. roxieoides* was described by Chamberlain from a specimen collected in east Sichuan. It is said to be allied to *R. roxieanum* but differs in the deep pink flowers and in the style glandular on the lower half. On these characters alone, the plant does not merit specific status.

R. roxieanum is closely allied to *R. cucullatum* but differs in that the leaves are usually shorter and narrower, with slightly convex or flat upper surface, and the indumentum on the lower surface is usually compact.

The species was first introduced by Forrest in 1913 (No. 10540—the Type number, and No. 10991). It was reintroduced by him under 16 different seed numbers. Rock sent seeds on 28 occasions. Kingdon-Ward introduced it once, and Yü four times. The species shows considerable variation, particularly in habit and height of growth, and in leaf size. In its native home it is a shrub 1–9 feet or rarely a tree 15 feet high. Several forms are in cultivation, including: Form 1. A compact rounded shrub, 3 feet high and as much across, with medium-sized lanceolate leaves. Form 2. A somewhat compact spreading shrub, 2 feet high and up to 3 feet wide with leaves up to 5 cm. long. Form 3. A broadly upright shrub, 3–4 feet high with medium-sized lanceolate leaves. Form 4. A very lax upright shrub, 3–4 feet high. The species is a slow grower with short annual growths and internodes, and many years are required before it reaches the flowering size. It varies a great deal in its freedom of flowering. The small compact forms are shy flowerers. Some of the other forms produce the flowers in moderation, whilst a few others are free-flowering and make a fine show with white flowers in compact trusses of 8–20. The species is hardy, and is successfully grown along the east coast.

Epithet. After Mrs. Roxie Hanna of Tali-fu, China, friend of George Forrest.
Hardiness 3. April–May.

R. roxieanum Forrest var. **oreonastes** (Balf. f. et Forrest) Davidian, comb. nov.

Syn. *R. recurvum* Balf. f. et Forrest var. *oreonastes* Balf. f. et Forrest in Notes Roy. Bot. Gard. Edin., Vol. 11 (1919) 113.

R. roxieanum Forrest var. *roxieanum* Oreonastes Group R. H. S. in Rhod. Handb. (1980) p. 60.

Forrest first collected this plant in August 1914 in the Kari Pass, Mekong-Yangtze Divide, north-west Yunnan. Subsequently it was found by him in north-west and mid-west Yunnan, and in south-west Sichuan. Rock collected it in several localities in north-west Yunnan. It grows in open stony pasture, amongst rocks, on open rocky slopes and cliffs, in open stony moorland, amongst scrub, on the margins of pine forests, and in fir forest, at elevations of 3,660–4,460 m. (12,000–14,623 ft.).

In this variety, the leaves are linear or linear-lanceolate, very narrow 2–8 mm. broad, and with markedly recurved margins. It shows a strong resemblance to *R. roxieanum* var. *recurvum*, but is usually distinguished by the shape and size of the leaves which are usually shorter (2.5–7.5 cm. long) and narrower.

The plant was first introduced by Forrest in 1914. It was reintroduced by him under four different seed numbers. Rock sent seeds on nine occasions. In its native home it grows 1–5 feet or rarely 10 feet high. In cultivation it is a compact rounded shrub, 1–2 feet or sometimes 3 feet high, densely filled with foliage. It is a slow grower, and takes many years to reach the flowering stage. Some plants are shy flowerers and hardly produce a few trusses every year; other plants are free-flowering with compact trusses of white flowers. The variety is hardy and a useful plant for the rock garden.

It was given an Award of Merit when shown by the Crown Estate Commissioners, Windsor, in 1973.

Epithet of the variety. Mountain-dwelling.
Hardiness 3. April–May.

R. roxieanum Forrest var. **parvum** Davidian, var. nov. See page 344.

This variety was first collected by Forrest in July 1921 in the Mekong-Salwin Divide, north-west Yunnan. It was found by him later in 1924 in the Mekong-Yangtze Divide, same region. In 1932 Rock collected it at Kaushu shan, Leilung, south-west Sichuan. It grows in open stony moorland, on terraced cliffs, in rocky meadows, on open rocky slopes, and in alpine region, at elevations of 3,660–4,575 m. (12,000–15,000 ft.).

The variety differs from the species in the small leaves, laminae 2.5–6 cm. long, 6 mm.–1.3 cm. broad, and in the dwarf habit of growth, 1–2 feet or sometimes 3 feet high.

It was first introduced by Forrest in 1924 (No. 25701—the Type number), and again later in the same year (No. 25987). Rock sent seeds in 1932 (No. 24501). Two distinct growth forms are in cultivation: Form 1. A compact, rounded or spreading shrub, 1–2 feet high and as much across, well-filled with foliage. Form 2. A broadly upright shrub 2–3 feet high. This form was successfully grown in the lower peat garden, the Royal Botanic Garden, Edinburgh. Unfortunately it has now been lost to cultivation. The variety is a slow grower, a shy flowerer, but is a beautiful foliage plant.

Epithet of the variety. Small.
Hardiness 3. April–May.

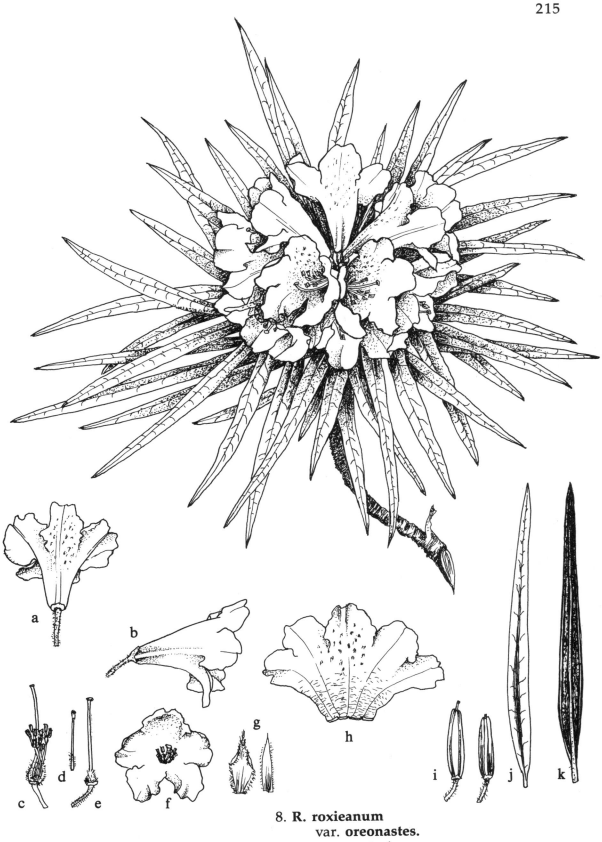

8. **R. roxieanum**
var. **oreonastes.**
nat. size.
a. flower. b. flower (side view). c. section. d. stamen. e. ovary, style. f. flower (front view).
g. flower-bud scales. h. petals. i. capsule. j. leaf (upper surface) k. leaf (lower surface).

R. roxieanum Forrest var. **recurvum** (Balf. f. et Forrest) Davidian, comb. nov.
     Syn. *R. recurvum* Balf. f. et Forrest in Notes Roy. Bot. Gard. Edin., Vol. 11 (1919)
110.

This plant was first collected by Forrest in July 1914 in the Kari Pass, Mekong-Yangtze Divide, north-west Yunnan. It was afterwards found by him and by Rock, McLaren's collectors, and Yü in the same region and mid-west Yunnan, also in the Tsarung Border, Yunnan-south-east Tibet. It grows in open stony pastures, on cliffs, rocky slopes, among rocks, in rhododendron thickets, among dwarf scrub, in and on the margins of pine forests, in shady side valleys, and in fir forest, at elevations of 3,355–4,423 m. (11,000–14,500 ft.).

The variety differs from the species in that the leaves are narrowly lanceolate or narrowly oblanceolate, usually 6 mm.–1.2 cm. broad, and markedly recurved at the margins.

The leaves (laminae) are usually 6–10 cm. long. The indumentum on the lower surface of the leaves is bistrate, upper layer Ramiform with long stem and narrow very long branches, lower layer Rosulate.

It was first introduced by Forrest in 1914 (No. 12947—the Type number) and again on three later occasions. Rock sent seeds under eight different seed numbers. Yü introduced it in 1937. In its native home it grows 2–10 feet high. Two distinct forms are in cultivation. Form 1. A compact rounded shrub 3–4 feet high and as much across, well-filled with dark green leaves. Although a shy flowerer, it is a most attractive foliage plant. Form 2. A broadly upright shrub 6–8 feet high, and provides an admirable display with its compact trusses of white flowers. Both forms are hardy and worthy of being widely grown.

Epithet of the variety. Recurved.
Hardiness 3. April–May.

R. russotinctum Balf. f. et Forrest in Notes Roy. Bot. Gard. Edin., Vol. 11 (1919) 129.
     Syn. *R. alutaceum* Balf. f. et W. W. Sm. var. *russotinctum* (Balf. f. et W. W. Sm.)
     Chamberlain in Notes Roy. Bot. Gard. Edin., Vol. 36 (1978) 119.

A rounded or broadly upright shrub, 1.50–2.44 m. (5–8 ft.) high, *branchlets* with long internodes, brown floccose, *rather densely or moderately glandular* with medium- and short-stalked glands, those below the inflorescences 3–4 mm. in diameter; leaf-bud scales persistent. *Leaves* oblong or lanceolate, lamina coriaceous, 5–11.5 cm. long, 1.5–3.2 cm. broad, apex obtuse or acute, base obtuse or rounded; upper surface dark green, matt, glabrous or with vestiges of hairs, midrib grooved, floccose, primary veins 12–18 on each side, deeply impressed; margin slightly recurved; *under surface covered with a thin or somewhat thick, woolly, rust-coloured, continuous, bistrate indumentum of hairs, upper layer detersile, falling off in large patches, Ramiform with very short stem, and very narrow, long branches, lower layer Rosulate, midrib* prominent, rather densely or moderately hairy, *rather densely or moderately glandular* with short-stalked glands; *petiole* 1–1.2 cm. long, grooved above, moderately or rather densely floccose, *glandular* with medium- and short-stalked glands. *Inflorescence* a lax racemose umbel of about 8 flowers, flower-bud scales deciduous; rhachis 7–8 mm. long, brown floccose, sparsely glandular with short-stalked glands; *pedicel* 1.3–1.8 cm. long, sparsely floccose, *glandular* with short-stalked glands. *Calyx* 5-lobed, minute, 0.5–1 mm. long, lobes triangular or ovate, *outside and margin* glabrous, *densely or moderately glandular* with short-stalked glands. *Corolla* campanulate, 2.4–3 cm. long, white flushed rose with few spots; lobes 5, 1–1.2 cm. long, 1–1.5 cm. broad, rounded, emarginate. *Stamens* 10, unequal, 1.3–2.6 cm. long, shorter than the corolla; filaments densely pubescent on the lower one-third to two-thirds of their length. *Gynoecium* 2.5–3 cm. long, as long as the corolla or shorter, longer than the stamens; *ovary* oblong or conoid, 5 mm. long, glabrous, *densely glandular* with short-stalked glands; style glabrous, eglandular. *Capsule:*—

This species was discovered by Forrest in June 1917 on the mountains north of Atuntze, north-west Yunnan. It was afterwards found by him and by Rock in other localities in the same region. The plant grows in open pine forests, and in rhododendron thickets, at elevations of 3,660–3,965 m. (12,000–13,000 ft.).

R. russotinctum is closely allied to R. tritifolium which it resembles in general features, but differs in that the branchlets, petioles, and midrib on the lower surface of the leaves are rather densely or moderately glandular, the ovary is glabrous, the corolla is usually smaller, the inflorescence is usually fewer-flowered, and the hairs of the upper layer of the indumentum on the lower surface of the leaves are Ramiform (in R. tritifolium they are very Long-rayed).

There is no record of the species in cultivation. Some plants in cultivation which have been labelled R. russotinctum, are in fact, forms of R. iodes.

Epithet. Tinged with red.

Not in cultivation.

R. triplonaevium Balf. f. et Forrest in Notes Roy. Bot. Gard. Edin., Vol. 13 (1920) 62.

A somewhat compact, rounded or spreading shrub, 92 cm.–4.27 m. (3–14 ft.) high; *annual growths and internodes short; branchlets* densely or moderately tomentose with a somewhat thin, rust-coloured or brown tomentum, *eglandular*, those below the inflorescences 5–6 mm. in diameter; leaf-bud scales deciduous or persistent. *Leaves* lanceolate, oblanceolate or oblong-lanceolate, *lamina* coriaceous, *6–17.5 cm. long*, 1.8–4.3 cm. broad, apex shortly acuminate or obtuse, base tapered or obtuse; upper surface dark green, shining or matt, glabrous or with vestiges of hairs, midrib grooved, primary veins 15–20 on each side, deeply impressed; margin recurved or flat; *under surface covered with a thin or somewhat thick*, rust- or cinnamon-coloured or brown, *continuous, bistrate indumentum of hairs, upper layer detersile, usually falling off in small patches, Long-rayed with very long or long ribbon-like arms, lower layer Radiate,* midrib prominent, densely or moderately tomentose, eglandular, primary veins concealed; *petiole* 0.6–1.5 cm. long, grooved above, densely or moderately tomentose with a somewhat thin, rust-coloured or brown tomentum, *eglandular. Inflorescence* a compact racemose umbel of 10–14 flowers, flower-bud scales persistent or deciduous; rhachis 0.5–1 cm. long, pubescent, eglandular; *pedicel* 0.8–1.8 cm. long, rather densely or moderately floccose, *eglandular. Calyx* 5-lobed, minute, 0.5–1 mm. long, lobes triangular, ovate or rounded, *outside* floccose or glabrous, *eglandular, margin* ciliate or eciliate, *eglandular. Corolla* campanulate, 2.7–3.8 cm. long, white flushed rose or pure white, with or rarely without a crimson blotch at the base, and with or without crimson spots; lobes 5, 1–1.4 cm. long, 1–1.8 cm. broad, rounded, emarginate. *Stamens* 10, unequal, 1.3–3 cm. long, shorter than the corolla; filaments densely or moderately pubescent at the base. *Gynoecium* 2.3–3 cm. long, shorter than the corolla, longer than the stamens; *ovary* oblong, conoid or slender, 4–5 mm. long, 7–8-celled, *densely tomentose* with dark brown or brown tomentum, *eglandular;* style glabrous, eglandular. *Capsule* oblong, 1.2–2 cm. long, 5–6 mm. broad, straight or slightly curved, moderately or sparsely floccose, *eglandular,* calyx-lobes persistent.

R. triplonaevium was discovered by the Abbé Soulié in 1903 at Tsekou, north-west Yunnan. It was later collected by Forrest in the same region and in south-east Tibet. Rock found it in north-west Yunnan. It grows in open mixed thickets, in rhododendron thickets, in open pine forests, in and on the margins of open conifer forests, at elevations of 3,355–3,660 m. (11,000–12,000 ft.).

The diagnostic features of the plant are the long lanceolate or oblanceolate leaves up to 17.5 cm. (7 in.) long, and the continuous indumentum of bistrate hairs on the lower surface of the leaves, upper layer detersile, usually falling off in small patches, Long-rayed with very long or long ribbon-like arms, lower layer, Radiate. The species is closely related to R. tritifolium but differs in that the pedicel, calyx, ovary and capsule are not glandular, and it is usually a somewhat compact, rounded or spreading shrub.

It was first introduced by Forrest in 1917 (No. 14492) and again in 1921 (No. 19574). Rock sent seeds in 1923 (No. 10923). In its native home it grows 3–14 feet high; in cultivation it is a somewhat compact, rounded or spreading shrub 3 feet high and is likely to grow taller. It is slow-growing, and many years are needed before it reaches the flowering size. Characteristic features are the short annual growths and internodes, and the compact trusses of 10–14 white flowers. The species is hardy, and has proved to be most attractive in flower. It is rare in cultivation, but would be well worth acquiring for every collection of rhododendrons.

Epithet. With triple moles.
Hardiness 3. April–May.

R. tritifolium Balf. f. et Forrest in Notes Roy. Bot. Gard. Edin., Vol. 13 (1920) 63.

A broadly upright shrub, 1.22–3.66 m. (4–12 ft.) high; *annual growths and internodes short*; branchlets densely or moderately tomentose with a thin rust-coloured or brown tomentum, eglandular, those below the inflorescences 5–8 mm. in diameter; leaf-bud scales deciduous or sometimes persistent. *Leaves* oblanceolate or lanceolate, lamina coriaceous, 8–19 cm. long, 2–4 cm. broad, apex shortly acuminate or acute, base tapered; upper surface dark green, matt or shining, glabrous or with vestiges of hairs, midrib grooved, primary veins 16–20 on each side, deeply impressed; margin slightly recurved or flat; *under surface covered with* a thin or somewhat thick, cinnamon- or rust-coloured, *continuous, bistrate indumentum of hairs*, the *upper layer detersile falling off in large or small patches, Long-rayed with very long or long ribbon-like arms, lower layer Radiate*, midrib prominent, rather densely or moderately tomentose, eglandular, primary veins concealed or slightly raised; petiole 1–1.6 cm. long, densely or moderately tomentose with a somewhat thin, rust-coloured or brown tomentum, eglandular. *Inflorescence* a compact or rarely lax racemose umbel of 10–15 flowers, flower-bud scales persistent or rarely deciduous; rhachis 0.7–1 cm. long, moderately or rather densely pubescent, eglandular; *pedicel* 1.4–2.5 cm. long, floccose, *moderately or sparsely glandular* with short-stalked glands. *Calyx* 5-lobed, minute, 0.5–1 mm. long, lobes triangular or ovate, *outside* sparsely or moderately puberulous, *sparsely or moderately glandular* with short-stalked glands, *margin* puberulous, *sparsely or moderately glandular* with short-stalked glands. *Corolla* funnel-campanulate or campanulate, 2.9–4 cm. long, white flushed rose, with or without a crimson blotch at the base, and with or without a few crimson spots; lobes 5, 1–1.4 cm. long, 1.5–2 cm. broad, rounded emarginate. *Stamens* 10, unequal, 1.5–2.6 cm. long, shorter than the corolla; filaments rather densely pubescent at the base. *Gynoecium* 2.5–3 cm. long, shorter than the corolla, longer than the stamens; *ovary* oblong or conoid, 4–5 mm. long, 5–7-celled, tomentose with a brown tomentum, *densely or moderately glandular* with short-stalked glands; style glabrous, eglandular. *Capsule* oblong, 1.4–2.3 cm. long, 5–6 mm. broad, straight or slightly curved, hairy, eglandular or *glandular* with short-stalked glands, calyx-lobes persistent.

This plant was first collected by Forrest in July 1917 in the Mekong-Salwin Divide, north-west Yunnan. It was afterwards found by him and by Rock in other localities in the same region. The plant grows in open pine forests, in open rhododendron thickets, in mixed thickets on bouldery slopes, and in cane brakes, at elevations of 3,355–3,965 m. (11,000–13,000 ft.).

R. tritifolium is closely allied to *R. triplonaevium* which it resembles in general features. The distinctions between them are discussed under the latter.

The plant was first introduced by Forrest in 1917 (Nos. 14208, 15043). It was reintroduced by him in 1921 (No. 19704). Rock sent seeds on three occasions. In its native home it grows 4–12 feet high; in cultivation it is a broadly upright shrub 4–5 feet in height. It is a slow grower with short annual growths and internodes, and requires several years to bloom. It is hardy, a robust grower, but is rare in cultivation.

Epithet. With polished leaves.
Hardiness 3. April–May.

TALIENSE SUBSERIES

General characters: shrubs or trees, 30 cm.–6.10 m. (1–20 ft.) high, branchlets eglandular or rarely glandular with short-stalked glands. Leaves oblong-lanceolate, lanceolate, oblong, elliptic, oblong-elliptic, oval, ovate or obovate, *lamina* 3.5–15 cm. long, 1.5–8.7 cm. broad; *under surface covered with a thick* or somewhat thick, *woolly or spongy* (in *R. doshongense* thin, plastered), *continuous, bistrate indumentum of hairs, upper layer Ramiform, lower layer Rosulate*, with or without a surface pellicle, (in *R. purdomii* indumentum absent); petiole eglandular or rarely glandular with short-stalked glands. Inflorescence a racemose umbel of 7–20 flowers; *pedicel* 0.8–4 cm. long, *eglandular. Calyx* 5-lobed (except in *R. clementinae* 6–7-lobed), minute, 0.5–1 mm. or rarely up to 3 mm. long, *eglandular.* Corolla campanulate or funnel-campanulate, 2–5.4 cm. long, creamy-yellow, white, white flushed rose, pink, rose or deep rose, with or without crimson spots; lobes 5 (except in *R. clementinae* 6–7). Stamens 10 (except in *R. clementinae* 12–14). *Ovary* conoid or oblong or rarely slender, 4–9 mm. long, 5–9-celled, *glabrous* or rarely hairy, *eglandular*; style glabrous, eglandular. *Capsule* oblong, oblong-oval or sometimes slender, 1–3.2 cm. long, 0.4–1.2 cm. broad, *glabrous, eglandular.*

KEY TO THE SPECIES

A. Corolla and calyx 5-lobed; stamens 10.
    B. Under surface of the leaves glabrous . . . . *purdomii*
    B. Under surface of the leaves covered with a continuous indumentum of hairs.
        C. Indumentum on the under surface of the leaves thick woolly, without a surface pellicle.
            D. Pedicel densely tomentose; leaf apex shortly acuminate or acute . . . . *taliense*
            D. Pedicel glabrous; leaf apex obtuse or almost rounded or slightly acute.
                E. Branchlets and petioles densely woolly; leaves oblong-lanceolate or oblong-obovate; indumentum on the under surface of the leaves fawn. *principis*
                E. Branchlets and petioles usually glabrous; leaves usually oval, oblong-oval, almost orbicular, elliptic or oblong-elliptic; indumentum on the under surface of the leaves cinnamon- or rust-coloured, brown or rarely fawn . . . *sphaeroblastum*
        C. Indumentum on the under surface of the leaves thin plastered, or thick spongy, with a surface pellicle (except in *R. doshongense*).
            F. Indumentum on the under surface of the leaves thin plastered . . . . *doshongense*
            F. Indumentum on the under surface of the leaves usually thick spongy, with a surface pellicle splitting or not splitting.
                G. Surface pellicle of the indumentum on the under surface of the leaves usually splitting into small or large patches; indumentum cinnamon- or rust-coloured, brown or fawn . . . . *flavorufum*
                G. Surface pellicle of the indumentum on the under surface of the leaves not splitting into patches; indumentum whitish, silvery-white, yellowish, brown or fawn.
                    H. Leaves usually ovate, ovate-elliptic or oblong-elliptic; indumentum on the under surface of the leaves often

brown, whitish or fawn; capsule oblong or oblong-
oval, 1–1.8 cm. long, usually straight; upper surface of
the leaves without small or large patches of white
sheen.
- I. Under surface of the leaves and midrib, and petiole
     eglandular; margin of leaves recurved . . . .
     . . . . *aganniphum*
- I. Under surface of the leaves and midrib, and petiole
     often glandular with short-stalked glands; margin
     of leaves usually flat . . . . *glaucopeplum*
- H. Leaves usually oblong-lanceolate; indumentum on the
     under surface of the leaves usually yellowish; capsule
     slender, 2–3.2 cm. long, curved; upper surface of the
     leaves often with small or large patches of white
     sheen . . . . *vellereum*
- A. Corolla and calyx 6–7-lobed; stamens 12–14 . . . . *clementinae*

DESCRIPTION OF THE SPECIES

R. aganniphum Balf. f. et Ward in Notes Roy. Bot. Gard. Edin., Vol. 10 (1917) 80.
    Syn. *R. aganniphum* Balf. f. et Ward var. *adenophyllum* W. W. Sm. nomen nudum.
    A broadly upright or somewhat rounded shrub, 30 cm.–3 m. (1–10 ft.) high,
branchlets glabrous or tomentose with a thin, whitish or fawn tomentum, eglandular or
rarely glandular with short-stalked glands, those below the inflorescences 3–5 mm. in
diameter; leaf-bud scales deciduous. *Leaves* ovate, ovate-elliptic, elliptic, ovate-oblong,
oblong-elliptic, oblong or oblong-lanceolate, lamina coriaceous, 3.5–8.5 cm. long, 1.5–4
cm. broad, apex obtuse, acute or shortly acuminate, base rounded or cordulate or
obtuse; upper surface dark green, matt or shining, slightly rugulose, glabrous or with
vestiges of hairs, midrib grooved, hairy or glabrous, eglandular, primary veins 12–15 on
each side, deeply impressed; margin recurved; *under surface covered with a thick or somewhat thick, spongy, brown, whitish, yellowish or fawn, continuous, bistrate indumentum of
hairs, upper layer Ramiform with medium or long stem, and medium or long narrow
branches, lower layer Rosulate with long or shorter, narrow or ribbon-like arms, with a silky
glossy surface pellicle (= skin), not splitting,* eglandular, *midrib* raised, densely hairy,
eglandular or rarely glandular with short-stalked glands, primary veins concealed; *petiole*
0.8–1.5 cm. long, grooved above, floccose or glabrous, *eglandular* or rarely glandular
with short-stalked glands. *Inflorescence* a racemose umbel of 8–12 flowers, flower-bud
scales deciduous; rhachis 0.4–1.4 cm. long, glabrous or rarely floccose, eglandular or
rarely glandular with short-stalked glands; *pedicel* 0.8–1.9 cm. long, glabrous or sometimes floccose, *eglandular*. *Calyx* 5-lobed, minute, 0.5–1 mm. long, lobes triangular or
ovate, *outside* glabrous, *eglandular, margin* glabrous or rarely hairy, *eglandular. Corolla*
funnel-campanulate or campanulate, 2.6–4.5 cm. long, white, white flushed rose, rose,
deep rose, purplish-pink or rarely creamy-white, with crimson spots; lobes 5, 1–1.5 cm.
long, 1.1–2.3 cm. broad, rounded, emarginate. *Stamens* 10, unequal, 1–2.2 cm. long,
shorter than the corolla; filaments densely pubescent on the lower one-third or up to
two-thirds of their length. *Gynoecium* 2–2.8 cm. long, shorter than the corolla, longer
than the stamens; *ovary* conoid or oblong, 4–8 mm. long, 6-celled, *glabrous, eglandular;*
style glabrous, eglandular. *Capsule* oblong or oblong-oval, 1–1.8 cm. long, 5–9 mm.
broad, straight or slightly curved, glabrous, *eglandular,* calyx-lobes persistent.

    R. aganniphum was discovered by Kingdon-Ward in July 1913 at Doker La, Tibet-
Yunnan frontier. Subsequently it was collected by him and by Forrest, Rock and Yü in

south-east Tibet, north-west Yunnan and south-west Sichuan. It grows in mixed scrub and rhododendron thickets, on open rocky slopes, in open situations amongst boulders, in open stony moist meadows, in open rocky pastures, on boulders and cliffs, in rocky moorland, in and on the margins of pine forests, on the margins of cane brakes, in rocky situations by streams, and in fir forest, at elevations of 3,400–4,575 m. (11,148–15,000 ft.). Kingdon-Ward records it as forming dense scrub 2–3 feet high at Doker La, and dense thickets 6–8 feet high in the Kari Pass, north-west Yunnan. According to Yü it is common in north-west Yunnan.

A distinctive feature of the species is the thick, spongy, continuous indumentum of hairs, the surface forming a silky glossy pellicle (= skin), on the lower surface of the leaves. The indumentum is bistrate, the upper layer is Ramiform with narrow branches; the lower layer Rosulate with long narrow or ribbon-like arms. *R. aganniphum* is closely allied to *R. flavorufum* to which it shows a certain degree of resemblance but differs in that the pellicle on the upper surface of the indumentum does not split into patches; and the indumentum is brown, whitish, yellowish or fawn. In *R. flavorufum* the pellicle on the upper surface of the indumentum usually splits into small or large patches; and the indumentum is usually dark brown, cinnamon- or rust-coloured. Moreover, in *R. aganniphum* the leaves are often smaller than those of its ally.

R. aganniphum was first introduced by Kingdon-Ward in 1913 (No. 768—the Type number). It was reintroduced by Forrest under nine different seed numbers. Rock sent seeds on four occasions. Yü introduced it a few times. In its native home it grows 1–10 feet high; in cultivation it is a broadly upright or somewhat rounded shrub 4–5 feet high, well-filled with foliage. Two distinct forms are in cultivation: Form 1. A plant with large ovate or ovate-elliptic leaves, laminae 7.8–8.5 cm. long, 3.5–3.8 cm. broad. Form 2. A plant with small elliptic leaves, laminae 3.5–4 cm. long, 1.5–2 cm. broad (Forrest No. 19773). This form has not been seen for some time, and is probably lost to cultivation. The species is slow-growing and requires many years to reach the flowering size. It is hardy, and a fairly robust grower. The flowers are white or white flushed rose in trusses of 8–12. The plant often produces oblong capsules containing good fertile seeds in plenty. It is rare in cultivation.

Epithet. Snowy.
Hardiness 3. May.

R. clementinae Forrest in Notes Roy. Bot. Gard. Edin., Vol. 8 (1915) 343.
Illustration. Bot. Mag. Vol. 158 t. 9392 (1935).

A somewhat compact rounded shrub, or tree, 92 cm.–4.58 m. (3–15 ft.) high, branchlets glabrous or rarely tomentose with a thin, whitish tomentum, eglandular, those below the inflorescences 0.6–1 cm. in diameter; leaf-bud scales deciduous. *Leaves* oval, oblong-oval, ovate, elliptic or oblong-elliptic, lamina coriaceous, 6–15 cm. long, 3.2–8.7 cm. broad, apex rounded or obtuse, recurved, base rounded or cordulate; upper surface dark green, (*in young leaves, bluish-green*) shining or matt, slightly rugulose, glabrous or with vestiges of hairs, midrib grooved, glabrous, eglandular, primary veins 12–18 on each side, deeply impressed; margin recurved; *under surface covered with a thick, spongy, fawn, whitish or silvery-white, continuous, bistrate indumentum of hairs, upper layer Ramiform with very short stem and long ribbon-like septate branches, lower layer Rosulate, with long ribbon-like or narrower arms,* with a *silky glossy pellicle* not splitting or splitting into very large patches, eglandular, midrib raised, densely hairy, eglandular, primary veins concealed; petiole 1–3 cm. long, grooved above, glabrous or rarely tomentose with a thin, whitish tomentum, eglandular. *Inflorescence* a racemose umbel of 7–15 flowers, flower-bud scales deciduous; rhachis 0.8–1.4 cm. long, glabrous, eglandular; pedicel 1.2–4 cm. long, glabrous, eglandular. *Calyx 6–7-lobed*, minute, 1 mm. long, lobes triangular or ovate, *outside and margin* glabrous, *eglandular. Corolla* campanulate, 3.6–5 cm. long, creamy-white, white, white flushed rose, bright rose, pink, deep pink or pur-plish-red, with or without crimson spots; *lobes 6–7*, 1.2–1.4 cm. long, 1.4–2.5 cm. broad, rounded, emarginate. *Stamens 12–14*, unequal, 1.1–2.8 cm. long, shorter than the corolla; filaments densely pubescent at the base or up to two-thirds of their length. *Gynoecium* 2.4–3.5 cm. long, shorter than the corolla, longer than the stamens; *ovary conoid or oblong, 6–9 mm. long, 6–9-celled, glabrous, eglandular;* style glabrous, eglandular. *Capsule* short stout or oblong-oval or oblong, 1.3–2 cm. long, 0.7–1.2 cm. broad, glabrous, eglandular, calyx-lobes persistent.

This species was discovered by Forrest in August 1913 on the mountains of the Chungtien plateau, north-west Yunnan. It was afterwards collected by him, Rock, and Yü in other localities in the same region and in south-west Sichuan. It grows in open thickets, in open situations amongst rocks, on rocky slopes, in open mixed thickets, on the margins of pine and conifer forests, in bouldery moorland, in alpine scrub, on ledges of cliffs, and in stony meadows, at elevations of 3,355–4,450 m. (11,000–14,590 ft.).

The diagnostic features of *R. clementinae* are the 6–7-lobed corolla, the 6–7-lobed calyx, and the 12–14 stamens. In these respects it is readily distinguished from all the other members of the Taliense Series. The indumentum on the lower surface of the leaves is bistrate. A characteristic feature of the Ramiform hairs of the upper layer is that the long ribbon-like branches are divided at short intervals by septae which are very similar to those of *R. pronum* in the Roxieanum Subseries.

R. clementinae was first introduced by Forrest in 1913 (No. 10857—the Type number, No. 11486). It was reintroduced by him under five different seed numbers. Rock sent seeds on six occasions. Yü introduced it in 1937. In its native home it is a shrub or tree 3–15 feet high; in cultivation it is a somewhat compact rounded shrub up to about 10 feet in height, with fairly thick branchlets. It is to be noted that the branchlets and petioles are usually glabrous. The species is slow-growing and also slow to reach the flowering size. It is a beautiful foliage plant with large oval to oblong-elliptic leaves, covered on the lower surface with a thick spongy fawn or whitish indumentum and with a silky surface pellicle. The young foliage, bluish-green in colour, is most distinctive and attracts attention. The plant is hardy, and blooms moderately, with large white flushed rose, or pink flowers in trusses of 7–15.

Epithet. After Clementine, wife of George Forrest.
Hardiness 3. April–May.

R. doshongense Tagg in Notes Roy. Bot. Gard. Edin., Vol. 15 (1927) 310.

A somewhat compact rounded, or broadly upright shrub, or tree, 60 cm.–4.58 m. (2–15 ft.) high, branchlets moderately or densely tomentose with a thin, whitish tomentum or glabrous, eglandular, those below the inflorescences 4–7 mm. in diameter; leaf-bud scales deciduous. *Leaves* oval, ovate, obovate, ovate-lanceolate, oblong-lanceolate or lanceolate, lamina coriaceous, 3.6–9 cm. long, 1.5–3.5 cm. broad, apex shortly acuminate, acute or obtuse, base obtuse or cordulate or rounded; upper surface dark green or olive-green, matt or shining, slightly rugulose, tomentose with a thin, whitish tomentum or with vestiges of hairs or glabrous, midrib grooved, tomentose eglandular, primary veins 10–15 on each side, deeply impressed; margin recurved; *under surface covered with a thin, plastered or somewhat plastered, glossy* fawn or whitish, *continuous, bistrate indumentum of hairs, upper layer a form of Ramiform, stem very short,* branches medium length, *lower layer Rosulate,* without pellicle, the *surface not splitting,* midrib raised, densely or moderately hairy, eglandular, primary veins concealed or slightly raised; petiole 0.5–1.5 cm. long, grooved above, densely or moderately tomentose with a thin, whitish tomentum, eglandular. *Inflorescence* a racemose umbel of 8–15 flowers, flower-bud scales deciduous; rhachis 0.6–1 cm. long, densely pubescent or glabrous, eglandular; pedicel 0.8–2 cm. long, glabrous or sparsely or moderately hairy, eglandular. *Calyx* 5-lobed, minute, 0.5–1 mm. long, lobes triangular or ovate, outside glabrous or sparsely hairy, *eglandular, margin* glabrous, *eglandular. Corolla* campanulate,

2.6–3.8 cm. long, pink, whitish-pink, pinkish-red, rose, white with 5 pink bands on the outside, or white, with or without a dark pink blotch at the base, and with crimson or purple spots; lobes 5, 0.8–1.2 cm. long, 1.3–2 cm. broad, rounded, emarginate. *Stamens* 10, unequal, 1–2.6 cm. long, shorter than the corolla; filaments glabrous or densely pubescent at the base or up to two-thirds of their length. *Gynoecium* 2–2.5 cm. long, shorter than the corolla, longer than the stamens; *ovary* conoid or oblong, 5–6 mm. long, 6-celled, *glabrous, eglandular;* style glabrous eglandular. *Capsule* oblong, 1–1.6 cm. long, 5–8 mm. broad, straight or slightly curved, *glabrous, eglandular,* calyx-lobes persistent.

R. doshongense was described by Tagg in 1927 from a specimen (No. 5863) collected by Kingdon-Ward in June 1924 at Doshong La, south-east Tibet. The species was first collected by Forrest in July 1918 at Bei-ma Shan, north-west Yunnan. Subsequently it was found by Forrest, Rock, and Ludlow, Sherriff and Elliot in other localities in the same region. It grows along the top ridges in alpine regions, in moist bouldery meadows, on rocks, and in spruce forests, at elevations of 3,660–4,118 m. (12,000–13,500 ft.).

R. doshongense is a distinct species and cannot be confused with the other species of its Subseries. The diagnostic feature of this plant is the thin, plastered indumentum on the lower surface of the leaves; this characteristic is particularly evident in plants in cultivation. In this respect it is readily distinguished from its nearest ally *R. aganniphum* in which the indumentum is thick and spongy with a distinct surface pellicle. *R. doshongense* also differs markedly from its ally in the structure of the hairs on the lower surface of the leaves.

The species was first introduced by Kingdon-Ward in 1924 (No. 5863—the Type number). Rock sent seeds in 1932 from north-west Yunnan (Nos. 23333, 23338). In its native home it is a shrub or tree, 3–15 feet high; in cultivation it is a somewhat compact rounded or broadly upright shrub, 2–4 feet high. Two distinct forms are in cultivation: Form 1. A rounded shrub 2 feet high with oval leaves, laminae 4–5 cm. long and as much broad. Form 2. A rounded shrub 3–4 feet high with oblong-lanceolate or lanceolate leaves, laminae 8–9 cm. long and 2–3.5 cm. broad. In both forms the thin, plastered, glossy indumentum on the lower surface of the leaves is a characteristic feature. The species is a slow grower and requires many years to produce the flowers. It is very hardy, a shy flowerer, with white or pink flowers in trusses of 8–15.

Epithet. From the Doshong La, S. E. Tibet.
Hardiness 3. April–May.

R. flavorufum Balf. f. et Forrest in Notes Roy. Bot. Gard. Edin., Vol. 11 (1919) 65.
    Syn. *R. schizopeplum* Balf. f. et Forrest in Notes Roy. Bot. Gard. Edin., Vol. 11 (1919) 131.
    R. fissotectum Balf. f. et Forrest, ibid. Vol. 13 (1920) 44.
    R. aganniphum Balf. f. et Ward var. *flavorufum* (Balf. f. et Forrest) Chamberlain, ibid. Vol. 36 (1978) 119.

A compact rounded, or broadly upright shrub, 30 cm.–3 m. (1–10 ft.) high, branchlets glabrous or floccose, eglandular, those below the inflorescences 0.4–1 cm. in diameter; leaf-bud scales deciduous. *Leaves* oval, oblong-oval, elliptic, ovate-elliptic, oblong, oblong-elliptic or oblong-lanceolate, lamina coriaceous, 4.5–12.5 cm. long, 1.9–6 cm. broad, apex rounded, obtuse or shortly acuminate, base rounded or cordulate or obtuse; upper surface dark green, shining or matt, slightly rugulose, glabrous or with vestiges of hairs, midrib grooved, floccose in its entire length or at the base or up to two-thirds of its length or glabrous, eglandular, primary veins 10–18 on each side, deeply impressed; margin flat or recurved; *under surface covered with a thick, brown, cinnamon- or rust-coloured or* fawn, continuous, *bistrate indumentum of hairs, upper layer Ramiform,* stem somewhat short, branches narrow medium length, *lower layer large Rosulate* with long narrow or ribbon-like arms, *with a surface pellicle splitting into small or large patches,* midrib raised, moderately or densely hairy, eglandular, primary veins slightly raised or concealed; petiole 0.8–1.5 cm. long, grooved above, floccose or glabrous, eglandular. *Inflorescence* a racemose umbel of 8–15 flowers, flower-bud scales deciduous; rhachis 0.4–1 cm. long, glabrous or floccose, eglandular; pedicel 0.8–2 cm. long, glabrous or sparsely floccose, eglandular. *Calyx* 5-lobed, minute, 0.5–1 mm. long, lobes triangular or ovate, *outside* glabrous, *eglandular, margin* glabrous or hairy, *eglandular. Corolla* campanulate, 2.5–5.4 cm. long, white, rose, deep rose, white flushed rose, or yellowish-white, with or rarely without crimson spots; lobes 5, 0.8–1.5 cm. long, 1.5–2.3 cm. broad, rounded, emarginate. *Stamens* 10, unequal, 1–2.6 cm. long, shorter than the corolla; filaments densely pubescent at the base or up to two-thirds of their length. *Gynoecium* 2–3 cm. long, shorter than the corolla, longer than the stamens; *ovary* conoid or oblong, 4–6 mm. long, 6–9-celled, *glabrous, eglandular;* style glabrous, eglandular. *Capsule* oblong or oblong-oval, 1–1.9 cm. long, 5–8 mm. broad, straight, *glabrous, eglandular,* calyx-lobes persistent.

This plant was first collected by Forrest in June 1917 on the mountains north of Atuntze, north-west Yunnan. Further gatherings by him, Rock and Yü show that the species is distributed in north-west Yunnan, south-east Tibet and south-west Sichuan. It grows in open situations amongst rocks, on cliffs, rocky slopes, in ravines, on screes, amongst boulders, on open bouldery slopes, in open thickets, in rhododendron thickets, on the margins of pine forests, in rocky moorland, and in alpine pasture, at elevations of 3,355–4,575 m. (11,000–15,000 ft.).

In 1919 *R. schizopeplum* Balf. f. et Forrest was described from a specimen (No. 14094) collected by Forrest in north-west Yunnan. It is identical with *R. flavorufum* under which it will now be placed in synonymy. *R. fissotectum* Balf. f. et Forrest, described in 1920 and relegated to synonymy under *R. schizopeplum* in *The Species of Rhododendron,* will now be referred to *R. flavorufum.*

The diagnostic features of *R. flavorufum* are the cinnamon- or rust-coloured or brown indumentum of hairs on the lower surface of the leaves splitting into a pattern of small or large patches. The isolated patches often fall off. The indumentum is bistrate, the upper layer Ramiform with narrow branches, the lower layer large Rosulate with long narrow or ribbon-like arms. It is to be noted that intergrading forms link the species with *R. aganniphum,* and some specimens could be given either name.

The species was first introduced by Forrest in 1917 (No. 14094—the Type number of *R. schizopeplum,* No.14345—the Type number of *R. flavorufum,* and No. 14368). It was reintroduced by him on 11 occasions. Yü sent seeds in 1937 (No. 10686). In its native home it grows 1–10 feet high; in cultivation it is a compact rounded, or broadly upright shrub 3–5 feet high with dark green foliage. The indumentum on the lower surface of the young leaf is at first yellowish, later it turns to cinnamon- or rust-coloured or brown. The characteristic splitting of the indumentum is usually evident under the young leaves. The species is a fairly vigorous grower, with rigid branchlets. It is hardy, but takes a very long time to flower. It is a shy flowerer, and hardly produces more than 1–2 trusses when it blooms.

Epithet. Yellow-red.
Hardiness 3. April–May.

R. glaucopeplum Balf. f. et Forrest in Notes Roy. Bot. Gard. Edin., Vol. 13 (1920) 46.

A broadly upright or somewhat compact rounded shrub, 92 cm.–2.44 m. (3–8 ft.) high, branchlets glabrous or moderately or densely floccose, eglandular, those below the inflorescences 4–6 mm. in diameter; leaf-bud scales deciduous. *Leaves* ovate, ovate-elliptic, elliptic or oblong-elliptic, lamina coriaceous, 4.8–9.5 cm. long, 2–3.8 cm. broad, apex acute or obtuse, base cordulate, rounded or obtuse; upper surface dark green, shining, slightly rugulose, glabrous or with vestiges of hairs, midrib grooved, hairy or glabrous, eglandular, primary veins 12–15 on each side, deeply impressed; margin slightly recurved or flat; *under surface covered with a somewhat thick, spongy,* white, fawn or yellowish, *continuous, bistrate indumentum of hairs, upper layer Ramiform* with somewhat short stem and narrow medium length branches, *lower layer large Rosulate with long or shorter narrow or ribbon-like arms with a surface pellicle* not splitting, *glandular with short-stalked glands* or eglandular, *midrib* raised, moderately or densely hairy, *glandular with short-stalked glands* or eglandular, primary veins concealed; *petiole* 0.6–1.5 cm. long, grooved above, glabrous or floccose or tomentose with a thin whitish tomentum, *glandular with short-stalked glands* or eglandular. *Inflorescence* a racemose umbel of 8–10 flowers, flower-bud scales deciduous; rhachis 5–6 mm. long, glabrous or sparsely floccose, eglandular; pedicel 1.4–2.3 cm. long, glabrous, eglandular. *Calyx* 5-lobed, minute, 0.5–1 mm. long, lobes triangular or ovate, *outside and margin* glabrous, *eglandular. Corolla* funnel-campanulate or campanulate, 3–3.5 cm. long, bright rose or white flushed rose, with crimson spots; lobes 5, 1–1.3 cm. long, 1.4–1.8 cm. broad, rounded, emarginate. *Stamens* 10, unequal, 1.3–2.3 cm. long, shorter than the corolla; filaments densely pubescent at the base or up to two-thirds of their length. *Gynoecium* 2.1–2.8 cm. long, shorter than the corolla, longer than the stamens; *ovary* oblong or conoid, 4–5 mm. long, 6-celled, *glabrous, eglandular;* style glabrous, eglandular. *Capsule* oblong, 1–1.5 cm. long, 5–8 mm. broad, straight or slightly curved, *glabrous, eglandular,* calyx-lobes persistent.

Forrest first collected this plant in July 1917 in the Mekong-Salwin Divide, north-west Yunnan. He found it again in 1918 on the mountains north-east of Chungtien in the same region, and on Ka-gwr-pw, Mekong-Salwin Divide, Tsarong, south-east Tibet. It grows in cane brakes, in thickets and rhododendron scrub, and in pine forests, at elevations of 3,355–4,270 m. (11,000–14,000 ft.).

R. glaucopeplum bears a strong resemblance to *R. aganniphum* in general characters, but differs in that the under surface of the leaves including midrib and petiole are often glandular with short-stalked glands, and the margins of the leaves are usually flat. The plant appears so distinct in cultivation, that its specific status will be retained.

The species was introduced by Forrest in 1918 (No. 16472). In cultivation it is a broadly upright or somewhat compact rounded shrub, 4–5 feet high with rigid branchlets, and well-filled with dark green foliage. The plant is hardy but takes a long time to reach the flowering stage. The flowers are white flushed rose in trusses of 8–10. The species is rare in cultivation.

Epithet. With a greyish covering.
Hardiness 3. April–May.

R. principis Bur. et Franch. in Journ. de Bot., Vol. 5 (1891) 93.

A small tree, *branchlets densely* brown *woolly,* eglandular, those below the inflorescences 0.6–1 cm. in diameter; leaf-bud scales deciduous. *Leaves* oblong-lanceolate or oblong-obovate, lamina coriaceous, 9–11.6 cm. long, 3.3–3.6 cm. broad, apex obtuse or slightly acute, base obtuse or rounded; upper surface dark green, somewhat shining, slightly rugulose, glabrous or with vestiges of hairs, midrib grooved, glabrous, eglandular, primary veins 15–18 on each side, deeply impressed; margin flat or slightly recurved; *under surface covered with a thick, woolly, fawn, continuous, bistrate indumentum of hairs, upper layer Ramiform with* long stem and *long somewhat ribbon-like branches, lower layer large Rosulate with long or shorter ribbon-like arms, without pellicle,* midrib raised, densely woolly, eglandular, primary veins concealed; *petiole* 1–1.8 cm. long, thick, grooved above, *densely* brown *woolly,* eglandular. *Inflorescence* a racemose umbel of *7–12 flowers,* flower-bud scales deciduous; rhachis 9 mm. long, pubescent, eglandular; pedicel 1–1.3 cm. long, glabrous, eglandular. *Calyx* 5-lobed, minute, 1 mm. long, lobes triangular or rounded, *outside* glabrous, *eglandular, margin* hairy or glabrous, *eglandular. Corolla* funnel-campanulate, 2.5–3.2 cm. long (colour unknown); lobes 5, 0.8–1 cm. long, 1.3–1.5 cm. broad, emarginate or entire. *Stamens* 10, unequal, 1.3–2.5 cm. long, shorter than the corolla; filaments rather densely pubescent at the base. *Gynoecium* 2.3–2.7 cm. long, shorter than the corolla, longer than the stamens; *ovary* conoid or oblong, 4–5 mm. long, sparsely hairy or *glabrous, eglandular;* style glabrous, eglandular. *Capsule:*—

R. principis is represented by a single gathering made by M. Bonvalot and Prince Henri d'Orléans in May 1890 between Lhassa and Batang, Tibet, growing in alpine region at an elevation of 3,000 m. (9,836 ft.).

The main features of the species are the densely brown woolly branchlets and petioles, the thick, woolly, bistrate indumentum on the lower surface of the leaves, upper layer Ramiform with long somewhat ribbon-like branches, lower layer large Rosulate with long or shorter ribbon-like arms, without a surface pellicle, the 7–12-flowered inflorescence, and the funnel-campanulate corolla 2.5–3.2 cm. long. The flower colour is unknown. It is allied to *R. vellereum* but differs in well-marked characters.

The plant has not been introduced into cultivation.

Epithet. Of the prince.

Not in cultivation.

R. purdomii Rehd. et Wils. in Pl. Wilsonianae, Vol. I (1913) 538.

A robust shrub, young branchlets puberulous; leaf-bud scales more or less persistent. *Leaves* oblong-lanceolate or oblong, lamina coriaceous, 6–8 cm. long, 2.5–3.5 cm. broad, apex acute or obtuse, base tapered or obtuse; upper surface light green, shining, slightly rugulose, glabrous, midrib grooved, glabrous, eglandular, primary veins 10–12 on each side, deeply impressed; margin recurved; *under surface glabrous,* midrib prominent, glabrous, eglandular, primary veins slightly raised; petiole 1–1.5 cm. long, grooved above, glabrous, eglandular. *Inflorescence* a racemose umbel of 10–12 or more flowers; rhachis about 1 cm. long, rufous-tomentose; pedicel 1–1.6 cm. long, densely or moderately hairy with fawn hairs, eglandular. *Calyx* 5-lobed, minute, 1 mm. long, lobes triangular or ovate, *outside and margin* sparsely pubescent or glabrous, *eglandular. Corolla* campanulate, 2–3 cm. long; lobes 5, 1 cm. long, 1–1.3 cm. broad, rounded, entire. *Stamens* 10, unequal, 1.3–2.5 cm. long, shorter than the corolla; filaments densely pubescent towards the base. *Gynoecium* 2–2.5 cm. long, shorter than the corolla, longer than the stamens; ovary conoid, 4–5 mm. long, 5-celled, sparsely or moderately hairy with whitish or brown hairs, eglandular; style glabrous, eglandular. *Capsule:*—

This plant is known from a single collection (No.4) made by W. Purdom in 1910 at Tai-pei-shan, in Shensi.

R. purdomii is an aberrant species in the Taliense Series on account of the completely glabrous lower surface of the leaves. It shows a certain degree of resemblance to *R. przewalskii* in the Lacteum Series, but differs markedly in distinctive features. Meanwhile it may be allowed to remain in its present Series until more is known of this plant.

The species has not been introduced into cultivation.

Epithet. After W. Purdom, collector in China, 1880–1921.

Not in cultivation.

R. sphaeroblastum Balf. f. et Forrest in Notes Roy. Bot. Gard. Edin., Vol. 13 (1920) 60.

A compact rounded, or broadly upright shrub, or tree, 60 cm.–6.10 m. (2–20 ft.) high, *branchlets glabrous* or rarely tomentose with a thin tomentum, eglandular, those below the inflorescences 5–9 mm. in diameter; leaf-bud scales deciduous. *Leaves oval, oblong-oval, almost orbicular, elliptic, oblong-elliptic* or rarely oblong-lanceolate, lamina coriaceous, 7–13.2 cm. long, 3.5–7 cm. broad, apex obtuse or almost rounded, base rounded or obtuse or cordulate; upper surface dark green, shining, slightly rugulose, glabrous or with vestiges of hairs, midrib grooved, glabrous, eglandular, primary veins 12–18 on each side, deeply impressed; margin flat; *under surface covered with a thick, woolly, cinnamon- or rust-coloured, brown* or rarely fawn, *continuous, bistrate indumentum of hairs, upper layer Ramiform with very short or long stem,* and *long ribbon-like branches, lower layer* small and large *Rosulate* hairs, *without pellicle,* midrib raised, densely woolly, eglandular, primary veins concealed; *petiole* 1–2.5 cm. long, thick, grooved above, *glabrous* or rarely tomentose with a thin tomentum, *eglandular. Inflorescence* a racemose umbel of 10–15 flowers, flower-bud scales deciduous; rhachis 0.8–1.5 cm. long, glabrous, eglandular; *pedicel* 1–2 cm. long, *glabrous,* eglandular. *Calyx* 5-lobed, minute, 1 mm. long, lobes triangular or ovate, *outside glabrous, eglandular, margin glabrous* or rarely hairy, *eglandular. Corolla* campanulate, 2.9–4 cm. long, white, creamy-white, white flushed rose, or pink, with or without crimson spots; lobes 5, 1–1.5 cm. long, 1.5–2.3 cm. broad, rounded, emarginate. *Stamens* 10, unequal, 1–2 cm. long, shorter than the corolla; filaments densely or moderately pubescent at the base or on the lower one-third of their length. *Gynoecium* 2–3 cm. long, shorter than the corolla, larger than the stamens; *ovary* conoid or oblong, 5–7 mm. long, 5–8-celled, *glabrous, eglandular;* style glabrous, eglandular. *Capsule* oblong or oblong-oval, 1–2 cm. long, 5–9 mm. broad, *glabrous, eglandular,* calyx-lobes persistent.

The discovery of this species has been wrongly credited to George Forrest. It was first collected by Wilson in July 1904 in Western China (No. 3957 = Seed No. 1863). The species was described in 1920 by Balfour f. et Forrest from a specimen (No. 17360 holotype) collected by Forrest in July 1918 in south-west Sichuan. Subsequently it was found by Forrest and Rock in the same region and in north-west Yunnan, and by Kingdon-Ward in Yunnan-Sichuan Border. It grows in open rocky meadows, in rhodo-dendron and mixed thickets, on rocky slopes, in open scrub, amongst boulders in ravines, in open forests, in conifer, spruce and *Abies* forests, at elevations of 3,355–4,600 m. (11,000–15,082 ft.). According to Kingdon-Ward, it is a big shrub, 20 feet high, forming thickets by itself in *Abies* forest and along the borders of meadows in the Yungning-Muli Pass at 15,000 feet. Rock records it as being a tree 15–20 feet high, forming forests in north-west Yunnan at elevations of 13,500–14,000 feet.

R. sphaeroblastum resembles *R. phaeochrysum* in the Lacteum Series in general features but differs in that the indumentum on the under surface of the leaves is thick woolly, bistrate, upper layer Ramiform hairs; in *R. phaeochrysum* the indumentum is thin, usually agglutinate, somewhat plastered, unistrate, the hairs are Long-rayed.

The species was first introduced by Wilson in 1904 (No. 3957 = Seed No. 1863). It was reintroduced by Forrest in 1918 (Nos. 16377, 17110), and again later under 17 seed numbers. Rock sent seeds on 12 occasions. In its native home it is a shrub or tree 2–20 feet high. Several forms are in cultivation, including: Form 1. A compact rounded shrub 5–6 feet high with large oval leaves and cinnamon-coloured indumentum on the lower surface. Form 2. A somewhat compact broadly upright shrub 7–8 feet high with large oblong-lanceolate leaves and brown indumentum on the lower surface. A charac-teristic feature of the species is the glabrous branchlets, petioles, pedicels, calyx, ovaries and capsules. The plant is hardy, a robust grower with thick branchlets. It is free-flowering, and provides an admirable display with its white flowers in trusses of 10–15. The species often produces large oblong or oblong-oval capsules containing good fer-tile seeds in plenty.

Epithet. With rounded buds.
Hardiness 3. April–May.

R. taliense Franch. in Bull. Soc. Bot. France, Vol. 33 (1886) 232.

A compact, rounded or spreading shrub, 1.22–3.66 m. (4–12 ft.) or rarely 60 cm. (2 ft.) high, *branchlets moderately or densely tomentose* with a thin, brown tomentum, *eglandular,* those below the inflorescences 5–7 mm. in diameter; leaf-bud scales deciduous. *Leaves* oblong-lanceolate, lanceolate, ovate-lanceolate or oblong-ovate, lamina coriaceous, 5–11 cm. long, 1.8–4 cm. broad, apex shortly acuminate or acute, base cordulate or rounded or obtuse; upper surface dark green, somewhat shining or matt, slightly rugulose, glabrous or with vestiges of hairs, midrib grooved, glabrous, eglandular, primary veins 12–18 on each side, deeply impressed; margin flat or slightly recurved; *under surface covered with a thick, woolly,* brown, *continuous, bistrate indumentum of hairs, upper layer Ramiform with very short stem and long somewhat ribbon-like branches, lower layer small and large Rosulate hairs, without pellicle,* midrib prominent, densely woolly, eglandular, primary veins concealed; *petiole* 0.8–1.5 cm. long, grooved above, *densely* or rarely moderately *tomentose with a thin, brown tomentum, eglandular. Inflorescence* a compact racemose umbel of 8–19 flowers, flower-bud scales deciduous; rhachis 1–1.2 cm. long, pubescent, eglandular; *pedicel* 1–2 cm. long, *densely tomentose, eglandular. Calyx* 5-lobed, 0.5–3 mm. long, lobes triangular or ovate, *outside* glabrous or rarely hairy, *eglandular, margin* glabrous or hairy, *eglandular. Corolla* campanulate, 2.5–3.5 cm. long, *creamy-yellow, pale yellow,* white or white flushed rose, with crimson spots; lobes 5, 0.9–1.2 cm. long, 1–2 cm. broad, rounded, emarginate. *Stamens* 10, unequal, 0.8–1.7 cm. long, shorter than the corolla; filaments densely pubescent at the base or up to one-half of their length. *Gynoecium* 2–2.5 cm. long, shorter than the corolla, longer than the stamens; *ovary* conoid, 4–5 mm. long, 5–7-celled, *glabrous, eglandular;* style glabrous, eglandular. *Capsule* oblong or sometimes oblong-oval, 1.3–2 cm. long, 4–7 mm. broad, *glabrous, eglandular,* calyx-lobes persistent.

R. taliense was discovered by the Abbé Delavay in June 1887 on Tsang chan mountain, above Tali, western Yunnan. It was afterwards found by Forrest, Rock, and McLaren's collectors in the same region and in north-west Yunnan. It grows in dry rocky situations on mountain meadows, in rocky pastures, in rhododendron thickets, in open scrub in side valleys, on cliffs, and on rocky slopes in ravines, at elevations of 3,050–3,660 m. (10,000–12,000 ft.).

The main features of the species are the thick, woolly, continuous, bistrate indumentum of hairs on the lower surface of the leaves, upper layer Ramiform with very short stem and long somewhat ribbon-like branches, lower layer small and large Rosulate hairs, the densely or moderately tomentose branchlets, petioles and pedicels, and the campanulate usually creamy-yellow corolla. *R. taliense* bears a resemblance to *R. sphaeroblastum* in some features, but differs markedly in distinctive features.

The species was first introduced by Forrest in 1910 (No. 6772). It was later reintroduced by him under Nos. 11579, 28237, 28253. (The last two numbers have been wrongly recorded as *R. flavorufum* in *The Rhododendron Handbook* 1980). Rock sent seeds in 1932 (No. 6253). In cultivation it is a compact, rounded or spreading shrub, 5–6 feet high and as much or more across, well-filled with dark green foliage. It is a robust grower with rigid branchlets, but is slow to reach the flowering size. The plant is hardy and makes a fine show with its creamy-yellow flowers produced freely in trusses of 8–19. It should be noted that usually the flowers open creamy-white but gradually turn to white. It often sets plentiful good fertile seeds in large oblong or oblong-oval capsules. The plant is rare in cultivation, but is worth being more widely grown. A magnificent compact spreading specimen, 5 feet high and about 6 feet across which was successfully grown in the Royal Botanic Garden, Edinburgh, has now ceased to exist.

Epithet. From Tali Range, Yunnan.
Hardiness 3. April–May.

R. vellereum Hutch. ex Tagg in The Species of Rhododendron (1930) 688.
      Syn. *R. principis Vellereum Group* R. H. S. in Rhod. Handb. (1980) p. 58.
Illustration. Bot. Mag. n.s. Vol. 168 t. 147 (1951).
A somewhat compact rounded shrub or bush or tree, 1.22–6.10 m. (4–20 ft.) high, *branchlets glabrous* or rarely tomentose with a thin, whitish tomentum, *eglandular,* those

below the inflorescences 4–6 mm. in diameter; leaf-bud scales deciduous. *Leaves* oblong-lanceolate or oblong-elliptic, lamina coriaceous, 5.5–13.5 cm. long, 2–5 cm. broad, apex acute, shortly acuminate or obtuse, base obtuse or rounded or cordulate; *upper surface* dark green, shining, smooth or slightly rugulose, glabrous or with vestiges of hairs, *often with small or large patches of white sheen*, midrib grooved, glabrous, eglandular, primary veins 14–20 on each side, deeply impressed; margin flat or slightly recurved; *under surface covered with a thick, spongy, silvery-white, yellowish or fawn, continuous, bistrate indumentum of hairs, upper layer Ramiform with long stem and long narrow branches, lower layer Rosulate usually with narrow arms, with a surface pellicle* not splitting or rarely splitting into small and large patches, midrib raised, moderately or densely hairy, eglandular, primary veins concealed; *petiole* 0.8–2 cm. long, grooved above, densely or moderately or sparsely tomentose above, glabrous below, *eglandular. Inflorescence* a racemose umbel of *12–20 flowers;* flower-bud scales deciduous; rhachis 0.5–1.6 cm. long, glabrous or hairy, eglandular; *pedicel* 1–3.5 cm. long, glabrous or rarely sparsely hairy, *eglandular. Calyx* 5-lobed, minute, 0.5–1 mm. long, lobes triangular or ovate, *outside* glabrous, *eglandular, margin* hairy or glabrous, *eglandular. Corolla* funnel-campanulate, 2.6–3.8 cm. long, white, white flushed pale pink, pale rose or pink, with or without carmine or purple spots; lobes 5, 0.8–1.2 cm. long, 1–2.3 cm. broad, rounded, emarginate. *Stamens* 10, unequal 1–2.8 cm. long, shorter than the corolla; filaments pubescent at the base. *Gynoecium* 2.3–3.4 cm. long, shorter than the corolla, longer than the stamens; *ovary* slender or oblong or rarely conoid, 4–6 mm. long, 5–8-celled, *glabrous, eglandular;* style glabrous, eglandular. *Capsule* slender, 2–3.2 cm. long, 4–5 mm. broad, curved, *glabrous, eglandular,* calyx-lobes persistent.

R. vellereum was discovered by Kingdon-Ward in 1924 above Nang Dzang, Tsangpo Valley, south-east Tibet. It was later found by him, and by Ludlow, Sherriff and together with Taylor or Elliot, in the same region and in south Tibet. It grows in *Picea,* rhododendron, and pine forests, in bamboo and rhododendron forest, in mixed conifer and deciduous forest, in holly, oak and conifer forest, among shrubs on stony river bank, on dry hillside amongst rocks, and by the side of lakes, at elevations of 2,898–4,575 m. (9,500–15,000 ft.). Kingdon-Ward records it as growing on sheltered slopes with birch, larch and other trees or as a bush covering whole hillsides above Nang Dzang, Tsangpo Valley. According to Ludlow, Sherriff and Taylor, it is common on rather dry stony hillside among other shrubs at Kyimdong Dzong.

The species is closely allied to *R. aganniphum* but is distinguished by the longer leaves and by their shape, by the slender and longer curved capsule, and often by the more spongy indumentum on the lower surface of the leaves. *R. vellereum* is also related to *R. principis* but differs markedly in that the branchlets are glabrous, the indumentum on the lower surface of the leaves is thick spongy with a distinct pellicle, the hairs of the indumentum are somewhat different, the inflorescence is 12–20-flowered, and the corolla is often larger.

The species was first introduced by Kingdon-Ward in 1925 (No. 5656), and again in 1933 (No. 10700). Ludlow, Sherriff and with Taylor or Elliot sent seeds on 11 occasions. In its native home it is a shrub or bush or tree, 4–20 feet high; in cultivation it is a somewhat compact rounded shrub, usually 5–6 feet high and densely filled with dark green foliage. Characteristic features are the thick spongy silvery-white, yellowish or fawn indumentum with a surface pellicle on the lower surface of the leaves, and often the small or large patches of white sheen on the upper surface of the leaves. The species is hardy, but requires several years before it starts flowering. It varies a great deal in its freedom of flowering. Some plants are shy flowerers and occasionally produce a few trusses; other plants bloom moderately or somewhat freely. The flowers are white or pale rose in large trusses of 12–20.

A clone 'Lost Horizon' was given an Award of Merit when shown by R. N. S. Clarke, Borde Hill, Sussex, in 1976.

Epithet. Fleecy.
Hardiness 3. March–May.

WASONII SUBSERIES

General characters: shrubs or rarely trees, 60 cm.–6.10 m. (2–20 ft.) high, branchlets eglandular or sometimes glandular with short-stalked glands; leaf-bud scales deciduous. Leaves lanceolate, oblong-lanceolate, oblong, oblanceolate, oblong-obovate, oblong-elliptic, elliptic, ovate or ovate-lanceolate, lamina 4.5–13.8 cm. long, 1.6–5.9 cm. broad; *under surface covered with a thick, woolly,* brown, cinnamon- or rust-coloured *continuous indumentum of hairs, or* with a *discontinuous, woolly indumentum in small or large patches,* hairs *unistrate or bistrate;* petiole 0.5–3 cm. long, eglandular or sometimes glandular with short-stalked glands. Inflorescence a lax racemose umbel of 4–12 flowers; pedicel 0.5–3.6 cm. long, moderately or densely tomentose, eglandular or sometimes glandular with short-stalked glands. Calyx 5-lobed, 0.5–3 mm. long, eglandular or sometimes glandular with short-stalked glands. Corolla campanulate or rarely funnel-campanulate, 2–4.3 cm. long, creamy-white, white, pink, white tinged pink, pinkish-purple, yellow or creamy-yellow, with or without a deep crimson blotch at the base, and with or without crimson spots; lobes 5. Stamens 10. Ovary oblong, conoid or rarely ovoid, 4–7 mm. long, 5–6-celled, densely or sometimes moderately tomentose or sometimes glabrous, eglandular or sometimes moderately or densely glandular with short-stalked glands. Capsule oblong or sometimes slender, 1.2–2.6 cm. long, 4–9 mm. broad, moderately or rather densely tomentose or sometimes glabrous, eglandular or sometimes moderately or densely glandular with short-stalked glands.

KEY TO THE SPECIES

A. Indumentum on the under surface of the leaves discontinuous, interrupted, in small or large patches.
  B. Indumentum on the under surface of the leaves bistrate, upper layer of hairs a form of Stellate (lower layer Rosulate); leaves oblanceolate; branchlets, petioles and pedicels densely rufous tomentose. From south-east Sichuan . . . . *coeloneurum*
                                                                                           (part)
  B. Indumentum on the under surface of the leaves unistrate, hairs Foliaceous or Ramiform; leaves lanceolate, oblong, oblong-elliptic or oblong-obovate; branchlets, petioles and pedicels moderately or densely floccose with brown or whitish hairs. From western Sichuan.
    C. Terminal leaf-bud ovate; leaves usually lanceolate or oblong-lanceolate; calyx minute, 1 mm. long; corolla 2.5–3.6 cm. long . . . . *inopinum*
    C. Terminal leaf-bud elongate, pointed; leaves oblong, oblong-elliptic or oblong-obovate; calyx 2–3 mm. long; corolla 3.4–4 cm. long . . . . . .
         . . . . *paradoxum*
A. Indumentum on the under surface of the leaves continuous, not interrupted, not in patches.
  D. Upper surface of the leaves markedly bullate; hairs of the indumentum somewhat Fasciculate . . . . *wiltonii*
  D. Upper surface of the leaves not bullate; hairs of the indumentum not Fasciculate.

E. Corolla yellow or creamy-yellow or creamy-white; hairs of the indumentum Long-rayed .... *wasonii*

E. Corolla pink, rose, white, white tinged pink or purplish; hairs of the indumentum Long-rayed or Ramiform.

    F. Leaves usually ovate or ovate-lanceolate; indumentum on the under surface of the leaves unistrate or bistrate.

        G. Indumentum on the under surface of the leaves unistrate, hairs Long-rayed; ovaries, and usually pedicels and calyx not glandular. From western Sichuan .... *wasonii* var. *rhododactylum*

        G. Indumentum on the under surface of the leaves bistrate, upper layer of hairs a form of Ramiform, lower layer Rosulate; ovary rather densely glandular with short-stalked glands, pedicels and calyx moderately or sparsely glandular with short-stalked glands. From Taiwan.... *pachysanthum*

    F. Leaves oval, almost orbicular, oblong-elliptic, elliptic, oblong, oblong-obovate, oblong-lanceolate or oblanceolate; indumentum on the under surface of the leaves bistrate.

        H. Hairs of the upper layer of the indumentum on the under surface of the leaves Ramiform; leaves oval, almost orbicular, oblong-elliptic, elliptic, oblong, oblong-obovate or oblong-lanceolate; branchlets moderately or sparsely tomentose or glabrous; tomentum of branchlets, petioles and pedicels pale fawn or whitish.

            I. Leaves oval, almost orbicular, oblong-elliptic or elliptic, base rounded or broadly obtuse, lamina usually 3–5.9 cm. broad............................ *weldianum*

            I. Leaves oblong, oblong-obovate or oblong-lanceolate, base often obtuse or cordulate, lamina usually 2–3.4 cm. broad............................... *rufum*

        H. Hairs of the upper layer of the indumentum on the under surface of the leaves a form of Stellate; leaves oblanceolate; branchlets densely tomentose; tomentum of branchlets, petioles and pedicels rufous................ *coeloneurum* (part)

DESCRIPTION OF THE SPECIES

R. coeloneurum Diels in Engl. Jahrb. XXIX (1900) 513.

A shrub or small tree, 3.66–4 m. (12–13 ft.) high, *branchlets densely rufous tomentose,* eglandular, those below the inflorescences 4–5 mm. in diameter; leaf-bud scales deciduous. *Leaves oblanceolate,* lamina coriaceous, 8–12 cm. long, 2.1–3.5 cm. broad, apex obtuse or acute, base cuneate or tapered; upper surface somewhat shining, slightly rugulose, glabrous, midrib grooved, moderately or sparsely hairy, eglandular, primary veins 10–14 on each side, deeply impressed; margin flat; under *surface covered with a thick woolly, rufous, continuous or discontinuous (patchy), bistrate indumentum of hairs, upper layer a form of Stellate, arms long somewhat broad ribbon-like, pointed, lower layer* whitish adpressed *Rosulate,* midrib prominent, densely or moderately tomentose, eglandular, primary veins raised; *petiole* 1.3–2 cm. long, grooved above, *densely rufous tomentose,* eglandular. *Inflorescence* a racemose umbel of 4–8 flowers, flower-bud scales deciduous; rhachis 4–5 mm. long, densely rufous tomentose, eglandular; *pedicel* 0.7–1 cm. long, *densely rufous tomentose,* eglandular. *Calyx* 5-lobed, minute, 1 mm. long, lobes triangular or rounded, *outside and margin densely rufous tomentose*, eglandular. *Corolla* funnel-campanulate, 4–4.3 cm. long, pink or purplish; lobes 5, 1–1.3 cm. long, 1.5–1.8 cm. broad, rounded, emarginate. *Stamens* 10, unequal, 2–3.6 cm. long, shorter than the corolla; filaments densely puberulous at the base. *Gynoecium* 4–4.2 cm. long, shorter than the corolla, longer than the stamens; *ovary* conoid, 4–5 mm. long, 5-celled, *densely tomentose*, eglandular; style glabrous, eglandular. *Capsule* cylindric, up to 2.5 cm. long, hairy.

The distribution of this species is restricted to south-east Sichuan. It was discovered by Bock and Rosthorn in 1891 at Nan Chuan. It was afterwards found by Tw at Chin-fu-shan, south of Nan Chuan. The plant grows in mixed forests at elevations of about 2,120 m. (6,951 ft.).

R. coeloneurum shows a certain degree of affinity with *R. wiltonii*, but differs in that the upper surface of the leaves is slightly rugulose (not bullate), the indumentum on the lower surface of the leaves is bistrate, the hairs of the upper layer are a form of Stellate, rufous, and the tomentum of the branchlets, petioles, pedicels and calyx is rufous in colour.

The species has not been introduced into cultivation.

Epithet. With impressed nerves.

Not in cultivation.

R. inopinum Balf. f. in Notes Roy. Bot. Gard. Edin., Vol. 15 (1926) 109.

A rounded shrub, 1.53–3 m. (5–10 ft.) high, *branchlets moderately or densely floccose with branched* brown *hairs*, eglandular or rarely glandular with long-stalked glands, those below the inflorescences 3–4 mm. in diameter, *terminal leaf-buds ovate*, leaf-bud scales deciduous. *Leaves lanceolate, oblong-lanceolate* or oblong-elliptic, lamina coriaceous, 5.3–10.5 cm. long, 1.6–3.6 cm. broad, apex acuminate or acute, base rounded or obtuse; upper surface olive-green or dark green, shining, slightly rugulose, glabrous or with vestiges of hairs, midrib grooved, glabrous or sparsely hairy, eglandular, primary veins 12–15 on each side, deeply impressed; margin slightly recurved or flat; *under surface* pale green, *with small patches of closely or widely separated woolly*, brown, *discontinuous, detersile unistrate indumentum, hairs Foliaceous with long stem, and medium, broad, flat, ribbon-like branches*, midrib prominent, hairy, eglandular, primary veins slightly raised; *petiole* 1–1.6 cm. long, grooved above, *moderately or densely floccose with branched* brown *hairs*, eglandular. *Inflorescence* a racemose umbel of 6–10 flowers, flower-bud scales deciduous; rhachis 6–8 mm. long, densely puberulous, eglandular; *pedicel* 0.8–2.1 cm. long, *moderately or densely floccose* with branched or unbranched brown hairs, eglandular. *Calyx* 5-lobed, *minute, 1 mm. long*, lobes ovate or triangular, outside and margin hairy, eglandular. *Corolla* campanulate, *2.5–3.6 cm. long*, creamy-white, white flushed pink, or pale yellow, with a deep crimson blotch at the base, and with crimson spots; lobes 5, 0.8–1.2 cm. long, 1.2–2 cm. broad, rounded, entire or emarginate. *Stamens* 10, unequal, 1–2.8 cm. long, shorter than the corolla; filaments rather densely puberulous at the base. *Gynoecium* 2.6–3.8 cm. long, as long as the corolla or longer, longer than the stamens; *ovary* oblong, 4–6 mm. long, 6-celled, *densely tomentose* with brown tomentum, eglandular; style glabrous, eglandular. *Capsule* oblong, 1.5–1.6 cm. long, 4–5 mm. broad, straight, moderately or rather densely tomentose with brown tomentum, eglandular, calyx persistent.

R. inopinum was described in 1926 from a plant raised in cultivation, from Wilson's seed No. 1886 in part, collected in western Sichuan. The herbarium specimen under this number is *Lonicera trichogynum*. It is to be noted that under the same number *R. wasonii* also appeared in cultivation.

The species resembles *R. paradoxum* in some features, particularly in the discontinuous small patches of unistrate indumentum closely or widely separated on the lower surface of the leaves, but is readily distinguished by the terminal ovate leaf-buds, usually by the shape of the leaves, and by the smaller calyx and corolla. It also differs in the Foliaceous hairs of the indumentum, with long stem, and medium, broad, flat, ribbon-like branches.

In cultivation *R. inopinum* is a rounded shrub with olive-green or dark green leaves. The plant is hardy outdoors, but along the east coast it should be given some protection from wind. The campanulate flowers are creamy-white or white flushed pink, with a crimson blotch at the base, and are produced freely in trusses of 6–10. The plant is uncommon in cultivation. There was a remarkable plant 5 feet high growing in the Royal Botanic Garden, Edinburgh; unfortunately it has now been lost to cultivation.

Epithet. Unexpected.

Hardiness 3. April–May.

R. pachysanthum Hayata in Icones Plant Formos. III (1913) 140.

A compact rounded shrub, 92 cm–1.22 m. (3–4 ft.) high, branchlets densely fawn tomentose, eglandular, those below the inflorescences 5–7 mm. in diameter; leaf-bud scales deciduous. *Leaves ovate, ovate-lanceolate* or lanceolate, lamina coriaceous, 5.8–11.8 cm. long, 2.5–4 cm. broad, apex acute, mucronate, base rounded; upper surface dark green, slightly rugulose, glabrous (in young leaves densely white-tomentose), eglandular, midrib grooved, hairy, eglandular, primary veins 12–15 on each side, deeply impressed; margin recurved; *under surface covered with a thick, woolly, cinnamon-coloured or rusty-brown, continuous, bistrate indumentum of hairs, upper layer a form of Ramiform, lower layer* whitish adpressed *Rosulate with long or short arms,* without pellicle, midrib prominent, densely tomentose, eglandular, primary veins slightly raised or obscured; petiole 1–2 cm. long, grooved above, densely fawn or whitish tomentose, eglandular. *Inflorescence* a racemose umbel of 8–10 or sometimes up to 20 flowers, flower-bud scales deciduous or persistent; rhachis 1–2 cm. long, puberulous, eglandular; *pedicel* 2.5–3 cm. long, rather densely hairy, *moderately or sparsely glandular* with short-stalked glands. *Calyx* 5-lobed, minute, 1 mm. long, lobes rounded or triangular, *outside* moderately or sparsely hairy, *sparsely glandular* with short-stalked glands, *margin* moderately or sparsely hairy, *moderately or sparsely glandular* with short-stalked glands. *Corolla* campanulate, 3.1–4 cm. long, *white with crimson spots;* lobes 5, 1–1.5 cm. long, 1.8–2.3 cm. broad, rounded, emarginate. *Stamens* 10, unequal, 1.3–2.8 cm. long, shorter than the corolla; filaments densely pubescent at the base. *Gynoecium* 2.8–3.5 cm. long, shorter than the corolla, longer than the stamens; *ovary* conoid or oblong, 4–5 mm. long, 5–6-celled, moderately or sparsely tomentose, *rather densely glandular* with short-stalked glands; style sparsely hairy at the base, or glabrous, sparsely glandular at the base with short-stalked glands or eglandular. *Capsule* cylindric, 1.5 cm. long, 5 mm. broad.

R. pachysanthum is a native of Taiwan (Formosa). It grows on grassy ridges above the tree line at elevations of 3,000–3,200 m. (9,836–10,492 ft.).

The species was described by Hayata in 1913. In *The Species of Rhododendron* 1930, it was relegated to synonymy under *R. morii* in the Maculiferum Subseries, Barbatum Series. From this species and Subseries, *R. pachysanthum* is very remote.

R. pachysanthum shows a strong resemblance to *R. wasonii* in height and habit of growth, in leaf shape and size, in the thick, woolly, cinnamon-coloured or rusty-brown indumentum on the lower surface of the leaves, in the 8–10-flowered inflorescence, in the minute calyx, in the campanulate corolla, and in other details. The main distinctions between them are that in *R. pachysanthum* the indumentum on the lower surface of the leaves is bistrate, the upper layer is a form of Ramiform, the lower layer Rosulate, the calyx is sparsely or moderately glandular with short-stalked glands, the corolla is white, and the ovary is rather densely glandular with short-stalked glands; whereas in *R. wasonii* the indumentum on the lower surface of the leaves is unistrate, with Long-rayed hairs, the calyx is usually eglandular, the corolla is yellow or creamy-yellow or creamy-white, and the ovary is eglandular. Moreover, they differ in their geographical distribution. *R. pachysanthum* comes from Taiwan (Formosa), but *R. wasonii* is a native of western Sichuan. However, *R. pachysanthum* is closely related to *R. wasonii*. It will now be placed in the Wasonii Subseries, Taliense Series.

The species was introduced by Patrick in 1972. In cultivation it is a compact rounded shrub about 3 feet high. It is a beautiful foliage plant with dark green leaves covered below with cinnamon-coloured or rusty-brown indumentum. The plant is hardy outdoors, with white flowers in trusses of 8–10.

Epithet. With thick flowers.

Hardiness 3. April–May.

R. paradoxum Balf. f. in Notes Roy. Bot. Gard. Edin., Vol. 15 (1926) 114.

A somewhat compact or broadly upright shrub, 1.22–2.14 m. (4–7 ft.) high, *branchlets rather densely or moderately hairy with long whitish hairs*, eglandular, those below the inflorescences 4–6 mm. in diameter, *terminal leaf-buds elongate, pointed*, leaf-bud scales deciduous. *Leaves oblong, oblong-elliptic or oblong-obovate*, lamina coriaceous, 5–11.5 cm. long, 2.3–4.6 cm. broad, apex rounded or obtuse, acuminate, base obtuse or rounded; upper surface dark green, somewhat matt, slightly rugulose, glabrous or with vestiges of hairs, midrib grooved, hairy or glabrous, eglandular, primary veins 12–15 on each side, deeply impressed; margin slightly recurved; *under surface pale green, with large or small patches of closely or widely separated, woolly*, brown, *discontinuous, detersile, unistrate indumentum, hairs somewhat Ramiform* with medium or long stem, and medium or long *somewhat broad, ribbon-like branches*, midrib prominent, hairy, eglandular, primary veins raised; *petiole* 1.2–2.5 cm. long, grooved above, *densely or moderately hairy with long whitish hairs*, eglandular. *Inflorescence* a racemose umbel of 8–10 flowers, flower-bud scales deciduous; rhachis 1–1.8 cm. long, pubescent, eglandular; *pedicel* 1.6–2.9 cm. long, *densely tomentose with long brown or white hairs*, eglandular. *Calyx* 5-lobed, *2–3 mm. long*, lobes ovate or triangular, outside and margin moderately or densely tomentose with brown tomentum, eglandular. *Corolla* campanulate, *3.4–4 cm. long*, white with a dark crimson blotch at the base breaking into spots; lobes 5, 1–1.5 cm. long, 1.6–2.6 cm. broad, rounded, emarginate. *Stamens* 10, unequal, 1.8–3.2 cm. long, shorter than the corolla; filaments rather densely puberulous at the base. *Gynoecium* 3–3.7 cm. long, as long as the corolla or shorter, longer than the stamens; *ovary* oblong, 5–6 mm. long, 6-celled, *densely* brown *tomentose*, eglandular; style glabrous, eglandular. *Capsule* narrow cylindric, 2–2.5 cm. long, about 4 mm. broad, brown tomentose.

R. paradoxum was described in 1922 from a plant raised in the Royal Botanic Garden, Edinburgh, from Wilson's seed No. 1353 in part, collected in 1908 in western Sichuan. The herbarium specimen under this number is *R. wiltonii* in part.

A distinctive feature of the plant is the detersile, large or small patches of woolly indumentum of hairs on the lower surface of the leaves. The species is closely related to *R. inopinum* to which it bears a certain degree of resemblance, but differs in that the terminal leaf-buds are elongate, pointed, the leaves are oblong, oblong-elliptic or oblong-obovate, the calyx is larger, and the corolla is usually larger. It also differs in the shape of the hairs of the indumentum on the lower surface of the leaves. *R. paradoxum* also resembles *R. wiltonii* to a certain extent, and might be a natural hybrid of it.

In cultivation *R. paradoxum* is a somewhat compact or broadly upright shrub 4–7 feet high, fairly well-filled with dark green foliage. It is hardy, a robust grower, and is easy to cultivate. The flowers are large, white with a dark crimson blotch at the base breaking into spots, in trusses of 8–10. The plant is rare in cultivation.

Epithet. Paradoxical.

Hardiness 3. April–May.

R. rufum Batalin in Act. Hort. Petrop. Vol. 11 (1891) 490.

A broadly upright or rounded shrub, or tree, 1.22–4.58 m. (4–15 ft.) high, branchlets glabrous or sparsely or moderately tomentose with a thin, whitish tomentum, eglandular, those below the inflorescences 4–7 mm. in diameter; leaf-bud scales deciduous. *Leaves oblong, oblong-obovate or oblong-lanceolate,* lamina coriaceous, 5–11 cm. long, *2–4 cm. broad,* apex obtuse, acute or shortly acuminate, *base obtuse, cordulate* or rounded; upper surface green, shining, not bullate, glabrous or with vestiges of hairs, eglandular, midrib grooved, glabrous, eglandular, primary veins 12–18 on each side, deeply impressed; margin slightly recurved or flat; *under surface covered with a thick, often loosely,* brown or rusty-brown, continuous, bistrate indumentum of *hairs, upper layer Ramiform* with long or medium stem and long narrow branches, *lower layer Rosulate,* without pellicle, midrib raised, moderately or densely hairy, eglandular, primary veins obscured; petiole 1–2.1 cm. long, thick, grooved above, rather densely or moderately tomentose with whitish tomentum, eglandular. *Inflorescence* a racemose umbel of 5–10 flowers, flower-bud scales deciduous or persistent; rhachis 5–8 mm. long, floccose, eglandular; pedicel 0.8–1.7 cm. long, moderately or densely floccose with brown or fawn hairs or rarely glabrous, eglandular or rarely glandular with short-stalked glands. *Calyx* 5-lobed, minute, 0.5–1 mm. long, lobes triangular or ovate, outside moderately or densely tomentose or rarely glabrous, eglandular or sometimes glandular with short-stalked glands, margin moderately tomentose or rarely glabrous, eglandular or sometimes glandular with short-stalked glands. *Corolla* funnel-campanulate or campanulate, 2–3.2 cm. long, white, pink or pinkish-purple, with or without purplish-pink stripes, and with or without crimson spots; lobes 5, 0.8–1 cm. long, 1–1.8 cm. broad, rounded, emarginate. *Stamens* 10, unequal, 1.1–2.9 cm. long, shorter than the corolla; filaments moderately or rather densely puberulous at the base. *Gynoecium* 1.9–3 cm. long, as long as the corolla or shorter, longer than the stamens; ovary conoid or ovoid, 4–5 mm. long, 5–6-celled, densely brown hairy or densely glandular with short-stalked glands; style glabrous or hairy at the base, eglandular. *Capsule* oblong, 1.6–2.5 cm. long, 5–7 mm. broad, straight or slightly curved, brown floccose or densely glandular with short-stalked glands, calyx-lobes persistent.

This species was discovered by G. N. Potanin in August 1885 in North Sichuan. It was afterwards collected by Rock and Fang in various localities in Kansu. The plant grows in *Abies* and *Picea* forests, among limestone rocks in *Abies* forests, and in woods, at elevations of 3,050–3,660 m. (10,000–12,000 ft.).

R. rufum is a distinctive species. Its main features are the oblong, oblong-obovate or oblong-lanceolate leaves, covered on the lower surface with a thick, often loosely, woolly, brown or rusty-brown continuous, bistrate indumentum of hairs, the upper layer Ramiform with long or medium stem and long narrow branches, the lower layer Rosulate, without pellicle. It is closely related to *R. weldianum;* the distinctions between them are discussed under the latter.

The species was first introduced by Rock from Kansu in 1925 (No. 13599). It was reintroduced by him in the same year and later from the same region under 22 different seed numbers. In its native home it is a shrub or tree 4–15 feet high; in cultivation it is a broadly upright or rounded shrub 4–5 feet in height. The indumentum on the under surface of the leaves is at first whitish but later turns brown or rusty-brown. The plant varies in its freedom of flowering. The white or pink flowers are often produced moderately in trusses of 5–10. The species is hardy outdoors, but to be able to grow it satisfactorily particularly along the east coast, protection from wind should be provided.

Epithet. Red.
Hardiness 3. April–May.

R. wasonii Hemsl. et Wils. in Kew Bull. (1910) 105.

Illustration. Bot. Mag. Vol. 153 t. 9190 (1927).

A broadly upright or somewhat compact rounded shrub or bush, 60 cm.–2.14 m. (2–7 ft.) high, branchlets densely or moderately tomentose with brown tomentum, moderately or sparsely glandular with medium- or short-stalked glands or eglandular, those below the inflorescences 5–7 mm. in diameter; leaf-bud scales deciduous. *Leaves ovate, ovate-lanceolate or broadly lanceolate*, lamina coriaceous, 5.5–10.3 cm. long, 2.5–4.5 cm. broad, apex shortly acuminate, acuminate or acute, base rounded or cordulate; *upper surface* dark green, shining, *not bullate*, with vestiges of hairs, eglandular, midrib grooved, with vestiges of hairs, eglandular, primary veins 12–15 on each side, deeply impressed; margin slightly recurved or flat; *under surface covered with a thick, woolly, brown or cinnamon-coloured (in young leaves white), continuous, unistrate indumentum of Long-rayed hairs with long or short, often somewhat broad ribbon-like arms*, without pellicle, midrib prominent, hairy, eglandular, primary veins slightly raised or obscured; petiole 0.5–1.8 cm. long, grooved above, densely or moderately tomentose with brown or fawn tomentum, moderately or sparsely glandular with short-stalked glands or eglandular. *Inflorescence* a racemose umbel of 6–10 flowers, flower-bud scales deciduous or persistent; rhachis 0.5–1 cm. long, rather densely or moderately pubescent, eglandular; *pedicel* 1–3.2 cm. long, densely brown tomentose, *eglandular* or rarely glandular with short-stalked glands. *Calyx* 5-lobed, 1–2 mm. long, lobes ovate or triangular, outside and margin densely or moderately tomentose with brown or fawn tomentum, *eglandular* or rarely glandular with short-stalked glands. *Corolla* campanulate, 2.6–4 cm. long, *yellow or creamy-yellow or creamy-white*, with or without reddish spots; lobes 5, 0.8–1.2 cm. long, 1–2.2 cm. broad, rounded, emarginate. *Stamens* 10, unequal, 1.2–2.8 cm. long, shorter than the corolla; filaments rather densely pubescent at the base. *Gynoecium* 2.5–3 cm. long, shorter than the corolla, longer than the stamens; *ovary* conoid, 4–7 mm. long, 5–6-celled, densely tomentose with brown or cinnamon-coloured tomentum, *eglandular*; style glabrous or hairy at the base, eglandular. *Capsule* oblong, 1.3–1.7 cm. long, 4–5 mm. broad, slightly curved, rather densely or moderately tomentose with brown tomentum, *eglandular*, calyx-lobes persistent.

R. wasonii was discovered by Wilson in May 1904 near Tatsienlu, western Sichuan. Subsequently it was found by him, and by F. T. Wang in other localities in the same region. It grows on rocks in coniferous forests, in woodlands, and in forests on cliffs and boulders, at elevations of 2,600–3,600 m. (8,525–11,803 ft.). Wilson records it as being a common low-growing species partial to rocks in the forests.

The diagnostic features of the species are the ovate, ovate-lanceolate or broadly lanceolate leaves, the non-bullate upper surface of the leaves, the thick woolly, brown or cinnamon-coloured continuous, unistrate indumentum of Long-rayed hairs on the lower surface of the leaves, and the yellow, creamy-yellow or creamy-white flowers. The species shows a certain degree of affinity with *R. wiltonii* but differs in well-marked characteristics. It is also closely allied to *R. pachysanthum*. The distinctions between them are discussed under the latter.

R. wasonii was first introduced by Wilson in 1904 (Nos. 1764, 1800, 1866). In its native home it grows 2–7 feet high; in cultivation it is a broadly upright or a somewhat compact rounded shrub 3–4 feet in height. It is a beautiful foliage plant with leaves dark green above, covered below with cinnamon-coloured indumentum. The plant is free-flowering, and is of great beauty with its yellow flowers in trusses of 6–10. An additional beauty is the young growth, with white indumentum on the lower surface of the leaves. Moreover, it has the advantage of flowering as a young plant. Although hardy, it requires a sheltered position along the east coast.

Epithet. After Rear-Adm. C. R. Wason, 1874–1941, friend of E. H. Wilson.

Hardiness 3. April–May.

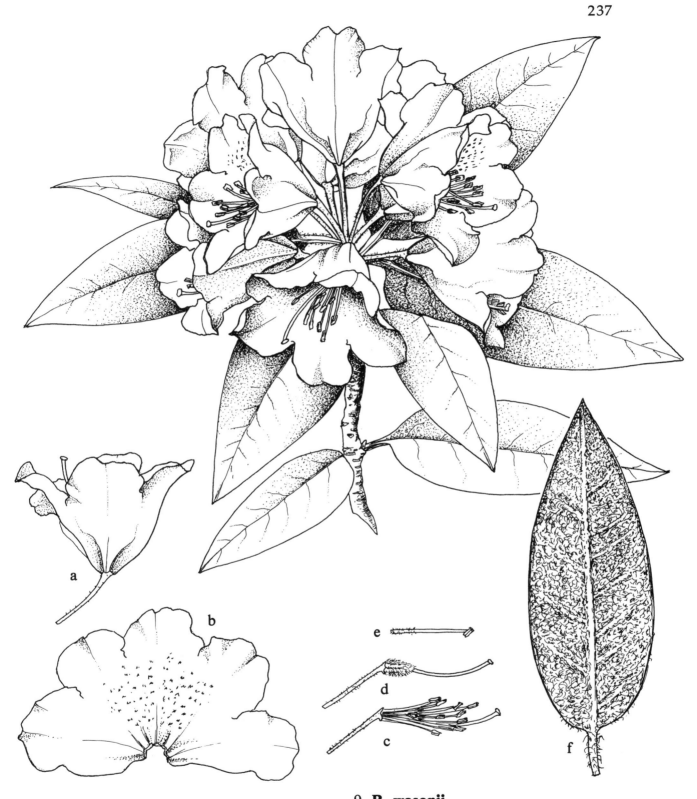

9. **R. wasonii.**
nat. size.

a. flower. b. petals. c. section.

d. ovary, style. e. stamen. f. leaf (lower surface).

R. wasonii Hemsl. et Wils. var. **rhododactylum** (Hort.) Davidian, comb. nov.
> Syn. *R. rhododactylum* Gardeners' Chronicle, Vol. LXXIII, Third Series (1923) 179.
> *R. wasonii* Hemsl. et Wils. 'Rhododactylum' R. H. S. in Rhod. Handb. (1980) p. 62.

This plant was first collected by Wilson in May 1904 near Tatsienlu, western Sichuan. It was later found by him at Mupin in the same region. It grows in coniferous forests and in woodlands, at elevations of 2,600–3,000 m. (8,525–9,836 ft.).

The variety differs from the species in that the corolla is pink, rose, rose-pink, white tinged pink or pinkish, with or without a crimson blotch at the base. Moreover, the leaves are very dark green, shining on the upper surface.

It was first introduced by Wilson in 1904 (No. 1876). Two growth forms are in cultivation: Form 1. A somewhat lax, broadly upright shrub 2–3 feet high. Form 2. A compact rounded shrub 4 feet high and as much across, well filled with dark green foliage. The variety is rare in cultivation, but would be well worth acquiring for every collection of rhododendrons.

The plant received an Award of Merit when exhibited as *R. rhododactylum* by Lady Aberconway and Hon. H. McLaren, Bodnant, in 1923, and again the same Award when shown as var. *rhododactylum* by the Crown Estate Commissioners, Windsor Great Park, in 1974.

Epithet of the variety. Tinged rosy-red finger-like.
Hardiness 3. April–May.

R. weldianum Rehd. et Wils. in Pl. Wilsonianae, Vol. I (1913) 532.

A rounded or broadly upright shrub, 1.53–6.10 m. (5–20 ft.) high, branchlets moderately or sparsely floccose, eglandular, those below the inflorescences 5–6 mm. in diameter; leaf-bud scales deciduous. *Leaves oval, almost orbicular, oblong-elliptic or elliptic,* lamina coriaceous, 6–13.8 cm. long, *2.7–5.9 cm. broad,* apex rounded, shortly acuminate or acute, *base rounded or broadly obtuse;* upper surface olive-green or pale green, shining, not bullate, glabrous, eglandular, midrib glabrous, eglandular, primary veins 10–20 on each side, deeply impressed; margin flat; *under surface covered with a thick, often loosely, woolly,* brown or rust-coloured *(in young leaves whitish), continuous, bistrate indumentum of hairs, upper layer Ramiform* with long or medium stem and long narrow branches, *lower layer Rosulate,* without pellicle, midrib prominent, densely or moderately hairy, eglandular, primary veins obscured or slightly raised; petiole 1–1.8 cm. long, thick, grooved above, moderately or rather densely tomentose with whitish or fawn tomentum, eglandular. *Inflorescence* a racemose umbel of 6–12 flowers, flower-bud scales deciduous; rhachis 5–7 mm. long, floccose, eglandular; *pedicel* 0.5–1.5 cm. long, *moderately or densely floccose,* glandular with short-stalked glands or eglandular. *Calyx* 5-lobed, minute, 0.5–1 mm. long, lobes triangular or ovate, outside glabrous or hairy, eglandular or sparsely glandular with short-stalked glands, margin glabrous or hairy, eglandular or moderately glandular with short-stalked glands. *Corolla* campanulate, 2.2–2.8 cm. long, white or white tinged pink or pink; lobes 5, 0.6–1 cm. long, 1–1.1 cm. broad, rounded, emarginate. *Stamens* 10, unequal, 0.6–2.2 cm. long, shorter than the corolla; filaments puberulous at the base. *Gynoecium* 2–2.8 cm. long, as long as the corolla or shorter, longer than the stamens; ovary conoid, 4–5 mm. long, 5–6-celled, moderately or densely tomentose with fawn tomentum, glandular with short-stalked glands or eglandular; style glabrous, eglandular. *Capsule* oblong, 2–2.5 cm. long, 5–9 mm. broad, slightly curved, brown floccose, glandular with short-stalked glands or eglandular, calyx-lobes persistent.

This plant was first collected by Wilson in October 1910 west of, and near Wench'uan Hsien, and near Sunpan Ting, western Sichuan. It was later found by Wm. Purdom, R. C. Ching, and Rock in various localities in west and south-west Kansu. The plant grows in woodlands, in dense forest, and in *Abies* forest, at elevations of 2,440–4,000 m. (8,000–13,111 ft.).

R. weldianum is closely allied to *R. rufum*. There is a strong resemblance between them in habit and height of growth, in the indumentum on the lower surface of the leaves, in the inflorescence, and in flower colour. When the extremes of these plants are compared, it will be seen that in *R. weldianum* the leaves are oval or almost orbicular, the apex and base are rounded, the corolla is small 2.2 cm. long, and the stamens are short 6 mm. long; whereas in *R. rufum* the leaves are oblong-lanceolate, the apex is acute, the base is obtuse, the corolla is large 3.2 cm. long, and the stamens are long 2.9 cm. in length. It may be remarked that although these distinctions are evident when the extremes are compared, the species are linked with intermediate forms. Nevertheless, the extremes are so distinct particularly in cultivation, that meanwhile it would be desirable to retain the name *R. weldianum*.

R. weldianum was first introduced by Wilson in 1910 (No. 4235—the Type number, and No. 4250). Rock sent seeds in 1925 (No. 13601). In its native home it is a shrub 5–20 feet high; in cultivation it is a rounded or broadly upright shrub 5 feet in height with olive-green or pale green leaves, upper surface shining. The flowers are white or white tinged pink in trusses of 6–12. A distinctive feature of the young growths is the whitish indumentum on the lower surface of the leaves. The species is hardy outdoors, but along the east coast it requires protection from wind for the best results to be obtained.

Epithet. After General S. M. Weld, a former President of the Massachusetts Horticultural Society.

Hardiness 3. April–May.

R. wiltonii Hemsl. et Wils. in Kew Bull., (1910) 107.

Illustration. Bot. Mag. Vol. 158 t. 9388 (1935).

A broadly upright shrub or bush, 92 cm.–5 m. (3–16 ft.) high, branchlets densely tomentose with brown or whitish tomentum, eglandular, those below the inflorescences 5–7 mm. in diameter; leaf-bud scales deciduous. *Leaves oblanceolate or oblong-obovate*, lamina coriaceous, 4.5–12.1 cm. long, 1.6–4 cm. broad, apex obtuse or shortly acuminate, base tapered or obtuse; *upper surface olive-green*, shining, *markedly bullate*, glabrous or with vestiges of hairs, eglandular, midrib grooved, hairy or glabrous, eglandular, primary veins 10–12 on each side, deeply impressed; margin recurved; *under surface covered with* a thick, woolly brown or cinnamon-coloured, *continuous unistrate indumentum of somewhat Fasciculate hairs with medium stout broad or somewhat narrow stem, and medium somewhat broad ribbon-like branches*, without pellicle, midrib prominent, hairy, eglandular, primary veins slightly raised; petiole 1–3 cm. long, grooved above, densely tomentose with brown or whitish tomentum, eglandular. *Inflorescence* a racemose umbel of 6–10 flowers, flower-bud scales persistent or deciduous; rhachis 5–8 mm. long, pubescent, eglandular; pedicel 1.5–3.6 cm. long, densely brown tomentose, eglandular. *Calyx* 5-lobed, 1–3 mm. long, lobes triangular or ovate, outside and margin densely brown tomentose, eglandular. *Corolla* campanulate, 3–4 cm. long, *pink or white*, with or without a crimson blotch at the base, and with or without red spots; lobes 5, 1–1.3 cm. long, 1.5–2.3 cm. broad, rounded, emarginate. *Stamens* 10, unequal, 1.5–3.2 cm. long, shorter than the corolla; filaments moderately or rather densely pubescent at the base. *Gynoecium* 3–3.6 cm. long, shorter than the corolla, longer than the stamens; *ovary* conoid or oblong, 4–7 mm. long, 5–6-celled, *densely* brown *tomentose, eglandular*; style glabrous or rarely hairy at the base, eglandular. *Capsule* oblong or slender, 1.2–2.6 cm. long, 4–6 mm. broad, slightly curved, brown tomentose, eglandular, calyx-lobes persistent.

Wilson discovered this species in May 1904 in western Sichuan when collecting for Messrs. Veitch. He found it again in 1908 and 1910 at Wa-shan and Mupin in the same region. Subsequently it was collected by F. T. Wang, and W. K. Hu on Mt. Omei and vicinity. It grows in thickets, in woodlands, and on rocky slopes, at elevations of 2,300–3,300 m. (7,541–10,820 ft.).

A diagnostic feature of R. *wiltonii* is the markedly bullate upper surface of the leaves. In this respect the species is readily distinguished from all the other members of its Subseries. Other distinctive characters are the oblanceolate or oblong-obovate leaves with olive-green upper surfaces, covered below with a thick woolly, continuous, unistrate indumentum of somewhat Fasciculate hairs with medium stout stem, and medium somewhat broad ribbon-like branches.

The species was first introduced by Wilson in 1904 (Nos. 1804, 1871). It was reintroduced by him in 1908 (No. 1353 in part), and in 1910 (No. 4264). In its native home it grows 3–16 feet high; in cultivation it is a broadly upright shrub usually up to 8 feet in height. It may be remarked that the leaves are very variable in size, laminae 4.5–12.1 cm. long, 1.6–4 cm. broad. The plant is hardy, but may take several years to bloom. The pink or white flowers are produced moderately or freely in trusses of 6–10.

The plant received an Award of Merit when exhibited by E. de Rothschild, Exbury, in 1957.

Epithet. After Sir Colville E. Wilton, b. 1870, Chinese Consular Service, Ichang. Hardiness 3. April–May.

1. *R. forrestii* var. *repens.*
Photo H. Gunn.

2. *R. forrestii* var. *repens.*
Photo H. Gunn.

3. *R. forrestii* var. *repens*
growing as a pot plant.

4. *R. chamaethomsonii.*
Photo H. Gunn.

5. *R. chamaethomsonii* var. *chamaethauma,*
rose form. Photo. J. T. Aitken.

6. *R. haematodes.* Photo H. Gunn.

7. *R. piercei*

8. *R. piercei.* Photo H. Gunn.

9. *R. chaetomallum.*
Photo J. T. Aitken.

10. *R. hillieri.*
Photo H. Gunn.

11. *R. catacosmum.*
Photo H. Gunn.

12. *R. pocophorum*

13. *R. hemidartum.*
Photo H. Gunn.

14. *R. mallotum.*
Photo H. Gunn.

15. *R. neriiflorum.*
Photo H. Gunn.

16. *R. phaedropum.*
Photo H. Gunn.

49. *R. macrophyllum,* a form.
West coast, U.S.A. Photo Britt Smith.

50. *R. macrophyllum,* a form.
West coast, U.S.A.
Photo Britt Smith.

51. *R. degronianaum* var. *heptamerum.*
Photo J. McQuire.

52. *R. degronianum*
in Kolak garden, California, U.S.A.
Photo E. & N. Kolak.

53. *R. adenogynum.*
Photo H. Gunn.

54. *R. adenogynum,* a form.

55. *R. adenogynum.*
Photo H. Gunn.

56. *R. bureavii.*
Photo J. McQuire.

57. *R. bureavioides.*
Photo H. Gunn.

58. *R. detonsum.*
Photo H. Gunn.

59. *R. nigroglandulosum.*
Photo T. Nitzelius.

60. *R. taliense.*
Photo H. Gunn.

61. *R. taliense.*
Photo H. Gunn.

62. *R. aganniphum*

63. *R. flavorufum.*
Photo H. Gunn.

64. *R. flavorufum,* leaf.
Photo Dr. George Smith.

65. *R. roxieanum*

66. *R. roxieanum.*
Photo H. Gunn.

67. *R. roxieanum* var. *oreonastes.*
Photo Dr. Florence Auckland.

68. *R. iodes.* Photo J. T. Aitken.

69. *R. iodes,* early stage,
indumentum yellow.
Photo H. Gunn.

70. *R. iodes,* later stage.
Photo J. McQuire.

71. *R. wasonii*

72. *R. wasonii* var. *rhododactylum.*
Photo H. Gunn.

73. *R. pachysanthum.*
Photo J. T. Aitken.

74. *R. cerasinum*

75. *R. cerasinum,*
white with a cherry-red band.
Photo H. Gunn.

76. *R. thomsonii.*
Photo H. Gunn.

77. *R. thomsonii,* a form. Photo H. Gunn.

78. *R. thomsonii* at Larachmhor,
Arisaig, Inverness-shire.
Photo I. Hedge.

79. *R. thomsonii* in Younger's Botanic Garden,
Benmore, Argyllshire.

80. *R. thomsonii* trunk at Blackhills, Morayshire.
Photo Dr. Florence Auckland.

82. *R. hookeri,* a form. Photo H. Gunn.

81. *R. hookeri*

83. *R. viscidifolium*

84. *R. meddianum.* Photo H. Gunn.

85. *R. cyanocarpum*

86. *R. hylaeum.*
Photo H. Gunn.

87. *R. stewartianum*

88. *R. stewartianum.* Photo H. Gunn.

89. *R. eclecteum*. Photo H. Gunn.

90. *R. eclecteum*. Photo H. Gunn.

91. *R. callimorphum.*
Photo A. Evans.

92. *R. callimorphum*. Photo A. Evans.

93. *R. callimorphum*

94. *R. caloxanthum.*
Photo H. Gunn.

95. *R. campylocarpum.* Photo A. Evans.

96. *R. campylocarpum.* Photo H. Gunn.

97. *R. selense*

98. *R. eurysiphon.*
Photo H. Gunn.

99. *R. setiferum.*
Photo Dr. Florence Auckland.

100. *R. wardii.*
Photo J. T. Aitken.

101. *R. wardii.*
Photo H. Gunn.

102. *R. wardii,*
Ludlow & Sherriff form.
Photo J. T. Aitken.

103. *R. souliei.* Photo H. Gunn

104. *R. puralbum.* Photo H. Gunn.

105. *R. williamsianum.* Photo A. Evans.

106. *R. williamsianum.*
Photo J. McQuire.

107. *R. leptothrium*

108. *R. hongkongense*

109. *R. championae.*
Photo H. Gunn.

110. *R. camtschaticum*

111. Young growth of *R. proteoides*.

112. Young growth of *R. recurvoides*.

113. Young growth
of *R. yakushimanum.*

114. Young growth
of *R. coelicum.*

115. Young growth
of *R. pocophorum.*

116. Young growth of *R. thomsonii.*

117. Young growth of *R. bureavii.*

118. Young growth
of *R. williamsianum.*

119. Natural regeneration of rhododendrons in
Younger's Botanic Garden, Benmore, Argyllshire.

120. Frost in winter
in the Royal Botanic Garden,
Edinburgh.

121. Frost in winter
in the rock garden
in the Royal Botanic Garden,
Edinburgh.

122. Winter at Larachmhor,
Arisaig, Inverness-shire.

123. Bracken, mulch.

124. Peat, mulch.

125. Wind damage.

126. Frost damage.

127. Shelter provided by a net.
Photo Dr. Florence Auckland.

128. A small rock garden in Edinburgh.

129. Dwarf rhododendrons in Mr. & Mrs. J. T. Aitken's garden, Edinburgh.

130. Rhododendrons in Mr. & Mrs. John Wood's garden, Edinburgh. The white spots are blossoms fallen from the apple tree.

131. Rhododendrons in Mr. & Mrs. H. Gunn's garden, Edinburgh.

132. Rhododendrons at Balbirnie (Glenrothes) Fife. Photo A. H. Cassells.

133. Rhododendrons in Mr. & Mrs. Adrian Palmer's garden, Manderston, Berwickshire.
Photo S. T. Clarke.

134. *R. ponticum* in Mr. & Mrs. Adrian Palmer's garden, Manderston, Berwickshire.
Photo D. Fullerton.

135. Rhododendrons at Dawyck, Peebles-shire.

136. Rhododendrons at Dawyck, Peebles-shire.

138. Rhododendrons on hillside,
Younger's Botanic Garden,
Benmore, Argyllshire.

137. Rhododendrons at Eglingham, Northumberland.
Photo Dr. Florence Auckland.

139. Rhododendrons on a damp misty day,
Younger's Botanic Garden, Benmore,
Argyllshire. Photo Mrs. Eileen Wood.

140. Autumn in Younger's Botanic Garden, Benmore, Argyllshire.

141. Rhododendrons at Inverewe, Wester Ross.

142. Stonefield Castle garden, Argyllshire.

143. Rhododendrons at Stonefield Castle, Argyllshire.

144. Rhododendrons at Brodick Castle, Isle of Arran.

145. Rhododendrons in
Corsock House garden,
Kirkcudbrightshire.

146. Rhododendrons in
Corsock House garden,
Kirkcudbrightshire.
Photo W. R. Hean.

147. Rhododendrons at
Galloway House,
Wigtownshire.

148. Rhododendrons at Lochinch, Wigtownshire.

149. Rhododendrons at entrance to Achamore House, Isle of Gigha. Photo Dr. Florence Auckland.

150. Rhododendrons in Deer Dell,
Mr. J. McQuire's garden,
Farnham, Surrey.

151. Rhododendrons in Deer Dell,
Mr. J. McQuire's garden,
Farnham, Surrey.

152. Rhododendrons at
Trengwainton, Cornwall.

153. Rhododendrons at Howth, Eire.

154. Rhododendrons in Mr. Cecil Smith's garden, Newburg, Oregon, U.S.A.

155. Rhododendrons in Mr. & Mrs. W. Berg's garden, Oregon, U.S.A.

156. Rhododendrons in Mr. Barfod's garden, Denmark.

157. Rhododendrons in Mr. Barfod's garden, Denmark.

158. *R. caucasicum* in East Turkey.

159. Collecting area in Bhutan.

160. Collecting area at Hpuginhka, North Burma.

161. Collecting area, Mt. Omei, Sichuan.

THOMSONII SERIES

General characters: shrubs or trees, 60 cm.–7.63 m. (2–25 ft.) or rarely up to 12.20 m. (40 ft.) high, branchlets glandular or eglandular. Leaves orbicular, oval, elliptic or oblong, lamina 1.5–18 cm. long; *under surface glabrous* or sometimes thinly hairy. Inflorescence terminal, racemose or umbellate, 3–15-, sometimes 1–2-, rarely 18–24-flowered; pedicel 0.6–4.8 cm. long. Calyx 0.5 mm.–2 cm. long. Corolla campanulate, tubular-campanulate, funnel-campanulate, bowl- or saucer-shaped, 2–6.3 cm. long, 5- or rarely 6-lobed, yellow, rose, pink, white, crimson or deep crimson. Stamens 10 or rarely 10–12. Ovary conoid, slender or oblong, 3–8 mm. long, densely glandular or eglandular, 5–10-celled; style eglandular or glandular at the base or up to one-half its length or throughout to the tip. Capsule slender, oblong, or short stout.

Distribution. Nepal, Sikkim, Bhutan, Assam, south, south-east and east Tibet, Upper Burma, north-east and east Upper Burma, west, north-west and mid-west Yunnan, west and south-west Sichuan.

This is a large Series of small, medium-sized and large shrubs, and trees. It is very variable in habit and height of growth, in the shape and size of the leaves, in the inflorescence, in the size of the calyx, in the shape, size and colour of the corolla, and in the shape and size of the capsule. Therefore, it is divided into six Subseries: Campylocarpum Subseries, Cerasinum Subseries, Selense Subseries, Souliei Subseries, Thomsonii Subseries, and Williamsianum Subseries. A characteristic feature of the Series is usually the orbicular, oval, ovate or oblong leaves, rounded at both ends, and glabrous on the under surface.

KEY TO THE SUBSERIES

A. Style glandular throughout to the tip.

    B. Corolla bowl- or saucer-shaped, yellow, white, pink or rose; calyx usually 4 mm.–1.2 cm. long .... *Souliei Subseries*

    B. Corolla campanulate, pink, rose, white, deep crimson or scarlet; calyx 1–5 mm. long or a mere rim.

        C. Leaves ovate or orbicular; compact, rounded or dome-shaped or spreading shrub; branchlets and usually petioles setulose-glandular; inflorescence 2–3- (rarely up to 5-) flowered; corolla pink or rose; young growths bronzy .... *Williamsianum Subseries*

        C. Leaves oblong, oblanceolate or sometimes oblong-obovate; usually a broadly upright shrub; branchlets and petioles not setulose-glandular; inflorescence 5–7-flowered; corolla deep crimson, scarlet or white; young growths bright green................. *Cerasinum Subseries*

A. Style eglandular or glandular at the base (rarely up to three-fourths its length but never throughout to the tip).

    D. Ovary eglandular .... *Thomsonii Subseries* (part)

    D. Ovary densely glandular.

        E. Branchlets and petioles usually not setulose-glandular; leaves usually obovate, oblong-obovate, orbicular, ovate, oval or broadly elliptic; corolla tubular-campanulate or campanulate.

            F. Leaves usually obovate or oblong-obovate; calyx large, usually 4 mm.–2 cm. long; style eglandular; capsule broadly oblong or short stout, straight; corolla usually deep crimson, rose or white............................... *Thomsonii Subseries* (part)

            F. Leaves orbicular, ovate, oval or broadly elliptic (except in *R. panteumorphum* oblong); calyx small, usually 0.5–3 mm. (sometimes up to 5 mm.) long; style glandular at the base or up to one-half its length or eglandular; capsule usually slender, often curved; corolla usually yellow, deep rose or white .... *Campylocarpum Subseries*

        E. Branchlets and petioles usually setulose-glandular; leaves usually oblong or elliptic; corolla funnel-campanulate or sometimes campanulate .... *Selense Subseries*

CAMPYLOCARPUM SUBSERIES

General characters: shrubs or rarely trees, 60 cm.–6.10 m. (2–12 ft.) high. Leaves orbicular, ovate, oval or broadly elliptic (in *R. panteumorphum* often oblong), lamina 2–10 cm. long, 1.4–5.6 cm. broad; *under surface glabrous.* Inflorescence terminal, umbellate or shortly racemose, 4–10-flowered; pedicel 1–3.5 cm. long, glandular. Calyx 0.5–6 mm. long, glandular. *Corolla* campanulate, 2.5–4.5 cm. long, *yellow, sulphur-yellow, lemon-yellow, pink, pale to deep rose, or white;* lobes 5. Stamens 10, filaments glabrous or puberulous at the base. Ovary slender, oblong or conoid, 4–6 mm. long, densely glandular; *style glandular at the base or up to one-half of its length or eglandular. Capsule slender* or oblong, curved or straight, glandular.

KEY TO THE SPECIES

A. Flowers yellow.
> **B.** Leaves elliptic or ovate or oblong.
>> **C.** Leaves elliptic or ovate. From the Himalayas .... *campylocarpum*
>> **C.** Leaves usually oblong (sometimes elliptic). From
>> S.E. Tibet and Yunnan......................... *panteumorphum*
> **B.** Leaves orbicular or more or less orbicular.
>> **D.** Average leaf length to breadth 5–4 cm................ *caloxanthum*
>> **D.** Average leaf length to breadth 4–3 cm................... *telopeum*

A. Flowers rose or pink or white.
> **E.** Flowers rose or pink .... *callimorphum*
> **E.** Flowers white .... *myiagrum*

DESCRIPTION OF THE SPECIES

R. callimorphum Balf. f. et. W. W. Sm. in Notes Roy. Bot. Gard. Edin., Vol. 10 (1917) 89.
> Syn. *R. cyclium* Balf. f. et Forrest in Notes Roy. Bot. Gard. Edin., Vol. 13 (1920) 39.
> *R. hedythamnum* Balf. f. et Forrest, ibid. Vol. 13 (1922) 261.

Illustration. Bot. Mag. Vol. 145 t. 8789 (1919).

A rounded or broadly upright shrub, 60 cm.–2.75 m. (2–9 ft.) high, branchlets glandular with short-stalked glands or rarely eglandular, those below the inflorescences 3–5 mm. in diameter. *Leaves orbicular, ovate* or broadly elliptic, lamina thinly leathery, 3–7 cm. long, 2–5.3 cm. broad, apex rounded or broadly obtuse, mucronate, base cordulate or truncate or rounded; upper surface dark green, glabrous or with scattered vestiges of hairs, glossy, midrib grooved, primary veins 9–12 on each side, deeply impressed; *under surface* glaucous, *glabrous,* midrib raised, sparsely or moderately glandular with minute glands; petiole 0.7–2.6 cm. long, glandular with short-stalked glands, hairy or glabrous. *Inflorescence* umbellate or shortly racemose, 5–8-flowered; rhachis 2–4 mm. long, glandular, hairy or glabrous; *pedicel* 1–3 cm. long, *glandular* with short-stalked glands. *Calyx* 5-lobed, 1–3 mm. long, lobes rounded or triangular, *outside glandular, margin gland-fringed. Corolla* campanulate or sometimes funnel-campanulate, 3–4.5 cm. long, *pink, pale to deep rose, or pale rose almost white,* with or without a crimson blotch at the base; lobes 5, 1–1.4 cm. long, 1.6–2.4 cm. broad, rounded, emarginate. *Stamens* 10, unequal, 1.3–3 cm. long; filaments glabrous or sometimes puberulous at the base. *Gynoecium* 2.6–3.5 cm. long; *ovary* slender or conoid, 4–5 mm. long, *densely glandular* with short- or long-stalked glands; style glandular at the base or eglandular. *Capsule slender,* cylindric, 1.4–2.2 cm. long, 4–6 mm. broad, moderately or slightly curved, glandular with short-stalked glands, calyx-lobes persistent.

Forrest discovered this species in August 1912 on the western flank of the Shweli-Salwin Divide, west Yunnan. He found it again later on several occasions in other localities in the same region. In 1919 Kingdon-Ward collected it in north-east Upper Burma. It grows on open rocky and on boulder strewn slopes, on ledges of cliffs, in open thickets, on the margins of rhododendron thickets, in cane brakes, amongst scrub, and in open rocky mountain pasture, at elevations of 2,745–3,355 m. (9,000–11,000 ft.).

In 1920 *R. cyclium* Balf. f. et Forrest was described from a specimen No. 18044 collected by Forrest in the N'Maikha-Salwin Divide, western Yunnan, and in 1922 *R. hedythamnum* Balf. f. et Forrest was founded on Forrest's No. 11601 from the western flank of the Tali Range, mid-western Yunnan. It is to be noted that in *The Rhododendron Year Book* 1951–52 p. 128, they were placed in synonymy under *R. callimorphum.*

R. callimorphum is easily recognised by the orbicular or ovate leaves, and campanu-

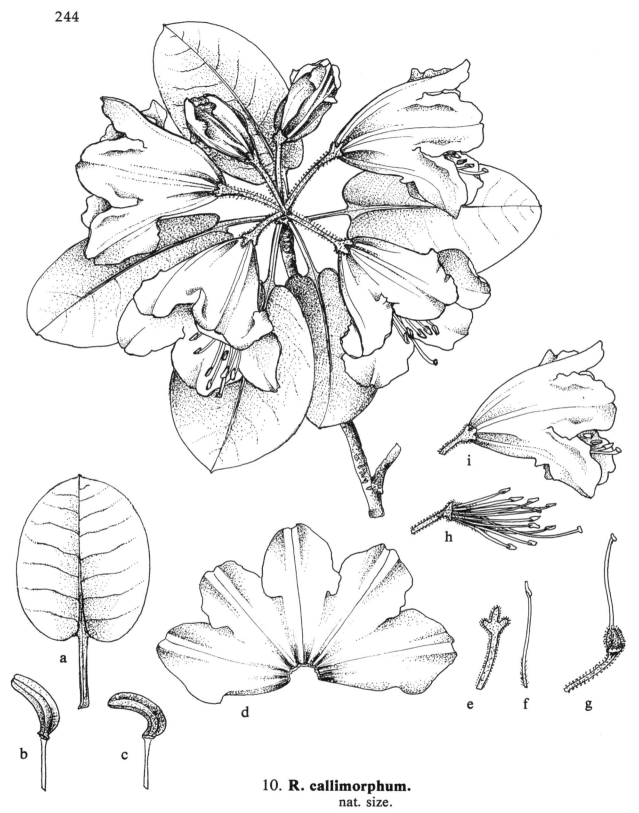

10. R. callimorphum.
nat. size.

a. leaf (upper surface).
b. capsule. c. capsule. d. petals. e. calyx.
f. stamen. g. ovary, style. h. section. i. flower.

late pink to deep rose flowers. It shows a certain degree of affinity with R. caloxanthum from which it is readily distinguished by the colour of the flowers; in R. caloxanthum the flowers are citron, yellow, pale sulphur-yellow or deep lemon-yellow.

The species was first introduced by Forrest in August 1912 (No. 9055). It was reintroduced by him on six occasions. Kingdon-Ward sent seeds in 1919 from north-east Upper Burma (Nos. 3408, 3721). R. callimorphum is a charming plant with neat habit of growth, and provides an admirable display with a profusion of flowers in trusses of 5–8. The species varies considerably in the size of the leaves. At one extreme the leaves (laminae) are small, 3 cm. long, and 2 cm. broad; at the other extreme they are large, 7 cm. long, and 5.3 cm. broad; these extremes are linked with several intermediates. A distinctive feature is the slender curved capsule up to 2 cm. long, containing fertile seeds in plenty. The species is hardy, but along the east coast and in gardens inland it should be given a sheltered position in order to obtain the best results.

Epithet. With a lovely shape.
Hardiness 3. April–May.

R. caloxanthum Balf. f. et Farrer in Notes Roy. Bot. Gard. Edin., Vol. 13 (1922) 238.
Syn. *R. campylocarpum* Hook. f. subsp. *caloxanthum* (Balf. f. et Farrer) Chamberlain in Notes Roy. Bot. Gard. Edin., Vol. 36 (1978) 116.

A rounded compact or bushy or broadly upright shrub, 60 cm.–2.5 m. (2–8 ft.) high, *branchlets glandular* with long- or short-stalked glands or rarely eglandular, those below the inflorescences 3–4 mm. in diameter. *Leaves orbicular, ovate* or broadly elliptic, lamina leathery, 3.2–8 cm. long, 2.5–5.6 cm. broad, apex rounded, mucronate, base truncate or cordate; *upper surface dark green*, glabrous, *glaucous, matt*, midrib grooved, primary veins 10–12 on each side, impressed; *under surface* pale glaucous green, papillate, *glabrous* or minutely hairy, midrib raised; *petiole* 1.1–2.8 cm. long, *sparsely or moderately glandular* with long- or short-stalked glands or eglandular, not hairy or rarely hairy. *Inflorescence* umbellate or shortly racemose, 4–9-flowered; rhachis 0.1–1.8 cm. long, glandular or eglandular, hairy or glabrous; *pedicel* 0.9–2.7 cm. long, *moderately or densely glandular* with short- or long-stalked glands, not hairy or rarely hairy. *Calyx* 5-lobed, small, 1–5 mm. long, lobes rounded, outside densely glandular or sometimes eglandular, margin glandular. *Corolla* campanulate, 2.5–4 cm. long, *citron, yellow, pale sulphur-yellow or deep lemon-yellow*, sometimes tinged pink, without or rarely with a purple patch at the base, *bud vermilion, crimson, red or rose*; lobes 5, 0.8–1.2 cm. long, 1.5–2.5 cm. broad, rounded, emarginate. *Stamens* 10, unequal, 1.4–3.5 cm. long; filaments glabrous or puberulous at the base. *Gynoecium* 2.3–3.4 cm. long; ovary oblong, conoid or slender, 4–6 mm. long, 5–7-celled, *densely glandular* with long- or short-stalked glands; style glandular on the lower one-fourth of its length or eglandular. *Capsule* oblong or slender, 1.7–2.5 cm. long, 5–7 mm. broad, curved or straight, *glandular*, calyx-lobes persistent.

This species was discovered by Farrer and E. H. M. Cox in May 1919 at Chimili and Hpimaw Passes, north-east Upper Burma. In July 1920 Farrer alone collected it in the Chawchi Pass, same region. Subsequently it was found by other collectors in north-east and east Upper Burma, north-west Yunnan, south-east and south Tibet, and in Yunnan-Tibet Border. It grows in mixed and rhododendron scrub in side valleys, on the margins of conifer forests, amongst alpine scrub in rocky meadows and slopes, on cliffs, and in thickets, at elevations of 2,745–4,150 m. (9,000–13,606 ft.). According to Farrer it is abundant in the Chawchi Pass, covering the open slopes and precipice ledges in dense masses of 2–3 feet in height.

R. caloxanthum is closely allied to R. campylocarpum which it resembles in the yellow flowers, but is readily distinguished usually by the orbicular leaves, upper surface glaucous and matt; in R. campylocarpum the leaves are usually elliptic or oblong-elliptic, upper surface is shining, not glaucous. R. caloxanthum is usually a smaller plant than its ally. Moreover, they usually differ in their geographical distribution. R. caloxanthum is a native of Upper Burma, north-west Yunnan and south-east Tibet, whereas *R. campylo-carpum* usually comes from Sikkim, Bhutan, and Assam.

The species was first introduced by Farrer and E. H. M. Cox in 1919 (No. 937—the Type number). Forrest sent seeds on four occasions. It was introduced by Kingdon-Ward in 1926 (No. 6868), and in 1953 from the North Triangle (No. 20927), also by Rock from north-west Yunnan in 1929 (No. 18405). It is undoubtedly one of the finest yellow-flowered rhododendrons in gardens. Three distinct forms are in cultivation: Form 1. A broadly upright shrub 5–6 feet high, with medium-sized leaves. Form 2. A rounded compact shrub 3 feet high with large leaves and large flowers, introduced by Farrer. Form 3. A rounded compact shrub 3–4 feet high with smaller leaves and smaller flowers, introduced by Kingdon-Ward from the North Triangle. All these forms are charming plants, free-flowering, and are greatly admired when adorned with yellow flowers in trusses of 4–9. A distinctive feature of the species is the vermilion, crimson, red or rose flower-bud. The plant is a somewhat slow grower, but one of its merits is that it flowers at a fairly young age.

It was given an Award of Merit when shown by Lionel de Rothschild, Exbury, in 1934.

Epithet. Of a beautiful yellow.

Hardiness 3. April–May.

R. campylocarpum Hook. f. Rhod. Sikkim Himal. t. 30 (1851).

Illustration. Bot. Mag. Vol. 83 t. 4968 (1857).

A compact rounded or spreading, or broadly upright or straggly shrub, or bush 92 cm.–3.66 m. (3–12 ft.) high, or rarely a tree 4.58–6.10 m. (15–20 ft.) high, *branchlets glandular* with short- or long-stalked glands, not hairy or rarely hairy, those below the inflorescences 3–4 mm. in diameter. *Leaves elliptic, oblong-elliptic,* ovate or sometimes oval, lamina leathery, 4–10 cm. long, 2.3–5.4 cm. broad, apex broadly obtuse or rounded, mucronate, base truncate, cordate or rarely rounded; *upper surface* dark or pale green, glabrous, *shining,* glossy, *not glaucous,* midrib grooved, eglandular or glandular, primary veins 10–15 on each side, impressed; *under surface* pale glaucous green or glaucous, papillate, *glabrous* or minutely hairy, midrib raised, glandular towards the base; petiole 0.8–2.4 cm. long, glandular with short- or long-stalked glands or eglandular, not hairy or sometimes hairy. *Inflorescence* umbellate or a racemose umbel of 6–10 flowers; rhachis 3–8 mm. long, glandular with short-stalked glands or eglandular, hairy or glabrous; *pedicel* 1.5–3.5 cm. long, *glandular* with short- or long-stalked glands. *Calyx* 5-lobed, minute, 1–1.5 mm. long, rarely more, lobes rounded or triangular, *outside glandular, margin gland-fringed. Corolla* campanulate, 2.5–4 cm. long, *yellow, pale or bright yellow, sulphur-yellow or lemon-yellow,* with or without a faint red or crimson blotch at the base; lobes 5, 1.1–2 cm. long, 1.5–2.5 cm. broad, rounded, emarginate. *Stamens* 10, unequal, 1.2–3.3 cm. long; filaments glabrous or puberulous at the base. *Gynoecium* 2.4–5 cm. long; *ovary slender* or rarely conoid, 4–6 mm. long, 5–7-celled, *densely glandular* with short- or long-stalked glands; *style glandular at the base or sometimes up to one-half of its length or eglandular. Capsule slender,* cylindric, 1.7–3 cm. long, 3–5 mm. broad, slightly or much curved, glandular, calyx-lobes persistent.

J. D. Hooker discovered this species in June 1848 in Sikkim-Himalaya. Further gatherings by various collectors show that the plant is distributed in Nepal, Sikkim, Bhutan, East Himalaya, Assam, south and south-east Tibet. It grows in rocky valleys, on open spurs, on rocky hill slopes, in mixed forest, among spruce, birch and other rhododendrons, in conifer, *Abies, Tsuga* and rhododendron forests, at elevations of 2,898–4,270 m. (9,500–14,000 ft.). J. D. Hooker records it as being abundant in rocky valleys and on open spurs in Sikkim. According to Ludlow, Sherriff and Taylor, it is very common on hillsides in south-east Tibet. In his field notes Kingdon-Ward describes it as being abundant at the Bhutan Frontier in Assam.

R. *campylocarpum* varies considerably in habit and height of growth. It is a compact rounded or spreading, or bushy or broadly upright or straggly shrub, 3–12 feet high. Ludlow, Sherriff and Hicks found a plant (No. 20626) in Bhutan growing as a tree, 15–20 feet high.

The affinity of the species is with *R. caloxanthum*. The distinctions between them are discussed under the latter. *R. campylocarpum* is sometimes confused with *R. wardii*. The main distinctions between them are that in *R. campylocarpum* the corolla is campanulate, the style is glandular at the base or sometimes up to one-half of its length or eglandular, the calyx is minute 0.5–1.5 mm. long, and the capsule is slender, usually much curved; whereas in *R. wardii* the corolla is cup- or saucer- or bowl-shaped, the style is glandular from the base throughout to the tip, the calyx is large 4 mm.–1.2 cm. long, and the capsule is short stout, or oblong usually straight.

R. campylocarpum was first introduced by J. D. Hooker in 1849. It was introduced on several occasions by R. E. Cooper, Kingdon-Ward, Ludlow and Sherriff, Spring-Smyth and other collectors. It flowered for the first time in 1856 growing in a cool frame in Messrs. Standish and Noble, Bagshot Nursery, Berkshire. Two distinct growth forms are in cultivation: Form 1. A compact rounded or spreading shrub 5–6 feet high and as much across, also known as "Hooker's form". Form 2. A broadly upright shrub up to 10–12 feet high or taller, which has been named in cultivation as "var. *elatum*". Both forms are free-flowering and make a fine show with trusses of 6–10 flowers. As the name "campylocarpum" suggests, a characteristic feature is the bent fruit, usually sickle-shaped. In view of the fact that the species comes from elevations of 9,500–14,000 feet, its hardiness varies in cultivation. Along the west coast it is perfectly hardy, but along the east coast and inland, to be able to grow it successfully, a sheltered position is essential.

A form with lemon-yellow flowers received a First Class Certificate when exhibited by Veitch and Sons, Chelsea, in 1892.

Epithet. With bent fruit.
Hardiness 3. April–May.

R. myiagrum Balf. f. et Forrest in Notes Roy. Bot. Gard. Edin., Vol. 13 (1920) 52.
Syn. *R. callimorphum* Balf. f. et W. W. Sm. var. *myiagrum* (Balf. f. et Forrest) Chamberlain in Notes Roy. Bot. Gard. Edin., Vol. 36 (1978) 116.

A somewhat compact rounded or spreading shrub, 92 cm.–1.83 m. (3–6 ft.) high, *branchlets glandular* with short-stalked glands, those below the inflorescences about 3 mm. in diameter. *Leaves* orbicular, ovate or broadly elliptic, lamina leathery, 2–7 cm. long, 1.5–4.8 cm. broad, apex rounded or rarely obtuse, mucronate, base cordulate or truncate; upper surface dark green, matt or somewhat glossy, glabrous, midrib grooved, primary veins 7–12 on each side, impressed; *under surface glabrous*, glaucous, papillate, midrib raised, minutely glandular towards the base; *petiole* 0.9–2.2 cm. long, *glandular* with short-stalked glands *or setulose-glandular*. *Inflorescence* an umbel of 4–5 flowers; *pedicel* 1.5–2.8 cm. long, *glandular with short- or long-stalked glands*. *Calyx* 5-lobed, small, *1–6 mm. long*, lobes oblong or rounded or triangular, *outside densely glandular, margin gland-fringed*. *Corolla* campanulate, 2.5–3.3 cm. long, *white*, spotted or unspotted, and with or without a crimson blotch at the base; lobes 5, 1–1.2 cm. long, 1.4–2 cm. broad, rounded, emarginate. *Stamens* 10, unequal, 1.3–3 cm. long; filaments glabrous or rarely puberulous at the base. *Gynoecium* 2.5–3.6 cm. long; *ovary* slender or conoid, 4–5 mm. long, *densely glandular* with short-stalked glands; style glandular at the base or rarely up to one-half its length or rarely eglandular. *Capsule slender*, 1.6–2 cm. long, 5 mm. broad, straight or slightly curved, *glandular* or with vestiges of glands, calyx-lobes persistent.

Forrest first collected this species in June 1919 in the N'Maikha-Salwin Divide, western Yunnan. He found it again later in various localities in north-east Upper Burma.

It grows in cane brakes, in thickets, and in scrub, at elevations of 3,050–3,965 m. (10,000–13,000 ft.).

The name *myiagrum* signifies "the fly-catcher", "it has . . . such glandular pedicels that in Yunnan they are often found plastered with small flies". The species is allied to *R. callimorphum*, but is readily distinguished by the white flowers, usually by the long-stalked glands on the pedicels and petioles, and often by the larger calyx.

R. myiagrum was first introduced by Forrest in 1925 from north-east Upper Burma (No. 27142). It was reintroduced by him from the same region in 1931 (No. 29647). In cultivation it is a somewhat compact rounded or spreading shrub up to 6 feet high and as much across. It is a pleasing shrub with white campanulate flowers produced freely in trusses of 4–5. The plant occasionally produces slender capsules containing plentiful fertile seeds. It is hardy, but along the east coast it should be given protection from wind for the best results to be obtained. The species is rare in cultivation, but is very desirable for inclusion in every collection of rhododendrons.

Epithet. The fly-catcher, alluding to the sticky pedicels.
Hardiness 3. April–May.

R. panteumorphum Balf. f. et W. W. Sm. in Notes Roy. Bot. Gard. Edin., Vol. 9 (1916) 257.
  Syn. *R. selense* Diels non Franch. in Notes Roy. Bot. Gard. Edin., Vol. 7 (1913) 295.
    R. telopeum Balf. f. et Forrest forma *telopeoides* Balf. f. ex Tagg in The Sp. of Rhod., (1930) 706.
    R. × *erythrocalyx* Balf. f. et Forrest *Panteumorphum Group* R. H. S. in Rhod. Handb. (1980) p. 56.

A somewhat compact or broadly upright shrub, 60 cm.–3 m. (2–10 ft.) high, *branchlets glandular* with short-stalked glands, not hairy or rarely floccose. *Leaves oblong,* oblong-elliptic or elliptic, *lamina* leathery, *3–7 cm. long,* 1.4–4.2 cm. broad, apex rounded or broadly obtuse, mucronate, base rounded or cordulate; *upper surface* dark green, *shining,* glossy, glabrous, midrib grooved, primary veins 10–12 on each side, impressed; under surface pale glaucous green, *glabrous* (or rarely with minute hairs), midrib raised; petiole 0.6–1.6 cm. long, glandular with short- or long-stalked glands or eglandular, not hairy or rarely floccose. *Inflorescence* terminal, umbellate or shortly racemose, 4–8-flowered; rhachis 3–5 mm. long, glandular or eglandular, hairy or glabrous; *pedicel* 1.3–2.2 cm. long, *glandular* with short-stalked glands, not hairy or rarely hairy. *Calyx* 5-lobed, small, 1–5 mm. long, lobes rounded or triangular, outside and margin glandular with short-stalked glands or rarely eglandular, not hairy or sometimes hairy. *Corolla* campanulate, 3–3.6 cm. long, *yellow or pale yellow;* lobes 5, 1–1.4 cm. long, 1.5–1.8 cm. broad, rounded, emarginate. *Stamens* 10, unequal, 1.6–3.1 cm. long; filaments puberulous at the base or glabrous. *Gynoecium* 2–3.4 cm. long; *ovary slender,* oblong or conoid, moderately or densely glandular with short-stalked glands, not hairy or rarely tomentose; style eglandular. *Capsule* slender or oblong, 1.4–1.8 cm. long, 4 mm. broad, curved, glandular with short-stalked glands, calyx-lobes persistent.

This plant was first collected by Forrest in September 1904 in the Mekong-Salwin Divide, north-west of Tsekou, south-east Tibet. It was later found by him, Rock, and McLaren's collectors in various localities in north-west Yunnan. The plant grows in marshy mountain meadows, in rhododendron scrub, in Larch forest, and in alpine regions, at elevations of 3,355–4,450 m. (11,000–14,590 ft.).

A diagnostic feature of this species is usually the small, oblong leaves by which it is readily distinguished from its nearest ally, *R. campylocarpum*. It further differs in that it is a Chinese or Tibetan species, whereas *R. campylocarpum* is predominantly a Himalayan species.

R. panteumorphum was introduced possibly by Forrest. In its native home it grows from 2 to 10 feet high. In cultivation it is a somewhat compact shrub, 3 feet high, fairly well-filled with foliage, and flowers freely. It is a pleasing shrub, and one of its merits is that it flowers when quite young. The plant is hardy, but along the east coast it requires a sheltered position in the garden. It is rare in cultivation, but is well worth acquiring for every collection of rhododendrons.

Epithet. Altogether beautiful.

Hardiness 3. April–May.

R. telopeum Balf. f. et Forrest in Notes Roy. Bot. Gard. Edin., Vol. 13 (1920) 61.

Syn. *R. campylocarpum* Hook. f. ssp. *caloxanthum* (Balf. f. et Farrer) Chamberlain *Telopeum Group* R. H. S. in Rhod. Handb. (1980) p. 33.

A somewhat compact rounded, or broadly upright shrub, 60 cm.–3 m. (2–10 ft.) or rarely a tree 4.58 m. (15 ft.) high, branchlets sparsely or moderately glandular with short-stalked glands, those below the inflorescences about 3 mm. in diameter. *Leaves orbicular, ovate* or broadly elliptic, lamina leathery, *2–5 cm. long, 1.5–3.5 cm. broad,* apex rounded or broadly obtuse, mucronate, base rounded or truncate or cordulate; *upper surface dark green,* glabrous, *glaucous, matt,* midrib grooved, primary veins 7–9 on each side, impressed; *under surface* pale glaucous green, papillate, *glabrous* or minutely hairy, midrib raised; petiole 0.8–1.8 cm. long, glandular with long- or short-stalked glands or eglandular. *Inflorescence* umbellate or shortly racemose, 4–5-flowered; rhachis 1–4 mm. long, glandular, hairy or glabrous; *pedicel* 1.1–2.5 cm. long, *glandular* with short-stalked glands. *Calyx* 5-lobed, 1–2 mm. long, lobes rounded or triangular, *outside glandular* or rarely eglandular, *margin glandular. Corolla* campanulate, 2.6–4 cm. long, *bright yellow, yellow, sulphur-yellow or creamy-white,* with or without a faint crimson blotch at the base; lobes 5, 1–1.5 cm. long, 1.5–2.2 cm. broad, rounded, emarginate. *Stamens* 10, unequal, 1.6–3 cm. long; filaments puberulous at the base or glabrous. *Gynoecium* 2.5–3.6 cm. long; *ovary* oblong, conoid or slender, 4–5 mm. long, *densely glandular* with short-stalked glands; style eglandular or sometimes glandular at the base. *Capsule* slender or oblong, 1.3–2 cm. long, 4–7 mm. broad, slightly or much curved, *glandular* with short-stalked glands, calyx-lobes persistent.

R. telopeum was first collected by Forrest in July 1919 in the Salwin-Kiu-Chiang Divide, south-east Tibet. It was afterwards found by him and Rock in the same region and in north-west Yunnan. In 1947, Ludlow, Sherriff and Elliot collected it at Doshong La, south-east Tibet. It grows at the margins of thickets, in scrub, in open conifer forests and cane brakes, and among cliffs and crags, at elevations of 3,660–4,423 m. (12,000–14,500 ft.).

The species is very variable in habit and height of growth. It is a somewhat compact rounded, or broadly upright shrub 2–10 feet high. In 1932 Rock found a plant (No. 22109) in the Province of Tsarung, south-east Tibet, growing as a tree 15 feet high.

R. telopeum is very similar to *R. caloxanthum* in general characters, but differs mainly in its smaller leaves. In this respect, however, these species are linked with intermediate forms. Nevertheless, the extremes of these forms—*R. telopeum* with very small leaves, lamina 2 cm. long and 1.5 cm. broad, and *R. caloxanthum* lamina 8 cm. long and 5.6 cm. broad—are so distinct, particularly in cultivation, that it would be desirable not to disturb the nomenclature.

R. telopeum was first introduced by Forrest in 1921 (No. 20023). It was reintroduced by him in 1922 (21875). In cultivation it is a somewhat compact rounded shrub 3–4 feet high, fairly well-filled with foliage. A characteristic feature is the distinctly glaucous, matt, upper surface of the leaves. The plant is free-flowering, and makes a fine show with its yellow flowers in trusses of 4–5. Occasionally it produces a few slender or oblong curved capsules containing fertile seeds. The plant is hardy, but like the other members of its Subseries, it requires a sheltered position along the east coast and inland. It is rare in cultivation, but is worth being more widely grown.

Epithet. Conspicuous.

Hardiness 3. April–May.

CERASINUM SUBSERIES

General characters: shrubs up to 3.66 m. (12 ft.) high, branchlets glandular or eglandular. Leaves oblong, oblanceolate or oblong-obovate, lamina 4–10 cm. long, 1.5–4 cm. broad; *under surface glabrous*. Inflorescence terminal, umbellate, 3–7-flowered; pedicel 1.3–2 cm. long, glandular. Calyx small, 1–5 mm. long, glandular. *Corolla* campanulate, 2.3–4.5 cm. long, *deep crimson, cherry-red, brilliant scarlet, white or creamy-white with a broad cherry-red or deep pink band round the summit*; lobes 5. Stamens 10, filaments glabrous. Ovary conoid, 5–8 mm. long, densely glandular; *style glandular throughout to the tip.* Capsule oblong, glandular.

KEY TO THE SPECIES

A. Corolla large, 3.5–4.5 cm. long; leaves (laminae) 5–10 cm. long, 1.8–4 cm. broad. . . . . *cerasinum*
A. Corolla small, 2.3 cm. long; leaves (laminae) 4–5 cm. long, 1.5 cm. broad. . . . . *bonvalotii*

DESCRIPTION OF THE SPECIES

R. bonvalotii Bur. et Franch. in Journ. de Bot., Vol. 5 (1891) 94.

A shrub, branchlets eglandular. *Leaves oblong*, lamina leathery, *4–5 cm. long, 1.5 cm. broad*, apex shortly acute, base obtuse; upper surface glabrous, midrib grooved, primary veins 12–14 on each side, deeply impressed; *under surface glabrous*, midrib raised; petiole 8 mm. long, eglandular. *Inflorescence* a terminal umbel of 5–6 flowers; rhachis 3 mm. long, glandular; pedicel 1.3–1.7 cm. long, glandular with short-stalked glands. *Calyx* 5-lobed, 3–5 mm. long, lobes unequal, ovate or rounded, outside glandular with short-stalked glands, margin gland-fringed. *Corolla* campanulate, *2.3 cm. long*, (rose?); lobes 5, 1 cm. long, 1.5 cm. broad, rounded, emarginate. *Stamens* 10, unequal, 1–1.5 cm. long; filaments glabrous. *Gynoecium* about 2 cm. long; ovary conoid, densely glandular; *style glandular throughout to the tip.* *Capsule:* not known.

R. bonvalotii is known from a single collection made by Bonvalot and Prince d'Orleans from the neighbourhood of Tatsienlu, south-west Sichuan. The date of collecting is unknown.

The main features of this plant are the small oblong leaves, laminae 4–5 cm. long, 1.5 cm. broad, the small campanulate corolla 2.3 cm. long, (rose?), and the style glandular throughout to the tip. It is closely related to R. cerasinum from which it differs in its smaller flowers, and smaller leaves.

The plant has not been introduced into cultivation.

Epithet. After Gabriel Bonvalot, who travelled with Prince Henri d'Orleans in Tibet and China.

Not in cultivation.

R. cerasinum Tagg in Notes Roy. Bot. Gard. Edin., Vol. 16 (1931) 188.

Illustration. Bot. Mag. Vol. 161 t. 9538 (1938).

A somewhat compact broadly upright or rounded shrub or bush, 1.22–3.66 m. (4–12 ft.) high, branchlets glandular with short-stalked glands or eglandular, those below the inflorescences 3–4 mm. in diameter. *Leaves* oblong, oblanceolate or sometimes oblong-obovate, *lamina* leathery, *5–10 cm. long, 1.8–4 cm. broad*, apex rounded or broadly obtuse, mucronate, base obtuse or somewhat rounded; upper surface dark green, glabrous, glossy, midrib grooved, primary veins 10–16 on each side, deeply impressed; *under surface* glaucous-green, *glabrous*, midrib prominent; petiole 0.7–2 cm. long, sparsely glandular with short-stalked glands or eglandular, hairy or glabrous. *Inflorescence* umbellate or shortly racemose, 3–7 *pendulous flowers;* rhachis 2–5 mm. long, sparsely glandular with short-stalked glands or eglandular, not hairy; *pedicel* 1.6–2 cm. long, *glandular* with subsessile or short-stalked glands, not hairy. *Calyx* 5-lobed or an undulate rim, 1–5 mm. long, lobes ovate or rounded or triangular, outside glandular with short-stalked glands or eglandular, margin glandular with short-stalked glands. *Corolla* campanulate, *3.5–4.5 cm. long*, fleshy, *brilliant scarlet or cherry-red or deep crimson, or white or creamy-white with a broad cherry-red or deep pink band round the summit*, with 5 *deep purple or coal-black nectar pouches at the base;* lobes 5, 1–1.2 cm. long, 1.5–2.6 cm. broad, rounded, emarginate. *Stamens* 10, unequal, 1.7–3.3 cm. long; filaments glabrous. *Gynoecium* 2.4–3.5 cm. long; ovary conoid, 5–8 mm. long, densely glandular with short-stalked glands; *style glandular throughout to the tip. Capsule* oblong, 2–2.5 cm. long, glandular with short-stalked glands, calyx-lobes persistent.

Kingdon-Ward discovered this species in June 1924 at Doshong La, south-east Tibet, forming dense tangled thickets by a stream. He records it (No. 5830) as being a shrub of 6–10 feet with brilliant scarlet flowers with five coal-black nectar pouches at the base, and he named the plant "Coals of Fire". In June 1926, he found the species at Seinghku Wang, Upper Burma growing in dense rhododendron thickets and on the edge of *Abies* forest, and he described it (No. 6923) as a stout, thickset bush as much as 10–12 feet high with white flowers with a broad deep pink band round the summit; he named the plant "Cherry Brandy". (The name was meant for a cherry-red form). Later in May 1928 Kingdon-Ward found the species in the Delei Valley, Assam, forming thickets practically impenetrable on ridges, and in forests; in his field note he records it (No. 8258) as a large shrub with ascending trunk sweeping up from the ground to a height of 10 feet, with deep crimson flowers. Subsequently, *R. cerasinum* was also collected by Ludlow, Sherriff and with Taylor or Elliot in various localities in south-east Tibet growing at the margins of *Picea* forest, in conifer forest, and on rocks. The species is found at elevations of 2,745–3,813 m. (9,000–12,500 ft.).

R. cerasinum is a distinctive species. A diagnostic character is the style glandular throughout to the tip. The species is related to *R. bonvalotii;* the distinctions between them are discussed under the latter. *R. cerasinum* agrees with the Thomsonii Subseries in the shape of the flowers but with the style glandular throughout to the tip as in the Souliei Subseries.

The plant was first introduced by Kingdon-Ward in 1924 (No. 5830). It was reintroduced by him in 1926 (No. 6923—the Type number), and in 1928 (No. 8258). In cultivation it is a somewhat compact broadly upright or rounded shrub, usually up to 5–6 feet high, fairly densely filled with dark green leaves. Characteristic features are the pendulous flowers and the five deep purple or coal-black nectar pouches at the base of the corolla. Three colour forms are in cultivation: Form 1. Deep crimson or cherry-red. Form 2. Brilliant scarlet. Form 3. White or creamy-white with a broad cherry-red or deep pink band round the summit. In the young stage of the plant, the flowers are partially hidden amongst the foliage, but later some adult plants bloom abundantly and provide an impressive display of colour. It may be noted that a few other forms are shy flowerers in some gardens and hardly produce more than a few flowers every year. The species seldom produces mature capsules with fertile seeds, and is difficult to root from cuttings. It is hardy outdoors, but like other species of its Series, it requires protection from wind.

A clone with creamy-white flowers with a cherry-red band round the margin (Kingdon-Ward No. 6923) was given an Award of Merit when shown by Lt.-Col. L. C. R.

Messel, Nymans, Sussex, in 1938, and again the same award to a clone with cherry-red flowers when exhibited by the Countess of Rosse and National Trust, Nymans Garden, in 1973.

Epithet. Cherry-coloured.

Hardiness 3. May–June.

SELENSE SUBSERIES

General characters: shrubs or rarely trees, 60 cm.–6.10 m. (2–20 ft.) high, *branchlets setulose-glandular or glandular* with short-stalked glands or eglandular. *Leaves oblong*, elliptic, oblong-oval to oval, lamina 2–12.5 cm. long, 0.8–5.3 cm. broad. Inflorescence terminal, umbellate or shortly racemose, 4–10- or sometimes 1–3-flowered; pedicel 0.7–3.5 cm. long, glandular with long- or short-stalked glands. Calyx 0.1–1 cm. long, usually glandular. *Corolla funnel-campanulate* or sometimes campanulate, 2.5–5 cm. long, rose, pink, white or creamy-white; lobes 5. Stamens 10; filaments puberulous at the base or rarely glabrous. *Ovary* slender, oblong or conoid, 3–7 mm. long, *densely glandular*, glabrous or rarely tomentose; style glandular at the base or rarely up to three-fourths its length or eglandular. *Capsule* oblong or *slender*, slightly or *much curved (sickle-shaped)* or rarely straight, glandular.

KEY TO THE SPECIES

A. Indumentum on the under surface of the leaves absent or a thin veil of hairs.
  B. Branchlets and usually petioles setulose-glandular.
    C. Ovary tomentose (glandular or eglandular); under surface of the leaves often with long-stalked glands. .... *dasycladoides*
    C. Ovary not tomentose (glandular); under surface of the leaves without long-stalked glands.
      D. Corolla unspotted or with a few spots, usually funnel-shaped or funnel-campanulate.
        E. Leaves (laminae) usually 2–4 cm. long; inflorescence 1–3-(rarely 4-) flowered, rarely more .... *martinianum* (part)
        E. Leaves (laminae) usually 5–12 cm. long; inflorescence 5–12-flowered.
          F. Under surface of the leaves markedly glaucous......
            .... *jucundum*
          F. Under surface of the leaves pale green.
            G. Leaves thin, chartaceous in texture, oval, oblong-oval, elliptic or oblong; calyx usually 1–2 mm. (sometimes 3–6 mm.) long........ *dasycladum*
            G. Leaves thick, coriaceous in texture, oblong; calyx 3 mm.–1 cm. long .... *setiferum*
      D. Corolla copiously spotted with crimson, campanulate........
        .... *eurysiphon* (part)
  B. Branchlets and petioles not setulose-glandular.
    H. Leaves (laminae) usually more than 7.5 cm. long and 4 cm. broad; leaf base usually cordate, sometimes rounded or obtuse; calyx 1 mm.–1 cm. long; corolla usually 3.5–4.5 cm. long (rarely less).
      I. Under surface of the leaves glabrous; leaves thin, chartaceous in texture .... *erythrocalyx*

    I. Under surface of the leaves with a thin veil of hairs; leaves coriaceous in texture . . . . *esetulosum*

  H. Leaves (laminae) usually less than 7.5 cm. long and 4 cm. broad; leaf base obtuse or rounded, not cordate; calyx 1–3 mm. long; corolla usually 2.2–3.5 cm. long.

    J. Corolla unspotted or with a few spots, funnel-shaped or funnel-campanulate.

      K. Leaves (laminae) usually more than 4 cm. long; inflorescence 4–8-(rarely 3-) flowered; pedicel usually 1–2 cm. long . . . . *selense*

      K. Leaves (laminae) usually 2–4 cm. long; inflorescence 1–3-(rarely 4-) flowered; pedicel 2.2–3.5 cm. long, rarely less . . . . *martinianum* (part)

    J. Corolla copiously spotted with crimson, campanulate . . . . *eurysiphon* (part)

A. Indumentum on the under surface of the leaves patchy-scurfy and with scattered tufts of dark brown hairs; or semi-agglutinate or non-agglutinate, discontinuous.

  L. Leaves (laminae) 3.2–6.2 cm. long; branchlets, petioles, and pedicels setulose-glandular and with short-stalked glands; corolla 3–3.5 cm. long; branchlets and often petioles not hairy . . . . *vestitum*

  L. Leaves (laminae) 7–10 cm. long; branchlets, petioles, and pedicels not setulose-glandular, only glandular with short-stalked glands; corolla 3.5–4.2 cm. long; branchlets and petioles hairy . . . . *calvescens*

DESCRIPTION OF THE SPECIES

R. calvescens Balf. f. et Forrest in Notes Roy. Bot. Gard. Edin., Vol. 11 (1919) 29.

    Syn. *R. duseimatum* Balf. f. et Forrest, ibid. Vol. 13 (1920) 41.

      R. selense Franch. subsp. *duseimatum* (Balf. f. et Forrest) Tagg in The Sp. of Rhod. (1930) 722.

      R. selense Franch. var. *duseimatum* (Balf. f. et Forrest) Cowan et Davidian in The Rhod. Year Book (1951–52) 152.

      R. calvescens Balf. f. et Forrest var. *duseimatum* (Balf. f. et Forrest) Chamberlain in Notes Roy. Bot. Gard. Edin., Vol. 36 (1978) 119.

A broadly upright or rounded shrub, 60 cm.–1.83 m. (2–6 ft.) high, *branchlets glandular* with short-stalked glands, hairy, those below the inflorescences 3–5 mm. in diameter; leaf-bud scales deciduous. *Leaves* oblong, oblong-elliptic, oblong-obovate or oblong-lanceolate, *lamina* coriaceous, *7–10 cm. long*, 2.6–4.3 cm. broad, apex obtuse or rounded, mucronate, base truncate, cordulate, or rounded; upper surface olive-green or dark green, matt or shining, glabrous or with vestiges of hairs, eglandular, midrib grooved, primary veins 10–15 on each side, deeply impressed; *under surface hairy* with semi-agglutinate or non-agglutinate, *thin discontinuous indumentum of hairs, glandular with small sessile glands,* midrib prominent, moderately or sparsely glandular with small sessile glands, hairy; petiole 0.6–1.8 cm. long, grooved above, sparsely glandular with small sessile glands or eglandular, hairy. *Inflorescence* terminal, shortly racemose, 5–8-flowered; rhachis 4–8 mm. long, eglandular, hairy; *pedicel* 1.3–2.3 cm. long, *glandular* with short-stalked glands, sparsely hairy or glabrous. *Calyx* 5-lobed, minute, 1 mm. long, lobes rounded, ovate or triangular, outside moderately or slightly glandular with short-stalked glands, glabrous, margin densely or sparsely glandular with short-stalked glands, glabrous. *Corolla* campanulate, *3.5–4.2 cm. long,* rose or pale rose or white flushed rose or white, without or with very few crimson spots, without a blotch or rarely with a crimson blotch at the base; lobes 5, 1.6–1.8 cm. long, 1.5–3 cm. broad, rounded, emarginate. *Stamens* 10, unequal, 1.2–3 cm. long; filaments puberulous at the base or glabrous. *Gynoecium* 3–3.5 cm. long, as long as the corolla or slightly shorter; *ovary* oblong, apex truncate, 4–5 mm. long, 5–6-celled, *moderately or densely glandular* with short-stalked glands, moderately or sparsely hairy; style glabrous, eglandular. *Capsule* oblong, 1.5–2 cm. long, 4–5 mm. broad, slightly curved or straight, furrowed, *glandular* with short-stalked glands, hairy, calyx-lobes persistent.

Forrest discovered this species in July 1917 on Doker-La, in the Mekong-Salwin Divide, Tsarong, south-east Tibet. Subsequently he found it in other localities in the same region, and in north-west Yunnan, also in north-east Upper Burma. It grows in open thickets, amongst scrub, and on the margins of pine forests and conifer forests, at elevations of 3,355–4,270 m. (11,000–14,000 ft.).

The main features of this plant are the large oblong to oblong-elliptic leaves, laminae 7–10 cm. long, with semi-agglutinate or non-agglutinate, thin discontinuous indumentum of hairs on the lower surfaces, and the fairly large campanulate corolla 3.5–4.2 cm. long. It is allied to *R. esetulosum* and *R. vestitum,* but differs from both in distinctive features.

The species was first introduced by Forrest in 1917 (No. 14331—the Type number, and No. 14464) and again on two other occasions. In cultivation it is a broadly upright or rounded shrub 3–4 feet high with rigid branchlets, and olive-green or dark green foliage. It is hardy, free-flowering, and provides a charming display with its rose or white flushed rose flowers in trusses of 5–8. The plant is rare in cultivation, but is a most desirable plant for every garden. There was a fine specimen growing in the Royal Botanic Garden, Edinburgh, 5 feet high and as much across, with white flowers which appeared freely in trusses of 5–6. Unfortunately this plant has now been lost to cultivation.

Epithet. Becoming hairless.
Hardiness 3. April–May.

R. dasycladoides Hand.-Mazz. Symb. Sin., VII (1936) 781.
A shrub, 2–4 m. (6½–13 ft.) high, *branchlets setulose-glandular,* those below the inflorescences 3–5 mm. in diameter. *Leaves oblong,* 3–7.6 cm. long, 1.8–3.3 cm. broad, apex obtuse or acute, mucronate, base cordulate or rounded; upper surface with vestiges of hairs, midrib grooved, primary veins 12–13 on each side, deeply impressed; *under surface often glandular with long-stalked glands,* minutely hairy or glabrous, midrib glandular with long-stalked glands; *petiole setulose-glandular. Inflorescence* umbellate or shortly racemose, 5–8-flowered; rhachis 3–5 mm. long, tomentose; *pedicel* 0.7–1.6 cm. long, *densely glandular* with long- or short-stalked glands or densely hairy. *Calyx* 5-lobed, 2–7 mm. long, lobes oblong or rounded, outside and margin glandular with short- or long-stalked glands or hairy. *Corolla* funnel-campanulate, 3.1–3.7 cm. long, pale pink, rose or pinkish-purple, with crimson spots; lobes 5, 1.4–1.7 cm. long, 1.7–2 cm. broad, rounded, emarginate. *Stamens* 10, unequal, 1.3–2.5 cm. long; filaments puberulous at the base. *Gynoecium* about 3 cm. long; *ovary* conoid, 4–6 mm. long, *tomentose, glandular* with long- or short-stalked glands *or eglandular;* style eglandular. *Capsule:* not seen.

This plant was first collected by Camillo Schneider in 1914 above Molien, south-west Sichuan. It was later found by Handel-Mazzetti, and by Rock in the same region. The plant grows at elevations of 3,050–4,875 m. (10,000–15,984 ft.).

R. dasycladoides is closely related to *R. dasycladum.* In both species the branchlets and petioles are setulose-glandular, and the under surface of the leaves is glabrous or minutely hairy. The main distinctions between them are that in *R. dasycladoides* the ovary is tomentose and glandular or eglandular, and long-stalked glands are often present on the under surface of the leaves which are oblong; whereas in *R. dasycladum* the ovary is not tomentose but is densely glandular, and long-stalked glands are absent on the under surface of the leaves which are oblong, oblong-oval, oval or elliptic.

There is no record of its occurrence in cultivation.

Epithet. Like *R. dasycladum.*

Not in cultivation.

R. dasycladum Balf. f. et W. W. Sm. in Notes Roy. Bot. Gard. Edin., Vol. 10 (1917) 98.
    Syn. *R. rhaibocarpum* Balf. f. et W. W. Sm. in Notes Roy. Bot. Gard. Edin., Vol. 10 (1917) 142.
       R. selense Franch. subsp. *dasycladum* (Balf. f. et W. W. Sm.) Chamberlain in Notes Roy. Bot. Gard. Edin., Vol. 36 (1978) 118.

A somewhat compact or broadly upright spreading shrub or sometimes a tree, 92 cm.–4.58 m. (3–15 ft.) high, *branchlets moderately or densely setulose-glandular,* hairy or glabrous, those below the inflorescences 3–5 mm. in diameter. *Leaves oblong, oblong-oval, oval or elliptic,* lamina thinly leathery, 3–12.5 cm. long, 1.5–4.7 cm. broad, apex obtuse or rounded, mucronate, base obtuse, cordulate, truncate or rounded; upper surface dark green, glabrous or with vestiges of hairs, midrib grooved, primary veins 9–16 on each side, deeply impressed; *under surface glabrous or with a thin veil of hairs,* midrib raised, glandular or eglandular, hairy or glabrous; *petiole* 0.8–2.5 cm. long, *setulose-glandular* or sometimes eglandular, hairy or glabrous. *Inflorescence* umbellate or shortly racemose, 5–10-flowered; rhachis 2–4 mm. long, slightly or moderately glandular, hairy or glabrous; *pedicel* 0.8–2.4 cm. long, *glandular* with long- or short-stalked glands. *Calyx* 5-lobed, 1–6 mm. long, lobes rounded or oblong or triangular, *outside moderately or densely glandular, margin fringed with* long- or short-stalked *glands. Corolla* funnel-campanulate, 2.5–3.6 cm. long, rose, pink, white or white flushed rose, with or without a crimson blotch at the base, spotted or unspotted; lobes 5, 0.8–1.6 cm. long, 1–2 cm. broad, rounded, emarginate. *Stamens* 10, unequal, 1–3.4 cm. long; filaments puberulous at the base. *Gynoecium* 2.4–3.7 cm. long; *ovary* slender or sometimes conoid, 3–7 mm. long, *densely glandular* with long- or short-stalked glands; style eglandular or glandular, not hairy or rarely hairy at the base. *Capsule* slender or rarely oblong, 1.5–2.8 cm. long, 3–5 mm. broad, slightly or much curved (sickle-shaped), *glandular* with short-stalked glands, not hairy or rarely hairy, calyx-lobes persistent.

This species was discovered by Forrest in July 1913 on the mountains in the north-east of the Yangtze bend, north-west Yunnan. It was afterwards found by him and by Kingdon-Ward, Rock, McLaren's collectors, and Yü in other localities in the same region and in mid-west Yunnan. The plant grows in open thickets, in open rocky situations, on bouldery slopes, on ledges of cliffs, in open scrub, in cane brakes, on the margins of pine and conifer forests, in pine forest, and in fir forest, at elevations of 3,050–3,965 m. (10,000–13,000 ft.). Yü records it as being very common at the margins of *Abies* forest at Atuntze, Dokerla, north-west Yunnan.

In 1917 *R. rhaibocarpum* Balf. f. et W. W. Sm. was described from a specimen No. 11312 collected by Forrest also on the mountains in the north-east of the Yangtze bend, north-west Yunnan; in *The Rhododendron Year Book* 1951–52 page 142, it was placed in synonymy under *R. dasycladum.*

The distinctive features of *R. dasycladum,* as the name suggests, are the setulose-glandular branchlets, usually the petioles and pedicels. The species is closely allied to *R. dasycladoides;* the distinctions between them are discussed under the latter.

The species was first introduced by Forrest in 1913 (No. 11312—the Type of *R. rhaibocarpum*). It was reintroduced by him under 10 different seed numbers. Rock sent seeds on eight occasions. Yü introduced it in 1937. In its native home it is a shrub 3–10 feet high, or sometimes a tree up to 15 feet. Three distinct forms are in cultivation:

Form 1. A somewhat compact medium-sized shrub, 5 feet high with oblong leaves, laminae 7.5 cm. long, and densely setulose-glandular branchlets and petioles. Form 2. A somewhat compact small shrub, 3 feet high with small, oval leaves, laminae 5 cm. long, and moderately glandular branchlets and petioles. Form 3. A broadly upright spreading large shrub, 10–12 feet high with elliptic leaves, laminae 6–6.5 cm. long, and glandular branchlets and petioles, known as *R. rhaibocarpum*. All these forms provide a fine display with white or white flushed rose flowers in trusses of 5–10. The larger forms often produce slender sickle-shaped capsules containing fertile seeds in plenty. The species is hardy outdoors, but is uncommon in cultivation.

Epithet. With hairy boughs.
Hardiness 3. April–May.

R. erythrocalyx Balf. f. et Forrest in Notes Roy. Bot. Gard. Edin., Vol. 12 (1920) 110.
   Syn. *R. beimaense* Balf. f. et Forrest in Notes Roy. Bot. Gard. Edin., Vol. 13 (1920) 32.
      R. cymbomorphum Balf. f. et Forrest, ibid. Vol. 12 (1920) 102.
      R. eucallum Balf. f. et Forrest, ibid. Vol. 13 (1920) 43.
      R. truncatulum Balf. f. et Forrest, ibid. Vol. 13 (1920) 63.
      R. erythrocalyx Balf. f. et Forrest subsp. *beimaense* (Balf. f. et Forrest) Tagg in The Sp. of Rhod. (1930) 716.
      R. erythrocalyx Balf. f. et Forrest subsp. *docimum* Balf. f. ex Tagg in The Sp. of Rhod. (1930) 716.
      R. erythrocalyx Balf. f. et Forrest subsp. *eucallum* (Balf. f. et Forrest) Tagg, ibid. (1930) 716.
      R. erythrocalyx Balf. f. et Forrest subsp. *truncatulum* (Balf. f. et Forrest) Tagg, ibid. (1930) 716.
      R. × erythrocalyx (Balf. f. et Forrest) (*R. selense* × *R. wardii*) Chamberlain in Notes Roy. Bot. Gard. Edin., Vol. 39 (1982) 280.

A broadly upright shrub, 92 cm.–2.44 m. (3–8 ft.) high, branchlets glandular with short-stalked glands or sometimes eglandular, those below the inflorescences 3–5 mm. in diameter. *Leaves* elliptic, oval, oblong-oval, oblong-elliptic or ovate, *lamina thin, chartaceous*, 3–10.6 cm. long, 2.1–5.3 cm. broad, apex rounded or broadly obtuse, with or without a beaked tip, mucronate, base cordulate or broadly obtuse or rounded; upper surface dark green, glabrous or with vestiges of hairs, midrib grooved, primary veins 10–16 on each side, deeply impressed; *under surface* pale green or pale glaucous green, *glabrous* or minutely hairy, midrib raised; petiole 1.1–3 cm. long, glandular with short-stalked glands or eglandular, not hairy or rarely hairy. *Inflorescence* umbellate or shortly racemose, 4–10-flowered; rhachis 0.3–1 cm. long, glandular; *pedicel* 1.3–3 cm. long, *glandular* with short-stalked glands. *Calyx* 5-lobed, usually unequal, 1–7 mm. long, lobes oblong, triangular or rounded, outside glandular, margin glandular, not hairy or sometimes hairy. *Corolla* campanulate or funnel-campanulate, 2.8–4.5 cm. long, creamy-white, creamy-yellow, creamy-yellow flushed rose, white, white flushed rose, pale rose, or rarely yellow, with or without a crimson blotch at the base, and with or without a few crimson spots; lobes 5, 0.8–1.8 cm. long, 1–2.5 cm. broad, rounded, emarginate. *Stamens* 10, unequal, 1.3–3.6 cm. long; filaments glabrous or puberulous at the base. *Gynoecium* 2.3–4.2 cm. long; *ovary* slender or oblong, 4–7 mm. long, *densely glandular* with short-stalked glands; style glandular at the base or on the lower one-third (or rarely up to one-half its length) or eglandular. *Capsule* oblong or slender, 1.4–1.7 cm. long, 4–6 mm, broad, slightly or much curved, glandular with short-stalked glands or with vestiges of glands, calyx-lobes persistent.

R. erythrocalyx was first collected by Forrest in June 1917 on Bei-ma-shan, north-west Yunnan. Subsequently it was found by him, and by Rock in other localities in the same region, and south-east Tibet, also in north-east Upper Burma. It grows in open thickets, in rhododendron thickets, amongst scrub, in pine forests, and on the margins of conifer forests and mixed forests, at elevations of 3,355–3,965 m. (11,000–13,000 ft.).

In 1920 four other species, *R. beimaense* Balf. f. et Forrest, *R. cymbomorphum* Balf. f. et Forrest, *R. eucallum* Balf. f. et Forrest, and *R. truncatulum*, Balf. f. et Forrest, were described from specimens which had been collected by Forrest in north-west Yunnan. In *The Rhododendron Year Book* 1951–52 page 144, they were placed under *R. erythrocalyx* in synonymy.

R. erythrocalyx is closely allied to *R. esetulosum* which it resembles in general features, but differs in that the lower surface of the leaves is glabrous, and the leaves are thin, chartaceous in texture; in *R. esetulosum* the lower surface of the leaves has a thin veil of hairs, and the leaves are thick, coriaceous.

The species was first introduced by Forrest in 1917 (Nos. 13936, 13938, 13951A), and again later on two occasions. Rock sent seeds in 1932 (No. 22226). In its native home it grows up to 8 feet high. In cultivation it is a broadly upright shrub of 5 feet; its distinctive features are the large oblong-oval leaves, laminae up to 10.6 cm. long, and large flowers up to 4.5 cm. in length. The species is rare in cultivation. It is hardy, flowers freely, and is worth being more widely grown.

Epithet. With a red calyx.
Hardiness 3. April–May.

R. esetulosum Balf. f. et Forrest in Notes Roy. Bot. Gard. Edin., Vol. 13 (1920) 42.
> Syn. *R. manopeplum* Balf. f. et Forrest in Notes Roy. Bot. Gard. Edin., Vol. 13 (1922) 275.

A broadly upright shrub, 1.22–1.83 m. (4–6 ft.) high, *branchlets glandular* with short-stalked glands, hairy or glabrous, those below the inflorescences 4–6 mm. in diameter. *Leaves* oblong, elliptic, ovate, or oblong-ovate, *lamina thick, coriaceous,* 5–9.4 cm. long, 2.3–5.1 cm. broad, apex shortly acute or broadly obtuse, mucronate, base rounded, truncate or cordulate; upper surface dark green, glabrous or with vestiges of hairs, midrib grooved, primary veins 12–14 on each side, deeply impressed; *under surface with a thin veil of hairs,* midrib prominent, glandular; petiole 1–2 cm. long, glandular with short-stalked glands or eglandular, hairy or glabrous. *Inflorescence* a racemose umbel of 8–10 flowers; rhachis 0.1–1 cm. long, glandular or eglandular, hairy or glabrous; *pedicel* 1–2.4 cm. long, *glandular* with short-stalked glands. *Calyx* 5-lobed, 0.1–1 cm. long, lobes rounded, oblong or triangular, outside glandular or eglandular, *margin fringed with glands.* *Corolla* broadly funnel-campanulate or campanulate, 3.1–5 cm. long, *creamy-white or white,* flushed or not flushed rose or purplish, spotted crimson or unspotted; lobes 5, 1.2–2 cm. long, 2–2.6 cm. broad, rounded, emarginate. *Stamens* 10, unequal, 1.1–3 cm. long; filaments puberulous at the base or up to one-half their length. *Gynoecium* 2.4–3.4 cm. long; *ovary* oblong or conoid, 4–6 mm. long, *densely glandular* with short-stalked glands; style glandular at the base or up to three-fourths its length (or rarely eglandular). *Capsule* oblong, 1.5–1.7 cm. long, 4–5 mm. broad, straight or curved, glandular with short-stalked glands or with vestiges of glands, calyx-lobes persistent.

This plant was discovered by Forrest in July 1918 on the mountains north-east of Chungtien, north-west Yunnan. It was later found by him in south-east Tibet and mid-west Yunnan. Rock collected it in 1923 in north-west Yunnan. It grows on bouldery slopes, and on the margins of thickets in side valleys, at elevations of 3,050–4,270 m. (10,000–14,000 ft.).

In 1922, *R. manopeplum* Balf. f. et Forrest was founded on a specimen (No. 18654) collected by Forrest in 1919 in Tsarong, south-east Tibet. It will be seen that the name was referred to *R. esetulosum* in *The Rhododendron Year Book* 1951–52, page 146.

The main features of *R. esetulosum* are the thick, coriaceous, large leaves, laminae up to 9.4 cm. long, the thin veil of hairs on the lower surfaces, and the large corolla up to 5 cm. long. The species is closely related to *R. erythrocalyx;* the distinctions between them are discussed under the latter.

R. esetulosum was first introduced by Forrest in 1918 (No. 16581—the Type number). Rock sent seeds in 1923 (No. 11094). The species was introduced to Sweden by Harry Smith. In cultivation it grows up to 5–6 feet high and attracts attention with its creamy-white or white flowers in trusses of 8–10. The plant is rare in cultivation, but is worthy of a place in every garden.

Epithet. Hairless.
Hardiness 3. April–May.

R. eurysiphon Tagg et Forrest in The Sp. of Rhod., (1930) 708; and in Notes Roy. Bot. Gard. Edin., Vol. 16 (1931) 191.

A broadly upright shrub, 92 cm.–1.53 m. (3–5 ft.) high, branchlets glandular with short-stalked glands or eglandular. *Leaves* oblong, oblong-oval or oblong-elliptic, *lamina leathery, rigid,* 2.6–7.5 cm. long, 1.3–2.8 cm. broad, apex rounded or broadly obtuse, mucronate, base rounded, cordulate or obtuse; upper surface dark green, glabrous, midrib grooved, primary veins 8–16 on each side, deeply impressed; margin recurved; *under surface* pale glaucous green, *glabrous,* minutely glandular or eglandular, midrib raised; petiole 0.5–1.2 cm. long, glandular with short-stalked glands or eglandular. *Inflorescence* terminal, umbellate or shortly racemose, 3–5-flowered; rhachis 3–5 mm. long, glandular or eglandular, tomentose or glabrous; pedicel 1.2–2.6 cm. long, glandular with short-stalked glands. *Calyx* 5-lobed, 2–4 mm. long, lobes rounded or triangular, *outside glandular, margin gland-fringed. Corolla campanulate,* 3–4 cm. long, creamy-white or very pale rose, flushed deep rose or deep magenta-rose, *copiously spotted with crimson;* lobes 5, 1.2–1.5 cm. long, 1.5–2 cm. broad, rounded, emarginate. *Stamens* 10, unequal, 1.3–3 cm. long; filaments puberulous at the base. *Gynoecium* 2.2–3.5 cm. long; ovary conoid, 3–5 mm. long, densely glandular with short-stalked glands; style eglandular. *Capsule* oblong, 1.2–1.6 cm. long, 4–6 mm. broad, slightly curved or straight, glandular with short-stalked glands, calyx-lobes persistent.

This species was discovered by Forrest in June 1922 in the Salwin-Kiu Chiang Divide, south-east Tibet, growing amongst scrub and in rhododendron thickets on stony slopes in side valleys at an elevation of 3,965 m. (13,000 ft.).

R. eurysiphon is a distinct species and cannot be confused with any species of its Subseries. It is allied to *R. selense* and *R. martinianum* but is distinguished by its campanulate corolla which is copiously spotted with crimson.

It was introduced into cultivation by Forrest in 1922 (No. 21694—the Type number). In its native home it grows 3–5 feet high; in cultivation it is a broadly upright shrub 3–4 feet in height, fairly well-filled with dark green foliage. It is a pleasing shrub with campanulate flowers produced freely in trusses of 3–5. The species is rare in cultivation. It is hardy, easy to grow, and is very desirable for inclusion in every collection of rhododendrons. In cultivation some plants which have been labelled *R. martinianum,* are, in fact, *R. eurysiphon.*

Epithet. With a broad tube.
Hardiness 3. May.

R. jucundum Balf. f. et W. W. Sm. in Notes Roy. Bot. Gard. Edin., Vol. 9 (1916) 242.
    Syn. *R. blandulum* Balf. f. et W. W. Sm. in Notes Roy. Bot. Gard. Edin., Vol. 10 (1917) 87.
        R. selense Franch. subsp. *jucundum* (Balf. f. et W. W. Sm.) Chamberlain, ibid. Vol. 36 (1978) 118.

A somewhat compact rounded, or broadly upright spreading shrub, 60 cm.–3 m. (2–10 ft.) high, or a tree up to 6.10 m. (20 ft.) high, branchlets not glandular, not setulose-glandular or sometimes setulose-glandular, hairy or glabrous, often warty those below the inflorescences 3–5 mm. in diameter. *Leaves* elliptic, oblong or oblong-elliptic, lamina leathery, 3.8–7.4 cm. long, 2–4 cm. broad, apex broadly obtuse or rounded, mucronate, base rounded or cordulate; upper surface dark green, glabrous or with vestiges of hairs, midrib grooved, primary veins 13–15 on each side, deeply impressed; *under surface markedly glaucous, glabrous* or minutely hairy, midrib raised, sparsely glandular towards the base with short-stalked glands or eglandular; *petiole* 0.9–2.2 cm. long, grooved above, not glandular, not setulose-glandular or rarely setulose-glandular, hairy or glabrous. *Inflorescence* umbellate or shortly racemose, *5–8-flowered;* rhachis 3–7 mm. long, glandular or eglandular, hairy or glabrous; *pedicel* 1–2.8 cm. long, *glandular* with long- and short-stalked glands, hairy or glabrous. *Calyx* 5-lobed, 1–6 mm. long, lobes oblong or rounded, outside glandular or eglandular, margin glandular, not hairy or sometimes hairy. *Corolla* funnel-campanulate or campanulate, 3–4 cm. long, pale rose, rose, pink, white or white flushed rose, with or without a crimson blotch at the base; lobes 5, 0.8–1.9 cm. long, 1.3–2.5 cm. broad, rounded, emarginate. *Stamens* 10, unequal, 1.3–2.5 cm. long; filaments puberulous at the base. *Gynoecium* 3–3.6 cm. long; *ovary* oblong or slender, 4–7 mm. long, *densely glandular* with long-stalked glands; style eglandular. *Capsule* oblong or slender, 1.3–2.2 cm. long, 3–6 mm. broad, slightly or much curved, glandular or with vestiges of glands, calyx-lobes persistent.

Forrest first collected this plant in July 1906 on the eastern flank of the Tali Range, western Yunnan. He found it again later on several occasions in other localities in the same region. It grows in open rocky situations, in meadows, amongst boulders, on the margins of pine forests and cane brakes, and in rhododendron forest, at elevations of 3,050–3,660 m. (10,000–12,000 ft.).

A diagnostic feature of this species is the very glaucous lower surface of the leaves by which it is readily distinguished from all the species in its Subseries. It may be remarked that this feature is markedly evident in plants in cultivation. However, in herbarium specimens that have been pressed, the glaucous characteristic tends to disappear. The species is allied to *R. martinianum* and *R. dasycladum*; besides the very glaucous lower surface of the leaves, it further differs from the former usually in the larger leaves and many-flowered inflorescence, and from the latter often in the esetulose-glandular branchlets and petioles and in the absence of a thin veil of hairs on the lower surface of the leaves.

R. jucundum was introduced by Forrest in 1917 (No. 15579). In its native home it is a shrub or tree 2–20 feet high; in cultivation it is a somewhat compact rounded or broadly upright spreading shrub 5–6 feet in height. It is a fairly fast grower and is easily recognised by the markedly glaucous lower surface of the leaves. The plant is hardy outdoors, free-flowering, and provides a fine display with its white or white flushed rose flowers in trusses of 5–8. It also has the merit of flowering at a young age. The plant is rare in cultivation but is worthy of being widely grown.

Epithet. Pleasant.
Hardiness 3. May–June.

R. martinianum Balf. f. et Forrest in Notes Roy. Bot. Gard. Edin., Vol. 11 (1919) 96.

A broadly upright or somewhat compact rounded or sometimes straggly shrub, 60 cm.–1.83 m. (2–6 ft.) high, *branchlets* moderately or sparsely setulose-glandular or sometimes eglandular, nodular, *thin,* those below the inflorescences 1.5–3 mm. in diameter. *Leaves* oblong, oblong-oval, elliptic or oblong-elliptic, *lamina* thinly leathery, *rigid, 1.9–4 cm.,* rarely 1.5 cm. (sometimes up to 5.4 cm.) long, 0.8–2.5 cm. broad, apex rounded or broadly obtuse, mucronate, base broadly obtuse or rounded; upper surfce glabrous or with vestiges of glands, midrib grooved, primary veins 8–10 on each side, deeply impressed; *under surface* glaucous or pale glaucous green, *glabrous* or rarely with tufts of hairs, punctulate with minute glands, midrib raised; petiole 3–7 mm. long, slightly or moderately glandular with long- or short-stalked glands. *Inflorescence* terminal, umbellate or shortly racemose, *1–3- or rarely 4-flowered;* rhachis 2–8 mm. long, glandular, hairy or glabrous; *pedicel* 2–3.5 cm. (rarely 1.5 cm.) long, *glandular* with long- or short-stalked glands, not hairy or rarely hairy. *Calyx* 5-lobed, 1–3 mm. long, lobes rounded or triangular, outside glandular or eglandular, margin usually gland-fringed. *Corolla* funnel-campanulate, 2.5–4 cm. (rarely 2 cm.) long, pink, pale rose, purple, white, or creamy-white faintly flushed pale rose, with or without crimson spots; lobes 5, 1.3–1.8 cm. long, 1.5–2.2 cm. broad, rounded, emarginate. *Stamens* 10, unequal, 1.5–3.2 cm. long; filaments puberulous at the base. *Gynoecium* 2.7–3.8 cm. long; *ovary* conoid or slender, 3–4 mm. long, 5–6-celled, *densely glandular* with short-stalked glands; style glandular at the base or eglandular. *Capsule* oblong or slender, 1.5–2.5 cm. long (rarely less), 5–7 mm. broad, curved or straight, glandular or with vestiges of glands, calyx-lobes persistent.

R. martinianum was discovered by Forrest in September 1914, in fruit, in western Yunnan. Subsequently it was collected by him, and by Farrer, Kingdon-Ward, and Rock, in the same region and in Upper Burma, also in east and south-east Tibet. It grows in open rocky pastures, in thickets and scrub, in alpine moorland and meadows, amongst rocks on the margins of conifer forests, amongst canes, on open ridges, in bamboo thickets on granite slabs, and amongst boulders, at elevations of 2,745–4,270 m. (9,000–14,000 ft.). Kingdon-Ward records it as forming tangled thickets 2 feet high in open places on granite ridges in mixed forest at Tara Tru Pass, Upper Burma.

The main features of this species are the thin branchlets, the small leaves, and the 1–3- (rarely 4-) flowered inflorescence. It is allied to *R. selense* which it resembles in some features, but differs in its smaller leaves, longer pedicels, and 1–3-flowered inflorescence.

R. martinianum was first introduced by Forrest in 1914 (No. 13301—the Type number, and No. 13439), and again later under six different seed numbers. Rock sent seeds on ten occasions. Kingdon-Ward introduced it three times. In its native home it grows up to 6 feet in height; in cultivation it is a broadly upright or somewhat compact rounded shrub, usually 3–4 feet high. Two forms are in cultivation: Form 1. A broadly upright shrub 4 feet high with small elliptic leaves, and somewhat small flowers. This form succeeded admirably outdoors in the Royal Botanic Garden, Edinburgh; it was somewhat rounded, 4 feet high, with clusters of 1–3 pink flowers, but unfortunately this plant has now ceased to exist. Form 2. A somewhat compact rounded shrub 2–3 feet high with larger oblong-oval leaves and larger flowers 4 cm. long. In 1924, Forrest introduced a very distinct form (No. 25614) with very small leaves, laminae 1.5–3 cm. long, and small pure white flowers 2–3 cm. long; unfortunately this plant is now possibly lost to cultivation. The species flowers freely, is easy to grow, and is a delightful plant. It produces good fertile seed occasionally. The plant is hardy outdoors, but along the east coast it requires a well-sheltered position. It is uncommon in cultivation, but is a most desirable plant for every garden.

Epithet. After J. Martin, gardener at Caerhays, Cornwall.
Hardiness 3. April–May.

R. selense Franch. in Journ. de Bot., Vol. 12 (1898) 257.
    Syn. *R. axium* Balf. f. et Forrest in Notes Roy. Bot. Gard. Edin., Vol. 13 (1920) 30.
        R. dolerum Balf. f. et Forrest, ibid. Vol. 13 (1920) 40.
        R. nanothamnum Balf. f. et Forrest, ibid. Vol. 13 (1920) 53.
        R. chalarocladum Balf. f. et Forrest, ibid. Vol. 13 (1922) 240.
        R. selense Franch. subsp. *axium* (Balf. f. et Forrest) Tagg in The Sp. of Rhod., (1930) 722.
        R. selense Franch. subsp. *dolerum* (Balf. f. et Forrest) Tagg, ibid. (1930) 722.
        R. selense Franch. subsp. *nanothamnum* (Balf. f. et Forrest) Tagg, ibid. (1930) 722.

11. **R. selense.** nat. size.
   a. leaf (lower surface). b. petals.
   c. capsule. d. flower. e. section.
   f. ovary, style. g. stamen.

R. selense Franch. subsp. *chalarocladum* (Balf. f. et Forrest) Tagg, ibid. (1930)
722.

A broadly upright or somewhat compact rounded shrub or bush, 60 cm.–1.83 m. (2–6 ft.) or sometimes 2.44–3 m. (8–10 ft.) high, *branchlets* glandular with short-stalked glands or sometimes eglandular, hairy or glabrous, those below the inflorescences *3–4 mm. in diameter*. Leaves oblong, obovate, oblong-oval or elliptic, lamina thinly leathery, 2.6–8.2 cm. long, 1.5–3.9 cm. broad, *apex broadly obtuse or rounded*, mucronate, *base broadly obtuse or rounded* or rarely cordulate; upper surface dark green, glabrous or with vestiges of hairs, midrib grooved, primary veins 10–15 on each side, deeply impressed; *under surface* green or pale glaucous green, *glabrous* or minutely hairy or sometimes with a thin veil of hairs, midrib raised; petiole 0.6–3 cm. long, glandular or eglandular, hairy or glabrous. *Inflorescence* umbellate or shortly racemose, *3–8-flowered*; rhachis 2–4 mm. long, glandular or eglandular, hairy or glabrous; *pedicel* 1–3 cm. long, *glandular* with short-stalked glands, hairy or glabrous. *Calyx* 5-lobed, 1–3 mm. long, lobes rounded or triangular, outside moderately or slightly glandular, *margin gland-fringed. Corolla funnel-campanulate*, 2.2–4 cm. long, pink, rose, white flushed rose, or rarely reddish-purple, *without* or rarely with a few *spots*, with or without a crimson blotch at the base; lobes 5, 0.9–1.7 cm. long, 1.2–2.2 cm. broad, rounded, emarginate. *Stamens* 10, unequal, 1.3–3.4 cm. long; filaments puberulous at the base. *Gynoecium* 2.2–4.2 cm. long; *ovary* slender or sometimes oblong, 4–5 mm. long, *densely glandular* with short-stalked glands, not hairy or sometimes sparsely hairy; style eglandular or sometimes glandular at the base. *Capsule slender* or sometimes oblong, 1.3–2.9 cm. long, 4–6 mm. broad, *curved* (*sickle-shaped*), glandular or with vestiges of glands, calyx-lobes persistent.

This species was discovered by the Abbé Soulié in June 1895 at Sie-La, Tsekou, Mekong-Salwin Divide, north-west Yunnan. Further gatherings by other collectors show that the species is distributed in north-west Yunnan, south-east Tibet, and south-west Sichuan. It grows in open pine forests, in *Abies* forest, spruce forest, in thickets, in rocky pastures, margins of scrub, and in open meadows, at elevations of 3,000–4,423 m. (9,836–14,500 ft.). Yü records it as being common in *Abies* forest at Atuntze, Dokerla, and in thickets in the Mekong-Salwin Divide, north-west Yunnan.

During the years 1920–22 Forrest collected a number of closely similar plants in the same regions, and these were described as *R. axium* Balf. f. et Forrest, *R. dolerum* Balf. f. et Forrest, *R. nanothamnum* Balf. f. et Forrest, and *R. chalarocladum* Balf. f. et Forrest. It will be noted that in *The Rhododendron Year Book* 1951–52 page 150, all these names were placed in synonymy under *R. selense*.

R. selense bears a certain degree of resemblance to *R. martinianum*. The distinctions between them are discussed under the latter.

The species was first introduced by Forrest in 1917 (Nos. 14057, 14458), and again later on five occasions. Kingdon-Ward sent seeds under No. 5414. Rock introduced it under 18 seed numbers. Yü sent seeds on three occasions. In its native home it grows 2–10 feet high; in cultivation it is a broadly upright or somewhat compact rounded shrub, usually 3–5 feet high. Features worth noting are the somewhat thin branchlets, usually the oblong or oblong-oval leaves, rounded or broadly obtuse at the apex, and the funnel-campanulate flowers. The species varies a great deal in its freedom of flowering. Some plants flower freely and make a fine show with white or rose flowers in trusses of 3–8, although other plants tend to be shy flowerers producing only a few trusses every year. A characteristic feature is the slender sickle-shaped capsule containing plentiful fertile seeds.

Epithet. From Sie-La, W. Yunnan.
Hardiness 3. April–May.

R. selense Franch. var. **pagophilum** (Balf. f. et Ward) Cowan et Davidian in The Rhodo-dendron Year Book (1951–52) 153.

Syn. *R. pagophilum* Balf. f. et Ward in Notes Roy. Bot. Gard. Edin., Vol.9 (1916) 256.
R. *selense* Franch. subsp. *pagophilum* (Balf. f. et Ward) Tagg in The Sp. of Rhod., (1930) 722.

This plant was first collected by Kingdon-Ward in June 1913 in the Ka-gwr-pw glacier valley, Tibet-Yunnan frontier. It was afterwards found by Forrest and Rock in various localities in north-west Yunnan and south-east Tibet. It grows in scrub, on boulder screes, in open situations amongst rocks, in shady situations in ravines, on rocky slopes, in alpine thickets and cane brakes, on the margins of pine forests and conifer forests, and in fir forest, at elevations of 3,660–4,880 m. (12,000–16,000 ft.). In his field notes, Kingdon-Ward describes it as being a scrub plant forming dense interlacing tangles 5–8 feet high on shady slopes with *Picea* on the Tibet-Yunnan frontier.

The variety differs from the species in the small flowers and small leaves. The colour of the flowers is often dark rose to dark crimson.

The plant was first introduced by Forrest in 1917 (No. 14009). It was reintroduced by him under four different seed numbers. Rock sent seeds on seven occasions. In its native home it grows 2–8 feet high; in cultivation it is a broadly upright shrub of 2–3 feet. Three colour forms are in cultivation: Form 1. White with a crimson blotch at the base. Form 2. Deep rose without markings. Form 3. Crimson. All these forms are charming plants and are well suited for small gardens. Form 3 is an unusually attractive sight when adorned with a profusion of crimson flowers. It may be remarked the foregoing 3 forms were successfully grown in the Royal Botanic Garden, Edinburgh, but in the course of years, they were lost to cultivation.

Epithet of the variety. Rock-loving.
Hardiness 3. April–May.

R. selense Franch. var. **probum** (Balf. f. et Forrest) Cowan et Davidian in The Rhododendron Year Book (1951–52) 153.

Syn. *R. probum* Balf. f. et Forrest in Notes Roy. Bot. Gard. Edin., Vol. 13 (1922) 288.
R. *metrium* Balf. f. et Forrest, ibid. Vol. 13 (1920) 52.
R. *selense* Franch. subsp. *probum* (Balf. f. et Forrest) Tagg in The Sp. of Rhod. (1930) 722.
R. *selense* Franch. subsp. *metrium* (Balf. f. et Forrest) Tagg, ibid. (1930) 722.

This variety was first collected by Forrest in July 1917 in the Mekong-Salwin Divide, north-west Yunnan. Subsequently it was found by him, and Rock, and by Ludlow, Sherriff and Elliot in the same region and in south-east Tibet. It grows in thickets, in pine forests, on the margins of conifer and rhododendron forests, in thick rain forest, and in open rhododendron scrub, at elevations of 3,050–3,965 m. (10,000–13,000 ft.).

In this variety the flowers are white without spots, with or without a crimson blotch at the base, and the under surface of the leaves is often glaucous.

The plant was first introduced by Forrest in 1918 (Nos. 16679, 16750) and again on three other occasions. Rock sent seeds in 1923 (No. 11065). In its native home it is a shrub 3–8 feet high. Ludlow, Sherriff and Elliot found a plant in thick rain forest at Kongbo, south-east Tibet, growing as a tree, 10–15 feet high. In cultivation it is a broadly upright or somewhat compact rounded shrub 3–4 feet high, well-filled with dark green foliage. It is hardy, and is of great beauty with its white flowers produced freely in trusses of 3–8. The plant is rare in cultivation but should be a valuable acquisition to every collection of rhododendrons.

Epithet of the variety. Excellent.
Hardiness 3. April–May.

R. setiferum Balf. f. et Forrest in Notes Roy. Bot. Gard. Edin., Vol. 11 (1919) 137.

Syn. *R. selense* Franch. subsp. *setiferum* (Balf. f. et Forrest) Chamberlain in Notes Roy. Bot. Gard. Edin., Vol. 36 (1978) 118.

A broadly upright shrub, 1.53–2.75 m. (5–9 ft.) high, *branchlets setulose-glandular* and with shorter-stalked glands, hairy or glabrous, those below the inflorescences 4–7 mm. in diameter. *Leaves oblong, lamina thick, coriaceous*, apex obtuse, shortly beaked, mucronate, base obtuse, rounded or truncate; upper surface dark green, glabrous or with vestiges of hairs, midrib grooved, primary veins 14–17 on each side, impressed; *under surface with a thin veil of hairs* and short-stalked or sessile glands, midrib raised, glandular, slightly or moderately hairy; *petiole* 0.8–1.7 cm. long, *setulose-glandular* and with shorter-stalked glands, slightly or moderately hairy. *Inflorescence* shortly racemose, 6–10-flowered; rhachis 5–8 mm. long, glandular, hairy; *pedicel* 1.3–2.1 cm. long, *glandular* with short-stalked glands, sparsely hairy. *Calyx* 5-lobed, *0.3–1 cm. long*, lobes oblong, outside glandular, margin fringed with glands and hairs. *Corolla* funnel-campanulate 3.1–3.5 cm. long, *creamy-white*, lined or not lined at base; lobes 5, 1.1–1.5 cm. long, 1.6–2 cm. broad, rounded, emarginate. *Stamens* 10, unequal, 1.8–3 cm. long; filaments puberulous at the base. *Gynoecium* 2.8–3.2 cm. long; *ovary* oblong, 4–5 mm. long, *densely glandular with long- and short-stalked glands*; style puberulous at the base, eglandular. *Capsule* oblong, 1.3–2.3 cm. long, 3–6 mm. broad, curved, *glandular*, calyx-lobes persistent.

R. setiferum is represented by a single gathering, Forrest No. 14066. It was found in June 1917 in the Mekong-Salwin Divide, north-west Yunnan, growing in open thickets and pine forests, at elevations of 3,660–3,965 m. (12,000–13,000 ft.).

The main features of this plant are the oblong leaves with a thin veil of hairs on the lower surface, the large calyx 0.3–1 cm. long, and the creamy-white corolla. It shows a certain degree of resemblance to *R. dascycladum* in general features but is readily distinguished by the thick leaves, coriaceous in texture, often by the thin veil of hairs on the lower surface, usually by the larger calyx, and by the creamy-white flowers.

The species was introduced by Forrest in 1917. In its native home it grows 5–9 feet high; in cultivation it is a broadly upright shrub of 8–9 feet, fairly well-filled with dark green leaves. It is hardy outdoors, flowers freely, and is easy to cultivate. The plant is rare in cultivation but is worth being more widely grown. A beautiful plant 8 feet high which was successfully grown in the Royal Botanic Garden, Edinburgh, has now been lost to cultivation.

Epithet. Bearing bristles.
Hardiness 3. April–May.

R. vestitum Tagg et Forrest in Notes Roy. Bot. Gard. Edin., Vol. 16 (1931) 210.

A broadly upright shrub, 60 cm–1.53 m. (2–5 ft.) high, *branchlets* moderately or sparsely *setulose-glandular and rather densely glandular with short-stalked glands*, not hairy, those below the inflorescences 3–4 mm. in diameter. *Leaves oblong, elliptic, obovate or oval, lamina leathery*, 3.2–6.2 cm. long, 1.5–3 cm. broad, apex rounded or broadly obtuse, mucronate, base rounded or broadly obtuse; upper surface glabrous, midrib grooved, primary veins 9–12 on each side, impressed; *under surface* with tawny or brown *patchy-scurfy indumentum of hairs and scattered tufts of hairs*, midrib raised, slightly or moderately glandular; *petiole* 5–9 mm. long, *setulose-glandular and glandular with short-stalked glands*, not hairy or sometimes hairy. *Inflorescence* umbellate or shortly racemose, 5–6-flowered; rhachis 2–5 mm. long, glandular, hairy; *pedicel* 0.9–1.5 cm. long, *setulose-glandular and with shorter-stalked glands*. *Calyx* 5-lobed, 1–2 mm. long, lobes rounded or triangular, outside glandular, margin gland-fringed. *Corolla* funnel-campanulate, 3–3.5 cm. long, white flushed rose, with a few crimson spots, and a crimson blotch at the base, deep rose in bud; lobes 5, 1–1.2 cm. long, 1.3–1.6 cm. broad. *Stamens* 10, unequal, 1.5–3 cm. long; filaments puberulous at the base. *Gynoecium* 3–3.5 cm. long; *ovary* conoid or oblong, 2–4 mm. long, *densely glandular* with long-stalked glands; style sparsely glandular at the base. *Capsule slender*, 1–1.5 cm. long, 3–4 mm. broad, straight or slightly curved, glandular, calyx-lobes persistent.

Forrest discovered this plant in June 1922 in the Salwin-Kiu Chiang Divide, southeast Tibet, growing in cane brakes in side valleys, at an elevation of 4,270 m. (14,000 ft.).

It is very similar to *R. selense* in general appearance, but differs in that the under surface of the leaves has an indumentum of patchy-scurfy and scattered tufts of tawny or brown hairs, and the branchlets, petioles and pedicels are setulose-glandular.

The species was introduced by Forrest in 1922 (No. 21877 = 22895—the Type number). In its native home it reaches a height of 4–5 feet; in cultivation it is a broadly upright shrub 2 feet high. The plant is now possibly lost to cultivation. It is doubtful whether the plants in cultivation under the name *R. vestitum* are correctly named.

Epithet. Clothed.

Hardiness 3. May–June.

SOULIEI SUBSERIES

General characters: shrubs or sometimes trees, 92 cm.–7.63 m. (3–25 ft.) high, branchlets glandular or eglandular. Leaves ovate, almost orbicular, ovate-elliptic, oblong-elliptic or oblong, lamina 3–12 cm. long, 1.8–5 cm. broad; *under surface glabrous.* Inflorescence terminal, umbellate or racemose umbel, 5–14-flowered; pedicel 1.5–4.8 cm. long, glandular. Calyx 0.2–1.2 cm. long, outside glandular or eglandular, margin glandular. *Corolla bowl- or saucer-shaped,* 2–4.4 cm. long, *yellow, pale yellow, pink, rose or white;* lobes 5. Stamens 10; filaments glabrous or puberulous at the base. Ovary conoid, 4–6 mm. long, densely glandular; *style glandular throughout to the tip.* Capsule short stout or oblong, 1.3–3.6 cm. long, straight or slightly curved, glandular, calyx-lobes persistent.

KEY TO THE SPECIES

A. Flowers yellow, pale yellow or lemon-yellow.

    B. Leaves almost orbicular, ovate, oblong-elliptic or sometimes oblong; under surface of the leaves pale green or pale glaucous green; corolla usually 3–4 cm. long. . . . . *wardii*

    B. Leaves usually oblong; under surface of the leaves markedly glaucous; corolla 2–3.8 cm. long . . . . *litiense*

A. Flowers rose, pink or white.

    C. Flowers rose, pink or white tinged pink. . . . . *souliei*

    C. Flowers pure white or rarely ivory-white . . . . *puralbum*

DESCRIPTION OF THE SPECIES

R. litiense Balf. f. et Forrest in Notes Roy. Bot. Gard. Edin., Vol. 12 (1920) 126.

    Syn. *R. wardii* W.W. Sm. var. *wardii Litiense Group* R.H.S. in Rhod. Handb. (1980) p. 32.

A broadly upright or somewhat compact rounded shrub or rarely a tree, 92 cm.–4.90 m. (3–16 ft.) high, branchlets glandular or eglandular, those below the inflorescences 3–6 mm. in diameter. *Leaves oblong,* oblong-oval, elliptic or rarely ovate, lamina leathery, 3–9.7 cm. long, 1.8–4.4 cm. broad, apex obtuse or rounded, mucronate, base truncate, cordulate or rounded; upper surface dark or paler green, glabrous, midrib grooved, primary veins 10–14 on each side, deeply impressed; *under surface* glabrous, minutely punctulate with glands, *markedly waxy glaucous*, midrib prominent; petiole 1–2.3 cm. long, glandular or eglandular, glabrous or sometimes floccose. *Inflorescence* umbellate or a racemose umbel of 5–7 flowers; rhachis 0.3–1 cm. long, sparsely or moderately glandular, floccose or glabrous; pedicel 1.5–4 cm. long, glandular with short-stalked glands. *Calyx* 5-lobed, 5–8 mm. long, lobes oblong or rounded, outside sparsely or moderately glandular with short-stalked glands, margin glandular. *Corolla bowl- or saucer-shaped*, 2–3.8 cm. long, *yellow or pale yellow*, without a blotch at the base, unspotted, outside eglandular; lobes 5, 1–1.6 cm. long, 1.8–2.6 cm. broad, rounded, emarginate. *Stamens* 10, unequal, 1–2 cm. long; filaments glabrous or rarely puberulous at the base. *Gynoecium* 2–2.6 cm. long; ovary conoid, 4 mm. long, densely glandular with long- and short-stalked glands; *style glandular throughout to the tip. Capsule* short stout, or oblong, 1.4–2 cm. long, 0.5–1 cm. broad, straight or slightly curved, glandular, calyx-lobes persistent.

This plant was first collected by Forrest in August 1914 in the Kari Pass, Mekong-Yangtze Divide, north-west Yunnan. It was afterwards found by him, by Handel-Mazzetti, and Rock in the same region and mid-west Yunnan. It grows in shady forests, in spruce forests, on the margins of pine forests, in rhododendron and mixed thickets, at elevations of 2,745–3,965 m. (9,000–13,000 ft.).

R. litiense bears a strong resemblance to *R. wardii* in general appearance. The main distinction between them is that in *R. litiense* the under surface of the leaves is markedly waxy glaucous, whereas in *R. wardii* the under surface is pale green. When the extremes of these two species are compared, it will be seen that in *R. litiense* the leaves are oblong, small, laminae 3–5 cm. long, and markedly waxy glaucous below, but in *R. wardii* the leaves are almost orbicular or broadly ovate, large, laminae 10–12 cm. long, pale green below. These extremes are so distinct, particularly in cultivation, that it would be desirable to retain the name *R. litiense*, although intergrading forms link the two species.

R. litiense was first introduced by Forrest in 1914 (No. 12969). It was reintroduced by him under six different seed numbers. Rock sent seeds on five occasions. In its native home it is a shrub or rarely a tree, 3–16 feet high. Three distinct forms are in cultivation with clear yellow flowers without markings: Form 1. A small broadly upright shrub 3 feet high, with small oblong leaves, laminae 3–4 cm. long, and small flowers 2 cm. long. This form which was grown in the Royal Botanic Garden, Edinburgh, has now been lost to cultivation. Form 2. A medium-sized somewhat compact rounded shrub 4–5 feet high, well-filled with ovate-oblong leaves, laminae 6 cm. long, and fairly large flowers 3.5 cm. long. Form 3. A tall broadly upright shrub 8–9 feet high, with large oblong-leaves, laminae 8–9 cm. long, and large flowers 3.8 cm. long. The species is free-flowering and is of great beauty with its bowl- or almost saucer-shaped flowers situated on long pedicels, in trusses of 5–7. Occasionally it produces one or two short stout or oblong capsules containing seeds in abundance. The plant is difficult to root from cuttings. It is hardy outdoors but along the east coast it requires a well-sheltered position in the garden.

The species received an Award of Merit when exhibited by L. de Rothschild, Exbury, in 1931, and a First Class Certificate when shown by Col. Lord Digby, Minterne, Dorset, in 1953.

Epithet. From Li-ti-ping, Yunnan.
Hardiness 3. May–June.

R. puralbum Balf. f. et W.W. Sm. in Notes Roy. Bot. Gard. Edin., Vol. 9 (1916) 266.
Syn. *R. wardii* W.W. Sm. var. *puralbum* (Balf. f. et W.W. Sm.) Chamberlain in Notes Roy. Bot. Gard. Edin., Vol. 36 (1978) 116.

A broadly upright or somewhat compact rounded shrub, 1.53–4.58 m. (5–15 ft.) high, branchlets sparsely glandular with short-stalked glands or eglandular, those below the inflorescences 3–5 mm. in diameter. *Leaves* ovate, ovate-oblong or oblong, lamina 5–12 cm. long, 2.4–5 cm. broad, apex obtuse, base truncate or cordulate or rounded; upper surface dark green, glabrous, midrib grooved, primary veins 9–12 on each side, deeply impressed; under surface pale glaucous green or pale green, glabrous, midrib raised; petiole 1.5–3 cm. long, glabrous. *Inflorescence* umbellate or shortly racemose, 5–8-flowered; rhachis 4–8 mm. long, glandular with short-stalked glands or eglandular, not hairy or rarely hairy; pedicel 2–5.3 cm. long, slightly or moderately glandular with short-stalked glands. *Calyx* 5-lobed, 0.5–1.1 cm. long, lobes unequal, oblong or rounded, outside glandular or eglandular, margin glandular. *Corolla* bowl- or saucer-shaped, 2.5–4 cm. long, *pure white or rarely ivory-white*, without or rarely with a dark crimson blotch at the base; lobes 5, 1.1–1.5 cm. long, 1.5–2.7 cm. broad, rounded, emarginate. *Stamens* 10, unequal, 1–2 cm. long; filaments glabrous or puberulous at the base. *Gynoecium* 1.8–3 cm. long; ovary conoid, 4–6 mm. long, densely glandular with long- or short-stalked glands; *style glandular throughout to the tip. Capsule* oblong, 1.3–3.6 cm. long, 5–8 mm. broad, slightly or moderately curved, glandular, calyx-lobes persistent.

Forrest discovered this plant in July 1913 on the mountains north-east of the Yangtze bend, north-west Yunnan. He found it again later in other localities in the same region. In 1938 Ludlow, Sherriff and Taylor collected it in Kongbo Province, south-east Tibet. It grows in rhododendron and mixed scrub, and on gravelly banks beside streams, at elevations of 3,355–4,270 m. (11,000–14,000 ft.).

The species is closely allied to *R. wardii* from which it is readily distinguished by the pure white or ivory-white flowers.

R. puralbum was first introduced by Forrest in 1913 (No. 10616—the Type number), and again in 1917 (No. 15417). In its native home it grows 5–15 feet high. Two distinct forms are in cultivation: Form 1. A somewhat compact rounded shrub 5–6 feet high, with large ovate leaves and large flowers 4 cm. long. Form 2. A broadly upright shrub 7–8 feet high, with smaller oblong leaves and smaller flowers 2.5 cm. long. This form which gave a fine display with its pure white flowers in the Royal Botanic Garden, Edinburgh, has now ceased to exist. The species is a fairly fast grower, and is exceedingly beautiful with its bowl-shaped pure white flowers produced freely in trusses of 5–8. Although hardy, it should be given protection from wind for the best results to be obtained. The species is rare in cultivation, but should be a most valuable acquisition to every collection of rhododendrons.

Epithet. Pure white.
Hardiness 3. May.

R. souliei Franch. in Journ. de Bot., Vol. 9 (1895) 393.
Syn. *R. cordatum* Lévl. in Bull. Geog. Bot., Vol. 24 (1914) 282.
Illustration. Bot. Mag. Vol. 141 t. 8622 (1915).

A compact rounded, or broadly upright shrub, or bush, or sometimes a tree, 1–5 m. (3⅓–16 ft.) high, branchlets sparsely glandular with short-stalked glands or eglandular, those below the inflorescences 3–5 mm. in diameter. *Leaves* ovate, ovate-elliptic, almost orbicular or oblong-elliptic, lamina leathery, 3.5–8.2 cm. long, 2.2–5 cm. broad, apex rounded or broadly obtuse, mucronate, base cordulate or truncate or rounded; upper surface dark green, shining, glabrous, midrib grooved, primary veins 8–14 on each side, deeply impressed; under surface pale glaucous green, glabrous, midrib prominent; petiole 1.5–2.5 cm. long, eglandular or sparsely glandular with short-stalked glands.

Inflorescence umbellate or shortly racemose, 5–9-flowered; rhachis 0.3–1 cm. long, glandular with short-stalked glands; pedicel 1.8–4.3 cm. long, glandular with short-stalked glands. *Calyx* 5-lobed, 2–8 mm. long, lobes unequal, oblong or rounded, outside moderately or sparsely glandular or eglandular, margin glandular. *Corolla bowl- or saucer-shaped*, 2.5–3.5 cm. long, *pink, rose, deep rose or white tinged pink*, without or rarely with a small crimson blotch at the base; lobes 5, 1–1.7 cm. long, 1.8–2.7 cm. broad, rounded, emarginate. *Stamens* 10, unequal, 1–2.4 cm. long; filaments glabrous. *Gynoecium* 1.8–2.5 cm. long; ovary conoid, 4–5 mm. long, densely glandular with short-stalked glands; *style glandular throughout to the tip. Capsule* oblong, 1.8–2.2 cm. long, 5–6 mm. broad, slightly curved, glandular with short-stalked glands, calyx-lobes persistent.

This species was discovered by the French missionary the Abbé Soulié, in July 1893 in the neighbourhood of Tatsienlu, western Sichuan. Ten years later, in 1903, Wilson found it in the same region when collecting for Messrs. Veitch. He collected it again in 1908 and 1910 when working on behalf of the Arnold Arboretum. E. E. Maire's specimens collected in 1911 and 1913 from the summit of Io-Chan and erroneously named by Léveillé *R. cordatum* are also *R. souliei*. Subsequently the species was found by Rock in south-west Sichuan, and by McLaren's collectors in the same region. It grows in thickets and woodlands, in oak and in spruce forests, and among boulders, at elevations of 3,000–4,550 m. (9,836–14,918 ft.).

R. souliei is closely related to *R. wardii* and *R. puralbum*, but is easily distinguished from both species by the pink, rose or white tinged pink flowers.

The species was first introduced by Wilson in 1903 (No. 3971). It was reintroduced by him in 1908 (No. 1222), and in 1910 (No. 4274). It may be remarked that some of the plants raised at Kew in 1909, flowered in 1913 when they were only four years old. In its native home *R. souliei* is a shrub 3–10 feet high or sometimes a tree up to 16 feet. Four distinct forms are in cultivation: Form 1. A tall broadly upright shrub 7–8 feet high, with medium-sized white tinged pink flowers. Form 2. A compact rounded shrub 5–6 feet high and as much across, well-filled with ovate leaves, and with large rose flowers. Form 3. A somewhat compact broadly upright shrub 3–4 feet high with fairly large pink flowers. Form 4. An upright shrub 4 feet high with small white tinged pink flowers. The species is undoubtedly one of the finest rhododendrons in cultivation. It is free-flowering, and is of exquisite beauty with its bowl-shaped flowers in trusses of 5–9. Some plants in a few gardens, with saucer-shaped 6-lobed corollas which have been labelled *R. souliei*, are in fact, hybrids, *R. souliei* × *R. vernicosum*. The species is hardy and is successfully grown in sheltered gardens along the west and east coasts. Like the other members of its Subseries, it is difficult to increase from cuttings.

As evidence of its merit as a garden plant, it is to be noted that a First Class Certificate was awarded three times to *R. souliei*: the first was given to a clone with pale rose flowers, deeper towards the margin, when shown by Messrs. J. Veitch, Chelsea, in 1909; the second went to a clone 'Exbury Pink' with flowers of a deeper shade of pink, when exhibited by L. de Rothschild, Exbury, in 1936; the third was awarded to a clone 'Windsor Park', flowers white with pink flush deepening at margins, and a small crimson blotch at the base of the three upper lobes, when shown by the Crown Estate Commissioners, Windsor Great Park, in 1951.

Epithet. After Père J. A. Soulié, 1858–1905, French Foreign Missions, Tibet.
Hardiness 3. May–June.

R. wardii W. W. Sm. in Notes Roy. Bot. Gard. Edin., Vol. 8 (1914) 205.
     Syn. *R. mussoti* Franch. nomen nudum.
          R. croceum Balf. f. et W.W. Sm. in Notes Roy. Bot. Gard. Edin., Vol. 10 (1917)
               93.
          R. astrocalyx Balf. f. et Forrest, ibid. Vol. 13 (1920) 30.

R. oresterum Balf. f. et Forrest, ibid. Vol. 13 (1920) 55.

R. prasinocalyx Balf. f. et Forrest, ibid. Vol. 13 (1920) 57.

R. gloeoblastum Balf. f. et Forrest, ibid. Vol. 13 (1922) 260.

Illustration. Bot. Mag. Vol. 178 t. 587 (1971).

A broadly upright or upright or bushy or lax rounded or compact rounded shrub, or tree, 60 cm.–7.63 m. (2–25 ft.) high, branchlets glandular or eglandular, those below the inflorescences 3–5 mm. in diameter. *Leaves* almost orbicular, ovate, oblong-elliptic or oblong, lamina leathery, 3–12 cm. long, 2–6.5 cm. broad, apex rounded or broadly obtuse, mucronate, base cordulate or truncate or rounded; upper surface dark or paler green, glabrous, midrib grooved, primary veins 10–15 on each side, deeply impressed; *under surface pale green or pale glaucous green,* glabrous, minutely punctulate with glands, midrib prominent; petiole 1–3.3 cm. long, eglandular or sometimes glandular. *Inflorescence* umbellate or a racemose umbel of 5–14 flowers; rhachis 0.3–2.2 cm. long, sparsely to densely glandular, floccose or glabrous; pedicel 1.6–4.8 cm. long, slightly or moderately glandular with short-stalked or sessile glands or rarely eglandular. *Calyx* 5-lobed, 0.4–1.2 cm. long, lobes usually unequal, rounded or oblong-oval or oblong, outside glandular or eglandular, margin glandular. *Corolla bowl- or saucer-shaped,* 2.4–4 cm. long, *yellow, pale yellow, pale cream, sulphur-yellow, primrose-yellow, bright yellow, pale lemon-yellow or lemon-yellow,* with or without a tiny or small or fairly large crimson or reddish-purple blotch at the base, in bud yellow or pale yellow, purple-crimson or red or flame-scarlet, outside somewhat glandular or eglandular; lobes 5, 0.8–2 cm. long, 1.3–3 cm. broad, rounded, emarginate. *Stamens* 10, unequal, 1–2 cm. long; filaments glabrous or rarely puberulous at the base. *Gynoecium* 2–2.9 cm. long; ovary conoid, 4–6 mm. long, densely glandular with short- or long-stalked glands; *style glandular throughout to the tip. Capsule* short stout, or oblong 1.5–2.5 cm. long, 0.5–1 cm. broad, straight or slightly curved, glandular with short-stalked glands, calyx-lobes persistent.

This well-known species is widely distributed in west and north-west Yunnan, south-east and east Tibet, and south-west Sichuan. It was first collected by the Abbé Soulié, (No. 1003) in June 1895 at Sie-La, east Tibet, and was named *R. mussoti* by Franchet. However, Franchet did not publish the name, although it is cited by Diels under his description of *R. stewartianum* in *Notes of the Royal Botanic Garden, Edinburgh,* Vol. V (1912) 212. In 1914 W. W. Smith described *R. wardii,* based upon Kingdon-Ward's Nos. 529 and 526 collected in the Doker La and at Atuntze, western Yunnan in June 1913, and he also cites Forrest's No. 10428 collected in July 1913 on the mountains in the north-east of the Yangtze bend, north-west Yunnan. Millais, in his book *Rhododendrons* (1917) p. 260 states that *R. wardii* was discovered by Forrest on the eastern flank of the Lichiang Range in 1906, but this appears to be a mistake; it is to be noted that no one has been able to discover a Forrest specimen of *R. wardii* collected before 1913.

R. wardii grows in very varied habitats. It is found in conifer and mixed forests, in rhododendron, *Abies,* pine, and spruce forests, in rhododendron thickets, in *Quercus-Ilex* thickets, amongst scrub, on rocky hillside, on bouldery slopes, on cliffs, amongst cane scrub, in rocky pastures, and sometimes in swampy ground in rain forest, at elevations of 2,745–4,875 m. (9,000–15,984 ft.). Kingdon-Ward records it as being a big shrubby bush or small tree up to 25 feet with pale lemon-yellow flowers, growing on steep grassy slopes wooded with conifers, in north-west Yunnan. According to Ludlow, Sherriff and Taylor, it is very common in clearings in *Abies* forest and open hillsides, in south-east Tibet.

Various plants apparently differing in minor details from *R. wardii,* have been given distinct specific names, namely, *R. croceum* Balf. f. et Forrest (1917), *R. astrocalyx* Balf. f. et Forrest (1920), *R. oresterum* Balf. f. et Forrest (1920), *R. prasinocalyx* Balf. f. et Forrest (1920), and *R. gloeoblastum* Balf. f. et Forrest (1922). It will be seen that in *The Rhododendron Year Book* 1951–52, page 160, all the foregoing names were placed in synonymy under *R. wardii.* It may be remarked that *R. oresterum* and *R. gloeoblastum* had already

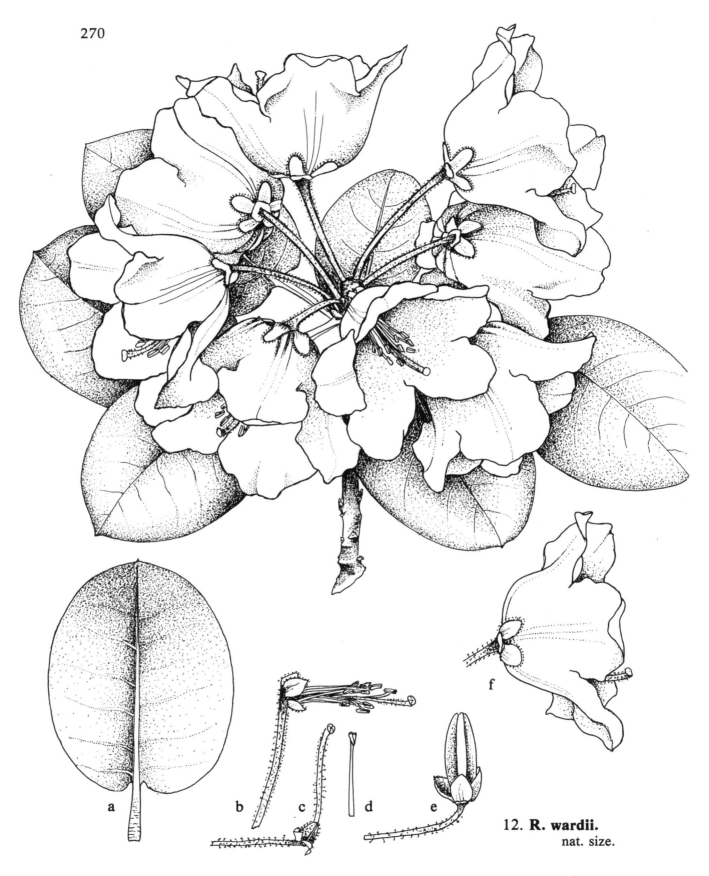

a. leaf (lower surface). b. section. c. ovary, style. d. stamen. e. capsule. f. flower.

12. **R. wardii.**
nat. size.

appeared in synonymy under *R. wardii* in *The Species of Rhododendron* 1930.

In view of its wide distribution, different habitats and altitudinal range, *R. wardii* varies considerably in general features, particularly in habit and height of growth, in leaf shape and size, and in flower size. It is closely allied to *R. souliei* and *R. puralbum*, but differs in the colour of its flowers. *R. wardii* is also related to *R. campylocarpum;* the distinctions between them are discussed under the latter.

The species was first introduced by Kingdon-Ward in 1913 (No. 529—the Type number), and by Forrest in the same year (Nos. 10428, 10680). It was reintroduced by Kingdon-Ward under three different seed numbers. Forrest sent seeds on eighteen other occasions. Ludlow, Sherriff with Taylor or Elliot introduced it five times, and Rock seventeen times. Several forms are in cultivation varying in many characters. It will be seen that the flower-buds are greenish-yellow or dark red, the corolla is bowl- or saucer-shaped, small, medium or large, 2.4–4 cm. long, and the colour varies from pale yellow, sulphur-yellow, yellow to lemon-yellow, with or without a tiny or small or fairly large crimson blotch at the base. The style, as in the other members of its Subseries, is glandular throughout to the tip. Some of the distinctive forms are: Form 1. A tall upright shrub 10 feet high, with large leaves and large clear yellow flowers. Form 2. A lax rounded or bushy shrub 5 feet high and as much across; leaves and flowers same as Form 1. Form 3. A compact rounded shrub 4 feet high and as much across; leaves and flowers same as Form 1. Form 4. A broadly upright shrub 5 feet high, with yellow flowers and a small crimson blotch at the base. Form 5. A shrub similar to Form 4, but with clear lemon-yellow flowers. Form 6. A clone similar to Form 4, but with lemon-yellow flowers and a large crimson blotch at the base, known as 'Ellestee'. Form 7. A small rounded shrub with small elliptic leaves and small flowers. Form 8. A rounded shrub 6 feet high, with very long pedicels 4.8 cm. long, flowers opening purple-crimson gradually fading to yellow. All these forms have been successfully grown in the Royal Botanic Garden, Edinburgh. Unfortunately some of them are now lost to cultivation.

R. wardii is a late-flowerer, the flowers appearing in May–June. It has the advantage of flowering as a young plant. The species flowers freely and provides an exceptionally fine display of colour, being one of the finest yellow-flowered rhododendrons in cultivation. A characteristic feature is the short stout or oblong capsule with a large leafy calyx at the base, containing fertile seeds in plenty. The plant is difficult to increase from cuttings. As it comes from elevations of 9,000–15,984 feet, its hardiness varies in cultivation. It is hardy outdoors but some forms introduced from lower elevations require well-sheltered positions along the east coast and inland.

Awards of Merit were received by several forms of *R. wardii:*

In 1926, as *R. croceum*, flowers bright yellow with a small crimson flash, when exhibited by A. M. Williams, Launceston, Cornwall.

In 1926, as *R. astrocalyx*, flowers flat, clear lemon-yellow, when shown by A. M. Williams, Launceston, Cornwall.

In 1931, as *R. wardii* (Kingdon-Ward No. 4170), flowers bright yellow, flushed green, when shown by Lionel de Rothschild, Exbury.

In 1959, as *R. wardii* 'Ellestee' (Ludlow, Sherriff and Taylor No. 5679), flowers lemon-yellow with a crimson blotch at the base, exhibited by Capt. Collingwood Ingram, Benenden, Kent.

In 1963, as *R. wardii* 'Meadow Pond' (Ludlow, Sherriff and Elliot No. 15764), flowers primrose-yellow with a crimson blotch at the base, exhibited by the Crown Estate Commissioners, Windsor Great Park.

The species was given an Award of Garden Merit in 1969.

Epithet. After F. Kingdon-Ward, 1885–1958, collector and explorer.

Hardiness 3. May–June.

THOMSONII SUBSERIES

General characters: shrubs or sometimes trees, 60 cm.–12.20 m. (2–40 ft.) high, branchlets glandular or eglandular. Leaves orbicular, oval, ovate, obovate, elliptic or oblong, lamina 2.7–18 cm. long, 1.5–9 cm. broad; *under surface glabrous* (except in *R. hookeri* and often in *R. stewartianum*). Inflorescence terminal, racemose or umbellate, 3–15- or rarely 18–24-flowered; pedicel 0.6–2.7 cm. long, glabrous, eglandular or sometimes glandular. Calyx 0.1–2 cm. long, eglandular or sometimes glandular, usually glabrous. *Corolla* campanulate or tubular-campanulate, 2.5–6.3 cm. long, *crimson or deep crimson* (except in *R. cyanocarpum, R. eclecteum, R. hylaeum, R. stewartianum,* and *R. thomsonii* var. *candelabrum*), 5 dark nectar pouches at the base. Stamens 10, often glabrous. Ovary conoid, 4–7 mm. long, eglandular or densely or moderately glandular; *style eglandular.* Capsule short stout or oblong, straight or sometimes slightly curved, 1–3 cm. long.

KEY TO THE SPECIES

A. Bead-like Fasciculate tufts of hairs present on the lateral veins on the under surface of the leaves. (Flowers crimson) . . . . *hookeri*
A. Bead-like Fasciculate tufts of hairs absent from the lateral veins on the under surface of the leaves.
    B. Flowers crimson or deep crimson.
        C. Leaves large, laminae usually 6–18 cm. long; calyx large, 4 mm.–2 cm. long; inflorescence 6–13-flowered; midrib on the under surface of the leaves hairy or glabrous; corolla 4–6.1 cm. long.
            D. Ovary eglandular.
                E. Leaves orbicular, ovate or broadly elliptic; calyx 6 mm.–2 cm. long, yellow, pale green, greenish-scarlet, or crimson. Species from Nepal, Sikkim, Bhutan, Assam, and south Tibet. . . . . *thomsonii*
                E. Leaves obovate or oblong-oval, sometimes oval, rarely oblong; calyx 4 mm.–1 cm. long, red. Species from western Yunnan and north-east Upper Burma . . . . *meddianum*
            D. Ovary densely or moderately glandular.
                F. Pedicel glandular; midrib on the under surface of the leaves glabrous; petiole long, 1–2 cm. in length. . . . . *meddianum* var. *atrokermesinum*
                F. Pedicel eglandular (rarely glandular); midrib on the under surface of the leaves usually hairy; petiole 3 mm.–1 cm. long, short for size of leaf . . . . *eclecteum* var. *brachyandrum*
        C. Leaves small, 2.7–8 cm. long; calyx small, 1–3 mm. long; inflorescence 3–5-flowered; midrib on the under surface of the leaves glabrous; corolla 2.5–4.2 cm. long.
            G. Leaves oval or almost orbicular, elliptic or oblong-elliptic; under surface of the leaves papillate; calyx 2–3 mm. long; ovary glandular or eglandular . . . . *lopsangianum*
            G. Leaves oblong or elliptic; under surface of the leaves epapillate; ovary eglandular . . . . *populare*

B. Flowers copper-red, white, pink, rose or yellow.

    H. Flowers copper-red; under surface of the leaves glandular, sticky to the touch; inflorescence 1–2-flowered .... *viscidifolium*

    H. Flowers white, pink, rose or yellow; under surface of the leaves eglandular (except in *R. hylaeum* minutely punctulate) not sticky to the touch; inflorescence 3–13- or sometimes 18–24-flowered.

        I. Leaves orbicular, oval, ovate or broadly elliptic; under surface of the leaves glabrous; petiole long, usually 2–3 cm. in length.

            J. Stem and branches with smooth, brown or fawn flaking bark; upper surface of the leaves dark green or olive-green; petiole rounded; corolla pink or rose-pink; calyx crimson, red, yellow or pale green. From Sikkim, Bhutan, Nepal, and south Tibet .... *thomsonii* var. *candelabrum*

            J. Stem and branches with rough bark; upper surface of the leaves bluish-green; petiole somewhat flat; corolla white or creamy-white flushed pale rose, or rich soft rose, or rarely pale pink; calyx greenish or pink. From Yunnan .... *cyanocarpum*

        I. Leaves usually oblong, oblanceolate, obovate or oblong-obovate; under surface of the leaves or midrib hairy or glabrous; petiole usually 3 mm.–2 cm. long, short for size of leaf or long.

            K. Stem and branches with smooth, brown, flaking bark; leaves oblong or oblanceolate; ovary eglandular or sometimes densely glandular; inflorescence 10–12- or sometimes 18–24-flowered .... *hylaeum*

            K. Stem and branches with rough bark; leaves usually obovate or oblong-obovate; ovary densely glandular; inflorescence 3–8- or sometimes 10–12-flowered.

                L. Under surface of the leaves glabrous, except midrib often hairy; petiole almost sessile, short, 3 mm.–1 cm. long, short for size of leaf (except in *R. eclecteum* var. *bellatulum*); inflorescence 6–12-flowered ... *eclecteum*

                L. Under surface of the leaves usually with a thin veil of hairs or farinose; petiole long, not sessile, 0.6–1.9 cm. long; inflorescence 3–7-flowered ...... *stewartianum*

DESCRIPTION OF THE SPECIES

R. cyanocarpum (Franch.) W. W. Sm. in Trans. Bot. Soc. Edin., Vol. 26 (1914) 274.

    Syn. *R. thomsonii* Hook. f. var. *cyanocarpum* Franch. in Journ. de Bot., IX (1895) 389.

        R. hedythamnum Balf. f. et Forrest var. *eglandulosum* Hand.-Mazz., Akad. Amzeig Wien, No. 19 . (1923).

        R. eriphyllum Balf. f. et W. W. Sm., nomen nudum.

        R. cyanocarpum (Franch.) W. W. Sm. var. *eriphyllum* Balf. f. et W. W. Sm. ex Tagg in The Sp. of Rhod. (1930) 738.

    Illustration. Bot. Mag. Vol. 168 t. 155 (1951).

    A broadly upright shrub or tree, 1.22–7.63 m. (4–25 ft.) high, *branchlets* glabrous, eglandular, *yellowish-green, glaucous,* those below the inflorescences 4–7 mm. in diameter. *Leaves* orbicular, oval or broadly elliptic, lamina thick, leathery, 5–12.6 cm. long, 4–9 cm. broad, apex rounded, mucronate, base rounded or cordulate or truncate; *upper surface bluish-green*, glabrous *midrib* grooved, *yellowish-green*, primary veins 10–15 on each side, deeply impressed; under surface glaucous pale green, glabrous or minutely hairy, *midrib* prominent, *yellowish-green*, primary veins slightly raised; *petiole* 1.5–3 cm. long, *stout, upper surface* somewhat *flat*, grooved above, *yellowish-green, glaucous*, sparsely glandular or eglandular. *Inflorescence* umbellate or shortly racemose, 6–10-flowered; rhachis 0.5–1 cm. long, eglandular; pedicel 1–2 cm. long, eglandular. *Calyx cup-shaped*, 5-lobed, 0.2–1.1 cm. long, greenish or pink, lobes unequal, rounded or truncate, eglandular, glaucous. *Corolla* campanulate or widely funnel-campanulate, 4–6 cm. long, *rosy-white, rich soft rose, pinkish-white, white flushed pale rose, pale pink, creamy-white flushed pale rose, or white*, without or sometimes with a few darker spots; lobes 5, 1.2–2.2 cm. long, 1.8–3.1 cm. broad, emarginate. *Stamens* 10, unequal, 2–4 cm. long; filaments glabrous. *Gynoecium* 3–4.5 cm. long; ovary conoid, 5–7 mm. long, eglandular, or rarely sparsely or moderately glandular, grooved; style glabrous. *Capsule* stout or oblong, 1–2.5 cm. long, 0.6–1 cm. broad, eglandular, *with a bluish glaucous bloom*, calyx-lobes persistent.

R. cyanocarpum was discovered by the Abbé Delavay who found it only in fruit, on Tsang chan, western Yunnan, and was described by Franchet in 1895 as *R. thomsonii* Hook. f. var. *cyanocarpum* Franch. Not much was known of this plant until Forrest collected it in flower in July 1906 on the eastern flank of the Tali Range. Subsequently it was found by him and by McLaren's collectors, Rock and others in various localities in west and north-west Yunnan. The plant was given specific status by W. W. Smith in 1914. It grows in moist mountain meadows, in open rocky pastures, in open rocky situations, in *Abies* and pine forests, and in rhododendron woodland and thickets, at elevations of 3,000–4,118 m. (9,836–13,500 ft.).

The diagnostic features of *R. cyanocarpum* are the rosy-white, rose, pink or white flowers, the leaves with bluish-green upper surfaces, and as the name implies, the capsules with a bluish glaucous bloom. Other distinctive features are the glaucous yellowish-green branchlets, the stout glaucous yellowish-green petioles with somewhat flat surfaces, and the yellowish-green midrib on both surfaces of the leaves.

The species was first introduced by Forrest in 1910 (Nos. 6775, 6779), and again later on four occasions. Rock sent seeds in 1922 (No. 6273). In its native home it is a shrub or tree, 4–25 feet high; in cultivation it is a broadly upright shrub up to 10 feet. It is a pleasing shrub, and makes a fine show with its rosy-white or rose campanulate flowers. Although it is hardy, a sheltered position should be provided along the east coast.

It was given an Award of Merit when shown by Lady Loder, Leonardslee, Sussex, in 1933.

Epithet. With blue fruits.
Hardiness 3. March–April.

R. eclecteum Balf. f. et Forrest in Notes Roy. Bot. Gard. Edin., Vol. 12 (1920).
Syn. *R. benemaculatum* Balf. f. nomen nudum.
A lax rounded spreading, or broadly upright or upright shrub, 60 cm.–3 m. (2–10 ft.) high, or sometimes a tree up to 4.58 m. (15 ft.) high, branchlets sparsely or moderately glandular or rarely eglandular, those below the inflorescences 3–7 mm. in diameter. *Leaves obovate or oblong-obovate or oblong, lamina almost sessile*, leathery, 5–14.5 cm. long, 2–6 cm. broad, apex rounded, base cordulate or obtuse or truncate; upper surface glabrous, glaucous, midrib grooved, primary veins 12–15 on each side, deeply impressed; *under surface glabrous, midrib* raised, *hairy* or glabrous; *petiole short, often broad, 0.3–1 cm. long*, grooved above, eglandular or sometimes glandular, not hairy or rarely hairy, more or less glaucous. *Inflorescence* umbellate or a racemose umbel of 6–12 flowers; rhachis 0.4–1.5 cm. long, eglandular or rarely glandular, not hairy or rarely hairy; pedicel 0.8–2 cm. long, eglandular or rarely glandular, more or less glaucous.

Calyx 5-lobed, variable in size, 0.2–2 cm. long, lobes rounded or ovate or oblong-oval, outside eglandular, margin eglandular or rarely glandular, not hairy or rarely hairy. *Corolla* tubular-campanulate, 3–5.3 cm. long, fleshy, white, white flushed rose, pink, deep pink, rose, pale yellow, yellow, purple, yellowish-red or red, with or without crimson spots; lobes 5, 0.9–1.8 cm. long, 1.2–2.4 cm. broad, rounded, emarginate. *Stamens* 10, unequal, 1.2–3.9 cm. long; filaments glabrous or puberulous at the base. *Gynoecium* 3–5.1 cm. long; *ovary* conoid, 4–6 mm. long, grooved, *densely or moderately glandular*, not hairy or rarely hairy; style eglandular. *Capsule* broadly oblong or short stout, 1.4–2.8 cm. long, 0.7–1.2 cm. broad, straight, glandular with short-stalked glands or rarely eglandular, glaucous or not glaucous, calyx-lobes persistent.

This species was discovered in fruit by Forrest in July 1917 on Ka-gwr-pw, Mekong-Salwin Divide, north-west Yunnan. Further gatherings by him and by Rock, Kingdon-Ward and Yü show that the species has a wide area of distribution extending from north-west Yunnan and north-east Upper Burma to south-east and east Tibet and south-west Sichuan. It grows in rhododendron thickets, amongst scrub on stony slopes, amongst boulders, in rocky meadows, on the margins of pine and mixed forests, and in spruce forest, at elevations of 3,000–4,423 m. (9,836–14,500 ft.). According to Yü it is common among thickets on open slopes in the Mekong-Salwin Divide.

R. eclecteum is a very variable plant particularly in habit and height of growth, in leaf size, and in flower colour, due to the various environmental conditions in which it is found. A diagnostic feature is the almost sessile leaf, with short petiole. In this respect and usually in the glabrous lower surface of the leaves, it is readily distinguished from its near ally, *R. stewartianum.*

The species was first introduced by Forrest in 1917 (No. 14485). It was reintroduced by him under 11 different seed numbers. Rock sent seeds on 27 occasions. The species was introduced by Kingdon-Ward (No. 6921) and by Yü (No. 19740). In its native home it is a shrub 2–10 feet or sometimes a tree up to 15 feet high. At least 10 different forms are in cultivation varying in leaf size, laminae 2–6 inches long, and in flower colour, namely, white, white flushed rose, pink, deep pink, rose, pale yellow, yellow, purple, yellowish-red or red, with or without crimson spots. It is to be noted that flower colour cannot be correlated with leaf size or with any other character. Some forms with white, pink, rose or yellow flowers are charming plants and attract attention. The species is hardy, free-flowering, and easy to cultivate. It has the merit of flowering at a moderately young age.

The species received an Award of Merit with primrose yellow flowers when exhibited by E. de Rothschild, Exbury, in 1949, and again the same Award for a clone 'Kingdom Come' with white flowers flushed yellow-green when shown by R. N. S. Clarke, Borde Hill, Sussex, in 1978.

Epithet. Picked out.

Hardiness 3. February–April.

R. eclecteum Balf. f. et Forrest var. **bellatulum** Balf. f. ex Tagg in The Sp. of Rhod., (1930) 739.

Syn. *R. anisocalyx* Balf. f. et Forrest, nomen nudum.

This plant was first collected by Forrest in June 1921 in the Loudre Pass, Mekong-Salwin Divide, north-west Yunnan. It was afterwards found by him in the same region and in south-east Tibet. Rock collected ample material in various localities in north-west Yunnan. It grows on the margins of thickets, on bouldery slopes, amongst rhododendron scrub on rocky slopes, in cane brakes, and in alpine regions among rocks, at elevations of 3,050–4,270 m. (10,000–14,000 ft.).

The variety differs from the species in that the petioles are long, the leaves are not subsessile, they are more or less oblong, base obtuse or rounded, and the pedicels are longer.

The plant was first introduced by Forrest in 1922 (Nos. 21839, 21887). Rock sent seeds under 13 different seed numbers. In cultivation it is a lax rounded spreading or broadly upright shrub, 3–5 feet high, and attracts attention with its white flushed rose or rose or pale yellow flowers. The plant is uncommon in gardens, but is worthy of being widely grown.

Epithet of the variety. Neat.

Hardiness 3. March–April.

R. eclecteum Balf. f. et Forrest var. **brachyandrum** (Balf. f. et Forrest) Tagg in The Sp. of Rhod., (1930) 739.

Syn. *R. brachyandrum* Balf. f. et Forrest in Notes Roy. Bot. Gard. Edin., Vol. 13 (1920) 32.

This variety was first collected by Forrest in July 1919 in the Salwin-Kiu Chiang Divide, south-east Tibet. Subsequently it was found by him in other localities in the same region, and in north-east Upper Burma. Rock collected it in north-west Yunnan and south-east Tibet. It grows in open rocky meadows, on rocky slopes, in rhododendron scrub among rocks and boulders, on the margins of conifer forests, in cane brakes, in open thickets, and in fir forest, at elevations of 3,660–4,270 m. (12,000–14,000 ft.).

In this variety the flowers are deep rose, deep rose-crimson, deep magenta-crimson or reddish-purple, with or without crimson markings.

The plant was first introduced by Forrest in 1919 (No. 18943–the Type number), and again on six other occasions. Rock introduced it under eight different seed numbers. In its native home it attains a height of 2–8 feet; in cultivation it is a lax rounded or broadly upright shrub 4–5 feet high. The flower colour varies in cultivation. Some plants are most effective with deep rose or deep rose-crimson flowers produced freely in trusses of 6–12. The variety is hardy, but is uncommon in cultivation.

Epithet of the variety. With short stamens.

Hardiness 3. March–April.

R. hookeri Nutt. in Hook. Kew Journ., Vol. 5 (1853) 359.

Illustration. Bot. Mag. Vol. 82 t. 4926 (1856).

A somewhat compact, broadly upright shrub, or bush or small tree, 2.44–6 m. (8–20 ft.) high; *stem and branches with smooth, brown, flaking bark;* branchlets eglandular, those below the inflorescences 4–5 mm. in diameter. *Leaves* oblong, oblong-obovate or oblong-oval, lamina leathery, 6.3–17 cm. long, 3–7.5 cm. broad, apex rounded or obtuse, mucronate, base obtuse or rounded or truncate; upper surface dark green, glabrous, midrib grooved, primary veins 9–15 on each side, deeply impressed; *under surface* pale glaucous green, glabrous except the *lateral veins studded with isolated bead-like Fasciculate hair tufts* which at first are white, ultimately brown, midrib raised; petiole 1.5–2.6 cm. long, eglandular. *Inflorescence* a racemose umbel of 8–15 flowers; rhachis 1.4—1.6 cm. long, eglandular; pedicel 0.7–1.6 cm. long, eglandular. *Calyx* 5-lobed, 0.5–2 cm. long, green, yellowish or reddish, lobes unequal, rounded or oblong, eglandular. *Corolla* tubular-campanulate or funnel-campanulate, 3.5–4.4 cm. long, *cherry-red, deep crimson or pink,* with or without faint spots, with *5 dark crimson nectar pouches at the base;* lobes 5, 1–1.4 cm. long, 1.6–2.2 cm. broad, rounded, emarginate. *Stamens* 10, unequal, 1.5–3 cm. long; filaments glabrous. *Gynoecium* 2.7–4 cm. long; ovary conoid, 5–7 mm. long, 7–8-celled, eglandular; style eglandular. *Capsule* oblong-obovate or broadly oblong, 2–2.5 cm. long, 0.8–1 cm. broad, calyx-lobes persistent.

R. hookeri was discovered by Booth in 1849 forming thickets on the Oola mountain, on the northern slopes of the Lablung Pass, in Bhutan. The plant does not appear to have been collected again until Kingdon-Ward found it in 1928 in the Delei Valley, Assam, and again in 1935 at Se La, Assam, also in 1938 at Poshing La, Assam, growing as a small tree. The plant is found at elevations of 2,440–3,660 m. (8,000–12,000 ft.).

A diagnostic feature of importance is the isolated bead-like Fasciculate tufts of hairs on the lateral veins on the lower surface of the leaves. No other species of Rhododendron has this type of hair. The species is related to *R. meddianum* and *R. thomsonii*, but is readily distinguished from both by well-marked characteristics.

R. hookeri was first introduced by Booth in 1849 and it flowered for the first time in Mr. Fairie's garden, Mosley Hall, near Liverpool. It was reintroduced by Kingdon-Ward in 1928 (No. 8238, pink form), and in 1938 (No. 13650, crimson form). In its native home it is a shrub or a small tree up to 20 feet high; in cultivation it is a somewhat compact, broadly upright shrub, usually up to 10 feet, fairly well-filled with large oblong-oval leaves. A distinctive feature is the smooth, brown, flaking bark of the stem and branches. Two flower colour forms are in cultivation, namely, crimson and pink. The species varies in freedom of flowering. It usually flowers moderately, but some plants are shy flowerers and hardly produce more than one or two trusses every year. The plant is hardy along the west coast, but along the east coast and gardens inland it tends to be somewhat tender and should be given a well-sheltered position in the garden. The species is not commonly to be seen in cultivation.

A form with darkest red flowers was given a First Class Certificate when shown by the Hon. H. D. McLaren, Bodnant, in 1933.

Epithet. After Sir J. D. Hooker, 1817–1911, a former Director of Kew, botanist and traveller in the Himalayas.

Hardiness 3. March–April.

R. hylaeum Balf. f. et Farrer in Notes Roy. Bot. Gard. Edin., Vol. 13 (1922) 265.
Syn. *R. faucium* Chamberlain in Notes Roy. Bot. Gard. Edin., Vol. 36 (1978) 124.
R. subansiriense Chamberlain, ibid. Vol. 36 (1978) 124.

A broadly upright or somewhat compact rounded shrub, or small tree, 1.22–13.73 m. (4–45 ft.) high; *stem and branches with smooth, brown flaking bark;* branchlets glandular or eglandular, those below the inflorescences 4–5 mm. in diameter. *Leaves oblong or oblanceolate,* lamina leathery, 6–17.5 cm. long, 2–5.8 cm. broad, apex rounded or obtuse, base obtuse, cordulate or tapered; upper surface dark or paler green, glabrous, midrib grooved, primary veins 16–18 on each side, deeply impressed; under surface pale green, glabrous, minutely punctulate with sessile glands, midrib prominent; petiole 1–2.4 cm. long, eglandular, more or less glaucous. *Inflorescence* a racemose umbel of 10–12 or sometimes 18–24 flowers; rhachis 1.3–4 cm. long, glandular or eglandular, hairy or glabrous; pedicel 0.8–1.5 cm. long, eglandular. *Calyx cup-like,* 4–8 mm. long, undulately 5-lobed, outside eglandular, hairy at the base or glabrous, margin eglandular, eciliate or sometimes ciliate. *Corolla* tubular-campanulate, 3.6–4.5 cm. long, fleshy, *pink, pale pink, rich pink, white tinged pink, rose, purplish-rose, scarlet (or rarely cream),* with darker spots, without or sometimes with dark red basal patches, without or sometimes with reddish streaks, 5 nectar pouches at the base; lobes 5, 1.3–1.5 cm. long, 1.6–2.5 cm. broad, deeply emarginate. *Stamens* 10, unequal, 2–3.5 cm. long; filaments glabrous. *Gynoecium* 3.5–4 cm. long; *ovary* conoid, 4–6 mm. long, 7–8-celled, *eglandular or densely glandular* with short-stalked glands, not hairy or densely hairy; style eglandular. *Capsule* oblong or broadly oblong, 1.4–2.5 cm. long, 0.6–1 cm. broad, straight, eglandular or glandular, slightly or moderately glaucous, calyx-lobes persistent.

This species was first collected by Farrer in May 1920 in the Chawchi Pass, north-east Upper Burma. Further gatherings by other collectors show that the plant is distributed in north-east Upper Burma, east and south-east Tibet, north-west Yunnan, and Assam. It grows in rhododendron forest, *Picea* forest, mixed forests, conifer forests, *Abies-Rhododendron* forest, in bamboo and deciduous forest, in thickets, on rocks, and on cliffs, at elevations of 2,135–3,813 m. (7,000–12,500 ft.). According to Ludlow, Sherriff and Elliot, it is very common in the west of Tongkuk Dzong, south-east Tibet, at 9,500 feet.

In 1978 *R. faucium* Chamberlain was described from a specimen No. 12289 collected by Ludlow, Sherriff and Elliot at Layoting, Tongyuk Chu, Pome province, south-east Tibet, and in the same year *R. subansiriense* Chamberlain was founded on Cox and Hutchison's No. 418 from south-east of Apa Tani valley, Subansiri division, Assam. When these Type specimens and all other specimens, also cultivated plants under these names are examined, it will be seen that in habit and height of growth, in the smooth, brown flaking bark of the stem and branches, in the shape and size of the leaves, calyx, and corolla, in the 10 stamens, and in the eglandular or glandular ovary, these plants are identical with *R. hylaeum*. The only distinction between *R. hylaeum* and *R. subansiriense* is that in *R. hylaeum* the corolla is pink, pale pink, rich pink, white tinged pink, rose, purplish-rose (or rarely cream), but in *R. subansiriense* the corolla is scarlet. On this slender distinction, *R. subansiriense* does not merit specific rank. Accordingly, *R. faucium* and *R. subansiriense* are now placed in synonymy under *R. hylaeum*.

R. hylaeum varies considerably in several features in view of its wide geographical distribution, altitudinal range and diverse habitats in which it is found. It is a small, medium- or large-sized shrub, or tree, 1.22–13.73 m. (4–45 ft.) high, the leaves (laminae) are 6–17.5 cm. long, 2–5.8 cm. broad, leaf base is obtuse, cordulate or tapered, the corolla is pink, pale pink to purplish-rose, scarlet, and the ovary is eglandular or densely glandular with short-stalked glands, not hairy or densely hairy.

It is allied to the species of the Thomsonii Subseries, but it also shows a certain degree of resemblance to the species of the Irroratum Series. Its main features are the smooth, brown flaking bark of the stem and branches, the oblong or oblanceolate leaves, laminae up to 17.5 cm. long, and the tubular-campanulate flowers.

The species was first introduced by Forrest in 1921 (No. 20961), and again in 1924 (No. 24660). Kingdon-Ward sent seeds in 1926 (No. 6833), in 1931 (No. 9322), and in 1950 (19452). It was introduced by Ludlow, Sherriff and Elliot in 1946 (Nos. 12019, 12045), and in 1947 (12208), also by Cox and Hutchison in 1965 (No. 418 under the name "*subansiriense*"). In its native home *R. hylaeum* is a shrub or tree 4–45 feet in height; in cultivation it is a broadly upright or somewhat compact rounded shrub of 5–18 feet. As it has been introduced from elevations of 7,000–12,500 feet, its hardiness varies in cultivation. Forrest's No. 24660 from 7,000–8,000 feet, and Cox and Hutchison's No. 418 from 8,400–9,200 feet, have proved tender and have failed to establish in some gardens along the east coast; they are suitable for a cool greenhouse or for well-sheltered gardens along the west coast. The species is a vigorous grower, and is an attractive sight with its tubular-campanulate flowers produced freely in trusses of 10–12. There was a remarkable plant growing freely in the Royal Botanic Garden, Edinburgh, 9 feet high, free-flowering with trusses of 10–12 pink flowers. Unfortunately this plant has now been lost to cultivation.

Epithet. Belonging to forests.
Hardiness 2–3. March–May.

R. lopsangianum Cowan in Notes Roy. Bot. Gard. Edin., Vol. 19 (1937) 250.
    Syn. *R. thomsonii* Hook. f. subsp. *lopsangianum* (Cowan) Chamberlain in Notes
    Roy. Bot. Gard. Edin., Vol. 39 (1982) 420.
An upright or compact shrub, *60 cm.–1.83 m. (2–6 ft.) high*, branchlets glandular or eglandular, those below the inflorescences 2–3 mm. in diameter. *Leaves* elliptic, oblong-elliptic, oval or almost orbicular, *lamina* leathery, *2.7–6 cm. long*, apex broadly obtuse or rounded, base obtuse or truncate or cordulate; upper surface dark green, eglandular or glandular along the grooved midrib, primary veins 9–12 on each side, deeply impressed; under surface papillate, glabrous, midrib raised; petiole 0.6–1 cm. long, glandular or eglandular. *Inflorescence* terminal, umbellate, 3–5-flowered; pedicel 0.7–2 cm. long, eglandular. *Calyx* 5-lobed, small, *2–3 mm. long*, crimson, lobes rounded,

outside eglandular, margin glandular. *Corolla* tubular-campanulate or funnel-campanulate, *3–4.2 cm. long,* fleshy, crimson, very deep crimson or dark crimson, outside with or without a glaucous bloom, 5 nectar pouches at the base; lobes 5, 0.6–1.3 cm. long, 1.1–2 cm. broad, emarginate. *Stamens* 10, unequal, 2.2–3.1 cm. long; filaments glabrous or puberulous at the base. *Gynoecium* 3–4 cm. long; ovary conoid, 5–7 mm. long, eglandular or glandular; style eglandular. *Capsule* oblong, 1.1–1.5 cm. long, 5 mm. broad, straight, eglandular, calyx-lobes persistent.

This species was discovered by Ludlow and Sherriff in May 1936 at Migyitun, Tsari Chu, south Tibet. It was later found by them in other localities in the same region, and with Taylor, was collected in Takpo Province, south-east Tibet. The plant grows on rocky hillsides, and hanging over cliffs, in rhododendron and *Abies* forest, at elevations of 2,593–4,270 m. (8,500–14,000 ft.). Ludlow, Sherriff and Taylor record it as being very common at Chubumbu La, Takpo Province, south-east Tibet.

R. lopsangianum is a remarkably distinct species. It is related to *R. thomsonii,* but differs markedly in that it is a smaller plant, the flowers are smaller, the calyx is small not forming a cup, and the leaves are usually much smaller.

The species was first introduced by Ludlow and Sherriff in 1936 (No. 2736). It was reintroduced by them, with Taylor, in 1938 (No. 6561). In cultivation it is a small upright or compact shrub 3–6 feet high with crimson flowers produced freely in trusses of 3–5. The plant is hardy in a sheltered position. It is rare in cultivation.

Epithet. After Nga-Wang Lopsang Tup-Den Gyatso, the late Dalai Lama of Tibet. Hardiness 3. April.

R. meddianum Forrest in Notes Roy. Bot. Gard. Edin., Vol. 12 (1920) 136.
Illustration. Bot. Mag. Vol. 163 t. 9636 (1942).

A broadly upright shrub, 92 cm.–2.44 m. (3–8 ft.) high, *branchlets eglandular,* thinly glaucous, those below the inflorescences 0.4–1 cm. in diameter. *Leaves oval, obovate or oblong-oval,* rarely oblong, lamina coriaceous, *5.5–11 cm. long,* 3.5–5.5 cm. or rarely 6.8 cm. broad, apex rounded or retuse, mucronate, base rounded, cuneate, obtuse or truncate; upper surface dark green, glabrous, glaucous, midrib grooved, primary veins 10–15 on each side, deeply impressed; under surface glabrous, midrib raised, primary veins conspicuous; petiole 1–2 cm. long, *broad,* grooved above, eglandular or rarely glandular, glaucous or not glaucous. *Inflorescence* umbellate or shortly racemose, 5–10-flowered; rhachis 2–5 mm. long, glandular or eglandular; *pedicel* 1–2 cm. long, reddish, *eglandular. Calyx* cup-shaped, 5-lobed, *4 mm.–1 cm. long,* fleshy, *red,* lobes unequal, rounded or ovate, eglandular. *Corolla tubular-campanulate,* 4–5.8 cm. long, fleshy, crimson, deep crimson, or almost black-crimson or scarlet, with or without a very few darker spots, without or sometimes with a dark blotch at the base, with or without a plum-like bloom on the exterior, 5 nectar pouches at the base; lobes 5, 1.3–2 cm. long, 2–2.6 cm. broad, rounded, emarginate. *Stamens* 10, unequal, 2.7–4.5 cm. long; filaments glabrous. *Gynoecium* 3.7–5 cm. long; *ovary* conoid, 4–5 mm. long, *eglandular,* grooved; style eglandular. *Capsule* short stout or oblong, 1.5–2 cm. long, 7 mm.–1 cm. broad, straight or slightly curved, eglandular, glaucous, calyx-lobes persistent.

Forrest discovered this plant in June 1917 in the Shweli-Salwin Divide, western Yunnan. He found it again later in other localities in the same region. In September 1925 he also collected it on the hills in north-east Upper Burma. It grows in open rhododendron scrub, on open rocky slopes, in thickets, and amongst scrub on the margins of forests, at elevations of 2,745–3,660 m. (9,000–12,000 ft.). It may be remarked that some of Forrest's earliest gatherings were lost in a steamer torpedoed on the way home during the World War 1914–18.

R. meddianum is often regarded as the counterpart of the Himalayan *R. thomsonii*. It is allied to *R. thomsonii,* but differs usually in the obovate or oblong-oval larger leaves, and the tubular-campanulate flowers. These combined characters, even though there is some overlapping, serve to distinguish the two species. They also differ in their geographical distribution. *R. meddianum* is a native of western Yunnan and north-east Upper Burma, but *R. thomsonii* comes from Nepal, Sikkim, Bhutan, Assam, and south Tibet.

R. meddianum was first introduced by Forrest in 1917 (No. 15767—the Type number), and again under four different seed numbers. In cultivation it is a broadly upright shrub up to 6–8 feet high. Two flower colour forms are grown in gardens, namely, crimson and scarlet. The species has proved to be of sturdy habit, with fairly stout branches, and is of great beauty with its large tubular-campanulate flowers. Although hardy, it requires a sheltered position along the east coast.

Epithet. After G. Medd, Agent I. F. Company, Bhamo, Upper Burma.
Hardiness 3. April–May.

R. meddianum Forrest var. **atrokermesinum** Tagg in The Sp. of Rhod., (1930) 742.

This plant was first collected by Forrest in April 1925 on the western flank of the N'Maikha-Salwin Divide, north-east Upper Burma. It grows amongst rhododendron scrub on rocky slopes, at elevations of 3,355 m. (11,000 ft.).

The variety differs from the species in that the ovary is densely glandular, the branchlets and pedicels are moderately glandular, the leaves and the flowers are often larger.

The plant was introduced by Forrest in 1925 (No. 26499—the Type number). It is hardy in a sheltered position, and blooms freely with deep purple-crimson or light red flowers with black-crimson spots. The plant is rare in cultivation.

It received an Award of Merit when exhibited by R. O. Hambro, Logan House, Stranraer, Wigtownshire, in 1954, and again the same Award for a clone 'Bennan' when shown by the National Trust for Scotland, Brodick Castle Gardens, in 1977.

Epithet of the variety. Black-crimson.
Hardiness 3. April–May.

R. populare Cowan in Notes Roy. Bot. Gard. Edin., Vol. 19 (1937) 251.

A shrub or tree, 92 cm.–4.58 m. (3–15 ft.) high, branchlets glandular or eglandular, those below the inflorescences 2–3 mm. in diameter. *Leaves oblong or elliptic*, lamina coriaceous, 3.5–8 cm. long, 1.5–3.5 cm. broad, apex broadly obtuse or rounded, mucronate, base obtuse or cordulate; upper surface glabrous, midrib grooved, floccose or glabrous, primary veins 8–12 on each side, deeply impressed; under surface epapillate or faintly papillate, glabrous, midrib raised; petiole 5–7 mm. long, sparsely or moderately floccose, eglandular. *Inflorescence* terminal, umbellate or shortly racemose, 3–7-flowered; rhachis 3–4 mm. long, hairy or glabrous; pedicel 0.6–1.2 cm long, eglandular. *Calyx* 5-lobed, 0.1–1 cm. long, crimson, lobes unequal, rounded or ovate, eglandular. *Corolla* tubular-campanulate or campanulate, *2.5–3.5 cm. long*, crimson or deep crimson, with or without deeper spots; lobes 5, 0.8–1 cm. long, 1.3–2 cm. broad, emarginate. Stamens 10, unequal, 1.4–2.6 cm. long; filaments glabrous. *Gynoecium* 2.5–3.5 cm. long; *ovary* conoid, 4–5 mm. long, *eglandular*, grooved; style eglandular. *Capsule* not known.

Ludlow and Sherriff discovered this plant in May 1936 at Natrampa, Chayul Chu, south Tibet. They found it again two days later at Lung, in the same region. It grows in rhododendron and bamboo forest, at elevations of 3,508–3,660 m. (11,500–12,000 ft.).

R. populare is closely allied to *R. lopsangianum* which it resembles in flower colour, but differs in that the leaves are oblong or elliptic, the lower surface of the leaves is epapillate or faintly papillate, and the ovary is eglandular.

The plant has not been introduced into cultivation.
Epithet. Popular.
Not in cultivation.

R. stewartianum Diels in Notes Roy. Bot. Gard. Edin., Vol. 5 (1912) 211.
> Syn. *R. aiolosalpinx* Balf. f. et Farrer in Notes Roy. Bot. Gard. Edin., Vol. 13 (1922) 227.
>> *R. niphobolum* Balf. f. et Farrer, ibid. Vol. 13 (1922) 277.
>> *R. stewartianum* Diels var. *aiolosalpinx* (Balf. f. et Farrer) Cowan et Davidian in The Rhod. Year Book (1951–52) 177.

A broadly upright or sometimes straggly shrub, or bush, 60 cm.–3 m. (2–10 ft.) high, branchlets eglandular or glandular, not hairy or rarely hairy, those below the inflorescences 3–4 mm. in diameter. *Leaves* obovate, oblong-obovate, oval or elliptic, lamina leathery, 5–12 cm. long, 2.5–6.5 cm. broad, apex rounded, base obtuse or rounded or truncate; upper surface bright green, glabrous, more or less glaucous, midrib grooved, primary veins 9–14 on each side, deeply impressed; *under surface with a thin veil of hairs or with farinose indumentum* or glabrous, midrib prominent, primary veins slightly raised; *petiole 0.6–1.9 cm. long,* not glandular or sometimes glandular, not hairy or rarely hairy. *Inflorescence* umbellate or shortly racemose, 3–7-flowered; rhachis 2–6 mm. long, glandular or eglandular, hairy or not hairy; pedicel 0.8–2.5 cm. long, glandular or eglandular. *Calyx* cup-shaped, 5-lobed, variable in size, 0.1–1.4 cm. long, lobes rounded, ovate or rarely oblong, outside eglandular, margin glandular or eglandular, not hairy or rarely hairy. *Corolla* tubular-campanulate, 3.6–5.4 cm. long, very variable in colour, pure white, white flushed rose, yellow, pale yellow, creamy-yellow, creamy-white, yellow flushed rose, pink, pale rose, deep rose margined deep crimson, purplish; or sometimes brilliant red or crimson, without or sometimes with a few crimson spots, without or rarely with a crimson blotch at the base; lobes 5, 1.2–1.5 cm. long, 1.8–2.5 cm. broad, rounded, emarginate. *Stamens* 10, unequal, 1.8–3.8 cm. long; filaments puberulous at the base or rarely glabrous. *Gynoecium* 3.1–4.1 cm. long; *ovary* conoid, 4–5 mm. long, *moderately or densely glandular,* rarely eglandular; style glabrous. *Capsule* oblong, 1.5–3 cm. long, 0.6–1 cm. broad, straight or slightly curved, glandular or with vestiges of glands, rarely eglandular, calyx-lobes persistent.

This species was discovered by Forrest in June 1904 on the ascent of the Tsedjiong Pass, Mekong-Salwin Divide, south-east Tibet when collecting for A. K. Bulley of Ness, Neston, Cheshire. Further gatherings by him and by other collectors show that the plant is distributed in south-east Tibet, north-west Yunnan, north-east and east Upper Burma, and Assam. It grows in meadows, in scrub, on rocky slopes, in rhododendron thickets, in cane brakes, in bamboo thickets, and in rhododendron forest, at elevations of 3,050–4,460 m. (10,000–14,623 ft.). Kingdon-Ward describes it as a tangled shrub, rising 6–8 feet from the ground, with interlacing stems more or less ascending, amongst thick bamboo brake along the summit of a granite ridge at Imaw Bum, north-east Upper Burma at 10,000 feet. Farrer records it as being particularly abundant, and flowering in the snow in the Chawchi Pass, north-east Upper Burma at 10,500 feet on May 15, 1920. According to Yü it is common in the Salwin-Kiu Chiang Divide, north-west Yunnan.

R. stewartianum varies considerably in height of growth, in the size of the leaves and calyx, and particularly in flower colour. It is allied to *R. eclecteum* which it resembles in some features, but is readily distinguished usually by the thin veil of hairs or farinose indumentum on the lower surface of the leaves, and by the long petiole.

The species was first introduced by Farrer in 1919 (No. 926) from north-east Upper Burma, and by Kingdon-Ward in the same year from that region (Nos. 3096, 3300). In cultivation it is a broadly upright shrub up to 4–5 feet high with bright green leaves, and with several colour forms, such as, pure white, white flushed rose, yellow, creamy-white, yellow flushed rose, pink and rose. Most forms are delightful plants and are of great beauty with their tubular-campanulate flowers in trusses of 3–7. It may be noted that Farrer came upon a plant in north-east Upper Burma with crimson flowers, whilst Rock collected a specimen in north-west Yunnan with brilliant red flowers. Unfortunately these two plants have not been introduced. In cultivation most forms are hardy, easy to cultivate, and succeed admirably along the west and east coasts. The species has the advantage of flowering at a fairly young age. Some plants occasionally produce one or two capsules containing seeds in plenty.

R. stewartianum was given an Award of Merit when shown by L. de Rothschild, Exbury, in 1934.

Epithet. After L. B. Stewart, 1876–1934, a former Curator, Royal Botanic Garden, Edinburgh.

Hardiness 3. February–April.

R. stewartianum Diels var. **tantulum** Cowan et Davidian in The Rhododendron Year Book (1951–52) 177.

Forrest first collected this plant in June 1922 in the Salwin-Kiu Chiang Divide, west of Si-K'ai, south-east Tibet. He found it again in June of that year in the same region. It grows on the margins of mixed thickets, on open stony slopes in side valleys, and in mixed scrub, at elevations of 3,355–3,660 m. (11,000–12,000 ft.).

The variety differs from the species in the minute calyx and in the small leaves.

It was introduced by Forrest in 1922 (No. 21918–the Type number, and Nos. 21708, 21781, 21787). In cultivation it is a broadly upright shrub, 3–4 feet high. It is hardy, free-flowering, and makes a fine show with its white, pale or deep rose flowers in trusses of 2–5.

Epithet. Very short calyx.
Hardiness 3. March–April.

R. thomsonii Hook. f. Rhod. Sikkim Himal., t. 12 (1851).
Syn. *R. thomsonii* Hook f. var. *flocculosa* C. B. Clarke in Hook. f. Fl. Brit. Ind., III, (1882) 468.
R. thomsonii Hook. f. var. *grandiflorum* Millais, Rhododendrons (1917) 253.
R. thomsonii Hook. f. var. *album* Millais, Rhododendrons (1917) 253.
Illustration. Bot. Mag. Vol. 83 t. 4997 (1857).

A rounded spreading, or broadly upright shrub, or bush, or tree, 1–6.10 m. (3⅓–20 ft.) high; *stem and branches with smooth, brown, fawn or pink flaking bark;* branchlets glandular or eglandular, thinly glaucous, those below the inflorescences 4–6 mm. in diameter. *Leaves orbicular or ovate or broadly elliptic,* lamina leathery, 4–10 cm. long, 3–7.5 cm. broad, apex rounded, mucronate, base rounded or cordulate or truncate; upper surface dark green or olive-green, glabrous, midrib grooved, primary veins 9–15 on each side, deeply impressed; under surface glaucous or pale glaucous green, glabrous, midrib raised, primary veins slightly raised; petiole 1–2.6 cm. long, glaucous green, eglandular or rarely glandular. *Inflorescence racemose umbel of 6–10 or rarely 12–13 flowers;* rhachis 0.5–1.8 cm. long, eglandular or rarely with a few glands, hairy or glabrous; pedicel 0.8–2.7 cm. long, glaucous or not glaucous, eglandular or rarely glandular. *Calyx cup-shaped,* 0.6–2 cm. long, yellow, whitish-green, pale green, greenish-scarlet, red, portwine-red, pale crimson or crimson, 5-lobed, lobes unequal, rounded or truncate, eglandular. *Corolla campanulate or tubular-campanulate,* 3.5–6 cm. long, fleshy, deep blood-red, deep crimson, crimson, pale vermilion, portwine-red, deep red or very deep rose, with or without spots on the upper posterior part, often with a bloom, *5 nectar pouches at the base;* lobes 5, 1.3–2 cm. long, 1.6–2.6 cm. broad, emarginate. *Stamens* 10, unequal, 2–4.5 cm. long; filaments glabrous or puberulous at the base. *Gynoecium* 3.2–5 cm. long; *ovary 5–7 mm long, conoid, eglandular, grooved, 6–10-celled;* style eglandular. *Capsule* short stout, or broadly oblong, 1.5–2.4 cm. long, 0.8–1 cm. broad, glaucous or not glaucous, *eglandular,* calyx-lobes persistent.

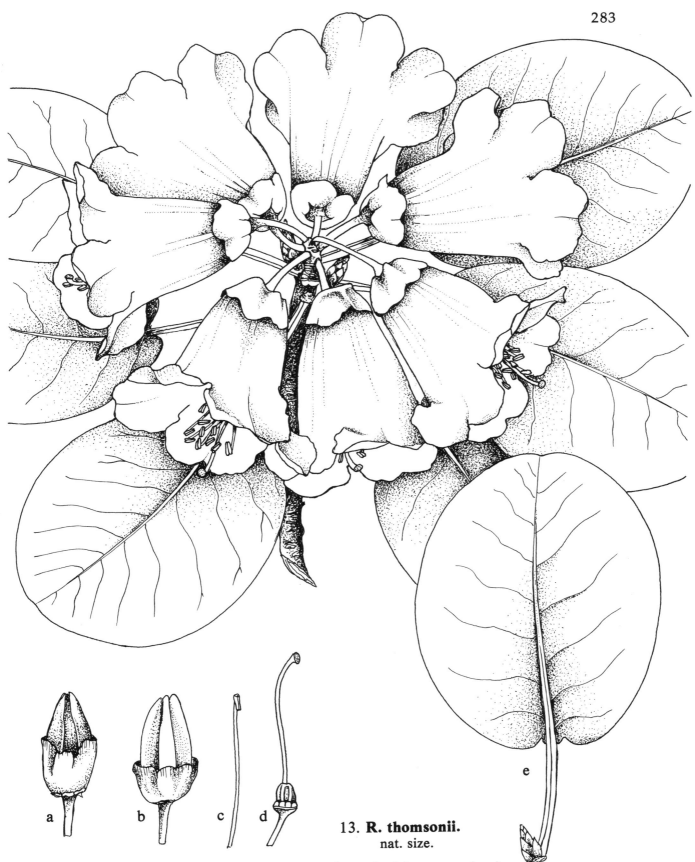

13. **R. thomsonii.**
nat. size.

a. capsule. b. capsule. c. stamen. d. ovary, style. e. leaf (upper surface).

This species was discovered by J. D. Hooker in 1849 in Sikkim Himalaya. Subsequently it was found by other collectors in Nepal, Sikkim, Bhutan, Assam, and south Tibet. It grows in scrub scattered on steep rocky exposed slopes, in *Abies* forest, in dense rhododendron and conifer forest, on open hillsides, and amongst bamboo on moist hillsides, at elevations of 2,440–4,270 m. (8,000–14,000 ft.). J. D. Hooker records it as being abundant at 11,000–13,000 feet in Sikkim. According to Cooper it grows profusely at Kopub Pumthang in Bhutan. In their field note, Ludlow, Sherriff and Hicks describe it as being common in conifer and bamboo forest at Rudo La, in East Central Bhutan. According to L. W. Beer, it is common in mixed woodland in east Nepal.

R. thomsonii is very variable in habit and height of growth. It is a small or large shrub, 3–12 feet high. Ludlow and Sherriff found a plant in Bhutan growing as a tree 20 feet in height. The species also varies in the size of the leaves, in the size and colour of the calyx, and in the size of the corolla. It is allied to *R. meddianum;* the distinctions between them are discussed under the latter.

The species was first introduced by J. D. Hooker in 1850. Cooper sent seeds in 1914 under three different seed numbers. Cave introduced it three times in 1920 and 1923. Ludlow, Sherriff, and with Taylor or Hicks sent seeds on four occasions. The species was also introduced by Beer, Lancaster and Morris. It first flowered in cultivation in 1857 in Mr. Methven's Stanwell Nurseries, Bonnington Road, Edinburgh. Several forms are in cultivation, including: Form 1. With large cup-shaped yellow or whitish-green calyx. Form 2. With small red calyx. Form 3. With small leaves, lamina 4 cm. (1½ in.) long and as much across. Form 4. With large leaves, lamina 10 cm. (4 in.) long and almost as much across. Form 5. With leaves dark green on the upper surface. Form 6. With leaves olive-green on the upper surface. All these forms are exceptionally fine garden plants. However, it should be noted that some of the old (pre 1930) introductions with dark green foliage, and laden with deep crimson flowers sometimes in tiers on the branches, are examples of perfection and great beauty. The inflorescence consists usually of 6–10 flowers, but rarely 12–13 flowers. The corolla is campanulate somewhat broad at the base, or tubular-campanulate narrowed at the base. An attractive feature of the species is the smooth, brown, fawn or pink flaking bark of the stem and branches. Other characteristic features are the glaucous-papillate lower surface of the leaves, and the five dark nectar pouches at the base of the corolla. Another distinctive feature in cultivation is the short stout or broadly oblong capsule with a large calyx, containing plentiful fertile seeds. The species is hardy outdoors, but along the east coast and in gardens inland, a well-sheltered position is essential.

It received an Award of Garden Merit in 1925. The species was given an Award of Merit when shown by the Crown Estate Commissioners, Windsor Great Park, in 1973.

Epithet. After Thomas Thomson, 1817–1878, a former Supt., Calcutta Botanic Garden.

Hardiness 3. April–May.

R. thomsonii Hook. f. var. **candelabrum** (Hook. f.) C. B. Clarke in Hook. Fl. Brit. Ind., III, (1882) 468.
>   Syn. *R. candelabrum* Hook. f. Rhod. Sikkim Himal. t. 29 (1849).
>   *R. thomsonii* Hook. f. var. *pallidum* Cowan in Notes Roy. Bot. Gard. Edin., Vol. 19 (1937) 253.
>   *R.* × *candelabrum* (Hook. f.) (*R. thomsonii* × *R. campylocarpum*) Chamberlain in Notes Roy. Bot. Gard. Edin., Vol. 39 (1982) 420.

This plant was first collected by J. D. Hooker in 1849 near Lachen, Sikkim. It was afterwards found by Cave in the same region, and by Ludlow and Sherriff in Central

Bhutan and south Tibet. Stainton collected it in two localities in the Arun Valley, Nepal. It grows in thick pine woods, in rhododendron forest, and amongst other shrubs, at elevations of 3,050–3,660 m. (10,000–12,000 ft.).

The variety differs from the species in that the corolla is pink or rose-pink, without or with magenta patches at the base, the ovary is moderately or sparsely glandular with short-stalked glands, and the calyx is small 1–4 mm. or rarely 8 mm. long.

The plant was introduced possibly by Ludlow and Sherriff from Bhutan in 1936 or 1937. It is hardy outdoors, and free-flowering.

Epithet of the variety. Like a candelabrum.

Hardiness 3. April–May.

R. viscidifolium Davidian in The Rhododendron and Camellia Year Book 1967 (104).

A broadly upright shrub, 60 cm.–2.44 m. (2–8 ft.) high, branchlets glabrous, glandular or eglandular, those below the inflorescences 2–4 mm. in diameter. *Leaves* evergreen, oval or rounded, lamina coriaceous, 4–9.7 cm long, 2.8–6.6 cm. broad, apex rounded, mucronate, base rounded or truncate or cordulate; upper surface green, glabrous, midrib grooved, primary veins 10–12 on each side, impressed; *under surface* not hairy, densely papillate, *glandular, sticky to the touch,* midrib raised; petiole 1–2.5 cm. long, glabrous, glandular or eglandular. *Most of the old leaves turn scarlet-crimson, bright red or bright yellow later in the season. Inflorescence* terminal, umbellate, *1–2-flowered;* rhachis 1–3 mm. long, hairy; pedicel 0.8–1 cm. long, reddish, glabrous, moderately or sparsely glandular or eglandular. *Calyx* cup-shaped, 5-lobed, divided to about the middle, 4–9 mm. long, green or copper-red, lobes rounded, outside glabrous, margin hairy. *Corolla* tubular-campanulate, fleshy, 3.6–4.6 cm. long, *copper-red, spotted crimson on the posterior side,* 5 crimson nectar pouches at the base; lobes 5, 1–1.6 cm. long, 1.5–2.3 cm. broad, rounded, emarginate. *Stamens* 10, unequal, 2.3–3.5 cm. long; filaments crimson, glabrous or puberulous at the base. *Gynoecium* 3.5–4.2 cm. long; ovary conoid, 7–8 mm. long, 6-celled, densely tomentose or densely or moderately glandular with short-stalked glands; style crimson, glabrous. *Capsule* oblong, 2 cm. long, 9 mm. broad, hairy, sparsely glandular, calyx-lobes persistent.

R. viscidifolium was discovered by Ludlow, Sherriff and Taylor at Lo La, Pachakshiri, south-east Tibet, in May 1938. It grows beside streams, usually on cliff faces near waterfalls at elevations of 2,745–3,355 m. (9,000–11,000 ft.).

In general appearance, *R. viscidifolium* shows a resemblance to the species of the Thomsonii Subseries, from all of which it is readily distinguished by the copper-red flowers. It agrees with *R. thomsonii* var. *candelabrum* in some respects, but differs markedly in the colour of the flowers, and in the glandular lower surface of the leaves sticky to the touch.

In cultivation, the plant was raised by Messrs. Gibson at Glenarn, from Ludlow, Sherriff and Taylor seed, but it has been incorrectly named *R. thomsonii* var. *pallidum.* The plant was probably raised from No. 6567, although the number quoted is 3750. The glandular lower surfaces of the leaves are sticky to the touch, this being a distinctive feature. It may be remarked that most of the leaves turn scarlet-crimson, bright red or bright yellow later in the season. The plant is hardy in a sheltered position. It was successfully grown in the Royal Botanic Garden, Edinburgh, but unfortunately it has now been lost to cultivation.

Epithet. With sticky leaves.

Hardiness 3. April–May.

WILLIAMSIANUM SUBSERIES

General characters: shrub, 60 cm.–1.53 m. (2–5 ft.) or rarely up to 2.44 m. (8 ft.) high, branchlets sparsely or moderately setulose-glandular. Leaves orbicular or ovate, lamina 1.5–4.2 cm. long, 1.3–4 cm. broad; *under surface glabrous* or punctulate with vestiges of hairs; petiole moderately or sparsely setulose-glandular or not setulose-glandular. Inflorescence 2–3- (rarely up to 5-) flowered. Calyx 5-lobed or a wavy rim, 1.5 mm. long. *Corolla campanulate* 3–4 cm. long, rose or pink; lobes 5–6. Stamens 10. Ovary 5–6-celled; *style glandular throughout to the tip.* Capsule oblong.

DESCRIPTION OF THE SPECIES

R. williamsianum Rehd. et Wils. in Sarg. Pl. Wilsonianae, I (1913) 538.
Illustration. Bot. Mag. Vol. 148 t. 8935 (1922).

A *compact, rounded or dome-shaped or spreading shrub,* 60 cm.–1.53 m. (2–5 ft.) or rarely up to 2.44 m. (8 ft.) high or more, *branchlets slender, sparsely or moderately setulose-glandular,* those below the inflorescences 1.5–3 mm. in diameter. *Leaves ovate or orbicular,* lamina leathery, 1.5–4.2 cm. long, 1.3–4 cm. broad, apex rounded or very broadly obtuse, mucronate, *base cordate or truncate;* upper surface bright green (*in young leaves bronzy*), glabrous, midrib grooved, primary veins 6–7 on each side, deeply impressed; under surface glaucous, papillate, glabrous or punctulate with vestiges of hairs, midrib raised, not hairy, not setulose or slightly setulose; *petiole* 0.7–1.5 cm. long, *moderately or sparsely setulose-glandular* or not setulose-glandular, the glands often extending to the margin of the leaf base. *Inflorescence* umbellate or a racemose umbel of *2–3* (rarely up to 5) *flowers;* rhachis 3–5 mm. long, eglandular; pedicel 1–2 cm. long, sparsely or moderately glandular with long-stalked glands or rarely eglandular. *Calyx* 5-lobed or a wavy rim, 1.5 mm. long, lobes rounded, glandular with long-stalked glands. *Corolla* campanulate, 3–4 cm. long, rose or pink, with or without spots; lobes 5–6, 1.2–1.4 cm. long, 1.5–2 cm. broad, rounded, emarginate. *Stamens* 10–12, unequal, 1.5–3 cm. long; filaments glabrous. *Gynoecium* 2.6–4 cm. long; *ovary* oblong-conoid, 4–5 mm. long, *rather densely glandular* with short- or long-stalked glands, not hairy, 5–6-celled; *style glandular throughout to the tip.* Capsule oblong, 1.5–1.8 cm. long, 4–5 mm. broad, straight, eglandular or sparsely glandular with short- or long-stalked glands, calyx-lobes persistent.

Wilson discovered this plant in June and October 1908 at Wa-shan, western Sichuan. He records it as being rare, growing in thickets covering a cliff, at an elevation of 2,800 m. (9,180 ft.). The species was later found by Fang in the same region.

R. williamsianum is a distinctive species and is unlikely to be confused with any other rhododendron. Its main features are the compact, rounded or dome-shaped or spreading habit of growth, the slender branchlets, the ovate or orbicular leaves with cordate or truncate base, and the inflorescence of usually 2–3 campanulate, rose or pink flowers.

The species was introduced by Wilson in 1908 (No. 1350—the Type number). In cultivation it is compact, densely branched and well-filled with bright green leaves. Along the east coast it grows up to 4–5 feet high, but along the west coast it reaches a height of 8 feet or more. The corolla has 5 or 6 lobes; both forms are often found on the same plant. Three distinct growth forms are found in gardens: Form 1. A small or large rounded shrub. Form 2. A dome-shaped shrub 3–4 feet high. Form 3. A dwarf spreading shrub. All these forms are exceedingly charming plants when laden with large rose or pink flowers in trusses of usually 2–3. A most remarkable feature is the young bronzy growths which, however, are liable to be destroyed by late frost. The

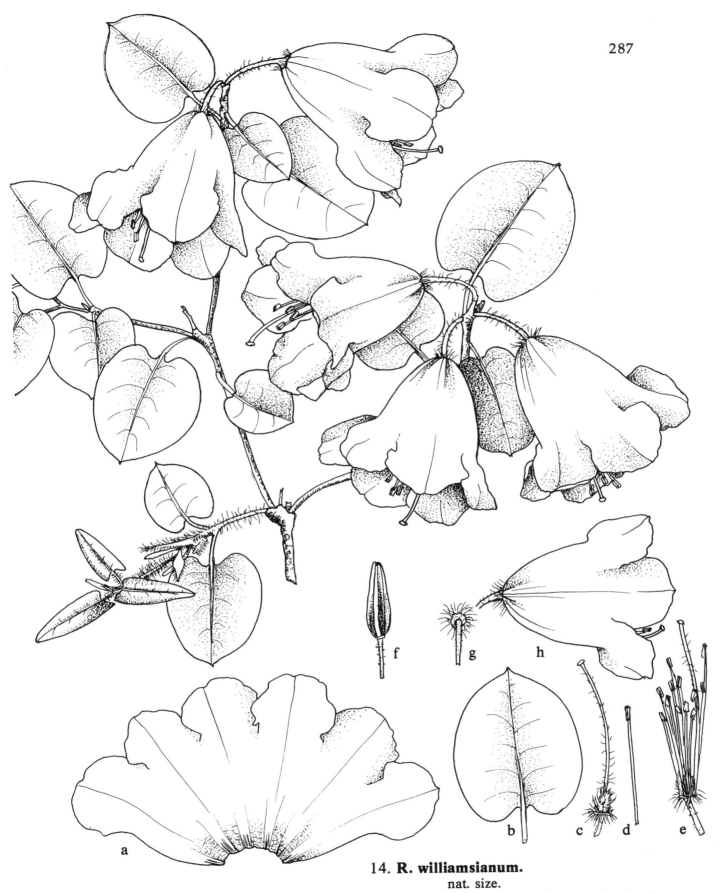

14. R. williamsianum.
nat. size.

a. petals. b. leaf (upper surface). c. ovary, style. d. stamen. e. section. f. capsule. g. calyx. h. flower.

species has the merit of flowering when quite small, and has proved to be easy to root from cuttings. It often produces a few oblong capsules containing seeds in plenty. As it has been introduced from a comparatively low elevation of 9,180 feet, it requires a well-sheltered position along the east coast. It should be noted that the dwarf form is a first class plant for the rock garden.

The species was given an Award of Merit when shown by Lord Aberconway, Bodnant, in 1938.

Epithet. After J. C. Williams, 1861–1939, of Caerhays, Cornwall.

Hardiness 3. April–May.

AZALEASTRUM

KEY TO THE SERIES

A. Branchlets, leaves, and the outside of calyx hairy with long appressed hairs; inflorescence 1–2-flowered from axillary buds along the branchlets of the previous year. Species from Canada and U.S.A. . . . . *Albiflorum Series*

A. Branchlets, leaves, and the outside of calyx not hairy or minutely puberulous, without long appressed hairs; inflorescence 1–8-flowered, axillary in the uppermost 1–4 leaves. Species from the Far East.

    B. Leaves deciduous, margins of the lamina crenulate; stamens 5, very unequal, dimorphic, the lower 3 stamens up to 1 cm. long, about as long as the corolla-lobes, filaments glabrous or sparsely puberulous at the base, their anthers oblong up to over 1.5 mm. long, the upper 2 stamens about half as long as the other 3, filaments 4 mm. long, densely pilose all along except at the base and the tips, their anthers much smaller, globose-ovoid, 0.5 mm. long; branchlets, petioles, pedicels, calyx margin, ovaries and capsules setulose-glandular . . . . *Semibarbatum Series*

    B. Leaves evergreen, margins of the lamina entire or rarely slightly serrulate; stamens 5–10, slightly unequal, isomerous, 1.3–5.4 cm. long, filaments pubescent at the base or up to three-fourths of their length, anthers oblong-oval; branchlets, petioles, pedicels, calyx margin, ovaries and capsules not glandular or glandular with short-stalked glands (except in *R. championae* and *R. vialii* bristly-glandular).

        C. Stamens 5; corolla rotate somewhat flat or almost bowl-shaped or tubular slightly widened towards the top, 1.6–3.2 cm. long; calyx 2–9 mm. long; ovary ovate or conoid, 1–3 mm. long; capsule ovoid or conoid, 4–6 mm. long; inflorescence 1–2-flowered . . . *Ovatum Series*

        C. Stamens 10, rarely 8, 11 or 13; corolla tubular-funnel-shaped, 2.5–7.8 cm. long; calyx minute 0.5–1 mm. long; ovary slender, 4 mm.–1.1 cm. long; capsule slender or sometimes oblong, 2–6.5 cm. long; inflorescence 1–8-flowered . . . . *Stamineum Series*

Open situations on the Lichiang Range. Photo J. F. Rock.

ALBIFLORUM SERIES

General characters: shrub, 75 cm.–1.83 m. (2½–6 ft.) high, *branchlets* moderately or rather densely *hairy with long, brown appressed hairs.* Leaves deciduous, oblong, oblong-elliptic to lanceolate, *lamina thin,* chartaceous, 3.2–7.5 cm. long, 1.3–2.5 cm. broad; *upper surface and midrib, and often lower surface and midrib, also petiole hairy with long, brown appressed hairs. Inflorescence 1–2-flowered* from *axillary* buds along the branchlets of the previous year, the flowers appearing after the leaves develop. Calyx large, 0.6–1.3 cm. long, outside moderately or rather densely hairy with long, appressed hairs. Corolla rotate-campanulate or campanulate. Stamens 10. Ovary 2–3 mm. long, densely glandular with long-stalked appressed glands, or densely hairy with long appressed hairs. Capsule ovoid, 0.7–1 cm. long, glandular with long-stalked appressed glands.

Distribution. Rocky Mountains from British Columbia and Alberta to Washington, Oregon and Colorado.

This Series contains only one species and is related to the Ovatum Series. The distinctive features are the long-pointed, undivided appressed hairs on the branchlets, leaves and on the outside of the calyx, the 1–2-flowered inflorescence from axillary buds along the branchlets of the previous year, the deciduous thin leaves, and pendulous flowers appearing after the leaves develop.

DESCRIPTION OF THE SPECIES

R. albiflorum W. J. Hooker in Fl. Bor. Am., Vol. 2 t. 133 (1834) 43.
    Syn. *Azalea albiflora* Kuntze.
        Azaleastrum albiflorum (Hooker) Rydberg, Mem. New York Bot. Gard. 1
        (1900) 297.

A. warrenii A. Nelson, Bot. Gaz. 56 (1913) 67.

R. warrenii (A. Nelson) MacBride, Contr. Gray Herb. n.s. 56 (1918) 55.

Illustration. Bot. Mag. Vol. 65 t. 3670 (1839).

A broadly upright shrub, 75 cm.–1.83 m. (2½–6 ft.) high with erect and ascending branches, *branchlets moderately or rather densely hairy with long, appressed brown hairs,* sparsely glandular with short-stalked glands or eglandular. *Leaves deciduous,* scattered or clustered at the end of short branchlets, oblong, oblong-elliptic, oblanceolate, lanceolate or obovate, *lamina thin, chartaceous,* 3.2–7.5 cm. long, 1.3–2.5 cm. broad, apex acute or obtuse, mucronate, *base* tapered or cuneate, *decurrent on the petiole; upper surface* bright green, *hairy with long, appressed brown hairs,* midrib grooved, hairy with long, appressed brown hairs, primary veins 6–8 on each side, deeply impressed; margin somewhat undulate or entire; under surface pale green, glabrous or sparsely hairy with long, appressed hairs, midrib prominent, hairy with long, appressed hairs or glabrous, primary veins raised; *petiole* 3–5 mm. long, flat above, *with a narrow wing on each side, hairy with long, appressed brown hairs,* glandular with short-stalked glands or eglandular. *Inflorescence 1–2-flowered from axillary buds along the branchlets* of the previous year, *flowers appearing after the leaves develop, pendulous,* flower-bud scales deciduous; rhachis 0.5–1 mm. long, hairy with long hairs, eglandular; pedicel 0.6–1.5 cm. long, hairy with long, brown hairs, rather densely or moderately glandular with short-stalked glands. *Calyx* 5-lobed, *0.6–1.3 cm. long,* lobes oblong or oblong-oval, *outside moderately or rather densely hairy with long, appressed brown hairs,* glandular with short-stalked glands or eglandular, margin fringed with short-stalked glands, glabrous. *Corolla* rotate-campanulate or campanulate, 1.3–2 cm. long, white, creamy-white or greenish-white, without or rarely with yellow or orange spots, hairy on the tube outside and inside; lobes 5, 0.8–1 cm. long, 0.6–1 cm. broad, ovate, oval or rounded, not emarginate. *Stamens* 10, unequal, 0.8–1.2 cm. long, shorter than the corolla; filaments pubescent in the lower half. *Gynoecium* 0.7–1.2 cm. long, shorter than, or sometimes as long as, the stamens, shorter than the corolla; *ovary* ovoid, 2–3 mm. long, 5-celled, *densely glandular with long-stalked appressed glands or densely hairy with long appressed hairs;* style hairy at the base or in the lower half or throughout to the tip, eglandular, stigma 5-lobed. *Capsule* ovoid, 0.7–1 cm. long, glandular with long-stalked appressed glands, shorter than the persistent calyx-lobes.

This species was discovered by Mr. Drummond in 1828 in the alpine woods of the Rocky Mountains in British Columbia, and was described by W. J. Hooker in 1834. Drummond records it as being a very beautiful and most distinct species, which would be a great ornament to our gardens. According to various collectors it is plentiful and forms thickets near the timber-line on the Rocky Mountains from British Columbia and Alberta to Washington, Oregon and Colorado, at elevations of 1,342–2,200 m. (4,400–7,213 ft.).

R. albiflorum is a unique species. A diagnostic feature is the pointed, undivided, appressed hairs on the branchlets, leaves and on the outside of the calyx. In this respect, the species is very similar to the Azalea Series. From this Series, however, *R. albiflorum* is very remote. Another distinctive character is the 1–2-flowered inflorescence from axillary buds along the branchlets of the previous year. Other well-marked characteristics are the deciduous thin leaves, the pendulous flowers appearing after the leaves develop, the leaf base decurrent on the petiole with a narrow wing on each side, and the large calyx.

The species was first introduced by Drummond in 1828. He sent seeds to Dr. Graham who was Regius Keeper of the Royal Botanic Garden, Edinburgh, where the species flowered for the first time outdoors in a border in July 1837.

It is unfortunate that *R. albiflorum* is very difficult almost impossible to grow in cultivation in its native home. On the contrary, in Scotland, it has adapted itself to its new environment, and has proved hardy, a fairly fast grower, and usually easy to cultivate, irrespective of differences in soil and climatic conditions. The plant was successfully grown in 1933 and for some years after, in a sheltered position in the Royal Botanic Garden, Edinburgh. The species grew very well in Andrew Harley's garden in Perthshire. In the *New Flora and Silva,* Vol. 9 (1937) page 128, Harley wrote: "*R. albiflorum* . . . gets a little overhead shade. It faces south and gets a great deal of sun, while the soil is rather poor and stony and inclined to dry out during summer. It was planted in this situation about eleven years ago as a small plant, and is now over 5 feet high . . . *R. albiflorum* with me is absolutely hardy and was quite untouched in the severe frost of May 1935 when many species and hybrids in my garden were severely damaged". In 1950 the species was satisfactorily grown at Tower Court, Ascot, Berks, in the South. At the present time, the plant succeeds admirably in the Royal Botanic Garden, Edinburgh. It was introduced as seed in 1950 from Seattle, Washington, and is now 4 feet high, growing in the lower peat bed, and is well-sheltered from wind, with a good amount of shade. The plant is hardy and blooms fairly freely. The species is uncommon in cultivation. A double-flowered form known as "f. *plenum*" has been collected.

Epithet. With white flowers.
Hardiness 3. June–July.

Forests in southeast Tibet. Photo J. F. Rock.

OVATUM SERIES

General characters: shrubs or trees, 60 cm.–7.63 m. (2–25 ft.) high, branchlets usually slender, young growths crimson-purple. Leaves evergreen, ovate, ovate-elliptic, oval, ovate-lanceolate, obovate, oblong-elliptic, lanceolate or oblong-lanceolate, lamina 2–10 cm. long, 1–3.1 cm. broad; *under surface glabrous,* midrib glabrous or sometimes rather densely minutely puberulous; petiole 0.3–2 cm. long, rather densely minutely puberulous. *Inflorescence axillary in the uppermost 1–4 leaves, 1–2-flowered;* pedicel 0.3–2.3 cm. long, usually moderately or densely glandular with short- or long-stalked glands. Calyx 5-lobed, 2–9 mm. long. *Corolla rotate somewhat flat, or almost bowl-shaped or tubular slightly widened towards the top,* 1.6–3.2 cm. long, white, pink, rose, purple, purplish-red, bright or deep magenta-rose or crimson; lobes 5. *Stamens 5.* Ovary 1–3 mm. long, 5-celled, setulose or setulose-glandular; style glabrous, eglandular. Capsule ovoid or conoid, 4–6 mm. long, 3–5 mm. broad, setulose or setulose-glandular, surrounded by the enlarged persistent calyx.

Distribution. Yunnan, north-east Upper Burma, Kweichow, Kwangtung, Hong Kong, Fokien, Taiwan, Kiangsi, Hupeh, Anhwei, Chekiang, and Chusan Islands.

This is a distinct Series of four species, and consists of shrubs and trees. The diagnostic features are the slender branchlets, the 1–2-flowered axillary inflorescence in the uppermost 1–4 leaves, usually the large calyx, the rotate corolla somewhat flat or bowl-shaped, (in *R. vialii* tubular, slightly widened towards the top), the five stamens, and the ovoid or conoid capsule surrounded by the enlarged persistent calyx. The Series is closely related to the Stamineum Series.

KEY TO THE SPECIES

A. Corolla rotate somewhat flat, or almost bowl-shaped, tube much shorter than the lobes; stamens puberulous on the lower one-half or three-fourths of their length.
  B. Leaves usually ovate, ovate-elliptic, oval or ovate-lanceolate, lamina as long as broad or up to twice longer than broad.
    C. Branchlets, pedicels and the outside of the flower-bud scales rather densely or moderately minutely puberulous (mealy); corolla white, pink, white tinged pink, rose, pale purple or very pale lilac, with or without pink or darker spots; leaves (laminae) usually 2–4.8 cm. long .... *ovatum*
    C. Branchlets, pedicels and the outside of the flower-bud scales glabrous; corolla white, with crimson spots; leaves (laminae) 3–8.4 cm. long... .... *hongkongense*
  B. Leaves lanceolate or oblong-lanceolate, lamina three times longer than broad .... *leptothrium*
A. Corolla tubular, slightly widened towards the top, tube much longer than the lobes; stamens glabrous .... *vialii*

DESCRIPTION OF THE SPECIES

R. hongkongense Hutch. in The Sp. of Rhod., (1930) 562.
  Syn. *Azalea myrtifolia* Champion in Bot. Mag. Vol. 77 sub. t. 4609 (1851).
  A broadly upright or somewhat lax shrub, much branched, 1.22–1.53 m. (4–5 ft.) high, branchlets rather densely or moderately glandular with short-stalked glands, glabrous. *Leaves* evergreen, *ovate, ovate-lanceolate, oval* or lanceolate, alternate, *lamina* coriaceous, slightly rigid, *3–8.4 cm. long,* 2–3 cm. broad, apex acute or obtuse, conspicuously mucronate, base obtuse or cuneate; *upper surface* dark green (*in young leaves crimson-purple*), glossy, glabrous, midrib grooved, rather densely minutely puberulous, primary veins 6–12 on each side, impressed; margin entire; *under surface* pale green, *glabrous,* midrib prominent, glabrous, primary veins slightly raised; petiole 0.4–2 cm. long, slightly grooved above, eglandular or sparsely glandular with short-stalked glands, rather densely minutely puberulous; (*young petioles crimson-purple*). *Inflorescence axillary* in the uppermost 1–4 leaves, *1–2-flowered, flower-bud scales* persistent during flowering, *glabrous outside;* rhachis 1 mm. long, densely minutely puberulous; *pedicel* 0.9–1.8 cm. long, crimson-purple, *moderately or rather densely glandular* with short-stalked glands, *glabrous. Calyx* 5-lobed, 2–5 mm. long, lobes ovate or rounded or oblong, one lobe often elongating, outside glabrous, glandular with short-stalked glands at the base or eglandular, margin glabrous, rather densely glandular with short-stalked glands or eglandular. *Corolla* rotate widely funnel-campanulate or almost bowl-shaped, 2–2.6 cm. long, 2.5–3.7 cm. broad, corolla-tube 4 mm. long, shorter than the lobes, *white, with crimson spots* at the base on the posterior side; lobes 5, 1.6–2 cm. long, 1–1.8 cm. broad, obovate, emarginate or rounded. *Stamens 5,* unequal, 1.3–2 cm. long, as long as the corolla or shorter; filaments pubescent on the lower one-half or three-fourths of their length. *Gynoecium* 2.4–3 cm. long, longer than the corolla; *ovary* conoid, 2 mm. long, 5-celled, *setulose-glandular,* glabrous; style glabrous, eglandular. *Capsule conoid,* 4–5 mm. long, 3–4 mm. broad, setulose-glandular, glabrous, *surrounded by the enlarged persistent calyx.*

This plant was first found by Lieut.-Col. Eyre of the Royal Artillery in March 1849 growing on rocks on Black Mountain, Hong Kong. It was afterwards collected in Kwangtung, in woods and on slopes, at elevations of 732–1,220 m. (2,400–4,000 ft.).

15. R. hongkongense.

nat. size.

a. leaf (lower surface) bud. b. capsule.
c. section. d. ovary, style. e. stamen. f. calyx. g. flower.

It may be remarked that in 1851 the plant was described as *Azalea myrtifolia* by J. G. Champion in *Bot. Mag.* Vol. 77 sub. t. 4609. It was later named *R. hongkongense* by Hutchinson with a brief description in *The Species of Rhododendron* 1930, page 562.

R. hongkongense shows a strong resemblance to *R. ovatum* in general features, but differs in that the branchlets, the outside of the flower-bud scales, and pedicels are glabrous, the leaves are often larger, and the flowers are always white.

The plant was recently introduced. It is tender along the east coast and is suitable for the greenhouse. It may succeed outdoors in well-sheltered gardens in mild areas along the west coast. In cultivation in the glasshouse it is a broadly upright somewhat lax shrub 3–4 feet high but is likely to grow taller. It is a vigorous grower, free-flowering, and provides an admirable display with its single or paired white bowl-shaped flowers, axillary in the uppermost 1–4 dark green leaves. An attractive feature is the crimson-purple young growths.

Epithet. From Hong Kong.
Hardiness 1. March–April.

R. leptothrium Balf. f. et Forrest in Notes Roy. Bot. Gard. Edin., Vol. 11 (1919) 84.
    Syn. *R. australe* Balf. f. et Forrest in Notes Roy. Bot. Gard. Edin., Vol. 12 (1920) 93.
        R. ngawchangense Philipson et Philipson in Notes Roy. Bot. Gard. Edin., Vol. 40 (1982) 228.
Illustration. Bot. Mag. n.s. Vol. 176 t. 502 (1967).
A broadly upright shrub or tree, 60 cm.–7.63 m. (2–25 ft.) high, *branchlets slender,* eglandular or sometimes glandular with short-stalked glands, rather densely or moderately minutely puberulous; young growths reddish. *Leaves* evergreen, *lanceolate or oblong-lanceolate, lamina chartaceous, 2.5–10 cm. long,* 1–3 cm. broad, apex acute or sometimes obtuse, conspicuously mucronate, base rounded or obtuse; upper surface dark green, glossy, glabrous, midrib grooved, rather densely or moderately minutely puberulous, *primary veins 6–15 on each side, raised;* margin entire or slightly serrulate; *under surface* pale green, *glabrous,* midrib prominent, rather densely minutely puberulous or glabrous, primary veins impressed or slightly raised; petiole 0.4–1.6 cm. long, slightly grooved above, eglandular, rather densely minutely puberulous. *Inflorescence axillary in the uppermost 1–4 leaves, 1-flowered,* flower-bud scales persistent during flowering, densely minutely puberulous outside (densely mealy); rhachis 1 mm. long, densely minutely puberulous; pedicel 1–2.3 cm. long, glandular with short-stalked glands, rather densely or moderately minutely puberulous. *Calyx* 5-lobed, 3–9 mm. long, lobes oblong, obovate, ovate or rounded, outside minutely puberulous at the base or glabrous, glandular with short-stalked glands at the base or eglandular, margin minutely puberulous or glabrous, minutely glandular or eglandular. *Corolla rotate* somewhat flat *or almost bowl-shaped,* 2–3.2 cm. long, 2.5–4 cm. broad, corolla-tube shorter than, or as long as, the lobes, rose, pale rose, deep rose, pale pink, purple, purplish-red or bright or deep magenta-rose, with or without crimson spots; lobes 5, 1.2–2 cm. long, 0.9–1.5 cm. broad, obovate or oval, emarginate or rounded. *Stamens 5,* unequal, 1.4–3 cm. long, as long as the corolla or shorter; filaments pubescent on the lower one-half or three-fourths of their length. *Gynoecium* 2.5–3.2 cm. long, longer than the corolla; *ovary* conoid, 2–3 mm. long, 5-celled, *setulose;* style glabrous, eglandular. *Capsule ovoid,* 5–6 mm. long, 4–5 mm. broad, *setulose, surrounded by the enlarged persistent calyx.*

R. leptothrium was discovered by Forrest in June 1912 on the flanks of volcanic mountain north-west of Tengyueh, western Yunnan. Subsequently it was found by him and by other collectors in the same area and in mid-west, north-west Yunnan, also in northeast Upper Burma. It grows in thickets, in scrub on cliffs, in pine forests, in open forests, on the margins of rhododendron forests, in open deciduous forests, and by streams, at elevations of 2,135–3,550 m. (7,000–11,803 ft.). Forrest records it as being very floriferous on slopes and cliffs in open gullies on the eastern flank of the N'Maikha-Salwin Divide.

The species is very closely allied to R. *ovatum* which it resembles in several features, but is readily distinguished by the lanceolate or oblong-lanceolate leaves, and often by the longer leaves.

R. *leptothrium* was first introduced by Forrest in 1912 (No. 9341), and again later under 18 different seed numbers. Rock sent seeds on five occasions. It first flowered in cultivation in May 1920 at Caerhays, Cornwall, and at Rowallane, Co. Down, N. Ireland. In its native home it is a shrub or tree, 2–25 feet high; in cultivation it reaches a height of 6 feet. As it has been introduced from elevations of 7,000–11,000 feet, its hardiness varies considerably in cultivation. Along the east coast some forms are tender and require the protection of a cool greenhouse, but a form possibly introduced from a high elevation is quite hardy outdoors in a sheltered garden; along the west coast it is successfully grown outdoors in mild areas. It is a broadly upright shrub with slender branchlets, and makes a fine show with its deep rose single axillary flowers produced with freedom.

Epithet. With thin leaves.
Hardiness 1–3. April–May.

R. ovatum. (Lindl.) Maxim. in Mém. Acad. Sci. St. Petersbourgh, ser. 7, XVI, No. 9 (1870) 45.

> Syn. *Azalea ovata* Lindl. in Journ. Hort. Soc. Lond. I (1846) 149.
>> R. *bachii* Lévl. in Fedde Repert. Vol. 12 (1913) 102.
>> R. *lamprophyllum* Hayata, Icon. Plant. Formos. III (1913) 135.
>> R. *ovatum* (Lindl.) Maxim. var. *prismaticum* Tam in Bull. Bot. Res. 2, 1 : 99 (1982).

> Illustration. Bot. Mag. Vol. 84 t. 5064 (1858), as *Azalea ovata*; ibid. Vol. 157 t. 9375 (1934), as R. *bachii*.

A shrub or bush or tree, 1–5 m. (3⅓–16 ft.) high, *branchlets slender*, glandular with short-stalked glands or eglandular, moderately or rather densely minutely puberulous; young growths reddish-brown. *Leaves* evergreen, *ovate, ovate-elliptic or ovate-lanceolate, lamina* coriaceous, 2–4.8 cm. or sometimes up to 6 cm. *long*, 1–2.4 cm. broad, apex acute, conspicuously mucronate, base rounded or broadly obtuse; upper surface dark green, glossy, glabrous, midrib grooved, rather densely or moderately minutely puberulous, *primary veins 6–10 on each side, raised;* margin entire or sometimes slightly serrulate; *under surface* pale green, *glabrous,* midrib prominent, glabrous, *primary veins impressed;* petiole 0.3–1.5 cm. long, slightly grooved above, eglandular or rarely glandular with short-stalked glands, rather densely minutely puberulous. *Inflorescence axillary* in the uppermost 1–3 leaves, *1-flowered,* flower-bud scales persistent during flowering, densely minutely puberulous outside (densely mealy); rhachis 1 mm. long, densely puberulous; pedicel 0.9–1.9 cm. long, glandular with short-stalked glands or eglandular, rather densely or moderately minutely puberulous. *Calyx* 5-lobed, 2–6 mm. long, lobes oblong, obovate, ovate or rounded, outside minutely puberulous in the lower half or glabrous, eglandular, margin glabrous, glandular with short-stalked glands or eglandular. *Corolla rotate somewhat flat or almost bowl-shaped,* 1.6–2.6 cm. long, 2.5–3 cm. broad, *corolla-tube rather wide,* shorter than the lobes, white, pink, white tinged pink, rose, pale purple or very pale lilac, with or without pink or darker spots; lobes 5, 1.3–1.6 cm. long, 1–1.4 cm. broad, obovate or oval, emarginate or rounded. *Stamens 5,* unequal, 1.3–2.3 cm. long, as long as the corolla or shorter; filaments pubescent on the lower one-half or three-fourths of their length. *Gynoecium* 2.3–3 cm. long, longer than the corolla; *ovary broadly ovate,* 2 mm. long, 5-celled, *setulose;* style glabrous, eglandular. *Capsule ovoid,* 4–6 mm. long, 4–5 mm. broad, *setulose, surrounded by the enlarged persistent calyx.*

This species was discovered by Fortune in 1843 in the Chusan Islands, south-east of Shanghai, and in Chekiang. Further gatherings by Henry, Wilson, Cavalerie, Forrest and other collectors show that it has a wide area of distribution extending from Chekiang, Anhwei, Hupeh, Kiangsi, Fokien, Taiwan to Kwangtung, Kweichow, mid-west Yunnan and north-east Upper Burma. It grows in woodlands, on cliffs, in thickets, in dense forests, and in mixed forests, at elevations of 175–2,745 m. (574–9,000 ft.). According to Wilson it is abundant in Kiangsi, 3–5 feet high. M. K. Li records it as being also abundant as a small tree in mixed forests in mid-west Yunnan.

It may be remarked that this species was originally described as *Azalea ovata* by Lindley in *Journ. Hort. Soc. London* I (1846) 149; it was later named *Rhododendron ovatum* by Maximowicz in *Rhod. As. Orient* (1870) 45.

In 1913 *R. bachii* Lévl. was described from a specimen (No. 2982) collected by Cavalerie in 1908 in Kweichow. It is identical with *R. ovatum* under which it will now be placed in synonymy.

The main features of *R. ovatum* are the small, ovate, ovate-elliptic or ovate-lanceolate leaves, the 1-flowered axillary inflorescence in the uppermost 1–3 leaves, the rotate somewhat flat, or almost bowl-shaped corolla, the 5 stamens, and the ovoid capsule. It is very closely related to *R. leptothrium;* the distinctions between them are discussed under the latter.

R. ovatum was first introduced by Fortune in 1844. It was introduced by Wilson in 1900 (No. 938), and in 1907 (Nos. 1391, 1690). It may be noted that the plant which was figured in the *Botanical Magazine* t. 5064 (1858) was raised from Fortune's seed as *Azalea ovata,* whilst Wilson's introduction is shown in t. 9375 (1934) as *R. bachii.* In cultivation the plant grows up to 5–6 feet high; in its native home it is a shrub or bush or tree 3–16 feet in height. Coming as it does from low elevations, the species is tender outdoors along the east coast and is suitable for a cool greenhouse; it succeeds outdoors along the west coast in Cornwall, and in the south. The plant is uncommon in cultivation.

Epithet. Egg-shaped.
Hardiness 1–3. May–June.

R. vialii Delavay et Franch. in Journ. de Bot. IX (1895) 398.

A shrub, 1.22–4.58 m. (4–15 ft.) high, *branchlets slender,* setulose-glandular or not setulose-glandular, rather densely minutely puberulous. *Leaves* evergreen, obovate, oblanceolate, lanceolate, oblong-lanceolate or oblong-elliptic, lamina 2.6–8 cm. long, 1.3–3.1 cm. broad, apex rounded or acute, slightly emarginate or often not emarginate, conspicuously mucronate, base cuneate or tapered or obtuse; upper surface bright green or dark green, glossy, glabrous, midrib grooved, rather densely minutely puberulous, primary veins 6–12 on each side, raised; margin entire; *under surface* pale green, *glabrous,* midrib prominent, glabrous, primary veins slightly raised or impressed; petiole 0.5–1.5 cm. long, slightly grooved above, not setulose-glandular or setulose-glandular, rather densely minutely puberulous. *Inflorescence axillary* in the uppermost 1–4 leaves, *1–2-flowered,* flower-bud scales persistent or deciduous during flowering, glabrous outside; rhachis 0.5–1 mm. long, minutely puberulous; *pedicel* 3–6 mm. long, *densely setulose-glandular,* glabrous. *Calyx* 5-lobed, 5–7 mm. long, crimson or pink, lobes oblong, oblong-oval or oval, outside not puberulous, setulose at the base, margin glabrous, glandular with short-stalked glands. *Corolla tubular, slightly widened towards the top,* 2.5–3.2 cm. long, *corolla-tube* 1.6–2.3 cm. long, *much longer than the lobes,* crimson or pink; lobes 5, 0.6–1 cm. long, 5–8 mm. broad, rounded, not emarginate. *Stamens 5,* unequal, 1.8–2.3 cm. long, as long as the corolla or shorter; *filaments glabrous. Gynoecium* 2.6–3.2 cm. long, longer than the corolla; *ovary* conoid, 1–2 mm. long, 5-celled, *setulose-glandular,* glabrous; style glabrous, eglandular. *Capsule*—

This plant was first collected by the Abbé Delavay in February 1891 near Kouangy, southern Yunnan. It was later found by Henry, Cavalerie, and C. W. Wang in other localities in south and west Yunnan. It grows in thickets and on rocks, at elevations of 1,220–1,830 m. (4,000–6,000 ft.). C. W. Wang records it as being abundant at Kwang-nan, west Yunnan.

R. vialii is a distinct species. The diagnostic features are the tubular corolla, 2.5–3.2 cm. long, the tube being much longer than the lobes, and the glabrous stamens. In these respects it is readily distinguished from all the other species in its Series. Another distinctive character is the densely setulose-glandular pedicels. The corolla is crimson or pink; crimson colour is absent in the other members of its Series.

R. vialii has not been introduced into cultivation. A plant which has been labelled *R. vialii* in cultivation, is in fact, *R. leptothrium*.

Epithet. After Père Paul Vial, French Missions in Yunnan.
Not in cultivation.

SEMIBARBATUM SERIES

General characters: shrub, 60 cm.–3 m. (2–10 ft.) high, *branchlets* rather densely or moderately *glandular with long-stalked glands. Leaves deciduous,* lamina thin, chartaceous, elliptic or ovate, 2–5 cm. long, 1–2.5 cm. broad, margin crenulate; under surface rather densely or moderately setulose; *petiole* densely pubescent, *setulose-glandular. Inflorescence 1-flowered, axillary* from lateral buds crowded at the ends of the branchlets, below the terminal bud which is a vegetative bud; flowers appear after the unfolding of the leaves; *pedicel* rather densely pubescent, *setulose-glandular.* Calyx 1–2 mm. long, margin setulose-glandular. Corolla rotate. *Stamens 5, very unequal, dimorphic. Ovary* densely *setulose-glandular. Capsule* ovoid or globose, *setulose-glandular.*

Distribution. Japan: Honshu, Shikoku and Kyushu.

This Series consists of one distinctive species. Its remarkable characters are the dimorphic stamens, the setulose-glandular features, the deciduous, thin, chartaceous leaves, the laminae with crenulate margins, and the rotate corolla. It shows a certain degree of affinity with the Ovatum Series.

DESCRIPTION OF THE SPECIES

R. semibarbatum Maxim in Bull. Acad. Sci. St. Pétersb., Vol. 15 (1870) 229.
    Syn. *Azalea semibarbata* (Maxim.) Kuntze, Rev. Gen. 2 (1891) 387.
        Azaleastrum semibarbatum (Maxim.) Makino, Bot. Mag. Tokyo 28 (1914) 338.
        Mumeazalea semibarbata Makino.
    Illustration. Bot. Mag. Vol. 152 t. 9147 (1928).
    An upright or bushy shrub, 60 cm.–3 m. (2–10 ft.) high; branches slender, spreading or ascending; *branchlets* rather densely or moderately pubescent, *glandular with long-*

stalked glands. Leaves deciduous, elliptic or ovate, *lamina thin, chartaceous,* 2–5 cm. long, 1–2.5 cm. broad, apex obtuse or sometimes acute, mucronate, base rounded or obtuse; upper surface dark green, glabrous or rarely hairy with long hairs, midrib grooved, rather densely or moderately pubescent, primary veins 6–10 on each side, deeply impressed; *margin crenulate,* setulose or esetulose; *under surface* pale green, *setulose* on the primary veins, eglandular, *midrib* prominent, rather densely pubescent, moderately or sparsely *setulose,* eglandular, primary veins slightly raised; *petiole* slender, 0.3–1.3 cm. long, slightly grooved above, densely pubescent, *setulose-glandular. Inflorescence 1-flowered, axillary* from lateral buds crowded at the ends of the branchlets, below the terminal bud which is a vegetative bud; flowers appear after the unfolding of the leaves, flower-bud scales persistent during flowering, glabrous outside; rhachis 0.5–1 mm. long, puberulous or glabrous; *pedicel* 3–6 mm. long, rather densely pubescent, *setulose-glandular. Calyx* 5-lobed, *1–2 mm. long,* lobes ovate or oblong-oval, outside puberulous or glabrous, *margin setulose-glandular. Corolla rotate,* with a short tube and spreading lobes, 1.5–2 cm. across, white, white flushed pink, or yellowish-white, with red spots at the base of the lobes, tube 4–6 mm. long; lobes 5, 5–6 mm. long, 4–6 mm. broad, rounded or obovate. *Stamens 5, very unequal, dimorphic,* exserted, *the lower* (= anterior) *3 stamens spreading* (curved) *up to 1 cm. long,* about as long as the corolla-lobes, filaments not puberulous or sparsely puberulous at the base, their *anthers oblong* up to over 1.5 mm. long; *the 2 upper* (= posterior) stamens *about half as long as the other three,* filaments 4 mm. long, densely pilose all along except at the base and the tips, *their anthers much smaller, globose-ovoid,* 0.5 mm. long. *Gynoecium* about 1 cm. long; *ovary* ovate or globose, 1 mm. long, 5-celled, not hairy, *densely setulose-glandular;* style glabrous, eglandular. *Capsule* ovoid or globose, 3–4 mm. long, 3–4 mm. broad, not hairy, *setulose-glandular,* calyx-lobes persistent.

Tschonoski, Maximowicz's Japanese collector, discovered this species in Japan. It was described by Maximowicz in 1870. The plant grows in thickets and woods on the mountains in Honshu, Shikoku and Kyushu.

R. semibarbatum is a distinctive species. A unique feature is the 5 dimorphic stamens; the anterior 3 stamens are long, glabrous or sparsely puberulous at the base with long oblong anthers, whilst the posterior 2 stamens are short, about half as long as the other 3, densely pilose, with much smaller globose-ovoid anthers. Another diagnostic character is the deciduous, thin, chartaceous leaf, the lamina with crenulate margins. Other remarkable features are the setulose-glandular branchlets, petioles, pedicels, calyx-margin, ovaries and capsules, the small calyx 1–2 mm. long, and the rotate corolla.

The plant was first introduced by Tschonoski who sent seeds to the Botanic Garden at St. Petersburg, where it flowered in a greenhouse in 1870. The species was reintroduced by Wilson in 1914 by means of seeds (No. 7733) sent to the Arnold Arboretum, U.S.A., and thence it arrived in Britain. The plant varies in hardiness; it is rare in cultivation.

Epithet. Partially bearded.

Hardiness 3. June.

STAMINEUM SERIES

General characters: small, medium-sized and large shrubs or trees, 92 cm.–13 m. (3–43 ft.) high, branchlets not bristly or sometimes bristly, eglandular or sometimes rather densely or moderately bristly-glandular. Leaves evergreen, elliptic-lanceolate, oblong-lanceolate, elliptic, oblong-elliptic, oblong-obovate, oblong, oblanceolate or lanceolate, lamina 3.4–18.5 cm. long, 1.2–6.3 cm. broad, apex acutely acuminate or acuminate; petiole 0.4–2.4 cm. long, glabrous, not bristly or sometimes bristly, eglandular or sometimes bristly-glandular. *Inflorescence axillary in the uppermost 1–3 leaves* (or rarely axillary and terminal), *1–8-flowered*; pedicel 0.6–3.8 cm. long, not bristly or sometimes moderately or densely bristly, eglandular or sometimes moderately or densely bristly-glandular. *Calyx* 5-lobed, *minute, 0.5–1 mm. long,* outside and margin eglandular or sometimes densely or moderately bristly-glandular. *Corolla tubular-funnel-shaped. 2.5–7.8 cm. long,* white, white flushed rose or pink, pink, rose, rose-red, purplish-rose, deep rose-magenta, lilac or rose-violet, with or without a yellow, pale green or green blotch at the base, and sometimes with deeper spots; lobes 5. Stamens 10, rarely 8, 11 or 13. Gynoecium 2.5–6 cm. long; *ovary slender,* 0.4–1.1 cm. long, 5–6-celled, glabrous or sometimes densely tomentose, not bristly or sometimes densely or moderately bristly, eglandular or sometimes densely or moderately bristly-glandular. *Capsule slender or sometimes oblong,* 2–6.5 cm. long, 0.2–1 cm. broad, glabrous or sometimes moderately or densely hairy, not bristly or sometimes bristly, not bristly-glandular or sometimes bristly-glandular.

Distribution. Burma, south-east and east Tibet, west and east Sichuan, Kweichow, Hupeh, Hunan, Kwangsi, Kwangtung, Hong Kong, Kiangsi, Anhwei, Chekiang, Fukien, Taiwan, Thailand, and Japan.

This Series consists of small, medium-sized and large shrubs or trees. A diagnostic feature of importance is the 1–8-flowered axillary inflorescence in the uppermost 1–3 leaves. Other distinctive characteristics are the tubular-funnel-shaped corolla 2.5–7.8 cm. long, the minute calyx 0.5–1 mm. long, and the slender corolla. The Series is closely allied to the Ovatum Series.

KEY TO THE SPECIES

A. Stamens and gynoecium much longer than the corolla.
    B. Pedicel, ovary and capsule glabrous.
        C. Midrib on the under surface of the leaves, and petiole not bristly. . . . . . .
        . . . . *stamineum*
        C. Midrib on the under surface of the leaves moderately or sparsely bristly;
          petiole moderately or sparsely bristly or not bristly . . . . *feddei*
    B. Pedicel, ovary and capsule densely or moderately hairy . . . . *cavaleriei*
A. Stamens shorter than the corolla; gynoecium usually as long as the corolla or
  shorter.
    D. Pedicel not bristly, not bristly-glandular.
        E. Ovary and capsule glabrous.
          F. Corolla 2.5–2.6 cm. long; leaves (laminae) 3.4–5.8 cm. long, 1.2–1.8
            cm. broad, lanceolate . . . . *esquirolii*
          F. Corolla 2.8–6.5 cm. long; leaves (laminae) usually 6–16.5 cm. long,
            usually 2–6.3 cm. broad, elliptic, obovate-elliptic, elliptic-
            lanceolate, oblong-lanceolate, oblanceolate or lanceolate.
            G. Each inflorescence 2–8-flowered.
              H. Corolla 2.8–3 cm. long; pedicel 0.6–1.1 cm long; stamens
                2–2.3 cm. long; gynoecium 2.5–2.6 cm. long . . . .
                . . . . *siamense*
              H. Corolla 3.5–6 cm. long; pedicel 1.1–3.2 cm. long;
                stamens 3–5.4 cm. long; gynoecium 3.5–5.7 cm. long.
                I. Margin of the leaves ciliate (bristly) . . . *pectinatum*
                I. Margin of the leaves not ciliate (not bristly).
                  J. Inflorescence 2–8-flowered; corolla 3.5–6 cm.
                    long; rhachis of the inflorescence 2–6 mm.
                    long; flower-bud scales usually densely or
                    moderately minutely puberulous outside. . .
                    . . . . *moulmainense*
                J. Inflorescence 2–3-flowered; corolla usually 5–
                    6 cm. long; rhachis of the inflorescence 1
                    mm. long; flower-bud scales glabrous
                    outside . . . . *ellipticum*
                                         (part)
            G. Each inflorescence usually 1-flowered.
              K. Flower-bud scales densely or rarely moderately
                minutely puberulous outside. . . . . *mackenzianum*
              K. Flower-bud scales glabrous outside.
                L. Corolla usually 5–6 cm. long; gynoecium 4.8–5.7
                  cm. long; stamens 3.2–5.4 cm. long. . . *ellipticum*
                                     (part)
                L. Corolla 3.5–4.3 cm. long; gynoecium 2.8–3.8 cm.
                  long; stamens 1.6–3.8 cm. long.
                  M. Leaves elliptic, elliptic-lanceolate or ovate-
                    lanceolate, 2–4.8 cm. broad; margin of the
                    flower-bud scales eglandular, densely or
                    moderately minutely puberulous . . . .
                    . . . . *wilsonae*
                M. Leaves oblanceolate or lanceolate, 1.9–2.9 cm.
                  broad; margin of the flower-bud scales
                  usually densely glandular with minute
                  glands, usually not puberulous. . . . .
                  . . . . *latoucheae*

E. Ovary densely tomentose; capsule moderately hairy.
    N. Under surface of the leaves and midrib esetulose; branchlets and petioles not bristly; pedicel esetulose; corolla 5–7.8 cm. long, white with a yellow blotch at the base; stamens 3.8–5.3 cm. long; gynoecium 5–5.9 cm. long . . . . *hancockii*
    N. Under surface of the leaves and midrib setulose; branchlets and petioles bristly; pedicel sparsely setulose; corolla 3–3.9 cm. long, violet; stamens 2–3 cm. long; gynoecium 2.8–3.3 cm. long . . .
    . . . . *tutcherae*
    (part)
D. Pedicel moderately or densely bristly, moderately or densely bristly-glandular.
    O. Branchlets and petioles bristly or moderately or rather densely bristly-glandular; under surface of the leaves and midrib bristly.
        P. Margin of the leaves (laminae) not bristly; inflorescence 1–2-flowered; calyx minute, 0.5 mm. long, lobes triangular or ovate, outside and margin not bristly-glandular; corolla 3–3.9 cm. long; stamens 2–3 cm. long; gynoecium 2.8–3.3 cm. long . . . .
        . . . . *tutcherae*
        (part)
        P. Margin of the leaves (laminae) rather densely bristly; inflorescence 2–6-flowered; calyx 0.3–1.3 cm. long, lobes lanceolate or linear, outside densely or moderately bristly-glandular, margin densely bristly-glandular; corolla 4.3–5.6 cm. long; stamens 3.5–5 cm. long; gynoecium 4.2–5.6 cm. long . . . . *championae*
    O. Branchlets and petioles not bristly, usually not bristly-glandular; under surface of the leaves and midrib not bristly.
        Q. Leaves (laminae) 4.8–9.5 cm. long; corolla pale lilac, rose or pink; ovary densely setulose or esetulose; shrub, 4–5.50 m. (13–18 ft.) high. Kwantung species. . . . . *henryi*
        Q. Leaves 10–14 cm. long; corolla white; ovary esetulose; tree, about 10 m. (33 ft.) high. Thailand species. . . . . *taiense*

DESCRIPTION OF THE SPECIES

R. cavaleriei Lévl. in Flore de Kouy-Tcheou (1914–15) 152.
    Syn *R. albicaule* Lévl. in Fedde Repert. XIII (1914) 148.
    A shrub or tree, 1.83–4 m. (6–13 ft.) high, branchlets slender, glabrous, eglandular, those below the inflorescences 2–3 mm. in diameter; leaf-bud scales deciduous. *Leaves* evergreen, oblanceolate, lanceolate or rarely elliptic-lanceolate, lamina 5.8–10 cm. long, 1.6–3.3 cm. or rarely 3.8 cm. broad, apex acutely acuminate, base tapered; upper surface green, glabrous, eglandular, midrib grooved, glabrous, eglandular, primary veins 12–14 on each side, deeply impressed; margin slightly recurved or flat; *under surface* pale green, *glabrous*, eglandular, midrib prominent, glabrous, eglandular, primary veins slightly raised; petiole 0.6–1.2 cm. long, grooved above, glabrous, eglandular. *Inflorescence axillary in the uppermost 1–3 leaves*, umbellate, *2–4-flowered*, flower-bud scales deciduous; rhachis 1–2 mm. long, glabrous, eglandular; *pedicel 1.9–2.5 cm. long, densely or moderately hairy*, eglandular. *Calyx* 5-lobed, minute, 0.5 mm. long, lobes triangular or ovate, outside and margin hairy or glabrous, eglandular. *Corolla narrowly tubular-funnel-shaped, 2.6–3 cm. long*, rose or white; lobes 5, small, 1.3–2 cm. long, *narrow 4–7 mm. broad*, oblong, entire. *Stamens* 10, unequal, 3–3.8 cm. long, *much longer than the corolla; filaments densely or moderately pubescent towards the lower half* or towards the base. *Gynoecium 3.5–4*

cm. long, *much longer than the corolla*, longer than the stamens; *ovary* slender, tapering into the style, 4 mm. long, 6-celled, *densely hairy, eglandular*; style glabrous, eglandular. *Capsule* slender, 3–3.8 cm. long, 4 mm. broad, ribbed, beaked by the lower end of the style, curved, *hairy*, eglandular, calyx persistent.

This species was first collected by P. J. Cavalerie in May 1899 in Kweichow. It was found by him again later in 1903 at Pin-fa in the same region. In 1933 W. T. Tsang collected it in Kwangsi. It grows in open forests, and is recorded as being fairly common in Kwangsi.

R. cavalerie is closely allied to *R. stamineum* which it resembles in general appearance, but differs in that the pedicel, ovary and capsule are densely hairy, and the stamens are usually pubescent in the lower half. Other characteristic features are the narrowly tubular-funnel-shaped corolla, and the long stamens and gynoecium, much longer than the corolla.

The plant has not been introduced into cultivation.

Epithet. After P. J. Cavalerie, b. 1869, a French collector in China.

Not in cultivation.

R. championae W. J. Hooker in Bot. Mag. Vol. 77 t. 4609 (1851). Also Illustration.

A broadly upright shrub or tree, 2.44–6 m. (8–20 ft.) high, *branchlets* moderately or sparsely *bristly, rather densely or moderately bristly-glandular*, those below the inflorescences 3–4 mm. in diameter; leaf-bud scales deciduous. *Leaves* evergreen, oblong, elliptic-lanceolate, oblong-lanceolate or lanceolate, lamina coriaceous, 7.8–18.5 cm. long, 2.3–6.2 cm. broad, apex acuminate or acutely acuminate, base rounded or obtuse; upper surface dark green, matt, bristly or not bristly, not bristly-glandular, midrib grooved, not bristly, eglandular, primary veins 14–20 on each side, deeply impressed; *margin* flat or slightly recurved, *rather densely bristly*, not bristly-glandular; *under surface* pale green, pubescent or not pubescent, *bristly, bristly-glandular* or not bristly-glandular, midrib raised, pubescent or not pubescent, moderately or rarely rather densely bristly, bristly-glandular or not bristly-glandular, primary veins raised; *petiole* 0.8–2.4 cm. long, grooved above, moderately or rather densely pubescent or not pubescent, *bristly* or not bristly, *moderately or rather densely bristly-glandular. Inflorescence axillary in the uppermost 1–3 leaves*, shortly racemose, *2–6-flowered*, flower-bud elongate, apex acuminate, flower-bud scales deciduous or persistent, outside and margin densely puberulous; rhachis 2–4 mm. long, pubescent or glabrous, eglandular; *pedicel* 1.5–3 cm. long, *moderately or densely bristly, densely or moderately bristly-glandular. Calyx* 5- or rarely 4-lobed, *0.3–1.3 cm. long*, lobes lanceolate or linear, *outside* not bristly, *densely or moderately bristly-glandular, margin bristly* or not bristly, *densely bristly-glandular. Corolla* tubular-funnel-shaped, 4.3–5.6 cm. long, pink, rose or white, with or without a yellow blotch at the base, and with or without ochre spots; lobes 5, large, 2.6–3.8 cm. long, 1.3–3.6 cm. broad, oblong or oblong-oval. *Stamens* 10, 4.8–5.4 cm. long, shorter than the corolla; filaments pubescent on the lower half or at the base. *Gynoecium* 4.2–5.6 cm. long, as long as the corolla or shorter, longer than the stamens; *ovary* slender, tapering into the style, 5 mm. long, 5–6-celled, *densely or moderately bristly, densely or moderately bristly-glandular*; style bristly at the base or not bristly, bristly-glandular at the base or not bristly-glandular. *Capsule* slender or oblong, 2.5–4 cm. long, 4–6 mm. broad, ribbed, beaked by the lower end of the style, straight or slightly curved, *bristly, bristly-glandular*, calyx-lobes persistent.

This plant was discovered by Captain and Mrs. Champion in April 1849, growing abundantly among rocks in a ravine at Fort Victoria, Hong Kong. Subsequently it was found by other collectors in the same region and in Kwangtung, Kwangsi, Fukien, Chekiang and Kiangsi. It grows among rocks, in ravines, in woods and in thickets, at elevations of up to 185 m. (607 ft.).

R. championae is a distinctive species and cannot be mistaken for any species of its

16. R. championae.
nat. size.

a. flower. b. capsule. c. bud. d. stamen. e. ovary, style.
f. calyx. g. leaf (lower surface).

17. R. championae.
nat. size.

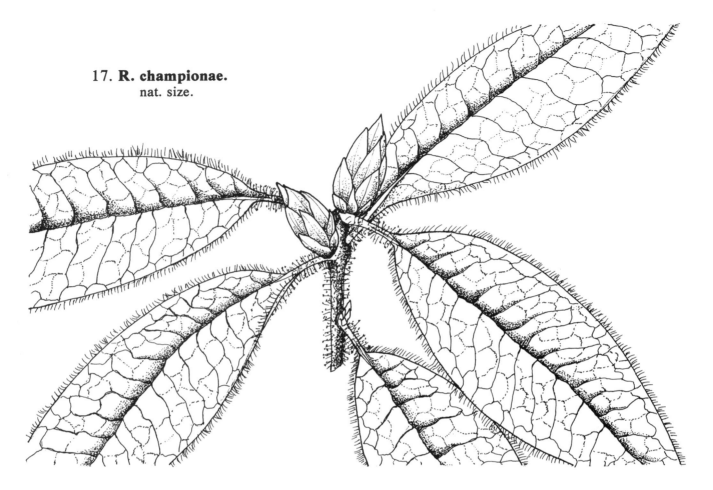

Series. The diagnostic features are the densely or moderately bristly and bristly-glandular branchlets, petioles, margins and lower surfaces of the leaves, pedicels, calyx, ovaries, and capsules. It is somewhat related to *R. henryi* but differs in well-marked characters.

The species was first introduced in 1881 from Hong Kong. It flowered for the first time at Kew in 1888. It is a tender plant and will grow outdoors only in well-sheltered gardens in mild areas along the west coast. The species has proved somewhat hardy in Cornwall. It is rare in cultivation.

Epithet. After Mrs. Champion, the wife of its discoverer, J. G. Champion, 1815–1854.

Hardiness 1–2. April–May.

R. ellipticum Maxim. in Bull. Acad. Petersb. XXXII (1888) 497.
   Syn. *R. leiopodum* Hayata, Ic. Plant Formos. III t. 24 (1913) 136.
      R. leptosanthum Hayata, Ic. Plant Formos. III (1913) 137.
A shrub up to 4.58 m. (15 ft.) high, branchlets slender, eglandular, those below the inflorescences 2–3 mm. in diameter; leaf-bud scales deciduous. *Leaves* evergreen, oblong-lanceolate or lanceolate, lamina coriaceous, 7.5–10.5 cm. long, 1.7–3.8 cm. broad, apex acutely acuminate, *base* tapered or obtuse, *decurrent on the petiole;* upper surface green, glabrous, eglandular, midrib grooved, glabrous, eglandular, primary veins 12–15 on each side, deeply impressed; margin slightly recurved or flat; *under surface* pale green, *glabrous, eglandular,* midrib prominent, glabrous, eglandular, primary

veins slightly raised; *petiole 1–2 cm. long*, grooved above, *narrowly winged on both sides, glabrous, eglandular. Inflorescence axillary in the uppermost 1–3 leaves*, umbellate, *1–3-flowered*, flower-bud elongate, apex acuminate, *flower-bud scales* deciduous or persistent, *outside glabrous, margin densely puberulous*; rhachis 1 mm. long, glabrous, eglandular; *pedicel 1.5–3 cm. long, glabrous, eglandular. Calyx* 5-lobed, minute, 0.5 mm. long, lobes triangular or ovate, *outside and margin glabrous, eglandular. Corolla* tubular-funnel-shaped, *5–6 cm.* or rarely 4.5 cm. *long*, pink or white; lobes 5, large 3–3.5 cm. long, 1.7–2.5 cm. broad, rounded, entire. *Stamens* 10 or rarely 8, 3.2–5.4 cm. long, shorter than the corolla; filaments rather densely puberulous towards the base. *Gynoecium 4.8–5.7 cm. long*, as long as the corolla or slightly shorter, longer than the stamens; *ovary* slender, apex truncate, 0.6–1 cm. long, 5–6-celled, *glabrous, eglandular*; style glabrous, eglandular. *Capsule* slender, 3–4 cm. long, 4–5 mm. broad, ribbed, beaked or not beaked by the lower end of the style, straight, *glabrous, eglandular*, calyx persistent.

This species was described by Maximowicz in 1888. Its area of distribution extends from Taiwan, South China to Japan, growing in forests, along streams, and on gravelly slopes in mixed forests, at elevations of 30–2,500 m. (98–8,197 ft.)

R. ellipticum is very closely allied to *R. moulmainense*, but differs in that the corolla is larger, usually 5–6 cm. long, the rhachis of the inflorescence is shorter, 1 mm. long, and the flower-bud scales are glabrous outside. It is also closely related to *R. latoucheae* to which it shows a strong resemblance in general features, but is distinguished by the larger corolla usually 5–6 cm. long, by the longer gynoecium 4.8–5.7 cm. long, and by the densely puberulous margin of the flower-bud scales.

The species was first introduced to California, U.S.A. from Taiwan, about 1969. In cultivation it is tender along the east coast, but should succeed in sheltered gardens on the west coast.

Epithet. Elliptic.
Hardiness 1–2. April–May.

R. esquirolii Lévl. in Fedde Repert. Vol. 12 (1913) 102.
  Syn. *R. vaniotii* Lévl. in Fedde Repert. Vol. 13 (1914) 148.
A shrub, 1 m. (3⅓ ft.) high, branchlets slender, glabrous, eglandular, those below the inflorescences 1–2 mm. in diameter; leaf-bud scales deciduous. *Leaves* evergreen, *lanceolate, lamina* coriaceous, *3.4–5.8 cm. long, 1.2–1.8 cm. broad*, apex acutely acuminate, base tapered or obtuse; upper surface green, glabrous, eglandular, midrib grooved, glabrous, eglandular, primary veins 10–15 on each side, deeply impressed; margin slightly recurved; *under surface* pale green, *glabrous, eglandular*, midrib prominent, glabrous, eglandular, primary veins slightly raised; petiole 4–6 mm. long, grooved above, glabrous, eglandular. *Inflorescence* axillary in the uppermost 1–3 leaves, umbellate or shortly racemose, *1–2-flowered*, flower-bud elongate, apex acuminate, *flower-bud scales* persistent, *outside* shining, *glabrous*, margin densely minutely puberulous or glabrous; rhachis 1–2 mm. long, glabrous, eglandular; *pedicel 1.4–1.6 cm. long*, glabrous, eglandular. *Calyx* 5-lobed, minute, 0.5 mm. long, lobes triangular or ovate, outside and margin glabrous, eglandular. *Corolla* tubular-funnel-shaped, *2.5–2.6 cm. long*, rose-violet; lobes 5, 1.4–1.5 cm. long, 0.9–1.3 cm. broad, rounded or oblong-oval, entire. *Stamens* 10, unequal, 1.5–2 cm. long, shorter than the corolla; filaments puberulous towards the base. *Gynoecium* 2.6–3.3 cm. long, as long as the corolla or slightly shorter or longer, longer than the stamens; *ovary very slender*, apex truncate, 5–7 mm. long, 5-celled, glabrous, eglandular; style glabrous, eglandular. *Capsule*:—

R. esquirolii was described by Leveillé in 1913 from a specimen collected by Cavalerie at Gan-chouen, Yunnan.

The diagnostic features of the species are the small lanceolate leaves, laminae 3.4–5.8 cm. long, 1.2–1.8 cm. broad, and the small corolla, 2.5–2.6 cm. long. In these respects it is readily distinguished from its near ally *R. moulmainense.*

The species has not been introduced into cultivation.

Epithet. After J. H. Esquirol, b. 1870, French missionary in China.

Not in cultivation.

R. feddei Lévl. in Fedde Repert. Vol. 12 (1913) 102.

A shrub or tree, 1–4 m. (3⅓–13 ft.) high, branchlets glabrous, eglandular, those below the inflorescences 3–4 mm. in diameter; leaf-bud scales deciduous. *Leaves* evergreen, lanceolate or oblanceolate, lamina coriaceous, 7.3–12.6 cm. long, 2–3.2 cm. broad, apex acutely acuminate, base tapered; upper surface green, matt, glabrous, eglandular, midrib grooved, glabrous, eglandular, primary veins 12–18 on each side, deeply impressed; margin slightly recurved; *under surface* pale green, *glabrous, eglandular, midrib* prominent, *moderately or sparsely bristly,* eglandular, primary veins slightly raised; *petiole* 1–1.3 cm. long, grooved above, *moderately or sparsely bristly* or not bristly, eglandular. *Inflorescence* axillary in the uppermost 1–3 leaves, shortly racemose, 2–5-flowered, flower-bud scales deciduous; rhachis 2–3 mm. long, glabrous, eglandular; pedicel 1.6–2.3 cm. long, glabrous, eglandular. *Calyx* 5-lobed, minute, 0.5–1 mm. long, lobes triangular or ovate, outside glabrous, eglandular, margin eciliate or ciliate, eglandular. *Corolla narrowly tubular-funnel-shaped,* 2.5–3 cm. long, white; lobes 5, small 1–1.6 cm. long, narrow 4–8 mm. broad, oblong, entire. *Stamens* 10, unequal, 3.2–4.3 cm. long, *much longer than the corolla;* filaments moderately or densely puberulous towards the lower one-third of their length. *Gynoecium* 4–5 cm. long, *much longer than the corolla,* longer than the stamens, *ovary* slender, tapering into the style, 5–6 mm. long, 6-celled, *glabrous, eglandular;* style glabrous, eglandular. *Capsule* slender, 2.5–3.4 cm. long, 2–3 mm. broad, ribbed, beaked by the lower end of the style, straight or slightly curved, glabrous, eglandular, calyx persistent.

This plant was first collected by J. Cavalerie in June 1903 at Pin-fa, Kweichow. It was afterwards found by him again and by Y. Tsiang in the same region, growing on the high mountains and on open hillsides.

R. feddei is very similar to *R. stamineum* in the shape and size of the leaves, in the shape, size and colour of the corolla, in the inflorescence, and in the long stamens and gynoecium, much longer than the corolla, but differs in that the midrib on the lower surface of the leaves is moderately or sparsely bristly, and the petiole is often bristly.

There is no record of the plant in cultivation.

Epithet. After F. Fedde, d. 1942, a German botanist.

Not in cultivation.

R. hancockii Hemsl. in Kew Bull. (1895) 107.

Illustration. Hemsl. in Hook. Icon. Plant., t. 2381 (1895).

A shrub or tree, 92 cm.–4.58 m. (3–15 ft) high, branchlets glabrous, eglandular, those below the inflorescences 2–4 mm. in diameter; leaf-bud scales deciduous. *Leaves evergreen, oblanceolate, elliptic-lanceolate, oblong-obovate, obovate, elliptic or oblong-lanceolate, lamina* coriaceous, 8.5–13.5 cm. long, 2.8–5 cm. broad, apex acuminate, base tapered or obtuse, decurrent on the petiole; upper surface green, glabrous, eglandular, midrib grooved, glabrous, eglandular, primary veins 12–23 on each side, deeply impressed; margin slightly recurved or flat; *under surface* pale green, *glabrous, eglandular,* midrib prominent, glabrous, eglandular, primary veins slightly raised; petiole 1–1.3 cm. long, grooved above, narrowly winged on both sides or not winged, glabrous or rarely sparsely setulose, eglandular. *Inflorescence axillary in the uppermost 1–3 leaves,* umbellate, *1-flowered,* flower-bud elongate, apex acuminate, flower-bud scales persistent or deciduous, outside glabrous or densely puberulous, margin densely or moderately puberulous, densely or moderately glandular with minute glands or eglandular; rhachis 1–2 mm. long, glabrous or puberulous, eglandular; pedicel 1.2–2.6 cm. long, glabrous or hairy, eglandular. *Calyx* 5-lobed, minute, 0.5 mm. long, lobes ovate or triangular, outside and margin glabrous or hairy, eglandular. *Corolla* tubular-funnel-shaped, *5–7.8 cm. long*, white, with a yellow blotch at the base, or sometimes pink; lobes 5, large, 4–4.3 cm. long, 2.6–3.4 cm. broad, rounded, entire. *Stamens* 10, unequal, 3.8–5.3 cm. long, shorter than the corolla; filaments densely pubescent towards the lower half or one-third of their length. *Gynoecium* 5–5.9 cm. long, as long as the corolla or shorter, longer than the stamens; *ovary* slender, tapering into the style, 6–7 mm. long, 5–6-celled, *densely tomentose*, eglandular; style glabrous or hairy at the base. *Capsule* oblong or slender, 4.6–6.5 cm. long: 0.9–1 cm. broad, ribbed, beaked by the lower end of the style, curved, *hairy*, eglandular, calyx persistent.

This species was described by Hemsley in 1895 from a specimen collected by Hancock in a mountain valley in Mengtse, southern Yunnan. It was later found by A. Henry, Tsai, Yang and others in the same region and in south-east Yunnan, also in Kwangsi. It grows in woods, in mixed forest, in pine forest, and on open slopes, at elevations of 1,500–2,000 m. (4,918–6,557 ft.).

The main features of the species are the obovate, oblong-obovate, elliptic to oblong-lanceolate leaves, laminae up to 13.5 cm. long and up to 5 cm. broad, the axillary 1-flowered inflorescence in the upper 1–3 leaves, the large corolla 5–7.8 cm. long, the densely tomentose ovary and the moderately hairy capsule.

R. hancockii is closely related to *R. ellipticum* which it resembles in general features, but is readily distinguished by the densely tomentose ovary, the moderately hairy capsule, and often by the 1-flowered inflorescence.

The plant has not been introduced into cultivation.

Epithet. After W. Hancock, 1847–1914, Chinese Imp. Customs.

Not in cultivation.

R. henryi Hance in Journ. Bot. Vol. 19 (1881) 243.

Syn. *R. dunnii* Wils. in Journ. Arnold Arboretum, Vol. VI No. 3 (1925) 170.

A shrub, 4–5.50 m. (13–18 ft) high, branchlets slender, glabrous or rarely minutely puberulous, eglandular or rarely sparsely setulose-glandular, those below the inflorescences 2–3 mm. in diameter; leaf-bud scales deciduous. *Leaves* evergreen, lanceolate, oblong-lanceolate, oblanceolate, elliptic-lanceolate or obovate-lanceolate, lamina coriaceous, 4.8–9.5 cm. long, 1.5–3.1 cm. or rarely 4.1 cm. broad, apex acuminate, base tapered or obtuse, decurrent on the petiole; upper surface green, glabrous, eglandular, midrib grooved, glabrous, eglandular, primary veins 10–15 on each side, deeply impressed; margin slightly recurved or flat, bristly or not bristly; *under surface* pale green, *glabrous*, not setulose, eglandular, midrib prominent, glabrous, not bristly, eglandular, primary veins slightly raised; petiole 0.8–1.3 cm. long, grooved above, narrowly winged on both sides or not winged, glabrous or rarely minutely puberulous, not bristly, eglandular or rarely setulose-glandular. *Inflorescence axillary* in the uppermost 1–3 leaves, shortly racemose, *3–5- or rarely 2-flowered, flower-bud oblong-oval*, flower-bud scales deciduous or persistent, outside glabrous, margin densely puberulous; rhachis 2–3 mm. long, glabrous, eglandular; *pedicel* 1.4–1.8 cm. long, *moderately or rather densely bristly or bristly-glandular*. *Calyx* 5-lobed, minute, 0.5–1 mm. long, lobes ovate or triangular, outside glabrous, eglandular, margin glabrous or rarely densely minutely puberulous, eglandular or rarely setulose-glandular. *Corolla widely tubular-funnel-shaped* with short tube, 3.8–5 cm. long, pale lilac, rose or pink; *lobes 5, large* 2.3–3.4 cm. long, 1.6–2 cm. broad, oblong-oval, entire. *Stamens* 10, unequal, 3.1–4.5 cm. long, shorter than the corolla; filaments moderately or densely pubescent towards the lower one-third of their length. *Gynoecium* 3.5–4.7 cm. long, as long as the corolla or shorter, longer than the stamens; *ovary* slender, tapering into the style, 5–6 mm. long, 5–6-celled, *densely setulose or esetulose*, eglandular; style glabrous, eglandular. *Capsule* slender, 4–6 cm. long, 3–6 mm. broad, ribbed, beaked by the lower end of the style, straight or slightly curved, esetulose or setulose, eglandular, calyx persistent.

B. C. Henry discovered this species in March 1881 at Tsing-ün North River near Canton, Kwangtung. Subsequently it was found by other collectors in the same region and in Kwangsi, Hunan, Fukien, Kiangsi and Chekiang. It grows in woods and forests at elevations of 300–800 m. (984–2,623 ft.).

R. henryi is related to *R. hancockii* to which it bears a certain degree of resemblance, but differs in that the pedicels are moderately or rather densely bristly or bristly-glandular, the inflorescence is 3–5- or rarely 2-flowered, the corolla is usually smaller 3.8–5 cm. long, the gynoecium is shorter 3.5–4.7 cm. long, and the ovary is densely setulose or esetulose.

There is no record of the plant in cultivation.

Epithet. After Rev. B. C. Henry, discoverer of the species.

Not in cultivation.

R. latoucheae Franch. in Bull. Soc. Bot. France, Vol. XLVI (1899) 210.

A shrub or tree, 1–3 m. (3⅓–10 ft.) high, branchlets slender, glabrous, eglandular, those below the inflorescences 2 mm. in diameter; leaf-bud scales deciduous or persistent. *Leaves* evergreen, *oblanceolate or lanceolate*, lamina coriaceous, 5.5–9.3 cm. long, 1.9–2.9 cm. broad, apex acutely acuminate, base tapered or obtuse; upper surface green, glabrous, eglandular, midrib grooved, glabrous, eglandular, primary veins 12–15 on each side, deeply impressed; margin slightly recurved or flat; under surface pale green, glabrous, eglandular, midrib prominent, glabrous, eglandular, primary veins slightly raised; petiole 0.5–1.1 cm. long, grooved above, tomentose with a thin, whitish tomentum or glabrous, eglandular. *Inflorescence axillary* in the uppermost 1–3 leaves, umbellate, *1-flowered*, flower-bud elongate, apex acuminate, *flower-bud scales* persistent, *outside glabrous, margin glabrous* or rarely densely minutely puberulous, *densely glandular with minute glands* or rarely eglandular; rhachis 1–2 mm. long, glabrous, eglandular; pedicel 1.5–3 cm. long, glabrous, eglandular. *Calyx* 5-lobed, minute, 0.5–1 mm. long, lobes triangular or ovate, outside and margin glabrous, eglandular. *Corolla widely tubular-funnel-shaped* with short tube, 3.5–4.3 cm. long, pink or purplish; lobes 5, large 2.3–3 cm. long, 1.5–2.5 cm. broad, rounded, emarginate. *Stamens* 10, unequal, 1.6–3.8 cm. long, shorter than the corolla; filaments densely pubescent towards the base. *Gynoecium* 3.4–3.8 cm. long, as long as the corolla or slightly longer, longer than the stamens; ovary slender, apex truncate, 7–8 mm. long, 5–6-celled, glabrous, eglandular; style glabrous, eglandular. *Capsule* slender, 2.5–3.4 cm. long, 3 mm. broad, ribbed, beaked by the lower end of the style, straight or slightly curved, glabrous, eglandular.

This plant was discovered by Madame de la Touche in 1898 in Fukien, and was described by Franchet in 1899. It was afterwards found by other collectors in the same region and in Kwangtung, Chekiang and Kiangsi. It grows in thickets, forests, and in hilly areas, at elevations of 150–600 m. (492–1,967 ft.).

R. latoucheae is closely allied to *R. wilsonae* which it resembles in general appearance, but differs in that the leaves are oblanceolate or lanceolate, and the margins of the flower-bud scales are usually glabrous and densely minutely glandular.

The plant has not been introduced into cultivation.

Epithet. After Madame de la Touche, collector in Fukien.

Not in cultivation.

R. mackenzianum G. Forrest in Notes Roy. Bot. Gard. Edin., Vol. 12 (1920) 132.

A shrub or tree, 1.53–12.20 m. (5–40 ft) or rarely 15.25 m. (50 ft.) high; stem and branches with smooth, brown, flaking bark; branchlets slender, glabrous, eglandular, those below the inflorescences 2–3 mm. in diameter; leaf-bud scales deciduous. *Leaves* evergreen, lanceolate, oblong-lanceolate or rarely elliptic-lanceolate, lamina coriaceous, 7.5–13.2 cm. long, 2–3.8 cm. or rarely 4.6 cm. broad, apex acutely acuminate, base tapered or obtuse; upper surface olive-green, shining, glabrous, eglandular, midrib grooved, glabrous, eglandular, primary veins 12–20 on each side, deeply impressed; margin flat or slightly recurved; under surface pale green, glabrous, eglandular, midrib prominent, glabrous, eglandular, primary veins slightly raised; petiole 0.8–1.8 cm. long, grooved above, glabrous, eglandular. *Inflorescence axillary* in the uppermost 1–3 leaves, umbellate or shortly racemose, *1- or sometimes 2-flowered*, flower-bud scales persistent, outside densely or rarely moderately minutely puberulous, margin densely minutely puberulous; rhachis 1–3 mm. long, puberulous or glabrous, eglandular; *pedicel* 1.8–2.8 cm. long, *glabrous, eglandular. Calyx* 5-lobed, minute, 0.5–1 mm. long, lobes triangular or ovate, outside and margin glabrous, eglandular. *Corolla tubular-funnel-shaped,* 4.4–6.5 cm. long, fragrant, white, white flushed rose, purplish-rose, purplish-pink, lilac-pink or deep rose-magenta, with a green or greenish-yellow or yellow blotch at the base; *lobes 5, large,* 2.4–3.5 cm. long, 2.1–2.7 cm. broad, rounded, entire. *Stamens* 10, unequal, 2.5–4.3 cm. long, shorter than the corolla; filaments puberulous on the lower half or one-third of their length. *Gynoecium* 4–6 cm. long, as long as the corolla or slightly shorter, longer than the stamens; *ovary* slender, apex truncate or tapering into the style, 0.6–1.1 cm. long, 5-celled, *glabrous, eglandular;* style glabrous, eglandular. *Capsule* 2.5–4.5 cm. long, 3–4 mm. broad, ribbed, beaked by the lower end of the style or rarely not beaked, straight or curved, glabrous, eglandular, calyx persistent.

This plant was first collected by Forrest in April 1918 in the Shweli-Salwin Divide, west Yunnan. It was afterwards found by other collectors in the same region, and in south-west, mid-west and north-west Yunnan, north-east Upper Burma, south-east Tibet, and Kwangsi. It grows in mixed forests, in pine forest, in mixed evergreen and deciduous forest, and in thickets, at elevations of 1,617–3,050 m. (5,300–10,000 ft.).

R. mackenzianum varies considerably in habit and height of growth. It is a shrub or tree 5–40 feet high. In 1949 Kingdon-Ward found an enormous plant of this species, growing as a tree 50 feet or more in height, at 6,000 feet, on the Mishmi Hills in Assam.

The species is very closely allied to *R. moulmainense* which it resembles in general appearance, but is readily distinguished usually by the one-flowered inflorescence.

It was first introduced simultaneously in 1919 by Forrest, Nos. 17819, 17832, and by Farrer, No. 801. It was reintroduced by Forrest on two other occasions. Kingdon-Ward sent seeds under Nos. 9275, 18540. In cultivation the species is tender along the east coast and requires greenhouse protection; it is fairly hardy along the west coast in well-sheltered gardens in mild areas. It is free-flowering, and is a charming plant where it can be grown.

Epithet. After Miss McKenzie of Rangoon.

Hardiness 1–2. April–May.

R. moulmainense W. J. Hooker in Bot. Mag. Vol. 82 t. 4904 (1856). Also Illustration.

Syn. *R. westlandii* Hemsl. in Journ. Linn. Soc. Vol. 24 (1889) 31.

R. oxyphyllum Franch. in Journ. de Bot. Vol. 12 (1898) 264.

R. leucobotrys Ridley in Journ. Fed. Mal. Stat. Mus. Vol. 4 (1909) 43.

R. klossii Ridley in Journ. Fed. Mal. Stat. Mus. Vol. 4 (1909) 43.

R. nematocalyx Balf. f. et W. W. Sm. in Notes Roy. Bot. Gard. Edin., Vol. 10 (1917) 124.

R. stenaulum Balf. f. et W. W. Sm. in Notes Roy. Bot. Gard. Edin., Vol. 10 (1917) 157.

Illustration. Bot. Mag. Vol. 164 t. 9656 (1944), as *R. stenaulum.*

A shrub or tree, 1.53–12.20 m. (5–40 ft.), rarely 92 cm.–1.22 m. (3–4 ft.) high, branchlets slender, glabrous, eglandular, those below the inflorescences 2–3 mm. in diameter; leaf-bud scales deciduous. *Leaves* evergreen, elliptic-lanceolate, oblong-lanceolate, elliptic, oblanceolate or lanceolate, lamina coriaceous, 5–16.5 cm. long, 1.7–6.3 cm. broad, apex acutely acuminate or rarely acuminate, base cuneate, tapered or obtuse; upper surface green or olive-green, somewhat shining or matt, glabrous, eglandular, midrib grooved, glabrous, eglandular, primary veins 9–20 on each side, deeply impressed; margin flat or slightly recurved; under surface pale green, glabrous, eglandular, midrib prominent, glabrous, eglandular, primary veins slightly raised; petiole 0.8–2 cm. long, not winged or slightly winged at the margins, grooved above, glabrous, eglandular. *Inflorescence axillary* in the uppermost 1–3 leaves, shortly racemose or umbellate, *2–8-flowered,* flower-bud scales deciduous or persistent, outside densely or sometimes moderately minutely puberulous or sometimes glabrous, margin densely minutely puberulous or sometimes glabrous; rhachis 2–6 mm. long, glabrous or densely or moderately puberulous, eglandular; *pedicel* 1.1–3.2 cm. long, *glabrous, eglandular. Calyx* 5-lobed, minute, 0.5–1 mm. long, lobes triangular or ovate, outside and margin glabrous, eglandular. *Corolla* tubular-funnel-shaped, 3.8–6 cm., rarely 3.5 cm. long, fragrant, white, white flushed yellow or pink, pink, rose, rose-red, purplish-rose or lilac, with or without a yellow or pale green blotch at the base; lobes 5, large, 2.1–4 cm. long, 1.6–2.8 cm. broad, rounded, entire. *Stamens* 10 or rarely 8, unequal, 3–4.5 cm. long, *shorter than the corolla;* filaments moderately or rather densely puberulous on the lower half or one-third or rarely glabrous. *Gynoecium* 3.5–5.3 cm. long, *as long as the corolla or slightly shorter,* longer than the stamens; *ovary* slender, tapering into the style, 4–8 mm. long, 5–6-celled, *glabrous, eglandular;* style glabrous, eglandular. *Capsule* slender, 2.5–5 cm. long, 2–7 mm. broad, ribbed, beaked by the lower end of the style, straight or curved, glabrous, eglandular, calyx persistent.

R. *moulmainense* was discovered by Thomas Lobb at Moulmein, on the Gerai Mountains, Burma, and was described by Hooker in 1856. Further gatherings show that the species has a large area of distribution, which extends from Burma, south-east and east Tibet, north-west, west and north-east Yunnan, Kweichow to Kwangsi and Thailand. It grows in thickets, on open hillsides, amongst scrub, on bouldery slopes, on cliffs, in open forests, pine forests, mixed forests, and in open deciduous forests, at elevations of 400–3,660 m. (1,311–12,000 ft.). Kingdon-Ward records it as being common on granite slopes in shady situations in north-east Yunnan, and on the foothills in north-east Upper Burma. According to other collectors it is also common in woods in Kweichow, and abundant in thickets in Kwangsi.

In 1889 the name R. *westlandii* Hemsl. was given to a plant from Kwangtung, Lantao island near Hong Kong. Moreover, in 1898 R. *oxyphyllum* Franch. was described from a specimen collected by Henri d'Orléans in 1895, and in 1917 R. *stenaulum* Balf. f. et W. W. Sm. was founded on Forrest's specimen No. 5530 collected in west Yunnan. The ample material now available shows that in height of growth, in the shape and size of the leaves, in the inflorescence, in the shape, size and colour of the flowers, and in all other morphological details, R. *westlandii,* R. *oxyphyllum* and R. *stenaulum* are identical with R. *moulmainense* under which they will now be placed in synonymy. R. *leucobotrys* Ridley, R. *klossii* Ridley, and R. *nematocalyx* Balf. f. et W. W. Sm. are also synonymous with R. *moulmainense.*

R. *moulmainense* is very variable in general features due to the various environmental conditions in which it is found. It is a shrub or tree, and grows from 3 to 40 feet high; the leaves are elliptic-lanceolate, elliptic, oblong-lanceolate or lanceolate, the laminae are 6–16.5 cm. long, 2.2–6.3 cm. broad, the corolla is 3.5–6 cm. long, and the capsule is 2.5–5 cm. long. The species is very closely related to R. *mackenzianum* but is readily distinguished by the 2–8-flowered inflorescence.

The plant was first introduced by Thomas Lobb, and it was first flowered by Messrs. Veitch of the Exeter and Chelsea Nurseries in their greenhouse in January 1856. Subsequently Forrest sent seeds under Nos. 5530—the Type number of R. *stenaulum,* 7673,

15756, 15998, 25849, 26047. The species was introduced by Kingdon-Ward in 1922 (Nos. 5425, 20679), by Yü in 1938 (No. 21047), and by Valder in December 1974–January 1975 (Nos. I 12, I 42A). As the plant has been introduced from low elevations of 5,902–8,000 feet, in cultivation it is tender along the east coast and is suitable for a cool greenhouse; along the west coast it succeeds in mild areas in well-sheltered gardens. It is worth noting that Forrest collected a plant of *R. moulmainense* (No. 20876) growing as a shrub of 12–20 feet at 11,000–12,000 feet in the Salwin-Kiu Chiang Divide, eastern Tibet. Unfortunately it has not been introduced into cultivation; otherwise, as it grows at a high elevation, it could have proved hardy outdoors along the east coast. The species flowers freely and provides a fine display with its white tubular-funnel-shaped flowers in axillary trusses of 2–8.

It was given an Award of Merit when shown simultaneously by L. de Rothschild, Exbury, and the Earl of Stair, Stranraer, in 1937.

Epithet. From Moulmein, Burma.
Hardiness 1–2. April–May.

R. pectinatum Hutch. in Gard. Chron. Vol. 101 (1937) 119.

A slender shrub or tree, 4–5 m. (13–16 ft.) high, branchlets glabrous. *Leaves* evergreen, subcoriaceous, elliptic or oblong-elliptic, 12–15 cm. long, 4.5–6 cm. broad, apex broadly acuminate, base acute; upper surface green, primary veins about 6 on each side, inconspicuous; *margin pectinate-ciliate;* petiole 2 cm. long, grooved above, glabrous. *Inflorescence axillary, 2–3-flowered, flower-bud scales glabrous outside,* margin minutely ciliolate; pedicel 2–3 cm. long, glabrous. *Calyx* slightly lobulate rim, occasionally long, green lobes. *Corolla* narrowly funnel-shaped, 5–5.5 cm. long, scented, glabrous, white, the dorsal lobe rich cream-yellow towards the base; lobes oblong-lanceolate, about 3 cm. long. *Stamens* 10–11, shorter than the corolla; filaments very slender, pubescent in the middle third. *Ovary* elongated and narrowly oblong, *glabrous;* style a little longer than the corolla, glabrous. *Capsule:—*

R. *pectinatum* was described by Hutchinson in 1937 from a cultivated plant grown under glass by Lionel de Rothschild at Exbury, under Forrest's seed No. 26022. It should be noted that Forrest's herbarium specimen under this number is in fruit, and is labelled *R. stamineum;* the margin of the leaves is not ciliate, and the specimen does not agree with the original description of *R. pectinatum.* This specimen was collected by Forrest in November 1924 in mid-west Yunnan.

The diagnostic feature of *R. pectinatum* is the ciliate margin of the leaves. In this respect it bears a resemblance to *R. championae.* It is also closely related to *R. moulmainense* but differs in the ciliate margin of the leaves, and usually in the flower-bud scales which are glabrous outside. *R. pectinatum* would appear to be a natural hybrid.

The plant is now possibly lost to cultivation.

It received an Award of Merit when exhibited by Lionel de Rothschild, Exbury, in 1935.

Epithet. Toothed like a comb.
Hardiness 1. April.

R. siamense Diels in Fedde Repert. IV (1907) 289.

A tree, branchlets slender, glabrous, eglandular, those below the inflorescences 2 mm. in diameter; leaf-bud scales deciduous. *Leaves* evergreen, elliptic-lanceolate or oblong-lanceolate, lamina coriaceous, 7–11 cm. long, 2.5–4.2 cm. broad, apex acuminate, base obtuse; upper surface green, somewhat shining, glabrous, eglandular, midrib grooved, glabrous, eglandular, primary veins 10–15 on each side, deeply impressed; margin flat; under surface pale green, glabrous, eglandular, midrib prominent, glabrous, eglandular, primary veins slightly raised; petiole 1–1.2 cm. long, not winged, grooved above, glabrous, eglandular. *Inflorescence axillary* in the uppermost 1–3 leaves, shortly racemose, *2–3-flowered*, flower-bud scales deciduous or persistent, outside minutely puberulous or glabrous, margin densely minutely puberulous; rhachis 1–3 mm. long, glabrous or puberulous, eglandular; *pedicel 0.6–1.1 cm. long*, glabrous, eglandular. *Calyx* 5-lobed, minute, 0.5 mm. long, lobes triangular or ovate (or rarely ligulate 3 mm. long), outside and margin glabrous, eglandular. *Corolla narrowly tubular-funnel-shaped, 2.8–3 cm. long*, white; lobes 5, small 1.4–1.5 cm. long, narrow 0.8–1 cm. broad, rounded, entire. *Stamens* 10, unequal, 2–2.3 cm. long, shorter than the corolla; filaments rather densely puberulous on the lower one-third or one-half. *Gynoecium 2.5–2.6 cm. long*, slightly shorter than the corolla, longer than the stamens; ovary slender, tapering into the style, 5 mm. long, 6-celled, glabrous, eglandular; style glabrous, eglandular. *Capsule:—*

This plant was first collected by Dr. C. C. Hosseus in March 1905 at Doi-Sutep, Thailand. It was afterwards found by Dr. A. F. G. Kerr in the same area, and is recorded as being common in evergreen jungle at 900–1,350 m. (2,951–4,426 ft.).

R. siamense is closely allied to *R. moulmainense* which it resembles in general appearance but is distinguished by the smaller corolla 2.8–3 cm. long which is narrowly tubular-funnel-shaped, by the shorter stamens and gynoecium, and usually by the shorter pedicels.

There is no record of the plant in cultivation.

Epithet. From Siam (Thailand).

Not in cultivation.

R. stamineum Franch. in Bull. Soc. Bot. France, Vol. XXXIII (1886) 236.
    Syn. *R. pittosporifolium* Hemsl. in Journ. Linn. Soc. Bot. XXVI (1889) 29.
        R. cavaleriei Lévl. var. *chaffanjonii* Lévl. in Bull. Soc. Agric. Sci. Arts Sarthe, 39: (1903) 49.
        R. chaffanjonii Lévl. MSS.
Illustration. Bot. Mag. Vol. 141 t. 8601 (1915).

A shrub or tree, 1–10 m. (3⅓–33 ft.) high, branchlets slender, glabrous, eglandular, those below the inflorescences 2–3 mm. in diameter; leaf-bud scales deciduous. *Leaves* evergreen, lanceolate, oblanceolate, obovate-lanceolate, elliptic-lanceolate or oblong-lanceolate, lamina coriaceous, 6–11 cm. long, 2–4.5 cm. broad, apex acutely acuminate, base tapered or obtuse; upper surface green, glabrous, eglandular, midrib grooved, glabrous, eglandular, primary veins 12–18 on each side, deeply impressed; margin slightly recurved or flat; under surface pale green, glabrous, eglandular, midrib prominent, glabrous, eglandular, primary veins slightly raised; petiole 0.8–1.5 cm. long, grooved above, glabrous, eglandular. *Inflorescence axillary in the uppermost 1–3 leaves*, shortly racemose, 2–8-flowered, flower-bud scales deciduous or persistent, outside glabrous or rarely densely minutely puberulous, margin densely minutely puberulous; rhachis 2–5 mm. long, glabrous or rarely hairy, eglandular; pedicel 2–3.8 cm. long, glabrous, eglandular. *Calyx* 5-lobed, minute, 0.5 mm. long, lobes triangular or ovate (or rarely ligulate 3 mm. long), outside and margin glabrous, eglandular. *Corolla narrowly tubular-funnel-shaped, 2.5–3.7 cm. long*, fragrant, white or rose, with a yellow blotch at the base; lobes 5, small 1.3–2 cm. long, *narrow 0.4–1 cm. broad*, oblong or sometimes oblong-oval, entire. *Stamens* 10 or rarely 13, 3.5–4.9 cm. long, unequal, *much longer than the corolla;* filaments moderately or sparsely puberulous at the base or up to one-half their length. *Gynoecium* 4–6 cm. long, *much longer than the corolla*, longer than the stamens; ovary slender, tapering into the style or apex truncate, 4–6 mm. long, 6-celled, glabrous, eglandular; style glabrous, eglandular. *Capsule* slender, 2–4.8 cm. long, 3–5 mm. broad, ribbed, beaked by the lower end of the style, straight or curved, glabrous, eglandular, calyx persistent.

R. stamineum was discovered by the Abbé Delavay in 1882 in north-east Yunnan,

near the border with Sichuan. Subsequently it was found by various collectors in the
same region and in western and eastern Sichuan, Hupeh, Kweichow, Hunan, Anhwei,
and Kwangsi. The plant grows in woods, forests, thickets, and in rocky shady ravines, at
elevations of 366–2,135 m. (1,200–7,000 ft.). It is recorded as being common in Anhwei
at 1,200 feet.

The diagnostic features of the plant are the long stamens and the long style, much
longer than the corolla. In these respects the species is readily distinguished from all the
other species of its Series except *R. cavaleriei* and *R. feddei*. Another distinctive feature is
the relatively small narrowly tubular-funnel-shaped corolla, 2.5–3.7 cm. long.

R. stamineum is closely allied to *R. cavaleriei* and *R. feddei*. The distinctions between
them are discussed under the latter two species.

It was first introduced by Wilson in 1900 (No. 887) when collecting seeds in Hupeh
for Messrs. Veitch. In 1908 he sent seeds (No. 567) during his first expedition for the
Arnold Arboretum, and in 1910 (No. 4268) from Sichuan during his second expedition for the same Arboretum. The species first flowered in cultivation in 1914 raised by
J. C. Williams at Caerhays, Cornwall, from Wilson's seed collected in 1900. In its native
home it is a shrub or tree, and grows from 3 to 33 feet high; in cultivation it is a shrub and
reaches up to about 10 feet. Coming as it does from low elevations of 1,200–7,000 feet, it
is tender along the east coast and in gardens inland and is suitable for a cool greenhouse; along the west coast it is somewhat hardy in mild areas in well-sheltered
gardens.

A form with white flowers and a yellow blotch at the base, grown in a cool greenhouse, was given an Award of Merit when shown by the Crown Estate Commissioners,
Windsor Great Park, in 1971.

Epithet. With prominent stamens.

Hardiness 1–2. April–May.

R. taiense Hutch. in Kew Bull. Misc. Inform. No. 1 (1938) 24.

A tree, about 10 m. (33 ft.) high, branchlets glabrous; leaf-bud scales glabrous
outside, margin shortly ciliate. *Leaves* evergreen, oblong-oblanceolate, *10–14 cm. long*,
3–3.5 cm. broad, glabrous, apex acutely acuminate, base acute, lateral veins about 10 on
each side; petiole 1.5 cm. long, grooved above. *Inflorescence* terminal, about 4-flowered,
flower-bud scales early deciduous; *pedicel* 1.5 cm. long, *glandular-pilose. Calyx* undulately lobed, short, glabrous. *Corolla* funnel-shaped, 4 cm. long, glabrous, *white*; lobes 5,
2 cm. long, oblong-elliptic. *Stamens* a little shorter than the corolla; filaments a little
pilose. *Ovary glabrous*; style as long as the corolla, glabrous. *Capsule*:—

R. taiense is represented by a single gathering by A. F. G. Kerr No. 15512 Holotype. It
was found in evergreen forest in Nakawn Sritamarat Province, Kao Luang, Thailand, at
an elevation of about 1,400 m. (4,590 ft.), and was described by Hutchinson in 1938.

It is closely related to *R. henryi* but differs in that the leaves are longer, usually
broader, and the corolla is white. Moreover, it differs in its geographical distribution.

The plant has not been introduced into cultivation.

Epithet. From Tai (the Siamese name for Siam).

Not in cultivation.

R. tutcherae Hemsl. et Wils. in Kew Bull. (1910) 117.

A tree, 12–13 m. (39–43 ft.) high, branchlets slender, *bristly* or not bristly, eglandular,
those below the inflorescences 2 mm. in diameter; leaf-bud scales deciduous. *Leaves*
evergreen, lanceolate or oblanceolate, lamina coriaceous, 7.3–14 cm. long, 1.5–3 cm.
broad, apex acutely acuminate, base tapered; upper surface green, glabrous,
eglandular, midrib grooved, glabrous, eglandular, primary veins 15–18 on each side,
deeply impressed; margin flat or slightly recurved, not bristly; *under surface* pale green,
setulose, eglandular, *midrib* prominent, *bristly*, eglandular, primary veins slightly raised;

petiole 0.8–1 cm. long, grooved above, *bristly,* eglandular. *Inflorescence* axillary in the uppermost 1–3 leaves and terminal, umbellate, *1–2-flowered,* flower-bud scales deciduous; rhachis glabrous or hairy, eglandular; *pedicel* 1.1–1.7 cm. long, elongating in fruit to 2 cm. long, *sparsely setulose,* eglandular. *Calyx* 5-lobed, minute, 0.5 mm. long, lobes triangular or ovate, outside and margin glabrous or hairy, eglandular. *Corolla* tubular-funnel-shaped, *3–3.9 cm. long, violet;* lobes 5, somewhat large, 2.2–2.8 cm. long, 1–1.4 cm. broad, oblong-elliptic or rounded, entire, (apex with or without a tuft of white hairs). *Stamens* 10, unequal, 2–3 cm. long, shorter than the corolla; filaments densely pubescent towards the lower one-third of their length. *Gynoecium* 2.8–3.3 cm. long, as long as the corolla or shorter, longer than the stamens; *ovary* slender, tapering into the style or apex truncate, 5–6 mm. long, 5-celled, *densely tomentose* with brown tomentum, eglandular; style glabrous, eglandular. *Capsule* slender, 2.5–3 cm. long, 3–4 mm. broad, ribbed, beaked or not beaked, curved, hairy, eglandular, calyx persistent.

This species was first collected by A. Henry about 1898 on the mountains south of Mengtze, south Yunnan, and was described by Hemsley and Wilson in 1910. In 1962 it was found by C. A. Wu in south-east Yunnan. It grows in forests at elevations of 1,750–2,000 m. (5,738–6,557 ft.), and is recorded as being frequent in south-east Yunnan.

R. tutcherae is allied to *R. hancockii* which it resembles in some respects, but differs in that the lower surface of the leaves and midrib, the branchlets, petioles and pedicels are setulose, the corolla is smaller 3–3.9 cm. long, violet, and the stamens and gynoecium are shorter. It also shows a certain degree of affinity with *R. championae,* but the latter is a rather densely bristly and bristly-glandular species.

There is no record of the species in cultivation.

Epithet. After Mrs. Tutcher, wife of W. J. Tutcher, Hong Kong B.G.

Not in cultivation.

R. wilsonae Hemsl. et Wils. in Kew Bull. (1910) 116.

A shrub or tree, 1–7 m. (3⅓–23 ft.) high, branchlets slender, glabrous, eglandular, those below the inflorescences 2 mm. in diameter; leaf-bud scales deciduous. *Leaves* evergreen, *elliptic, elliptic-lanceolate or ovate-lanceolate,* lamina coriaceous, 5–10 cm. long, 2–4.8 cm. broad, apex acuminate or acutely acuminate, base obtuse or cuneate; upper surface green, reticulate, shining, glabrous, eglandular, midrib grooved, glabrous, eglandular, primary veins 12–14 on each side, deeply impressed; margin flat or slightly recurved; under surface pale green, glabrous, eglandular, midrib prominent, glabrous, eglandular, primary veins slightly raised; petiole 0.8–1.2 cm. long, grooved above, glabrous, eglandular. *Inflorescence axillary* in the uppermost 1–3 leaves and terminal, umbellate, *1-flowered, flower-bud* elongate, apex acuminate, *flower-bud scales* persistent, *outside glabrous,* margin densely or moderately minutely puberulous; rhachis 1–2 mm. long, glabrous, eglandular; pedicel 1.6–2 cm. long, glabrous, eglandular. *Calyx* 5-lobed, minute, 0.5 mm. long, lobes triangular or ovate, outside and margin glabrous, eglandular. *Corolla widely tubular-funnel-shaped, 3.5–3.6 cm. long, tube short, lobes nearly three times as long as the tube,* fragrant, pink or purple, with or without deeper spots; lobes 5, 2.5–2.8 cm. long, 1.5–1.6 cm. broad, oblong-oval entire. *Stamens* 10, unequal, 1.6–2.5 cm. long, shorter than the corolla; filaments puberulous at the base or on the lower half. *Gynoecium* 2.8–3.6 cm. long, as long as the corolla or shorter, longer than the stamens; ovary slender, tapering into the style, 7 mm. long, 5-celled, glabrous, eglandular; style glabrous, eglandular. *Capsule* slender, 2.3–4.5 cm. long, 3–5 mm. broad, ribbed, beaked by the lower end of the style, curved or straight, glabrous, eglandular, calyx persistent.

Wilson discovered this species in 1900 in west Hupeh. Later in 1930, Y. Tsiang collected it at Van-ching-shan, in Kweichow. It is found in woods and in densely shaded ravines, at elevations of 400–2,000 m. (1,311–6,557 ft.). According to Y. Tsiang it is common as a small tree growing in woods at 1,475 feet in Kweichow. Wilson records it as being one of the most beautiful and distinct rhododendrons.

The distinctive features of R. *wilsonae* are the elliptic, elliptic-lanceolate or ovate-lanceolate leaves, the one-flowered inflorescence, and the relatively small corolla 3.5–3.6 cm. long, with a short tube, the lobes being nearly three times as long as the tube. The species bears a certain degree of resemblance to R. *mackenzianum* in general features, but is distinguished by the smaller corolla, usually by the shape of the leaves, and by the flower-bud scales glabrous outside.

R. *wilsonae* was first introduced by Wilson in 1900 (No. 317—the Type number), and again in the same year (No. 886) when collecting for Messrs. Veitch. It first flowered in 1912 at Caerhays, Cornwall. In its native home it is a shrub or tree, 3–23 feet high; in cultivation it grows up to about 8 feet. Along the east coast the species is tender and is suitable for a cool greenhouse, but a few plants have proved fairly hardy outdoors and have somewhat survived the cold winters; along the west coast and in the south, it succeeds outdoors in sheltered gardens and makes a fine show with its pink or purple flowers.

It received an Award of Merit (plant grown in the greenhouse) when exhibited by the Crown Estate Commissioners, Windsor Great Park, in 1971.

Epithet. After Mrs. Wilson, d. 1931, wife of E. H. Wilson.

Hardiness 1–2. April–May.

CAMTSCHATICUM

CAMTSCHATICUM SERIES

General characters: *low or prostrate shrubs,* 10–30 cm. (4 in.–1 ft.) high, young branchlets pubescent or glabrous, glandular with long-stalked glands or eglandular. *Leaves deciduous,* short-petioled or sessile, obovate, oval, ovate, oblong-obovate or spathulate-obovate, lamina thin, chartaceous, 0.5–5 cm. long, 0.3–1.8 cm. or sometimes up to 2.5 cm. broad; upper surface not setulose (rarely setulose), primary veins 2–3 on each side, ascending; margin crenulate, bristly or setulose-glandular; under surface with prominent midrib which is bristly or setulose-glandular, primary veins conspicuous, ascending at a narrow angle, bristly or setulose-glandular; petiole short 1–2 mm. long or absent. *Inflorescence 1–2 or rarely 3-flowered produced at the ends of the young leafy shoots and not in special buds;* pedicel 1–2.5 cm. long, bearing leafy bracts. Calyx 5-lobed, 0.5–1.8 cm. long, outside and margin bristly-glandular. *Corolla rotate,* 1.5–2.5 cm. long, *tube on the lower side split to the base or nearly so,* carmine-purple, rose-purple, reddish-purple, pink or rarely white. Stamens 10, unequal. Ovary ovate or ovoid, 2 mm. long, 5-celled, densely pubescent, style pubescent at the base or sometimes in the lower half. Capsule oblong-ovoid or oval, 0.7–1 cm. long, pubescent.

Distribution. Kamtschatka, Manchuria, the Aleutian Islands, Alaska, southward to Saghalien, the Kurile Islands, and northern Japan.

This is a small distinct Series of three species. The main diagnostic features of importance are the low or prostrate habit of growth, the 1–2- or rarely 3-flowered inflorescence produced at the ends of the young leafy shoots and not in special buds, and the rotate corolla with the tube on the lower side split to the base or nearly so.

KEY TO THE SPECIES

A. Corolla moderately or rather densely pubescent outside; margins and under surface of the leaves bristly, not setulose-glandular (rarely margins setulose-glandular) . . . . *camtschaticum*
A. Corolla glabrous outside; margins and under surface of the leaves not bristly, only setulose-glandular.
    B. Corolla-lobes longer than the tube; corolla 1.8–2.3 cm. long, lobes 1.2–1.8 cm. long; calyx 8 mm.–1 cm. long; leaves 8 mm.–1 cm. broad . . . *glandulosum*
    B. Corolla-lobes as long as, or shorter than, the tube; corolla about 1.5 cm. long, lobes 6 mm. long; calyx 5 mm. long; leaves 3–6 mm. broad . . . *redowskianum*

DESCRIPTION OF THE SPECIES

R. camtschaticum Pallas in Fl. Ross. Vol. I t. 33 (1784) 48.
    Syn. *Rhodothamnus camtschaticus* (Pallas) Lindley, Paxton's Flower Garden 1 : t. 22 (1853).
    Therorhodion camtschaticum (Pall.) Small, N. Amer. Fl. 29 (1) : 45 (1914).
    R. camtschaticum Pallas var. *pallasianum* Komar. in Flora Peninsul. Kamtsch. II (1929) 360.
    Illustration. Bot. Mag. Vol. 134 t. 8210 (1908).

A low growing or prostrate or cushion shrub, 10–30 cm. (4 in.–1 ft.) high, with procumbent or upright branches, and spreads by means of underground suckers; young branchlets pubescent and hairy with very long hairs, glandular with very long-stalked glands or eglandular. *Leaves deciduous, short-petioled or sessile,* obovate, oblong-obovate or spathulate-obovate, *lamina thin, chartaceous,* 1.6–5 cm. long, 0.8–1.8 cm. or sometimes up to 2.5 cm. broad, apex rounded or obtuse, mucronate, base tapered or cuneate, decurrent on the petiole, or obtuse not decurrent; upper surface dark green or bright green or olive-green, not setulose or rarely setulose, midrib slightly raised, pubescent, primary veins 2–3 on each side, slightly raised, ascending; *margin crenulate, bristly* or rarely setulose-glandular; under surface pale green, *midrib* prominent, *bristly, primary veins conspicuous,* ascending at a narrow angle, *bristly,* not glandular; petiole short, 1–2 mm. long or absent, flat above, with a narrow wing on each side, bristly. *Inflorescence 1–2 or rarely 3-flowered produced at the ends of the young leafy shoots and not in special buds; pedicel* 1–2.5 cm. long, moderately or rather densely pubescent, glandular with very long-stalked glands, and *bearing leafy bracts,* margins setulose-glandular. *Calyx* 5-lobed, green, *large, 1–1.8 cm. long,* lobes oblong, strongly nerved, outside and margin bristly-glandular. *Corolla rotate,* 1.8–2.5 cm. long, *tube on the lower (anterior) side split to the base or nearly so,* one-third as long as the lobes, carmine-purple, rose-purple, reddish-purple or pink, spotted within, *outside moderately or rather densely pubescent;* lobes 5, 1.6–2 cm. long, 0.5–1.1 cm. broad, oblong, oblong-oval or obovate, apex rounded. *Stamens* 10, unequal, purple-red, 0.8–1.9 cm. long, shorter than the corolla; filaments densely pubescent at the base. *Gynoecium* 1.8–2.3 cm. long, as long as the corolla or slightly longer; ovary ovate or ovoid, 2 mm. long, 5-celled, densely pubescent, eglandular; style purplish-red, pubescent at the base, eglandular. *Capsule* oblong-ovoid, 0.5–1 cm. long, pubescent.

R. camtschaticum was discovered by Pallas in Kamtschatka, along the shores of the sea of Okhotsk, and it was described by him in 1784. It has a wide area of distribution and extends from Kamtschatka, the Aleutian Islands, Alaska, southward to Saghalien, the Kurile Islands, and northern Japan. According to Pallas, it occurs in muddy mountainous places; it also grows in rock crevices, on the top of hills, in gravelly loam, in dry

18. **R. camtschaticum.**
nat. size.

a. young growth, flower-bud, flower. b. capsule. c. stamens. d. ovary, style. e. calyx.
f. petals. g. leaf (upper surface). h. leaf (lower surface).

rocky tundra, in boggy places, and in the alpine zone of forest regions.

The distinctive features of this species are the 1–2- or rarely 3-flowered inflorescence, produced at the ends of the young leafy shoots and not in special buds, the pedicels bearing leafy bracts, and the rotate corolla with the tube on the lower (anterior) side split to the base or nearly so. Other characteristics are the deciduous, thin, chartaceous leaves, short-petioled or sessile, and the large oblong calyx.

R. camtschaticum was first introduced in 1799. Although reintroduced many times, it is still uncommon in cultivation. It is very difficult in the south of England. The plant does not tolerate high summer temperatures and dryness at the roots. It requires cold gardens along the east coast, and cool, moist conditions about the roots in summer. The species flourishes in several gardens in Scotland, and succeeds admirably in the Royal Botanic Garden, Edinburgh. Two distinct growth forms occur in cultivation: Form 1. A compact cushion plant, up to 6 inches high and as much or more across. Form 2. A low growing plant a few inches high with procumbent branches. The species is a slow grower and spreads by means of underground suckers. It varies in its freedom of flowering; some plants are shy flowerers and hardly produce more than a few flowers every year, whilst other plants make a fine show with a profusion of flowers. Two colour forms are grown in gardens: 1. Reddish-purple. 2. Pink. The germination from seed is sometimes up to 8–10 per cent.

The species was given an Award of Merit when shown by G. Reuthe, Keston, Kent, as *Rhodothamnus kamtschaticus* in 1908.

Epithet. From Kamtschatka.

Hardiness 3. May–June.

R. camtschaticum Pallas var. **albiflorum** Koidzumi in Tokyo Botanical Magazine, Vol. XXXI (1917) 34.

    Syn. *Therorhodion camtschaticum* (Pall.) Small f. *albiflorum* Nakai in Trees & Shrubs Jap. I (1922) 31.

The variety differs from the species in its white flowers.

It was described by G. Koidzumi in 1917 from a plant growing on Mt. Nutakkamshipe, Yezo, Japan. Within recent years it was also found on Kodiak Island, Alaska. The plant is rare in cultivation.

Epithet. With white flowers.

Hardiness 3. May–June.

R. glandulosum (Standley ex Small) Millais Rhod. (1917) 173.

    Syn. *Therorhodion glandulosum* Standley in N. Amer. Flora Vol. XXIX (1914) 45.

        R. camtschaticum Pallas subsp. *glandulosum* (Standley ex Small) Hult. Fl. Kamtschatka 4 (1930) 15.

A low shrub forming dense clumps about 10 cm. (4 in.) high, copiously branched, *young branchlets glabrous*, sparsely glandular with long-stalked glands or eglandular. *Leaves* deciduous, short-petioled or sessile, spathulate, oval, ovate, obovate or oblong-obovate, lamina thin, chartaceous, 0.8–2 cm. long, 0.8–1 cm. broad, apex rounded, obtuse or acute, mucronate, base tapered or cuneate, decurrent on the petiole, or obtuse not decurrent; upper surface dark green or bright green, somewhat shining, not setulose, midrib slightly raised, pubescent, primary veins 2–3 on each side, slightly raised, ascending; *margin crenulate, setulose-glandular, not bristly; under surface* pale green, midrib prominent, *setulose-glandular, not bristly,* primary veins conspicuous, ascending at a narrow angle, *setulose-glandular, not bristly*; petiole short, 1–2 mm. long or absent, flat above, with a narrow wing on each side, *setulose-glandular, not bristly. Inflorescence* 1-flowered produced at the ends of the young leafy shoots and not in special buds; pedicel 1–2 cm. long, glabrous, rather densely setulose-glandular, and bearing leafy bracts, margins setulose-glandular. *Calyx* 5-lobed, large, 0.8–1 cm. long, lobes oblong, lanceolate or rarely oblong-elliptic, strongly nerved, outside and margin setulose-glandular. *Corolla* rotate, 1.8–2.3 cm. long, tube on the lower (anterior) side split to the base or nearly so, one-third as long as the lobes, rose-purple, *outside glabrous;* lobes 5, 1.2–1.8 cm. long, 0.5–1.1 cm. broad, oblong or oblong-oval, apex rounded. *Stamens* 10, unequal, purple-red, 0.8–1.8 cm. long, shorter than the corolla; filaments densely pubescent at the base. *Gynoecium* 1.8–2 cm. long, as long as the corolla or slightly shorter; ovary ovate, 2 mm. long, 5-celled, densely pubescent, eglandular; style purple-red, rather densely pubescent at the base, eglandular. *Capsule* oval, 7–9 mm. long, pubescent with short white hairs.

This species is known from a single collection (No. 1725) made by F. A. Walpole, on August 4, 1901, at the foot of Kigluaik Mountains, near Oogluk Bay, Imuruk Basin, in the vicinity of Port Clarence, Alaska.

R. glandulosum is very similar to *R. camtschaticum* in general appearance, but differs in that the corolla is glabrous outside, the lower surface and margins of the leaves, and the petiole are setulose-glandular, the young branchlets are not pubescent, not hairy, and the calyx is often smaller.

The plant has not been introduced into cultivation.

Epithet. Glandular.

Not in cultivation.

R. redowskianum Maxim. in Prim. Fl. Amur. (1859) 189.

Syn. *Therorhodion redowskianum* (Maxim.) Hutch. in Kew Bull. (1921) 204.

Illustrations. Maxim. Prim. Fl. Amur. (1870), 48 t. 2, figs. 21–25; Kew Bull. (1921) 204, fig 1.

A low shrublet, about 10 cm. (4 in.) high, branched from the base, young branchlets setulose-glandular. *Leaves* deciduous, short-petioled or sessile, spathulate-oblanceolate, *lamina* thin, chartaceous, *0.5–1.5 cm. long, 3–6 mm. broad,* apex obtuse, base tapered or cuneate, decurrent on the petiole, or obtuse not decurrent; upper surface glabrous; margin ciliate-glandular; under surface with conspicuous venation; petiole short or absent. *Inflorescence* 1–3-flowered produced at the ends of the young leafy shoots and not in special buds; pedicel finely pubescent, sparsely glandular with long-stalked glands, and bearing also a few leafy bracts. *Calyx* 5-lobed, *lobes* linear-oblong, *5 mm. long,* 1–2 mm. broad, apex obtuse, outside finely puberulous, ciliate-glandular. *Corolla* almost rotate, about *1.5 cm. long,* tube on the lower (anterior) side split to the base, *tube 7–8 mm. long,* rose-purple, *outside glabrous; lobes 5, 6 mm. long,* 5 mm. broad, broadly oblong, margin crenulate. *Stamens* 10, a little longer than the corolla-tube; filaments pubescent on the lower third; anthers broad for their length. *Gynoecium hardly 1 cm. long,* shorter than the corolla; ovary densely pubescent; style 5 mm. long, abruptly curved, pubescent on the lower half, stigma discoid. *Capsule:—*

This plant was discovered by the Russian traveller Redowsky in Manchuria, and was described by Maximowicz in 1859. It is also found in East Siberia and Korea.

R. redowskianum is closely allied to *R. camtschaticum* which it resembles in general features, but differs in that the corolla is glabrous outside, it is smaller about 1.5 cm. long, the lobes are as long as, or shorter than the tube, the calyx is smaller, the leaves (laminae) are shorter and narrower, and the gynoecium is shorter.

There is no record of the species in cultivation.

Epithet. After J. Redowsky, d. 1805, a Russian collector.

Not in cultivation.

The Destruction in 1965 of the Famous Rhododendron Glasshouse in the Royal Botanic Garden, Edinburgh

The Rhododendron Glasshouse provided shelter to a large number of rhododendrons which are not hardy outdoors along the east coast. It consisted of a centre area possessing several large-sized species, with surrounding borders which were given to medium-sized and small rhododendrons.

At the north border there was a fine specimen of *R. nuttallii*, the largest-flowered of all rhododendrons. It was 9 feet high, with beautiful deep purple-red young growths, and large tubular-bell-shaped flowers, 6 inches long, pale yellow with an orange blotch.

Along the same border we found a beautiful plant of *R. polyandrum* 10 feet high with lanceolate leaves and tubular-funnel-shaped, white flushed pink flowers. Nearby, a noteworthy feature was a splendid specimen of *R. parryae*, a spreading shrub 5 feet high and 6 feet across, with large white flowers with a yellowish-orange blotch. This plant received a First Class Certificate in 1957.

In the centre area an outstanding feature was a magnificent specimen of *R. arboreum*, 20 feet high, with leaves silvery-white beneath, and compact trusses of crimson flowers which appeared freely in February or March. The plant was raised from seed sent by Wallich from Nepal presumably in 1818.

Close by, there was a fine plant of *R. sinogrande* (Forrest No. 20818), 15 feet high with large trusses of creamy-white flowers with a crimson blotch. It first flowered on 6th April 1920. Forrest discovered the species in western Yunnan in 1912. It has the largest leaf of all rhododendrons, up to 2½ feet in length and 1 foot in width.

Nearby grew a plant of *R. elliottii* (Kingdon-Ward No. 7725) 12 feet high, which seldom failed to display the beauty of its bell-shaped crimson flowers with darker spots, in June.

Another remarkable plant growing here was *R. kyawii*, a rounded, spreading shrub 15 feet high and 10 feet across, with beautiful foliage and large trusses of tubular-bell-shaped crimson flowers which appeared in July. The species is rare in cultivation, but is a most desirable rhododendron wherever it can be grown.

A short distance nearby, we came upon *R. giganteum* 5 feet high with large, broadly elliptic almost rounded leaves, dark green above, covered below with a silvery-white plastered indumentum, introduced by Kingdon-Ward in 1953 from The Triangle, North Burma. The continuous plastered indumentum served to distinguish the plant from *R. protistum* with glabrous leaves.

The later-flowering rhododendrons included a perfect specimen of *R. facetum*, one of the finest of the crimson-flowered species. It was introduced by Farrer (No. 1022) and was known as "Farrer's form" with leaves 8 inches in length and flowers produced freely in June–July. According to our records, this form is now possibly extinct in cultivation. It is a great pity that this form was not propagated by grafting or from seed.

An outstanding feature in the centre area was a superb specimen of *R. grande* 20 feet high, which was worthy of special notice for its handsome foliage and beautiful trusses of large, creamy-white flowers with a deep purple blotch.

Very near to *R. grande*, was *R. megacalyx*, a noteworthy species 9 feet high with large fragrant white flowers, discovered by Kingdon-Ward in East Upper Burma where in rain forest it reaches a height of 25 feet. The species would now appear to be rare in cultivation.

Mention must be made of a splendid specimen of *R. cubittii*, 12 feet high, with flaking bark. In March it provided a wealth of colour with its large, widely funnel-shaped, white flowers tinged with pink.

Here we also found growing an excellent plant of *R. falconeri* 18 feet high with beautiful brown flaking bark, large leaves rugulose above, with rust-coloured wool beneath and large trusses of bell-shaped flowers. The species was first introduced from the Himalayas in 1850 where it attains a height of 50 feet.

An exceptionally charming sight in March was a large plant of *R. protistum* (Kingdon-Ward No. 8069) 18 feet high, which first produced large trusses of deep rose-crimson flowers in 1954. It was planted by Sir William W. Smith himself when the seedling was 12 inches high.

Close by there was a remarkable plant of *R. griersonianum*, rounded, somewhat compact, 6 feet high and as much across which covered itself with bright rose flowers in May.

An outstanding feature in the centre area was a superb plant of *R. griffithianum* (Cooper No. 2315), 20 feet high with smooth, brown, flaking bark, handsome foliage, and large, bell-shaped, white flowers of exquisite beauty.

Special reference must be made to the 8 distinctive forms of *R. crassum* growing in the Glasshouse (See Vol. I p. 263). These were magnificent plants with large fragrant flowers (one form was pink) with a yellowish blotch, varying considerably in habit and height 5–12 feet high, in leaf shape and size, in the size of the corolla and size of the calyx. The species was remarkable for its long flowering period. One of these plants flowered in May, others in June and July, whilst another opened its flowers in August.

A charming sight in June was a broadly upright somewhat compact, spreading plant of *R. maddenii*, 12 feet high with smooth, brown flaking bark and large sweetly scented white flowers produced with great freedom. The species was discovered by J. D. Hooker in 1849 at Choongtam in Sikkim. This particular plant in the Glasshouse was undoubtedly the finest *R. maddenii* in general cultivation.

Near the west entrance at the corner there was a fine specimen of *R. delavayi* 9 feet high and was most attractive when covered with very compact trusses of deep crimson flowers. It was lifted and planted outdoors on the south side of the woodland garden exposed to the south-west wind. It survived for only two winters.

Next to *R. delavayi* we came upon *R. lukiangense* 9 feet high, which made a grand show with its deep rose flowers with crimson spots. The species was discovered by the Abbé Soulié in 1895 in north-west Yunnan. It is now rare in cultivation.

Another remarkable plant growing here was a large plant of *R. johnstoneanum* 8 feet high which gave a fine display with its creamy-white flowers in April.

Other interesting species along the west border that were destroyed included *R. scottianum*, 4 feet high, a rare plant in the Maddenii Series, and *R. genestierianum* in the

Glaucophyllum Series.

At the south end of the west border an interesting feature was another magnificent plant of *R. parryae*, broadly upright, 8 feet high, with large white flowers with a yellowish-orange blotch, of exquisite beauty.

Along the east border, there was an excellent plant of *R. hardingii* (Irroratum Series), introduced by Forrest from mid-west Yunnan. It was 8 feet high and provided a wealth of colour with its large white flowers in trusses of 8–14. The species is rare in cultivation. Why was this plant not propagated from cuttings or from seed or by grafting? It often produced short stout or oblong capsules containing seeds in plenty.

A beautiful plant of *R. chrysodoron* (Forrest No. 25446—the Type number), 6 feet high, gave a fine display with its yellow flowers in February or March, as did a fine plant of *R. ciliicalyx*, 9 feet high, with lovely reddish-brown flaking bark and beautiful widely funnel-shaped white flowers.

Along the east border near the entrance, an unusual sight was a splendid specimen of *R. eximium*, 8 feet high, with smooth, brown flaking bark, the upper surface of the young leaves up to one year old or more densely hairy with rust-coloured woolly hairs, the lower surface including the primary veins of the adult leaves covered with a continuous indumentum of hairs. The species *R. eximium* has been confused with *R. falconeri*. Any person in the Glasshouse would easily have distinguished at first sight *R. eximium* from *R. falconeri* growing nearby.

In the same border, towards the north end, there was a superb specimen of *R. dalhousiae*, one of J. D. Hooker's finest discoveries in the Himalayas. The plant was 10 feet high, and made a grand show in May with its large, tubular-bell-shaped yellow flowers.

Among the later-flowering rhododendrons an exceptionally fine sight in June was a plant of *R. eriogynum* (Forrest No. 13508—the Type number), now known as *R. facetum*, 12 feet high, with a profusion of bell-shaped crimson flowers.

A noteworthy plant growing nearby was *R. carneum* of the Maddenii Series, with pink flowers produced freely in April–May. The species is rare in cultivation.

Other plants growing along the east border included a small plant of *R. zeylanicum*, three specimens of *R. supranubium* that provided a mass of colour in May with widely funnel-shaped, white flowers tinged with pink, and the rare evergreen Azalea, *R. scabrum* with scarlet flowers.

Also destroyed were three plants of the rare species *R. lasiopodum*, the rare *R. peramoenum*, *R. horlickianum* (Kingdon-Ward No. 9403—the Type number), *R. xanthostephanum*, *R. oldhamii*—an Azalea, a fine specimen of *R. veitchianum*, and a rounded somewhat compact form of *R. iteophyllum*.

In a bed at the north side of the centre area was an interesting specimen of *R. taronense*, Maddenii Series, rare in cultivation. It was 4 feet high with white flowers with a yellow blotch which appeared freely in April–May.

The early-flowering rhododendrons included another form of *R. cubittii* trained on the wall, which provided an exceptionally fine sight in March with its large white flowers tinged with pink.

Special mention must be made of a superb plant of *R. formosum*, 12 feet high, which covered itself with white flowers in May. This plant was given an Award of Merit in 1960 in London when exhibited by the Royal Botanic Garden, Edinburgh.

Finally, witness the fate that befell R. 'William Wright Smith' 6 feet high with large tubular-bell-shaped, creamy-yellow flowers. It is indeed unbelievable that the person who named this plant after Sir William Wright Smith, was himself involved in ordering the destruction of the same famous plant after Sir William's death.

To sum up the foregoing remarks. The famous Rhododendron Glasshouse in the Royal Botanic Garden, Edinburgh, had undoubtedly the finest collection of the cream of tender rhododendrons not only in Britain but also throughout the world. What remains is the sad residue of a once magnificent collection.

Unplaced Species

balangense *Fang* Q
chihsinianum *Chun et Fang* Q
chunienii *Chun et Fang* Q
dimidiatum *Balf. f.* Possibly R. callimorphum
    hybrid Q
hoii *Fang* Q
huidongense *T. L. Ming.* Possibly a small-leaved
    form of R. facetum Q
kiangsiense *Fang* Q
lanatoides *Chamberlain.* Doubtful Q
lapidosum *T. L. Ming* Q
leishanicum *Fang et S. S. Chang* Q
lungchiense *Fang* Q
maximowiczianum *Lévl.* Q
potanini *Batalin* Q
pubicostatum *T. L. Ming* Q
pulchroides *Chun et Fang* Q
tawangense *Sahni et Naithani* Q
urophyllum *Fang* Q
versicolor *Chun et Fang* Q
yulingense *Fang* Q

Recently Described Little-known Species

R. barkamense *Chamberlain* Q
R. hangzhouense *Fang. & M.Y. He* Q
R. medoense *Fang. & M.Y. He* Q
R. mitriforme *Tam* Q
R. sanidodeum *Tam* Q
R. tianlinense *Tam* Q
R. xinganense *G.Z. Li* Q
R. detampullum *Chun ex Tam* Q
R. huguangense *Tam* Q
R. kaliense *Fang. & M.Y. He* Q
R. linearicupulare *Tam* Q
R. shiwandashanense *Tam* Q
R. subestipitatum *Tam* Q

List of Synonyms

ADENOGYNUM Diels *Adenophorum Group* R.H.S. = ADENOGYNUM
adenophorum Balf. f. et W. W. Sm. = ADENOGYNUM
adenopoda Lévl., nomen nudum = DECORUM
adenostemonum Balf. f. et W. W. Sm. = POGONOSTYLUM
admirabile Balf. f. et Forrest = LUKIANGENSE
adoxum Balf. f. et Forrest = VERNICOSUM
aemulorum Balf. f. = MALLOTUM
AGANNIPHUM Balf. f. et Ward var. AGANNIPHUM = AGANNIPHUM
AGANNIPHUM Balf. f. et Ward var. *adenophyllum* W. W. Sm., nomen nudum = AGANNIPHUM
AGANNIPHUM Balf. f. et Ward var. *flavorufum* (Balf. f. et Forrest) Chamberlain = FLAVORUFUM
agetum Balf. f. et Forrest = NERIIFLORUM var. AGETUM
aiolopeplum Balf. f. et Forrest = DRYOPHYLLUM
aiolosalpinx Balf. f. et Farrer = STEWARTIANUM
aischropeplum Balf. f. et Forrest = ROXIEANUM
albicaule Lévl. = CAVALERIEI
album Buchanan-Hamilton = ARBOREUM forma ALBUM
algarvense Page, nomen nudum = PONTICUM
ALUTACEUM Balf. f. et W. W. Sm. var. ALUTACEUM = ALUTACEUM
ALUTACEUM Balf. f. et W. W. Sm. var. *iodes* (Balf. f. et Forrest) Chamberlain = IODES
ALUTACEUM Balf. f. et W. W. Sm. var. *russotinctum* (Balf. f. et Forrest) Chamberlain = RUSSOTINCTUM
anisocalyx Balf. f. et Forrest, nomen nudum = ECLECTEUM var. BELLATULUM
ANNAE Franch. *Laxiflorum Group* R.H.S. = LAXIFLORUM
ANTHOSPHAERUM Diels subsp. *hylothreptum* (Balf. f. et W. W. Sm.) Tagg = ANTHOSPHAERUM
araliaeforme Balf. f. et Forrest = VERNICOSUM forma ARALIIFORME
ARBOREUM Sm. subsp. ARBOREUM = ARBOREUM
ARBOREUM Sm. var. *album* Lindl. = ARBOREUM forma ALBUM
ARBOREUM Sm. var. *angustifolium* Hort.? = ARBOREUM
ARBOREUM Sm. subsp. *campbelliae* (Hook. f.) Tagg = CAMPBELLIAE
ARBOREUM Sm. var. *cinnamomeum* (Wall. ex G. Don) Lindl. = CINNAMOMEUM
ARBOREUM Sm. subsp. *cinnamomeum* (Wall. ex G. Don) Tagg = CINNAMOMEUM
ARBOREUM Sm. var. *cinnamomeum* (Wall. ex G. Don) Lindl. *Campbelliae Group* R.H.S. = CAMPBELLIAE
ARBOREUM Sm. subsp. *delavayi* (Franch.) Chamberlain = DELAVAYI
ARBOREUM Sm. var. *kingianum* (Watt ex W. Watson) Hook. f. = ZEYLANICUM
ARBOREUM Sm. subsp. *kingianum* (Watt ex W. Watson) Tagg = ZEYLANICUM
ARBOREUM Sm. var. *limbatum* W. J. Hooker = ARBOREUM forma ROSEUM
ARBOREUM Sm. var. *nilagiricum* (Zenker) C. B. Clarke = NILAGIRICUM
ARBOREUM Sm. subsp. *nilagiricum* (Zenker) Tagg = NILAGIRICUM
ARBOREUM Sm. var. *paxtoni* Paxt.? = ARBOREUM hybrid
ARBOREUM Sm. var. *peramoenum* (Balf. f. et Forrest) Chamberlain = PERAMOENUM
ARBOREUM Sm. var. *roseum* Lindl. = ARBOREUM forma ROSEUM
ARBOREUM Sm. subsp. *zeylanicum* (Booth) Tagg = ZEYLANICUM
ARBOREUM Sm. *'Doctor Bowman'* = DELAVAYI var. ALBOTOMENTOSUM
argenteum Hook. f. = GRANDE
ARGYROPHYLLUM Franch. subsp. ARGYROPHYLLUM = ARGYROPHYLLUM
ARGYROPHYLLUM Franch. subsp. *argyrophyllum Cupulare Group* R.H.S. = ARGYROPHYLLUM var. CUPULARE
ARGYROPHYLLUM Franch. subsp. *hypoglaucum* (Hemsl.) Chamberlain = HYPOGLAUCUM
ARGYROPHYLLUM Franch. var. *leiandrum* Hutch. = ARGYROPHYLLUM
ARGYROPHYLLUM Franch. subsp. *nankingense* (Cowan) Chamberlain = ARGYROPHYLLUM var. NANKINGENSE
ARGYROPHYLLUM Franch. subsp. *omeiense* (Rehd. et Wils.) Chamberlain = ARGYROPHYLLUM var. OMEIENSE
ashleyi Coker = MAXIMUM
asmenistum Balf. f. et Forrest = CLOIOPHORUM
asteium Balf. f. et Forrest = MESOPOLIUM
astrocalyx Balf. f. et Forrest = WARDII

aucklandii Hook. f. = GRIFFITHIANUM
AUREUM Georgi var. AUREUM = AUREUM
AUREUM Georgi var. *hypopitys* (Pojarkova) Chamberlain = HYPOPITYS
australe Balf. f. et Forrest = LEPTOTHRIUM
axium Balf. f. et Forrest = SELENSE
azalea albiflora Kuntze = ALBIFLORUM
azalea myrtifolia Champion = HONGKONGENSE
azalea ovata Lindl. = OVATUM
azalea semibarbata (Maxim.) Kuntze = SEMIBARBATUM
azalea warrenii A. Nelson = ALBIFLORUM
azaleastrum albiflorum Rydb. = ALBIFLORUM
azaleastrum semibarbatum Makino = SEMIBARBATUM
bachii Lévl. = OVATUM
baeticum Boissier et Reuter = PONTICUM
BARBATUM Wall. ex G. Don var. *smithii* Nutt. ex W. J. Hooker = MACROSMITHII
batemanii Hook. f. = natural hybrid between CAMPANULATUM and ARBOREUM (?)
BEANIANUM Cowan var. *compactum* Cowan = PIERCEI
beimaense Balf. f. et Forrest = ERYTHROCALYX
benemaculatum nomen nudum = ECLECTEUM
blandulum Balf. f. et W. W. Sm. = JUCUNDUM
brachyandrum Balf. f. et Forrest = ECLECTEUM var. BRACHYANDRUM
BRACHYCARPUM D. Don ex G. Don subsp. BRACHYCARPUM = BRACHYCARPUM
BRACHYCARPUM D. Don ex G. Don subsp. *fauriei* (Franch.) Chamberlain = FAURIEI
BRACHYCARPUM D. Don ex G. Don var. *roseum* Koidzumi = BRACHYCARPUM
BRACHYCARPUM D. Don ex G. Don subsp. *tigerstedtii* Nitzelius = BRACHYCARPUM var.
    TIGERSTEDTII
brettii Hemsl. et Wils. = LONGESQUAMATUM
burriflorum Balf. f. et Forrest = DIPHROCALYX
californicum W. Hooker = MACROPHYLLUM
CALLIMORPHUM Balf. f. et W. W. Sm. var. CALLIMORPHUM = CALLIMORPHUM
CALLIMORPHUM Balf. f. et W. W. Sm. var. *myiagrum* (Balf. f. et Forrest) Chamberlain = MYIAGRUM
CALOPHYTUM Franch. var. CALOPHYTUM = CALOPHYTUM
CALOPHYTUM Franch. var. *openshawianum* (Rehd. et Wils.) Chamberlain = OPENSHAWIANUM
CALVESCENS Balf. f. et Forrest var. CALVESCENS = CALVESCENS
CALVESCENS Balf. f. et Forrest var. *duseimatum* (Balf. f. et Forrest) Chamberlain = CALVESCENS
CAMPANULATUM D. Don subsp. CAMPANULATUM = CAMPANULATUM
CAMPANULATUM D. Don var. *aeruginosum* (Hook. f.) Cowan et Davidian = AERUGINOSUM
CAMPANULATUM D. Don subsp. *aeruginosum* (Hook. f.) Chamberlain = AERUGINOSUM
CAMPANULATUM D. Don var. *wallichii* (Hook. f.) Hook f. = WALLICHII
CAMPYLOCARPUM Hook. f. subsp. CAMPYLOCARPUM = CAMPYLOCARPUM
CAMPYLOCARPUM Hook. f. subsp. *caloxanthum* (Balf. f. et Farrer) Chamberlain =
    CALOXANTHUM
CAMPYLOCARPUM Hook. f. subsp. *caloxanthum* (Balf. f. et Farrer) Chamberlain *Telopeum Group*
    R.H.S. = TELOPEUM
CAMTSCHATICUM Pallas subsp. *glandulosum* (Standley ex Small) Hult. = GLANDULOSUM
CAMTSCHATICUM Pallas var. *pallasianum* = CAMTSCHATICUM
candelabrum Hook. f. = THOMSONII var. CANDELABRUM
× *candelabrum* (Hook. f.) Chamberlain, THOMSONII × CAMPYLOCARPUM = THOMSONII var.
    CANDELABRUM
CATAWBIENSE Michaux var. *album* Hort.? = CATAWBIENSE
CATAWBIENSE Michaux var. *compactum* Hort.? = CATAWBIENSE
CATAWBIENSE Michaux forma *tomopetalum* Rehder = CATAWBIENSE
caucaseum Sims = CAUCASICUM
CAUCASICUM Pallas var. *stramineum* W. Hooker = probably CAUCASICUM hybrid
CAVALERIEI Lévl. var. *chaffanjonii* Lévl. = STAMINEUM
CHAETOMALLUM Balf. f. et Forrest var. *glaucescens* Tagg et Forrest = CHAETOMALLUM
chaffanjonii Lévl. MSS = STAMINEUM
chalarocladum Balf. f. et Forrest = SELENSE
CHAMAETHOMSONII (Tagg et Forrest) Cowan et Davidian var. *chamaedoron* (Tagg et Forrest)
    Chamberlain = CHAMAETHOMSONII var. CHAMAETHAUMA
CHAMAETHOMSONII (Tagg et Forrest) Cowan et Davidian var. CHAMAETHOMSONII =
    CHAMAETHOMSONII
chawchiense Balf. f. et Farrer = ANTHOSPHAERUM
chengianum Fang = HEMSLEYANUM

chionophyllum Diels = HYPOGLAUCUM
chlanidotum Balf. f. et Forrest = CITRINIFLORUM
chlorops Cowan = DECORUM hybrid
chrysanthum Pallas = AUREUM
chrysanthum Pallas var. *nikomontanum* Komatsu = × *nikomontanum* (Komatsu) Nakai
CITRINIFLORUM Balf. f. et Forrest var. CITRINIFLORUM = CITRINIFLORUM
CITRINIFLORUM Balf. f. et Forrest subsp. *aureolum* Cowan = CITRINIFLORUM
CITRINIFLORUM Balf. f. et Forrest subsp. *horaeum* (Balf. f. et Forrest) Cowan = HORAEUM
CITRINIFLORUM Balf. f. et Forrest var. *horaeum* (Balf. f. et Forrest) Chamberlain = HORAEUM
CITRINIFLORUM Balf. f. et Forrest subsp. *rubens* Cowan = HORAEUM var. RUBENS
CLOIOPHORUM Balf. f. et Forrest subsp. *asmenistum* (Balf. f. et Forrest) Tagg = CLOIOPHORUM
CLOIOPHORUM Balf. f. et Forrest subsp. *leucopetalum* (Balf. f. et Forrest) Tagg = CLOIOPHORUM
    var. LEUCOPETALUM
CLOIOPHORUM Balf. f. et Forrest subsp. *mannophorum* (Balf. f. et Forrest) Tagg = CLOIOPHORUM
    var. MANNOPHORUM
CLOIOPHORUM Balf. f. et Forrest subsp. *roseotinctum* (Balf. f. et Forrest) Tagg = CLOIOPHORUM
    var. ROSEOTINCTUM
coccinopeplum Balf. f. et Forrest = ROXIEANUM
cordatum Lévl. = SOULIEI
coryphaeum Balf. f. et Forrest = PRAESTANS
CRINIGERUM Franch. var. CRINIGERUM = CRINIGERUM
croceum Balf. f. et W. W. Sm. = WARDII
cupressens Nitzelius = PHAEOCHRYSUM
CYANOCARPUM (Franch.) W. W. Sm. var. *eriphyllum* Balf. f. et W. W. Sm. ex Tagg =
    CYANOCARPUM
cyclium Balf. f. et Forrest = CALLIMORPHUM
cymbomorphum Balf. f. et Forrest = ERYTHROCALYX
dabanshanense Fang et Wang = PRZEWALSKII
decipiens Lacaita = natural hybrid, FALCONERI × HODGSONII
DEGRONIANUM Carrière var. *yakushimanum* (Nakai) Kitamura = YAKUSHIMANUM
dendritrichum Balf. f. et Forrest = UVARIFOLIUM
DICHROANTHUM Diels subsp. DICHROANTHUM = DICHROANTHUM
DICHROANTHUM Diels subsp. *apodectum* (Balf. f. et W. W. Sm.) Cowan = APODECTUM
DICHROANTHUM Diels subsp. *herpesticum* (Balf. f. et Ward) Cowan = HERPESTICUM
DICHROANTHUM Diels subsp. *scyphocalyx* (Balf. f. et Forrest) Cowan = SCYPHOCALYX
DICHROANTHUM Diels subsp. *scyphocalyx* Balf. f. et Forrest *Herpesticum Group* = HERPESTICUM
DICHROANTHUM Diels subsp. *septendrionale* Tagg ex Cowan = SCYPHOCALYX var.
    SEPTENDRIONALE
dichropeplum Balf. f. et Forrest = PHAEOCHRYSUM
dolerum Balf. f. et Forrest = SELENSE
dumicola Tagg et Forrest = BAINBRIDGEANUM
dunnii Wils. = HENRYI
duseimatum Balf. f. et Forrest = CALVESCENS
ECLECTEUM Balf. f. et Forrest var. ECLECTEUM = ECLECTEUM
edgari Gamble, Darjeeling List = CAMPANULATUM
emaculatum Balf. f. et Forrest = BEESIANUM
epipastum Balf. f. et Forrest = MESOPOLIUM
eriogynum Balf. f. et W. W. Sm. = FACETUM
eriphyllum Balf. f. et W. W. Sm. nomen nudum = CYANOCARPUM
eritimum Balf. f. et W. W. Sm. = ANTHOSPHAERUM var. ERITIMUM
eritimum Balf. f. et W. W. Sm. subsp. *chawchiense* (Balf. f. et Farrer) Tagg = ANTHOSPHAERUM
eritimum Balf. f. et W. W. Sm. subsp. *gymnogynum* (Balf. f. et Forrest) Tagg = ANTHOSPHAERUM var.
    ERITIMUM
eritimum Balf. f. et W. W. Sm. subsp. *heptamerum* (Balf. f.) Tagg = ANTHOSPHAERUM var.
    ERITIMUM
eritimum Balf. f. et W. W. Sm. subsp. *persicinum* (Hand.-Mazz.) Tagg = ANTHOSPHAERUM
ERYTHROCALYX Balf. f. et Forrest subsp. *beimaense* (Balf. f. et Forrest) Tagg = ERYTHROCALYX
ERYTHROCALYX Balf. f. et Forrest subsp. *docimum* Balf. f. ex Tagg = ERYTHROCALYX
ERYTHROCALYX Balf. f. et Forrest subsp. *eucallum* (Balf. f. et Forrest) Tagg = ERYTHROCALYX
ERYTHROCALYX Balf. f. et Forrest subsp. *truncatulum* (Balf. f. et Forrest) Tagg = ERYTHROCALYX
× *erythrocalyx* (Balf. f. et Forrest) (SELENSE × WARDII) Chamberlain = ERYTHROCALYX
× *erythrocalyx* Balf. f. et Forrest *Panteumorphum Group* R.H.S. = PANTHEUMORPHUM
euanthum Balf. f. et W. W. Sm. = VERNICOSUM forma EUANTHUM
eucallum Balf. f. et Forrest = ERYTHROCALYX

euchaites Balf. f. et Forrest = NERIIFLORUM var. EUCHAITES
EUDOXUM Balf. f. et Forrest var. EUDOXUM = EUDOXUM
EUDOXUM Balf. f. et Forrest subsp. EUDOXUM = EUDOXUM
EUDOXUM Balf. f. et Forrest subsp. *asteium* (Balf. f. et Forrest) Tagg = MESOPOLIUM
EUDOXUM Balf. f. et Forrest subsp. *brunneifolium* (Balf. f. et Forrest) Tagg = BRUNNEIFOLIUM
EUDOXUM Balf. f. et Forrest var. *brunneifolium* (Balf. f. et Forrest) Chamberlain = BRUNNEIFOLIUM
EUDOXUM Balf. f. et Forrest subsp. *epipastum* (Balf. f. et Forrest) Tagg = MESOPOLIUM
EUDOXUM Balf. f. et Forrest subsp. *glaphyrum* (Balf. f. et Forrest) Tagg = GLAPHYRUM
EUDOXUM Balf. f. et Forrest subsp. *mesopolium* (Balf. f. et Forrest) Tagg = MESOPOLIUM
EUDOXUM Balf. f. et Forrest var. *mesopolium* (Balf. f. et Forrest) Chamberlain = MESOPOLIUM
EUDOXUM Balf. f. et Forrest subsp. *pothinum* (Balf. f. et Forrest) Tagg = TEMENIUM
EUDOXUM Balf. f. et Forrest subsp. *temenium* (Balf. f. et Forrest) Tagg = TEMENIUM
EUDOXUM Balf. f. et Forrest subsp. *trichomiscum* (Balf. f. et Forrest) Tagg = TRICHOMISCUM
exquisetum T. L. Ming = possibly SIKANGENSE
FABERI Hemsl. subsp. FABERI = FABERI
FABERI Hemsl. subsp. *prattii* (Franch.) Chamberlain = PRATTII
faberioides Balf. f. = FABERI
FALCONERI Hook. f. subsp. FALCONERI = FALCONERI
FALCONERI Hook. f. var. *eximia* Hook. f. = EXIMIUM
FALCONERI Hook. f. var. *eximium* (Nutt.) Hook. f. = EXIMIUM
FALCONERI Hook. f. subsp. *eximium* (Nutt.) Chamberlain = EXIMIUM
FALCONERI Hook. f. var. *macabeanum* Watt Mss. = MACABEANUM
FARGESII Franch. var. *album* Wils., nomen nudum = FARGESII
faucium Chamberlain = HYLAEUM
FAURIEI Franch. var. *rufescens* Nakai = BRACHYCARPUM
fissotectum Balf. f. et Forrest = FLAVORUFUM
FLOCCIGERUM Franch. subsp. *appropinquans* (Tagg et Forrest) Chamberlain = FLOCCIGERUM var. APPROPINQUANS
fokienense Franch. = SIMIARUM
fordii Hemsl. = SIMIARUM
FORRESTII Balf. f. ex Diels subsp. *forrestii Repens Group* R.H.S. = FORRESTII var. REPENS
FORRESTII Balf. f. ex Diels subsp. *papillatum* Chamberlain = FORRESTII var. REPENS
(? FORRESTII × HAEMATODES) Chamberlain = CHAETOMALLUM var. CHAMAEPHYTUM
FORTUNEI Lindl. subsp. FORTUNEI = FORTUNEI
FORTUNEI Lindl. subsp. *discolor* (Franch.) Chamberlain = DISCOLOR
FORTUNEI Lindl. subsp. *discolor* Franch. *Houlstonii Group* R.H.S. = HOULSTONII
FORTUNEI Lindl. var. *houlstonii* (Hemsl. et Wils.) Rehd. et Wils. = HOULSTONII
foveolatum Rehd. et Wils. = CORIACEUM
franchetianum Lévl. = DECORUM
FULVASTRUM Balf. f. et Forrest subsp. FULVASTRUM = FULVASTRUM
FULVASTRUM Balf. f. et Forrest subsp. *mesopolium* (Balf. f. et Forrest) Cowan = MESOPOLIUM
FULVASTRUM Balf. f. et Forrest subsp. *trichophlebium* (Balf. f. et Forrest) Cowan = TEMENIUM
FULVASTRUM Balf. f. et Forrest subsp. *trichomiscum* (Balf. f. et Forrest) Cowan = TRICHOMISCUM
× *Geraldii* (Hutch.) Ivens = SUTCHUENENSE var. GERALDII
GIGANTEUM Forrest ex Tagg var. *seminudum* Tagg et Forrest = PROTISTUM
giraudiasii Lévl. = DECORUM
GLISCHRUM Balf. f. et W. W. Sm. subsp. GLISCHRUM = GLISCHRUM
GLISCHRUM Balf. f. et W. W. Sm. var. *adenosum* Cowan et Davidian = ADENOSUM
GLISCHRUM Balf. f. et W. W. Sm. subsp. *glischroides* (Tagg et Forrest) Chamberlain = GLISCHROIDES
GLISCHRUM Balf. f. et W. W. Sm. subsp. *rude* (Tagg et Forrest) Chamberlain = RUDE
gloeoblastum Balf. f. et Forrest = WARDII
gracilipes Franch. = HYPOGLAUCUM
GRANDE Wight var. *roseum* Hook. f. = natural hybrid of GRANDE
gratum T. L. Ming = possibly BASILICUM
GRIFFITHIANUM Wight var. *aucklandii* (Hook. f.) Hooker = GRIFFITHIANUM
gymnanthum Diels = LUKIANGENSE
gymnogynum Balf. f. et Forrest = ANTHOSPHAERUM var. ERITIMUM
haematocheilum Craib = OREODOXA
HAEMATODES Franch. subsp. HAEMATODES = HAEMATODES
HAEMATODES Franch. var. *calycinum* Franch. = HAEMATODES
HAEMATODES Franch. subsp. *chaetomallum* (Balf. f. et Forrest) Chamberlain = CHAETOMALLUM
HAEMATODES Franch. subsp. *chaetomallum* (Balf. f. et Forrest) Chamberlain *Glaucescens Group* = CHAETOMALLUM
HAEMATODES Franch. var. *hypoleucum* Franch. = HAEMATODES

hedythamnum Balf. f. et Forrest = CALLIMORPHUM
hedythamnum Balf. f. et Forrest var. *eglandulosum* Hand.-Mazz. = CYANOCARPUM
helvolum Balf. f. et Forrest = DRYOPHYLLUM
× *hemigymnum* Tagg et Forrest (POCOPHORUM × ECLECTEUM) Chamberlain = CHAETOMALLUM var. HEMIGYMNUM
heptamerum Balf. f. = ANTHOSPHAERUM var. ERITIMUM
hexamerum Hand.-Mazz. = DECORUM
× HILLIERI Davidian = HILLIERI
HUNNEWELLIANUM Rehd. et Wils. subsp. HUNNEWELLIANUM = HUNNEWELLIANUM
HUNNEWELLIANUM Rehd. et Wils. subsp. *rockii* (Wils.) Chamberlain = ROCKII
hylothreptum Balf. f. et W. W. Sm. = ANTHOSPHAERUM
Hymenanthes Makino var. *heptamerum* (Maxim.) Makino = DEGRONIANUM var. HEPTAMERUM
Hymenanthes japonica Blume = DEGRONIANUM var. HEPTAMERUM
intortum Balf. f. et Forrest = DRYOPHYLLUM
IRRORATUM Franch. subsp. IRRORATUM = IRRORATUM
IRRORATUM Franch. subsp. *pogonostylum* (Balf. f. et W. W. Sm.) Chamberlain = POGONOSTYLUM
jangtzowense Balf. f. et Forrest = APODECTUM
JAPONICUM (Blume) Schneider var. JAPONICUM = JAPONICUM
japonicum (Blume) Schneider (1912), not (A. Gr.) Suringer (1908) = DEGRONIANUM var. HEPTAMERUM
japonicum (Blume) Schneider var. *pentamerum* Hutch. = DEGRONIANUM
KAMTSCHATICUM Pallas = CAMTSCHATICUM
KAMTSCHATICUM Pallas subsp. *glandulosum* (Standley ex Small) Hult. = GLANDULOSUM
kansuense Millais = possibly ROXIEANUM
KENDRICKII Nutt. var. *latifolium* Hooker = KENDRICKII
kialense Franch. = PRZEWALSKII
kingianum Watt ex W. Watson = ZEYLANICUM
kingii Millais = ZEYLANICUM
kirkii Millais = DISCOLOR
klossii Ridley = MOULMAINENSE
kuluense Chamberlain = ADENOSUM
lacteum Rehd. et Wils. pro parte, non Franch. = GALACTINUM
LACTEUM Franch. var. *macrophyllum* Franch. = FICTOLACTEUM
lamprophyllum Hayata = OVATUM
LANATUM Hook. f. var. *luciferum* Cowan = LUCIFERUM
lancifolium Hook. f. = BARBATUM
lancifolium Moench, nomen illegit = PONTICUM
lapidosum T. L. Ming = POGONOSTYLUM?
leei Fang = PRATTII
leiopodum Hayata = ELLIPTICUM
leptosanthum Hayata = ELLIPTICUM
leucobotrys Ridley = MOULMAINENSE
leucolasium Diels = HUNNEWELLIANUM
leucopetalum Balf. f. et Forrest = CLOIOPHORUM var. LEUCOPETALUM
leucostigma Lévl., nomen nudum = DECORUM
levistratum Balf. f. et Forrest = DRYOPHYLLUM
limprichtii Diels = OREODOXA
liratum Balf. f. et Forrest = APODECTUM
longifolium Nutt. = GRANDE
LONGIPES Rehd. et Wils. var. LONGIPES = LONGIPES
LONGIPES Rehd. et Wils. var. *chienianum* (Fang) Chamberlain = CHIENIANUM
lophophorum Balf. f. et Forrest = PHAEOCHRYSUM
lucidum Franch. non Nutt. = VERNICOSUM
LUKIANGENSE Franch. subsp. *admirabile* (Balf. f. et Forrest) Tagg = LUKIANGENSE
LUKIANGENSE Franch. subsp. *adroserum* (Balf. f. et Forrest) Tagg = ADROSERUM
LUKIANGENSE Franch. subsp. *ceraceum* (Balf. f. et W. W. Sm.) Tagg = CERACEUM
LUKIANGENSE Franch. subsp. *gymnanthum* (Diels) Tagg = LUKIANGENSE
MACULIFERUM Franch. subsp. MACULIFERUM = MACULIFERUM
MACULIFERUM Franch. subsp. *anhweiense* (Wils.) Chamberlain = ANHWEIENSE
magorianum Balf. f. = hybrid of a species in the Adenogynum Subseries, Taliense Series
mairei Lévl. = LACTEUM
mandarinorum Diels = DISCOLOR
mannophorum Balf. f. et Forrest = CLOIOPHORUM var. MANNOPHORUM
manopeplum Balf. f. et Forrest = ESETULOSUM
MAXIMUM Linn. var. *album* Pursh = MAXIMUM
MAXIMUM Linn. var. *purpureum* Pursh = MAXIMUM

MEDDIANUM Forrest var. MEDDIANUM = MEDDIANUM
megaphyllum Balf. f. et Forrest = BASILICUM
metrium Balf. f. et Forrest = SELENSE var. PROBUM
metternichii Sieb. et Zucc. var. *heptamerum* Maximovicz = DEGRONIANUM var. HEPTAMERUM
?metternichii Sieb. et Zucc. var. *intermedium* Sugimoto = YAKUSHIMANUM
metternichii Sieb. et Zucc. var. *metternianum* Wada, nomen nudum = DEGRONIANUM
metternichii Sieb. et Zucc. var. *micranthum* Nakai = DEGRONIANUM
metternichi nom. illegit f. *pentamerum* Maxim. = DEGRONIANUM
metternichii Sieb. et Zucc. subsp. *pentamerum* (Maximovicz) Sugimoto = DEGRONIANUM
metternichii Sieb. et Zucc. var. PENTAMERUM Maxim. forma *angustifolium* Makino = MAKINOI
metternichii Sieb. et Zucc. var. *yakushimanum* (Nakai) Ohwi = YAKUSHIMANUM
metternichii Sieb. et Zucc. subsp. *yakushimanum* (Nakai) Sugimoto = YAKUSHIMANUM
MICROGYNUM Balf. f. et Forrest *Gymnocarpum Group* R.H.S. = GYMNOCARPUM
microterum Balf. f. nomen nudum = COLLETUM
mollyanum Cowan et Davidian = MONTROSEANUM
monbeigii Rehd. et Wils. = UVARIFOLIUM
mumeazalea semibarbata Makino = SEMIBARBATUM
mussoti Franch. nomen nudum = WARDII
myrtifolium Lodd. (non Schott et Kotschy) = PONTICUM
nanothamnum Balf. f. et Forrest = SELENSE
nebrites Balf. f. et Forrest = HIMERTUM
nematocalyx Balf. f. et W. W. Sm. = MOULMAINENSE
NERIIFLORUM Franch. subsp. NERIIFLORUM = NERIIFLORUM
NERIIFLORUM Franch. subsp. *agetum* (Balf. f. et Forrest) Tagg = NERIIFLORUM var. AGETUM
NERIIFLORUM Franch. subsp. *euchaites* (Balf. f. et Forrest) Tagg = NERIIFLORUM var. EUCHAITES
NERIIFLORUM Franch. subsp. *neriiflorum Euchaites Group* R.H.S. = NERIIFLORUM var. EUCHAITES
NERIIFLORUM Franch. subsp. *phaedropum* (Balf. f. et Farrer) Tagg = PHAEDROPUM
NERIIFLORUM Franch. subsp. *phoenicodum* (Balf. f. et Farrer) Tagg = NERIIFLORUM var. EUCHAITES
ngawchangense Philipson et Philipson = LEPTOTHRIUM
niphargum Balf. f. et Ward = UVARIFOLIUM
niphobolum Balf. f. et Farrer = STEWARTIANUM
nishiokae Hara = SUCCOTHII
NIVEUM Hook. f. var. *fulva* Hook. f. = NIVEUM
nobile Wall. non Hort., nomen nudum = NILAGIRICUM
nobile Hort. = hybrid between CAMPANULATUM and ARBOREUM?
oblongum Griff. = GRIFFITHIANUM
ochrocalyx Franch. nomen nudum = MIMETES
officinale Salisb. = AUREUM
ombrochares Balf. f. et Ward = TANASTYLUM
ORBICULARE Decaisne subsp. ORBICULARE = ORBICULARE
ORBICULARE Decaisne subsp. *cardiobasis* (Sleumer) Chamberlain = CARDIOBASIS
OREODOXA Franch. var. OREODOXA = OREODOXA
OREODOXA Franch. var. *shensiense* Chamberlain = OREODOXA
oresterum Balf. f. et Forrest = WARDII
OVATUM (Lindl.) Maxim. var. *prismaticum* Tam = OVATUM
oxyphyllum Franch. = MOULMAINENSE
pagophilum Balf. f. et Ward = SELENSE var. PAGOPHILUM
pankimense Cowan et Ward = KENDRICKII
parviflorum Dumont de Courset = PONTICUM
peregrinum Tagg = hybrid, GALACTINUM × possibly WATSONII
persicinum Hand.-Mazz. = ANTHOSPHAERUM
perulatum Balf. f. et Forrest = COMISTEUM
PHAEOCHRYSUM Balf. f. et W. W. Sm. var. PHAEOCHRYSUM = PHAEOCHRYSUM
PHAEOCHRYSUM Balf. f. et W. W. Sm. var. *agglutinatum* (Balf. f. et Forrest) Chamberlain = AGGLUTINATUM
PHAEOCHRYSUM Balf. f. et W. W. Sm. var. *levistratum* (Balf. f. et Forrest) Chamberlain = DRYOPHYLLUM
phoenicodum Balf. f. et Farrer = NERIIFLORUM var. EUCHAITES
pilovittatum Balf. f. et W. W. Sm. = DELAVAYI
pittosporaefolium Hemsl. = STAMINEUM

POCOPHORUM Balf. f. ex Tagg var. POCOPHORUM = POCOPHORUM
POCOPHORUM Balf. f. ex Tagg var. *hemidartum* (Balf. f. ex Tagg) Chamberlain = HEMIDARTUM
poecilodermum Balf. f. et Forrest = ROXIEANUM
poliopeplum Balf. f. et Forrest = HIMERTUM
PONTICUM Linn. var. *album* Sweet = PONTICUM forma ALBUM
PONTICUM Linn. var. *brachycarpum* Boissier = PONTICUM
PONTICUM Linn. subsp. *artvinense* nomen nudum = × *Sochadzea* (PONTICUM × CAUCASICUM)
PONTICUM Linn. subsp. *baeticum* (Boissier et Reuter) Hand.-Mazz. = PONTICUM
porphyroblastum Balf. f. et Forrest = CUCULLATUM
pothinum Balf. f. et Forrest = TEMENIUM
prasinocalyx Balf. f. et Forrest = WARDII
PRINCIPIS Bur. et Franch. *Vellereum Group* R.H.S. = VELLEREUM
probum Balf. f. et Forrest = SELENSE var. PROBUM
procerum Salisb. nomen nudum = MAXIMUM
prophantum Balf. f. et Forrest = KYAWII
PROTISTUM Balf. f. et Forrest var. PROTISTUM = PROTISTUM
PROTISTUM Balf. f. et Forrest var. *giganteum* (Forrest ex Tagg) Chamberlain = GIGANTEUM
puniceum Roxburgh = ARBOREUM
purpureum (Pursh) G. Don = MAXIMUM
purshii G. Don = MAXIMUM
rasile Balf. f. et W. W. Sm. = DIAPREPES
recurvum Balf. f. et Forrest = ROXIEANUM var. RECURVUM
recurvum Balf. f. et Forrest var. *OREONASTES* = ROXIEANUM var. OREONASTES
regale Balf. f. et Ward = BASILICUM
reginaldii Balf. f. = OREODOXA
repens Balf. f. et Forrest = FORRESTII var. REPENS
repens Balf. f. et Forrest var. *chamaedoron* Tagg et Forrest = CHAMAETHOMSONII var. CHAMAETHAUMA
repens Balf. f. et Forrest var. *chamaedoxa,* nomen nudum = CHAMAETHOMSONII var. CHAMAETHAUMA
repens Balf. f. et Forrest var. *CHAMAETHAUMA* Tagg = CHAMAETHOMSONII var. CHAMAETHAUMA
repens Balf. f. et Forrest var. *chamaethomsonii* Tagg et Forrest = CHAMAETHOMSONII
REX Lévl. subsp. REX = REX
REX Lévl. subsp. *arizelum* (Balf. f. et Forrest) Chamberlain = ARIZELUM
REX Lévl. subsp. *fictolacteum* (Balf. f.) Chamberlain = FICTOLACTEUM
rhaibocarpum Balf. f. et W. W. Sm. = DASYCLADUM
rhantum Balf. f. et W. W. Sm. = VERNICOSUM forma RHANTUM
rhododactylum Hort. = WASONII var. RHODODACTYLUM
rhodothamnus camtschaticus Lindl. = CAMTSCHATICUM
roseotinctum Balf. f. et Forrest = CLOIOPHORUM var. ROSEOTINCTUM
rotundifolium Arm. David = ORBICULARE
ROXIEANUM Forrest var. ROXIEANUM = ROXIEANUM
ROXIEANUM var. *roxieanum Oreonastes Group* R.H.S. = ROXIEANUM var. OREONASTES
ROXIEANUM Forrest var. *cucullatum* (Hand.-Mazz.) Chamberlain = CUCULLATUM
roxieoides Chamberlain = ROXIEANUM
rubropunctatum Hayata non Léveillé et Van = HYPERYTHRUM
SANGUINEUM Franch. subsp. SANGUINEUM = SANGUINEUM
SANGUINEUM Franch. var. SANGUINEUM = SANGUINEUM
SANGUINEUM Franch. subsp. *aizoides* Cowan = CITRINIFLORUM
SANGUINEUM Franch. subsp. *atrorubrum* Cowan = HAEMALEUM var. ATRORUBRUM
SANGUINEUM Franch. subsp. *cloiophorum* (Balf. f. et Forrest) Cowan = CLOIOPHORUM
SANGUINEUM Franch. var. *cloiophorum* (Balf. f. et Forrest) Chamberlain = CLOIOPHORUM
SANGUINEUM Franch. subsp. *consanguineum* Cowan = SANGUINEUM var. CONSANGUINEUM
SANGUINEUM Franch. subsp. *didymoides* (Tagg et Forrest) Cowan = SANGUINEUM var. DIDY-MOIDES
SANGUINEUM Franch. subsp. *didymum* (Balf. f. et Forrest) Cowan = DIDYMUM
SANGUINEUM Franch. subsp. *haemaleum* (Balf. f. et Forrest) Cowan = HAEMALEUM
SANGUINEUM Franch. var. *haemaleum* (Balf. f. et Forrest) Chamberlain = HAEMALEUM
SANGUINEUM Franch. subsp. *himertum* (Balf. f. et Forrest) Cowan = HIMERTUM
SANGUINEUM Franch. var. *himertum* (Balf. f. et Forrest) Chamberlain = HIMERTUM
SANGUINEUM Franch. subsp. *leucopetalum* (Balf. f. et Forrest) Cowan = CLOIOPHORUM var. LEUCOPETALUM
SANGUINEUM Franch. subsp. *melleum* Cowan = CITRINIFLORUM
SANGUINEUM Franch. subsp. *mesaeum* Balf. f. ex Cowan = HAEMALEUM var. MESAEUM

SANGUINEUM Franch. subsp. *sanguineoides* Cowan = SANGUINEUM var. SANGUINEOIDES
schizopeplum Balf. f. et Forrest = FLAVORUFUM
SELENSE Franch. subsp. SELENSE = SELENSE
selense Diels non Franch. = PANTEUMORPHUM
SELENSE Franch. subsp. *axium* (Balf. f. et Forrest) Tagg = SELENSE
SELENSE Franch. subsp. *chalarocladum* (Balf. f. et Forrest) Tagg = SELENSE
SELENSE Franch. subsp. *dasycladum* (Balf. f. et W. W. Sm.) Chamberlain = DASYCLADUM
SELENSE Franch. subsp. *dolerum* (Balf. f. et Forrest) Tagg = SELENSE
SELENSE Franch. subsp. *duseimatum* (Balf. f. et Forrest) Tagg = CALVESCENS
SELENSE Franch. var. *duseimatum* (Balf. f. et Forrest) Cowan et Davidian = CALVESCENS
SELENSE Franch. subsp. *jucundum* (Balf. f. et W. W. Sm.) Chamberlain = JUCUNDUM
SELENSE Franch. subsp. *metrium* (Balf. f. et Forrest) Tagg = SELENSE var. PROBUM
SELENSE Franch. subsp. *nanothamnum* (Balf. f. et Forrest) Tagg = SELENSE
SELENSE Franch. subsp. *pagophilum* (Balf. f. et Ward) Tagg = SELENSE var. PAGOPHILUM
SELENSE Franch. subsp. *probum* (Balf. f. et Forrest) Tagg = SELENSE var. PROBUM
SELENSE Franch. subsp. *setiferum* (Balf. f. et Forrest) Chamberlain = SETIFERUM
semnum Balf. f. et Forrest = PRAESTANS
serpens Balf. f. et Forrest = PORPHYROPHYLLUM
sheltonae Hemsl. et Wils. = VERNICOSUM forma SHELTONAE
sigillatum Balf. f. et Forrest = DRYOPHYLLUM
silvaticum Cowan = LANIGERUM var. SILVATICUM
SIMIARUM Hance subsp. *youngae* (Fang) Chamberlain = YOUNGAE
simulans (Tagg et Forrest) Chamberlain = MIMETES var. SIMULANS
smithii Nutt. ex W. J. Hooker = MACROSMITHII
smithii Nutt. ex W. J. Hooker *Argipeplum Group* R.H.S. = ARGIPEPLUM
speciosum Salisbury, nomen illegit = PONTICUM
SPERABILE Balf. f. et Farrer var. SPERABILE = SPERABILE
SPERABILE Balf. f. et Farrer var. *chimiliense* Tagg et Forrest, nomen nudum = SPERABILE var.
    WEIHSIENSE
spooneri Hemsl. et Wils. = DECORUM
stenaulum Balf. f. et W. W. Sm. = MOULMAINENSE
stenophyllum Makino non Hook. f. = MAKINOI
STEWARTIANUM Diels var. *aiolosalpinx* (Balf. f. et Farrer) Cowan et Davidian = STEWARTIANUM
subansiriense Chamberlain = HYLAEUM
syncollum Balf. f. et Forrest = PHAEOCHRYSUM
TANASTYLUM Balf. f. et Ward var. TANASTYLUM = TANASTYLUM
TELOPEUM Balf. f. et Forrest forma *telopeoides* Balf. f. ex Tagg = PANTEUMORPHUM
TEMENIUM Balf. f. et Forrest subsp. TEMENIUM = TEMENIUM
TEMENIUM Balf. f. et Forrest var. TEMENIUM = TEMENIUM
TEMENIUM Balf. f. et Forrest subsp. *albipetalum* Cowan = GLAPHYRUM var. DEALBATUM
TEMENIUM Balf. f. et Forrest subsp. *chrysanthemum* Cowan = FULVASTRUM
TEMENIUM Balf. f. et Forrest subsp. *dealbatum* Cowan = GLAPHYRUM var. DEALBATUM
TEMENIUM Balf. f. et Forrest var. *dealbatum* (Cowan) Chamberlain = GLAPHYRUM var.
    DEALBATUM
TEMENIUM Balf. f. et Forrest subsp. *gilvum* Cowan = FULVASTRUM var. GILVUM
TEMENIUM Balf. f. et Forrest var. *gilvum* (Cowan) Chamberlain = FULVASTRUM var. GILVUM
TEMENIUM Balf. f. et Forrest var. *gilvum* (Cowan) Chamberlain *Chrysanthemum Group* =
    FULVASTRUM
TEMENIUM Balf. f. et Forrest subsp. *glaphyrum* (Balf. f. et Forrest) Cowan = GLAPHYRUM
TEMENIUM Balf. f. et Forrest subsp. *rhodanthum* Cowan = TRICHOMISCUM
theiophyllum Balf. f. et Forrest = DRYOPHYLLUM
therorhodion camtschaticum (Pall.) Small = CAMTSCHATICUM
therorhodion camtschaticum (Pall.) Small forma *albiflorum* Nakai = CAMTSCHATICUM var.
    ALBIFLORUM
therorhodion glandulosum Standley = GLANDULOSUM
therorhodion redowskianum Hutch. = REDOWSKIANUM
THOMSONII Hook. f. subsp. THOMSONII = THOMSONII
THOMSONII Hook. f. var. *album* Millais = THOMSONII
THOMSONII Hook. f. var. *cyanocarpum* Franch. = CYANOCARPUM
THOMSONII Hook. f. var. *flocculosa* C. B. Clarke = THOMSONII
THOMSONII Hook. f. var. *grandiflorum* Millais = THOMSONII
THOMSONII Hook. f. subsp. *lopsangianum* (Cowan) Chamberlain = LOPSANGIANUM
THOMSONII Hook. f. var. *pallidum* Cowan = THOMSONII var. CANDELABRUM

torquatum Balf. f. et Farrer = CLOIOPHORUM var. MANNOPHORUM
TRAILLIANUM Forrest et W. W. Sm. var. TRAILLIANUM = TRAILLIANUM
TRAILLIANUM Forrest et W. W. Sm. var. *dictyotum* (Balf. f. ex Tagg) Chamberlain = DICTYOTUM
trichophlebium Balf. f. et Forrest = TEMENIUM
truncatulum Balf. f. et Forrest = ERYTHROCALYX
vaniotii Lévl. = ESQUIROLII
venosum Nutt. = FALCONERI
vicinum Balf. f. et Forrest = DRYOPHYLLUM
waldemeria argentea Klotzch. = GRANDE
wallaceanum Millais, Rhododendrons = imperfectly known, possibly a synonym of a species in the
    Taliense Subseries
WARDII W. W. Sm. var. WARDII = WARDII
WARDII W. W. Sm. var. *puralbum* (Balf. f. et W. W. Sm.) Chamberlain = PURALBUM
WARDII W.W. Sm. var. *wardii Litiense Group* R.H.S. = LITIENSE
warrenii (A. Nels.) MacBride = ALBIFLORUM
WASONII Hemsl. et Wils. 'Rhododactylum' R.H.S. = WASONII var. RHODODACTYLUM
wattii Cowan = NILAGIRICUM
westlandii Hemsl. = MOULMAINENSE
windsorii Nutt. = ARBOREUM
windsorii Nutt. var. *leucanthum* Hort.? = ARBOREUM forma ALBUM
× *xanthanthum* (Tagg et Forrest) Chamberlain = CHAETOMALLUM var. XANTHANTHUM
xanthoneuron Lévl. = DENUDATUM
xenosporum Balf. f. nomen nudum = ADENOGYNUM hybrid
YAKUSHIMANUM Nakai subsp. YAKUSHIMANUM = YAKUSHIMANUM
YAKUSHIMANUM Nakai subsp. *makinoi* (Tagg) Chamberlain = MAKINOI

New Taxa

Rhododendron heftii Davidian, sp. nov. See Vol. II page 149.

Species R. *wallichii* Hook. f. affinis sed foliis crassis infra glabris vel nonnunquam puberulis, supra atroviridis nitidis, corollis immaculatis albis recedens.

Frutex compactus, 1.83–3 m. altus, ramulis purpureis glabris vel floccosis eglandulosis, sub inflorescentia 3—5 mm. diametro, perulis deciduis. Folia sempervirentia; lamina crassa coriacea, late elliptica fere orbiculare, ovalia vel oblongo-elliptica, 7—11.8 cm. longa, 3.6–6.8 cm. lata, apice rotundata et mucronata, basi leviter cordata vel rotundata, supra atroviridis nitens glabra, costa media sulcata glabra, venis primariis 10—15 impressis, infra pallide viridis, glabra vel nonnunquam puberula, costa media prominente, venis primariis elevatis; petiolus 1.3—2.6 cm. longus purpureus rotundatus supra sulcatus, glaber, eglandulosus. Inflorescentia racemoso-umbellata 6—9-flora; rhachis 1.3–2 cm. longa, puberula vel glabra; pedicelli 1.4–2.4 cm. longi glabri. Calyx 5-lobatus minutus 0.5–1 mm. longus, lobis ovatis vel rotundatis, extra glabris, margine glabris vel puberulis. Corolla campanulata, 3.8–4.5 cm. longa immaculata eburnea; lobi 5, 1.2–1.5 cm. longi, 2–2.3 cm. lati, rotundati emarginati. Stamina 10 inaequalia, 1.3–3.4 cm. longa, corollae breviora; filamenta basi puberula. Gynoecium 3.6–4 cm. longum, corollae leviter brevius; ovarium tenue, 6–7 mm. longum, 6–7-loculare, glabrum, eglandulosum; stylus glaber, eglandulosus. Capsula gracilis vel anguste oblonga, 2–2.5 cm. longa, 5–6 mm. lata, paulo vel moderate curvata, costata, glabra, eglandulosa, calyce persistente.

Nepal. Arun Valley. Maghung Khola, E. of Num. 11,000 ft. Height 10 ft. Amongst hillside shrubs. Corolla and filaments white. 7.5.56. John D. A. Stainton No. 245 (Holotype in Herb. Brit. Mus. Nat. Hist.).

Rhododendron poluninii Davidian, sp. nov. See Vol. II page 155.

Species R. *tsariensi* Cowan affinis sed foliis lanceolatis oblongo-lanceolatis vel oblongis majoribus, lamina 6.2–8 cm. longa, infra indumento ferrugineo, inflorescentia 5–11-flora, corolla eburnea vel eburnea roseo-tincta differt.

Frutex 1.53–1.83 m. altus; ramuli dense tomentosi, tomento ferrugineo, eglandulosi, sub inflorescentia 4–5 mm. diametro, perulis deciduis. Folia sempervirentia; lamina coriacea, lanceolata, oblongo-lanceolata vel oblonga, 6.2–8 cm. longa, 2.6–2.8 cm. lata, apice breviter acuta vel obtusa et mucronata, basi rotundata vel leviter cordata, supra atroviridis nitens glabra, costa media sulcata dense tomentosa, venis primariis 10–12 impressis, margine recurva vel plana, infra indumento crasso lanato ferrugineo continuo unistratoso (in foliis juvenilibus flavido), costa media prominente dense tomentosa, venis primariis occultis; petiolus 1–1.6 cm. longus rotundatus supra sulcatus dense tomentosus tomento ferrugineo eglandulosus. Inflorescentia terminalis racemoso-umbellata 5–11-flora, bracteis deciduis; rhachis 4–5 mm. longa, dense tomentosa, eglandulosa; pedicelli 0.9–1.1 cm. longi crassi dense tomentosi tomento brunneo, eglandulosi. Calyx minutus, 0.5–1 mm. longus 5-lobatus, lobis triangularibus, extra et margine dense tomentosis eglandulosis. Corolla tubuloso-campanulata, 3.5–3.8 cm. longa, eburnea vel roseo-tincta postice kermesino-maculata; lobi 5, 1–1.2 cm. longi, 1.3–1.6 cm. lati, rotundati, emarginati. Stamina 10 inaequalia, 1.4–2 cm. longa; filamenta versus trientem inferiorem dense pubescentia. Gynoecium 2.9–3.4 cm. longum, corollae brevius; ovarium conoideum vel oblongo-ovale, 4–5 mm. longum, 5-loculare, dense tomentosum, tomento pallide brunneo vel brunneo, eglandulosum; stylus glaber eglandulosus. Capsula oblonga vel conoidea, 1–1.3 cm. longa, 3–5 mm. lata, recta, dense tomentosa, tomento ferrugineo, eglandulosa, calyce persistente.

Central Bhutan. Dunshinggang. Black Mountain. Alt. 13,000 ft. 20.5.1937. F. Ludlow—G. Sherriff No. 3089.

S. Tibet F. Ludlow & G. Sherriff?

Holotype, cultivated specimen in Herb. Hort. Bot. Edin.

Rhododendron tsariense Cowan var. **magnum** Davidian, var. nov. See Vol. II page 157.

A planta typica foliis majoribus ad 8.5 cm. longus, habitu magnus ad 3 m. altus differt.

Bhutan. Lhabja Pumthang. Altitude 12,500 ft. Bush 8–10 ft., veined leaves. 22/9/14. R. E. Cooper No. 2148 (Holotype in Herb. Hort. Bot. Edin.).

Bhutan. Weitang. Bumthang Chu. Altitude 13,500 ft. Corolla pale pink, or white suffused pale pink, rose at base of tube outside. Leaves under surface bright rusty brown. 29.5.1949. F. Ludlow, G. Sherriff, & J. H. Hicks No. 18998.

Rhododendron tsariense Cowan var. **trimoense** Davidian, var. nov. See Vol. II page 157.

A planta typica foliis infra ramulis petiolis pedicellis calycis et ovariis pallide brunneis vel fere albidis, foliis plerumque ovatis vel orbicularis differt.

South Tibet. Trimo. Nyam Jang Chu. Altitude 11,000 ft. Shrub. Seed collected. In rhododendron and fir forest. 17.11.36. F. Ludlow, G. Sherriff No. 2894 (Holotype in Herb. Brit. Mus. Nat. Hist. Details of the description are based on a cultivated plant under Ludlow & Sherriff No. 2894).

Rhododendron delavayi Franch. var. **albotomentosum** Davidian, var. nov. See Vol. II page 75.

Syn. *R. arboreum* Sm. 'Doctor Bowman', Journ. American Rhododendron Society, Vol. 38 Number 2 Spring 1984 pp. 85–86.

A planta typica foliis infra albotomentosis, ramulis et petiolis immaculatis albis, corollis coccineis differt.

West Central Burma. Mount Victoria. 10,000 ft. A large veteran tree, or a shrub, according to exposure, and fate in the grass fires. Many in full bloom. Flowers of an intense glowing scarlet, no spots. The leaf buds exude a sticky gum under leaf surface, pure white, the indumentum looser than in the form found below 5,000 ft. Found on the extreme summit with Q-semecarpaefolia the hardiest and most fire resistant tree here. 9.4.1956. Kingdon-Ward No. 21976 (Holotype in Herb. Brit. Mus. Nat. Hist.).

Rhododendron fictolacteum Balf. f. var. **miniforme** Davidian, var. nov. See Vol. II page 170.

A planta typica foliis, inflorescentiis et floribus minoribus differt.

N. W. Yunnan. Mekong-Yangtze Divide east of A. Wa. Lat. 27° 25'N. Long. 99° 18'E. Alt. 13,000 ft. Shrub of 20 ft. In immature fruit. In rhododendron thickets and mixed forests. June 1924. George Forrest No. 25512 (Holotype in Herb. Hort. Bot. Edin.).

S. Eastern Tibet. Tsarong. Salwin-Kiu Chiang Divide. N.W. of Si-chi-to. Lat. 28° 48'N. Long. 98° 15'E. Alt. 13,000 ft. Shrub of 8–12 ft. In fruit. In rhododendron thickets. Oct. 1922. George Forrest No. 22888.

N. W. Yunnan. Oct. 1924. George Forrest No. 25896 = Forrest No. 25512. Same locality and altitude.

Northwestern Yunnan. Mount Ta-Pao, between Wei-Hsi and the Mekong. Alt. 3,850 m. Tree, 4.5–6 m.; fls. white. In fir forest. September–October, 1929. J. F. Rock No. 18451.

South-east Tibet. Province of Tsarung. Forests and alpine regions of the Solo-la. Altitude 13,500 ft. Shrub 6–8 feet. Flowers pink. August–October 1932. Joseph F. Rock No. 22660.

Rhododendron scyphocalyx Balf. f. et Forrest var. **septendrionale** Tagg ex Davidian, var. nov. See page 135.

Syn. *R. dichroanthum* Diels subsp. *septendrionale* Tagg ex Cowan in Notes Roy. Bot. Gard. Edin., Vol. 20 (1940) 87.

A planta typica ovariis, calycis et plerumque pedicellis eglandulosis, foliis oblanceolatis differt.

N. E. Upper Burma. Western flank of the Salwin-Kiu Chiang Divide. Lat. 27° 18'N. Long. 98° 40'E. Alt. 13–14,000 ft. Shrub of 3½–4 ft. Flowers yellowish, heavily flushed rose. On alpine meadows and moorland. July 1924. George Forrest No. 25750 (Holotype in Herb. Hort. Bot. Edin.).

N. W. Yunnan. Mekong-Salwin Divide. Lat. 27°N. Long. 99° 2'E. Alt. 13–14,000 ft. Rhod. aff. *R. citriniflorum* Balf. fil. Shrub of 3 ft. Flowers yellow, flushed rose at extreme base. On ledges of cliffs and on boulders in ravines. July 1924. George Forrest No. 25577.

N. W. Yunnan. Mekong-Salwin Divide. Lat. 27°N. Long. 99° 2'E. Alt. 14,000 ft. Rhod. Shrub of 4 ft. Flowers lemon-yellow, ruddy at base exterior. On alpine moorland. July 1924. George Forrest No. 25579.

N. W. Yunnan. Rhod. aff. *R. citriniflorum* = F No. 25577. Same locality and altitude. Oct. 1924. George Forrest No. 25787.

Rhododendron roxieanum Forrest var. **parvum** Davidian, var. nov. See page 214.

A planta typica foliis minoribus, laminis 2.5–6 cm. longis, 6 mm.–1.3 cm. latis, habitu parvus differt.

N. W. Yunnan. Mekong-Salwin Divide. Lat. 27° 30'N. Long. 98° 56'E. *R. roxieanum*. Shrub of 2 ft. Flowers white, with few or no markings. Open stony woodland. Alt. 14,500 ft. July 1921. G. Forrest No. 19780.

N. W. Yunnan. Chao-ü Shan. Mekong-Yangtze Divide. Lat. 27° 5'N. Long. 99° 35'E. Roxieanum form. Shrub of 3 ft. Flowers white, spotted crimson. On terraced cliffs and rocky meadows. Alt. 13,000 ft. July 1924. G. Forrest No. 25701 (Holotype in Herb. Hort. Bot. Edin.).

N. W. Yunnan. = Forrest No. 25701. Same locality and altitude. Oct. 1924. G. Forrest No. 25940.

N. W. Yunnan. Chao-ü Shan. Mekong-Yangtze Divide. *R. roxieanum* form. Shrub of 2 ft. Flowers in bud only, deep rose. On open rocky slopes. Alt. 12–13,000 ft. Oct. 1924. G. Forrest No. 25987.

S. W. Sichuan. Kaushu shan, Leilung (Leirong). *R. pronum* Tagg et Forrest. Shrub 1 foot. Flowers white. Alpine region. Alt. 15,000 feet. October 1932. J. F. Rock No. 24501.

Lepidote:

Rhododendron mucronulatum Turcz. var. **chejuense** Davidian, var. nov.

A planta typica habitu nanus, 10–30 cm. altus differt.

Cheju island, Korea. 4,500–6,000 ft. May 1976. Mr. and Mrs. Warren Berg and Mr. Hideo Suzuki. (Holotype, cultivated specimen in Edinburgh).

The variety differs from the species in that it is a dwarf plant, 10–30 cm. high.

This plant was first collected by Mr. and Mrs. Warren Berg and Hideo Suzuki in May 1976 on the island of Cheju, Korea. They found it growing in abundance on Mt. Halla at elevations of 4,500–6,000 feet (1,373–1,830 m.). The plant was introduced by them into cultivation in 1976. It is hardy outdoors, free-flowering, and it has the added advantage of producing the flowers quite young when raised from seed.

Epithet. From Cheju island, Korea.

Hardiness 3. March. Plate 159. See Vol. II.

Series **Argyrophylla** Davidian, Ser. nov. See Vol. II page 83.

Frutices vel arbores, 92 cm.–12 m. alti; ramuli moderate vel dense tomentosi, tomento tenui. Folia sempervirentia, oblongo-lanceolata, lanceolata, oblanceolata, oblonga vel obovata; lamina 4–20.5 cm. longa, 0.8–6.9 cm. lata, infra indumento tenui pannoso continuo unistrato, vel crasso lanato continuo bistrato. Inflorescentia laxa, racemoso-umbellata 4–20-flora vel nonnunquam 30-flora. Calyx 5-lobatus, 1–2 mm. vel raro 3–5 mm. longus. Corolla infundibuliformi-campanulata, campanulata vel nonnunquam tubuloso-campanulata, 2–5.3 cm. longa; lobi 5 vel raro 6–7. Stamina 10–12 vel nonnunquam 13–15 vel raro 8–9. Ovarium dense tomentosum vel raro glabrum. Capsula oblonga vel raro gracilis.

Typus Seriei: *R. argyrophyllum* Franch.

Subseries **Campanulata** Davidian, Subser. nov. See Vol. II page 146.

Frutices vel nonnunquam arbores, 30 cm.–5.50 m. alti; ramuli glabri vel nonnunquam floccosi. Foliorum lamina 5–15.8 cm. longa, 2.2–2.8 cm. lata, infra indumento continuo unistrato (in *R. aeruginoso* bistrato excepto), vel infra floccosa vel glabra; petiolus glaber vel nonnunquam floccosus. Inflorescentia racemoso-umbellata 5–18-flora, pedicelli glabri vel floccosi. Calyx 0.5–2 mm. vel raro 3 mm. longus, glaber vel floccosus. Corolla 2.1–5 cm. longa, lavandulacea, lilacina, purpurea, rosea vel alba. Ovarium 4–8 mm. longum, glabrum vel dense tomentosum. Capsula 1.4–3.8 cm. longa, glabra.

Typus Subseriei: *R. campanulatum* D. Don.

Subseries **Lanata** Davidian, Subser. nov. See Vol. II page 151.

Frutices vel nonnunquam arbores, 30 cm.–7.63 m. alti; ramuli dense tomentosi. Foliorum lamina 1.8–14 cm. longa, 1–5.4 cm. lata, infra indumento crasso (in *R. flinckii* tenui excepto) lanato continuo unistrato; petiolus dense tomentosus. Inflorescentia racemoso-umbellata 2–20-flora, pedicelli dense tomentosi. Calyx 0.5–2 mm. longus, dense tomentosus vel glaber. Corolla late campanulata vel campanulata, 2.6–5 cm. longa, pallide lutea, viridulo-flavida, rosea vel alba. Stamina 10. Ovarium 4–6 mm. longum, dense tomentosum. Capsulo 1–2.5 cm. longa, dense vel moderate tomentosa.

Typus Subseriei: *R. lanatum* Hook. f.

Series **Fulgensia** Davidian, Ser. nov. See Vol. II page 215.

Frutices vel nonnunquam arbores parvi, 60 cm.–6 m. alti, cortice brunneo papyraceo textus; ramuli glabri eglandulosi. Folia obovata, ovalia, oblongo-obovata vel elliptica; lamina 5.3–13.5 cm. longa, 2.4–7 cm. lata; infra indumento crasso lanato continuo unistrato, vel infra glabra; petiolus glaber, eglandulosus. Inflorescentia compacta, 8–15-flora, pedicelli glabri, eglandulosi. Calyx 1–3 mm. longus, glaber. Corolla tubuloso-campanulata, 2–3.5 cm. longa, kermesina vel coccinea. Stamina 10. Ovarium glabrum, eglandulosum. Corolla 0.7–3 cm. longa, glabra, eglandulosa.

Typus Seriei: *R. fulgens* Hook. f.

Series **Griersoniana** Davidian, Ser. nov. See Vol. II page 247.

Frutex laxus, 1.53–3 m. altus; gemmae foliorum longe, conice, angustate. Folia sempervirentia, lanceolata; lamina 6.4–20 cm. longa, 1.2–5.3 cm. lata; infra indumento crasso lanato continuo vel interrupto. Inflorescentia racemoso-umbellata 5–12-flora; alabastra magna, longa, conica, angustata. Corolla infundibuliformis, 5–8 cm. longa, coccinea, miniata vel rosea, 5-lobata. Stamina 10. Ovarium dense tomentosum. Capsula oblonga.

Typus Seriei: *R. griersonianum* Balf. f. et Forrest.

Series **Parishia** Davidian, Ser. nov. See page 139.

Frutices vel arbores, 1.22–12.20 m. alti; ramuli glabri vel moderate vel dense floccosi pilis stellatis. Folia oblonga, oblongo-ovalia, elliptica, obovata, oblanceolata vel lanceolata; lamina 6–28 cm. longa, 1.7–11 cm. lata, infra glabra vel moderate tomentosa, vel nonnunquam indumento continuo vel interrupto, pilis stellatis; petiolus glaber vel dense vel sparsim floccosus, pilis stellatis. Inflorescentia racemoso-umbellata 5–16-flora, pedicelli moderate vel dense floccosi pilis plerumque stellatis vel glabris. Calyx 0.5–5 mm. vel nonnunquam 0.9–2 cm. longus. Corolla tubuloso-campanulata vel nonnunquam campanulata, 2.5–6 cm. longa, kermesina, coccinea, roseo-kermesina, rosea, nonnunquam purpurea vel alba; lobi 5. Stamina 10. Ovarium 3–9 mm. longum, dense vel nonnunquam moderate tomentosum, pilis stellatis. Capsula 1.2–4 cm. longa, moderate vel dense floccosa, pilis stellatis.

Typus Seriei: *R. parishii* C. B. Clarke.

Series **Sherriffia** Davidian, Ser. nov. See page 175.

Frutices vel arbores, 1.53–6 m. alti. Folia ovalia, obovata, elliptica vel oblonga; lamina 3.3–6 cm. longa, 1.5–4 cm. lata, infra indumento crasso lanato continuo unistrato. Inflorescentia laxa racemoso-umbellata 3–6-flora. Calyx 2 mm.–1.4 cm. longus, kermesinus vel coccineus. Corolla campanulata vel tubuloso-campanulata, 2.8–4 cm. longa, kermesina vel coccinea, 5-lobata. Ovarium glabrum. Capsula 1.3–1.4 cm. longa, glabra.

Typus Seriei: *R. sherriffii* Cowan.

Subseries **Williamsiana** Davidian, Subser. nov. See page 286.

Frutex compacta vel rotundata, 60 cm.–1.63 m. vel raro ad 2.44 m. altus; ramuli sparsim vel moderate setuloso-glandulosi. Folia orbiculare vel ovata; lamina 1.5–4.2 cm. longa, 1.3–4 cm. lata, infra glabra; petiolus moderate vel sparsim setuloso-glandulosus vel eglandulosus. Inflorescentia 2–3- (raro ad 5-) flora. Calyx 5-lobatus annularis tantum, 1.5 mm. longus. Corolla campanulata, 3–4 cm. longa, rosea, 5–6-lobata. Stamina 10. Ovarium 5–6-loculare; stylus omnino glandulosus.

Typus Subseriei: *R. williamsianum* Rehd. et Wils.

Synopsis of Elepidote Rhododendron Species and Some of their Characteristics

Q = not in cultivation

Species	Series	Subseries	Height	Flower colour	Hardiness	Month of Flowering
aberconwayi	Irroratum	—	30 cm.–2.44 m. (1–8 ft.)	White, white tinged pink	3	April–May
aberrans Q	Lacteum	—	60 cm.–4.50 m. (2–15 ft.)	White, white flushed rose	—	—
adenogynum	Taliense	Adenogynum	46 cm.–5.50 m. (1½–18 ft.)	Rose, magenta-rose, reddish-purple, pink, white tinged pink or rose, white, rarely creamy-white	3	April–May
adenopodum	Ponticum	—	1.22–3 m. (4–10 ft.)	Pale rose	3	April–May
adenosum	Barbatum	Glischrum	2–5 m. (6½–16 ft.)	White tinged pink, white	3	April–May
adroserum	Irroratum	—	92 cm.–4.58 m. (3–15 ft.)	Light-coloured at base, towards margins heavily flushed deep magenta-rose, white tinged pink	3	April–May
aeruginosum	Campanulatum	Campanulatum	30 cm.–2.75 m. (1–9 ft.)	Lilac, rose, deep rose, light to dark purple, reddish-purple, purple-rose, pink	3	April–May
aganniphum	Taliense	Taliense	30 cm.–3 m. (1–10 ft.)	White, white flushed rose, rose, deep rose, purplish-pink, rarely creamy-white	3	May
agapetum	Parishii	—	1.83–10.68 m. (6–35 ft.)	Crimson-scarlet, deep crimson	1–3	May–June
agastum	Irroratum	—	1.22–6 m. (4–20 ft.)	Rose, deep rose, pale rose, white tinged pink	3	March–May
agglutinatum	Lacteum	—	60 cm.–4.58 m. (2–15 ft.)	White, creamy-white, white flushed rose or pink	3	April–May
albertsenianum	Neriiflorum	Neriiflorum	1.22–2.14 m. (4–7 ft.)	Bright crimson-rose, scarlet-crimson	3	April–May
albiflorum	Albiflorum	—	75 cm.–1.83 m. (2½–6 ft.)	White, creamy-white, greenish-white	3	June–July
alutaceum	Taliense	Adenogynum	1.83–4.27 m. (6–14 ft.)	Rose, deep rose	3	April–May
anhweiense	Irroratum	—	92 cm.–3.66 m. (3–12 ft.)	White, white tinged pink, pink	3	April–May
annae	Irroratum	—	1–2 m. (3⅓–6½ ft.)	Rose, white flushed rose, creamy-white flushed rose	1–3	April–June
anthosphaerum	Irroratum	—	1.53–9 m. (5–30 ft.)	Bright rose-magenta, deep rose-magenta, crimson-rose, deep crimson-magenta, purple, lilac, pale lavender-blue, peach colour, pink	3	March–May
anthosphaerum var. eritimum	Irroratum	—	1.53–12 m. (5–40 ft.)	Deep plum-crimson, crimson	3	March–May
aperantum	Neriiflorum	Sanguineum	8–60 cm. (3 in.–2 ft.) sometimes 92 cm. (3 ft.), rarely 1.53–1.83 m. (5–6 ft.)	Deep crimson, crimson, rose-crimson, rose, pink, yellow, orange, creamy-white, white, white flushed rose	3	April–May

Species	Series	Subseries	Height	Flower colour	Hardiness	Month of Flowering
aperantum var. subpilosum	Neriiflorum	Sanguineum	30–46 cm. (1–1½ ft.)	White	3	April–May
apodectum	Neriiflorum	Sanguineum	30–2.44 m. (1–8 ft.)	Deep crimson, crimson, deep rose flushed orange, pale or deep orange flushed rose, bright cherry-scarlet, deep crimson flushed orange	3	May–June
araiophyllum	Irroratum	—	1.22–9 m. (4–30 ft.)	White, creamy-white, white flushed rose	2–3	April–May
arboreum	Arboreum	—	1.22–18.30 m. (4–60 ft.)	Deep crimson, crimson, scarlet, red	1–3	Feb.–May
arboreum forma album	Arboreum	—	3–6 m. (10–20 ft.)	White	2–3	Feb.–May
arboreum forma roseum	Arboreum	—	3–9 m. (10–30 ft.)	Rose	2–3	Feb.–May
argipeplum	Barbatum	Barbatum	1.83–4.58 m. (6–15 ft.)	Crimson, scarlet	3	March–April
argyrophyllum	Argyrophyllum	—	1–12 m. (3⅓–39 ft.)	White, pink, rose, white flushed rose	3	May
argyrophyllum var. cupulare	Argyrophyllum	—	Up to 3 m. (10 ft.)	White, pink, rose, white flushed rose	3	May
argyrophyllum var. nankingense	Argyrophyllum	—	2.44–10 m. (8–33 ft.)	Deep pink	3	May
argyrophyllum var. omeiense Q	Argyrophyllum	—	Up to 2 m. (6½ ft.)	White, pink, rose, white flushed rose	—	—
arizelum	Falconeri	—	1.83–7.63 m. (6–25 ft.) rarely 12.20 m. (40 ft.)	Pale or deep yellow, pale creamy, pale creamy-white, white, pale or deep rose, pink	3	April–May
arizelum var. rubicosum	Falconeri	—	2.44–3 m. (8–10 ft.)	Crimson, carmine	3	April–May
asterochnoum Q	Fortunei	Calophytum	Small tree	White suffused rose	—	—
aureum	Ponticum	—	10–30 cm. (4–12 in.)	Yellow	3	April–May
auriculatum	Auriculatum	—	1.83–10 m. (6–33 ft.)	White, rose-pink, creamy-white	3	July–August
bainbridgeanum	Barbatum	Crinigerum	60 cm.–2.75 m. (2–9 ft.)	Creamy-yellow, white, creamy-white flushed or not flushed rose, reddish-purple, pink	3	March–April
balfourianum	Taliense	Adenogynum	92 cm.–4.58 m. (3–15 ft.)	Pale or deep rose, pink, white	3	April–May
balfourianum var. aganniphoides	Taliense	Adenogynum	60 cm.–5 m. (2–16 ft.)	Pale or deep rose	3	April–May
barbatum	Barbatum	Barbatum	2.44–18.30 m. (8–60 ft.)	Crimson, scarlet	3	Feb.–April
basilicum	Falconeri	—	2.44–9.15 m. (8–30 ft.)	Pale yellow, creamy-white, pink	3	April–May
bathyphyllum	Taliense	Roxieanum	92 cm.–1.53 m. (3–5 ft.)	White, white flushed rose, creamy-white flushed rose	3	April–May
beanianum	Neriiflorum	Haematodes	92 cm.–3 m. (3–10 ft.)	Deep crimson, crimson	3	March–May
beesianum	Lacteum	—	1.83–9 m. (6–30 ft.)	White, white flushed rose, pink, rose, deep rose, purple, red	3	April–May
bijiangense Q	Neriiflorum	Neriiflorum	About 1 m. (3⅓ ft.)	Reddish-purple	—	—
bonvalotii Q	Thomsonii	Cerasinum	Shrub	Rose?	—	—
brachycarpum	Ponticum	—	1.22–3 m. (4–10 ft.)	White, white flushed pink, creamy-white flushed pink along the middle of the petals	3	June–July
brachycarpum var. tigerstedtii	Ponticum	—	1.22–3 m. (4–10 ft.)	White	3	June–July
brevinerve Q	Irroratum	—	Up to 5 m. (16 ft.)	Purple	—	—
brunneifolium	Neriiflorum	Sanguineum	92 cm.–1.22 m. (3–4 ft.)	Rose-crimson	3	April–May
bureavii	Taliense	Adenogynum	1.22–7.63 m. (4–25 ft.)	Rose, reddish, white, white flushed rose, creamy-white flushed rose	3	May
bureavioides	Taliense	Adenogynum	1.22–3 m. (4–10 ft.)	Rose	3	May
callimorphum	Thomsonii	Campylocarpum	60 cm.–2.75 m. (2–9 ft.)	Pink, pale to deep rose, pale rose almost white	3	April–May

Species	Series	Subseries	Height	Flower colour	Hardiness	Month of Flowering
calophytum	Fortunei	Calophytum	4.58–15 m. (15–49 ft.)	White, white tinged pink, pink, rose, rosy-white, purple	3	March–April
caloxanthum	Thomsonii	Campylocarpum	60 cm.–2.5 m. (2–8 ft.)	Citron, yellow, pale sulphur-yellow, deep lemon-yellow, sometimes tinged pink	3	April–May
calvescens	Thomsonii	Selense	60 cm.–1.83 m. (2–6 ft.)	Rose, pale rose, white flushed rose, white	3	April–May
campanulatum	Campanulatum	Campanulatum	30 cm.–5.50 m. (1–18 ft.), sometimes up to 9.15 m. (30 ft.)	Lavender-blue, pale lavender-blue, bluish-purple, pale purple, lilac, mauve, various shades of mauve, rose, rosy-purple, white, white tinged lilac	3	April–May
campbelliae	Arboreum	—	3–12.20 m. (10–40 ft.)	Purplish-rose, reddish, pink, purple, scarlet crimson	2–3	April–May
campylocarpum	Thomsonii	Campylocarpum	92 cm.–3.66 m. (3–12 ft.)	Yellow, pale or bright yellow, sulphur-yellow, lemon-yellow	3	April–May
camtschaticum	Camtschaticum	—	10–30 cm. (4 in.–1 ft.)	Carmine-purple, rose-purple, reddish-purple, pink	3	May–June
camtschaticum var. albiflorum	Camtschaticum	—	10–30 cm. (4 in.–1 ft.)	White	3	May–June
cardiobasis	Fortunei	Orbiculare	1.22–3 m. (4–10 ft.)	White, red	3	April–May
catacosmum	Neriiflorum	Haematodes	1.22–2.75 m. (4–9 ft.)	Crimson, crimson-rose, pink	3	April–May
catawbiense	Ponticum	—	92 cm.–3 m. (3–10 ft.)	Rose, lilac-purple, pink, white	3	May–June
caucasicum	Ponticum	—	30 cm.–1 m. (1–3⅓ ft.)	Pale cream, white flushed lemon-yellow, very pale lemon flushed pink, pale lemon	3	April–May
cavaleriei Q	Stamineum	—	1.83–4 m. (6–13 ft.)	Rose, white	—	—
ceraceum	Irroratum	—	2.10–4.58 m. (7–15 ft.)	Magenta-rose, dark magenta-crimson, crimson-purple, red	2–3	March–April
cerasinum	Thomsonii	Cerasinum	1.22–3.66 m. (4–12 ft.)	Brilliant scarlet, cherry-red, deep crimson, white, creamy-white with a broad cherry-red or deep pink band round the summit	3	May–June
cerochitum Q	Irroratum	—	3–6 m. (10–20 ft.)	Deep rose, rose	—	—
chaetomallum	Neriiflorum	Haematodes	60 cm.–3 m. (2–10 ft.)	Deep crimson, crimson, black-crimson, deep carmine, scarlet, deep rose, pink	3	March–May
chaetomallum var. chamaephytum Q.	Neriiflorum	Haematodes	30–60 cm. (1–2 ft.)	Deep crimson	—	—
chaetomallum var. hemigymnum	Neriiflorum	Haematodes	Up to 1.83 m. (6 ft.)	Bright crimson	3	April–May
chaetomallum var. xanthanthum	Neriiflorum	Haematodes	92 cm.–1.53 m. (3–5 ft.)	Creamy-yellow, flushed or striped and often margined pale rose or crimson	3	April–May
chamaethomsonii	Neriiflorum	Forrestii	30–92 cm. (1–3 ft.), rarely 15 cm. (6 in.)	Deep crimson, crimson	3	March–May
chamaethomsonii var. chamaethauma	Neriiflorum	Forrestii	60–92 cm. (2–3 ft.)	Deep crimson, crimson, deep crimson-rose, deep scarlet, rose-red, rose, apple green, shell pink, pale pink	3	March–May
championae	Stamineum	—	2.44–6 m. (8–20 ft.)	Pink, rose, white	1–2	April–May
chienianum Q	Argyrophyllum	—	3–10 m. (10–33 ft.)	Purple, pinkish	—	—
chionanthum	Neriiflorum	Haematodes	60–92 cm. (2–3 ft.)	White	3	April–May
cinnamomeum	Arboreum	—	3–7.63 m. (10–25 ft.)	White	2–3	April–May

Species	Series	Subseries	Height	Flower colour	Hardiness	Month of Flowering
circinnatum Q	Taliense	Adenogynum	6.10–7.63 m. (20–25 ft.)	—	—	—
citriniflorum	Neriiflorum	Sanguineum	30 cm.–1.53 m. (1–5 ft.)	Bright lemon-yellow, yellow, yellow margined rose, yellowish flushed rose	3	April–May
clementinae	Taliense	Taliense	92 cm.–4.58 m. (3–15 ft.)	Creamy-white, white, white flushed rose, bright rose, pink, deep pink, purplish-red	3	April–May
cloiophorum	Neriiflorum	Sanguineum	30 cm.–1.53 m. (1–5 ft.)	Rose, yellowish towards the base, yellowish, flushed rose or deep rose, rose, rose-crimson, white, tinged and margined rose, orange-red	3	April–May
cloiophorum var. leucopetalum	Neriiflorum	Sanguineum	92 cm.–1.22 m. (3–4 ft.)	Pure white	3	April–May
cloiophorum var. mannophorum Q	Neriiflorum	Sanguineum	60 cm.–1.22 m. (2–4 ft.)	Rose, yellowish flushed rose or deep rose, orange-red	—	—
cloiophorum var. roseotinctum	Neriiflorum	Sanguineum	30–60 cm. (1–2 ft.)	Rose	3	April–May
codonanthum	Taliense	Adenogynum	30 cm.–1.22 m. (1–4 ft.)	Bright yellow	3	April–May
coelicum	Neriiflorum	Haematodes	92 cm.–1.83 m. (3–6 ft.)	Deep scarlet, deep crimson	3	April–May
coeloneurum Q	Taliense	Wasonii	3.66–4 m. (12–13 ft.)	Pink, purplish	—	—
colletum	Lacteum	—	1.53–7.63 m. (5–25 ft.)	Pale rose, white flushed rose, pink, red	3	April–May
comisteum	Taliense	Roxieanum	60 cm.–1.22 m. (1–4 ft.)	Soft rose, deep soft rose, pale rose	3	April–May
cookeanum	Parishii	—	1.22–8 m. (4–26 ft.)	White, pink, red-purple	3	May–July
coriaceum	Falconeri	—	1.22–7.63 m. (4–25 ft.)	White, white flushed rose, rose	3	April–May
coryanum	Argyrophyllum	—	2.44–6.10 m. (8–20 ft.)	Creamy-white, white	3	April–May
crinigerum	Barbatum	Crinigerum	92 cm.–6.10 m. (3–20 ft.), rarely 60 cm. (2 ft.)	White, white flushed rose, white heavily flushed and margined rose, white with rose bands, pink, reddish-purple, red	3	April–May
crinigerum var. euadenium	Barbatum	Crinigerum	Up to 1.83 m. (6 ft.)	White tinged pink, white	3	April–May
cruentum Q	Taliense	Adenogynum	92 cm.–1.22 m. (3–4 ft.)	White, white flushed rose	—	—
cucullatum	Taliense	Roxieanum	60 cm.–1.53 m. (2–5 ft.), rarely 3 m. (10 ft.)	White, white flushed rose	3	April–May
cyanocarpum	Thomsonii	Thomsonii	1.22–7.63 m. (4–25 ft.)	Rosy-white, rich soft rose, pinkish-white, white flushed pale rose, pale pink, creamy-white flushed pale rose, white	3	March–April
dasycladoides Q	Thomsonii	Selense	2–4 m. (6½–13 ft.)	Pale pink, rose, pinkish-purple	—	—
dasycladum	Thomsonii	Selense	92 cm.–4.58 m. (3–15 ft.)	Rose, pink, white, white flushed rose	3	April–May
davidii Q	Fortunei	Davidii	1–6 m. (3⅓–20 ft.)	Rose, light purple, bright rosy-red, lilac	—	—
decorum	Fortunei	Fortunei	92 cm.–9.15 m. (3–30 ft.), rarely up to 15.25 m. (50 ft.)	White, white flushed rose, pink, rose	3	May–June
degronianum	Ponticum	—	92 cm.–2 m. (3–6 ft.)	Pink, rose, deep rose, reddish or rarely white	3	April–May
degronianum var. heptamerum	Ponticum	—	92 cm.–4 m. (3–13 ft.)	Pink, rose, deep rose	3	April–May
delavayi	Arboreum	—	92 cm.–12.20 m. (3–40 ft.)	Deep crimson, crimson, bright cherry-crimson, scarlet	1–3	March–May
delavayi var. albotomentosum	Arboreum	—	Up to 12.20 m. (40 ft.)	Scarlet	1–3	March–May

Species	Series	Subseries	Height	Flower colour	Hardiness	Month of Flowering
delavayi var. album	Arboreum	—	Up to 3 m. (10 ft.)	Pure white	1–2	April–May
denudatum Q	Argyrophyllum	—	2–3.66 m. (6½–12 ft.)	Rose	—	—
detersile Q	Taliense	Adenogynum	92 cm.–1.22m. (3–4 ft.)	Reddish	—	—
detonsum	Taliense	Adenogynum	2.44–3.66 m. (8–12 ft.)	Rose-pink, pink	3	April–May
diaprepes	Fortunei	Fortunei	1.22–7.62 m. (4–25 ft.)	White or white flushed rose, base green or not green	3	June–July
dichroanthum	Neriiflorum	Sanguineum	60 cm.–2.44 m. (2–8 ft.)	Yellowish-rose, orange, yellowish-white flushed rose, orange-red, rosy-red, pinkish-red	3	May–June
dictyotum	Lacteum	—	1.22–3.66 m. (4–12 ft.)	White, white flushed rose	3	April–May
didymum	Neriiflorum	Sanguineum	30–92 cm. (1–3 ft.)	Black-crimson, dark crimson	3	June–July
dignabile Q	Lacteum	—	60 cm.–6.10 m. (2–20 ft.)	Pink, cream, lemon-yellow, white	—	—
dimitrum	Neriiflorum	Neriiflorum	1.22–2.75 m. (4–9 ft.)	Deep rose, white heavily flushed rose, pink	3	April–May
diphrocalyx	Barbatum	Glischrum	92 cm.–4.58 m. (3–15 ft.)	Deep wine-crimson, deep crimson-rose, light crimson, rose, bright red	3	April–May
discolor	Fortunei	Fortunei	1.22–8 m. (4–26 ft.)	White, pink, rosy-pink	3	June–July
doshongense	Taliense	Taliense	60 cm.–4.58 m. (2–15 ft.)	Pink, whitish-pink, pinkish-red, rose, white with 5 pink bands on the outside, white	3	April–May
dryophyllum	Lacteum	—	60 cm.–7.63 m. (2–25 ft.)	White, creamy-white, white flushed rose, pink, pinkish-purple	3	April–May
dumosulum	Lacteum	—	30 cm.–1.21 m. (1–4 ft.)	White faintly flushed rose	3	April–May
eclecteum	Thomsonii	Thomsonii	60 cm.–3 m. (2–10 ft.)	White, white flushed rose, pink, deep pink, rose, pale yellow, yellow, purple, yellowish-red, red	3	Feb.–April
eclecteum var. bellatulum	Thomsonii	Thomsonii	92 cm.–1.53 m. (3–5 ft.)	White flushed rose, rose, pale yellow	3	March–April
eclecteum var. brachyandrum	Thomsonii	Thomsonii	60 cm.–2.44 m. (2–8 ft.)	Deep rose, deep rose-crimson, deep magenta-crimson, reddish-purple	3	March–April
elegantulum	Taliense	Adenogynum	92 cm.–1.53 m. (3–5 ft.)	Pale purplish-pink	3	May
elliottii	Parishii	—	2.44–4.58 m. (8–15 ft.)	Crimson, scarlet-crimson, scarlet, deep rose	1–3	May–July
ellipticum	Stamineum	—	Up to 4.58 m. (15 ft.)	Pink, white	1–2	April–May
epapillatum Q	Irroratum	—	5.19 m. (17 ft.)	Pale pink	—	—
erastum Q	Neriiflorum	Forrestii	6–9 cm. (2½–3½ in.)	Clear rose	—	—
erosum	Barbatum	Barbatum	2.44–9.15 m. (8–30 ft.)	Rose-pink, very deep crimson	3	March–April
erubescens	Fortunei	Oreodoxa	1–3.66 m. (3⅓–12 ft.)	White, rose-carmine outside, rose	3	March–April
erythrocalyx	Thomsonii	Selense	92 cm.–2.44 m. (3–8 ft.)	Creamy-white, creamy-yellow, creamy-yellow flushed rose, white, white flushed rose, pale rose, rarely yellow	3	April–May
esetulosum	Thomsonii	Selense	1.22–1.83 m. (4–6 ft.)	Creamy-white or white, flushed or not flushed rose or purplish	3	April–May
esquirolii Q	Stamineum	—	1 m. (3⅓ ft.)	Rose-violet	—	—
euchroum Q	Neriiflorum	Neriiflorum	30–60 cm. (1–2 ft.)	Bright brick-red	—	—

Species	Series	Subseries	Height	Flower colour	Hardiness	Month of Flowering
eudoxum	Neriiflorum	Sanguineum	30 cm.–1.83 m. (1–6 ft.)	Crimson-rose, rose, magenta-rose, creamy-white faintly flushed rose, white flushed rose, dark red	3	April–May
eurysiphon	Thomsonii	Selense	92 cm.–1.53 m. (3–5 ft.)	Creamy-white or very pale rose, flushed deep rose or deep magenta-rose, copiously spotted with crimson	3	May
exasperatum	Barbatum	Barbatum	1.53–4.58 m. (5–15 ft.)	Brick-red, rose-pink, scarlet	3	March–May
eximium	Falconeri	Falconeri	1.53–9.15 m. (5–30 ft.)	Rose, pink	2–3	April–May
faberi	Taliense	Adenogynum	1–6 m. (3⅓–20 ft.)	White	3	May
facetum	Parishii	—	1.53–12.20 m. (5–40 ft.)	Crimson, deep crimson, scarlet-crimson, scarlet, crimson-rose, deep rose	1–3	June–July
faithae Q	Fortunei	Fortunei	4–8 m. (13–26 ft.)	White	—	—
falconeri	Falconeri	—	3–12.20 m. (10–40 ft.), sometimes up to 15.25 m. (50 ft.)	Creamy-white, yellowish, sometimes white or pinkish	3	April–May
fargesii	Fortunei	Oreodoxa	1–6 m. (3⅓–20 ft.)	White, pink, rose, deep rose, deep rosy-red	3	Feb.–March–April
farinosum Q	Argyrophyllum	—	1.22–2 m. (4–6½ ft.)	White	—	—
fauriei	Ponticum	—	92 cm.–3 m. (3–10 ft.)	White or yellowish, flushed pink along the middle of the lobes	3	June–July
feddei Q	Stamineum	—	1–4 m. (3⅓–13 ft.)	White	—	—
fictolacteum	Falconeri	—	1.83–12.20 m. (6–40 ft.)	White, white flushed rose, pink, crimson-rose, creamy	3	April–May
fictolacteum var. miniforme	Falconeri	—	92 cm.–6.10 m. (3–20 ft.)	White, white flushed rose	3	April–May
flavorufum	Taliense	Taliense	30 cm.–3 m. (1–10 ft.)	White, rose, deep rose, white flushed rose, yellowish-white	3	April–May
flinckii	Campanulatum	Lanatum	1.53–2.44 m. (5–8 ft.)	Yellow	3	April–May
floccigerum	Neriiflorum	Neriiflorum	60 cm.–2.44 m. (2–8 ft.)	Deep crimson, crimson, scarlet, carmine, bright rose, reddish-pink, lemon-yellow margined or flushed rose or bright crimson, yellow flushed pink	3	March–May
floccigerum var. appropinquans	Neriiflorum	Neriiflorum	1.53–3 m. (5–10 ft.)	Deep crimson, crimson, scarlet, bright rose, yellow flushed pink	3	March–May
floribundum	Argyrophyllum	—	1.83–6.10 m. (6–20 ft.)	Pink, rose, pinkish-purple, purplish-lavender	3	April–May
formosanum	Argyrophyllum	—	1.83–5.50 m. (6–18 ft.)	White, pink	2–3	April–May
forrestii	Neriiflorum	Forrestii	3–45 cm. (1 in.–1½ ft.)	Deep crimson, crimson, scarlet, light rose-crimson, carmine	3	April–May
forrestii var. repens	Neriiflorum	Forrestii	3–45 cm. (1 in.–1½ ft.)	Deep crimson, crimson, scarlet, light rose-crimson, carmine	3	April–May
forrestii var. tumescens	Neriiflorum	Forrestii	15–45 cm. (6 in.–1½ ft.)	Deep crimson, crimson, bright pink, pinkish-purple	3	April–May
fortunei	Fortunei	Fortunei	1.83–9.15 m. (6–30 ft.)	Pale rose, lilac, pink	3	May–June
fulgens	Fulgens	—	60 cm.–4.58 m. (2–15 ft.)	Deep blood-red, deep scarlet, scarlet, crimson, cherry-red	3	March–April
fulvastrum	Neriiflorum	Sanguineum	60 cm.–1.53 m. (2–5 ft.)	Pale lemon-yellow, creamy-yellow, yellow, rarely yellow tinged pink	3	April–May
fulvastrum var. gilvum	Neriiflorum	Sanguineum	92 cm.–1.22 m. (3–4 ft.)	Pale yellow, yellow	3	April–May

Species	Series	Subseries	Height	Flower colour	Hardiness	Month of Flowering
fulvoides	Fulvum	—	1.22–7.62 m. (4–25 ft.)	White, white flushed rose or pink, pink, deep rose	3	March–April
fulvum	Fulvum	—	92 cm.–12.20 m. (3–40 ft.)	White, white flushed rose, pink, rose, deep rose	3	March–April
galactinum	Falconeri	—	3.66–8 m. (12–26 ft.)	White, white tinged rose	3	April–May
giganteum	Grande	—	6–30.50 m. (20–100 ft.)	Deep rose-crimson, deep crimson, deep purple-crimson	1–3	Feb.–April
glanduliferum Q	Fortunei	Fortunei	—	White	—	—
glandulosum Q	Camtschaticum	—	About 10 cm. (4 in.)	Rose-purple	—	—
glaphyrum	Neriiflorum	Sanguineum	30–92 cm. (1–3 ft.)	White flushed rose, deep rose, pale yellow faintly flushed rose on margins, pale yellow flushed very faintly rose	3	April–May
glaphyrum var. dealbatum	Neriiflorum	Sanguineum	60–76 cm. (2–2½ ft.)	White	3	April–May
glaucopeplum	Taliense	Taliense	92 cm.–2.44 m. (3–8 ft.)	Bright rose, white flushed rose	3	April–May
glischroides	Barbatum	Glischrum	1.83–4.58 m. (6–15 ft.)	White flushed deep rose, pale rose, creamy-white	3	March–April
glischroides var. arachnoideum	Barbatum	Glischrum	1.83 m. (6 ft.)	White flushed deep rose	3	April–May
glischrum	Barbatum	Glischrum	1.22–9.15 m. (4–30 ft.)	Plum-rose, white, white flushed deep rose, rose, deep rose-purple, pink	3	April–May
globigerum	Taliense	Roxieanum	92 cm.–1.83 m. (3–6 ft.)	White	3	April–May
grande	Grande	—	3–15.25 m. (10–50 ft.)	Pale yellow, lemon-yellow, creamy-white, white	1–3	Feb.–April
griersonianum	Griersonianum	—	1.22–3 m. (4–10 ft.)	Bright geranium-scarlet, rich carmine almost vermilion, bright rose	2–3	June–July
griffithianum	Fortunei	Griffithianum	92 cm.–15.25 m. (3–50 ft.)	White or white flushed pink, rarely yellow inside towards the base	2–3	April–May
gymnocarpum	Neriiflorum	Sanguineum	60 cm.–1.53 m. (2–5 ft.)	Deep claret-crimson, deep crimson	3	April–May
habrotrichum	Barbatum	Glischrum	92 cm.–3.66 m. (3–12 ft.)	Pale rose, white, deep rose, white flushed rose-crimson or rose	3	April–May
haemaleum	Neriiflorum	Sanguineum	30 cm.–1.83 m. (1–6 ft.)	Black-crimson, black carmine, dark carmine, nearly black	3	April–May
haemaleum var. atrorubrum	Neriiflorum	Sanguineum	Up to about 60 cm. (2 ft.)	Dark carmine	3	April–May
haemaleum var. mesaeum	Neriiflorum	Sanguineum	23 cm.–1.53 m. (9 in.–5 ft.)	Black-crimson, black carmine, dark carmine, nearly black	3	April–May
haematodes	Neriiflorum	Haematodes	30 cm.–1.22 m. (1–4 ft.), rarely 5–8 cm. (2–3 in.)	Deep crimson, crimson, scarlet, rarely black-crimson or rose	3	May–June
hancockii Q	Stamineum	—	92 cm.–4.58 m. (3–15 ft.)	White, sometimes pink	—	—
haofui Q	Argyrophyllum	—	4–6 m. (13–20 ft.)	White, sometimes flushed rose	—	—
hardingii	Irroratum	—	1.53–2.44 m. (5–8 ft.)	White flushed rose-pink, white	1–3	April–May
heftii	Campanulatum	Campanulatum	1.83—3 m. (6–10 ft.)	Pure ivory-white	3	April–May
hemidartum	Neriiflorum	Haematodes	60 cm.–1.83 m. (2–6 ft.)	Deep rich crimson, crimson, scarlet, light red	3	April–May
hemsleyanum	Fortunei	Fortunei	2.14–8 m. (7–26 ft.)	White or white tinged pink outside, with or without a yellowish-green flush towards the base	3	May–June–July
henryi Q	Stamineum	—	4–5.50 m. (13–18 ft.)	Pale lilac, rose, pink	—	—

Species	Series	Subseries	Height	Flower colour	Hardiness	Month of Flowering
herpesticum	Neriiflorum	Sanguineum	15–60 cm. (6 in.–2 ft.)	Orange, deep crimson, orange flushed rose or crimson, yellow flushed rose or crimson	3	May–June
hillieri	Neriiflorum	Haematodes	30 cm.–1.83 m. (1–6 ft.)	Bright rose-crimson, crimson-rose, light crimson, crimson, rose	3	April–May
himertum	Neriiflorum	Sanguineum	45–92 cm. (1½–3 ft.)	Yellow, lemon-yellow, bright yellow	3	April–May
hirtipes	Barbatum	Glischrum	92 cm.–7.62 m. (3–25 ft.), rarely 30–45 cm. (1–1½ ft.)	Rose-pink, pink, or white flushed pink, with or without pink and white bands outside	3	April–May
hodgsonii	Falconeri	—	3–12.20 m. (10–40 ft.)	Crimson, crimson-purple, port wine, deep cerise, magenta, deep purple, purple, pinkish-red, rose, deep pink, pink, deep lilac	3	April–May
hongkongense	Ovatum	—	1.22–1.53 m. (4–5 ft.)	White	1	March–April
hookeri	Thomsonii	Thomsonii	2.44–6 m. (8–20 ft.)	Cherry-red, deep crimson, pink	3	March–April
horaeum	Neriiflorum	Sanguineum	15 cm.–1.53 m. (6 in.–5 ft.)	Deep crimson, rose-crimson, carmine, deep yellowish-crimson, orange-crimson, yellow heavily margined crimson, pale rose margined deeper	3	May–June
horaeum var. rubens	Neriiflorum	Sanguineum	60–92 cm. (2–3 ft.)	Red, crimson	3	May–June
houlstonii	Fortunei	Fortunei	1.50–4.58 m. (5–15 ft.)	Pink, with or without narrow mixed green and red bands on the posterior side	3	April–June
huianum Q	Fortunei	Fortunei	2–9 m. (6½–30 ft.)	Lilac, deep lilac, light violet, pale red, purplish, pale rose	—	—
hunnewellianum	Argyrophyllum	—	1.83–5.50 m. (6–18 ft.)	White tinged pink	3	March–May
hylaeum	Thomsonii	Thomsonii	1.22–13.73 m. (4–45 ft.)	Pink, pale pink, rich pink, white tinged pink, rose, purplish-rose, scarlet, (rarely cream)	2–3	March–May
hyperythrum	Ponticum	—	92 cm.–2.44 m. (3–8 ft.)	White, pink	3	April–May
hypoglaucum	Argyrophyllum	—	1–6.10 m. (3⅓–20 ft.)	White, pink, white flushed rose	3	May
hypopitys Q	Ponticum	—	About 1 m. (3⅓ ft.)	Yellow	—	—
imberbe	Barbatum	Barbatum	1.83–3 m. (6–10 ft.)	Red, scarlet	3	Feb.–April
inopinum	Taliense	Wasonii	1.53–3 m. (5–10 ft.)	Creamy-white, white flushed pink, pale yellow	3	April–May
insigne	Argyrophyllum	—	1.60–6 m. (5–20 ft.)	Pale or deep pink, red, white flushed rose or red down the middle of the lobes	3	May–June
iodes	Taliense	Roxieanum	60 cm.–4.58 m. (2–15 ft.)	White, white flushed rose	3	April–May
irroratum	Irroratum	—	92 cm.–9 m. (3–30 ft.)	Yellowish-white, white, creamy-yellow, deep rose, pink	3	March–May
jucundum	Thomsonii	Selense	60 cm.–6 m. (2–20 ft.)	Rose, pink, white	3	May–June
kendrickii	Irroratum	—	1.83–7.62 m. (6–25 ft.)	Pink, rose, scarlet, crimson	1–3	April–May
kwangfuense Q	Fortunei	Oreodoxa	3–4 m. (10–13 ft.)	Rose	—	—
kyawii	Parishii	—	3–7.63 m. (10–25 ft.)	Deep crimson, crimson, crimson-scarlet	1–3	June–July
lacteum	Lacteum	—	1.22–9 m. (4–30 ft.)	Yellow, pale yellow or clear canary yellow, sometimes tinged pink, rarely pure white	3	April–May
lampropeplum	Taliense	Roxieanum	60 cm.–1.22 m. (2–4 ft.)	White faintly flushed rose, creamy-white	3	April–May

Species	Series	Subseries	Height	Flower colour	Hardiness	Month of Flowering
lanatum	Campanulatum	Lanatum	30 cm.–3 m. (1–10 ft.)	Yellow, pale yellow, pale sulphur-yellow, lemon-yellow	2–3	April–May
lanigerum	Arboreum	—	2.44–6.10 m. (8–20 ft.)	Rose-purple	3	Feb.–April
lanigerum var silvaticum	Arboreum	—	Up to about 2.44 m. (8 ft.)	Crimson	3	Feb.–April
latoucheae Q	Stamineum	—	1–3 m. (3⅓–10 ft.)	Pink, purplish	—	—
laxiflorum	Irroratum	—	1.22–6 m. (4–20 ft.)	White or creamy-white, flushed or not flushed rose	3	April–May
leptopeplum Q	Irroratum	—	2.75–4.27 m. (9–14 ft.)	Rose, white flushed rose, creamy-white flushed rose	—	—
leptothrium	Ovatum	—	60 cm.–7.63 m. (2–25 ft.)	Rose, pale rose, deep rose, pale pink, purple, purplish-red, bright or deep magenta-rose	1–3	April–May
litiense	Thomsonii	Souliei	92 cm.–4.90 m. (3–16 ft.)	Yellow, pale yellow	3	May–June
longesquamatum	Barbatum	Maculiferum	2–6 m. (6½–20 ft.)	Pink, rose, rosy-red	3	May
longipes Q	Argyrophyllum	—	1–2.5 m. (3⅓–8 ft.)	Pale rose	—	—
lopsangianum	Thomsonii	Thomsonii	60 cm.–1.83 m. (2–6 ft.)	Crimson, very deep crimson, dark crimson	3	April
luciferum	Campanulatum	Lanatum	1.22–7.62 m. (4–25 ft.)	Palest lemon, very pale lemon-cream, pale lemon-yellow, lemon-yellow, pale yellow	3	April–May
lukiangense	Irroratum	—	92 cm.–6 m. (3–20 ft.)	Rose, deep rose, pale rose-pink, pinkish-purple	3	March–April
macabeanum	Grande	—	3–15.25 m. (10–50 ft.)	Yellow, pale yellow, yellowish-white, pale greenish-yellow	3	March–May
mackenzianum	Stamineum	—	1.53–12.20 m. (5–40 ft.)	White, white flushed rose, purplish-rose, purplish-pink, lilac-pink, deep rose-magenta	1–2	April–May
macrophyllum	Ponticum	—	1.83–3.66 m. (6–12 ft.), sometimes 9 m. (30 ft.)	Pink, rose, rose-purple	3	May–June
macrosmithii	Barbatum	Barbatum	1.22–7.63 m. (4–25 ft.)	Scarlet, crimson, deep red	3	Feb.–April
maculiferum	Barbatum	Maculiferum	1–10 m. (3⅓–33 ft.)	White, pink, white flushed pink	3	April–May
magnificum	Grande	—	3–18.30 m. (10–60 ft.)	Crimson-purple, rosy-purple	1–3	Feb.–April
makinoi	Ponticum	—	92 cm.–2.44 m. (3–8 ft.)	Pink, rose	3	May–June
mallotum	Neriiflorum	Haematodes	1.53–4.58 m. (5–15 ft.)	Scarlet-crimson, deep crimson, crimson	3	March–April
martinianum	Thomsonii	Selense	60 cm.–1.83 m. (2–6 ft.)	Pink, pale rose, purple, white, creamy-white faintly flushed pale rose	3	April–May
maximum	Ponticum	—	1.22–3.66 m. (4–12 ft.), sometimes up to 12.20 m. (40 ft.)	White, white tinged pink, pink, light rose, rose, purplish	3	July
meddianum	Thomsonii	Thomsonii	92 cm.–2.44 m. (3–8 ft.)	Crimson, deep crimson, almost black-crimson, scarlet	3	April–May
meddianum var. atrokermesinum	Thomsonii	Thomsonii	1.53–2.44 m. (5–8 ft.)	Deep purple-crimson, light red	3	April–May
mengtszense Q	Irroratum	—	6 m. (20 ft.)	Purple-red	—	—
mesopolium	Neriiflorum	Sanguineum	46 cm.–1.53 m. (1½–5 ft.)	Pale rose, rose, rose margined and lined a deeper shade, bright pink, rarely crimson	3	April–May
microgynum	Neriiflorum	Sanguineum	92 cm.–1.22 m. (3–4 ft.)	Dull soft rose	3	April–May

Species	Series	Subseries	Height	Flower colour	Hardiness	Month of Flowering
mimetes	Taliense	Adenogynum	92 cm.–2.14 m. (3–7 ft.)	White, white faintly flushed and margined rose, pinkish-purple	3	May
mimetes var. simulans	Taliense	Adenogynum	1.53 m. (5 ft.)	White, pinkish-purple	3	May
miniatum Q	Sherriffii	—	1.53–4.58 m. (5–15 ft.)	Deep crimson, very deep rose	—	—
monosematum	Barbatum	Maculiferum	1.53–6.10 m. (5–20 ft.)	White, white flushed rose-pink, pink, reddish-purple	3	March–April
montroseanum	Grande	—	3–15.25 m. (10–50 ft.)	Pink, deep pink, pale mauve, rosy-purple, white	2–3	March–May
morii	Barbatum	Maculiferum	1.53–7.63 m. (5–25 ft.)	White, white tinged rose	3	April–May
moulmainense	Stamineum	—	1.53–12.20 m. (5–40 ft.), rarely 92 cm.–1.22 m. (3–4 ft.)	White, white flushed yellow or pink, pink, rose, rose-red, purplish-rose, lilac	1–2	April–May
myiagrum	Thomsonii	Campylocarpum	92 cm.–1.83 m. (3–6 ft.)	White	3	April–May
nakotiltum	Lacteum	—	92 cm.–3.66 m. (3–12 ft.)	Pale rose, white flushed rose	3	April–May
nankotaisanense Q	Barbatum	Maculiferum	Small shrub	—	—	—
neriiflorum	Neriiflorum	Neriiflorum	60 cm.–3 m. (2–10 ft.)	Deep crimson, crimson, scarlet, carmine, deep rose	3	April–May
neriiflorum var. agetum	Neriiflorum	Neriiflorum	Up to 1.83 m. (6 ft.)	Deep crimson, crimson, scarlet, deep rose	3	April–May
neriiflorum var. euchaites	Neriiflorum	Neriiflorum	2.44–6 m. (8–20 ft.)	Deep crimson, crimson, scarlet	3	April–May
nigroglandulosum	Taliense	Adenogynum	2–5 m. (6½–16 ft.)	Deep pink at first, later yellowish-pink	3	April–May
nilagiricum	Arboreum	—	2.44–12 m. (8–39 ft.)	Rose, deep crimson, crimson-rose, pink	1–3	April–May
ningyuenense Q	Irroratum	—	Medium-sized shrub	Whitish-rose	—	—
niveum	Arboreum	—	2.75–6.10 m. (9–20 ft.)	Lilac, mauve, purplish-lilac	3	April–May
ochraceum Q	Neriiflorum	Neriiflorum	Up to 3 m. (10 ft.)	Crimson	—	—
openshawianum Q	Fortunei	Calophytum	2–6 m. (6½–20 ft.)	White, purplish-white	—	—
orbiculare	Fortunei	Orbiculare	1.5–3 m. (5–10 ft.)	Rose, rosy-red, deep red, reddish-purple	3	April–May
oreodoxa	Fortunei	Oreodoxa	1.5–5 m. (5–16 ft.)	Pale rose, pink, rarely carmine	3	Feb.–March–April
ovatum	Ovatum	—	1–5 m. (3⅓–16 ft.)	White, pink, white tinged pink, rose, pale purple, very pale lilac	1–3	May–June
pachysanthum	Taliense	Wasonii	92 cm.–1.22 m. (3–4 ft.)	White	3	April–May
pachytrichum	Barbatum	Maculiferum	1.22–6 m. (4–20 ft.)	White, pale pink, pale rose, deep purple, red	3	March–April
panteumorphum	Thomsonii	Campylocarpum	60 cm.–3 m. (2–10 ft.)	Yellow, pale yellow	3	April–May
papillatum Q	Irroratum	—	Small shrub	Pale cream	—	—
paradoxum	Taliense	Wasonii	1.22–2.14 m. (4–7 ft.)	White	3	April–May
parishii Q	Parishii	—	6–8 m. (20–26 ft.)	Deep red, with darker bands along the petals	—	—
parmulatum	Neriiflorum	Sanguineum	60 cm.–1.22 m. (2–4 ft.)	White, pale yellow, pale creamy-yellow, whitish-pink, white flushed crimson	3	April–May
pectinatum	Stamineum	—	4–5 m. (13–16 ft.)	White, the dorsal lobe rich cream-yellow towards the base	1	April
pennivenium	Irroratum	—	2.44–6 m. (8–20 ft.)	Rose-crimson, deep crimson	2–3	April–May
peramoenum	Arboreum	—	1.22–12.20 m. (4–40 ft.)	Deep rose-crimson, rose-crimson, bright cherry-scarlet, bright scarlet-crimson, black-crimson	1–3	March–May
phaedropum	Neriiflorum	Neriiflorum	92 cm.–6 m. (3–20 ft.), rarely 60 cm. (2 ft.)	Crimson, scarlet, salmon-rose, tawny-orange, straw-yellow	3	March–May

Species	Series	Subseries	Height	Flower colour	Hardiness	Month of Flowering
phaeochrysum	Lacteum	—	92 cm.–6 m. (3–20 ft.)	White, white flushed rose, creamy-white, rarely yellow, purple, pinkish	3	April–May
piercei	Neriiflorum	Haematodes	1.22–1.53 m. (4–5 ft.)	Crimson	3	March–May
pingianum	Argyrophyllum	—	4–7 m. (13–23 ft.)	Pale purple, purple, pink, pinkish-purple	3	May
planetum	Fortunei	Davidii	1.22–4.58 m. (4–15 ft.)	Pink	3	March–April
platypodum Q	Fortunei	Fortunei	2–8 m. (6½–26 ft.)	Pinkish-red, pink	—	—
pocophorum	Neriiflorum	Haematodes	92 cm.–3 m. (3–10 ft.)	Deep crimson, crimson, crimson-scarlet, red	3	March–April
pogonostylum Q	Irroratum	—	1.22–6 m. (4–20 ft.)	Pink, light yellow, white, white flushed pink, red	—	—
poluninii	Campanulatum	Lanatum	1.53–1.83 m. (5–6 ft.)	Creamy-white, creamy-white slightly tinged pink	3	April–May
pomense Q	Lacteum	—	60 cm.–1.22 m. (2–4 ft.)	Pink	—	—
ponticum	Ponticum	—	1–4.60 m. (3⅓–15 ft.)	Deep mauve, mauve, lavender, purple, rosy-purple, lilac-purple, pinkish-purple, pink	4	June–July
ponticum forma album	Ponticum	—	1–3 m. (3⅓–10 ft.)	Pure white	4	June–July
populare Q	Thomsonii	Thomsonii	92 cm.–4.58 m. (3–15 ft.)	Crimson, deep crimson	—	—
porphyrophyllum Q	Neriiflorum	Forrestii	6–60 cm. (2½ in.–2 ft.)	Pale or deep rose	—	—
praestans	Grande	—	1.22–9 m. (4–30 ft.)	White flushed rose, creamy-white, white, yellow, deep magenta-rose	3	April–May
praeteritum	Fortunei	Oreodoxa	3 m. or more (10 ft.)	Pink, white flushed pink	3	Feb.–March–April
praevernum	Fortunei	Davidii	1.83–4.58 m. (6–15 ft.)	White, white tinged pink, rose, with a large dark purple or crimson blotch at the base	3	March–April
prattii	Taliense	Adenogynum	1–6.40 m. (3⅓–21 ft.)	White	3	April–May
preptum	Falconeri	—	1.83–9.15 m. (6–30 ft.)	Yellowish-white, pale yellow, pale creamy-white	3	April–May
principis Q	Taliense	Taliense	Small tree	—	—	—
pronum	Taliense	Roxieanum	8–60 cm. (3 in.–2 ft.)	Creamy-yellow, white, pink	3	May
proteoides	Taliense	Roxieanum	30–92 cm. (1–3 ft.), rarely 8–15 cm. (3–6 in.)	Pale creamy-yellow, creamy-white, pale yellow, yellow, white	3	April–May
protistum	Grande	—	6–30.50 m. (20–100 ft.)	Creamy-white flushed rose, crimson-purple, rosy-crimson	1–2	Feb.–March
przewalskii	Lacteum	—	92 cm.–4.58 m. (3–15 ft.)	White, rose-pink	3	April–May
pseudochrysanthum	Barbatum	Maculiferum	30 cm.–3 m. (1–10 ft.)	White, white tinged pink, pink with deeper rose lines outside	3	April–May
pudorosum	Grande	—	1.83–12.20 m. (6–40 ft.)	Bright pink, pink, rose, mauve-pink	3	March–April
puralbum	Thomsonii	Souliei	1.53–4.58 m. (5–15 ft.)	Pure white, rarely ivory-white	3	May
purdomii Q	Taliense	Taliense	Shrub	—	—	—
pyrrhoanthum	Neriiflorum	Forrestii	30–92 cm. (1–3 ft.)	Crimson	3	April–May
ramsdenianum	Irroratum	—	1.83–12.20 m. (6–40 ft.)	Crimson, scarlet-crimson, rose	3	April–May
recurvoides	Taliense	Roxieanum	60–92 cm. (2–3 ft.)	Rose, white, white tinged pink	3	April–May
redowskianum Q	Camtschaticum	—	About 10 cm. (4 in.)	Rose-purple	—	—
rex	Falconeri	—	3–12.20 m. (10–40 ft.)	Rose, white, pink, creamy-white	3	April–May
ririei	Argyrophyllum	—	3–12.20 m. (10–40 ft.)	Purplish, lilac-purple, reddish-purple	3	Feb.–April
rockii Q	Argyrophyllum	—	3.66–6 m. (12–20 ft.)	Pale rose, pinkish-purple	—	—

Species	Series	Subseries	Height	Flower colour	Hardiness	Month of Flowering
rothschildii	Falconeri	—	2.44–6 m. (8–20 ft.)	Pale yellow, pale creamy-white	3	April–May
roxieanum	Taliense	Roxieanum	92 cm.–2.75 m. (3–9 ft.), rarely 4.58 m. (15 ft.)	Creamy-white, white, white flushed rose, pink, rose, rarely yellow	3	April–May
roxieanum var. oreonastes	Taliense	Roxieanum	30 cm.–1.53 m. (1–5 ft.), rarely 3 m. (10 ft.)	White	3	April–May
roxieanum var. parvum	Taliense	Roxieanum	30–60 cm. (1–2 ft.), sometimes 92 cm. (3 ft.)	White	3	April–May
roxieanum var. recurvum	Taliense	Roxieanum	60 cm.–3 m. (2–10 ft.)	White	3	April–May
rude	Barbatum	Glischrum	1.83–2.75 m. (6–9 ft.)	Purplish-crimson or pinkish-purple, with darker bands outside	3	April–May
rufum	Taliense	Wasonii	1.22–4.58 m. (4–15 ft.)	White, pink, pinkish-purple, with or without purplish-pink stripes	3	April–May
russotinctum Q	Taliense	Roxieanum	1.50–2.44 m. (5–8 ft.)	White flushed rose	—	—
sanguineum	Neriiflorum	Sanguineum	30 cm.–1.22 m. (1–4 ft.), rarely up to 2.44 m. (8 ft.)	Deep crimson, crimson, rose-crimson, carmine, scarlet	3	March–May
sanguineum var. consanguineum	Neriiflorum	Sanguineum	60–92 cm. (2–3 ft.)	Crimson, carmine	3	April–May
sanguineum var. didymoides	Neriiflorum	Sanguineum	60–92 cm. (2–3 ft.)	Rose, yellow flushed and margined crimson, orange-red, rarely red	3	April–May
sanguineum var. sanguineoides	Neriiflorum	Sanguineum	30 cm.–1.83 m. (1–6 ft.)	Red	3	April–May
schistocalyx	Parishii	—	1.83–6 m. (6–20 ft.)	Rose-crimson, crimson	2–3	April–May
scyphocalyx	Neriiflorum	Sanguineum	92 cm.–1.53 m. (3–5 ft.)	Yellowish-crimson, rose-orange, coppery yellow, orange, deep crimson, orange flushed crimson	3	May–June
scyphocalyx var. septendrionale	Neriiflorum	Sanguineum	46 cm.–1.53 m. (1½–5 ft.)	Yellow flushed rose at the base, lemon-yellow	3	May–July
selense	Thomsonii	Selense	60 cm.–1.83 m. (2–6 ft.), sometimes 2.44–3 m. (8–10 ft.)	Pink, rose, white flushed rose, rarely reddish-purple	3	April–May
selense var. pagophilum	Thomsonii	Selense	60 cm.–2.44 m. (2–8 ft.)	White, deep rose, crimson	3	April–May
selense var. probum	Thomsonii	Selense	92cm.–4.58 m. (3–15 ft.)	White	3	April–May
semibarbatum	Semibarbatum	—	60 cm.–3 m. (2–10 ft.)	White, white flushed pink, yellowish-white	3	June
semnoides	Falconeri	—	2.44–6 m. (8–20 ft.)	White flushed rose, creamy-white	3	April–May
serotinum	Fortunei	Fortunei	2.50–3 m. (8–10 ft.)	White, slightly flushed rose outside, with a red blotch at the base	3	July— September, sometimes June
setiferum	Thomsonii	Selense	1.53–2.75 m. (5–9 ft.)	Creamy-white	3	April–May
shepherdii	Barbatum	Barbatum	3–3.66 m. (10–12 ft.)	Deep scarlet, bright red	3	March–April
sherriffii	Sherriffii	—	1.53–6 m. (5–20 ft.)	Rich deep carmine	3	March–April
siamense Q	Stamineum	—	Tree	White	—	—
sidereum	Grande	—	1.83–12.20 m. (6–40 ft.)	Creamy-white, yellow, lemon-yellow	2–3	April–May
sikangense	Parishii	—	3–5 m. (10–16 ft.)	Purple	3	May–June
simiarum	Argyrophyllum	—	1–6 m. (3⅓–20 ft.)	Pink, white	2–3	April–May
sinofalconeri Q	Falconeri	—	6.10 m. (20 ft.)	Pale yellow	—	—
sinogrande	Grande	—	3–15.25 m. (10–50 ft.)	Creamy-white, creamy-yellow, yellow, white	1–3	April–May
sinogrande var. boreale	Grande	—	3–12.20 m. (10–40 ft.)	Creamy-yellow	3	April–May

Species	Series	Subseries	Height	Flower colour	Hardiness	Month of Flowering
smirnowii	Ponticum	—	50 cm.–6.10 m. (1½–20 ft.)	Pink, deep pink, rose-red, rose-purple	3–4	May–June
souliei	Thomsonii	Souliei	1–5 m. (3⅓–16 ft.)	Pink, rose, deep rose, white tinged pink	3	May–June
spanotrichum Q	Irroratum	—	6 m. (20 ft.)	Crimson	—	—
sperabile	Neriiflorum	Neriiflorum	92 cm.–2.44 m. (3–8 ft.)	Scarlet, crimson, deep crimson	3	April–May
sperabile var. weihsiense	Neriiflorum	Neriiflorum	1.53–1.83 m. (5–6 ft.)	Scarlet, crimson	3	April–May
sperabiloides	Neriiflorum	Neriiflorum	60 cm.–1.22 m. (2–4 ft.)	Deep to light crimson	3	April–May
sphaeroblastum	Taliense	Taliense	60 cm.–6.10 m. (2–20 ft.)	White, creamy-white, white flushed rose, pink	3	April–May
spilotum	Barbatum	Glischrum	92 cm.–1.53 m. (3–5 ft.)	Pink, white tinged pink	3	April–May
stamineum	Stamineum	—	1–10 m. (3⅓–33 ft.)	White or rose, with a yellow blotch at the base	1–2	April–May
stewartianum	Thomsonii	Thomsonii	60 cm.–3 m. (2–10 ft.)	Pure white, white flushed rose, yellow, pale yellow, creamy-yellow, creamy-white, yellow flushed rose, pink, pale rose, deep rose margined deep crimson, purplish, sometimes brilliant red or crimson	3	Feb.–April
stewartianum var. tantulum	Thomsonii	Thomsonii	92 cm.–1.22 m. (3–4 ft.)	White, pale or deep rose	3	March–April
strigillosum	Barbatum	Maculiferum	2–7 m. (6½–23 ft.)	Crimson, scarlet, deep red, red, rose-pink, rarely white	3	Feb.–April
succothii	Fulgens	—	60 cm.–6 m. (2–20 ft.)	Crimson, scarlet	3	March–April
sutchuenense	Fortunei	Davidii	2–6 m. (6½–20 ft.)	Light or deep rose, rose-pink, white tinged pink, pink, without a blotch at the base	3	Feb.–April
sutchuenense var. geraldii	Fortunei	Davidii	Up to about 3.66 m. (12 ft.)	Light or deep rose, rose-pink, white tinged pink, pink, with a large crimson or reddish blotch at the base	3	Feb.–April
taiense Q	Stamineum	—	About 10 m. (33 ft.)	White	—	—
taliense	Taliense	Taliense	1.22–3.66 m. (4–12 ft.)	Creamy-yellow, pale yellow, white, white flushed rose	3	April–May
tanastylum	Irroratum	—	92 cm.–12.20 m. (3–40 ft.)	Crimson, deep crimson, cherry-crimson, black-crimson, purple-crimson, crimson-magenta	2–3	April–May
telopeum	Thomsonii	Campylocarpum	60 cm.–3 m. (2–10 ft.), rarely 4.58 m. (15 ft.)	Bright yellow, yellow, sulphur-yellow, creamy-white	3	April–May
temenium	Neriiflorum	Sanguineum	30 cm.–1.22 m. (1–4 ft.)	Deep crimson, crimson, carmine, light to dark purplish-crimson, purplish-red	3	April–May
thayerianum	Irroratum	—	1.83–4 m. (6–13 ft.)	White tinged pink, white, or deeply flushed on the outside down the lobes	3	June–July
thomsonii	Thomsonii	Thomsonii	1–6.10 m. (3⅓–20 ft.)	Deep blood-red, deep crimson, crimson, pale vermilion, port wine, red, deep red, very deep rose	3	April–May
thomsonii var. candelabrum	Thomsonii	Thomsonii	1–5 m. (3⅓–16 ft.)	Pink, rose-pink	3	April–May
traillianum	Lacteum	—	92 cm.–9 m. (3–30 ft.)	White, white flushed rose, pink, rose	3	April–May
trichomiscum	Neriiflorum	Sanguineum	60 cm.–1.22 m. (2–4 ft.)	Pale rose-pink, purplish, orange-red	3	April–May

Species	Series	Subseries	Height	Flower colour	Hardiness	Month of Flowering
trilectorum Q	Neriiflorum	Forrestii	23–30 cm. (9 in.–1 ft.)	Pale yellow or pale lemon-yellow, flushed pale pink	—	—
triplonaevium	Taliense	Roxieanum	92 cm.–4.27 m. (3–14 ft.)	White flushed rose, pure white	3	April–May
tritifolium	Taliense	Roxieanum	1.22–3.66 m. (4–12 ft.)	White flushed rose	3	April–May
tsariense	Campanulatum	Lanatum	60 cm.–3.66 m. (2–12 ft.)	Pink, white, white tinged pink	3	March–May
tsariense var. magnum	Campanulatum	Lanatum	2.44–3 m. (8–10 ft.)	Pink, white tinged pink	3	April–May
tsariense var. trimoense	Campanulatum	Lanatum	1.22–3 m. (4–10 ft.)	Pink, white tinged pink	3	April–May
tutcherae Q	Stamineum	—	12–13 m. (39–43 ft.)	Violet	—	—
ungernii	Ponticum	—	1–6.10 m. (3⅓–20 ft.)	Pale rose, pink, white	3	June–July
uvarifolium	Fulvum	—	1.22–10.68 m. (4–35 ft.)	White, white flushed rose, pale rose, pink	3	March–April
uvarifolium var. griseum	Fulvum	—	1.22–9 m. (4–30 ft.)	White	3	March–April
vellereum	Taliense	Taliense	1.22–6.10 m. (4–20 ft.)	White, white flushed pale pink, pale rose, pink	3	March–May
venator	Parishii	—	1.53–3 m. (5–10 ft.)	Scarlet, deep crimson	3	May–June
vernicosum	Fortunei	Fortunei	92 cm.–7.62 m. (3–25 ft.)	White, rose-lavender, deep or pale rose, pink, pinkish-purple, purplish-red, carmine-purple	3	April–May
vernicosum forma araliiforme	Fortunei	Fortunei	1.22–1.53 m. (4–5 ft.)	White, deep or pale rose, pink	3	April–May
vernicosum forma euanthum	Fortunei	Fortunei	2.44–3 m. (8–10 ft.)	White in the lower half inside, pink above	3	April–May
vernicosum forma rhantum	Fortunei	Fortunei	1.83–3 m. (6–10 ft.)	Pale rose	3	April–May
vernicosum forma sheltonae	Fortunei	Fortunei	2.44–3.66 m. (8–12 ft.)	Purplish-red, carmine-purple	3	April–May
vesiculiferum	Barbatum	Glischrum	1.53–3 m. (5–10 ft.)	Purplish-rose, pinkish-purple, almost white	3	April–May
vestitum	Thomsonii	Selense	60 cm.–1.53 m. (2–5 ft.)	White flushed rose	3	May–June
vialii Q	Ovatum	—	1.22–4.58 m. (4–15 ft.)	Crimson, pink	—	—
viscidifolium	Thomsonii	Thomsonii	60 cm.–2.44 m. (2–8 ft.)	Copper-red	3	April–May
wallichii	Campanulatum	Campanulatum	92 cm.–5 m. (3–16 ft.)	Mauve, pale mauve, pale lilac, pinkish, pink, pinkish-mauve, white faintly flushed purple, sometimes white	3	April–May
wardii	Thomsonii	Souliei	60 cm.–7.63 m. (2–25 ft.)	Yellow, pale yellow, pale cream, sulphur-yellow, primrose-yellow, bright yellow, pale lemon-yellow, lemon-yellow	3	May–June
wasonii	Taliense	Wasonii	60 cm.–2.14 m. (2–7 ft.)	Yellow, creamy-yellow, creamy-white	3	April–May
wasonii var. rhododactylum	Taliense	Wasonii	60 cm.–1.22 m. (2–4 ft.)	Pink, rose, rose-pink, white tinged pink or pinkish	3	April–May
watsonii	Grande	—	1.53–10 m. (5–33 ft.)	White, white tinged pink	3	March–April
weldianum	Taliense	Wasonii	1.53–6.10 m. (5–20 ft.)	White, white tinged pink, pink	3	April–May
wightii	Lacteum	—	60 cm.–4.60 m. (2–15 ft.)	Yellow, pale sulphur-yellow, pale lemon-yellow, lemon-yellow, rarely white tinged pink	3	April–May
williamsianum	Thomsonii	Williamsianum	60 cm.–1.53 m. (2–5 ft.), rarely up to 2.44 m. (8 ft.)	Pink, pale rose, rose	3	April–May
wilsonae	Stamineum	—	1–7 m. (3⅓–23 ft.)	Pink, purple	1–2	April–May
wiltonii	Taliense	Wasonii	92 cm.–5 m. (3–16 ft.)	Pink, white	3	April–May

Species	Series	Subseries	Height	Flower colour	Hardiness	Month of Flowering
wuense Q	Taliense	Wasonii	About 5.50 m. (18 ft.)	—	—	—
yakushimanum	Ponticum	—	30 cm.–2.5 m. (1–8 ft.)	Pure white, very pale pink	3	May
youngae Q	Argyrophyllum	—	3–5 m. (10–16 ft.)	Purple, pink, whitish, purplish	—	—
zeylanicum	Arboreum	—	1.83–10.68 m. (6–35 ft.)	Crimson, pink	1–3	May–July

Lepidote

Species	Series	Subseries	Height	Flower colour	Hardiness	Month of Flowering
mucronulatum var. chejuense	Dauricum	—	10–30 cm. (4 in.–1 ft.)	Rose, rose-purple, pale rose-purple	3	March

List of Lepidote Rhododendron Species, Varieties and Synonyms

ANTHOPOGON SERIES

R. anthopogon D. Don

R. anthopogon D. Don var. **album** Davidian

R. anthopogonoides Maxim.

R. cephalanthum Franch.
    Syn. *R. chamaetortum* Balf. f. et Ward in Notes Roy. Bot. Gard. Edin., Vol. 9 (1916) 218.

R. colletianum Aitch. et Hemsl.

R. crebreflorum Hutch. et Ward
    Syn. *R. cephalanthum* Franch. var. *crebreflorum* (Hutch. et Ward) Cowan et Davidian in Rhod. Year
        Book (1947) 70.
        R. cephalanthum Franch. subsp. *cephalanthum Crebreflorum* Group R.H.S. in Rhod. Handb.
        (1980) p. 4.

R. hypenanthum Balf. f.
    Syn. *R. haemonium* Balf. f. et Cooper in Notes Roy. Bot. Gard. Edin., Vol. 9 (1916) 283.
        R. anthopogon D. Don var. *haemonium* (Balf. f. et Cooper) Cowan et Davidian in Rhod. Year
        Book (1947) 68.
        R. anthopogon D. Don subsp. *hypenanthum* (Balf. f.) Cullen in Notes Roy. Bot. Gard. Edin., Vol.
        37 (1979) 327.

R. kongboense Hutch.

R. laudandum Cowan

R. laudandum Cowan var. **temoense** Ward ex Cowan et Davidian
    Syn. *R. temoense* Ward. nomen nudum.

R. nmaiense Balf. f. et Ward
    Syn. *R. cephalanthum* Franch. var. *nmaiense* (Balf. f. et Ward) Cowan et Davidian in Rhod. Year Book
        (1947) 71.

R. platyphyllum Franch. ex Balf. f. et W.W. Sm.
    Syn. *R. cephalanthum* Franch. var. *platyphyllum* Franch. MSS. ex Diels in Notes Roy. Bot. Gard.
        Edin., Vol. 7 (1912) 211, nomen nudum.
        R. cephalanthum Franch. subsp. *platyphyllum* (Franch. ex Balf. f. et W.W. Sm.) Cullen in Notes
        Roy. Bot. Gard. Edin., Vol. 37 (1979) 327.

R. pogonophyllum Cowan et Davidian

R. primuliflorum Bur. et Franch.
    Syn. *Azalea fragrans* Adams in Mem. Acad. Sci. St. Petersburg ii (1808) 332.
        R. fragrans (Adams) Maxim. in Rhodo. As. Or. (1870) non Paxton.
        R. acraium Balf. f. et W.W. Sm., in Notes Roy. Bot. Gard. Edin., Vol. 9 (1916) 209.
        R. clivicola Balf. f. et W.W. Sm., ibid., p. 221.
        R. cremnophilum Balf. f. et W.W. Sm., ibid., p. 223.
        R. gymnomiscum Balf. f. et Ward, ibid., p. 230.
        R. lepidanthum Balf. f. et W.W. Sm., ibid., p. 245.
        R. praeclarum Balf. f. et Farrer, ibid., p. 261.
        R. tsarongense Balf. f. et Forrest, ibid., Vol. 11 (1919) 150.
        R. adamsii Rehder in Rehd. & Wils. Monog. Azal. (1921) 190.
        R. primuliflorum Bur. et Franch. var. *lepidanthum* (Balf. f. et W.W. Sm.) Cowan et Davidian in
        Rhod. Year Book (1947) 79.

R. primuliflorum Bur. et Franch. var. **cephalanthoides** (Balf. f. et W.W. Sm.) Cowan et Davidian
    Syn. *R. cephalanthoides* Balf. f. et W.W. Sm. in Notes Roy. Bot. Gard. Edin., Vol. 9 (1916) 216.

R. radendum Fang

R. rufescens Franch.
    Syn. *R. daphniflorum* Diels in Act. Hort. Gothob. I (1924) 180.

R. sargentianum Rehd. et Wils.

R. trichostomum Franch.
  Syn. *R. fragrans* Franch. in Bull. Soc. Bot. France, XXXIV (1887) p. 284 (non Maxim.), forma
    parviflora Franch.
    R. ledoides Balf. f. et W.W. Sm., in Notes Roy. Bot. Gard. Edin., Vol. 9 (1916) 243.
    R. sphaeranthum Balf. f. et W.W. Sm., ibid., p. 278.
    R. trichostomum Franch. var. *ledoides* (Balf. f. et W.W. Sm.) Cowan et Davidian in Rhod. Year
      Book (1947) 84.
    R. trichostomum Franch. *Ledoides Group* R.H.S. in Rhod. Handb. (1980) p. 4.
R. trichostomum Franch. var. **hedyosmum** (Balf. f.) Cowan et Davidian
  Syn. *R. hedyosmum* Balf. f. in Notes Roy. Bot. Gard. Edin., Vol. 9 (1916) 234.
R. trichostomum Franch. var. **radinum** (Balf. f. et W.W. Sm.) Cowan et Davidian
  Syn. *R. radinum* Balf. f. et W.W. Sm. in Notes Roy. Bot. Gard. Edin., Vol. 9 (1916) 268.
    R. trichostomum Franch. *Radinum Group* R.H.S. in Rhod. Handb. (1980) p. 4.

BOOTHII SERIES
BOOTHII SUBSERIES
R. boothii Nutt.
R. chrysodoron Tagg ex Hutch.
  Syn. *R. butyricum* Ward, nomen nudum.
R. dekatanum Cowan
R. mishmiense Hutch. et Ward
  Syn. *R. boothii* Nutt. *Mishmiense Group* R.H.S. in Rhod. Handb. (1980) p. 26.
R. sulfureum Franch.
  Syn. *R. theiochroum* Balf. f. et W.W. Sm. in Notes Roy. Bot. Gard. Edin., Vol. 9 (1916) 282.
    R. cerinum Balf. f. et Forrest, ibid. Vol. 13 (1922) 240.
    R. commodum Balf. f. et Forrest, ibid. Vol. 13 (1922) 252.

MEGERATUM SUBSERIES
R. leucaspis Tagg
R. megeratum Balf. f. et Forrest
  Syn. *R. tapeinum* Balf. f. et Farrer in Notes Roy. Bot. Gard. Edin., Vol. 12 (1920) 164.

CAMELLIIFLORUM SERIES
R. camelliiflorum Hook. f.
  Syn. *R. sparsiflorum* Nutt. in Hooker's Kew Journ., Vol. 5 (1853) 363.
    R. cooperi Balf. f. in Notes Roy. Bot. Gard. Edin., Vol. 10 (1917) 91.

CAMPYLOGYNUM SERIES
R. campylogynum Franch.
  Syn. *R. caeruleo-glaucum* Balf. f. et Forrest in Notes Roy. Bot. Gard. Edin., Vol. 13 (1920) 34.
    R. glauco-aureum Balf. f. et Forrest, ibid., p. 46.
    R. damascenum Balf. f. et Forrest, ibid., (1922) 254.
    R. cerasiflorum Ward, Gard. Chron. Ser. 3, XCIII (1933) 277, nomen nudum.
    R. rubriflorum Ward, Rhod. Assoc. Year Book Supp. (1934) 240, nomen nudum.
R. campylogynum Franch. var. **celsum** Davidian
  Syn. *R. campylogynum* Franch. *Celsum Group* R.H.S. in Rhod. Handb. (1980) p. 25.
R. campylogynum Franch. var. **charopoeum** (Balf. f. et Farrer) Davidian
  Syn. *R. charopoeum* Balf. f. et Farrer in Notes Roy. Bot. Gard. Edin., Vol. 13 (1922) 245.
    R. campylogynum Franch. *Charopoeum Group* R.H.S. in Rhod. Handb. (1980) p. 25.
R. campylogynum Franch. var. **myrtilloides** (Balf. f. et Ward) Davidian
  Syn. *R. myrtilloides* Balf. f. et Ward in Notes Roy. Bot. Gard. Edin., Vol. 13 (1922) 276.
    R. campylogynum Franch. *Myrtilloides Group* R.H.S. in Rhod. Handb. (1980) p. 25.
R. cremastum Balf. f. et Forrest
  Syn. *R. campylogynum* Franch. var. *cremastum* (Balf. f. et Forrest) Davidian in Rhod. & Camell. Year
    Book (1954) No. 8, p. 83.
    R. campylogynum Franch. *Cremastum Group* R.H.S. in Rhod. Handb. (1980) p. 25.

CAROLINIANUM SERIES
R. carolinianum Rehder
  Syn. *R. minus* Michaux var. *minus Carolinianum Group* R.H.S. in Rhod. Handb. (1980) p. 15.
R. chapmanii A. Gray
  Syn. *R. minus* Michaux var. *chapmanii* (A. Gray) Duncan & Pullen, Brittonia 14(1962)297.
R. minus Michaux
  Syn. *R. punctatum* Andrews, Bot. Rep. I, t.36 (1798).
    R. cuthbertii Small in Torreya II (1902) 9.

CILIATUM SERIES
R. amandum Cowan
R. burmanicum Hutch.
R. ciliatum Hook. f.
R. crenulatum Hutch. ex Sleumer
R. fletcherianum Davidian
R. valentinianum Forrest ex Hutch.

CINNABARINUM SERIES
R. cinnabarinum Hook. f.
R. cinnabarinum Hook. f. var. **aestivale** Hutch.
    Syn. *R. cinnabarinum* Hook. f. ssp. *cinnabarinum 'Aestivale'* R.H.S. in Rhod. Handb. (1980) p. 22.
R. cinnabarinum Hook. f. var. **blandfordiiflorum** (W. J. Hooker) Hutch.
    Syn. *R. blandfordiiflorum* W. J. Hooker in Bot. Mag. Vol. 82 t.4930 (1856).
        R. cinnabarinum ssp. *cinnabarinum Blandfordiiflorum Group* R.H.S. in Rhod. Handb. (1980)
        p. 22.
R. cinnabarinum Hook. f. var. **breviforme** Davidian
R. cinnabarinum Hook. f. var. **pallidum** W. J. Hooker
    Syn. *R. cinnabarinum* Hook. f. ssp. *xanthocodon Pallidum Group* R.H.S. in Rhod. Handb. (1980) p. 22.
R. cinnabarinum Hook. f. var. **purpurellum** Cowan
    Syn. *R. cinnabarinum* Hook. f. ssp. *xanthocodon Purpurellum Group* R.H.S. in Rhod. Handb. (1980)
        p. 22.
R. cinnabarinum Hook. f. var. **roylei** (Hook. f.) Hutch.
    Syn. *R. roylei* Hook. f. Rhod. Sikkim Himal. t.17 (1849).
        R. cinnabarinum Hook. f. ssp. *cinnabarinum Roylei Group* R.H.S. in Rhod. Handb. (1980) p. 22.
R. cinnabarinum Hook. f. var. **roylei** (Hook. f.) Hutch. forma **magnificum** W. Watson
    Syn. *R. cinnabarinum* Hook. f. ssp. *cinnabarinum Roylei Group 'Magnificum'* R.H.S. in Rhod. Handb.
        (1980) p. 22.
R. concatenans Hutch.
    Syn. *R. cinnabarinum* Hook. f. ssp. *xanthocodon Concatenans Group* R.H.S. in Rhod. Handb. (1980)
        p. 22.
R. keysii Nutt.
    Syn. *R. igneum* Cowan in Notes Roy. Bot. Gard. Edin., Vol. 19 (1937) 235.
R. keysii Nutt. var. **unicolor** Hutch.
    Syn. *R. keysii 'Unicolor'* R.H.S. in Rhod. Handb. (1980) p. 22.
R. tamaense Davidian
    Syn. *R. cinnabarinum* Hook. f. subsp. *tamaense* (Davidian) Cullen in Notes Roy. Bot. Gard. Edin.,
        Vol. 36 (1978) 113.
R. xanthocodon Hutch.
    Syn. *R. cinnabarinum* Hook. f. subsp. *xanthocodon* (Hutch.) Cullen in Notes Roy. Bot. Gard. Edin.,
        Vol. 36 (1978) 113.

DAURICUM SERIES
R. dauricum Linn.
R. dauricum Linn. var. **album** D.C. Prod. VII (1839) 725.
    Syn. *R. dauricum* Linn. var. *albiflorum* Nakai, Fl. Sylv. Koreana (1919) 37.
R. dauricum Linn. var. **sempervirens** Sims in Bot. Mag. Vol. 44 t.1888 (1817).
    Syn. *R. dauricum* Linn. var. *atrovirens* Hort. (1817).
        R. ledebourii Pojarkova in Komarov, Flora USSR Vol. XIII (1952) 722.
R. mucronulatum Turcz.
    Syn. *R. dauricum* Turcz. var. *mucronulatum* (Turcz.) Maxim., Rhodo. Asiae Orient (1870) 44.
        R. taquetii Lévl., in Feddes Rep. XII (1913) 101.
        R. mucronulatum Turcz. var. *ciliatum* Nakai, Fl. Sylv. Koreana VIII (1919) 35.
R. mucronulatum Turcz. var. **acuminatum** Hutch.
R. mucronulatum Turcz. var. **albiflorum** Nakai
R. mucronulatum Turcz. var. **chejuense** Davidian
R. sichotense Pojark.

EDGEWORTHII SERIES
R. edgeworthii Hook. f.
    Syn. *R. bullatum* Franch. in Bull. Soc. Bot. France, XXXIV (1887) 281.
        R. sciaphyllum Balf. f. et Ward in Notes Roy. Bot. Gard. Edin., Vol. 10 (1917) 146.
R. pendulum Hook. f.
R. seinghkuense Hutch.

FERRUGINEUM SERIES
R. ferrugineum Linn.
R. ferrugineum Linn. var. **album** D. Don
R. ferrugineum Linn. var. **atrococcineum** Bean
R. hirsutum Linn.
R. hirsutum Linn. var. **albiflorum** Schroet.
R. hirsutum var. **latifolium** Hoppe
R. kotschyi Simonk.
   Syn. *R. myrtifolium* Schott & Kotschy, not Lodd.
      R. ferrugineum Linn. var. *myrtifolium* (Schott & Kotschy) Schroeter
      R. ferrugineum Linn. subsp. *myrtifolium* (Schott & Kotschy) Hayek
      R. ferrugineum Linn. subsp. *kotschyi* (Simonkai) Hayek, Prod. Fl. Balc. 2:17 (1928).

GLAUCOPHYLLUM SERIES
GENESTIERIANUM SUBSERIES
R. genestierianum Forrest
R. micromeres Tagg

    GLAUCOPHYLLUM SUBSERIES
R. brachyanthum Franch.
R. brachyanthum Franch. var. **hypolepidotum** Franch.
   Syn. *R. hypolepidotum* Balf. f. et Forrest in Notes Roy. Bot. Gard. Edin., XIII (1922) 266.
      R. charitostreptum Balf. f. et Ward in Notes Roy. Bot. Gard. Edin., XIII (1922) 244.
      R. brachyanthum Franch. subsp. *hypolepidotum* (Franch.) Cullen in Notes Roy. Bot. Gard. Edin., XXXVI (1978) 114.
R. charitopes Balf. f. et Farrer
R. glaucophyllum Rehder
   Syn. *R. glaucum* Hook. f. Rhod. Sikkim Himal. t. 17 (1849).
R. glaucophyllum Rehder var. **album** Davidian
R. luteiflorum Davidian
   Syn. *R. glaucophyllum* Rehder var. *luteiflorum* Davidian in Journ. Roy. Hort. Soc., Vol. 85 (1960) 369.
R. pruniflorum Hutch.
   Syn. *R. tsangpoense* Ward var. *pruniflorum* (Hutch.) Cowan et Davidian in Rhod. Year Book No. 3 (1948) 90.
      R. sordidum Hutch. in Rhod. Soc. Notes III, No. 5, (1929–31) 286.
R. shweliense Balf. f. et Forrest
R. tsangpoense Ward
   Syn. *R. charitopes* Balf. f. et Farrer ssp. *tsangpoense* (Ward) Cullen in Notes Roy. Bot. Gard. Edin., Vol. 36 (1978) 114.
R. tsangpoense Ward var. **curvistylum** Ward ex Cowan et Davidian
   Syn. *R. curvistylum* Ward, Plant Hunting on Edge of the World (1930) 375, nomen nudum.
      R. tsangpoense Ward ssp. *tsangpoense Curvistylum* Group R.H.S. in Rhod. Handb. (1980) p. 24.
R. tubiforme (Cowan et Davidian) Davidian
   Syn. *R. glaucophyllum* Rehder var. *tubiforme* Cowan et Davidian in Rhod. Year Book No. 3 (1948) 86.

HELIOLEPIS SERIES
R. bracteatum Rehd. et Wils.
R. desquamatum Balf. f. et Forrest
   Syn. *R. catapastum* Balf. f. et Forrest in Notes Roy. Bot. Gard. Edin., Vol. 13 (1920) 36.
      R. rubiginosum Franch. *Desquamatum* Group R.H.S. in Rhod. Handb. (1980) p. 15.
      R. leprosum Balf. f. nomen nudum.
R. fumidum Balf. f. et W.W. Sm.
R. heliolepis Franch.
   Syn. *R. brevistylum* Franch. in Journ. de Bot. Vol. 7 (1898) 261.
      R. oporinum Balf. f. et Ward in Notes Roy. Bot. Gard. Edin., Vol. 10 (1917) 129.
      R. plebeium Balf. f. et W.W. Sm. ibid., p. 136.
      R. porrosquameum Balf. f. et Forrest, ibid., Vol. 13 (1920) 57.
      R. heliolepis Franch. var. *brevistylum* (Franch.) Cullen, ibid., Vol. 36 (1978) 110.
R. invictum Balf. f. et Farrer
R. pholidotum Balf. f. et W.W. Sm.
R. rubiginosum Franch.
   Syn. *R. leclerei* Lévl. in Feddes Repert. Vol. 12 (1913) 284.
      R. stenoplastum Balf. f. et Forrest in Notes Roy. Bot. Gard. Edin., Vol. 13 (1920) 60.
      R. squarrosum Balf. f. ibid., Vol. 17 (1930) 266, nomen nudum.

LAPPONICUM SERIES
  CUNEATUM SUBSERIES
R. cuneatum W.W. Sm.
    Syn. *R. ravum* Balf. f. et W.W. Sm. in Notes Roy. Bot. Gard. Edin., Vol. 9 (1916) 270.
      R. cinereum Balf. f. in Millais Rhod. (1917) 145, nomen nudum.
      R. cheilanthum Balf. f. et Forrest in Notes Roy. Bot. Gard. Edin., Vol. 11 (1919) 32.

  LAPPONICUM SUBSERIES
R. alpicola Rehd. et Wils.
    Syn. *R. alpicola* Rehd. et Wils. var. *strictum* Rehd. et Wils. in Pl. Wilsonianae I (1913) 506.
      R. oreinum Balf. f. in Notes Roy. Bot. Gard. Edin., Vol. 13 (1920) 54.
R. amundsenianum Hand.-Mazz.
R. bulu Hutch.
R. burjaticum Malyschev
R. capitatum Maxim.
R. chryseum Balf. f. et Ward
    Syn. *R. muliense* Balf. f. et Forrest in Notes Roy. Bot. Gard. Edin., Vol. 11 (1919) 101.
      R. chamaezelum Balf. f. et Forrest, ibid., Vol. 13 (1922) 241.
      R. rupicola W.W. Sm. var. *chryseum* (Balf. f. et Ward) Philipson et Philipson, ibid., Vol. 34 (1975) p. 62.
      R. rupicola W.W. Sm. var. *muliense* (Balf. f. et Forrest) Philipson et Philipson, ibid., p. 63.
R. compactum Hutch.
R. complexum Balf. f. et W.W. Sm.
R. dasypetalum Balf. f. et Forrest
R. diacritum Balf. f. et W.W. Sm.
    Syn. *R. pycnocladum* Balf. f. et W.W. Sm. in Notes Roy. Bot. Gard. Edin., Vol. 9 (1916) 267.
R. drumonium Balf. f. et Ward
R. edgarianum Rehd. et Wils.
    Syn. *R. vicarium* Balf. f. in Notes Roy. Bot. Gard. Edin., Vol. 12 (1920) 176.
R. fastigiatum Franch.
    Syn. *R. nanum* Lévl. in Feddes Repert. Vol. XII (1913) 285.
R. fimbriatum Hutch.
    Syn. *R. hippophaeoides* Balf. f. et W.W. Sm. var. *hippophaeoides Fimbriatum Group* R.H.S. in Rhod. Handb. (1980) 16.
R. flavidum Franch.
    Syn. *R. primulinum* Hemsl. in Gard. Chron. 47 (1910) 4.
      R. flavidum Franch. var. *psilostylum* Rehd. et Wils. in Sargent Plantae Wilsonianae, Vol. 1 (1913) 513.
      R. psilostylum (Rehd. et Wils.) Balf. f. in Notes Roy. Bot. Gard. Edin., Vol. 11 (1919) 104.
R. fragariflorum Ward
R. hippophaeoides Balf. f. et W.W. Sm.
R. idoneum Balf. f. et W.W. Sm.
R. impeditum Balf. f. et W.W. Sm.
    Syn. *R. semanteum* Balf. f. nomen nudum.
      R. nivale Hook. f. subsp. *australe* Philipson et Philipson in Notes Roy. Bot. Gard. Edin., Vol. 34 (1975) 54. Type Forrest No. 25707—*R. impeditum.*
R. intricatum Franch.
    Syn. *R. blepharocalyx* Franch. in Journ. de Bot. Vol. 9 (1895) 396.
      R. peramabile Hutch. in Gard. Chron. Vol. 91 (1932) 366.
R. lapponicum (L.) Wahlenb.
    Syn. *Azalea lapponica* L., Sp. Pl. (1753) 151.
R. litangense Balf. f.
R. lysolepis Hutch.
R. microleucum Hutch.
    Syn. *R. orthocladum* Balf. f. et Forrest var. *microleucum* (Hutch.) Philipson et Philipson in Notes Roy. Bot. Gard. Edin., Vol. 34 (1975) 45.
R. nigropunctatum Bureau et Franch.
R. nitidulum Rehd. et Wils.
    Syn. *R. nitidulum* Rehd. et Wils. var. *omeiense* Philipson et Philipson in Notes Roy. Bot. Gard. Edin., Vol. 34 (1975) 25.
R. nitidulum Rehd. et Wils. var. **nubigenum** Rehd. et Wils.
R. nivale Hook. f.
R. oresbium Balf. f. et Ward
    Syn. *R. nivale* Hook. f. subsp. *boreale* Philipson et Philipson in Notes Roy. Bot. Gard. Edin., Vol. 34 (1975) 52. Type Rock No. 9312.

R. orthocladum Balf. f. et Forrest
R. paludosum Hutch. et Ward
R. parvifolium Adams
    Syn. *R. lapponicum* (L.) Wahlenb. *Parvifolium Group* R.H.S. in Rhod. Handb. (1980) p. 19.
R. parvifolium Adams var. **albiflorum** (Herder) Maxim.
R. polifolium Franch.
R. polycladum Franch.
R. ramosissimum Franch.
    Syn. *R. yaragongense* Balf. f. in Notes Roy. Bot. Gard. Edin., Vol. 13 (1920) 64.
R. rupicola W.W. Sm.
    Syn. *R. achroanthum* Balf. f. et W.W. Sm. in Notes Roy. Bot. Gard. Edin., Vol. 9 (1916) 208.
        R. propinquum Tagg in Rhod. Soc. Notes Vol. III (1925) 30, nomen nudum.
R. russatum Balf. f. et Forrest
    Syn. *R. cantabile* Balf. f. ex Hutch. in Bot. Mag. Vol. 148 t.8963 (1922).
        R. osmerum Balf. f. et Forrest in The Species of Rhododendron (1930) 425, nomen nudum.
        R. luridum Ward, Rhod. Year Book (1932) 248, nomen nudum.
R. scintillans Balf. f. et W.W. Sm.
    Syn. *R. orthocladum* Balf. f. et Forrest var. *longistylum* Philipson et Philipson in Notes Roy. Bot. Gard.
        Edin., Vol. 34 (1975) 44.
        R. polycladum Franch. *Scintillans Group* R.H.S. in Rhod. Handb. (1980) p. 17.
        R. gemmiferum Philipson et Philipson in Notes Roy. Bot. Gard. Edin., Vol. 39, No. 1 (1980) 80.
R. sclerocladum Balf. f. et Forrest
R. setosum D. Don
R. spilanthum Hutch.
R. stictophyllum Balf. f.
    Syn. *R. batangense* Balf. f. in Notes Roy. Bot. Gard. Edin., Vol. 13 (1920) 31.
R. tapetiforme Balf. f. et Ward
R. telmateium Balf. f. et W.W. Sm.
R. thymifolium Maxim.
R. tsai Fang
R. verruculosum Rehd. et Wils.
R. violaceum Rehd. et Wils.
R. websterianum Rehd. et Wils.
    Syn. *R. hippophaeoides* Balf. f. et W.W. Sm. var. *occidentale* Philipson et Philipson in Notes Roy. Bot.
        Gard. Edin., Vol. 34 (1975) 20.
        R. websterianum Rehd. et Wils. var. *yulongense* Philipson et Philipson, ibid., p. 23.
R. yungningense Balf. f. ex Hutch.
    Syn. *R. glomerulatum* Hutch. in Gard. Chron. Vol. 91 (1932) 438.
        R. minyaense Philipson et Philipson in Notes Roy. Bot. Gard. Edin., Vol. 34 (1975) 45.

LEPIDOTUM SERIES
BAILEYI SUBSERIES
R. baileyi Balf. f.
    Syn. *R. thyodocum* Balf. f. et Cooper in Notes Roy. Bot. Gard. Edin., Vol. 11 (1919) 148.

LEPIDOTUM SUBSERIES
R. cowanianum Davidian
R. lepidotum Wall. ex G. Don
    Syn. *R. salignum* Hook. f. Rhod. Sikk. Himal. t.23A (1851).
        R. sinolepidotum Balf. f. in Notes Roy. Bot. Gard. Edin., Vol. 10 (1917) 155.
        R. lepidotum Wall. ex G. Don var. *chloranthum* W. J. Hooker in Bot. Mag. Vol. LXXX t.4802
        (1854).
        R. cremnastes Balf. f. et Farrer in Notes Roy. Bot. Gard. Edin., Vol. 13 (1922) 253.
R. lepidotum Wall. ex G. Don var. **album** Davidian
R. lepidotum Wall. ex G. Don var. **elaeagnoides** (Hook. f.) Franch.
    Syn. *R. elaeagnoides* Hook. f. Rhod. Sikk. Himal., t.23B (1851).
R. lepidotum Wall. ex G. Don var. **minutiforme** Davidian
R. lepidotum Wall. ex G. Don var. **obovatum** Hook. f.
    Syn. *R. obovatum* Hook. f. Rhod. Sikk. Himal., 6, t.23 (1849).
R. lowndesii Davidian

MADDENII SERIES
CILIICALYX SUBSERIES
R. carneum Hutch.

R. ciliicalyx Franch.
    Syn. *R. missionarum* Léveillé in Bull. Inter. Geog. Bot. XXIV (1915) 20.
        R. pseudociliicalyx Hutch. in Notes Roy. Bot. Gard. Edin., Vol. 12 (1919) 54.
        R. atentsiense Hand.-Mazz. in Anz. Akad. Wien. No. 18 (1921) 8.
        R. yungchangense Cullen in Notes Roy. Bot. Gard. Edin., Vol. 36 (1978) 123.
R. ciliipes Hutch.
R. coxianum Davidian
R. cubittii Hutch.
    Syn. *R. veitchianum* Hook. *Cubittii Group* R.H.S. in Rhod. Handb. (1980) p. 10.
R. cuffeanum Craib ex Hutch.
R. dendricola Hutch.
R. fleuryi Dop
R. formosum Wallich
    Syn. *R. gibsonii* Paxton, Mag. of Bot. Vol. 8, t.217 (1841).
        R. formosum Wallich var. *salicifolium* C. B. Clarke in Hook. f. Fl. Brit. India, Vol. III (1882) 473.
R. horlickianum Davidian
R. inaequale (C. B. Clarke) Hutch.
    Syn. *R. formosum* Wall. var. *inaequalis* C. B. Clarke in Hook. f. Fl. Brit. India, Vol. III (1882) 473.
        R. formosum Wall. var. *inaequale* [(C. B. Clarke) Hutch.] Cullen in Notes Roy. Bot. Gard. Edin.,
        Vol. 36 (1978) 108.
R. iteophyllum Hutch.
    Syn. *R. formosum* Wall. var. *formosum Iteophyllum Group* R.H.S. in Rhod. Handb. (1980) p. 8.
R. johnstoneanum Watt ex Hutch.
    Syn. *R. formosum* Wall. var. *johnstonianum* Brandis, Indian Trees (1906) 411.
R. lasiopodum Hutch.
R. ludwigianum Hosseus
R. lyi Léveillé
R. notatum Hutch.
R. pachypodum Balf. f. et W.W. Sm.
    Syn. *R. pilicalyx* Hutch. in Notes Roy. Bot. Gard. Edin., Vol. 12 (1919) 66.
R. parryae Hutch.
R. roseatum Hutch.
R. rufosquamosum Hutch.
R. scopulorum Hutch.
R. scottianum Hutch.
R. smilesii Hutch.
R. supranubium Hutch.
    Syn. *R. pseudociliipes* Cullen in Notes Roy. Bot. Gard. Edin., Vol. 36 (1978) 122.
R. surasianum Balf. f. et Craib
R. taronense Hutch.
    Syn. *R. dendricola* Hutch. *Taronense Group* R.H.S. in Rhod. Handb. (1980) p. 8.
R. veitchianum Hook.
    Syn. *R. formosum* Wall. var. *veitchianum* (Hooker) Kurz in Journ. Asiat. Soc. 46(2):276 (1887).
R. walongense Ward

MADDENII SUBSERIES
R. brachysiphon Balf. f.
R. calophyllum Nutt.
R. crassum Franch.
    Syn. *R. maddenii* Hook. f. subsp. *crassum* (Franch.) Cullen in Notes Roy. Bot. Gard. Edin., Vol. 36
        (1978) 107.
R. excellens Hemsl. et Wils.
R. maddenii Hook. f.
    Syn. *R. jenkinsii* Nutt. in Hooker's Kew Journ. Bot. V (1853) 361.
        R. maddenii Hook. f. varieties *aciphyllum, platyphyllum, undulatum,* and var. *longiflora* W.
        Watson.
R. manipurense Balf. f. et Watt
    Syn. *R. maddenii* Hook. f. var. *obtusifolium* Hutch. in Bot. Mag. Vol. 134 t.8212 (1908).
R. odoriferum Hutch.
R. polyandrum Hutch.

MEGACALYX SUBSERIES
R. basfordii Davidian
R. dalhousiae Hook. f.
R. goreri Davidian

R. grothausii Davidian
R. headfortianum Hutch.
R. kiangsiense Fang
R. levinei Merrill
R. liliiflorum Léveillé
R. lindleyi T. Moore
    Syn. *R. bhotanicum* C. B. Clarke in Hook. f. Fl. Brit. India, Vol. III (1882) 475.
R. megacalyx Balf. f. et Ward
R. nuttallii Booth
    Syn. *R. sinonuttallii* Balf. f. et Forrest in Notes Roy. Bot. Gard. Edin., Vol. 13 (1920) 60.
R. nuttallii Booth var. **stellatum** Hutch.
R. rhabdotum Balf. f. et Cooper
    Syn. *R. dalhousiae* Hook. f. var. *rhabdotum* (Balf. f. et Cooper) Cullen in Notes Roy. Bot. Gard. Edin.,
        Vol. 36 (1978) 107.
R. taggianum Hutch.

MICRANTHUM SERIES
R. micranthum Turcz

MOUPINENSE SERIES
R. dendrocharis Franch.
R. moupinense Franch.
R. petrocharis Diels

SALUENENSE SERIES
R. calostrotum Balf. f. et Ward
    Syn. *R. rivulare* Ward in Gard. Chron. Ser. 3, LXXXVI (1929) 503, non Handel-Mazzetti (1921).
        R. riparium Ward in Notes Roy. Bot. Gard. Edin., Vol. 16 (1931) 180.
        R. kingdonii Merrill in Sunyatsenia 3 (1937) 256.
        R. calostrotum Balf. f. et Ward subsp. *riparioides* Cullen in Notes Roy. Bot. Gard. Edin., Vol. 36
        (1978) 112.
R. calostrotum Balf. f. et Ward var. **calciphilum** (Hutch. et Ward) Davidian
    Syn. *R. calciphilum* Hutch. et Ward in Notes Roy. Bot. Gard. Edin., Vol. 16, (1931) 179.
        R. calostrotum Balf. f. et Ward. subsp. *riparium* (Ward) Cullen in Notes Roy. Bot. Gard. Edin.,
        Vol. 36 (1978) 112.
R. chameunum Balf. f. et Forrest
    Syn. *R. cosmetum* Balf. f. et Forrest in Notes Roy. Bot. Gard. Edin., Vol. 13 (1920) 38.
        R. charidotes Balf. f. et Farrer in Notes Roy. Bot. Gard. Edin., Vol. 13 (1922) 242.
        R. colobodes Balf. f. nomen nudum.
        R. sericocalyx Balf. f. nomen nudum.
        R. pamprotum Balf. f. et Forrest, nomen nudum.
        R. humifusum Balf. f. nomen nudum.
        R. saluenense Franch. subsp. *chameunum* (Balf. f. et Forrest) Cullen in Notes Roy. Bot. Gard.
        Edin., Vol. 36 (1978) 112.
R. keleticum Balf. f. et Forrest
    Syn. *R. calostrotum* Balf. f. et Ward subsp. *keleticum* (Balf. f. et Forrest) Cullen in Notes Roy. Bot.
        Gard. Edin., Vol. 36 (1978) 112.
R. nitens Hutch.
R. prostratum W.W. Sm.
    Syn. *R. prostratum* W.W. Sm. ssp. *chameunum Prostratum Group* R.H.S. in Rhod. Handb. (1980) p. 21.
R. radicans Balf. f. et Forrest
    Syn. *R. calostrotum* Balf. f. et Ward ssp. *keleticum Radicans Group* R.H.S. in Rhod. Handb. (1980) p. 21.
R. saluenense Franch.
    Syn. *R. amaurophyllum* Balf. f. et Forrest in Notes Roy. Bot. Gard. Edin., Vol. 13 (1922) 230.
        R. humicola Balf. f. nomen nudum.

SCABRIFOLIUM SERIES
R. hemitrichotum Balf. f. et Forrest
R. mollicomum Balf. f. et W.W. Sm.
R. mollicomum Balf. f. et W.W. Sm. var. **rockii** Tagg.
    Syn. *R. mollicomum Rockii Group* R.H.S. in Rhod. Handb. (1980) p. 13.
R. racemosum Franch.
    Syn. *R. racemosum* Franch. var. *rigidum* Rehnelt in Gartenfl., LVII (1908) 561.
        R. motsouense Lévl. in Feddes Repert., XIII (1914) 148.

R. *iochanense* Lévl., nomen nudum.

R. *crenatum* Lévl. in Bull. Geogr. Bot. XXV (1915) 20.

R. scabrifolium Franch.

R. spiciferum Franch.

Syn. R. *pubescens* Balf. f. et Forrest in Notes Roy. Bot. Gard. Edin., Vol. 12 (1920) 153.

R. *scabrifolium* Franch. var. *spiciferum* (Franch.) Cullen in Notes Roy. Bot. Gard. Edin., Vol. 36 (1978) 110.

R. spinuliferum Franch.

Syn. R. *scabrifolium* Franch. var. *pauciflora* Franch. in Journ. de Bot., XII (1898) 262.

R. *duclouxii* Lévl. in Bull. Soc. Agri. Sarthe, XXXIX (1903) 46.

R. *fuchsiaeflorum* Lévl. in Feddes Repert., XII (1913) 284.

TEPHROPEPLUM SERIES

R. auritum Tagg

R. chrysolepis Hutch. et Ward

R. tephropeplum Balf. f. et Farrer

Syn. R. *spodopeplum* Balf. f. et Farrer in Notes Roy. Bot. Gard. Edin., Vol. 13 (1922) 299.

R. *deleiense* Hutch. et Ward, ibid. Vol. 16 (1931) 172.

R. xanthostephanum Merr.

Syn. R. *aureum* Franch. in Journ. de Bot. IX (1895) 394.

R. *messatum* Balf. f. nomen nudum.

TRICHOCLADUM SERIES

R. caesium Hutch.

R. lepidostylum Balf. f. et Forrest

R. lithophilum Balf. f. et Ward

R. mekongense Franch.

Syn. R. *chloranthum* Balf. f. et Forrest in Notes Roy. Bot. Gard. Edin., Vol. 12 (1920) 98.

R. *semilunatum* Balf. f. et Forrest, ibid. Vol. 13 (1922) 292.

R. melinanthum Balf. f. et Ward

Syn. R. *mekongense* Franch. var. *melinanthum* (Balf. f. et Ward) Cullen in Notes Roy. Bot. Gard. Edin., Vol. 36 (1978) 115.

R. rubrolineatum Balf. f. et Forrest

Syn. R. *mekongense* Franch. var. *rubrolineatum* (Balf. f. et Forrest) Cullen in Notes Roy. Bot. Gard. Edin., Vol. 36 (1978) 115.

R. rubroluteum Davidian

R. trichocladum Franch.

Syn. R. *xanthinum* Balf. f. et W.W. Sm. in Trans. Bot. Soc. Edin., XXVII (1916) 87.

R. *brachystylum* Balf. f. et Ward in Notes Roy. Bot. Gard. Edin., Vol. 13 (1922) 236.

R. *oulotrichum* Balf. f. et Forrest ibid. p. 281.

R. *lophogynum* Balf. f. et Forrest ex Hutch. in The Species of Rhododendron (1930) 750.

R. trichocladum Franch. var. **longipilosum** Cowan.

Syn. R. *mekongense* Franch. var. *longipilosum* (Cowan) Cullen in Notes Roy. Bot. Gard. Edin., Vol. 36 (1978) 115.

R. viridescens Hutch.

Syn. R. *mekongense* Franch. var. *mekongense Viridescens Group* R.H.S. in Rhod. Handb. (1980) p. 27.

TRIFLORUM SERIES
AUGUSTINII SUBSERIES

R. augustinii Hemsl.

Syn. R. *augustinii* Hemsl. var. *yui* Fang in Contri. Biol. Lab. Soc. China, XII (1939) 78.

R. *augustinii* Hemsl. var. *azureus* Chen ex Laum. in Rev. Horte, XXXI, 46, t. (1948).

R. augustinii Hemsl. var. **chasmanthum** (Diels) Davidian

Syn. R. *chasmanthum* Diels in Notes Roy. Bot. Gard. Edin., Vol. 5 (1912) 212.

R. *augustinii* Hemsl. forma *grandifolia* Franch. in Journ. de Bot., XII (1898) 261.

R. *augustinii* Hemsl. forma *subglabra* Franch. in Journ. de Bot., XII (1898) 261.

R. *chasmanthoides* Balf. f. et Forrest in Notes Roy. Bot. Gard. Edin., Vol. 13 (1922) 246.

R. *augustinii* Hemsl. subsp. *chasmanthum* (Diels) Cullen in Notes Roy. Bot. Gard. Edin., Vol. 36 (1978) 109.

R. bergii Davidian

Syn. R. *augustinii* Hemsl. var. *rubrum* Davidian in The Rhododendron and Camellia Year Book (1963) 165.

R. *augustinii* Hemsl. subsp. *rubrum* (Davidian) Cullen in Notes Roy. Bot. Gard. Edin., Vol. 36 (1978) 109.

R. bivelatum Balf. f.
R. hardyi Davidian
> Syn. *R. augustinii* Hemsl. subsp. *hardyi* (Davidian) Cullen in Notes Roy. Bot. Gard. Edin., Vol. 36 (1978) 109.

R. hirsuticostatum Hand.-Mazz.
R. trichanthum Rehder
> Syn. *R. villosum* Hemsl. et Wils. in Kew Bull. Misc. Inform. (1910) 119.

HANCEANUM SUBSERIES

R. afghanicum Aitch. et Hemsl.
R. hanceanum Hemsl.
R. hanceanum Hemsl. 'Nanum'
> Syn. *R. hanceanum* Hemsl. var. *nanum* Hort.
> *R. hanceanum* Hemsl. *Nanum Group* R.H.S. in Rhod. Handb. (1980) p. 23.

TRIFLORUM SUBSERIES

R. ambiguum Hemsl.
> Syn. *R. chengshienianum* Fang in Icones Plantarum Omeiensium I, No. 1 (1942).

R. bauhiniiflorum Watt ex Hutch.
> Syn. *R. triflorum* Hook. f. var. *bauhiniiflorum* (Watt. ex Hutch.) Cullen in Notes Roy. Bot. Gard. Edin., Vol. 36 (1978) 109.

R. flavantherum Hutch. et Ward
R. kasoense Hutch. et Ward
R. keiskei Miq.
> Syn. *R. laticostum* Ingram in R.H.S. Rhod. Year Book, No. 25 (1971) 30–31.
> *R. trichocalyx* Ingram, ibid., p. 33.

R. lutescens Franch.
> Syn. *R. costulatum* Franch. in Journ. de Bot., IX (1895) 399.
> *R. lemeei* Lévl. in Feddes Repert., XIII (1914) 339.
> *R. blinii* Lévl. in Bull. Acad. Geogr. Bot., XXIV (1915) 21.

R. triflorum Hook. f.
> Syn. *R. deflexum* Griffith, Notulae 4: 303 & t.519 (1854).

R. triflorum Hook. f. var. **mahogani** Hutch.
> Syn. *R. triflorum* Hook. f. var. *triflorum Mahogani Group* R.H.S. in Rhod. Handb. (1980) p. 12.

R. wongii Hemsl. et Wils.

YUNNANENSE SUBSERIES

R. amesiae Rehd. et Wils.
R. apiculatum Rehd. et Wils.
R. bodinieri Franch.
R. concinnoides Hutch. et Ward
R. concinnum Hemsl.
> Syn. *R. yanthinum* Bur. et Franch. in Journ. de Bot., V (1891) 94.
> *R. coombense* Hemsl. in Bot. Mag. Vol. 135, t.8280 (1909).
> *R. atroviride* Dunn, Journ. Linn. Soc. XXXIX (1911) 484, nomen nudum.
> *R. yanthinum* Bur. et Franch. var. *lepidanthum* Rehd. et Wils. in Pl. Wils., I (1913) 519.
> *R. laetevirens* Balf. f., Hutch. in The Species of Rhododendron (1930) 781, nomen nudum.
> *R. subcoombense* Balf. f. nomen nudum.
> *R. concinnum* Hemsl. forma *laetevirens* Cowan in Bot. Mag. Vol. 147, t.8912 (1938).
> *R. concinnum* Hemsl. var. *lepidanthum* (Rehd. et Wils.) Rehd. in Journ. Arn. Arb., XX, No. 4 (1939) 424.
> *R. hutchinsonianum* Fang in Acta Phytotax., II (1953) 83.

R. concinnum Hemsl. var. **benthamianum** (Hemsl.) Davidian
> Syn. *R. benthamianum* Hemsl. in Kew Bull. (1907) 319.

R. concinnum Hemsl. var. **pseudoyanthinum** (Balf. f. ex Hutch.) Davidian
> Syn. *R. pseudoyanthinum* Balf. f. ex Hutch. in The Species of Rhododendron (1930) 783.

R. davidsonianum Rehd. et Wils.
> Syn. *R. charianthum* Hutch. in Bot. Mag. Vol. 142, t.8665 (1916).

R. hormophorum Balf f. et Forrest
> Syn. *R. chartophyllum* Franch. forma *praecox* Diels in Notes Roy. Bot. Gard. Edin., Vol. 5 (1912) 217.
> *R. yunnanense* Franch. *Hormophorum Group* R.H.S. in Rhod. Handb. (1980) p. 11.

R. hypophaeum Balf. f. et Forrest
R. longistylum Rehd. et Wils.
R. oreotrephes W.W. Sm.
> Syn. *R. timeteum* Balf. f. et Forrest in Notes Roy. Bot. Gard. Edin., Vol. 12 (1920) 166.

R. *artosquameum* Balf. f. et Forrest, ibid. Vol. 13 (1922) 234.
R. *cardioeides* Balf. f. et Forrest, ibid. p. 239.
R. *depile* Balf. f. et Forrest, ibid. p. 255.
R. *hypotrichotum* Balf. f. et Forrest, ibid., p. 268.
R. *oreotrephoides* Balf. f. nomen nudum.
R. *phaeochlorum* Balf. f. et Forrest in Notes Roy. Bot. Gard. Edin., Vol. 13 (1922) 284.
R. *pubigerum* Balf. f. et Forrest, ibid., p. 289.
R. *trichopodum* Balf. f. et Forrest, ibid., p. 304.
R. *siderophylloides* Hutch. in Journ. Roy. Hort. Soc., LX (1935) 326.

R. oreotrephes W.W. Sm. 'Exquisetum'
Syn. R. *exquisetum* Hutch. in Gard. Chron. XCII (1932) 9.

R. polylepis Franch.
Syn. R. *harrovianum* Hemsl. in Gard. Chron., XLVII (1910) 4.

R. rigidum Franch.
Syn. R. *caeruleum* Lévl. in Feddes Repert., XII (1913) 284.
R. *rarosquameum* Balf. f. in Notes Roy. Bot. Gard. Edin., Vol. 10 (1917) 137.
R. *sycnanthum* Balf. f. et W.W. Sm. ibid., p. 162.
R. *hesperium* Balf. f. et Forrest, ibid. Vol. 13 (1922) 263.
R. *eriandrum* Lévl., Tagg in Rhod. Soc. Notes, III (1928) 228, nomen nudum.
R. *eriandrum* Lévl. ex Hutch. in The Species of Rhododendron (1930) 798.

R. searsiae Rehd. et Wils.

R. siderophyllum Franch.
Syn. R. *rubro-punctatum* Lévl. et Vant in Feddes Repert., IX (1911) 448.
R. *leucandrum* Lévl. in Feddes Repert., XII (1913) 103.
R. *jahandiezii* Lévl. ibid., XIII (1914) 340.
R. *ioanthum* Balf. f. in Notes Roy. Bot. Gard. Edin., Vol. 13 (1922) 270.
R. *obscurum* Franch. ex Balf. f. ibid., p. 278.

R. suberosum Balf. f. et Forrest

R. tatsienense Franch.
Syn. R. *tapelouense* Lévl. in Bull. Geogr. Bot., XXV (1915) 20.
R. *stereophyllum* Balf. f. et W.W. Sm. in Notes Roy. Bot. Gard. Edin., Vol. 10 (1916) 159.
R. *leilungense* Balf. f. et Forrest, ibid. Vol. 13 (1922) 273.
R. *heishuense* Fang in Acta Phytotax., II, 83, pl. IX (1933).

R. vilmorinianum Balf. f.

R. yunnanense Franch.
Syn. R. *chartophyllum* Franch. in Journ. de Bot. IX (1895) 398.
R. *sequini* Lévl. in Feddes Repert., XIII (1914) 148.
R. *aechmophyllum* Balf. f. et Forrest in Notes Roy. Bot. Gard. Edin., Vol. 13 (1922) 226.
R. *pleistanthum* Balf. f. ex Hutch. in The Species of Rhododendron (1930) 806.
R. *strictum* Lévl., nomen nudum.

R. zaleucum Balf. f. et W.W. Sm.
Syn. R. *erileucum* Balf. f. et Forrest in Notes Roy. Bot. Gard. Edin., Vol. 12 (1920) 108.

R. zaleucum Balf. f. et W.W. Sm. var. **flaviflorum** Davidian

UNIFLORUM SERIES
R. imperator Hutch. et Ward
Syn. R. *patulum* Ward in Gard. Chron. Vol. 88 (1930) 298.
R. *uniflorum* Hutch. et Ward var. *imperator* (Hutch. et Ward) Cullen in Notes Roy. Bot. Gard. Edin., Vol. 36 (1978) 113.
R. *pemakoense* Patulum Group R.H.S. in Rhod. Handb. (1930) p. 21.

R. ludlowii Cowan
R. monanthum Balf. f. et W.W. Sm.
Syn. R. *sulfureum* Diels in Notes Roy. Bot. Gard. Edin., Vol. 7 (1912) 66, non Franchet.

R. pemakoense Ward
R. pumilum Hook. f.
R. uniflorum Hutch. et Ward

VACCINIOIDES SERIES
R. asperulum Hutch. et Ward
R. emarginatum Hemsl. et Wils.
R. euonymifolium Lévl.
R. insculptum Hutch. et Ward
R. kawakamii Hayata
R. santapaui Sastry, Kataki, P. Cox, Patricia Cox & P. Hutchison
R. vaccinioides Hook. f.

VIRGATUM SERIES
R. virgatum Hook. f.
    Syn. *R. oleifolium* Franch. in Bull. Soc. Bot. France, XXXIII (1886) 235.
       R. virgatum Hook. f. subsp. *oleifolium* (Franch.) Cullen in Notes Roy. Bot. Gard. Edin., Vol. 36
        (1978) 113.
       R. sinovirgatum Balf. f. nomen nudum.

General Index

Index of Rhododendrons